Music in the Human Experience

Music in the Human Experience: An Introduction to Music Psychology, Second Edition, is geared toward music students yet incorporates other disciplines to provide an explanation for why and how we make sense of music and respond to it—cognitively, physically, and emotionally. All human societies in every corner of the globe engage in music. Taken collectively, these musical experiences are widely varied and hugely complex affairs. How did human beings come to be musical creatures? How and why do our bodies respond to music? Why do people have emotional responses to music? *Music in the Human Experience* seeks to understand and explain these phenomena at the core of what it means to be a human being.

New to this edition:

■ Expanded references and examples of non-Western musical styles
■ Updated literature on philosophical and spiritual issues
■ Brief sections on tuning systems and the acoustics of musical instruments
■ A section on creativity and improvisation in the discussion of musical performance
■ New studies in musical genetics
■ Greatly increased usage of explanatory figures

Donald A. Hodges, formerly the Covington Distinguished Professor of Music Education, is now Professor Emeritus at the University of North Carolina, Greensboro.

Music in the Human Experience

An Introduction to Music Psychology

Second Edition

Donald A. Hodges
University of North Carolina at Greensboro

Routledge
Taylor & Francis Group

NEW YORK AND LONDON

First published 2020
by Routledge
52 Vanderbilt Avenue, New York, NY 10017

and by Routledge
2 Park Square, Milton Park, Abingdon, Oxon, OX14 4RN

Routledge is an imprint of the Taylor & Francis Group, an informa business

First edition published by Routledge 2011

Library of Congress Cataloging-in-Publication Data
Names: Hodges, Donald A., author.
Title: Music in the human experience : an introduction to music psychology /
   Donald A. Hodges.
Description: Second edition. | New York ; London : Routledge, 2019.
Identifiers: LCCN 2019020375 (print) | LCCN 2019022266 (ebook) |
   ISBN 9781138579804 (hardback) | ISBN 9781138579828 (pbk.)
Subjects: LCSH: Music—Psychological aspects.
Classification: LCC ML3830 .H47 2019 (print) | LCC ML3830 (ebook) |
   DDC 781.1/1—dc23
LC record available at https://lccn.loc.gov/2019020375
LC ebook record available at https://lccn.loc.gov/2019022266

ISBN: 978-1-138-57980-4 (hbk)
ISBN: 978-1-138-57982-8 (pbk)
ISBN: 978-0-429-50777-9 (ebk)

Typeset in Times New Roman
by Apex CoVantage, LLC

www.routledge.com/cw/hodges

Contents

PART II: PERCEIVING, UNDERSTANDING, AND RESPONDING TO MUSIC

Media Tutorials

This symbol will appear throughout the book whenever there is a Media Tutorial program that supplements the text. In the line next to the media icon, the superscript MT will appear along with the number of the program. For example,^{MT6.3} indicates that Media Tutorial program 6.3 *The Hearing Process* is available online at www.routledge.com/cw/hodges. **Please note that the tutorials in the original CD were called multimedia modules (MM) and this is how they are still referenced online. However, in the text they are now referred to as media tutorials (MT).**

5. Acoustical Foundations of Music
    MT5 Physical Acoustics

6. Musical Hearing
    MT6.1 Ear Anatomy
    MT6.2 Sound Localization
    MT6.3 The Hearing Process
    MT6.4 Hearing Damage

7. Psychoacoustics and the Perception of Music
    MT7.1 The Critical Band
    MT7.2 The Perception of Pitch
    MT7.3 Wave Form Generator
    MT7.4 Pitch Discrimination
    MT7.5 The Perception of Loudness
    MT7.6 Equal Loudness Contours
    MT7.7 The Perception of Timbre
    MT7.8 The Perception of Duration

8. Music Cognition
    MT8.1 Gestalt Principles of Musical Organization
    MT8.2 Auditory Stream Segregation
    MT8.3 Musical Fusion and Fission
    MT8.4 Tchaikovsky: Symphony No. 6
    MT8.5 Musical Memory
    MT8.6 Expectancy Theory
    MT8.7 Gap-Fill Melody
    MT8.8 Changing Note Patterns

Illustrations

Preface

WELCOME to the second edition of *Music in the Human Experience: An Introduction to Music Psychology*. In the years since the publication of the first edition in 2011, the field of music psychology has continued to grow and develop, mostly at a steady pace but with occasional spurts in certain areas. My intent has been to reflect those changes throughout the second edition in at least six ways:

1.   On almost every page there are minor revisions that clarify the text, correct errors, update references, and so on.
2.   Revised and updated sections are found throughout the book. Here are just two examples:
     ■   In Chapter 9: Music and the Brain, there is an additional paragraph on music and Alzheimer's Disease with references from 2003, 2014, 2015, and 2019.
     ■   In a discussion of performance anxiety in Chapter 15: Music and Health, there is a paragraph, accompanied by images, about a performance simulator developed by Aaron Williamon and his group.
3.   The text and figures are more inclusive of non-Western and non-classical music genres. In addition to the global perspective in Chapter 4, examples of inclusiveness occur throughout the book, including:
     ■   Figures of musicians or dancers from Africa, Belgium, China, Egypt, Greece, India, Korea, Mexico, Mongolia, Peru, Scotland, and Sweden. Images from America include Inuit, Native Americans, mariachi musicians, a gospel choir, and jazz and rock musicians.
     ■   In Chapter 16: Music in Social Contexts, a heading has been changed from "Music in American Society" to "Music in Society," to reflect a broader global view. Later in the same chapter under the heading "The Influence of Music in the Workplace," the economic impact of music around the world is described.
4.   There are new or significantly revised sections in five of the chapters.
     ■   Chapter 2
         – (new) Is music psychology encroaching on music philosophy's territory?
     ■   Chapter 5
         – (new) Tuning systems (in Western and non-Western music)
         – (new) Acoustics of the voice and musical instruments
         – (new) Room acoustics

- Chapter 12
  – The section entitled "Is Musicality Inherited or Acquired?" is revised and updated to include current information on genetics.
  – (new) Religious and Spiritual Aspects
- Chapter 13
  – (new) A new section entitled "Musical Creativity" includes subsections on memory and creativity, divergent and convergent thinking, flow, and improvisation.

5. The number of figures has been increased significantly from 87 in the first edition to 148 in the second edition. Not only are there considerably more images but a greater emphasis has been placed on explanatory rather than simply decorative images. Here are examples from just three chapters:

- Chapter 2 contains a discussion of biological differences among humans and other animals. Figure 2.1 depicts a bird syrinx and a human larynx, illustrating the difference between vocal production in the two species.
- In Chapter 5, new figures include an organ "split" keyboard, vocal folds, open and closed pipes, parts of a violin, comparison of vibratory rates of a bass drum and a gong, an undercut arch in a marimba bar, and overtones of a timpani.
- In Chapter 9, there are figures comparing myelinated and unmyelinated neurons, depictions of four types of neurons, a neural network, and DTI fiber tracts.

6. References have been expanded, updated, and culled to reflect a current state of the literature.

With all these changes, teachers and students alike will find a resource that reflects traditional and modern scholarship in music psychology.

ORGANIZATION

Music in the Human Experience is divided into three sections. In Part I (Chapters 1–4), readers are provided with a broad overview of the field, setting the stage for more detailed discussions that follow. The opening chapter includes a model of music psychology, a modicum of history and background on some of the early pioneers, and information on the major books published over the past 150 years. Music psychology and music philosophy share many mutual concerns and some of those interactions are sketched out. You explore how it is we came to be musical creatures in the first place, and in the final chapter in this section you will read about the many roles music plays all over the globe.

The second part of the book (Chapters 5–11) traces the arc of the musical experience beginning with music as sound outside the body, moving through the ear and the brain, to the mind where we make sense of music and respond to it, physically and emotionally. Although you do not necessarily need to read these chapters in order, in many ways they are additive. That is, each chapter informs the ones that follow. Be certain to use the supplementary Media Tutorials; if a picture is worth a thousand words, these aural and visual examples will be of considerable use to you in understanding the contents of these chapters.

Part III (Chapters 12–16) explores what it means to be a musical person. You will examine whether musicians have a distinctive personality type and how music influences their sense of identity and their preferences. In the following two chapters, you will review the literature on music performance skills and on music learning. Next, you will have the opportunity to learn how music plays a significant role in health. Finally, you will read about music in a variety of social contexts.

SUPPLEMENTARY FEATURES

■ *Review material*
   – *Discussion questions*. Ten questions follow each chapter. These not only provide an occasion to review key ideas, but also afford you an opportunity to reflect on how the material informs your understanding of music and how it might impact your future career or engagement with music.
   –*Extensive glossary*. At the end of the book is an extensive glossary that contains brief explanations of nearly 450 terms. These are useful aids while you read the chapters, for example, when you re-encounter a term that was introduced in a previous chapter, and can be helpful as you review for exams.
■ *Companion website*: www.routledge.com/cw/hodges
   – *Brief quizzes* over key points in each chapter are available online. These quizzes are a quick way for you to make certain you identified main points and can be helpful in reviewing for class exams.
   – *Flash cards* are also posted online. Glossary terms and other key concepts are presented so that you can test yourself over key terms and ideas.
   – *Supplemental reading lists* for each chapter are available online.
   – *Media Tutorials*. Media Tutorials created by David Sebald are a truly unique aspect of this book. The first edition was accompanied by a CD, but these programs are now online. They include 32 multimedia movies incorporating over 200 individual modules. Included are photographs, drawings, animations, sound files, and many interactive media files that illustrate key concepts of the text. Figure P.1 shows the menu of programs.

In MT5, Physical Acoustics (Fig. P.2a) you will learn about the acoustical basis of timbre. Then, you can use the Wave Form Generator, MT7.3 (Fig. P.2b) to create and manipulate

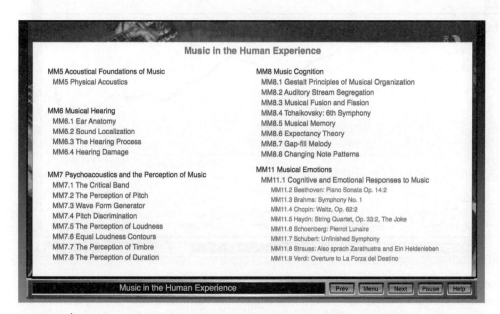

FIGURE P.1 | Menu for Media Tutorials. In the original CD, these were called multimedia modules (MM) as shown here. However, in the text they are now referred to as media tutorials (MT).

your own timbres by using slider bars to alter the first 12 harmonics of a complex tone. After choosing the amount of energy present in each harmonic, you can see the wave shape and musical notation of the harmonics and hear the resultant sound. Using the Wave Form Generator, you can investigate the results of changes in a complex wave shape and conduct exercises such as the missing fundamental experiment.

(a)

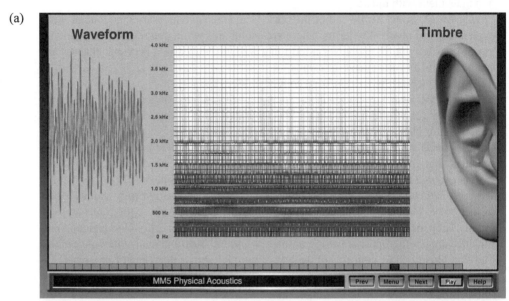

(b)

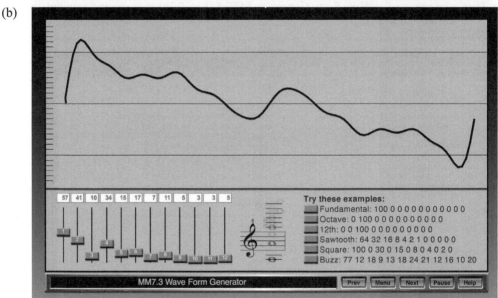

FIGURE P.2 | Learning About Timbre. (a) A screen shot from the section in physical acoustics on musical timbre (MT5). (b) A screen shot of the Wave Form Generator (MT7.3) showing the complex wave shape that results from manipulating the energy in the first 12 harmonics. The relative intensity of each frequency is indicated by the shadings in the musical notation.

Many musical examples are used to illustrate specific concepts. In P. 3a, you can see and hear how Beethoven delayed the cadence in a phrase repetition of his Piano Sonata in C Major. In P. 3b you can see and hear how Bach created the appearance of two melodies emerging from a single line by alternating pitches.

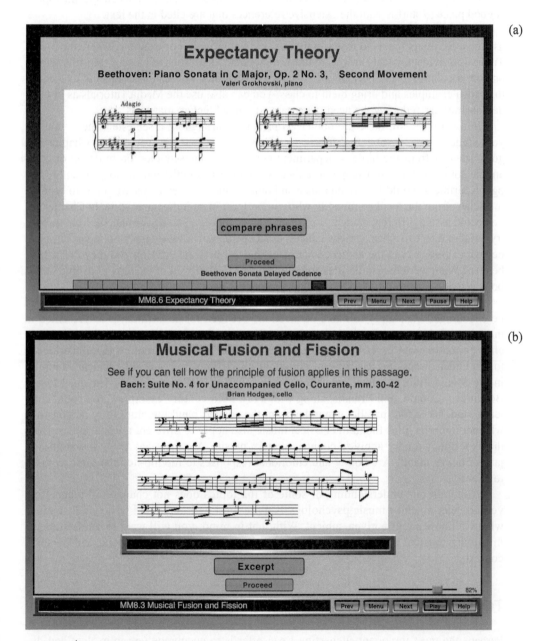

FIGURE P.3 | Musical Examples. (a) Beethoven Piano Sonata in C Major is used as an example of musical expectancy in MT8.6. (b) Bach Suite No. 4 for Unaccompanied Cello illustrates musical fission (MT8.3).

TO THE TEACHER

How one uses the book and additional features may depend significantly on the level and background of your students. With younger or less experienced students, you may wish to focus more literally on the text. With more advanced students, you may wish to assign outside readings that provide additional details and more in-depth discussions on specific topics. A good place to start is with the extensive references that are cited in the text.

The Media Tutorials will be a valuable teaching and learning tool. I recommend that you use them for assignments to foster individual student growth. For example, where the Media Tutorials provide musical excerpts to illustrate specific ideas, such as closure, gap-fill melody, or how a composer can play on a listener's expectations, you can ask students to identify their own examples and bring them to class. You can also use the Media Tutorials as in-class demonstrations, reducing the need to prepare additional lecture materials.

In a similar vein, there are numerous instances throughout a semester where you and your students can investigate different ideas beyond the text. For example, in Chapter 3, a guest speaker from the biology department could give a presentation on birdsong or other animal sound making. In Chapter 4, a faculty member from ethnomusicology or anthropology departments could lecture on music and other cultures. Even better would be to bring in musicians from the local community who can perform in an indigenous style. In Chapter 16, you could assign different students to attend various concerts and performances, from a country western dance to a heavy metal concert or an opera, with an assignment to report on social behaviors among both the audience members and the performers. How did they dress, talk, behave? What were the similarities and differences? Virtually all of the topics covered in this book provide opportunities for creating explorations.

As noted in the previous suggestion for using the Media Tutorials, students should be encouraged constantly to make connections between research findings as presented in the text and their own musical experiences. You could assign different students for each class period to bring in recordings or provide live musical demonstrations that illustrate the topics under discussion. Because of copyright restrictions, many of the musical examples in the Media Tutorials are from the standard repertoire—Bach, Vivaldi, Haydn, Mozart, Beethoven, Chopin, and Brahms, along with a few 20th-century examples. You could challenge students to find parallel examples from the concert band literature or to demonstrate whether the principles found in classical music also apply to different musical styles. Does the expectancy theory apply to country western music? Are there any event hierarchies in jazz or heavy metal? Are bodily and emotional responses to rap/hip-hop the same as those to Mozart?

Although our understanding of some of the topics does not change too much from year to year, much of music psychology is quite fluid with rapid and frequent changes in what we know about a given subject. With that in mind, you will want to guide students in finding musical connections that place the material into current social and personal contexts.

TO THE STUDENT

Perhaps the most important suggestion I can offer is to encourage you to explore and discover with enthusiasm, and to be open to stretching preconceptions to accommodate new understandings. Refer to the Media Tutorials to supplement your reading. Participate in class discussions, and review the online interactive quizzes and flash cards. Follow through with projects by taking it upon yourself to investigate the recommended supplemental readings that are posted online. The world of music psychology is a rich treasure trove of powerful, meaningful experiences; I hope you will find great delight in exploring music in the human experience.

Acknowledgments

D AVID Sebald wrote the text for the first half of Chapter 5: Acoustical Foundations of Music. He also created the Media Tutorials for Chapter 5 and the Wave Form Generator. Although I wrote the text for the remaining Media Tutorials, David turned them into wonderful programs that significantly enhance the text. Taken together, these multimedia programs are a marvelous tool for student learning. Thank you, David.

I want to thank Constance Ditzel, my editor at Routledge, her assistant Peter Sheehy, and the entire team at Routledge, for their work in producing this book. They make an arduous process much easier. I am also grateful for the anonymous reviewers who provided valuable feedback on the first edition and gave many useful suggestions to improve the second edition.

Finally, I would like to thank my wife, Diana Allan, for her love and support. She is a marvelous sounding board for my thoughts, always has good ideas of her own, and makes the work of writing worthwhile.

Part I

Introducing Music Psychology

WELCOME to the world of music psychology. It is my pleasure to serve as your guide as we explore this diverse and fascinating field of study. Four chapters provide the initial introduction, connections between philosophy and music psychology, a look at the evolutionary basis for human musicality, and a broad survey of musical behaviors from around the globe. In Chapter 1: *What is Music Psychology?*, you will be introduced to a model of music psychology and then we will go on a brief tour of major disciplines that contribute to the field. You will also be directed to Appendix A, a listing of selected major works in music psychology from the 19th century to the present that provide a sense of how scholars have addressed different topics over time.

When music psychologists conduct research, they do so from a philosophical orientation, whether explicit or implied. In Chapter 2: *Philosophical Issues in Music Psychology*, we will explore relationships between the two disciplines. Although philosophical orientations are not always readily apparent, they can have a significant impact on how we interpret and understand research findings. Some topics, such as beauty and human nature, are best, or perhaps only, understood from a combined perspective of philosophy and psychology.

Do you think that human musicality has an evolutionary basis? Are we musical creatures because music provided a survival benefit? Do other animals make music? That is, are bird songs and whalesongs really music? We will investigate these issues in Chapter 3: *How We Came to be Musical*.

Human beings in every place and at all times have participated in musical activities. In Chapter 4: *Music Around the World and Across Time*, we will review the archaeological evidence for ancient music making and read about the kinds of musical behaviors that characterize different cultural groups around the world.

The goal of these first four chapters is to help you understand what music psychology is and to place it in a broad context. Armed with this knowledge, the study of more particular aspects of music psychology such as music perception and cognition will be more meaningful.

Chapter 1

What Is Music Psychology?

LET us begin our journey into the world of music psychology by considering how an old soldier described his experience during the Second Boer War in South Africa (1899–1902):

> I was in a Highland Regiment, as you know—the Scots Guards—and I'll tell you something: there is nothing in the world like the sound of the bagpipes to raise a man's morale, to lift his spirits, and give him strength. However tired and thirsty we were, the bagpipes at the front of the column only had to strike up and within seconds you felt your feet lift off the ground, your step lighten, your spirits rise, and every man-Jack was marching strong, in rhythm to the pipes.
>
> (Worth, 2013, pp. 250–251; see Fig. 1.1)

FIGURE 1.1 | Bagpipes Band at the 2017 AFL Grand Final Parade on September 29, 2017, in Melbourne, Victoria.

How are we to account for this power of music to enliven weary soldiers? Gaston (1968) implied that there are rational explanations when he wrote, "Music is not mystical; it is mysterious" (p. 10). We may not have the answers yet, but it is the work of the music psychologist to provide scientifically based answers. So, our first glimmer of what music psychology is all about is that music psychologists ask and answer questions. Here are a few illustrative questions they might seek to answer:

- How did human beings come to be musical creatures?
- Do some animals make music, too? (Are bird*song* and whale*song* really music?)
- Are there universals in music such that all people, everywhere, organize musical sounds in similar ways?
- How does our sense of hearing work?
- Are there specific parts of the brain devoted to music, just as there might be for language or mathematics?
- How and why do our bodies respond to music and can we harness these reactions to affect changes in health or behavior?
- Can we explain why people have such strong emotional responses to music?
- Do different kinds of musicians have different kinds of personalities?
- How is it that music can bring people together and unite them or conversely divide them into different cliques?
- What is happening inside a pianist's mind as he or she plays a Beethoven sonata?
- How can harp music restore balance to a young patient's vital signs in the middle of surgery?
- How can a person have a cognitive disorder and still excel at playing the guitar?

As we will explore later, all human societies—in every place on the planet and at all times in history—engage in musical behaviors. In fact, human beings all over the world engage in music to such an extent that many consider music to be a species-specific trait (Blacking, 1973). Taken collectively, these musical experiences are widely varied, hugely complex affairs and it is the job of music psychologists to understand and explain this phenomenon that seems to be so central to what it means to be a human being.

The sample questions given above are just the tip of the iceberg. Interested scholars have pondered and conducted research on hundreds (thousands?) of such questions. In the earliest days, dating even back to the ancient Greeks, most of the questions were approached philosophically, although Pythagoras did conduct experiments as early as the sixth century BC. More recently, researchers have utilized very sophisticated laboratory technologies, statistical analyses, and other means to arrive at answers. It is the job of the music psychologist to bring some order to the myriad pieces of information that need to be connected into a coherent understanding of all the ways we are musical. As a guide to exploring topics that range over a broad range of human knowledge, we will use a model developed by Charles Eagle (1996).

As you can see in Figure 1.2, Eagle arrayed a broad range of disciplines around a central core. Quantum physics tells us that everything that exists, exists in a state of vibration. Even though the chair you are sitting on as you read this page feels solid, if you move down to the molecular, and even deeper quantum level, there is more space than matter and the matter is in constant movement. Some vibrations are perceived as sound—nominally those between 20 and 20,000 cycles per second for humans—and some sounds are perceived as music. The model indicates that we can consider music from a number of disciplines but also from an interdisciplinary standpoint. Thus, we might say more formally that music psychology is a multidisciplinary and interdisciplinary study of music in the human experience.

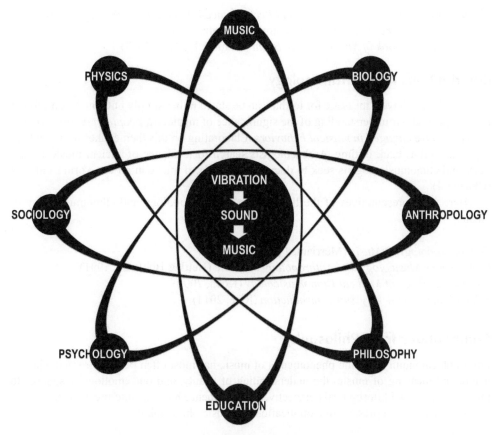

FIGURE 1.2 | Descriptive Model of the Interdisciplinary World of Music Psychology.

A BRIEF TOUR OF THE MODEL OF MUSIC PSYCHOLOGY

As an expansion of the foregoing definition of music psychology, let us take a brief tour around the model, looking briefly at the major disciplines involved. We will start with Biology on the upper right and move clockwise around the outside, finishing with Music.

Contributions from Biology

Musical experiences are bodily experiences and understanding them requires investigations into such biological topics as the brain, hearing, vision, emotions, motor mechanisms, and physiological responses, such as heart rate changes (Chapters 3, 6, 9, 10, 13, and 15). BioMusic is a term used to study animal sound making, such as birdsong, and the relationship this has with human music.

Here are representative publications in the biology of music:

Biomusicology: Neurophysiological, Neuropsychological and Evolutionary Perspectives on the Origins and Purposes of Music (Wallin, 1991)

The Biology of Musical Performance and Performance-related Injury (Watson, 2009)
The Biological Foundations of Music (Zatorre & Peretz, 2001)
The Oxford Handbook of Music and the Brain (Thaut & Hodges, 2019)

Contributions from Anthropology

Anthropologists have a message for us that can be stated rather simply but which is profound in its impact on our understanding of the significance of music: *All people in all times and in all places have engaged in musical behaviors*. Elaborating on this theme takes us around the world as well as back in time. Archaeologists search for evidence of ancient musical practices, and ethnomusicologists seek to document the role of music in all the world's cultures (Chapter 4).

Here are representatives of the literature in the anthropology and ethnomusicology of music:

The Anthropology of Music (Merriam, 1964)
Comparative Musicology and Anthropology of Music (Nettl & Bohlman, 1991)
Oxford Handbook of Medical Ethnomusicology (Koen, 2008)
Ethnomusicology: A Very Short Introduction (Rice, 2014)

Contributions from Philosophy

Philosophical inquiry into the phenomenon of music has most often been concerned with the nature and meaning of music, the understanding of beauty, and our emotional responses to music (Chapter 2). Philosophical perspectives may influence how one interprets scientific data.

Here are some representative publications in music philosophy:

In Search of Beauty in Music: A Scientific Approach to Musical Esthetics (Seashore, 1947)
Aesthetics and Psychobiology (Berlyne, 1971)
Music and Mind: Philosophical Essays on the Cognition and Meaning of Music (Fiske, 1990)
A Concise Survey of Music Philosophy (Hodges, 2017)

Contributions from Education

Music has been part of the American educational system since 1838, when Lowell Mason convinced the Boston School Board to accept it as part of the curriculum (Birge, 1928). Although there is no national curriculum for music, the *National Standards for Music Education* (2014) specify what students should know and be able to do in music. Music is considered a core academic subject (Camera, 2015). Those who are interested in conducting research on the role of music in the broader educational context might belong to the Music Special Interest Group (SIG) of the American Educational Research Association (AERA). The purpose of this group is "to improve the quality of research conducted in the music education field" (2007). Researchers who wish to study music in the context of the other arts disciplines can become affiliated with two additional AERA SIGs: Arts and Learning and Arts-Based Approaches to Educational Research. In all of this, there is a central focus on music teaching and learning (see Chapter 14).

Here a few representative publications in music education relevant to music psychology:

The MENC Handbook of Research on Music Learning, 2 vols. New York: Oxford University Press. (Colwell & Webster, 2011)

The Oxford Handbook of Music Education, 2 vols. Oxford, UK: Oxford University Press. (McPherson & Welch, 2012)
Music and Music Education in People's Lives (McPherson & Welch, 2018)
The Routledge International Handbook of Music Psychology in Education and the Community (Hallam, Creech, & Hodges, 2020)

Contributions from Psychology

Psychologists explore an immense number of topics related to music. Psychologists from each of the major approaches (e.g., behavioral, cognitive, developmental, Freudian, Gestalt, humanistic, etc.) contribute unique understandings of musical experiences. Psychologists are interested in the perception and cognition of music. They want to know how we make sense of musical experiences. Other important topics include the musical personality, special musicians (e.g., musical savants, Williams Syndrome musicians, etc.), the development of musicality, performance anxiety, affective responses to music, musical aptitude, and music teaching and learning (Chapters 7, 8, 11, 12, 13, and 14).

Here are some representative publications from the field of psychology:

Psychology of Music (Tan, Pfordresher, & Harré, 2010)
The Oxford Handbook of Music Psychology (Hallam, Cross, & Thaut, 2016)
Psychology of Music (Hallam, 2018)
The Psychology of Music: A Very Short Introduction (Margulis, 2019)

Contributions from Sociology

Some sociologists are interested in the role music plays in social interactions. They tell us that each individual has the potential to respond to music of the surrounding culture. No condition of age, race, gender, mental or physical state, or socioeconomic status prohibits one from a meaningful musical experience. The sociology of music takes us into business and economics, politics, religion, the military, youth culture, and the entertainment and media industries (Chapter 16).

Here are some representative publications in the sociology of music:

The Sociology of Music (Dasilva, Blasi, & Dees, 1984)
Music, Culture, and Society (Scott, 2000)
The Social and Applied Psychology of Music (North & Hargreaves, 2008)
Music: A Social Experience (Cornelius & Natvig, 2012)

Contributions from Physics

Acoustics, a branch of physics, is the science of sound and provides a fundamental basis for understanding the sonic aspects of music (Chapter 5). From acoustics, further investigations lead to psychoacoustics (a branch of psychophysics; Chapter 7) or how the mind interprets (musical) sound. Practical applications of acoustics are made in architecture and engineering, and the physics of musical instruments leads to ergonomics and biomechanics.

Here are some sample books on the physics of music:

Introduction to the Physics and Psychophysics of Music (Roederer, 1975)
The Physics of Music (Wood, 1980)
Measured Tones: The Interplay of Physics and Music (Johnston, 2002)
The Jazz of Physics (Alexander, 2016)

Contributions from Music

Many musicians would perhaps rather compose, conduct, perform, or analyze music than investigate it scientifically. However, music researchers have made many significant contributions to the understanding of the phenomenon of music in a variety of fields.

Music theorists have led the way in showing how structural elements of music influence our perceptions (Chapter 8). Ethnomusicologists explore the ways all human cultures are musical (Chapter 4). Although in the United States the term "musicology" frequently is used synonymously with the phrase "music history," in fact musicologists are expanding their purview into such interdisciplinary fields as comparative musicology, evolutionary musicology, and cognitive musicology. Those interested in musical performance have investigated a variety of related topics such as the acquisition of motor skills and strategies for learning music (Chapter 13). Music therapists investigate the role of music in a wide variety of client populations, such as cognitively or physically impaired individuals (Chapter 15). Music educators have had a particular involvement with music psychology, in particular emphasizing music-teaching learning processes (Chapter 14).

Here are three representative books in music theory and musicology:

Tonal Pitch Space (Lerdahl, 2001)
Hearing in Time: Psychological Aspects of Musical Meter (London, 2012)
Applied Musicology (Ockelford 2013a)

Here are some examples of music therapy literature:

Music in Therapy (Gaston, 1968)
Music, Health, and Wellbeing (MacDonald, Kreutz, & Mitchell, 2012)
Music Therapy Research, 3rd ed. (Wheeler & Murphy, 2016)

Music educators have made significant contributions to the literature in music psychology:

Sociology: *Advances in Social-Psychology and Music Education Research* (Ward-Steinman, 2011)
Anthropology: *Multicultural Perspectives in Music Education* (Anderson & Campbell, 1996)
Biology: *Neurosciences in Music Pedagogy* (Gruhn & Rauscher, 2007)
Physics: *Improving Music Acoustics for Music Teaching* (Geerdes, 1991)
Psychology: *Music Psychology in Education* (Hallam, 2005)

Taking Figure 1.2 and this brief tour of disciplines into account, let us revisit the definition given previously: Music psychology is a multidisciplinary and interdisciplinary study of music in the human experience. It is natural to wonder why the field is called music *psychology* if so many other disciplines are involved. This is a direct result of the work of Carl Seashore, who is considered by many to be the father of modern music psychology (e.g., Thaut, 2009). Seashore (1938) believed that the proper study of musical behavior encompassed physics, physiology, psychology, anthropology, philosophy, and metaphysics. He said that while the whole field might be called the "science of music," psychologists tend to take over the field for want of a sponsor and so the field has come to be dominated by psychologists and thus called music psychology (pp. 373–375).

Some music psychologists conduct research on very particular and specialized topics, while others try to synthesize all these disparate fields into one coherent view of musical

behavior. The purpose of this introductory book on music psychology is to provide an overview of the field in a way that balances detailed research findings with broad conclusions. So
much relevant literature is now available—with much of it involving sophisticated statistical
analyses or complicated equipment such as brain imaging machines—that in-depth coverage
of all the topics is not possible. However, sweeping generalities without sufficient support
from objective research findings are also insufficient. Throughout the book, numerous references will guide the reader to more details if they are desired.

A VERY BRIEF HISTORY OF MUSIC PSYCHOLOGY

No one has yet written a definitive history of music psychology (but see Gjerdingen, 2002, for
a nice overview). Though such an endeavor is far beyond the scope of this book, the purpose
of this section is to provide a brief glimpse at how the discipline has developed. The scientific
study of music psychology starts at least with the ancient Greeks. Pythagoras (580–500 BC)
was a philosopher and mathematician whose work influenced Plato (427–327 BC) and Aristotle (384–322 BC) (Haar, 2007; Shlain, 1991). He conducted a series of experiments with
a monochord that laid the groundwork for music theory. Over the next millennium, ancient
scholars such as Galen (ca. 131–203), Rhazes (860–923), Ibn Hindu (10th–11th c.), Mai-
monides (1135–1204), and Zarlino (1517–1590) incorporated music as part of their medical
practices (Campbell, 1926; Pratt & Jones, 1987).

   In the seven liberal arts of the ancient Greek educational system, later adopted by the
Romans, scholars included music in the upper quadrivium along with arithmetic, geometry,
and astronomy; in other words, they classified it as a mathematical science. The remaining three disciplines, called the trivium, included grammar, rhetoric, and dialectic. Boethius
(480–524) later described and codified this educational system (Powell, 1979). In *De institutione musica*, Boethius articulated mathematical ideas about music that he based largely
on the work of Pythagoras, Plato, and Aristotle. Music's beauty derived from the purity of
numbers and carried theological implications as well. This treatise was highly influential
throughout the middle ages.

   Modern music psychology began in earnest in the 19th century, particularly in Germany
and England. Graziano and Johnson (2006) presented an in-depth look at the contributions
of Richard Wallaschek that provides insights into the amount of activity underway at that
time. In addition to Wallaschek, German scholars making contributions to music psychology included Gustav Theodor Fechner (1801–1887), Hermann von Helmholtz (1821–1894),
Theodor Billroth (1829–1894), Wilhelm Wundt (1832–1920), Ernst Mach (1838–1916), Carl
Stumpf (1848–1936), Theodor Lipps (1851–1914), and Robert Lach (1874–1958). British
psychologists James Sully (1843–1923) and Edmund Gurney (1847–1888), along with neurologists William Gowers (1845–1915) and John Hughlings Jackson (1835–1911), also made
important contributions. Collectively, these pioneers utilized an interdisciplinary approach
that included the integration of neurology, philosophy and aesthetics, psychology, ethnomusicology, and comparative musicology. Generally, they divided their efforts into *Musikpsychol-
ogie* (music psychology)—emphasizing mental processes and a more global view of musical
behaviors, and *Tonpsychologie* (tone psychology)—focusing more upon physiology, sensation, and the perception of individual musical elements.

   Contemporary with the last of these German and English scholars was Carl Seashore
(1866–1949; Fig. 1.3), who, as was mentioned previously, is credited by many as being the
father of modern music psychology. Born in Sweden, Seashore came to the United States
with his family in 1870 and spent more than 40 years in the Psychology and Physiology

FIGURE 1.3 | Music Psychologist Carl E. Seashore (1866–1949).

departments at the University of Iowa (Matthews, 2007). Seashore is recognized as the father of music psychology for at least the following reasons: (a) He was very productive. A brief biography at his alma mater's website (Gustavus Adolphus College, 2007) indicates that he published 237 books and articles. (b) Beyond his prodigious output was his extremely broad range of interest in important topics such as musical aesthetics, hearing, perception, musical performance, vibrato, and many others. (c) While other psychologists included music among a variety of topics, he tended to concentrate his research on music. (d) He developed the first standardized tests of musical aptitude that were widely used. (e) Finally, and perhaps most importantly, he laid out an interdisciplinary vision for the field and brought many disparate disciplines together under an umbrella called the psychology of music.

AN OVERVIEW OF THE LITERATURE IN MUSIC PSYCHOLOGY

Since the time of Seashore, there has been an incredible growth in the discipline known variously as psychology of music, music psychology, or music cognition. The literature in music psychology is extensive, encompassing as it does anthropology, sociology, psychology, biology, physics, philosophy, and other fields. Appendix A contains a chronological listing of some of the major books in music psychology. This list should not be considered exhaustive in that decisions on which books to include were inevitably subjective. However, the list does give some indication of the breadth of the field and readers are encouraged to peruse it to gain a better understanding of the scope of music psychology.

An examination of citations in Appendix A indicates a steady growth in scholarly output in music psychology. Except for the decade of the 1940s, which saw WWII, there has been a steady increase throughout the last century, with a dramatic increase in the past 30 years (see Figure 1.4).

CONCLUSION

Among music psychologists' many roles, three are interrelated. First, they must conduct rigorous research on specific topics. In so doing, they must use the very best scientific techniques available to derive explicit answers to precise questions. Second, they must place the results of these experiments into a broader context. They must ask, "How do my findings fit in

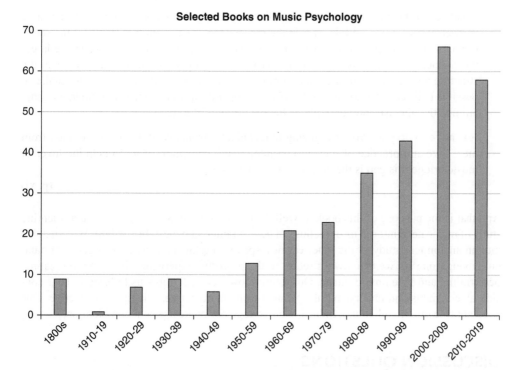

FIGURE 1.4 | Publication of Selected Music Psychology Books From the 1800s to 2019.

with what we already know about this subject?" These first two roles generally continue to alternate, as one outcome of an experiment is a new set of questions, which leads to further research, and the process continues. The third role music psychologists must play is to weave together the disparate threads coming from all the different disciplines into a coherent view of the human musical experience.

Some readers may be concerned that the scientific study of music will destroy or diminish the experience of beauty in music. For anyone with such concerns, it might be helpful to read what Seashore wrote in the preface to his *Psychology of Music* (1938).

> Upon invitation from my Alma Mater to give the so-called academic address at an anniversary celebration last year, I chose as my subject *The Power of Music*. This had been the subject of my class oration when graduating from the academy fifty-one years before. Half a century ago the adolescent lover of music began his oration as follows:

> Music is the medium through which we express our feelings of joy and sorrow, love and patriotism, penitence and praise. It is the charm of the soul, the instrument that lifts mind to higher regions, the gateway into the realms of imagination. It makes the eye to sparkle, the pulse to beat more quickly. It causes emotions to pass over our being like waves over the far-reaching sea.

> That was what the music I lived in meant to me half a century ago. It was the expression of the genuine thrill of young enthusiasm. Considering what music meant to me then and what it means to me now after a life career in the science of music, there comes to me an analogy from astronomy. Then I was a stargazer; now I am an astronomer. Then the youth felt the power of music and gave expression to this feeling in the way he loved and

wondered at the stars before he had studied astronomy. Now the old man feels the same "power of music," but thinks of it in the manner that the astronomer thinks of the starry heavens. Astronomy has revealed a macrocosm, the order of the universe in the large; the science of music has revealed a microcosm, the operation of law and order in the structure and operation of the musical mind. It is a wonderful thing that science makes it possible to discover, measure, and explain the operations of the musical mind in the same attitude that the astronomer explains the operation of the stars.

It is not easy to pass from stargazing to technical astronomy. It is not easy to pass from mere love and practice of music to an intelligent conception of it. To help the lover of music bridge this gap is the purpose of this volume.

(p. xi)

And that is the purpose of this book as well. What Seashore was getting at is that a scientific study of music need not rob us of feelings of awe, wonder, and ineffable delight. We can delve into an anatomical study of the inner ear or a spectrographic analysis of a singer's formant; but having done so, we can always return to the powerful experiences involved in creating, performing, and listening to music. Our return, however, will allow us to bring to bear considerable insights and understandings gleaned from an objective, scientific perspective. One need not rule out the other and, indeed, the two together make a potent combination.

DISCUSSION QUESTIONS

1. Some sample questions that music psychologists investigate are given at the beginning of the chapter. As you begin your study of music psychology, what questions do you have that you would like to have answered? What do you think should be the core questions, that is, what questions should receive the most focused attention from music psychologists?

2. Imagine you were conversing with a friend. How would you describe the field of music psychology?

3. Considering the model of music psychology presented in Figure 1.2, discuss the interrelatedness of the various disciplines that contribute to music psychology.

4. Vibration, sound, and music are placed in the center of the model (Figure 1.2). How do the three relate to each other and why are they in the center?

5. Not every possible discipline relevant to understanding the phenomenon of music is included in the model (Figure 1.2). Consider economics and religion, for example. What contributions might they make? Can you think of other disciplines that might make useful contributions?

6. Although practical and historical reasons were given for how this discipline got its name, it seems odd that a field of study with so many foundational disciplines would be called music *psychology*. Can you think of a better, more appropriate name?

7. What are the advantages and disadvantages of having most of the research in music psychology conducted by individuals who, although they might be accomplished amateur musicians, are not necessarily professionally trained musicians?

8. What observations can you make about the literature in music psychology from perusing Appendix A? Likewise, if you conduct an online search on specific topics in music psychology, what observations can you make about the periodical literature in music psychology?

9. Do you agree with Seashore that the study of music psychology does not need to rob you of the appreciation of musical beauty? Do you think learning about music psychology will enhance or detract from the joy you find in music?
10. Based on the brief overview provided in this chapter, can you speculate on how the study of music psychology might inform your future career? Do you see the types of topics mentioned so far as irrelevant, supplementary, or central to your future in music?

Chapter 2

Philosophical Issues in Music Psychology

WHAT is music? What does music mean? Why do we have music? Philosophers from the ancient Greeks to today have written about the nature and value of music and their ideas have had an enormous impact on music psychology. Chapter 1 contained a brief description of connections between philosophy and music, however, this is an area that is still somewhat under-utilized in much of the music psychology literature. In fact, no one has written a "philosophy of music psychology" book.

The chapter is organized into two main sections. The first section deals with the larger issue of human nature. That is, how does music fit into a general conception of human nature? Is it rather unimportant in the grand scheme of things or is it central to what it means to be a human being? The second section includes five examples of how music philosophy and music psychology interface.

HUMAN AND MUSICAL NATURE

Philosophers have long considered human nature. That is, what is it that makes us human? Are we different from other animals? If we are different, what is it about human beings that makes us unique, and how do our musical behaviors fit into this uniqueness? Is music separate from humanness, or is there evidence to support a view of music as an integral part of human nature?

If we attempt to specify the ways in which human beings are unique and different from other animal species, we must quickly conclude that most, if not all, differences are in degree, not in kind (Gazzaniga, 2008). That is, other animals may possess a particular trait similar to humans, but not to the same extent. For example, if we say that language is a distinctive characteristic of humankind, it is possible to point to communication among dolphins or the sign language learned by apes in certain experiments as rudimentary forms of the same behavior. Or, if we say that social organizations are a human trait, a parallel might be found in the behaviors of bees or ants. We have elaborate rituals connected with death, but elephants have been observed engaging in what might be called a burial ceremony. Music may even have its animal counterpart in whalesong or birdsong—to a degree (see Chapter 3 for more details). However, it is the *degree* of human involvement in such behaviors as language, social organizations, rituals, and music that separates us from other animals.

If human beings are different from animals primarily in degree and not necessarily in kind of behaviors, how then can we be described? What is the nature of human nature? Such a question has engaged philosophers, scientists, and artists for centuries and will not be answered completely in these pages. However, in order to set the stage for subsequent discussions, ten ways in which human beings are unique will be introduced. Following the more general discussion, some brief remarks about the relationship of music to each unique trait will be made. The ten topics are: biological differences, adaptability, cultural development, symbolic behaviors, love, religion, play, technology, knowledge, and aesthetic sensitivity. Throughout this section, citations are kept to a minimum, as these topics will be elaborated upon in subsequent chapters.

Biological Differences

Biologically, humans are a distinct species, although the genetic variance between great apes and us is exceedingly small (Varki & Gagneux, 2017). Biological differences between us and other animals have consequences. For example, while we have a larynx, birds have a syrinx (Fig. 2.1), resulting in substantial disparities in our vocalizations. Human beings also differ from other animals in the degree to which our behavior is controlled by inborn instructions. We inherit reflexes such as eye blink and startle responses, basic expressive responses such as smiling, and life-sustaining actions such as suckling and swallowing. However, more complex behavior patterns are learned. We do inherit reflexes and many predispositions, such as personality traits, that influence our behaviors but not instincts, if they are defined as relatively complex patterns of behavior that are essentially not modifiable over time (Lefrançois, 2006).

Anatomical variations and relative freedom from instincts notwithstanding, the single most important difference between humans and other animals is our brain power. Those behaviors that make us distinctively human—language, art, religion, technology, and so on—are all generated from an enormous reservoir of potential. We start life with a voracious appetite for learning and there seem to be few limitations on what or how much might be learned. Thus, it is our human biological potential that makes music possible. We are musical creatures because of our physical and mental make-up.

Adaptability

Most animals have a physical specialty—jaguars have blinding speed and eagles have incredible eyesight. In contrast, human beings are mental specialists. In order to survive, we came to

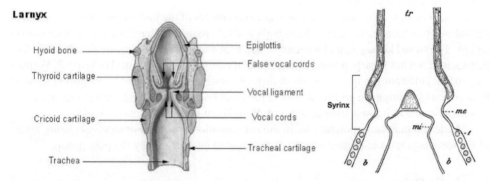

FIGURE 2.1 | Larynx and Syrinx. Because a syrinx (right panel) is located where the trachea (*tr*) branches into two bronchial tubes (*b*) that connect to the lungs, birds can localize the sound on either side, alternate back and forth between two sounds rapidly, or even produce two sounds at once. air flowing through the syrinx vibrates the external (*me*) and internal (*mi*) tympanic membranes, producing sound.

rely on quick wits and an ability to gain an advantage primarily through mental means, rather than through a particular physical skill.

Tremendous intellectual capabilities, combined with a lack of predetermined behavior patterns and a lack of reliance on a specific physical trait have given us freedoms that no other animals have. We have a freedom to become or to do nearly anything that we can conceive. We have explored every possible climate—from deserts to arctic regions, from the depths of oceans to outer space. While other animals are destined to lead a lifestyle appropriate for their species, we have adapted ourselves to live as nomads, nuns, and whalers.

Adaptability is a hallmark of our artistic behaviors, too. Our plasticity has led us to create sand paintings and stained-glass windows, limericks and novels, square dances and grand ballet, huge stone monuments and miniature ivory carvings. We have sitars, gamelan orchestras, tubas, and panpipes. We have the musical background to 15-second television commercials and four-hour Chinese operas. We are in art, as in all things, highly adaptable creatures.

Cultural Development

Another of the clearly distinguishing marks of humanity is our reliance on cultural development. Biological evolution originally shaped human beings, however, around 35,000 years ago we began to override the system. We did this by changing our environment rather than having it change us (Dubos, 1974). Animals trying to exist in arctic climates developed various protective devices to combat the frigid temperatures, such as heavy fur coats and thick layers of blubber. Humans living in the same situation did not grow thick coverings of hair (though they did undergo some minor changes, such as the development of a slightly thicker layer of subcutaneous fat). Rather, they modified the environment; they created parkas, igloos, and eventually heaters to survive the bitter cold. It should be remembered, however, that biological evolutionary processes are still active, as witnessed in current global climate changes and their potential impact on human behavior (Muehlenbein, 2015).

Human culture includes all of our socially transmitted behavior patterns. Thus, our political, social, educational, economic, and religious institutions are a part of culture, as are all other products of human thought (Portin, 2015; Richerson & Boyd, 2008). Also included in every culture are ways of enriching the sensory environment. We modify and experiment with sights, sounds, tastes, smells, and textures. This interaction with the sensory environment leads to art, a primary aspect of culture.

Human beings are automatically biological members of the human race but must learn to behave as other humans do. Learning to walk and talk requires interactions with other human beings. The stored knowledge of a society allows each individual to become enculturated into that society. Art has clearly played a major role in cultural development (Hodgson & Verpooten, 2015). Different groups of people in different times and places can be identified through their artworks. Studying a group's artworks provides unique insights into its character. In fact, it is not possible to know a tribe or nation fully without considering its artworks.

Music can play an important role in the enculturation process. For example, being aware of the top songs is an important way for a teenager to be accepted by the peer group.

Symbolic Behaviors

One readily identifiable mark of human uniqueness is our highly developed capacity for symbolic behavior. Language, for example, makes it possible for us to communicate a wealth of ideas—from the functionality of the phone book to the imagery of poetry. However, while language is indispensable to human lifestyles, it is, nonetheless, inadequate for expressing the full range of human thought and feeling.

In addition to language, we have developed a broad range of nonverbal symbolic behaviors, including mathematical symbols and computer languages, body language, and art. Symbols such as hairstyle, body adornments, and mode of dress can communicate an enormous amount of information about an individual or a group of people. We often express religious tenets in a powerful way through symbols, such as the Jewish star or the Christian cross. Nonverbal forms of communication would be unnecessary if we could express everything we wanted to with words. However, nonverbal communication not only supplements and extends verbal communication, as in the use of gesticulations while speaking, but also provides for distinct modes of expression.

Visual arts provide ways of knowing and feeling that are not possible through any other means. What we gain through art can be discussed, analyzed, or shared verbally, but cannot be experienced verbally. Thus, rock carvings, totem poles, and portraits are artistic symbols that give humankind tremendously powerful means of communicating and sharing. Many forms of music are symbolic also, as we express our deepest fears, griefs, and joys.

Love

Perhaps more than any other attribute thus far discussed, love demonstrates the truth of an earlier statement: Differences between humans and other animals are those of degree more than of kind. Any animal observer can certainly attest to the fact of loving behaviors among animals. Thus, rather than speculate on whether human beings love more than do other animals, it suffices to say that human beings have a tremendous need to love and to be loved.

In fact, love is so important to human beings that without it we suffer severe physical and psychological consequences. Many illnesses can be traced to dysfunctions in the giving and receiving of love. Because it is so crucial to us, we have developed many ways of sharing and expressing love. We murmur terms of endearment and struggle to articulate inner feelings in poetic verse. The sense of touch is vitally important in our expressions of love. Music, too, is an often-used vehicle.

From the singing of lullabies to the crooning of love ballads, from the use of funeral dirges and wedding songs, music is a powerful means of communicating love from one to another. Alma maters, national anthems, and hymns are examples of ways we use music to express love of school and friends, love of country, and love of a deity.

Play

Human beings spend enormous amounts of time engaging in activities that do not seem at first glance to be necessary for biological survival. We could list many activities under the generic term "play": athletic contests, reading, watching television, daydreaming, and visiting with one another are just a few examples.

Celebrations are a formalized style of play. All over the world, human beings find almost any excuse to celebrate. Besides obvious celebrations such as birthdays, weddings, and religious holidays, we celebrate the coming of spring, important battles, and the gathering of the harvest. Celebrations are very much a part of human nature; likewise, singing and dancing are integral parts of celebrations. Indeed, it is difficult to think of celebrations that have no music.

That art and celebrations are interrelated is supportive of a particular viewpoint of the nature of art. In this view, art is a type of creative play (Pfeiffer, 1969). Human beings are quite naturally intrigued by the surprise, adventure, and experimentation that come with the manipulation of objects, ideas, and sensory materials. Our very creativity is born of this sense of adventure and it brings us pleasure. In music, manipulating and experimenting with sounds is at the root of compositional activity and improvisation.

Humor is a special kind of play. Whether physical comedy as in slapstick, or mental humor as in puns, we take great delight in twists and variations on the expected. There are many pieces of music, such as Mozart's *Musical Joke*, in which the unexpected likewise is intended to elicit a mirthful response.

Religion

Clearly, we humans are marked by our spiritual nature. The need to consider a power beyond our own is so universal that it is deeply ingrained in human nature. While each of us must wrestle with the eternal questions—Who put us here? Why are we here? What is the meaning of life?—societies have deemed the issues important enough that certain members of the community are assigned responsibility for such matters. Priest, shaman, rabbi, prophet, pastor, monk, muezzin—all pursue answers to spiritual questions. Religious practices have been with us for a long time. The Neanderthals left behind artifacts connected with burial rituals that indicate some sense of concern for the spirits of the dead perhaps as early as 120,000 years ago (Petit, 2011). Even from the beginnings, so far as we have any knowledge of it, and certainly in nearly all the practices since then, music has been a part of religious worship. This is so because language is inadequate to express fully our spiritual feelings; music can take us beyond the confines of words. Perhaps music and religion are so intertwined because both are concerned primarily with internal feelings rather than external facts. Whatever the reasons, religious beliefs and the expression of these beliefs through music are a ubiquitous fact of human nature (Fig. 2.2).

Technology

From the time we learned to control and use fire to the time of computerization, humankind has been most conspicuous by our technological inventions. We are a tool-making species and we seem always to be seeking ways to do a task easier, faster, better. Tools have extended our capabilities far beyond our physical limitations. Certain animals have been observed using tools—such as chimpanzees using a stick to dig termites from a mound (Fuentes, 2018)—but

FIGURE 2.2 | Hindu Musicians and a Gospel Choir. Nearly all worship traditions utilize music as an expression of faith.

in keeping with the theme of this chapter, it is a matter of degree, not necessarily the kind of behavior that distinguishes humans.

It is entirely resonant with our nature that we extend our toolmaking into other areas of life than work. Consider athletics, for example; we are constantly improving athletic "tools" that, within the rules, will give us an edge on the competition. Tools are used in music, too. In fact, all instruments are tools used to create sounds beyond the scope of the human voice (Vandervert, 2016).

There is another connection between art and tools. Tools have always been made with an eye to something beyond functional design. Spear points and axe handles are created with attention to shape. Jugs—tools for carrying water—are shaped in a manner and with a flair that are not necessary for utilitarian purposes but seem to be necessary for human pleasure. Farb (1978) even states explicitly that, "the great advances in technology would obviously have been impossible without the human urge to explore new directions in artistic creativity" (p. 75).

Music technology is an obvious aspect of the modern music landscape as computer software and electronic instruments such as synthesizers and drum machines, sequencers, and so on are widely used. As one example, consider that electronic music technologies are so prevalent in the pit orchestras for musicals that the number of players has been drastically reduced. The most recent union contract for Broadway theaters, lasting until 2019, stipulates that the minimum number of musicians hired ranges from 3–19, depending on the particular theater (Broadway Memorandum of Agreement, 2016–2019). In addition, a joint labor-management committee meets quarterly to discuss electronic music technologies as they pertain to the life of Broadway musicians.

Aesthetic Sensitivity

By nature, human beings are predisposed to seek out and to create beauty. The variety of ways we have done so is nothing short of staggering. We have decorated our own bodies in nearly every way conceivable (though future generations will find still more ways). What we have done to our bodies we have done to clothes, food, and dwellings. Beyond the decoration of our surroundings, human beings have always and everywhere explored every mode of sensory experience with an aesthetic sensitivity that is supremely characteristic of our species.

The manipulation of sound, sight, space, and movement—the arts—has given us tremendous insights into the human condition and brought us much pleasure in the process. To be human is to have the potential of perceiving and responding to artistic experiences with a depth of feeling. We are as much aesthetic creatures as we are physical, social, intellectual, emotional, and religious beings. As we will explore in Chapter 4, various cultural groups place different emphases on aesthetic musical experiences, some hardly acknowledging them at all and others making them central to communal life.

Knowledge

One of the unique traits of humankind is a natural propensity for seeking knowledge. Conceptions of the human infant as a *tabula rasa* (blank slate) or as a passive organism only learning from interactions with the environment are wrong. We are active seekers of knowledge. It is basic to human nature to be curious, to wonder, to explore, to discover.

We gain knowledge through all the sense modalities. We learn about our world by touch; for the blind, this becomes an important avenue of information. Babies, in particular, explore their world through taste; everything goes immediately to the mouth. Smelling may seem like a less important means of gathering knowledge, but we can "know" something about another person through her perfume or the hint of woodworking on his clothes. Because the olfactory lobes are in close proximity to the site of long-term memory storage, odors often trigger strong remembrances of past events or places. Vision and hearing are also primary means of gathering knowledge.

We learn some of the first things we know through hearing. Our sense of hearing begins to function in the last few months of fetal development and babies recognize the sounds of their mother's voice within a few days, if not sooner. What the baby "knows" about mother is not facts, but feelings—feelings associated with security and pleasure. This is an important concept to remember—that knowledge involves far more than facts. Because some philosophers have recognized music as a special way of knowing, this notion is explored in more detail in a following section.

These, then, are some of the ways we are unique. While this is but a brief introduction, the significant role that music plays in human nature should already be apparent. Music is not a trivial, extraneous aspect of being human; rather, musicality is at the core of what it means to be human. Based on this premise, we now consider five examples of how music philosophy influences music psychology: general philosophical approaches, the science of beauty, a philosophical paradigm shift in music psychology, music as a way of knowing, and music psychology's encroachment on music philosophy's territory.

THE INTERFACE OF MUSIC PHILOSOPHY AND MUSIC PSYCHOLOGY

General Philosophical Approaches

Philosophers have developed hundreds of competing ideas over the several thousand years that they have been writing about music (Hodges, 2017). Many of them are exceedingly complex and difficult to understand. Reducing philosophical views on music to a few paragraphs removes the richness and variety from a broadly diverse field. Nevertheless, for the purposes of this chapter, it is worthwhile to recognize four main approaches to the nature, meaning, and value of music—absolutism, referentialism, formalism, and expressionism that can be combined into three main positions. We will then see how these positions influence music psychologists.

Absolutists believe that the meaning of music resides exclusively within the music itself. The focus of attention is on relationships among the musical elements of melody, rhythm, harmony, form, and so on. Referentialists find meaning in extramusical referents. That is, music has value as it points to images, actions, emotions, and other things outside the music. Absolute and referential meanings can coexist in the same musical experience; the difference is on which aspect is primary. Absolutists recognize that there may be extramusical referents, but for them these external associations are irrelevant or secondary. Likewise, referentialists recognize the necessity of internal musical processes, but these have meaning only to the degree that they refer to something of value outside the music.

Formalists argue that one derives meaning through an understanding of the creative musical processes within the music and that this musical meaning is primarily intellectual or cognitive. Expressionists believe that the value of music comes from its expression of human feelings and emotions. Formalists are absolutists, in that both find meaning within the music itself (see Table 2.1). Expressionists can be either absolutists or referentialists. An absolute

TABLE 2.1 | Simplified Chart of Music Philosophies.

	Absolutism (meaning is found within the music itself)	Referentialism (meaning is found in extramusical referents)
Formalism (meaning is in musical relationships and is primarily intellectual)	**Absolute Formalism** (meaning is found in the music and is primarily intellectual)	*
Expressionism (meaning is found in the expression of human feelings)	**Absolute Expressionism** (meaning is found in external referents expressed in and through the music)	**Referential Expressionism** (meaning derives from expressiveness of external referents)

*There is no position labeled referential formalism because the two are antithetical; formalists find meaning in the music itself and referentialists find it outside the music. Although Meyer uses the term referential expressionism (1956, p. 3), the far more commonly used term is simply expressionism.

expressionist finds value in expressiveness derived from internal musical processes; a referential expressionist derives value from expressiveness that arises from external associations.

From these viewpoints, philosophers have derived three main positions: absolute formalism, absolute expressionism, and referentialism. Although each is illustrated in the following discussion with a separate example, it is important to note that the music does not determine the philosophical position. Rather, the individual adopts a philosophical position that can be applied to all music (at least of a particular style such as classical music).

- *Absolute Formalism.* Certain music is valued for the clarity of its formal structure. Considering the Bach *Goldberg Variations* from this position, the focus is on the music and in the listener's recognition and appreciation of interrelationships among the different voices. The response is more intellectual than feelingful. Thus, Glenn Gould (1956) described one section as counterpoint "in which a blunt rusticity disguises an urbane maze of *stretti*" (p. 6).
- *Absolute Expressionism.* Proponents of this viewpoint maintain the focus on the music but place more value on its expressive nature as expressed in and through the music. Here's how Duke Ellington described a shift in style when Charlie Parker and Dizzy Gillespie started playing very difficult, complex, and rapid passages: "Because of the speed of execution, the old tonal values were sacrificed (it was no longer possible to play with the former expressive vibrato), and the new music had a shrill, cooler sound. Soon it was fashionable to play 'cool' rather than 'hot'" (Ellington, 1973, p. 421).
- *Referentialism.* In this position, the shift is away from the music and onto what the music points to outside itself. After writing *Where Were You (When the World Stopped Turning)* in response to the terrorist attacks of September 11, 2001, Alan Jackson was quoted as saying, "The song is really a lot of those emotions and things that I witnessed on television and through other people. Those were real heartbreaking emotions" (Mansfield, 2002).

Rather than taking separate exemplars of each viewpoint, another way is to consider the same piece of music from all three perspectives. Let us take William Dawson's *Negro Folk Symphony* (1964). Because Dawson wished to write authentic folk music in a symphonic format (Southern, 1975), one could find the primary value of this work to be in the musical relationships and compositional techniques (absolute formalism position). Later, following a trip to West Africa, he added African musical traits to the spiritual and jazz aspects (Baptiste, 2007), so one could focus on the expressive nature of the music as found in the melodies, harmonies, and rhythms (absolute expressionism). Finally, one could be moved primarily by the external references to the black experience of slavery in America (referentialism). In closing this section, it should be noted that the brevity of presentation should be taken as only a hint of the richness, complexity, and profundity of numerous philosophies of music and that there are numerous additional viewpoints such as symbolism, phenomenology, pragmatism, social philosophy, praxialism, and postmodernism. Nevertheless, these brief descriptions should allow us to proceed with connections to music psychology.

Leonard Meyer provided an excellent model of how philosophical views can shape or inform music psychology. At the very outset of *Emotion and Meaning in Music* (1956), he presented brief discussions of the meaning of music in terms of the positions just described. He took the position that (absolute) formalist and absolute expressionist views could coexist; "thinking and feeling need not be viewed as polar opposites but as different manifestations of a single psychological process" (1956, p. 39). By eliminating the referentialist position, Meyer staked a claim that the meaning of music is found in a focus on the music itself. Whether or not one agrees with Meyer, at least he has made his position clear. One must then read and understand his work in this context.

Alf Gabrielsson (2009) also began one of his chapters from a philosophical stance. Before discussing the relationship between musical structure and perceived expression, he reviewed absolutism and referentialism. For his particular purposes, the focus was on referential meanings. The concern of the moment is not that Meyer wrote from an absolutist position and that Gabrielsson wrote from a referentialist perspective. Rather, what is to be noted is that these are two examples of music psychologists who situated their work within a philosophical context. Ideally, all music psychologists would be as explicit in situating their work within a philosophical framework.

The Science of Beauty

One of the primary concerns of music psychologists has been *aesthetics*, or the particular branch of philosophy that deals with art (Lacey, 1990). That is, they are interested in whether there are underlying explanations for why listeners find some music appealing. Are there logical principles that undergird experiences of beauty in music and our emotional responses to it?

Experimental Aesthetics In 1876, Gustav Fechner, building on ideas that can be traced back to Plato, wrote a book that established experimental aesthetics as the second oldest topic in experimental psychology (North & Hargreaves, 1997a). Later, Carl Seashore wrote a book entitled *In Search of Beauty, a Scientific Approach to Musical Esthetics* (1947). More than 25 years after that, Daniel Berlyne, another influential figure in this field, wrote two influential books on the science of beauty: *Aesthetics and Psychobiology* (1971) and *Studies in the New Experimental Aesthetics* (1974). The subtitle for the second book speaks clearly to the issue of a scientific approach toward aesthetic philosophy: *Steps Toward an Objective Psychology of Aesthetic Appreciation*. As we will see later in this chapter, neuroscientists are now involved in what is called neuroaesthetics.

There is a considerable amount of literature beyond Berlyne's pioneering work. For example, North and Hargreaves (1997a) wrote a chapter entitled *Experimental Aesthetics and Everyday Music Listening* (also see Chapter 3 in North & Hargreaves, 2008) and Russell

(1986) wrote an article entitled *Experimental Aesthetics of Popular Music Recordings: Pleasingness, Familiarity and Chart Performance*. There is even a journal entitled *Empirical Studies of the Arts*. Because the work of Berlyne and others is discussed subsequently (see Chapter 11), a detailed examination will not be made at this point. Suffice it to say, however, that music psychologists have studied at least certain aspects of the aesthetic experience in order to bring us to a deeper level of understanding.

The Golden Mean and Mathematical Influences. One of the mathematical principles that provides a rational explanation for beauty is the *Fibonacci Series*. Leonardo Pisano (1170–1250?) is credited with discovering this mathematical principle (Kramer, 1973; Powell, 1979). The Fibonacci Series is 0, 1, 1, 2, 3, 5, 8, 13, 21, 34, 55. . . . Starting with 0 and 1, each subsequent number is obtained by adding the two previous numbers; thus, $0+1=1$, $1+1=2$, $1+2=3$, $2+3=5$, and so on. If you continue this series, the ratios derived by dividing any number by the one following gradually center around 0.618 or what is known as the *golden mean*.

In nature, we find that spirals found in conch shells are derived from the Fibonacci series (Rath & Naik, 2005; see Fig. 2.3); the number and arrangement of flowers often follow the series, for example in plants with two groups of three petals each or poppy seeds with 13 ridges, sunflowers with 55 and 89 spirals, and so on (Mitchison, 1977). The golden mean is found in architecture (McWhinnie, 1989), such as the Parthenon in Athens, the Pantheon in Rome, and the United Nations in New York. Similar ratios are found in numerous paintings, as many of da Vinci's works are based on them, along with paintings by Seurat, Mondrian, and other modern artists (McWhinnie, 1986). In music, the proportions of a violin follow the Fibonacci series, as luthiers have employed ratios in making violins much as architects have done in designing buildings.

Many composers have specifically used the golden mean in their compositions, as the climax frequently comes roughly two-thirds through the movement. Sandresky (1981) addressed the use of the golden mean by Dufay in three motets written in 1420, 1431, and 1453. All three employ a tenor (the primary melody) derived from the same scheme, a two-part cantus firmus based on the number 13. Although these compositions range over a span of 33 years, all three have important moments (e.g., a unique motive, entry of the cantus firmus, a cadence, or some definitive sign) to designate the golden mean. Sandresky presented considerable analytic data on the use of Fibonacci numbers as underlying structural elements in the motets. In similar fashion, Powell (1979) provided elaborate mathematical and geometric

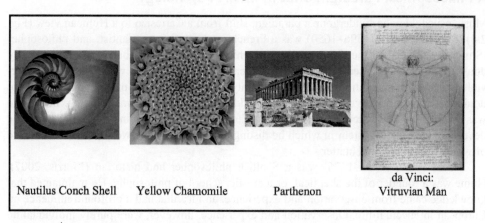

Nautilus Conch Shell   Yellow Chamomile   Parthenon   da Vinci: Vitruvian Man

FIGURE 2.3 | Fibonacci Patterns. Examples can be found in nature, architecture, and art.

explanations for the Fibonacci series and Golden Mean in motets by de la Halle, Machaut, and Dufay. He further stated that Boethius (480–524) provided mathematical explanations in his *De institutione musica* and that any well-educated Middle Ages or Renaissance composer could have known about these principles.

Many composers since the Middle Ages have employed the Fibonacci series and the golden mean in their compositions, including Bach, Mozart, Beethoven, and Chopin. For example, in the *Fugue in d minor, BWV 565*, Bach divided the seven interludes such that while two are divided in halves, the rest are divided within 0.02% and 0.7% of the golden mean (Voloshinov, 1996). This practice has continued with modern composers. In discussing the music of Bartok, Kramer (1973), referring to earlier work by Lendvai, stated that in the *Sonata for Two Pianos and Percussion*:

> the golden mean is evident from the largest level [the whole piece is 6432 eighth-note beats long, divided at its golden mean into the first movement (3974) and the second plus third movements $(771 + 1687 = 2458)$] down to the smallest level (the 17-bar introduction is elaborately subdivided on many levels according to golden mean ratios).
>
> (p. 119)

There are numerous examples of music composed with mathematical models other than the golden mean. Hofstadter (1979) wrote a Pulitzer Prize winning book on relationships among music by Bach, graphic drawings by Escher, and mathematical proofs by Gödel. Rothgeb (1966) discussed mathematical principles underlying twelve-tone music. In a book on connections between music and mathematics, Rothstein (2006) included a chapter on the pursuit of beauty, and the composer Xenakis (1992) included a chapter on philosophy in a book on mathematics and composition. Mathematics and geometry can be used to explain and understand certain aspects of music (Ashton, 2003; Benson, 2006; Hall, 2008).

The point of this discussion is not to suggest that all music is composed rigidly according to mathematical formulas. Rather, it reveals some of the rational principles that undergird musical compositions. While some composers may have used the golden mean or other mathematical algorithms intentionally (e.g., serialism), other composers may have come to the notion more intuitively. How strongly these ideas influence music perception and cognition has yet to be explicated fully by music psychologists.

A Philosophical Paradigm Shift in Music Psychology

Music psychology has undergone a paradigm shift from a Cartesian to a Humean view (Fig. 2.4). René Descartes (1596–1650) was a French mathematician, scientist, and philosopher (Smith, 2007). Called the father of modern philosophy, Descartes began by methodically doubting knowledge based on authority, the senses, and reason. He was in favor of observations and experimentation and found certainty in the observation that although he might doubt the existence of everything else, he could not doubt that he was thinking. In this, he was assured that he existed. Expressed in the famous statement "I think, therefore I am", he developed a dualistic system in which he distinguished radically between mind, the essence of which is thinking, and matter.

David Hume (1711–1776) was a Scottish philosopher and historian (Morris, 2007). Hume was a founder of the skeptical, or agnostic, school of philosophy. He maintained that knowledge came from observation and experience, an idea that had a profound influence on European intellectual life. Observation and experience, however, were purely individual he insisted. A person's perceptions of objects were just that—perceptions. No underlying reality

FIGURE 2.4 | Philosophers René Descartes and David Hume.

could ever be proved, because every individual's perceptions are unique—even if they agree with someone else's. The "someone else" is also only a perception of the senses.

In the Cartesian view, there is only one Truth and this Truth lies external to human perception. In the Humean view, there are many truths; each person constructs his or her own reality or truth. Campbell and Heller (1980) wrote eloquently about how adopting a Cartesian or Humean viewpoint influences the outcome of music psychology experiments. Suppose, for example, an experiment is being conducted in which listeners are asked to determine whether an instrumentalist is in-tune, sharp, or flat relative to a standard tone. From a Cartesian viewpoint, there is a correct answer that can be determined by a machine (e.g., an electronic tuner); truth is an external, objective reality. If a listener were to judge a tone as sharp while the tuner measured it as flat, the listener would then be "wrong" according to a Cartesian view. From a Humean viewpoint on the other hand, a listener's judgment is given an equivalent status to the readout from the tuner. In fact, in several experiments, listeners actually preferred a solo performance sharp relative to the accompaniment (e.g., Madsen & Geringer, 1976).

According to the Humean view, the inner, subjective reality of the listener is an equivalent truth to external, objective reality. There are as many "truths" as there are listeners, as each has his/her own perceptual reality. There are many music psychology experiments in which there are discrepancies between internal/subjective perceptions and external/objective measurements. How the results are viewed depends upon the philosophical perspective taken. Campbell and Heller (1980) argue that earlier music psychology research was dominated by a Cartesian view but that contemporary researchers should adopt a Humean view. They list at least four advantages of this paradigm shift:

1. As indicated previously, varying realities are seen as equivalent rather than placed on an "objective-subjective" hierarchy.
2. The basis of human music making is seen as evocation rather than message transmission.
3. Implicit rules shared by performers and listeners are used as models of music learning, perception, and development.
4. Performer initiated information that is not notated and is thus decoded on the basis of implicit rules is given equal status to notated information.

Can music exist independent of human apprehension of the sounds? Philosophers have long discussed this notion, phrased and rephrased in many different ways. To the extent that music is a phenomenon of the human mind, adopting a Humean viewpoint—recognizing the validity of human perceptions—is critical to the advancement of the work of music psychology.

Music as a Way of Knowing

Langer (1967, 1972, 1982) and other philosophers have posited that music is a special way of gaining insights into the human condition. Data from cognitive neuroscience substantiates music as a neural system that is dissociated at least partially from other neural systems such as language or mathematics. Another way to characterize this notion is to think of music as a human knowledge system. A *knowledge system* is a mode of sharing, expressing, understanding, and knowing information about our inner and outer worlds and for understanding relationships within and between the two. All animals rely on knowledge systems to function in the environment; the term *human* applied to knowledge systems simply designates the particular ways of knowing that characterize human beings.

The musical knowledge system is a way of knowing that arises from innate brain structures and represents a unique means of functioning in the environment that is no better or worse than that provided by other knowledge systems. All human beings, with the exception of those born with limitations in music processing skills (see Chapter 9), are endowed with an ability to process the music of their culture. However, individuals vary in their facility of operating within musical systems. Although it is convenient to discuss each knowledge system separately, in reality there are many interconnections. Music, in fact, has rich connections with other knowledge systems; multiple connections among many of the knowledge systems can be seen in an experience such as opera that involves a combination of music, words, costumes, staging, movement, dance, and an exploration of inter- and intrapersonal relationships.

Each human being, then, has built-in systems for knowing his or her inner and outer worlds. Through these systems one can discover, understand, share, and express an infinite variety of thoughts and feelings. Each knowledge system may be more or less appropriate for dealing with a particular thought or feeling. For example, joy can be known in a variety of ways through the linguistic, musical, spatial, bodily, and personal knowledge systems but perhaps less so through the mathematical knowledge system. One might experience joy at solving a difficult mathematical problem, but the notion of logically deducing the constituents of joy or of representing joy by a mathematical formula seems improbable. Mathematics takes center stage, however, when the central issue is space and time as they relate to an understanding of the universe.

If one assumes agreement on the foregoing, that music does indeed represent a knowledge system, it then becomes legitimate to ask: What does one know, understand, share, or express through music? Most societies recognize and understand what is to be gained through language and mathematics knowledge systems; a widely accepted notion that a basic education consists of reading, writing, and arithmetic is but one example. But, what is gained through music?

Before presenting a partial list of possibilities, two brief caveats must be stated at this point: (1) The given list is not meant to be exhaustive; such an exercise would be tedious and unnecessary. (2) While it is convenient to discuss each item separately, there is, of course, a significant amount of intertwining. Ten items are presented here merely for the purposes of stimulating thinking; these represent only a few of the things we know, discover, understand, experience, share, or express through music:

1. *Feelings.* Central to any discussion of music as a knowledge system must be the idea of feelings. From one end of the continuum dealing with vague, unlabeled moods to the other end dealing with crystallized emotions such as grief or joy, music is connected intrinsically with feelings.
2. *Aesthetic experiences.* Human beings often seek out beauty and find pleasure in their innate responsiveness to the organized sounds that we call music.
3. *The ineffable.* Precisely because music is a nonverbal form of expression, it is a powerful means to express or to know that which is difficult or impossible to put into words. Love and spiritual awareness are two of the most common human experiences that are frequently known through music.
4. *Thoughts.* Musical thought is just as viable as linguistic, mathematical, or visual thought. It can be a potent means of expressing ideas and of knowing truth.
5. *Structure.* Closely allied to the idea of thinking is structure. The human mind seeks patterns, structure, order, and logic. Music provides a unique way of structuring sounds across time, as well as a providing a means of structuring the expression of thoughts, feelings, and human experience.
6. *Time and space.* Time and space are elemental ingredients of the universe. All human knowledge systems provide ways of dealing with time and space. As indicated in number 5, music is a means of organizing sounds across time. Although music occurs in *real* time, it deals more with *felt* time. Music is a primary means of experiencing space in time. Marching bands, music in dance, and antiphonal choral performances are only three examples.
7. *Self-knowledge.* Maslow's (1968) description of the role of music in intrinsic, and especially peak, learning experiences provides an excellent model for how music allows for insights into our private, inner worlds.
8. *Self-identity.* Many gain their sense of self through a variety of musical activities and experiences.
9. *Group knowledge and identity.* Group knowledge through music can be divided into two types of experiences: (a) Music helps cement the bonding of those members of a group—insiders—who share common ideas, beliefs, and behaviors. (b) Music helps isolate and separate outsiders from insiders. Group identity through music is both inclusive and exclusive.
10. *Healing and wholeness.* From more specific applications of music in therapy and medicine to more general interactions, music has profound effects on human beings. Music provides a vehicle for the integration of body, mind, and spirit.

All ten of these, and the many others that could be listed, can be subsumed under the idea that music provides knowledge of the human condition, that is, the condition of being human.

Tait and Haack (1984) used a simpler framework when they characterized the human experience as one of thinking, feeling, and sharing. One aspect of being human is that while we may experience common thoughts and feelings, no one else can share in another person's unique inner world. Thus, while all may experience loneliness, exultation, anger, or grief, each person's experience is unique. The power of music, and the other arts as well, is that it allows us to share, to express, to discover, to understand, in short, to know grief in a way that encompasses the notion of corporate grief, while speaking directly to our own personal, private sense of grief. Reimer (1989) characterized this way of knowing by saying that music provides knowledge *of* grief not knowledge *about* grief.

Bruner (1969) and Eisner (1985) wrote about art as a mode of knowing and perhaps the most important thing we can learn through music is about ourselves and about all of human nature. Throughout this book, we will explore evidence provided by music psychologists that music is an important way of knowing.

Is Music Psychology Encroaching on Music Philosophy's Territory?

After everything we have covered in this chapter, it would be extreme to suggest that music psychology can replace music philosophy. Nevertheless, there are some hints here and there that music psychologists may be more effective in answering some questions that have traditionally been answered by music philosophers. Clearly not everyone would agree—most especially philosophers!—but at the very least, data from music psychology experiments can inform philosophical thinking. Consider five examples:

1. *Music cognition.* As previously stated, countless experiments have demonstrated that a host of neural networks subserve musical processing and behaviors. We are born with musical capacities; as newborns we can process and respond to music appropriately even within a few hours of birth (Perani et al., 2010; Stefanics, 2009). While some neural networks are shared with other cognitive domains such as language, there are also distinctive musical networks (Norman-Haignere, Kanwisher, & McDermott, 2015). Thus, while philosophers have long held that musicality is a human birthright, music psychologists are demonstrating that fact scientifically (see Chapter 9 for additional details).

2. *Emotion.* As you read earlier in this chapter, there is a schism between those philosophers who find more value in intellectual understandings of music (formalists) and those who value the emotional expression of music (expressionists). Music psychologists have conducted numerous experiments on emotional responses to music. They have identified cognitivist (perception without feeling) and emotivist (feeling musical emotions) positions (Juslin, Liljeström, Västfjäll, & Lundqvist, 2010). While research is ongoing, a more nuanced understanding is developing, involving psychophysiological (e.g., heart rate changes) and brain responses. We will explore this is in some detail in Chapter 10.

3. *Beauty.* For centuries, philosophers considered beauty a central aspect of aesthetic experience. Recently, however, that position has changed for some who contend that the notion of beauty is outmoded, unnecessary, and irrelevant. For example, Ludwig Wittgenstein (1967) said, "It is remarkable that in real life, when aesthetic judgments are made, aesthetic adjectives such as 'beautiful', 'fine', etc. play hardly any role at all" (p. 3). In direct contrast, many music psychology experiments have demonstrated that beauty remains a very important concept in aesthetic experiences for most people (Istók, 2009).

4. *Aesthetics.* Although aesthetic experiences have long been important in music philosophy, more recently there are some who consider aesthetic experiences unnecessary (e.g., Regelski, 2005). Furthermore, there are those who feel that neuroscience has nothing to offer in the way of explaining aesthetic experiences to art (e.g., Tallis, 2008). In contrast, the term "neuroaesthetics" refers to how we can account for aesthetic experiences in the brain (Brattico, 2019; Hodges, 2016b) and many experiments support the notion of aesthetic experiences (e.g., Brattico, Bogert, & Jacobsen, 2013; Sachs, Ellis, Schlaug, & Loui, 2016; Trost, Ethofer, Zentner, & Vuillemumier, 2012). Recall, too, the previous contributions from experimental psychology. While there is a long way yet to go in having

a full scientific explanation, Huron (2009) stated that, "cognitive neuroscience is poised to overtake philosophical aesthetics: rather than *influencing* aesthetic philosophy, aesthetic philosophy is receding to a sideline 'advisory' role, while cognitive science takes an unaccustomed leadership position" (p. 151).

5. *Music at the core of being human.* Numerous philosophers have posited that music is at the core of what it means to be human. For example, in answering the question "what is the value of music?" Graham (2000) said that it "assists us in understanding better what it is to be a human being" (p. 87). What can music psychology contribute to this discussion? In essence, this entire book is part of an answer. However, let us look at one particular experiment. Wilkins, Hodges, Laurienti, Steen, and Burdette (2014) asked participants to listen to six musical examples—exemplars of classical music, country, rap, rock, Chinese opera, and a participant's pre-reported favorite song. Brain scans demonstrated that regardless of what style was their favorite or whether it had lyrics, highly preferred music strongly activated networks in the brain, called the default mode network (DMN). The DMN, in poetic rather than scientific terms, supports our sense of humanity. It is implicated in sense of self, autobiographical memories, emotional processing, and empathy for others. Thus, it may be that people all over the world derive great pleasure from whatever music they prefer because it taps into what makes them human.

The point of these five examples is not to suggest that music philosophy is no longer useful or needed and that music psychology is now the predominate mode. Rather, a more useful take-away would be that music psychologists and music philosophers should seek opportunities to work together more closely and that by doing so we might advance our understanding at a much greater pace. It is not a matter of either/or, but both/and. In some ways this would be a return to older times when philosophical and psychological concerns were not seen as separate pursuits but rather parts of a larger conjoined effort (Reed, 1997).

CONCLUSION

From these brief examples, one can see that philosophy can and ought to have a significant impact on the field of music psychology. Readers of this book are encouraged to keep philosophical views in mind as they delve into a scientific understanding of the phenomenon of music.

DISCUSSION QUESTIONS

1. What is your personal view about human nature vis-à-vis other animals? Are we "just another animal" or are we, somehow, separate and distinct from the other animals?
2. Based on the discussion of human nature, how important is music to the notion of what it means to be human?
3. The ten aspects of human nature presented in this chapter were not meant to be an exhaustive list. Can you think of other attributes that characterize human nature? What connections do they have, if any, to music?
4. Identify a specific piece of music and explain its meaning and value from each of the philosophical positions described in this chapter. With which viewpoint do you resonate most strongly?

5. Imagine that you are part of a three-person team of researchers investigating listeners' emotional responses to music. What difference would it make if one of you were an absolute formalist, one were an absolute expressionist, and one were a referentialist?

6. Examine some of the music you are currently studying or performing. Can you find any evidence of the golden mean or other underlying mathematical structures?

7. Do you think it is possible to study musical beauty scientifically? Why is it necessary to understand beauty from a scientific standpoint? Or is it?

8. Should music psychologists conduct all their experiments from a Humean perspective? If your answer is "no," give an example of an experiment that should be viewed from a Cartesian standpoint.

9. What does it mean to say, "music provides insights into the human condition"? Identify specific musical compositions or musical situations (e.g., a garage band rehearsal) and discuss how they shed light on what it means to be human.

10. Do you agree or disagree with the notion that music philosophers and music psychologists ought to work together more frequently?

Chapter 3

How We Came to Be Musical

IN considering the nature of human musicality, one might reasonably wonder why we are musical at all and how we came to be this way. Oddly enough, there are frequent statements in the literature that make it appear as if there is no known reason for music. Here are just a few: "Musical skills are not essential so far as we know" (Brown, 1981, p. 8). "Reactions to music are not obviously of direct biological significance" (Dowling & Harwood, 1986, p. 202). One "might ask why evolution should have provided us with such complex innate machinery, for which there is no evident survival value" (Lerdahl & Jackendoff, 1983, pp. 232–233). "Why do we respond emotionally to music, when the messages therein seem to be of no obvious survival value?" (Roederer, 1982, p. 38). "Why do we have music, and let it occupy our lives with no apparent reason?" (Minsky, 1981, p. 41). In fairness, most of these authors went on to provide a rationale for the existence of music. However, Steven Pinker (1997) caused the most ruckus with comments such as: "As far as biological cause and effect are concerned, music is useless. . . . music could vanish from our species and the rest of our lifestyle would be virtually unchanged" (p. 528). "I suspect music is auditory cheesecake" (p. 534).

These statements are puzzling since it is becoming increasingly clear that every human being has "a biologic guarantee of musicianship" (Wilson, 1986b, p. 2). This is so because genetic instructions create a brain and body that are predisposed to be musical. Just as we are born to be linguistic, with the specific language to be learned determined by the culture, so we are born with the means to be responsive to the music of our culture. If music does not confer any survival benefits, why would it be provided for in our neurophysiological structures? Why would it have developed to the point where it is a universal trait of our species if it were irrelevant to our existence? Traits that are common among all people give evidence of a biological rather than cultural basis for that behavior (Turner & Ioannides, 2009).

A place to begin looking for answers is with the central focus of evolutionary theory. Attributes that confer survival benefits upon members of a species, whether arrived at through genetic mutation or adaptation to the environment, are passed on to offspring. The notion of *natural selection* or *survival of the fittest* is that certain members of a species, by virtue of these attributes, are more likely to live longer and to produce more offspring; thus, the attributes they possess are more likely to be promoted until all members of the species possess the same attributes (Patterson, 2004). In this way, the cheetah got its speed and the giraffe its long neck. The cornerstone of evolution theory is that traits that promote survival become genetically encoded. What survival values does music provide? In what way does being musical make it more likely that the individual possessor will survive long enough to mate and thus to transmit these musical genes? The discussion begins with a brief consideration of Plotkin's theory of primary and secondary heuristics.

Plotkin (1994) calls the natural tendency for an organism to perpetuate itself through progeny the primary heuristic. Secondary heuristics are more generalized attributes (e.g., language) in which the particulars that are not inherited (e.g., French, Swahili, or English) need to be shaped by environmental circumstances. They provide organisms with the ability to respond to unpredictable changes. Species unable to make appropriate adaptations to changing environments are doomed to extinction. Many animals adapted a "physical specialty" such as great speed or superior vision as a survival mechanism, while human beings became mental specialists. As primates and early hominid forebears explored ever more divergent habitats, a basic means of solving unforeseen problems was necessary. Unlike many species that tend to remain in a more or less stable habitat (even if they migrate they tend to move back and forth to familiar destinations), early humans gradually moved into every possible habitat on the globe. Doing so forced us to respond to myriad challenges and we became admirably equipped to do just that. Eventually our intelligence led us to change the environments instead of adapting to them. In fact, some argue that biological evolution gave way to cultural adaptations around 35,000 years ago (Dubos, 1974).

Plotkin states that "one would expect intelligence to take the form of skill- or domain-specific intelligences, with learning, memory and thinking machinery focused upon specific areas of function" (1994, p. 189). Modern cognitive neuroscientists recognize both general intelligence and domain-specific intelligences that represent ways of solving problems presented by living in a complex and changing world (Barbey, 2018). Thus, people are generally adept at many cognitive tasks and may have special abilities in selected domains. Our concern in this chapter is how and why humans came to be such musical creatures and what purposes music serves. We continue by looking at rhythm.

RHYTHM, A FUNDAMENTAL LIFE PROCESS

One of the tenets of quantum physics is that everything that exists is in a state of vibration. Some of these vibrations are periodic, others are aperiodic or irregular. Our concern, at the moment, is the nature of periodic patterns in the universe. "Quantum field theory, the unification between special relativity and quantum mechanics, states that all matter and its interactions are composed of harmonious vibrations of fields. One is left with the vision that the entire universe is a symphonic orchestra of those fields" (Alexander, 2016, p. 120).

At the macroscopic end of the scale, geophysicists talk about the "hum of the Earth," a continuous vibration of the earth even in the absence of seismic activity of earthquakes (Kurrle & Widmer-Schnidrig, 2008). Those who study *helioseismology*, or the vibratory rates of the sun, tell us that the sun also rings like a bell (Stanford Solar Center, 2018). *Asteroseismologists* apply the same techniques to remote stars (Belkacem et al., 2009; Montgomery, 2008). In fact, NASA's Chandra X-Ray Observatory has detected sound waves emanating from a black hole, as illustrated in Figure 3.1 (Chandra, 2003). This black hole is 250 million light years from earth and the sound waves being emitted may have remained roughly constant for about 2.5 billion years. This is a frequency that is a quadrillion times slower than we can hear and is the lowest frequency detected from any object in the universe. Before continuing, it should be noted that vibrations in space cannot be heard (even if they were within the frequency range of human hearing) because vibrations cannot be transmitted in a vacuum.

At the microscopic end of the scale, our brains monitor more than 100 oscillations a day in our bodies, including undulations in body temperature, blood sugar, white corpuscle count, and so on (Reinberg & Ashkenazi, 2003). Researchers have listened to sounds produced by the vibrations of single cells (Kestenbaum, 2004) and Susumu Ohno created an algorithm that

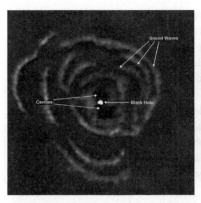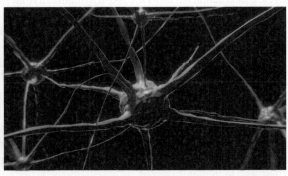

FIGURE 3.1 | Illustration of Ripples in Perseus, and a Single Brain Cell. Left panel: Illustration of Ripples in Perseus. An artist's illustration depicts the sound waves (ripples) in the hot gas that fills the Perseus Cluster. The ripple features were discovered by using a special image-processing technique to bring out subtle changes in brightness. These sound waves are thought to have been generated by cavities blown out by jets from a supermassive black hole (bright white spot) at the center of the Perseus Cluster. Right panel: A single brain cell in the foreground connected to other brain cells.

turned DNA strands into sound (Ohno, 1993; Ohno & Ohno, 1986). Others have turned the sounds of DNA into music (Ge & Li, 2012; Takahashi & Miller, 2007) and you can listen to samples on the internet (Alexjander, 2007).

One way to connect the macro to the micro universe is through string theory, a major tenet of quantum physics. The idea is that the smallest particles in the universe are made of loops of vibrating strings, just like a violin string (Witten, 2002). Also, like a violin string, each particle or string has many different harmonics and the various harmonics correspond to different elementary particles. Astrophysicist Alexander (2016) said, "our universe resembles a finely tuned instrument" (p. 190). While string theory is not universally accepted, it is integral to our current best understanding of how all matter in the universe is unified.

On a human scale, we cannot perceive vibrations at the macro and microscopic ends of a time continuum but the periodicities we can perceive create a rhythmic environment. Seasons of the year, phases of the moon, and periods of daylight and dark follow in regular, timely patterns. Our bodies, too, operate on rhythmic patterns. Heart and breathing rates are two of the more obvious bodily processes that are periodic. Chronobiologists, those who study rhythms in living things, believe that rhythm is such an important part of life that a lack of it can indicate illness. For example, complex forms of dysrhythmia may be a symptom of autism, manic-depression, or schizophrenia; dysrhythmia can also indicate dyslexia or other learning disabilities (Jansiewicz et al., 2006; Reinberg & Ashkenazi, 2003).

The human body consists of multiple oscillators creating rhythms that drive the body and control behavior. The suprachiasmatic nucleus (SCN) in the hypothalamus is "much like the conductor of an orchestra" (Kumar, 2017, p. 177) coordinating numerous timekeepers in the body. Rhythmic patterns that range in cycles from less than one second to more than a year are identified as follows: *ultradian rhythms* are those with a cycle of less than 24 hours, such as heart rate or brain waves; *circadian rhythms* are about 24 hours in cycle, such as in awake/asleep patterns; and *infradian rhythms*, have cycles longer than 24 hours, as in seasonal cycles. Interaction rhythms are those dynamic rhythm patterns that occur between two or more individuals. These rhythm patterns may vary from microbits, which are studied by means of slow-motion film, to macrobits, covering days and weeks of interactions among individuals.

The impact of rhythmic experiences on infants is widespread (Ciccone, 2015). Rhythm is a critical factor in language acquisition, and infants who receive stimulation through rocking or other body movements gain weight faster, develop vision and hearing acuity faster, and acquire regularity of sleep cycles at a younger age. Integration into environmental rhythms begins at birth with the onset of rhythmic breathing and continues as the baby gradually adapts to the rhythmic cycles of the world into which it has been born. Over the next months, the patterns of family life, particularly the parent's cycle of activity and rest, will condition and shape the baby's social rhythms. This is highly important, since nearly all social interactions are rhythmically based.

Social interactions are highly rhythmic and these rhythmic exchanges are pervasive in human behavior (Bassetti & Bottazzi, 2015). Researchers have discovered that "persons involved in social interactions unconsciously move 'in space' with one another through a rhythmic coordination of gestures and movements which exhibit all the characteristics of a dance" (Montagu & Matson, 1979, p. 150). Rhythmic synchrony is central to human sociality and sense-making. For example, in conversation we engage in turn-taking by means of utterances (e.g., uh-huh and OK) and gestures (e.g., head nodding and other body movements) involving exquisitely timed responses (Levinson & Torreira, 2015). Such rhythmic body movements influence affect, attitudes, and cognition. According to Koch (2014),

> the results from our findings indicate that dynamic movement and movement qualities are an important research topic with potentially far reaching implications for clinical and health-related questions, but also for social cognition, interaction, communication, thinking, learning, memory, research methods, and in any case – as demonstrated here – for affect and attitudes as core themes of social embodiment research.
>
> (p. 10)

Social connectedness in terms of coordination between two or more in rhythmic movement influences people's feelings of relationship to others (Marsh, Richardson, & Schmidt, 2009).

Recently, some have been concerned that social media is causing a diminution of such personal interactions. However, when researchers analyzed 362 million messages exchanged by 4.2 million users on Facebook over a two-year period, they found daily and weekly temporal patterns (Golder, Wilkinson, & Huberman, 2007).

The rhythmic aspects of human behavior are so powerful that entrainment is possible (Clayton, Sager, & Will, 2005; Cross & Morley, 2009; Dissanayake, 2009a, Osborne, 2009). Entrainment occurs when two or more persons become attuned to the same rhythm. Non-human examples of entrainment include crickets chirping or frogs croaking in synchrony and a school of fish or a flying "V" of migrating birds changing directions suddenly. Human entrainment has been demonstrated experimentally when two people in conversation produced brain wave tracings that were synchronized (Pérez, Carreiras, & Duñabeitia, 2017). Entrainment may also operate in riots and other large crowd behaviors. Musical entrainment probably occurs at nearly any concert, but is particularly evident in overt audience behaviors such as at rock concerts. Thus, "the image of the totality of life as an orchestral beating, throbbing, surging polyrhythm is scientifically more accurate than that of rhythmicity being a barely perceptible undulation upon the placid sea of life" (Brown, 1982, p. 4).

In the midst of all these biological, environmental, and social rhythms, it is important to consider the fact that human beings are much more time-independent than other living things.

Plants thrive or wither depending on the time of year. Likewise, many animals, especially the cold-blooded ones, are dependent upon time cycles (light/dark, heat/cold) for their existence. Human beings, instead, rely on homeostasis to provide an internal environment that is relatively constant and somewhat independent of external events. Thus, our internal body temperature varies only one or two degrees above or below 98.6, whether it is blazing-hot summer or bone-chilling winter. At the same time, "strategies were acquired by the brain in its fundamental operations of knowing, learning and remembering, which mediate the relationship between the internal environment of mind and the external environment of the world. They supply psychological sameness, as homeostasis provides biological sameness" (Campbell, 1986, pp. 55–56). Psychological homeostasis involves stability in hormones and neurotransmitters (Tavassoli, 2009).

Hearing is a primary sense through which we create a stable, inner world of time. Millions of years ago when dinosaurs ruled the earth, mammals, then just small forest creatures, were forced to hunt at night for safety's sake (Prugh & Golden, 2014). Hunting at night requires a keen sense of hearing. Sound events occurring across time must be ordered to become meaningful A rustling of leaves may indicate a predator approaching or prey retreating. Thus, evolution provided us with a remarkable capacity to interpret sounds that are time-ordered:

> To hear a sequence of rustling noises in dry leaves as a connected pattern of movements in space is a very primitive version of the ability to hear, say, Mozart's *Jupiter Symphony* as a piece of music, entire, rather than as momentary sounds which come and then are no more.
>
> (Campbell, 1986, pp. 263–264)

The foregoing illustrates some of the ways we are rhythmic creatures and how our ability to deal with time-ordered behavior may have evolved. It does not yet tell us, however, specifically why musical behaviors were necessary. Some aspects of rhythmic and time-ordered behavior are just as true of speech as they are of music. What advantages did music confer on human beings so that it has become a species-specific trait? Because evolution works too stingily to assign only one function to each trait, there are several possible ways music may have conferred survival benefits on humankind. These are organized under five headings: natural soundscapes, parent-infant bonding, the acquisition of language, music as a way of knowing, and social organization.

NATURAL SOUNDSCAPES

Earth is not a silent planet. It is filled with an immense variety of *geophanies* (the sounds of inanimate nature such as waterfalls, thunderstorms, and wind), *biophanies* (the sounds of animals), and *anthrophonies* (sounds made by humans) (Krause, 2002). These sounds of nature are at once both familiar and mysterious. We have all heard many animal and nature sounds either in the wild or at least on television. But perhaps many of us have not stopped to consider how these natural soundscapes and human musicality intersect. As a context for the subsequent discussion, consider just a few examples of non-human sounds:

- Male and female mosquitoes alter their wing beats while in flight to bring their tones in tune with each other as part of a mating duet (Robert, 2009). Frequency matching occurs in higher harmonics at the lowest common integer multiple frequency (e.g., 1200 Hz for 300 and 400 Hz fundamentals).

- Ants make a chirping sound by scraping an appendage along ridges on their posteriors (Barbero, Thomas, Bonelli, Balletto, & Schönrogge, 2009). Queens make different sounds from worker ants; their ridges are spaced farther apart and the frequencies they emit are lower. Queen sounds cause worker ants to display more on-guard, attentive behaviors.
- Male tree-hole frogs, living in the rainforest of Borneo, actively adjust their calls over a wide frequency range to match varying resonating characteristics of water-filled logs where they build their nests (Lardner & Lakim, 2002). Further research has shown that females routinely select males that do the best job of emitting a resonant sound. In a related study, researchers demonstrated that female túngara frogs selectively attended to the songs of males of their species, but not of other frog species (Hoke, Ryan, & Wilczynski, 2008). An area deep in the brains of these female frogs actually blocks the sounds of non-túngara males.
- Mice emit ultrasonic vocalizations at frequencies from 20,000–91,000 Hz (Kalcounis-Rueppell, Metheny, & Vonhof, 2006). Mice in the wild vocalize differently than mice in captivity and the variety of whistles and barks they use indicate individual and contextual vocalizations.
- Just as we can recognize one person from another by the sound of his or her voice, so can horses. Proops, McComb, and Reby (2009) demonstrated that domesticated horses matched the sound of a whinny with the correct face of a horse it knew from its own herd.
- Male humpback whales (Fig. 3.2) create extended vocalizations that are common to a pod (Gray et al., 2001). Over a breeding season this song is varied so that by the next season it is completely changed (Payne, 2000). Whale vocalizations utilize many features that bear similarities to human music, such as improvisation, imitation, rhythm patterns, phrases, pitch intervals, formal structures, and even rhyming schemes.
- Fish choruses recorded off the coast of Australia covered a wide range of frequencies and were either intermittent, suggesting fewer fish, or continuous, indicating a larger group of fish (Parsons, Salgado Kent, Recalde-Salas, & McCauley, 2017). Choruses were seasonal, occurring mostly in late spring and early fall, and diurnal, appearing primarily at sunrise, sunset or both.

FIGURE 3.2 | Male Humpback Whales Create and "Sing" Extended Songs.

- Oscine songbirds make up nearly half of the 9,000 species of birds. Similar to whales, they invest their songs with many of the same characteristics as human music (Gray et al., 2001; Whaling, 2000). Finches, particularly the zebra finch, make up more than half the subjects of songbird studies (Williams, 2004). Although males are the primary singers, a practice of antiphonal singing, called duetting, occurs between males and females (Slater, 2000). In duetting, a male and female bird alternate phrases in an exchange so tightly interwoven it can sound as if only one bird is singing. In an unusual display of sound-making, the club-winged manakin actually "sings" with its wings (Bostwick, Riccio, & Humphries, 2012; Koeppel, 2012). The male knocks its wing feathers together at speeds up to 107 times per second, creating a sound as a means of attracting a mate. One feather on each wing has seven ridges and another feather acts like a plectrum, plucking the ridges to create a violin-like sound at a pitch around $F_\sharp$ or G two octaves above middle C.
- It has long been thought that humans are the only species that can selectively entrain to a rhythmic beat. However, recent work has shown that a cockatoo named Snowball and a parrot named Alex actually moved in time to human music, adjusting their movements to the beat as the music increased or decreased in tempo (Fitch, 2009; Patel, Iversen, Bregman, & Schulz, 2009). Rhythmic entrainment occurs in species capable of vocal mimicry, primarily parrots (Schachner, Brady, Pepperberg, & Hauser, 2009).
- Griesser (2008) has shown that jays have a variety of calls to signal others about a predatory hawk in the area. One call indicates that the jay is hiding from a hunting hawk, another call urges other jays to gather in response to a perched hawk, and a third call warns of a diving hawk attack. Vervet monkeys have at least 30 distinct calls, including ones for large cats, for birds of prey, and for snakes (Hauser, 1997).
- Ape vocalizations range from high-pitched squeals to pant-hoots to duetting, although singing, in general, is practiced perhaps by as little as 11% of primate species (Geiss-mann, 2000). Bonobos are subjects of intensive cognitive science research and successfully communicate with humans through sign language and lexigrams (Rumbaugh & Fields, 2000). Recently a group of Bonobos began interacting with humans in musical ways, using instruments and exhibiting other abilities that researchers consider to be "musical" (Great Ape Trust, 2009).

The sonic world in which we evolved was filled with an incredible array of detectable patterns. Modern living has detached us from the sounds of nature, but the very survival of our ancient ancestors depended upon their ability to detect patterns in these sounds, derive meaning from them, and adjust their behavior accordingly. Wind and water noises, bird calls, monkey screeches, and tiger growls all had meaning. Beyond this, many (if not all) animal sounds were suffused with an "emotional" content (Hauser, 2000). They screamed in pain, roared a challenge, or offered enticements for mating. Darwin contended that human musicality arose out of the emotional content of animal sound-making when he said that "musical tones and rhythm were used by our half-human ancestors, during the season of courtship, when animals of all kinds are excited not only by love, but by the strong passions of jealousy, rivalry, and triumph" (1897/nd, p. 880).

Based on Darwin's reasoning, the fact that some animal vocalizations are undoubtedly concerned with mate attraction, and that it is predominantly the males who vocalize in most species, some have posited that music's primary role in evolution is sexual selection. Miller (2000), in particular, contended that sexual selection was a primary survival benefit conferred by musical behaviors. Males could advertise their prowess and desirability through music, thus attracting more females. However, others (e.g., Cross, 2009b; Fitch, 2006) disagree with this position, and feel that insufficient data are available to support such a view in humans.

Early humans would have heard sounds in their habitats not in isolation but holistically as a sound tapestry. Krause's (1987,1998, 2002) niche hypothesis likens the sounds of nature to a symphonic score. A spectrogram of the sounds of the forest or around a pond shows that each species produces sounds that occupy particular frequency and temporal niches (see Figure 3.3). These sounds are important—mating calls, for example—and they would not be very effective if they were lost among all the other sounds. Thus, each animal has learned over the millennia to create sounds that occupy particular strata in the overall soundscape, insuring that those for whom the sounds are intended can identify them.

Growing up in a particular sonic environment—growing up both in the sense of the individual and of the generations over thousands of years—it is quite natural that we would attempt to mimic the sounds of nature. With our great brains, we moved easily from mimicry to elaboration, extension, synthesis, and eventually to the creation of novel sounds. Thus, we occupy our own niche in the natural order of sounds, but we are not content to remain in that niche. As a dramatic example, Krause (1987, 2002) finds that where it once took 20 hours of field recordings to acquire one hour of usable material it now takes 2,000 hours; the reason for this is that it is nearly impossible to find natural habitats that are not invaded and inundated by human sounds.

Much of the earliest music would have been vocal or other bodily sounds, and many of the earliest instruments would have been biodegradable, having been made of reeds, wood, or skins, and thus lost in the mists of time. Nevertheless, there are evidences of early music. Scientific evidence has documented the use of flint blades for musical purposes perhaps 40,000 years ago (Cross, Zubrow, & Cowan, 2002). Atema (Gray et al., 2001) recently demonstrated a 53,000-year-old bone flute made from an animal leg bone. This is not a simple "toy" such that any child could make out of a hollow tube. Rather, it is a fipple flute (similar to a recorder), requiring a plug in the head joint with an air channel venting through an air hole

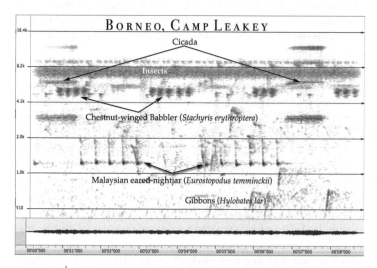

FIGURE 3.3 | A Nine-Second Spectrogram of the Biophony in an Old-Growth Habitat in Borneo Illustrating Krause's Niche Hypothesis. Each species occupies a temporal (along the X axis) and frequency (along the Y axis) niche that separates it from the others. Insects occupy a continuous, frequency band between 4,000 and 8,000 Hz, while the chestnut-winged babbler appears four times and the Malaysian eared-nightjar sounds below that. The lowest sounds along the bottom are gibbons.

and tone holes properly spaced down the length of the tube. This is a startling demonstration that even at that early stage in our development we had the brain power to figure out complex problems. Moreover, this was obviously important enough to have invested a considerable amount of time and energy to get it right. No doubt, there were many unsuccessful attempts along the way. (See Chapter 4 for a review of additional ancient musical artifacts.)

Merker (2019) posited a theory based on hedonic reversal. That is, among songbirds, responses to other birdsongs range from boredom and indifference at one end to interest/curiosity and surprise in mid-range, and caution, fear, and terror in "danger zone" responses. Among humans, aesthetic judgments result in a hedonic reversal at the upper end from danger zone to awe and being moved or impressed. Shifting from fear to being moved indicates a replacement of a tendency to escape with a tendency to yield or surrender. Shivers, chills, goosebumps, and tears that normally occur in a fear state now accompany a positive aesthetic experience.

PARENT-INFANT BONDING

In consideration of the survival benefits music has to offer, the evolutionary advantage of the smile, like music a universally innate human trait, provides a useful analogy. From a more recent, cultural development standpoint, the smile has taken on many diverse meanings. However, from a biological evolutionary standpoint, the primary survival benefit may have been the bonding of parent and infant (Parsons, Young, Murray, Stein, & Kringelbach, 2010). Likewise, music has many widely diverse cultural meanings today. However, at its roots it may also have had survival benefits in connection with parent-infant bonding. The first step in arriving at this conclusion is to look at the evolutionary history of the brain.

Over a period of 3.5 million years, the brain has grown from about 450 cubic centimeters (cm^3) in *Australopithecines* to about 1350 cm^3 and three pounds weight in modern *homo sapiens* (Roth & Dicke, 2005). In the womb, the brain of the fetus grows at the rate of 580,000 brain cells per minute (Brotherson, 2005) and at its peak around the 34th week of gestation nearly 40,000 new synapses are formed every second (Tau & Peterson, 2010). At birth, the brain is 12% of the total body weight, but even then it is incompletely developed. It takes the next six years for the brain to reach 90% of its adult size, when it will represent approximately two percent of body weight. This is in contrast to rhesus monkeys, for example, that are born with a brain that is already 75% of its eventual adult size. If the human fetus were carried "full term" in terms of brain development, the head would be too large to pass through the birth canal. The evolutionary solution to this problem was that we are now born with our brains incompletely developed. At birth the skull bones are not yet knit together, allowing for additional increase in brain mass.

The result of this post-partum brain development is an increased period of dependency of infants on their parents (Cross & Morley, 2009; Dissanayake, 2009b). Compared with any other animal species, human infants are more helpless and for far longer periods. The fact that human mothers most often give birth to single babies rather than litters means that more time may be devoted to the individual child. While the baby is in this stage, s/he is growing, developing, and learning at a tremendous rate. Nearly 75% of a newborn's cerebral cortex is uncommitted to specific behaviors (Springer & Deutsch, 1989). This uncommitted gray matter, called association areas, allows for the integration and synthesis of sensory inputs in novel ways. It is in this way that human ingenuity is possible.

Most human behaviors are not instinctive, but acquired, and it is during this period of extended infant dependency that we acquire many important human behaviors. Parents and newborns confer many important physiological and psychological benefits on each other and perhaps chief among the many behaviors that are first observed at this point are loving behaviors. Babies learn to love almost immediately and in turn are nurtured by love. The importance of these loving interactions cannot be overstated.

In the late 19th and early 20th centuries, records kept in American and European foundling homes indicated that infants under one year of age who were placed in these foundling homes suffered a death rate of nearly 100%. This syndrome was so prevalent that many homes would enter "condition hopeless" into the records when the baby was first received, because they knew that the child was destined to perish (Farb, 1978; Montagu, 1977, 1978; Montagu & Matson, 1979). For a long time, the authorities were unable to trace the cause of the malady; it seemed not to lie in poor diet nor in lack of clothing or shelter. Eventually, the cause of and cure for the problem was discovered in a German foundling home. Soon after the hiring of an elderly woman, the babies began to survive. This lady merely spent time every day loving each infant. They had been dying from lack of love. In recent years, researchers have seen similar situations, as children who do not receive adequate personal attention often develop cognitive and affective disorders (Chugani et al., 2001).

Love and affection are communicated to a baby in a number of ways. Speaking, singing, and touching are three primary modes of communicating with infants. Some psychologists have coined the term "motherese" in reference to the particular kind of speech patterns mothers use with their infants (Kuhl & Rivera-Gaxiola, 2008), also referred to as infant-directed speech (IDS) (Powers & Trevarthen, 2009; see Fig. 3.4). The musical aspects of IDS are critically important, not only as an aid to language acquisition, but especially in the communication of emotions. Long before youngsters begin to talk, they are adept at deciphering the emotional content of speech, largely due to the musical characteristics of IDS. In IDS, it is the prosodic, or pitch, timbral, dynamic, and rhythmic aspects to which the baby responds, certainly not the verbal content. "You are an ugly baby" spoken in a soft, sing-song fashion will elicit a far more positive response than "you are a beautiful baby" shouted in an angry tone.

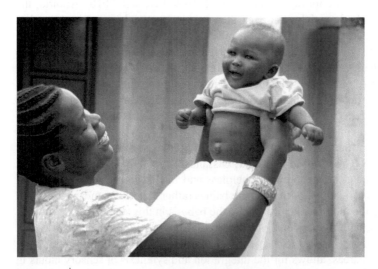

FIGURE 3.4 | Infant-Directed Speaking and Singing Has Particular Characteristics that Are Fairly Consistent Around the World. Since babies do not understand words, they respond to the prosodic or musical aspects of speech and singing.

West, King, and Goldstein (2004) nicely encapsulate both the advantages of IDS and the evolutionary basis:

> In summary, musical speech to infants has many important functions, as it predicts the behavior of caregivers, organizes infant attention, facilitates associative learning, and regulates social interactions. Infant-direct speech and singing create a framework in which adults and babies, despite being very different organisms, can learn about each other and establish the earliest building blocks of communication. As any parent can tell you, not all close encounters between parent and child are mutually satisfying. What infants want can be fantastically puzzling and if music helps in only a small percentage of interactions, it serves a conspicuously important function.
>
> (pp. 381–382)

Of course, the communication system is a two-way affair. Babies, too, are learning to give love as well as receive it. Neonates imitate vocal sounds with rhythmic expressions within 45 minutes after birth (Mazokopaki & Kugiumutzakis, 2009). Vocalizations are a primary way babies express their feelings (Panksepp & Trevarthen, 2009; Powers & Trevarthen, 2009). Even in the first few days, babies begin to establish a relationship with their parents through their cries. In the first few months of life, they develop a wider range of crying styles that form a particular kind of infant language. The development of variations in crying styles is important to emotional development, in providing cues to parents regarding their state, and in practicing for the eventual development of language. Babies learn to cry to gain attention and to express an increasing range of feelings. Because their vocalizations are nonverbal, it is once again the manipulation of pitch, timbre, rhythm, and dynamics that forms the basis of their communications system.

Survival benefits of musical behaviors in terms of parent-infant bonding may be summarized in three steps: (1) As the human brain increased in size over millions of years, it was necessary for birth to occur before the brain reached full development. Likewise, this increased the period of post-partum infant dependency to the point where human infants are essentially helpless for an extended length of time. (2) During the period of infant dependency, it is critically important for the baby to receive love and affection. Research shows that infants may suffer permanent psychological and emotional impairment without enough love. (3) Musical elements are primary means of communicating love and affection to a newborn. These elements include rhythmic behaviors such as rocking, patting, and stroking and modulation of pitch, timbre, dynamics, and rhythm in both speaking and singing. As the cranial capacity and length of infant dependency were being increased, there were survival benefits in building in responsiveness to nonverbal forms of communication. Even if the earliest examples of these behaviors are termed "pre-musical," cultural adaptations could easily have taken advantage of the inherent possibilities once the responsiveness was built in.

Imagine a small tribe of people living many thousands of years ago. A mother sits cradling a newborn baby in her arms. This baby will be completely dependent upon her for all the basic necessities of life—food, clothing, shelter, protection—for nearly two years and somewhat dependent upon her for many years after that. If the baby were not responsive to anything related to musical or pre-musical behaviors, how would the mother communicate love? And, if the mother could not communicate love, how would the baby survive? And, if the baby could not survive, how could the species survive? Fortunately, the baby has an inborn capacity to respond to a wide range of pre-musical expressions. A large part of this inborn response mechanism must deal with some notion of pleasure. Warmth, assurance, security, contentedness, even nascent feelings of happiness, are all a part of what is being shared with the baby. If these responses to pre-musical activities were wired into the brain, is it not understandable that music still brings us deep pleasure long after various cultures have developed these pre-musical behaviors into bagpipes, grand opera, and gamelan orchestras?

THE ACQUISITION OF LANGUAGE

A third means of conferring survival benefits through music is in the acquisition of language. Acquiring language skills is one of the most important steps to be taken for the survival of the human species and attributes that assisted in this process would have been selected for their advantages. The musical aspects of language have already been mentioned; melodic contour, timbre variations, and rhythm are of primary importance to speech. One of the outcomes of the parent-infant dyad discussed previously is that the baby becomes motivated to recognize and respond to sound patterns that will later become necessary for speech perception. When parents communicate with their infants, their "talk" quite naturally emphasizes the melodic, timbral, and rhythmic aspects used in the native tongue. Correspondingly, the native language shapes the melodic contour of infant vocalizations (Mampe, Friederici, Christophe, & Wermke, 2009).

Simultaneously with the acquisition of the mechanics of listening to and producing speech, infants are learning other useful information through the musical aspects of communication. They are learning that there are important nonverbal messages to be sent and received. Almost any utterance can be spoken with an infinite variety of shadings and resultant meanings. Through such means as body language, context, and primarily through the musical aspects of speech (prosody), one can express the "real" meaning behind the words. In terms of biological evolution, equipping the brain with neural systems that have the ability to produce and interpret both verbal and nonverbal messages was a crucial step in our survival. See Chapter 8 for more details on music and language.

One survival benefit of the "musical" aspects of the brain may be in the acquisition of language. Interchanges with adults who use infant-directed speech motivate the baby to pay attention to the melodic contours, timbres, and rhythms of speech. The baby is also learning to perceive and emit sound with both emotional and cognitive content.

MUSIC AS A WAY OF KNOWING

The foregoing discussion of music's role in the acquisition of language may have seemed to place it in a secondary or supporting role. But remembering that there may be multiple functions for the same attribute, a fourth survival benefit of music is that it provides a unique mode of knowing: It has immense value in and of itself.

Music as a unique mode of knowing was discussed in the previous chapter. Perhaps the most important thing human beings have learned through music is how to deal with feelings, and in the context of this chapter, it is important to note that music may provide a means of conferring survival benefits through the socialization of emotions. When group living is mandatory for survival, as it is for human beings, learning to react to others with sensitivity has clear evolutionary advantages. Lions hunt in groups; however, after a kill has been made each individual fights for his or her share. The biggest and strongest get the most to eat. This display of aggression at feeding time necessitates a subsequent period of licking and rubbing—"making up." This is necessary to keep the social bonds of the pride in place (Joubart, 1994).

Listening to the daily news is all one needs to do to realize that human beings still have to deal with many aggressive behaviors in our societies. We need to find ways to separate actions from feelings. How does one feel anger without acting on it? How does one avoid giving in to loneliness and despair? These are extreme examples, but at all levels of feeling it is important to learn how to feel deeply without always resorting to action. Music is one of the most powerful outlets for expressing emotions. One can learn to cope with grief, frustration, and anger or to express joy and love through musical experiences. Thus, music's unique way for us to know may be a survival mechanism.

SOCIAL ORGANIZATION

A fifth avenue of approach to the possibility of survival benefits conferred by musical behaviors has to do with social organization (Cross & Morley, 2009). For prehistoric societies, cooperation was vital for hunting, gathering, protection (from the elements, animals, and enemies), and for the creation of the family unit; a social network was necessary for survival of the human species. Music may have conferred survival benefits in two ways related to social organization: (1) Music is a powerful unifying force; (2) music is a powerful mnemonic device.

Consider, once again, a prehistoric tribe. Survival is possible to the extent that members of the tribe are committed to each other as a group. If the group scatters at the first sign of danger, the individuals will have a much more difficult time of coping. Behaviors that help promote the notion of corporate identity would be of immense value. One of music's strongest attributes is that it brings people together for a common purpose. To develop a feeling of unity, some common ideas, goals, visions, dreams, and beliefs must be shared. What better way to share them than through music and dance (see Fig. 3.5)?

Members of a tribe are often bound by common religious beliefs and these are frequently expressed through music. Members of one tribe must band together to fight off members of another tribe. Music gives courage to those going off to battle and it gives comfort to those who must stay behind. Much of the work of a tribal community requires the coordination of many laborers; music not only provides for synchrony of movement but also for relief from tedium. These are only a few of the many ways music may have supplied a unifying force to early communities.

Memory is also of crucial importance to the survival of a society. Not only is memory of a technological nature important—when best to plant? where best to find game? how best to start a fire?—but also memory of the things that make the society unique and special. Who are we? Where did we come from? What makes us better than our enemies who live on the other side of the river? Music is one of the most effective mnemonic devices; it enables preliterate societies to retain information, not just facts but the feelings that accompany the facts, as well (Brandt, 2009; Mithen, 2006). Poems, songs, and dances are primary vehicles for the transmission of a heritage. Music, along with the other arts, is uniquely suited to expressing meanings that cannot be communicated adequately in words. This ability allows for groups to bond and for the fittest to survive (Balter, 2009b).

FIGURE 3.5 │ Developing a Feeling of Unity Through Music and Dance. Top left panel: Mariachi musicians at a restaurant. Top right panel: An orchestra playing Swedish folk music with dancers performing traditional folk dances. Bottom left panel: African street musicians. Bottom right panel: Musicians from Bombay in the 19th century.

CONCLUSION

As these discussions have shown, the evolutionary process provided human beings with an innate capacity for musical responsiveness. Some of the attributes necessary for musical behaviors came as we developed more sophisticated means of living in synchrony with our rhythmic environment. Our sense of hearing conferred advantages as a means of dealing with time-ordered events. More specifically, music may have provided survival benefits by helping to establish parent-infant bonds, by aiding in the acquisition of language, by providing a unique way of knowing, and by playing important roles in social organization. Speaking only of music may have made it seem more important than it is in the overall scheme of human development. The notion that music is the most important attribute necessary for survival is patently absurd. However, the opposite notion—that music is nonessential—is no less misleading. Speaking of an outpouring of artistic expression among human beings 30–35,000 years ago, Pfeiffer (1980) said: "It represents activity as basic for the survival of the human species as reproducing, getting food, or keeping predators at bay" (p. 74).

What has been put forward is an attempt to account for the ubiquitous presence of musical behaviors in human beings. Aside from the fact that this discussion might be interesting to some, it carries a vital message for all. The message is that music is no mere fluke; we are not musical because of a quirk of nature. We are musical because music, like language and all the other knowledge systems we possess, played and continues to play an essential role in shaping our humanity. If music is an inherent system, put there because of its importance, it must be valuable for us still to engage in musical behaviors. Musicians (performers, educators, therapists, et al.) know that music is significant through direct experience and involvement; additional support now comes in the form of a plausible theory of music's evolutionary development (see also Balter, 2004; Cross, 2009b; Cross & Morley, 2009; Dissanayake, 2009b; Fitch, 2006; Hauser & McDermott, 2003; Mithen, 2006; Patel, 2008).

DISCUSSION QUESTIONS

1. If you were on a debate team, assigned to argue the position that music has no survival value, what arguments would you make to support your case?
2. Are you aware of any environmental rhythms that have an influence on your actions, thoughts, and feelings?
3. Do you have someone such as a twin, close friend, or spouse, with whom you frequently feel "entrained?" Describe circumstances in which you feel in synchrony with another human being.
4. Do any of your social interactions feel musical? Can you describe social exchanges that seem to have a rhythmical basis?
5. Animals frequently engage in sophisticated sonic experiences. Much of this is for courtship and mating rituals, signaling, and so on. We humans perceive some of these sounds as musical, but is any of it music? What is your definition of music?
6. Have you had any experiences dealing with an infant? If so, comment on the musical nature of those interactions. What would it mean to have *amusical* interactions with a baby or to use *amusical* infant-directed speech?
7. If you speak more than one language, do you feel a different rhythmicity to your speech in one language compared to another? If you listen to someone speaking in a language you do not understand, does the flow of the speech seem more or less rhythmic than your own language? When listening to speech you do not understand, can you detect the emotional tone from the prosodic aspects? How confident are you in that judgment?
8. Music as a unique mode of knowing was discussed in Chapter 2 as well as in this chapter. In light of Pinker's comment— "music could vanish from our species and the rest of our lifestyle would be virtually unchanged"—what information would be missing from our sense of self, of others, and of interactions between our inner and outer worlds if music were deleted from our daily existence?
9. Think of small (e.g., family, neighborhood), medium (e.g., school, work, church or synagogue), and large (e.g., political party, nation) social organizations. What roles does music play, if any, in cementing bonds of affiliation? Can you think of examples where music is used in inclusionary and exclusionary ways, that is, to keep insiders in and outsiders out?
10. Do you think the case for an evolutionary basis of human musicality is weak, moderate, or strong?

Chapter 4

Music Around the World and Across Time

MUSIC is a universal trait of humankind and throughout the ages it has played a significant role in the lives of people in every part of the globe (Cross & Morely, 2009). As Ackerman (1995) put it, "At some point in our past it was important enough that all human beings born, no matter whether Bengalese, Inuit, or Quechua, no matter whether blind, left-handed, or freckled, were not merely *capable* of making music; they *required* music to add meaning to their lives" (p. 210). This can be illustrated by imagining an internal soundtrack for each of the following vignettes:

Fortaleza, Brazil: Nighttime revelers parade down the street by the light of flickering torches. The movements of the *cabocolinhos* (the dancers) are accompanied by drums, *caracaxa* (scraped gourds), and flutes (Olsen, 1980).

Bayonne, New Jersey: A lonely, confused teenager sits brooding in his room. He wears headphones connected to an iPod that is playing his favorite rap songs.

Sakaka, Saudi Arabia: As a nervous bride makes last-minute preparations, she can hear the strains of the professional orchestra hired to entertain the wedding guests. The *Nawba*, a suite of pieces, is being played on the *ud* (lute), *nay* (flute), and *duff* (tambourine) (Pacholczyk, 1980).

Madrid, Spain: Thousands of voices roar as the matador strides into the arena, followed by the banderilleros and picadores. Their measured pace is timed to a pasodoble played by the band. Subsequent phases of the bullfight will be introduced or accompanied by the blaring of trumpets.

Roulers, Belgium: A nun sits in a corner of the convent garden. She is strumming lightly on a guitar and humming softly to herself.

Mazar-e-Sharif, Afghanistan: Mourners gather from all parts of the village at a mass burial for fallen soldiers. Their dirges are accompanied by the sound of a *ritchak*, a two-stringed lute whose sound box is made of a discarded, rectangular gasoline can (Malm, 1967).

Yenyuan, China: Peasant families have been assembled to hear speeches given by visiting political dignitaries. The ceremonies begin with the appropriate, state-approved music played over loudspeakers.

As stated in Chapter 1, anthropologists and ethnomusicologists have a message for us that can be put rather simply but is profound in its impact on our understanding of the significance of music. The message is this: *All people in all times and in all places have engaged in musical behaviors* (see Fig. 4.1). There is much to be said in elaboration of this statement, of course, and that is the purpose of this chapter.

FIGURE 4.1 | All People in All Times and in All Places Have Engaged in Musical Behaviors. Top left: Peruvian musicians. Top right: Korean musicians playing traditional instruments. Bottom left: Apache musician. Bottom right: Mongolian musician.

In the field of anthropology, music can be studied along with the many other products and processes of various cultural groups. In addition, there are music specialists, known as *ethnomusicologists*, who study "music in its social and cultural contexts" (Society for Ethnomusicology, 2018). Although anthropologists who study music and ethnomusicologists study the same behaviors from different perspectives, the two groups may be moving closer together. Feld and Fox (1994) stated that ethnomusicologists are moving toward a more anthropological perspective. Increasingly, they consider music in its social context. Also, according to Reyes (2009), ethnomusicologists consider that, "music is not only a human creation, but a social act" (p. 13).

Moving into the 21st century, Becker (2009) also believed that insights from the psychology, biology, and the neuroscience of music can inform ethnomusicologists. While ethnomusicologists have tended to eschew a scientific approach, she felt it would be useful as a probe to understand musical experiences. Titon (2009a) agreed that the different disciplines have much to gain from talking with each other, however, he interjected several notes of caution in that the sciences tend to take a more reductionist approach, while ethnomusicologists take a more expansionist approach. "As a discipline, ethnomusicology moves away from isolation and toward relationship. [Ethnomusicologists focus on] music *and* culture, music *as* culture, people *making* music, *musical being-in-the-world*" (p. 502). Or, as Clayton et al. (2005) put it, ethnomusicology is experiencing "an ongoing shift towards a paradigm that sees the business of ethnomusicology as the investigation of musicking as embodied, interactive, communicative behavior" (p. 39).

There is a significant body of literature in the field. Beyond general books, such as *The Cultural Study of Music* (Clayton, Herbert, & Middleton, 2003), *Ethnomusicology: A Very Short Introduction* (Rice, 2014), and *Thinking Musically* (Wade, 2009), there are numerous books on the music of a specific culture, region, or country, such as *Music in Mainland Southeast Asia* (Douglas, 2009). In addition, many articles can be found in such journals as *Asian Music, Ethnomusicology, Ethnomusicology Forum, The World of Music*, and *Yearbook for Traditional Music*. Other journals focus on a particular music, including *African Music, American Music*, and *Popular Music*. Ethnomusicologists also publish in a wide variety of anthropology, sociology, and areas studies journals. A great deal of their work is in ethnography, gathering empirical data on specific cultural groups that are published as field notes or case reports.

TIME LINE OF EARLY ARTISTIC BEHAVIORS

One of the more fascinating relationships between anthropology and art is the inquiry into art's beginnings. This is an important topic to study because the individuals who created the earliest known art are essentially the same as we are, biologically and psychologically. As noted previously, it appears that biological evolution stopped among human beings or at least greatly slowed down, approximately 35,000 years ago (Dubos, 1974). From that time to this, humankind has adapted to the environment primarily through cultural changes, not biological evolution. Thus, being essentially the same creatures as our ancient forebears, we are able to respond to the expressions inherent in their art. Furthermore, we can learn a great deal about our own creative impulses by studying humankind's first efforts at art.

Examples of prehistoric art are shrouded in the mists of time, and often there are controversies as to whether a specific finding was created by human beings, including early progenitors such as *homo erectus* and *Neanderthals*, or by a quirk of nature (Balter, 2009b). The time line that follows is not meant to be exhaustive. Rather, it is simply included to give some hint of how long art has been with us, and the extent to which we have engaged in it. For, wherever we find evidence of art we find evidence of human beings and wherever we find human beings we find evidence of art (Henshilwood & Marean, 2003).

500,000 years ago: Archaeologists have found shiny quartz crystals in caves in China (Prideaux, 1973). Engravings on fossils found in an Indonesian riverbank are dated between 430,000 and 540,000 years ago (Goldberg, Weiner, Bar-Yosef, Xu, & Liu, 2001). *Homo erectus* may have collected objects of beauty as early as this time. The *Venus of Tan-Tan* is a piece of quartzite dated at between 300,000–500,000 years old. Bednarik (2003) argued that grooves carved in it and the fact that it was coated with red paint represented early attempts at creating a figurine that symbolically resembles a person.

200,000 years ago: Hand axes and other tools and utensils were shaped far more beautifully than was required for utilitarian purposes (Mithen, 2006).

100,000 years ago: Pieces of engraved red ochre found in South Africa may represent an early artistic tradition (Balter, 2009a). The incisions may also represent early examples of symbolic expression. These pieces are similar to ones dated from 82,000 (Bouzouggar et al., 2007) and 77,000 years ago (Henshilwood et al., 2002), suggesting sustained behavior over many millennia.

70,000 years ago: Cave paintings from 70,000 years ago include a depiction of a bow. Many anthropologists believe that initially the bow may have been used as both a musical instrument and a weapon (Kending & Levitt, 1982; Mumford, 1966); see Fig. 4.2.

60,000 years ago: Artifacts found in a cave in Lebanon—including ocher-colored spear-points, daggers, and hand axes buried with fossilized remains of deer and other animals—indicate ceremonies, accompanied by dancing and singing (Constable, 1973).

53,000 years ago: Prehistoric bone flutes made in France and Slovenia resemble modern-day recorders (Gray et al., 2001). Others (e.g., Morley, 2006), claim the earliest bone flutes date from around 43,000 years ago.

40,000 years ago: Remains, such as human skeletons buried with flowers, show spiritual concerns with death around 40,000 years ago (Petit, 2011). Burial rituals apparently included both music and dance. There are also indications that Neanderthals used pigments for cosmetics. Lithophones, rock percussion instruments, such as chimes and gongs made of boulders, stalactites, and stalagmites, have been found in the presence of cave art and dated at 20,000–40,000 years old (Dams, 1985; Lewis-Williams, 2002; Mithen, 2006). Portable lithophones, such as Paleolithic flint blades have also been identified (Cross et al., 2002). In both cases, researchers made a diagnosis of use-wear patterns related to acoustical properties of sound production (Blake & Cross, 2008).

35,000 years ago: Cro-Magnons fashioned and wore jewelry. Ice-age art flourished in caves from 10,000–35,000 years ago (Whitley, 2009) and a figurine has been dated at the end of this period (Conrad, 2009). Bone and ivory flutes dated at 35,000 years old provide concrete evidence of a well-established musical tradition in southwestern Germany (Conrad, Malina, & Münzel, 2009) and in France (d'Errico et al., 2003); see Fig. 4.3. The vast amount of art found, and its continuity for over 35,000 years, speaks to its importance.

30,0000 years ago: Flutes and bullroarers or thundersticks have been found in southern France, the Pyrenees, and Russia (Morley, 2006). Although it is impossible to reconstruct the

FIGURE **4.2** | Mouth Bow. Mouth or musical bows are used in many different cultures. Bows are not only used as weapons for hunting or war but also as a musical instrument. Sometimes the tip of the musical bow is placed on a hollow gourd that serves as a resonator. Otherwise, the mouth serves as a resonator. The bow string may be plucked, bowed, or struck.
Source: Dargie, 2007

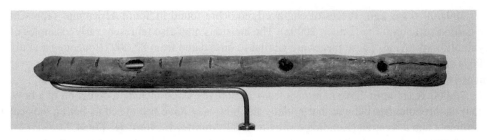

FIGURE 4.3 | Prehistoric Flute. Hohle Fels Flute from around 35,000 years ago made from a vulture's wing bone with five finger holes.

music that would have been heard that long ago, the positioning of the tone holes on the flutes indicates that these were no mere duck calls. Rather, they were more sophisticated musical instruments with richer tonal characteristics resulting from reed or lip-reed voicing (d'Errico et al., 2003). Early humans were creating music of artistic significance (Wilford, 1986).

25,000 years ago: The first appearance of a pipe held by a Pan-like figure occurs in a Magdalenian cave painting (Prideaux, 1973). A hollow bone flute with two or three holes was found in Czechoslovakia, dated around 25,000 years ago (Putman, 1988).

20,000 years ago: Flutes, rattles, and bone and rock percussion instruments indicate that Cro-Magnons engaged in festival and ritual events around 20,000 years ago (Farb, 1978). Musical instruments have also been found in Africa and Western Asia going back 15,000–20,000 years. These include boomerangs, bullroarers, whistles, flutes, and trumpets.

20,000 to 18,300 years ago: Ceramic fragments from the Hunan province in China are the oldest known examples of pottery (Boaretto et al., 2009; Wu et al., 2012).

10,000 years ago: Flutes and whistles dating back to 10,000 years ago have been found in Colorado (Stanford, 1979). Also, decorated pottery and rock carvings have been found in caves in Brazil (von Puttkamer, 1979).

6,000 years ago: Rock carvings in Utah may be 6,000 years old (Smith & Long, 1980). Many of the figures shown are musicians and dancers. Literary references to musical behavior and fragments of instruments attest to a rich musical life in Mesopotamia and India.

5,000 years ago: Egyptian bas-reliefs allow us to describe an entire orchestra, including wind, string, and percussion instruments, harps, and singers (Farmer, 1969; Jenkins, 1970). From the details provided, such as hand-positions, some speculations can be made about the sounds produced. Also, some of the actual instruments have survived. Diggings in South America show the Mayan civilization to be over 4,000 years old (Hammond, 1982). Artifacts include art, architecture, jewelry, pottery, weapons, tools, and musical instruments, such as clay ocarinas with five tone holes. Rock paintings of musicians were found in Tanzania (Leakey, 1983). During this period, the Chinese selected their rulers by means of formal examinations in the "six arts," which included music, archery, charioteering, reading, writing, and mathematics (Lee, 2000).

3,800 years ago: The oldest known example of musical notation was a cult song inscribed on Syrian clay tablets in cuneiform (Claiborne, 1974; West, 1994).

2,500 years ago: Ancient Chinese civilizations equated each season of the year with a musical tone or musical instrument. Also, a huge set of bells has been found made out of cast bronze (Shen, 1987; Stickney, 1982).

1,200 years ago: Remote caves in Guatemala were covered with paintings of musicians (Stuart & Garrett, 1981). Frescoes in Egyptian tombs and Greek vases contain depictions of musicians (see Fig. 4.4).

FIGURE 4.4 | Egyptian Fresco and Greek Vase Painting. Left panel: Egyptian dancers and flutists from 1420–1375 BC. Right panel: Greek music lesson with the teacher on the right, a student on the left and a boy in-between, from approximately 510 BC.

Some of the earliest examples of writing give us clues to ancient musical practices. Most of the early writing samples are business records, historical accounts and the like; however, many contain creative efforts, including hymns, that corroborate the ideas about humankind's artistic nature gained from a study of prehistoric art (Claiborne, 1974). Clay tablets from Sumer and Asia Minor (2000 BC) discuss the place of music in ritual, the organizations of cult musicians, and so on. The Bible contains many references to the use of music in worship, war, healing, and so forth (Kraeling & Mowry, 1969). Records indicate the use of hand signs to indicate changes in the music of Pharaonic Egypt, in Indian Vedic chants, Jewish music, and Byzantine and Roman chants (Sadie, 1988).

The records we have of humankind's earliest artistic behaviors must represent only a tiny fraction of all our ancestors' creative output. Many musical artifacts, such as drums made of wood and leather or flutes made of bamboo, were biodegradable and are no longer in existence. Far more prevalent were musical processes involving singing and body percussion that, of course, would have left no trace. Enough remains, however, to establish clearly that human beings have always and everywhere been artistic creatures.

PREHISTORIC CAVE AND ROCK ART

One of the most glorious examples of artistic creativity of any epoch is the magnificent cave art from all over the world (Lewis-Williams, 2002; Whitley, 2009). Archeologists have investigated caves in Africa (Henshilwood, d'Errico, & Watts, 2009), Australia (Aubert, 2012), France (White et al., 2012), Germany (Conard, 2003), Spain (Hoffmann et al., 2018), Indonesia (Aubert et al., 2014), and many other places that contain hundreds of paintings, drawings, engravings, and smaller figurine carvings of bone, stone, and clay dating back to as early as 100,000 years ago (see Fig. 4.5). In what ways does the existence of cave art relate to the importance of music? Not only do these paintings demonstrate that early human beings were capable of creating expressive works, but the tremendous amount of it indicates that art was an important part of their lives. If these hundreds of thousands of paintings and carvings have been preserved in the deep recesses of remote caves where they have been protected from the elements, how much more art must have been produced in the open air and subsequently destroyed? If early humans were this adept and active in the visual arts, could one

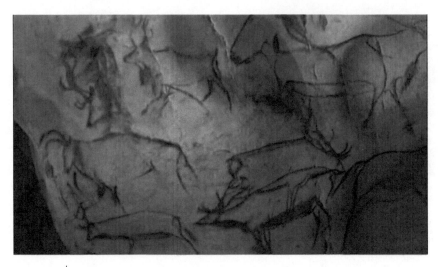

FIGURE 4.5 | Deer Drawing from the Chauvet Cave, France. The drawing may be 30,000–32,000 years old.

not suppose, by inference, that they were equally involved in other expressive, artistic modes, such as music?

In support of this contention, there are several important points to consider. The presence of musical instruments and depictions of musicians and dancers provide the strongest support. Whistles, flutes, and mammoth bones that may have been used as drums or xylophones have been found in the caves (Kunej & Turk, 2000). Analyses of caves show that those places where the acoustics are best suited for human singing and chanting are accompanied by many paintings; those places where the acoustics are poor have few or no cave paintings (Cross & Morley, 2009; Morley, 2006). "Thus, the best places to view the artwork of the cave appear to have been the best places to hear music or chants" (Allman, 1994, p. 216). Archaeoacoustics is the study of acoustical properties of caves (Scarre & Lawson, 2006) and the particular role of music in those caves (Morley, 2006).

Another point is that there are various indicators that religious ceremonies were held in the same rooms that contain paintings. It is also likely that these rooms are where the largest number of people could gather. Given the strong connection that music and religion have had throughout human history, it is likely that music was heard in these caves during Cro-Magnon times. "Indeed rituals and celebrations are mainly based on singing and music, and why would the Paleolithic tribes choose preferably resonant locations for painting if it were not for making sounds and singing in some kinds of ritual celebrations related with the pictures?" (Reznikoff, 2008, p. 4138). Further support comes from a film of a present-day Australian aborigine executing a cave painting (Mumford, 1966). As both priest and artist, each gesture of the painting is accompanied by songs and ritual dances, which appear to take a much more important place in the ceremony than the wall decoration itself.

We can never know, of course, exactly when or where the first music was made. What is important is to take note of the evidence we do have. Human beings are artistic creatures by nature. Art does not occur only when a certain amount of leisure time is available; art does not occur after the "important business" of life is taken care of or after a certain level of technology has been reached. Art occurs as part and parcel of human life.

ART AND TECHNOLOGY

Another way of documenting the artistic nature of humankind is through an examination of the development of technology. A popular misconception of the chronology of art and technology is that as our skill in making tools improved, we were able to do more work at a faster pace, and thus gain leisure time that could then be spent on creative or artistic activities. Nothing could be further from the truth.

Anthropologists agree that solving artistic and creative problems often led to inventions that later were seen to have utilitarian uses. An excellent example can be seen in the historical development of ceramics. The first example of pottery is thought to have come from China more than 18,000 years ago (Boaretto et al., 2009). However, the first kilns existed more than 8,000 years earlier (Vandiver, Soffer, Klima, & Svoboda, 1989). If the early kiln was not used to fire pottery, what was its use? Many examples of modeled clay figures have been found—bison, bears, foxes, lions, and human figures. These are not childlike "mudpies" dried in a fire, but mixtures of earth and clay materials calculated to make the heat spread evenly to produce a new, rock-hard material. Whether these figures were created as art objects or used in some ancient ritual, clearly an artistic use of a technological invention predates other uses by thousands of years.

Another example of technology dating from Cro-Magnon times involves stone blades. One particular type of finely chipped stone blade is called a "laurel leaf" because of its shape (Aubry et al., 2008). One specimen is eleven inches long and only four-tenths of an inch thick, too thin, and too fragile to be used for hunting. It must have been used for ceremonial purposes or perhaps as an object of admiration. Perhaps a master craftsman turned it out just to show to what extremes his skills could go. Speaking specifically of this laurel leaf blade, Prideaux (1973) says:

> Clearly, to produce an object of such daring proportions required craftsmanship bordering on art, and many archeologists think this masterpiece and others like it may have been just that—works of art that served an esthetic or ritual function rather than a utilitarian one and may even have been passed, as highly prized items, from one man or group to another.
>
> (p. 61)

Other similar objects, such as knives, have been found that show no signs of wear, indicating that they were not used for cutting or slicing. Some of these are richly decorated.

Contemporary Bushmen have been observed putting the tip of a hunting bow on a dry melon shell and tapping on the string with a reed to make music (Dargie, 2007). Australian aborigines developed spears, long wooden poles with an "elbow" joint called an atlatl, that were also used for beating out rhythms for dancing (Mumford, 1966). Metallurgy, appearing some 10,000 years ago was used for making decorative art objects such as jewelry, along with tools (Roberts, 2011). Without trying to create an exhaustive list, the point surely has been made that artistic and technological problem-solving are part of the same process. Human beings are as much artists as tool makers.

The technology of the compact disc (CD) provides an excellent contemporary example of the interrelationships between art and technology, how it is not technology and then art, but both simultaneously. CD players produce their amazing quality of sound by means of an incredible sampling rate of 44,100 times per second (Pohlmann, 1992). This means that each second of sound is sliced into 44,100 pieces. Each "slice" is then given a number that represents the sound characteristics of that portion of the music. The disc on which this information is stored can hold up to 2 billion bits of information. During playback, the newest CD players sample the information stored on the disc at up to four times the sampling rate, thus making certain that none of the bits of information is lost and that all are used in the reproduction of the musical message. This technology, first used for musical applications, was later linked with computers for the storage of other kinds of information. Currently, each CD-ROM can hold up to 250,000 pages of text—along with accompanying graphics, soundtracks, and movies—making encyclopedias, dictionaries, and other reference works instantaneously available to the computer screen. In talking about the role of music in these space-age advancements, Elmer-Dewitt (1987) said: "Without the CD music market, data CDs would not exist. . . . Every time Bruce Springsteen and Stevie Wonder sell a compact disc, it's good news for the data side" (p. 71). Of course, online download services such as iTunes are making even the CD obsolete.

Electronic music instruments such as the synthesizer, computer, and MIDI (musical instrument digital interface) devices provide an excellent illustration of the connection between art and technology. Here are instruments of incredible sophistication, instruments that are being improved at a tremendously rapid pace, and instruments that are drastically changing our experiences with music. Musical uses of electronic technology did not wait until such engineering was perfected. Composers and performers have, in fact, been at the cutting edge, pushing technology to provide them with ever more advanced tools for creating and manipulating sounds.

Bronowski (1973) believed that art and technology arise out of a common capacity to draw conclusions from past experiences and visualize the future. Both art and technology enable us to move our minds through time and space. "Man is unique not because he does science, and he is unique not because he does art, but because science and art equally are expressions of his marvelous plasticity of mind" (p. 412).

INVARIANTS

As used by Dubos (1981), the term *invariants* applies to particular aspects of human behavior that are universal, but whose actual realizations vary widely from group to group. Invariants occur because of the biological and psychological unity of humankind. All people have the same invariant needs, but the expressions of those needs are culturally determined. Invariants include such things as language, shelter, food, clothing, and so on. At least four invariants bear a special relationship to music: religion, celebrations and rites, altered states of consciousness, and dance (discussed subsequently in the section on music as an invariant).

Religion

All human groups engage in some type of religious worship (Ember & Ember, 1973). Furthermore, music, along with other practices such as prayer and exhortation (preaching), is used the world over in spiritual exercises such as chanting, hymn singing and meditation with the accompaniment of suitable music. Perhaps we intertwine music and religion so inextricably because in both we are concerned with the ineffable. Music helps us to experience and express spiritual concerns in a way that words cannot. "It is not the business of a composer to preach over the dead, but his requiem mass may help make death vivid and significant as no verbal account can" (Broudy, 1968, p. 13).

Celebrations

Human beings seem to feel the need periodically to set aside mundane tasks and worries and so all over the world people celebrate (Fuller, 2004). At these times, they congregate to participate in holidays, festivals, ceremonies, spectacles, pageants, rites of passage, fairs, carnivals, parades, extravaganzas, jubilees, commemorations, coronations, and other rites and observances. These occasions provide for a heightened focus as well as a release of the human spirit, a means of transcending daily routines. "Probably it is through their monuments, their ceremonies, and their rites that societies best express their ideals and reveal what they would like to become" (Dubos, 1974, pp. 201–202). Celebrations are also where communal ideas can be overturned, as well (Turner, 1982).

Nearly as common as celebrations themselves is the presence of music in celebrations. While we cannot say that there are no celebrations without music, it would be a difficult task to name very many. Conversely, it is a simple task to provide many, many examples of the ways in which music is used in celebrations, ranging from marching bands on parade to aborigine fertility dances (see Fig. 4.6). Music, especially when accompanied by dancing, seems to be a powerful way of expressing joy, thanksgiving, and all the other feelings connected with the idea of celebrating.

Altered States of Consciousness

Music also has a special connection with a human invariant that is sometimes a part of celebrations, sometimes a part of religious worship, but can also be a private affair. In many different ways, human beings everywhere seek altered states of consciousness, which can include ordinary sleep, hypnotic states, trance, or drug-induced hallucinations (Fábián, 2012). A survey of 4,000 cultures indicated that over 90% of these groups practiced some kind of institutionalized altered-state ritual (Hooper, 1981, 1982). To this inventory must be added the individual journeys many take via such means as prayer, meditation, daydreaming, or drugs. Music has an important role to play in both group and private activities designed to bring persons to altered states of consciousness (List, 1984). Chanting to a mantra or whirling to the feverish pounding of drums are examples of ways to reach altered states with the aid of music (Becker, 2004; Farb, 1978). This serves a very practical purpose for adolescent

FIGURE 4.6
Cultural Celebration
in Uganda.

males in central African tribal societies who follow their bush schooling with several days of continuous dancing to drum rhythms that induces an altered state of consciousness; this allows them to undergo circumcision without benefit of anesthesia. More generally, often in the name of dance and accompanied by music, virtually all of the world's children will spin themselves to the point of dizziness and collapse in their experimentation with altered states of consciousness.

MUSIC: A HUMAN INVARIANT

Music making is also a human invariant and, as with the previously discussed invariants, is quite diverse. Numerous anthropological and ethnomusicological studies provide ample evidence of the universality of music (Mithen, 2006). However, this fact gives rise to an important question: If music is a universal phenomenon of humankind, what is universal about it? Asked another way: Are there aspects of all music (the product) and all music making (the process) that are common to all peoples? Ethnomusicologists have debated this issue to a considerable extent (e.g., Boiles, 1984; List, 1984; Merriam, 1964; Nettl, 1977, 1983, 2000, 2005; Nketia, 1984).

One of the first difficulties is that of defining terms. Although many societies have a word for music as well as for a variety of musical activities, other groups, such as the Hausa of Nigeria or the Southern Paiute of Nevada, engage in many musical activities but have no single word that refers specifically to music (Besmer, 1983; Cross & Morley, 2009; Dissanayake, 2009b, Waterman, 1993). Societies that do have a word for music often mean different things by it (Rice, 2014). Even in the ancient Greek roots of Western civilization music meant not just the sound/time art of today but the arts of melody, dance and poetry under the guidance of their various muses (Merker, 2000). Similarly, *muzika* in Bulgaria only refers to instrumental music (Rice, 2014), *ngoma* in Bantu means drumming, singing, dancing, and festivity, and *saapup* among the Blackfoot indicates singing, dancing, and ceremony (Nettl, 2000).

If there is no agreement on what exactly music is or is named, there does seem to be agreement that the intent to make music is universal (Nettl, 2005). Cross (2009a) coined the phrase *floating intentionality* to refer to the fact that humans intend to incorporate music into many diverse situations and contexts. To many peoples, music is a process, not a product (Wade, 2009). Making music is the central focus, not music as an external, independent object. Furthermore, it is making music in a social context that is at the heart of most of the world's conceptions of what is musical (see Figure 4.7). As John Blacking (1995a) put it, "Every musical performance is a patterned event in a system of social interactions, whose meaning cannot be understood or analyzed in isolation from other events in the system" (p. 227).

Specific universal traits of music or music making are similarly difficult to identify. One could speak of structural elements, such as the fact that music is organized into units and that these have a beginning and an end. It consists of manipulating one or more of the elements of pitch, rhythm, timbre, or form in some organized fashion that societal groups recognize as music. The octave appears to be universal, probably because of the biomechanics of the inner ear (Turner & Ioannides, 2009). Common, but not universal, is the use of repeated beat patterns, the use of pitches separated by discrete intervals, and musical scales of five to seven pitches (Monmaney, 1987). For each of these, however, there are exceptions. For example, a considerable amount of *shakuhuchi* (bamboo flute) music of Japan, is not organized with metrical pulses (Osborne, 2009). Rather, phrases are based on how long the player chooses to extend the breath. Pitch glides are also used, countering commonly utilized discrete pitches. Exceptions for other musical elements, such as repeated beat patterns, exist as well.

FIGURE 4.7 | Chinese Musicians Performing in an Outdoor Gathering Space in Beijing. This was not a formal concert setting with an audience. Rather it took place in a setting where many people gathered to play chess, perform exercises, chat, sew, and in general spend time together. Although they were intent on their activity of choice, the overarching theme appeared to be the social nature of the pursuit.

Other universals include singing lullabies to infants, dancing to music, and music for warfare (McDermott, 2008). Not only is the singing of lullabies universal, apparently there are common, cross-cultural characteristics in those songs, as well. In one experiment, Western adult listeners were able to identify which of two song pairs was a lullaby when presented with lullabies and paired songs from around the world (Trehub, Unyk, & Trainor, 1993). Similarly, although much of the emotional expression of music is undoubtedly culturally specific, scholars recently discovered that a native African population, the Mafa, could recognize expressions of happy, sad, and scared/fearful in Western music, suggesting that these emotions were universally understood through music (Fritz et al., 2009). This confirmed results of earlier studies in which Western listeners perceived similar emotions in Hindustani ragas as native Indians did (Balkwill & Thompson, 1999) and Japanese listeners identified intended emotions in Japanese, Western, and Hindustani music (Balkwill, Thompson, & Matsunaga, 2004) and in Western music (Adachi, Trehub, & Abe, 2004). However, Gregory and Varney (1996) found differences in affective ratings between European and Asian listeners. It is likely that there are many emotional expressions, particularly more subtle ones, that are not easily understood by those outside a given culture (Davies, 2010).

Singing is universal (Lomax, 1968) and the use of musical instruments may be nearly so (Wade, 2009). Musical instruments are tools that allow us to extend our sound production capabilities beyond what we can accomplish with our voices, whistling, or body percussion. Just as cars, planes, and boats extend our locomotion capabilities, so do the hundreds of musical instruments extend our music-making capabilities in terms of range, timbre, dynamics, technique, and so on.

Generally, musical instruments may be divided into four major categories: *idiophones* (struck instruments such as xylophones, gongs, and bells and shaken instruments such as rattles), *membranophones* (drums), *aerophones* (wind instruments), and *chordophones* (stringed instruments) (Hornbostel & Sachs, 1992). More recently, two additional categories have been recognized: *electrophones* (mechanical and electrical instruments) and *corpophones* (hand clapping, finger snapping, body slapping, etc.) (Wade, 2009).

Some musical instruments are relatively simple from a modern technological standpoint. Other instruments represent major technological achievements and state-of-the-art engineering. An Indian sitar or a MIDI synthesizer are technologically more complex than an Orff xylophone, for example. The issue, however, is not one of greater technology creating better instruments, but simply different ones. Each culture's music does, and has always done, just what its users want it to do. Music written for the piano does not necessarily do a better job of pleasing listeners today than harpsichord music did in the 17th century or than music played on the *mbira* (thumb piano) does for the Shona.

Another way of looking at universals in music is to look at what role music plays in various societies. In his landmark text, *The Anthropology of Music*, Merriam (1964) makes it clear that while music is a universal trait of humankind, the role of music is not the same for all people. Accordingly, he differentiates between uses and functions of music. "Uses of music" refer to the relatively specific ways in which music is employed, for example, as an expression of love or an invocation to the gods. The "functions of music" are the more basic reasons or purposes for those uses of music. Generally, contemporary ethnomusicologists have moved away from such distinctions between functions and uses of music. Rather, they are more concerned with how different societies and cultures engage in musical activities, or as Wade (2009) put it "People make music meaningful and useful in their lives" (p. 1). Speaking of the current era in ethnomusicology, Nettl (2005) states that, "emphasis seems to have moved from primary focus on musical styles and sound to the other sectors of Merriam's model, to the ideas about music that motivate people to make certain musical choices and decisions, and to things for which people use music, and things that music does for them" (p. 442).

It is impossible, then, to create any sort of definitive list, because the functions/uses/ roles are not mutually exclusive or discrete. One of the difficulties is the extreme variation among human societies. For example, songs, dances, and stories are extremely important to the !Kung culture (Leakey, 1981). They have few possessions apart from musical instruments. Other cultures do not emphasize music nearly to that degree. Thus, the role that music plays varies greatly and many of these roles may overlap and occur simultaneously within the same musical experience.

Table 4.1 includes three lists. Even if these are not the exact roles of music that are universal to all human societies, they are at least representative of much of the world's music. The biological and psychological unity of humankind assures that music will be a human invariant, and that its various uses and purposes also approach invariant status. Yet, the inherent power of individuality assures that the music of one group may be markedly different from the music of another group as specific uses and sounds of music vary around the world. What follows are exemplars of these roles. Hundreds more could be given, but the intent is merely to give a broad sampling of the world's music.

Emotional Expression (Merriam); Regulation of an Individual's Emotional, Cognitive, or Physiological State (Clayton)

One function of music that seems to be widespread among different cultural groups is that of emotional expression. Music can also be used to regulate emotions, by lifting one up when feeling depressed or calming when frightened or nervous. The Kaingana of Brazil mourn

TABLE 4.1 | Functions and Roles of Music.

Merriam (1964)	Music provides the function of: 1. emotional expression 2. aesthetic enjoyment 3. entertainment 4. communication 5. symbolic representation 6. physical response 7. enforcing conformity to social norms 8. validation of social institutions and religious rituals 9. contribution to the continuity and stability of culture 10. contribution to the integration of society
Gregory (1997)	Traditional roles of music are: 1. lullabies 2. games 3. work music 4. dancing 5. storytelling 6. ceremonies and festivals 7. battle 8. communication 9. personal symbol 10. ethnic or group identity 11. salesmanship 12. healing 13. trance 14. personal enjoyment 15. court music 16. religious music
Clayton (2009)	Functions of music include: 1. regulation of an individual's emotional, cognitive, or physiological state 2. mediation between self and other 3. symbolic representation 4. coordination of action

with a series of death chants (Sullivan, 1984). These are sung not only at funerals, but also at any time one might think about death. Song provides a way of ritual remembering, so that the living will not forget the departed. These songs are so powerful and have such an effect on the singers that they later wash their mouths out with muddy water as a means of ridding themselves of such potent medicine.

Aesthetic Enjoyment (Merriam)

This is a difficult function to assess owing to the lack of a consistent or universal definition of "aesthetic." A first step is not so difficult, in that many cultures around the world do share aesthetic views similar to our own Western views, namely that art (or specifically music) can be viewed or contemplated apart from a more utilitarian function ("art for art's sake"), that a concept of beauty is integrally bound up with the notion of art, and so on (for more on aesthetic experiences in Western music see Chapter 11). However, Merriam goes to some lengths to illustrate that there are cultures that do not share similar views, at least in so much as we are able to translate complex and abstract concepts cross-culturally. For example, Hausa musicians do not create music for aesthetic purposes but to be appropriate for particular situations or to be socially useful (Besmer, 1983). It may be, however, if we are willing to grant the broadest possible definition to the aesthetic function, or even perhaps more appropriately, to grant culturally defined definitions, that peoples all over the world do share some common traits with regard to the contemplation, appreciation, and/or evaluation of both art products and processes. Precisely what these traits are, or how they might be verbalized, is still in need of further scholarly attention.

One example of the aesthetic function of music is found in India, where there are a number of transmission systems known as *gharana* (Deshpande, 1973). Each *gharana* has an artistic discipline that follows certain laws (*kaydas*). The origin of each *gharana* is in the vocal or instrumental quality (*swara*) of its founder. The *swara* and *laya* (musical time) are two of the most important aesthetic principles in these musical traditions. While one style might emphasize *swara* to the neglect of *laya*, and vice versa, aesthetic judgments are made on a proper balance being maintained between the two. For example, the *gharana* known as "Alladiya Khan" or Jaipur style is prized by people in that gharana because of the near-perfect integration of the two facets.

Entertainment (Merriam); Personal Enjoyment, Games (Gregory)

By comparison to the function of aesthetic enjoyment, the function of entertainment or enjoyment seems much easier to document and to accept as clearly universal. Musical behaviors are fun; they bring pleasure. People enjoy making music, listening to others make it, or doing things, such as dancing, to music. The function of entertainment most often coexists with other functions and it is clearly one that pervades many musical behaviors. For example, the most common form of entertainment among the Kassena-Nankani of northern Ghana is the *jongo*, a dance suite that is also performed on many social occasions (Robertson, 1985). *Jongo* is frequently performed with a set of four cylindrical drums (*gulu*), an hourglass drum (*gunguna*), and a set of seven flutes (*wia*). *Jongo* is danced only by adults, but it is widely imitated by children. Before the children are allowed to play instruments, they practice imitating the sounds using various body parts. A common sight is the drumming of a rhythm pattern on another's buttocks, which often elicits peals of laughter. Adults take great delight in ending a dance performance with a gesture that challenges another to outdo their performance.

Children and even adults engage in musical games all over the world. At one time, American television broadcast a program called *Name That Tune*, where contestants vied to identify songs in the fewest possible notes. Yupik children, from Southwest Alaska, play many musical games (Morley, 2006). These include the juggling game, the string-figure game, and jump-rope songs. Jugglers sing satirical or indelicate songs while juggling stones with one hand. Similar type songs are sung throughout Alaska, Canada, Greenland, and Siberia. In the string-figure game, a child sings while winding a string around hands and feet in time to the rhythm and syllables of the song. Jump-rope songs take a question and answer format (see Fig. 4.8). The rope holders ask the question and the jumpers try to answer the question without becoming entangled in the ropes. In *The Games Black Girls Play*, Gaunt (2006) details similar jump-rope games played on the streets of America today and Marsh (2008) describes the musical playground from a global perspective.

FIGURE 4.8 | Often, the Game of Jump-Rope Is Accompanied by Singing or Chanting Rhymes. Left panel: Alaskan children playing jump-rope. Right panel: Girls playing jump-rope on an American city street.

Communication (Merriam, Gregory)

Music communicates. Many groups in Africa use talking drums (*atumpan* in Akan, *kalangu* in Hausa, *gan gan* or *dun dun* in Yoruba, etc.) for long-distance communication (Menuhin & Davis, 1979). What, how, and to whom it communicates are culturally determined issues. Within each musical language, a variety of communications are possible. Persons who are conversant with not only the musical language, but with other cultural practices as well, are better able to share in the communications processes of that culture. Persons who are not fully a part of the cultural experience may extract some of the "messages" being communicated, but are likely to be more or less limited in their ability to receive the full communication. Music may suffer, by comparison to verbal language, from the lack of specific external referents, but it has precisely the corresponding advantage of ambiguity (i.e., each person is free to derive personal meanings from a musical experience). Speaking of talking drums, Ong (1977) comments:

> That is to say, to understand African drum talk, one must know the spoken language being used—for one drummer will drum his native Duala, another Yaounde, another Lokele—and, in addition, one must discover the way in which the language is adapted or styled for the drums. A drum language is not understood *ipso facto* when one knows the spoken language it reproduces: drum language has to be specially learned even when the drums speak one's own mother tongue.
>
> (p. 411)

A Sufi religious brotherhood in Morocco known as *Gnawa* uses music in very specific forms of communication (Schuyler, 1981). For example, in the game *txabia* (a form of hide-and-seek), the *m'allem* (master) plays musical clues on the *ginbri*, a three-stringed lute. These musical clues tell the seeker where to find a hidden object or how to perform a secret task, such as carrying out all the necessary preparations for a tea ceremony. Although it looks completely mystifying to an outsider, the process relies on using two basic melodies in a fashion similar to the Western game of "hot and cold." One melody translates as "it's not there" and the other as "there it is"; however, the words are not sung during the game. The musical code is further complicated by any number of possible variations that give specific refinements to the message.

Symbolic Representation (Merriam, Clayton); Personal Symbol (Gregory)

Music is a means of symbolizing many aspects of culture. On one level, song texts may be used symbolically, in the way that pre-Civil War slaves expressed their longings for freedom in symbolically laced spirituals. On different levels, music may symbolize other cultural values and behaviors. Initiation rites of boys of the Barasana (Columbia) require a great deal of musical accompaniment (Sullivan, 1984). Air blown from the long flutes that are played during the ceremony symbolize the life-giving breath of ancient ancestors. The air blown over the initiates turns them into strong adults. Moreover, the length and shape of the instruments represents the body of a mythical ancestor, Manioc-stick Anaconda, whose dismembered limbs are said to have formed the original Barasana people.

Physical Response (Merriam); Dancing (Clayton)

Dance, another human invariant (Bond, 2009; Hanna, 1984), is closely related to the three previously mentioned invariants—religion, celebrations, and altered states of consciousness (Dissanayake, 2009a)—and rarely exists, if at all, without music. The very nature of music's rhythmic structure elicits a ready physical response from all groups. Physical activities other than dance are often accompanied by music, such as walking or marching, working, games or sports, and children's play. Among the Hawaiians, music and dance are inseparable (Keali'inohomoku, 1985). In this culture, formal dance, the hula, requires training at the hands of a master. Candidates are selected on the basis of talent and dedication, but are not discriminated against by virtue of gender or age. Hawaiian dance accompanies the music in a way that will express the all-important text through "enhanced speech" or recitative by a chanter. Chanters undergo rigorous training and can achieve an exalted position within the society. The poetry that serves as the basis for the chant covers a wide variety of subject matters, including recollections of past heroes and events, sacred prayers and incantations, and personal expressions of love, humor, or grief.

Enforcing Conformity to Social Norms (Merriam); Mediation Between Self and Other (Clayton)

Children in every society need to learn appropriate, socially approved behaviors. Music is one of the most common and most effective means of helping to shape these behaviors. Through the use of music, young children learn right and wrong behaviors, through music they are initiated into adulthood, and adults even express disapproval of inappropriate behaviors through protest songs. Among the Venda of South Africa there is an initiation school (*domba*) that prepares young women for marriage, childbirth, and motherhood (Blacking, 1973, 1995b). Through the music and dance of the domba, the girls learn much of what they need to know to carry out these adult roles. In a series of songs and stylized dance steps, such as the *khulo* where the girls sing in imitation of a pattern played on the reed pipes (*mutavha*) by the men, they enact various stages of the reproductive cycle.

Validation of Social Institutions and Religious Rituals (Merriam); Ceremonies and Festivals; Religious Music (Gregory)

Public ceremonies, military campaigns, significant family events such as birthdays, initiation ceremonies and rites of passage, marriages, and funerals, are all validated through music (Dissanayake, 2009a; Merker, 2009). A great deal of the social fabric of many societies receives strength and support through music. Indeed, many social institutions would be woefully incomplete, and thus invalidated, if the music were missing. This is also true for religious rituals and observances.

Music in Vietnamese Buddhist temple ceremonies invites the congregation to enter a state of peaceful contemplation (Van Khe, 1984). In the Vietnamese tradition, music accompanies many parts of the service, including the chanting of verbal formulae (*mantras*), chanting prayers or teachings of Buddha (*xuong*), and chanting highly elaborate melismas (*tan*) accompanied by a small gong (*tang*) and a wooden drum (*mo gia tri*), and chanting for the purification of the souls of the dead (*khai xa hac*). Other instruments may be used during funeral ceremonies; these may be played by lay musicians and may include the oboe (*ken*), flute (*sao*), and lute (*dannguyet* or *dan nhi*).

Contribution to the Continuity and Stability of Culture (Merriam); Ethnic or Group Identity (Gregory)

Music is a major vehicle for maintaining a social history. This is true for all societies, but most especially for those who rely on an oral tradition. Learning songs and dances of the group is a major way of enabling youngsters to learn who they are and where they have come from. Myths, legends, folktales, and accounts of important battles and conquests, are all passed from one generation to the next via song and dance.

With painstaking care over many years, Chinese musicologists have collected more than 180,000 folksongs, and they estimate that there may be as many as 120,000 more yet to be gathered (Ling, 1984). These songs represent a people scattered over 30 provinces, encompassing remote mountain ranges and offshore islands. An important facet of these songs is that many of them provide direct links to the ancient Chinese cultures of 2,000 years ago or more. Many of these are field songs, sung by peasants at work in the rice paddies. A recently unearthed pottery sculpture, dated from the first or second century AD, depicts farmers in a rice field, one of whom plays a drum. The continuity and stability of Chinese culture over several thousand years is due, in no insignificant way, to these songs. For example, these songs provided an important means of preserving ancient traditions and values during the Cultural Revolution of 1966–76.

Contribution to the Integration of Society (Merriam)

Although music can be experienced individually, it is first and foremost a group activity. Singing and dancing invite group participation. Individuals are integrated into the group as they join in the corporate activities of music making. Music provides a rallying point that focuses on social unity. For outsiders to become accepted as a full member of the group, it will be necessary for them to partake of the social acts of singing and dancing. An ethnomusicologist describes the experiences of her daughter in northern Ghana and in Washington, DC: "In both of these settings, Vanessa's inclusion into a new peer group was partly dependent on her mastery of certain song and dance formulae that identified her as an insider, even though she was a newcomer to these cultural traditions" (Robertson, 1985, p. 95).

As a result of the Diaspora, the Jewish world has historically been divided into Ashkenazic and Sephardic communities (Bahat, 1980). Jews exiled into primarily Northern European locations are identified as *Ashkenazi* (after the Old Hebrew name for Germany). Jews who were displaced into Persia, India, Spain, and the Mediterranean Basin are known as *Sephardi* (Old Hebrew for Spain). During their centuries of exile, the Jews faced the problem of retaining their cultural identity while living in foreign lands. This has resulted in a pluralism of Jewish musical styles. Within the more European-influenced Ashkenazic styles there is considerable diversity, as between Russian and German Jews, for example. Likewise, there is the variety of North African and Babylonian Jewish music within Sephardic styles.

The inclusive and exclusive aspects of the power of music to integrate members of a society may be seen in this situation. On the one hand, music centered on Jewish liturgy or holidays and festivals enabled a scattered people to maintain their cultural identity over vast distances of time and space. On the other hand, modern Israel had a difficult time integrating all the subcultures into one ethnic whole. "If we start with the assumption that the aim in Israel is to achieve a unified national culture, the questions that inevitably arise are how far should one attempt to blend the unique and deeply rooted musical heritages of the many and varied ethnic communities, and what are the means whereby this is to be achieved?" (Hofmann, 1982, p. 148).

Perhaps national anthems provide clearer examples of the role of music in integrating societies. The parade of athletes at the opening ceremony or the national anthems played for the gold medal winners at the Olympic Games are good examples of the way in which music serves to represent national identity.

Lullabies (Gregory)

All over the world, mothers and other infant caregivers sing to their babies (Trehub & Trainor, 1998). These songs may be used to soothe a fussy baby, to help a baby fall asleep, to promote parent-infant bonding, to impart important family or cultural values and attitudes, and so on. Perhaps it is not so much the text of the song or the quality of the performance, but the style and manner of singing that make a lullaby successful. Curtis (1921) described a scene in the Yuma desert near the border of Mexico in which he came upon a young Indian girl. On her lap she held a baby strapped in a cradle-board. She crooned the words *Kashmam, 'asow' − wa* (sleep, child), alternating with *loo-loo-loo-loo* crooned in a soft, low voice.

Work Music (Gregory); Coordination of Action (Clayton)

Music has often accompanied workers in their labors. Sailors sang sea shanties to coordinate hauling in sails. Slaves sang as they chopped, hoed, planted, and dug. Fishermen sang as they brought in their nets. Washerwomen sang as they scrubbed and rinsed. Members of the Frafra tribe in Barotseland, Ghana, play on the *dagomba* (a one-stringed fiddle) and shake rattles to accompany workers who are cutting grass (Nketia, 1974). The workers swing their machetes rhythmically in such a way that the cutting sounds are timed to fall on the main beats of the music. Another example is found in the guise of four postal workers in Ghana hand canceling stamps (Titon, 2009b). They whistle an improvised melody over the rhythmic thumping caused by their hand stamping. The tune is based on a hymn entitled "Bompata" by the Ghanaian composer Akyeampong.

Storytelling (Gregory)

Telling stories through music is a powerful means of communicating messages beyond the story itself. Wandering musicians go by many names, such as troubadour, minstrel, minnesinger, bard, wait, stadtpfeifer, or griot. These storytellers are entertainers who pass on gossip, news, and political commentary. In another instance of musical storytelling, health care professionals use songs in the villages of Uganda to transmit important health messages

(Silver, 2001). Villagers rely on oral traditions, and they have long used songs as a storytelling device. In this case, they impart information on appropriate health care, with lyrics on such topics as hygiene, nutrition, and sanitation. Commonly, one can hear children sing these health-message songs as they play and walk to and from school. Lyrics are simple and direct and teach the people what to do in the case of illness. Here in an example of song lyrics translated from Iteso (Silver, 2001, p. 51).

> If their eyes are pale, and they're feeling very weak,
> > to the hospital, to the hospital;
> If their hips are small, and they're looking pretty thin,
> > to the hospital, to the hospital;
> If their fever's high, and they're having lots of chills,
> > to the hospital, to the hospital;

Battle (Gregory)

Songs have accompanied soldiers into battle from time immemorial. Whether it is the sound of Scottish bagpipes, Apache war dances (Fig. 4.9), or the fife and drum of the American Revolution, music is a staple of warfare. It is not hard to imagine why this is so. Music can give warriors courage, it can remind them who and what they fight for, and it can prepare them for death. Crow (1897) translated two ancient English songs that were sung during the Danish Invasions of the tenth century. During raid after raid, English patriots used poem and song to strengthen ties of kinship, to fan the flames of home, hearth, and country, to mourn fallen heroes, and to celebrate victories. Music in the military is not simply a practice of past history; even today the US military, for example, expends enormous sums of money on music (Graham, 2004–2005).

FIGURE 4.9 | Apache War Dance. War dances are usually performed by men, with the degree of participation by women varying from tribe to tribe.

Salesmanship (Gregory)

Modern advertising is routinely accompanied by music (North & Hargreaves, 2005). This is not a new phenomenon or restricted to Madison Avenue, however. Southern (1997) wrote of black street vendors in 19th-century America who sold such wares as hominy and strawberries. Although the cries were often as much shout as song, some vendors gained recognition for the quality of their singing. Ahmed (2000) recalled the sound of street vendors in Cairo selling tomatoes, old clothes, and furniture. Likewise, singing vendors sell a variety of food products all over the world (Bebey, 1999).

Healing, Trance (Gregory)

As indicated earlier in the section on altered states of consciousness, music plays a particular role in enabling people to reach a different state of mind (Sacks, 2006). Music and dance are often a means of transport, putting people in a trance or leading to ecstasy (Becker, 2004; Dissanayake, 2009a, Rouget, 1985). Singing, drumming, clapping, marching, and dancing are often a central focus of religious and social ceremonies (Freeman, 2000). Music has also been used as part of healing rituals throughout the world. For example, members of the !Kung tribe participate in the Giraffe Dance for hours until they reach an extreme emotional state called *kia* (Katz, 1982). Once they have achieved *kia*, they can heal others. Jankowsky (2007) makes the point that in *stambeli* (a ritual healing process in sub-Saharan Tunisia), the music does not heal. Rather the music is used to contact the spirits who are manifested through possession, and it is they who affect the healing.

In Chibale, Zambia, music refers to *inyimbo* (songs and singing), *malimba* (one-note xylophones or musical instruments in general), and *ngoma* (drums, dancing, and ritual) (IJzermans, 1995). As much as 14% of the population is possessed, and most are members of a cult led by a possession leader, the *shin'anga*. During large gatherings, the possessed hold rituals where they make music continuously. A healing ritual, dealing with serious illnesses, is called *Mwami*. For less complicated illnesses, people go to the local health clinic for medical treatments.

Court (Gregory)

Music is used to accompany all manner of courtly and political rituals and ceremonies. The pageantry surrounding the crowning of a king or queen, the induction of an American president, or recognition of nearly any public official is unthinkable without music. Courtly music precedes, accompanies, and concludes the pomp and circumstance of all manner of royal and official ceremonies. Court musicians among the Hausa of Nigeria are ranked higher than other kinds of musicians (Besmer, 1983). Japanese court musicians trace their lineage back from student to teacher to the eighth century (Garfias, 1985). Douglas (2007) described a current situation in Myanmar in which the government sponsors and promotes court music from an earlier time as a means of reconstructing and preserving the pre-colonial heritage (pre-1885). For example, at an exchange concert in Rangoon, the Asian Fantasy Orchestra based in Japan presented an eclectic concert of contemporary and traditional music. Midway through, a traditional Burmese *saing waing* orchestra performed a 19th-century classical song written by revered court composer Myawadi U Sa. Although Myanmar is more open to foreign trade and tourism than before, the government sponsorship of traditional culture reinforces state-sanctioned notions of national identity. Music and culture of the 19th-century

Burmese court has become a symbol for the current political regime, providing an imprimatur of legitimacy.

Reading these descriptions from around the world is not nearly as effective as listening to the music, or even better, participating in it. Readers are encouraged to check for world music collections in local libraries or online for recordings and video footage. Also, you are encouraged to seek out musicians in your local community who perform on indigenous instruments, sing, or dance to music outside traditional Western musical styles.

CONCLUSION

Anthropological and ethnomusicological perspectives of musical behaviors indicate that the relationship between music and human societies is a symbiotic one. Blacking (1973) described this eloquently in a pair of opposing chapters: "Humanly Organized Sound" and "Soundly Organized Humanity." In the first chapter, Blacking stated that music is a product of human behavior due to biological processes and cultural agreement. Aural perceptions and the brain's ability to create and perceive patterns of sounds combine with cultural agreement to give us music. Music, then, is "sound that is organized into socially accepted patterns" (p. 25). Above all, music exists because human beings impose a sonic order on the sounds that nature provides rather than passively accept them.

Having stressed that music is humanly organized sound, Blacking then wrote about "Soundly Organized Humanity." He acknowledged that music affects physiological processes but concentrated more on the effects of music on social behaviors. Basing his comments on a thorough study and analysis of music from many different cultures, he asserted that one of the main functions of music is to help organize human social behaviors. In particular, music helps in the age-old problem of learning how to be human. Music does not change societies in the same way as developments in technology or changes in political organizations, but it serves an equally important role as it reinforces, enhances, and clarifies common human experiences and feelings.

The anthropological significance of music can be presented rather simply: All people in all times and in all places have engaged in musical behaviors. The documentation for this statement began with an examination of prehistoric art. Through inferences from the visual arts, depictions of musicians and dancers, and through actual musical instruments, we know that music was part of our behavioral repertoire from the earliest times. This evidence is corroborated and extended through the study of the history of technology and the earliest examples of writing.

A study of cultures worldwide provides abundant evidence that musical behaviors are a human invariant. Being musical is a hallmark of humanity. Musical styles and practices found around the world vary widely, perhaps because the overriding role of music in culture is a symbiotic one with cultural patterns shaping music and music influencing social behaviors.

Reck (1977) attempted a massive undertaking when he wrote about *Music of the Whole Earth*. One of his opening remarks eloquently expresses the anthropological significance of music.

> The earth is also full of a variety of musics, musics that can be as different as men are from men, or societies from societies, or the frozen ice lands of the north from the steaming tropical jungles, yet they are somehow tied together by that wonderful common denominator, the human being. Men and women everywhere have eyes, noses, ears, voices,

and hands, inventive and inquisitive brains, and (perhaps most important) a capacity for feeling. For art, and music is an art, concerns a depth of expression which somehow reaches beneath the surface of our being and touches on mysteries essential to the core of what we are; and all the scientific inquiry and philosophizing of recent and distant centuries (even the superrationalism of our computers) has not been able to put "that," the feeling, its mysteries and importance, into words or equations.

(p. 1)

DISCUSSION QUESTIONS

1. What reactions or responses do you have when you hear music from other cultures with which you are unfamiliar? Does it make you uncomfortable? Curious? Confused? Excited?
2. How would you describe what ethnomusicologists do? Why is their work important?
3. What are the implications of archaeological findings concerning music? What kinds of biodegradable musical artifacts can you imagine that are no longer in existence? Does the connection between music and cave art, circumstantial though most of it is, suggest that music was also heard in other living spaces (e.g., tents, huts, etc.) that are no longer in existence?
4. When you shop for a car are you more attracted to the form (e.g., color, shape, materials such as leather seats, etc.) or the function (gas mileage, trunk space, etc.)? Discuss the relation of form and function and other relationships between art and technology as a means of contextualizing music. In what ways are they the same and in what ways are they distinct?
5. Discuss *functional* and *aesthetic* musical processes and experiences. Are they necessarily antithetical?
6. Discuss human invariants other than the ones presented in the chapter. Can you think of invariants that have a special relationship to music besides religion, celebrations, altered states of consciousness, and dance?
7. In the previous chapter, various writers were quoted giving the opinion that music has no biological function and provides no survival value such that we have evolved to be musical. Does the discussion in the current chapter on music as an invariant provide any information to contradict those ideas?
8. Also, in the previous chapter, the notion of whether non-human animals have music was discussed. Given that chapter and the information presented in this chapter, how would you define music? Or, do you take the position that music either cannot or should not be defined?
9. Do you agree or disagree with the following? We make scientific progress, improving step-by-step over time. Furthermore, some societies are more technologically advanced than others. In music, however, we do not improve in the sense that today's music is *better* than the music of earlier times. In addition, no one culture's music is better than any other culture's music.
10. Given the enormous variety of musical expressions found around the world, who qualifies to be identified as a *musician*? What does it mean to be musical?

Part II

Perceiving, Understanding, and Responding to Music

THIS section of the book contains seven chapters dealing with acoustics, hearing, psycho-acoustics, music cognition, the brain, bodily responses, and emotional responses to music. Essentially, we will trace a sound wave from outside the body, through the hearing system, and then consider how the mind/brain organizes those sounds, how the body responds, and how we form our emotional responses to music.

The study of acoustics is fundamental for all musicians, but is particularly relevant for an understanding of music psychology. In Chapter 5: *Acoustical Foundations of Music*, you will learn about sound—how to measure and describe it, how the environment affects it, and what some of the practical applications of acoustics are in tuning systems, instrument acoustics, and room acoustics. The emphasis is on what happens to sound outside the body. In Chapter 6: *Musical Hearing*, you will learn how sound is processed by the hearing mechanism. We look first at the anatomy of the ear, track the information sent from the ear to the brain, and take a closer look at the auditory cortex in the brain. Be certain to use the Multimedia Tutorials, as they will greatly enhance the text.

In Chapter 8: *Psychoacoustics and the Perception of Music*, you will discover the ways the mind organizes the musical elements of pitch, loudness, timbre, and duration. In Chapter 9: *Music Cognition*, the discussion moves to a higher level. Here, we will explore how we derive meaning from larger units such as melodies, or how we process musical form. We will discuss musical memory, expectancy theory, and hierarchical strategies for deriving structural knowledge of musical sounds as they occur across time. In short, we attempt to answer the question: How do listeners make sense of the music they hear?

Chapter 9: *Music and the Brain* begins with a brief introduction to the brain, with a focus on issues that are critical to understanding music—plasticity, pruning, and critical periods. Then we will cover supporting information on the musical brain that comes from ancillary disciplines and from indirect approaches. A major focus of the chapter is on neuroimaging studies of musicians. We review current imaging technologies that are used in studying the musical brain and present findings on perception and cognition, affective responses, musical performance, and music learning.

Musical experiences do not occur entirely in the mind; they occur in the body as well. In Chapter 10: *Bodily Responses to Music*, we explore physiological responses to music, such as heart rate, and physical responses, such as facial gestures. There is abundant evidence to document that the body responds vigorously to musical experiences. These bodily responses also serve a principal role in our feelingful responses to music, which we explore in Chapter 11: *Musical Emotions*. Three major positions have come to dominate current thinking—the cognitivist position, the emotivist position, and an alternative viewpoint, the aesthetic trinity theory.

Although these seven chapters of necessity must be presented in linear fashion, a primary value of music psychology is in developing a coherent view of the musical experience. By the end of Part II, you should have a clearer understanding of how we perceive, understand, and respond to music.

Chapter 5

Acoustical Foundations of Music^{MT5}

MUSIC psychology is concerned primarily with how some sounds are recognized as music *inside* the human organism. Recognition and organization of sound is subjective and is usually referred to as psychoacoustics. Yet from a strictly physical perspective, music is based on measurable phenomena that occur *outside* the human organism. Although even a cursory understanding of music requires an integration of the two viewpoints, this chapter focuses more on how sound and music work from the physical perspective—acoustics^{MT5}, as opposed to *psychoacoustics* (see Chapter 7). The first portion of the chapter covers basic acoustic principles. The last portion deals with some practical applications—tuning systems, acoustics of musical instruments and the voice, and room acoustics.

WHAT IS SOUND?

From a physical perspective, sound is nothing more than mechanical pressure variances traveling as waves through an elastic molecular medium. These pressure variances propagate in all directions from anything that vibrates mechanically and that is in contact with the medium. For a better understanding, some of this explanation's terms will be defined in subsequent discussions. Before proceeding, however, it should be noted that even in physics encyclopedias and dictionaries, varying definitions exist for each of the terms that follow. Those chosen or paraphrased here best fit the purposes of this chapter. For further investigation of these terms and basic acoustics, the reader is referred to the following readily available sources: Bartholomew (1990), Culver (1969), Dainith (2010), Johnston (2002), McGraw-Hill (2005), Rigden (1996), and Thewlis (1962).

The word "wave" refers to a disturbance from a state of equilibrium that propagates energy through a medium. Dropping a pebble into a pond creates a visual example as waves ripple out from the center. The water is not moving from the center, only the wave deformations of the water's level, which is potential energy. In sound, waves can be either transverse, where the disturbance is at right angles to the wave's travel (like a displacement in a violin string) or longitudinal, where the disturbance is in the same direction as the wave's travel (like the traveling compressions/rarefactions in a clarinet's air column). The waves that travel in air from a source to an ear are always longitudinal.

The word "medium" in the natural sciences refers to any distributed system that has the capacity to propagate a wave. When considering sound phenomena, we can restrict the meaning further to refer to any molecular substance that contacts the source of mechanical vibrations. In reality this meaning encompasses quite literally everything of a physical, molecular nature. Of course, air is the most common example; but water is also an example. The wooden bridge that contacts a violin string is an example, too. What would be a non-example? Quite literally, nothing. A molecular vacuum doesn't contain enough physical matter to transmit mechanical disturbances. Thus, there is no sound in outer space because there is no molecular medium through which vibrations can travel.

The word "elastic" refers to an object's ability to return to its original shape after having been deformed by some external force. Therefore, an elastic medium is a substance in which the molecular positions can be deformed but in which they tend to return to their original rest position. Every physical substance has some elasticity, even something as seemingly unyielding as solid steel—consider the elasticity of a steel spring. Liquids, too, are elastic. Push the surface of water down and it easily reforms to its flat, rest position. *All* physical substances are elastic to some degree.

Why is this so? For nearly a century, it has been known that all physical substances— even the atoms that comprise them—are mostly empty space (Rutherford, 1911). Even solids contain empty space within their molecular lattices, and though the molecule positions are tightly bound, the space between them can be changed if enough force is applied. In a gas or gas mixture like air, the molecules are not so tightly bound but instead are constantly moving about, colliding with each other, and rebounding. In fact, in air at standard temperature (0° Celsius) and pressure (101325 pascals; Lide, 2008) or STP, air molecules take up only about 0.1% of the total space, and within this space they are moving at a speed of approximately 500 meters per second or 1,118 miles per hour—faster than the speed of sound. It is also noteworthy that even though they take up only a thousandth of the space they inhabit, a cubic centimeter of air contains 27,000,000,000,000,000,000 (27 quintillion) of these gyrating molecules. They're small!

Air is elastic. Its molecules can easily be compressed (pushed closer together) or rarefied (pulled further apart), but they will always spring back to a "normal" average distance apart. We can extrapolate this "normal" distance from the 0.1% volume figure stated in the previous paragraph and see that at STP each moving molecule will be on average about 10 molecular widths from its neighbor (see Figure 5.1). Remember, of course, that in an actual block of air, these molecules would be in constant motion careening and colliding at high velocity.

Any vibrating body surrounded by air will compress these gyrating air molecules slightly closer together when it thrusts forward, and it will pull them further apart when it moves backward. In Figure 5.2, imagine that the left wall of the block is vibrating. As the wall moves inward, it pushes the air molecules together—a compression, and as it moves outward it pulls them farther apart—a rarefaction. These pressure changes radiate out from the vibrating body at about 1,120 feet per second. The tine of a tuning fork or the body of a guitar acts just like this.

Although the two previous figures show how a gas transmits waves of compression and rarefaction, they should not be taken as accurate scale. Humanly audible compression-rarefaction cycles are much longer than the one shown in the graphics. The sound waves that we can perceive measure between a half-inch for the highest frequencies to about 50 feet for the lowest frequencies. Scaled to an actual molecular level, the cycle shown in the graphic would measure 0.00000013 inches and would theoretically produce a frequency of approximately 103,384,610,000 cycles per second. This frequency would produce the note G, 28 octaves and a fifth above middle C.

Also, the amount of compression in the graphic shows an approximate doubling (200%) in number of molecules from least dense to most dense region. Again, the illustration is for concept clarity and should not be taken literally. In reality, the pressure changes do not need to be anywhere near that large for human perception. In a typical conversation at one meter, the

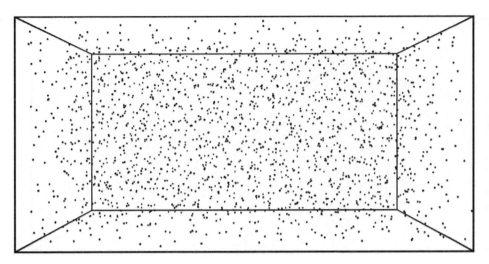

FIGURE 5.1 | A Block of 2,000 Air Molecules at STP. This illustration gives a fairly accurate idea of each molecule's size relative to the space it occupies. Actual distance varies with pressure and temperature.

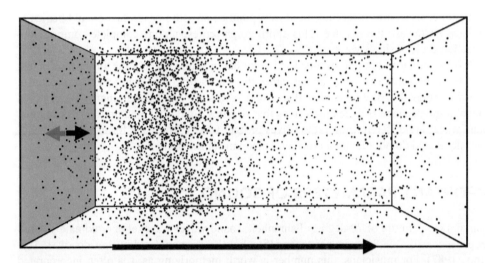

FIGURE 5.2 | A Vibrating Object in a Block of Air Molecules. The same block of 2,000 air molecules at STP showing a vibrating object (at left) causing compression of air molecules followed by rarefaction.

actual difference between highest compression or rarefaction to ambient pressure is less than 0.0001%, one ten thousandth of one percent. Theoretically, a fast-reacting barometer would show an air pressure change from 29.921242 inches of mercury to 29.921270.

It is common to illustrate the traveling pressure changes on a graph where the horizontal axis represents passage of time and the vertical axis represents pressure. Such a graph is superimposed on the molecular illustration in Figure 5.3 below. As you move from left to right along the dark, curving line, the pressure or density of molecules increases to a maximum point of compression. As the line turns and heads back toward the midline, molecular density

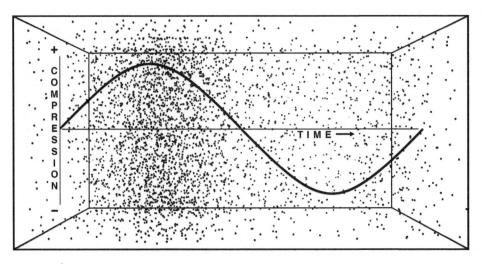

FIGURE 5.3 | A Typical Graph of a Compression-Rarefaction Cycle.

begins to decrease until it reaches the lowest point of pressure or rarefaction and begins to turn back up toward the midline. This entire graph represents one complete compression-rarefaction cycle, a single wave.

It is important to draw from this discussion that in sound it is not the air molecules that travel from the source to your ear but rather the waves of compression and rarefaction of those molecules. Finally, remember that sound waves are mechanical energy—a physical change in the distance between molecules that requires a physical medium for propagation. Sound waves are different from radio waves or light waves. These are forms of electromagnetic energy and do not require a molecular medium for transmission.

IMPORTANT PARAMETERS OF SOUND

In air at a temperature of 70 degrees Fahrenheit, sound waves travel at approximately 1,128 feet per second or 343.8 meters per second (Sytchev, Vasserman, Kozlov, Spiridonov, & Tsymarny, 1987). For musicians, this number is worth memorizing as it is often incorporated into useful algorithms related to sound in musical settings. However, in a broader context the speed of sound is highly dependent on several environmental factors.

The most significant of these factors is the physical makeup of the transmitting medium. For example, the speed of sound in water is 4,756 feet per second, and in steel it is 16,732 feet per second. Why? In general, the stiffer the medium the faster sound travels and, although it may seem counter-intuitive, the denser the medium, the slower sound travels (Walker, 2002). Formula 1 below shows how the speed of a traveling sound wave is related to stiffness and density.

Formula 1:

$$Speed = \sqrt{\frac{\text{coefficient stiffness}}{\text{density}}}$$

Temperature also affects the speed of sound in air, although the changes are quite small. In general, the higher the temperature the faster the speed, that is, the faster the air pressure wave moves across a space. The actual change equates to about 1 foot per second for every 1 degree change Fahrenheit or about 0.6 meters per second for every degree Celsius as shown in Formula 2 below.

Formula 2:

$$speed = 331.5 * \sqrt{\frac{1 + \text{temperature}}{273.15}}$$

There are also some factors worth mentioning that do *not* have an effect on the speed of sound. In contrast to temperature, air density has no appreciable effect. Although the speed of sound can indeed vary with altitude, the change is due to temperature differences, not density. Likewise, neither frequency nor amplitude changes within the range of human perception affect the speed of sound. Thus, sound waves propagate at the same speed whether the source is vibrating fast or slow; whether it is vibrating a little or a lot; and whether it is in the thin air

TABLE 5.1 | Speed of Sound in Various Materials.

Material	Meters/second	Feet/second
Aluminum	5,000	16,000
Brass	3,480	11,400
Brick	4,176	13,700
Concrete	3,200–3,600	10,500–11,800
Copper	3,901	12,800
Cork	366–518	1,200–1,700
Diamond	12,000	39,400
Glass	3,962	13,000
Glass, Pyrex	5,640	18,500
Gold	3,240	10,630
Hardwood	3,962	13,000
Iron	5,130	16,830
Lead	1,158	3,800
Lucite	1,840	8,790
Rubber	40–150	130–492
Steel	6,100	20,000
Water	1,433	4,700
Wood (hard)	3,960	13,000
Wood	3,300–3,600	10,820–11,810

Examples of the speed of sound in various materials at room temperature. These are approximate figures as the actual composition and other factors of these materials would vary from sample to sample.

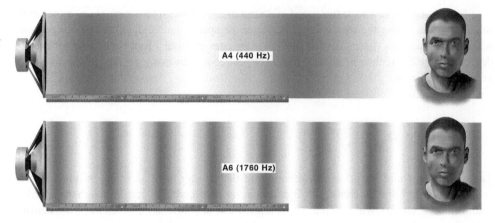

FIGURE 5.4 | Low Frequency Sound Waves Travel at the Same Speed as High Frequency Waves. The difference in pitch is a result of their lengths.

at the top of Mt. Everest or the dense air of the Antarctic shoreline (assuming the temperature is the same).

While it may be interesting to note the effects that these environmental factors have or do not have on the speed of sound, most people do not experience sound while immersed in a steel or water environment. Likewise, temperature varies little under normal listening conditions. For most practical purposes we can use 1,128 feet per second as a constant measure of the speed of sound.

Sound is initiated by a physically vibrating object immersed in or contacting a molecular medium. Since the speed of propagating sound waves is constant, we can deduce that the faster the object's vibrations, the smaller the distance must be between each compression-rarefaction cycle and the higher the frequency. As illustrated in Figure 5.4, if a middle C (C^3) and a C two octaves higher (C^5) sounded at the same time, the resulting sound waves would travel an equal distance and arrive at a listener's ear at the same time. The difference between the two is in the length of the waves.

In sustained sounds, molecular displacement is usually repetitive and highly regular. This means that it repeats the same way at very evenly spaced time intervals—say, every 440th of a second for the note A3 (A440). This regularity is called *periodic* motion. When compression waves repeat like this, the sound they produce has an identifiable pitch to humans—a musical tone. If there is no regularity, then the vibrations are *aperiodic*, that is, random, and produce noise.

The waves that convey sound can be extremely long or extremely short; however, there is a practical limit to this range. At the short end of the scale, compression waves cannot be shorter than the average empty space between molecules. Since this distance in air is only about 0.1 micron (one millionth of a meter) and since sound travels at 343.8 meters per second, a bit of math shows that in air, sound beyond 343,800,000,000 cycles per second is theoretically impossible. And, even that number is far beyond the bounds of physical practicality. The number is derived from a common equation, shown in Formula 3 below, which relates frequency, wavelength, and the speed of sound:

Formula 3:

$$frequency = \frac{speed\ of\ sound}{wavelength}$$

On the long end of the scale, if any limitation exists, it is not as clear. Eventually, however, as compression waves get longer, sound phenomena transmute into something more closely related to seismic phenomena or changes in weather.

For human hearing, we need not worry about this broad spectrum of physical possibility. Our ears respond to only a tiny fraction of the range, nominally between 20 cycles per second and 20,000 cycles per second. Put in spatial terms, our hearing range is about an inch in a theoretical range of some ten miles. Even our limited range is significantly shortened by age and health conditions, and within this shortened range, humans are most sensitive to the frequencies between 1,000 and 5,000 cycles per second (Howard & Angus, 2006, p. 83).

MEASURING AND DESCRIBING SOUND

Acoustics deals primarily with the physical description and quantification of sound phenomena. Since sound is based on the transfer of mechanical energy through waves, a discussion of sound should focus on the properties of these waves and how they interact with each other and with external factors.

The two primary descriptors applied to waves are frequency and amplitude. Combinations of two or more frequencies or amplitudes give rise to secondary descriptors, namely, phase and waveform. Considerations of changes that occur to any of these descriptors as they continue are measured against the scale of time. In textbooks these descriptors are often limited to the four shown in Table 5.2 and are discussed co-equally because they mesh well with similar descriptors based on human perception:

Frequency

In acoustics, frequency is a measurement of the number of periodic waves that pass a given point in a given span of time. Human perception of frequency is called pitch. It must be emphasized that though *frequency* and *pitch* focus on the same natural phenomenon, they are not equivalent terms. Frequency is objective, quantifiable, and external to the human organism, while pitch is an internal, subjective reaction to frequency primarily but influenced by other phenomena as well. Relationships among frequency, pitch, and other variables are discussed in Chapter 7: Psychoacoustics and Music Perception.

The most common unit for frequency in sound waves is cycles per second (cps) or the equivalent term hertz (Hz) named after Heinrich Hertz, a German physicist of the 19th century. Hertz is the more frequently used term currently.

In some situations, a logarithmic measurement called cents may be preferable to compare two frequencies (as in "A meantone major third is 14 cents flatter than an equal-tempered major third.") While performing musicians do not normally use this terminology, music psy-

TABLE 5.2 | Commonly Accepted Descriptors of Sound.

Physical	Perceptual
Frequency	Pitch
Amplitude	Loudness
Waveform	Timbre
Time	Duration

chologists do find it useful in experiments dealing with tuning and intonation (as in "This violinist was 8 cents sharp compared to the standard.") A cent is 1/1200th of an octave or 1/100 of an equal-tempered semitone.

A single wave cycle is measured from a point of equilibrium through maximum compression (crest), equilibrium, maximum rarefaction (trough) and back to equilibrium as illustrated in Figure 5.5 below.

The time that it takes to complete this cycle is said to be the wave's *period*. Assuming that waves are periodic (i.e., evenly spaced), period and frequency bear a reciprocal relationship as shown in Formulas 4 and 5 below.

Formula 4:

$$frequency = \frac{1\ second}{period}$$

or

Formula 5:

$$period = \frac{1\ second}{frequency}$$

To illustrate this, the frequency of a tone with a wave period of 1/440th of a second (or 0.00227273 seconds) is 440 Hz. The period of a 440 Hz tone is 1/440th of a second.

The physical distance that a wave covers in one cycle is referred to as its *wavelength*. Because speed of sound is relatively constant within a medium, wavelength is inversely related to frequency; that is, the greater the frequency, the smaller the wavelength. This relationship is shown in Formulas 6 and 7 below:

Formula 6:

$$frequency = \frac{speed\ of\ sound}{wavelength}$$

or

Formula 7:

$$wavelength = \frac{speed\ of\ sound}{frequency}$$

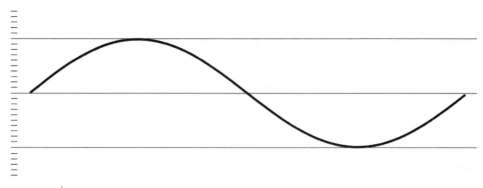

FIGURE 5.5 | A Single Wave Cycle.

A few examples derived from the above formulas are shown in Table 5.3:

TABLE 5.3 | Wavelengths of Various Frequencies.

A 20 Hz tone's wavelength = 56.4 feet.

A 440 Hz tone's wavelength = 2.564 feet.

A 1000 Hz tone's wavelength = 1.128 feet.

A 20,000 Hz tone's wavelength = 0.0564 feet (or 0.67 inches.).

Relating frequency to wavelength can be useful to instrument makers. Most wind instruments require a resonant air column half as long as the wavelength of the fundamental frequency they want to sound at fullest length. The air column inside a common C flute (without a B foot) is 2.16 feet long because its lowest note, C (261 Hz), produces a wavelength of 4.32 feet. Among orchestral winds, clarinet is the lone exception to this relationship because the closed, cylindrical pipe that is its air column needs to be only one-third as long as the fundamental frequency's wavelength.

Amplitude

Amplitude is a measure of how much energy is contained in the compression or rarefaction of molecules that make up sound waves. The greater the difference from normal pressure, the more energy is present. This is true whether the change is positive or negative, thus the measurement is always an absolute, that is, positive number. Sound pressure does not equate directly to the energy or intensity of a sound. Sound pressure decreases in an inverse relationship with the distance from a sound source, but sound energy decreases with an inverse-squared relationship with the distance from the source.

The most common unit for instantaneous measurements of sound pressure is the pascal. Although instantaneous measurements of sound pressure may be useful in some applications such as checking peak sound levels, it is generally more useful to state an average sound pressure level (SPL) over a period of time. This averaging is done through the mathematical equation known as root mean square (RMS) shown in Formula 8 in which many instantaneous measurements are taken; each measurement is squared; an average is taken of these squares; and the square root is taken from this average:

Formula 8:

$$rms = \sqrt{\frac{x_1^2 + x_2^2 + x_n^2}{n}}$$

When comparing sound pressure levels to other sound pressure levels, the decibel (dB) scale is used. This term was coined in honor of Alexander Graham Bell, inventor of the telephone, hence the capital B in the abbreviation. The decibel scale is a base 10 logarithmic scale in which each numeric increase of 10 represents a ten-fold increase in energy. This means that a 10 decibel increase equals 10 times the energy, a 20 decibel increase equals 100 times the energy and a 30 decibel increase equals 1,000 times the energy. Although the range of human frequency perception—a ratio of approximately 1:1000—can be expressed easily on a linear scale, a logarithmic scale is preferable in dealing with the far greater range of human amplitude perception—a ratio of 1:1,000,000,000,000 (one to one trillion).

It is important to emphasize that while many people use the term decibels as if it were an absolute measurement, it is not. It is a relative statement of how one sound pressure level compares to another. Only when a reference SPL is specified does it become absolute. Often a sound pressure of 0.00002 pascals is implied when the "threshold of hearing" is stated as 0 dB. This at least gives some concrete meaning to often seen tables such as Table 5.4.

Sound energy, or intensity, is usually measured in watts per square meter. Like SPLs, intensities can be compared using the decibel scale, but there is a difference in what the decibels refer to. This difference can be shown in Formulas 9 and 10 below, where P = pascals and I = intensity:

Formula 9:   Formula 10:

$$dB_{(pressure)} = 20\log\left(\frac{P_1}{P_2}\right) \qquad\qquad dB_{(energy)} = 10\log_{10}\left(\frac{I_1}{I_2}\right)$$

As in SPLs, decibel comparison of intensities has no external meaning unless a reference point is specified. Often this reference is implied using 10^{-12} watts per square meter (0.000000000001 W/m²) as 0 dB, the threshold of hearing. Table 5.5 below illustrates the relationship between SPL dB and intensity dB using their implied reference points for 0 dB. The magnitude difference between the two measures of sound amplitude is obvious. Each level of change in pressure is matched by that level squared in intensity. A doubling of sound

TABLE 5.4 | Commonly Stated Decibel Levels Associated with Various Acoustic Conditions.

120 dB = threshold of pain

90 dB = typical wind instrument

80 dB = classical guitar

60 dB = conversation at three feet

50 dB = classroom during a test

30 dB = quiet music practice room

10 dB = anechoic sound chamber

0 dB = threshold of hearing

TABLE 5.5 | Comparing the Arithmetic Progression of Sound Pressure to the Logarithmic Progression of Sound Intensity.

decibels	SPL (pascals)	Intensity (W/m²)
120	20	1
100	2	0.01
80	0.2	0.0001
60	0.02	0.000001
40	0.002	0.00000001
20	0.0002	0.0000000001
0	0.0002	0.000000000001

energy can be represented by a 3 dB increase whereas a doubling of SPL is represented by a 6 dB increase.

Loudness refers to human perception of amplitude and can be somewhat loosely quantified in phons or sones. Two tones of equal amplitude are not necessarily perceived as being equally loud. Phons (pronounced fones) are used as a psychological measurement of loudness level. If a listener adjusts a tone of 500 Hz so that it seems to match loudness in a 1,000 Hz standard tone known to be 60 dB$_{SPL}$, the adjustable tone is said to be 60 phons. Sones are used in psychoacoustical scaling experiment; by convention, the loudness of any tone at 40 phons is said to be one sone (Hedden, 1980).

Our sense of loudness is instigated by amplitude, but is not directly proportional to it. It is often confounded by biological and psychoacoustical factors such as our perception of frequency. The equal loudness contours shown in Figure 5.6 below (sometimes called Fletcher-Munson curves) illustrate the fact that in order to create a sensation of equivalent loudness, more amplitude is required at high and low frequencies than at our most sensitive range of 1,000 to 5,000 Hz (Davis & Jones, 1988).

To compensate for this uneven perception of amplitude throughout the audible frequency range, decibel measurements for audio are usually adjusted with a filter that roughly inverts the frequency response shown by the middle lines of the chart above. This is known as A-weighting (dBA). A-weighting applies a smooth 40 decibel increase in sensitivity as frequency approaches 1,000 Hz. For loud sounds, C-weighting (dBC) can be used, though it is not as common. C-weighting applies a flatter response curve similar to an inversion of the top lines of the chart above.

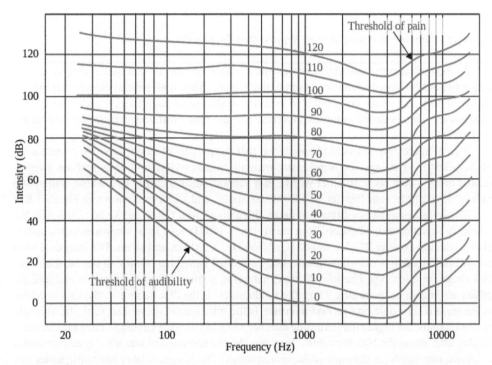

FIGURE 5.6 | Equal Loudness Contours. Also Known as Fletcher-Munson Curves.

Waveform (Signal Shape)

In periodic vibrations and particularly in music, waveform is a graphic or mathematical representation of one complete vibration cycle. Vibration of any object or medium follows physical principles that can be described with mathematical formulas. Consider, for example, the simple periodic motion of a swinging pendulum. Observation of its back and forth vibration shows that the momentum slows at the top of each displacement and accelerates through its center equilibrium point. This natural inertia of any vibrating object can be simulated using as a sine function as shown in Formula 11:

Formula 11:

$$displacement = Amplitude * \sin(2 * \pi * time)$$

Figure 5.7 is a graphic of a single cycle generated by this formula:

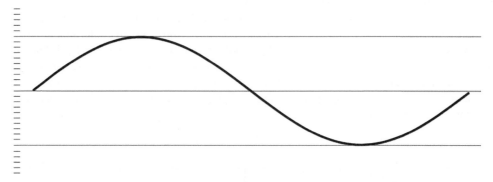

FIGURE 5.7 | Simple Harmonic Motion Represented Graphically.

A *sinewave* like the one above represents a simple vibration—one that is composed of a single frequency. However, nature is rarely that simple. Almost all natural objects that vibrate do so not only as a whole body but also in many smaller parts that generate additional higher frequencies. This is called complex vibration and the many different frequencies are called *partials*.

It is an interesting physical phenomenon that the partials of essentially one-dimensional bodies like violin strings and wind instrument air columns vibrate in parts that are integer-related to the whole body. In other words, they vibrate simultaneously as a whole, and in two halves, three thirds, four fourths, five fifths, six sixths, and so forth as shown in Figure 5.8.

These fractional parts vibrate two times, three times, four times, and so on, faster than the whole, or fundamental, vibration. That means that a 440 Hz tone from a musical instrument is also producing tones at 880 Hz, 1,320 Hz, 1,760 Hz, 2,200 Hz, and so on. The integer-related partials produced by a one-dimensional body are often called harmonics, to denote their special integer relationship. The lowest (first) harmonic is often called the fundamental and the others are known as overtones. Thus, the fundamental is the first harmonic, the first overtone is the second harmonic, the second overtone is the third harmonic, and so forth. In naturally created sounds, the higher the harmonic number, the less energy it contains. They fade to inaudibility after about the 10th harmonic. Together, the phenomenon of integer-related harmonics is known commonly as the *natural harmonic series*. The integer related harmonic series can be notated as shown in Figure 5.9. The numbers under the staff show the integer relationship of the harmonics and below that the frequencies as used in the equal tempered scale.

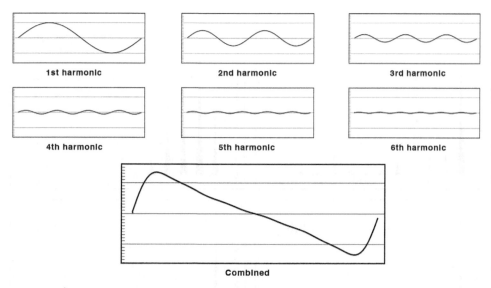

FIGURE 5.8 | Six Integer-Related Partials (Harmonics) Combined Into a Single Complex Vibration. When sound engineers talk about a "sawtooth" wave or a "square" wave, they are really referring to the particular combination of frequencies and their intensities that combine to make a sawtooth or square shape.

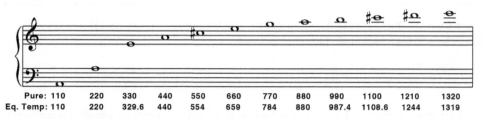

Pure:	110	220	330	440	550	660	770	880	990	1100	1210	1320
Eq. Temp:	110	220	329.6	440	554	659	784	880	987.4	1108.6	1244	1319

FIGURE 5.9 | The So-Called "Natural" Harmonic Series.

The word "natural" applied to this integer relationship is somewhat of a misnomer. The "natural" harmonic series is by no means the only harmonic series we hear in nature or even in music. Vibrating plates like drumheads, cymbals, and even bells, are essentially two-dimensional, and they produce non-integer related partials when they vibrate. A typical vibrating timpani head, on which waves travel from center to rim and also around various radial sectors, will produce partials something like this: 1, 1.59, 2.13, 2.3, 2.65, 2.92, 3.16, 3.6, and so on (Moravcsik, 1987, p. 190). The waveform they create is much more complex and their tones less distinct than wind and string instruments.

Timbre is how we perceive a waveform's complexity. The multiple vibration phenomenon means that any tone we hear from a musical instrument is almost always a combination of many frequencies, even though we identify it as a single frequency—usually the fundamental. As shown in Figure 5.10, it is the relative strength of the harmonics that allows us to identify the body of a tone as that of a violin, oboe, flute, clarinet, and so on.

All tones—no matter how complex they sound—can be reduced to a collection of individual frequencies represented by simple sine waves. This fact is known as the Fourier theorem, after a famous French mathematician. The process of reducing a complex tone into

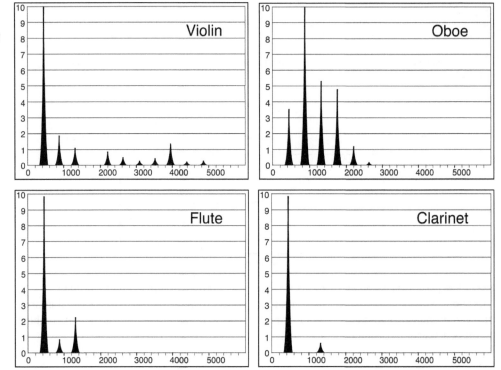

FIGURE 5.10 | Fourier Series of A-440 Played by Four Orchestral Instruments Showing their Characteristic Distribution of Harmonic Strength.

its constituent partials and strengths is known as Fourier analysis or sometimes harmonic analysis. It can be performed easily by any modern computer with a digital signal processor and inexpensive software. Applying the analysis to the same tone played on several instruments clearly shows that it is the varying strengths of overtones that form the basis for our perception of timbre.

Time

Sound is a temporally based phenomenon. It takes time for pressure waves to travel from a source to a receiver. All sounds last for a finite amount of time. All of the previously mentioned parameters—frequency, amplitude, and waveform—tend to change throughout a sound's duration. Therefore, time itself becomes an important descriptor of sound. Time can be measured in absolute units of hours, minutes, seconds, or milliseconds, although in musical situations we often use relative units of measures, beats, and parts of a beat. These are called relative because the actual time that any beat-expressed event takes must be related to how fast the beat is.

Changes that occur over the course of a single sound—for example an individual tone played by a musical instrument—are described as the sound's *envelope*. The term can be applied to any time-based mutation but is most commonly used for changes in amplitude and waveform. Envelopes are a major factor in helping listeners identify and infer meaning from the sound. The changes are measurable and are characteristic of particular instruments and performance styles. For example, consider a guitar and a clarinet each playing A-440. The spectrographs from Fourier analyses included in Figure 5.11 look quite similar so if waveform were the only basis for discrimination, it might be easy to mistake one instrument for the other. But when an amplitude envelope is applied to the two waveforms, the difference becomes easily distinguishable.

Often envelopes are broken down into four parts for more specific discussion: *attack, decay, sustain,* and *release* as shown in Figure 5.12. Sometimes we lump these parts back together under the term *ADSR*, an acronym synonymous with envelope.

In an amplitude envelope, the attack portion refers to the length of time that a sound takes to rise from nothing to initial peak intensity. While the actual time varies greatly depending on the instrument and on the performance style, it is usually measured in milliseconds as Table 5.6 shows:

TABLE 5.6 | Attack Times of Various Instruments.

Orchestra bells (brass mallet)	0.4 ms
Snare drum	4 ms
Marimba (yarn mallet)	20 ms
Oboe	25 ms
Violin	55 ms
Cello (slow attack)	130 ms
Alto Sax (breath attack)	500 ms

Musical tones tend to "settle in" after they reach the first peak amplitude. This is referred to as the decay portion of an amplitude envelope. The sustain portion is not necessarily constant but can contain changes in amplitude as crescendo, diminuendo and vibrato are applied. The release portion is the length of time that it takes the sound to fall to nothing after the note is released. While the concept of an envelope's parts may be helpful in describing and measuring a tone, the divisions are not always clear cut. The two graphic examples used in Figure 5.11 illustrate this.

Envelopes also apply to changes in waveform over time and thus our perception of timbre. One excellent example of this, shown in Figure 5.13, is how a vibraphone waveform mutates from an overtone-rich metallic sound in its attack to a nearly pure sinewave as it subsides.

HOW ENVIRONMENT AFFECTS SOUND

Many physical explanations of how sound works limit their coverage to the parameters discussed above: frequency, amplitude, waveform, and time. While these parameters provide a basic theoretical framework for understanding the acoustical nature of sound, what reaches our ears is not quite so simple. In reality the sound we hear is complicated by the environment in which it travels. Even when we listen to music through isolating headphones, environmental factors are almost always present in the form of artificially produced reverbs, choruses,

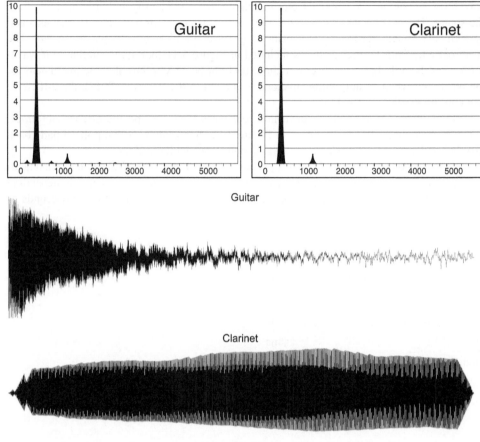

FIGURE 5.11 | Amplitude Envelopes of Two Instruments. Although the spectrographs of the instruments shown here are similar, their amplitude envelopes allow a listener to clearly distinguish them.

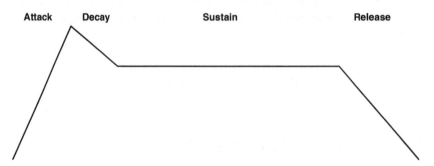

FIGURE 5.12 | A Graphic Representation of a Generic Amplitude Envelope Showing the Common Subdivisions.

delays, equalizers, and similar audio processors. This sonic sweetening is added to make the sound more "real" or at least not unpleasantly dry and characterless.

The major environmental factor affecting sound as it travels is the presence of physical obstacles. Except for experimental situations, people always experience sound in a setting

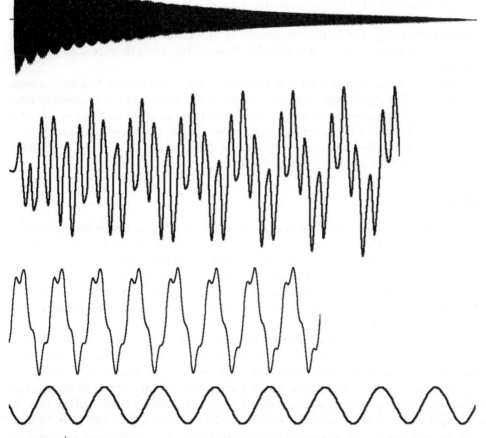

FIGURE **5.13** | This Representation of a Vibraphone Envelope Shows How the Waveform Changes Over Time. The top graphic shows a full six seconds of tone. The second graphic magnifies the waveform at its start; the third at about one second; and the bottom graphic at about five seconds.

that contains some kind of barriers: walls, ceilings, objects, other audience members, or perhaps just the ground beneath their feet. Whatever the obstructions are, they greatly affect the sound that the listener receives.

When a sound wave meets a barrier only a few things can happen to it. It can be *transmitted* through the barrier; it can be *absorbed* by the barrier; it can be *reflected* by the barrier; it can be *diffracted* around the barrier; it can be *refracted* (its direction of travel bent) through the barrier. In all likelihood, most or all of these things will happen simultaneously to some degree depending on the type and composition of the barrier.

In addition to being affected by barriers, sound waves can be affected by other sound waves, a set of phenomena known as *interference*. The following are a few specifics of what happens to sound when it meets barriers or other sounds:

Transmission and Absorption

Although we think of air as only a transmitter of sound, it is also an absorber. As sound waves travel, the mechanical energy present in their compressions and rarefactions eventually transforms into heat energy and dissipates—luckily for us. Conversely, barriers that we think of as absorbers of sound are also transmitters (see Figure 5.14). The difference is only a matter of degree.

Sound absorption is greater for high frequency sounds than for low frequency sounds. In air the loss of energy through absorption alone—that is not counting loss caused by other factors such as distance and humidity—is proportional to the square of the frequency. In other words, for each doubling of frequency, absorption quadruples (Khenkin, nd). Knowing this, recording engineers often reduce the amplitude on the upper end of the sound's frequency spectrum to help make its source seem further away.

Reflection

When sound waves hit a barrier the energy that is not absorbed or transmitted through the material is reflected. Both the size of the environment and the placement of the listener affect the time delay between perception of the direct sound and the first reflection. If the time delay is short the effect is that of a "fatter" sound—another phenomenon that many current recording engineers like to emulate. As the delay grows beyond about 30 milliseconds, the effect becomes a more distinct echo. Our brains can quite accurately infer the size of the environment from this initial delay

Incidentally, solid objects are not the only type of barrier that causes sound reflection. The change of impedance, or springiness, at the end of an enclosed tube of air also reflects traveling compressions and rarefactions back up the tube. At some point along this air column, the traveling initial wave and the traveling reflected wave meet with a 180-degree phase differential. This is a node point where the pressure is effectively at zero all the time. At another point along the tube, an antinode point, the two waves reinforce each other for maximum pressure changes. In woodwind instruments, a small vent at this point will force the air column to vibrate in parts, effectively moving its vibration frequency to the next higher harmonic.

FIGURE 5.14 | Representation of Sound Waves in Air (Left) and Entering a Solid (Right). Some of the energy is transmitted while some is transformed into heat. Notice that the waves in the solid are spaced further apart, but are traveling faster so the frequency remains the same.

In an auditorium or any other performance environment, echoes and re-echoes continue to bounce from the back wall, the side walls, ceiling, floor, seats, and any other objects so many times that what we hear morphs from echo into reverberation. The length of the reverberation, that is the time it takes to fade by 60 dB, allows our brains to infer the "liveness" of the environment or in other words an image of the room size, configuration, and barrier materials. A certain amount of reverberation is a necessary part of a pleasurable listening experience, although too much can be confusing and annoying as anyone who has listened to a marching band in an enclosed stadium can verify.

Diffraction

Unlike light waves, sound waves can diffract, that is, bend around corners. This is because a pressure disturbance of air molecules tends to spread in all directions. If a traveling wave passes the edge of a wall, some of its energy at the edge spreads around the corner rather than continuing in a straight trajectory. This is more pronounced for long waves than for short waves, so a person standing behind a barrier will notice more attenuation of high sounds than of low sounds (See Figure 5.15). This of course affects timbre perception of complex waveforms. It is also why placement of a subwoofer in an audio room is of less importance than placement of mid-range and high-range speaker; the low sound is perceived as less directional.

Refraction

As was mentioned previously in this chapter, sound waves travel at different speeds through different media, yet the frequency we hear remains the same. This implies that as sound energy transfers from one material into and through another, its wavelength changes. For example, a 1,000 Hz tone that has a wavelength of 1.128 feet as it travels through air will suddenly have a wavelength of 4.75 feet when it hits water. If a wave hits a barrier at an angle, the speed change forces a directional change commonly called refraction. It is the same phenomenon as seeing a pencil "bend" when it is immersed in a glass of water.

Even a difference in air temperature is enough to cause a slight refraction of sound waves because sound travels faster at higher temperatures and slower at low temperatures. Under the right conditions this can cause a listener farther away from a sound source to hear it better than one who is closer.

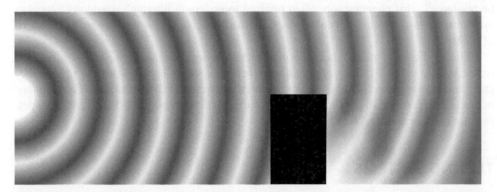

FIGURE 5.15 | Representation of Sound Waves Traveling Past the Edge of a Wall. Waves tend to reform after the barrier. Long waves reform better than short waves.

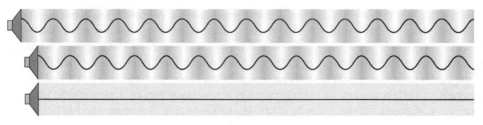

FIGURE 5.16 | Destructive Interference of Two Like Frequencies That Are 180 Degrees Out of Phase. Under controlled conditions they would cancel each other out (lowest panel).

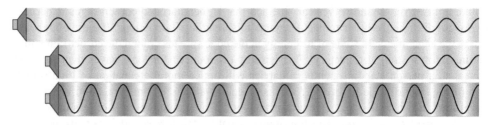

FIGURE 5.17 | Constructive Interference of Two Like Frequencies in Phase. Under controlled conditions the two waves would reinforce each other (lowest panel).

Interference

Sound is caused by traveling compressions and rarefactions. If one source of a single frequency sound were to be placed a half wavelength behind the source of an identical single frequency sound, the two sounds would theoretically cancel each other to silence because the compression of one wave would reach the listener at the same time as the rarefaction of the other wave. Figure 5.16 shows a graphic representation of this.

Conversely, if the two sources were separated by any multiple of a full wavelength, the two sounds would reinforce each other as shown in Figure 5.17.

Real world environments with reverberation and multiple frequencies complicate sound interference. For example, two *complex* tones, even under the controlled conditions shown in Figs. 5.16 and 5.17, would have some harmonics cancelled or attenuated while others would be reinforced. This phenomenon, often referred to as "comb filtering" would not cancel or reinforce the tone but rather would change the waveform and thus the listener's perception of timbre.

Enclosed environments can cause interference because copies of the original traveling waves bounce off walls, floor, and ceiling. When they reflect back toward the source, they can cause standing waves, that is, points at which the pressure changes seem to be stationary, not traveling. Poorly designed enclosures often exhibit dead spots (nodes) or overly live spots (antinodes) because of reflected interference.

TUNING SYSTEMS

Human hearing is such that most of us can detect as many as 240 different pitches within an octave in mid-rage frequencies (Gill & Purves, 2009). This leads to so many variations in tuning systems worldwide that any attempt to describe them succinctly would be doing them a disservice. Even within Western music there are dozens of tuning systems. What follows is a grossly simplified overview that can only hint at tuning in Western music and tuning systems worldwide.

Tuning in Western Music

The most common way to discuss tuning in Western music is to take a chronological approach. In our brief survey, we will look at Pythagorean, Just, Meantone, and Equal-Tempered tuning systems. For those wanting to know more, there are many excellent sources that provide considerably more detail (e.g., Barbour, 1951; Donahue, 2005; Isacoff, 2009; Jorgensen, 1991).

Pythagorean Scale. Around 550 BC, Pythagoras conducted experiments on a monochord, which was a hollow box with a string strung over two bridges and fixed at either end. A third bridge was movable and was used to divide the string in various lengths. Placing the movable bridge along the string at integers (i.e., one-half the length, one-third, one-fourth, and so on) created a series of ratios. When the string was divided at half its length (a ratio of 2:1), each half sounded one octave higher than the string vibrating as a whole. A ratio of 2:1 produces an octave, 3:2 is a fifth, 4:3 is a fourth, and so on.

A Pythagorean scale is based on a 3:2 ratio (a perfect, beatless fifth). A series of ascending perfect fifths, with resulting pitches lowered to fit within an octave gives us the 12 half steps of the chromatic scale. However, the ratios become very complicated (e.g., with C as a starting point, E–F = 256:243, F–F♯ = 2187:2048, etc.), resulting in two sizes of half steps. Not only that, enharmonic pitches (e.g., E♯ and F) are not equivalent. As long as music was monophonic, the Pythagorean scale worked very well; however, it is less useful for polyphonic music and for modulating between keys.

Just Intonation. In an attempt to overcome the complexities of the Pythagorean scale, ratios were simplified during the 15th and 16th centuries by using only whole number ratios (e.g., 3:2, 4:3, 5:4, etc.). However, this caused different sizes of whole steps, along with other problems, and once again it was less satisfactory for the development of polyphony.

Meantone Tuning. Because thirds were increasingly used during the 16th through 18th centuries—and Pythagorean and Just thirds sound "out of tune"—attempts were made to temper some of the intervals. Although meantone tuning was an improvement and did allow for "nearby" modulations, it also created different enharmonic pitches. For example, G♯ and A♭ and D♯ and E♭ were sometimes represented by divided (split) keys on keyboards during this time (Fig. 5.18). Performances comparing meantone to equal temperament can be heard on the internet.

Equal Temperament. In equal temperament, the octave is divided into 12 equal parts. The use of equal temperament, promoted by J.S. Bach's Well-Tempered Clavier (WTC Bk I in 1722 and Bk II in 1738–42), allows for free modulations, the use of chromaticism, and transposition. Note that Bach did not invent equal-temperament, but the WTC is the first collection to take full advantage of the new system.

Using a measurement system whereby 100 cents = one half step, you can use the following chart to compare these tuning systems (Table 5.7). Notice the disparities, particularly at mi, la, and ti.

Here are three primary musical consequences of equal-tempered tuning:

1. Because equal temperament is an artifact (i.e., it does not occur naturally) some musical instruments are built "out of tune." For example, brass players playing on valve instruments have to employ a number of devices to overcome tuning problems inherent in the

FIGURE 5.18
The Keyboard of a
Harpsichord by Bernhard
von Tucher (Germany).
The keyboard has "divided
black keys" in order to play
different enharmonic pitches
(e.g., G♯ or A♭) depending on
the key.

TABLE 5.7 | Different Tuning Systems with Diatonic Tones Shown in Cents Values.

	do	re	mi	fa	so	la	ti	do
Pythagorean	0	204	408	498	702	906	1110	1200
Just	0	204	386	498	702	884	1088	1200
Meantone	0	204	386	503	697	890	1083	1200
Equal Temperament	0	200	400	500	700	900	1100	1200

difference between the natural harmonic series (i.e., Pythagorean overtones) and equal temperament. Depending on the musical context, they may have to "lip" pitches up or down (i.e., adjust the embouchure), use valve slides, employ alternate fingerings, or, for horn players, adjust the hand in the bell.

2. Many claim that performers, especially singers performing *a capella* and string players in a string quartet or performing alone, tend to modify equal temperament by raising and lowering various intervals (e.g., raising the leading tone). The extent to which this actually occurs is not extensively studied, however. Howard (2007a) found that singers singing *a capella* tended to modify their tuning toward Just intonation. Singing music that shifts tonality in a non-equal tempered system necessarily means that the pitch center will drift and that the singers will have to modify their intonation to accommodate different keys (Howard, 2007b). In an earlier study, Nickerson (1949) studied solo and ensemble performances by accomplished string quartet players and found that Pythagorean intonation was typical of both unaccompanied and ensemble performances. Loosen (1993) examined how eight professional violinists performed an unaccompanied C major scale. He found that Pythagorean and equal-tempered scales were both appropriate for the performances, but that Just intonation was less successful.

3. For most performers, the advantages of equal temperament outweigh any disadvantages. As indicated previously, the considerable usage of modulations, chromaticism, and transposition in Western music is aided significantly by equal-tempered tuning.

Other scalar systems do occur in Western music, of course, but the vast majority of music is based on the 12-tone scale.

Non-Western Tuning Systems

Given the previously mentioned acuity of human hearing, it is not surprising that there is a bewildering array of tuning systems worldwide. Within this assortment of possibilities, however, the most common arrangements are five (pentatonic) or seven (heptatonic) pitches per octave. Often, the octave is divided into more than five or seven pitches (e.g., 24 pitches per octave in Arab music), but only five or seven are used in a given melody (Wade, 2009). As always, however, there are exceptions. For example, Sotho melodies and harmonies in South Africa are often based on a six-note scale (Allingham, 1999). Tetrachords are often used. A tetrachord consists of four scalar notes with an interval of a fourth separating the first from the last. Sometimes a lower and upper tetrachord are combined to form a heptatonic (seven-note) scale.

The following examples are brief glimpses into some of the tuning systems found in world music:

Thailand. Tuning in traditional Thai music involves seven equidistant pitches per octave (Morton & Duriyanga, 1976). Generally, melodies employ five of these pitches in a pentatonic scale with the other two used as passing tones or decorations. Measurements taken from fixed-pitch Thai instruments support this equidistant scalar structure of seven pitches.

Arab music. In Arab music, the octave is divided into 24 equivalent intervals (Touma, 2009). The function of any given tone depends not upon an absolute pitch but upon its position within a scale. Tones as sung or played may vary as much as a fourth above or below a notated pitch, depending upon the instrument or singer. Arab music contains as many as 70 modes, which are based on heptatonic scales.

India. Indian classical music is based on a foundation of 12-note heptatonic scales (Iyler, 2018). North Indian music has a system of ten heptatonic scales, while South Indian music employs 72 heptatonic scales. Pitches consist of notes from the 12 tones within an octave and microtones that are smaller than a semitone. Ragas (North Indian Hindustani) and ragam (South Indian Karnatic) are scale-like melodies, with 200 main patterns and their numerous, intricate, and complex variations.

Ghana. Musicians in northwestern Ghana use nine types of xylophone called gyil (plural: gyili or gyile) which may have from 12 to 18 slats or bars (Mensah, 1962). Tuning systems include anhemitonic (no half steps) pentatonic scales (approximately the intervals of the black keys on a piano), a pentatonic scale with intermittent major and minor thirds, and a scale with a perfect fourth, a minor third, a major second, and two minor seconds.

Uganda. Musicians use both free and fixed-key xylophones, some with a few and others with more than 20 keys (Bae, 2001; Teffera, 2011). Free-key xylophones have keys that are independent from each other and from the frame. Tuning ranges from four-note (tetra) to seven-note (heptatonic) scales.

Norway. The hardingfele is a Norwegian fiddle that employs a drone, along with four or five resonating strings (Cronshaw, 1999). The resonating strings can be arranged in 24 different tunings. Different regions feature different playing styles, and by favoring varying modalities (i.e., different tunings), performers can create different moods and inflections.

These few examples may serve to illustrate the variety and complexity of tuning systems used around the world. Numerous examples of these and other styles can be heard on the internet.

ACOUSTICS OF THE VOICE AND MUSICAL INSTRUMENTS

As described in Chapter 4, musical instruments can be divided into the following categories: idiophones, membranophones, aerophones, chordophones, electrophones, and corpophones. To this we must add the voice. There are so many variations throughout the world that detailed discussions are impossible in this limited format. Therefore, what follows is a very rudimentary introduction to basic acoustics of the voice and musical instruments. More detailed explanations can be found in many resources (e.g., Backus, 1977; Benade, 2012; Berg & Stork, 2005; Bilbao, 2009; Butler, 1992; Chaigne & Kergomard, 2016; Colwell, Hewitt, & Fonder, 2017; Fletcher & Rossing, 2012; Hall, 2002; Hartmann, 2013; Howard & Angus, 2006; Jeans, 1961; Olson, 1967; Parker & Smith, 2013; Roederer, 1973; Rossing, 2000, 2001; Rossing &Fletcher, 2004).

The Voice

At the simplest level, singing involves expelling air from the lungs through the trachea, setting the vocal cords into vibratory motion (Fig. 5.19). The vocal cords are mucosal membranes whose length can be adjusted by attached muscles. Although lengthening the strings of a violin lowers the pitch, lengthening the vocal cords raises the pitch as the increased tension and decreased mass of the cords overcompensates for the increased length. For normal speaking, male vocal cords have a fundamental frequency of 80–240 Hz, females from 140–500 Hz, and children from 170–600 Hz (Handel, 1989).

Vocal cords produce complex vibrations that consist of a fundamental and many overtones. Acting as a resonator, the oral cavity is shaped by vowel formation (also involving the articulators—lips, tongue, and soft palate) which affects timbre and intonation. The nasal

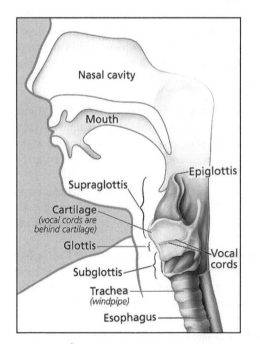
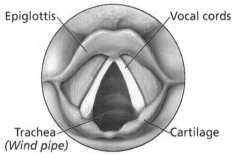

FIGURE 5.19 | Illustration of the Human Vocal Tract (Left) and the Vocal Cords (Right).

cavity and maxillary sinuses (on the sides of the nose below the cheeks and above the teeth) may also play an important role as they enhance the singer's formant (Sundberg et al., 2007). However, this notion is controversial, as noted by Titze, who wrote "The fact that the sensations are felt in the face is an indication of effective conversion of aerodynamic energy to acoustic energy, rather than sound resonation in the sinuses or the nasal airways" (Titze, 2001, p. 519). An early experiment supports the contention that nasal resonance adds little to the quality of the singing voice (Vennard, 1964). Singers' nasal passages were blocked and listeners could tell no difference in the quality of sound compared to normal singing. With evidence on both sides of the issue, "the role of nasal resonances in singing is unclear" (Gramming, Nord, Sundberg, & Elliot, 1993, p. 35). Perhaps some of the disagreement can be resolved by saying that the role of nasal resonance may depend upon the individual singer and the repertoire or style being sung.

In any musical instrument there are formant regions that amplify frequencies that fall within certain bands due to characteristics of the instrument (size, shape, etc.). In the voice, formants are created by the size and shape of the oral cavity, tongue placement, and vowel formation. The so-called singer's formant is around 2.9 KHz. An orchestra's energy is 25 dB less in this frequency range than at lower frequencies; thus, the solo singer's voice can be projected above the orchestra (Backus, 1977).

Aerophones

Two factors unite all wind instruments: (1) They all use air as an energy source to generate sound. (2) They all involve columns of air vibrating inside a hollow tube, producing standing waves. The vibrating entity varies according to the following:

- Flutes: the air column is split along the edge of a tone hole. Some of the vibrations travel down the length of the hollow tube. Keys shorten or lengthen the tube, raising and lowering the pitch respectively.
- Single reeds: the player's breath sets a reed vibrating against a mouthpiece and the vibrating air column travels down the length of the instrument, venting when keys are lifted or air holes left open.
- Free reeds: a reed inside a frame is set into motion by a player's breath or bellows (e.g., accordion or reed organ).
- Double reeds: air passes between two reeds, setting them in motion.
- Trumpet and horn-like instruments: Breath sets the player's lips into vibration and again the vibrating column of air travels throughout the length of the instrument

Two additional acoustical concepts are important: open/closed pipes and cylindrical/conical bores. Open pipes are open to the air at both ends (e.g., a transverse flute, all brass instruments). Closed pipes are open at only one end (e.g., woodwind instruments except the flute). When the air is directed down the length of the instrument in longitudinal waves—to the end or near the bell, or to the farthest open tone hole—standing waves are set in motion, with molecules of air moving back and forth between nodes at a frequency matching the fundamental pitch being played. Nodes are points at which the wave reverses itself; antinodes are where the amplitude is the greatest (Fig. 5.20). The length of the standing wave is determined by the length of the pipe.

Cylindrical pipes have a bore or inner diameter that remains the same for the length of the pipe; conical pipes have a bore that increases along its length. The clarinet and some brass instruments (e.g., trumpet and trombone) are primarily cylindrical; the rest are conical.

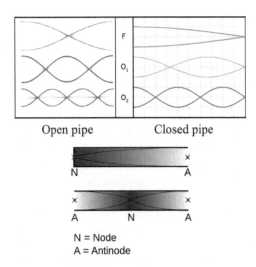

N = Node
A = Antinode

FIGURE **5.20**

Open and Closed Pipes. Top left: The fundamental and first two overtones in an open pipe. Top right: The fundamental and first two overtones in a closed pipe. Bottom: Nodes and antinodes.

Cylindrical instruments usually have a brighter, more penetrating tone and conical instrumentals have a mellower, darker tone. For example, the trumpet and cornet are the same length and produce the same fundamental pitch. However, the trumpet with its bright tone is approximately two-thirds cylindrical, while the mellower cornet is about 70% conical.

Keyboards are normally divided between aerophones (organs) and chordophones (pianos). Some have even considered pianos as a percussion instrument. Mbiras, kalimbas, and similar instruments are considered plucked idiophones. Most musical instrument museums use the Hornbostel-Sachs system, but there are serious reservations about how well it works, since some instruments cannot be accurately classified by a system based on "initial vibration" (Weisser & Quanten, 2011). For example, the piano is classified as a chordophone because vibrating strings produce the initial sound, however, the soundboard has a stronger effect on the sound perceived. Nevertheless, pianos, organs, and other keyboard instruments do share some acoustical characteristics with other classifications.

Chordophones

String instruments include all those that produce a sound by a vibrating string; in the West this includes violin, viola, cello, bass, guitar (lute, banjo, ukulele, etc.), piano, and harpsichord. Around the world, there are numerous examples such as the sitar (India), erhu (China), or guitarrón (Mexico). In each case, sound is produced by a string that is set into motion by bowing, plucking, or striking.

The perceived pitch (fundamental frequency or f_0) produced by a given string is determined by the mass per unit length (determined by the thickness, type of material, etc.), the length of the string, and the amount of tension it is under. For example, as shown in Figure 5.21, the strings of a violin are anchored at the top end as they cross the nut and are wound onto the pegs in the scroll. At the lower end they are anchored by the tail piece. They are raised slightly above the fingerboard by the bridge. Tuning is primarily done by turning the peg that increases or decreases the tension of each string; tightening the tuning peg raises the pitch. Once the string is set in vibration, the sound is amplified by the body of the violin; vibrations are transferred through the bridge to the top of the violin and the sound post transmits the vibrations from the top plate (belly) to the back plate. The air inside the violin body is also amplifying the sound and the f holes allow this sound to be projected to the outside.

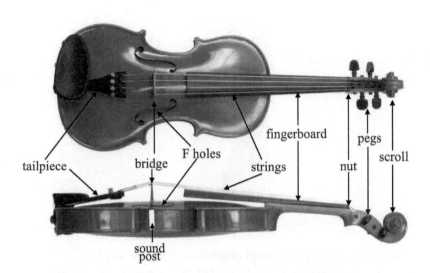

FIGURE 5.21 |
Components
of a Violin.

*Acoustical
Foundations
of Music*^{MT5}

fingerboard

pegs

F holes

scroll

tailpiece

bridge

strings

nut

sound
post

Idiophones, Membranophones, and Corpophones

Idiophones include those instruments that are struck, such as gongs, bells, xylophones and marimbas, and those that are shaken like rattles. Membranophones, mostly drums, produce sound by a vibrating membrane. Corpophones refer to body percussion. These three classifications are combined in this discussion for three reasons: (1) they share many acoustical properties, (2) there are so many different idiophones and membranophones that it is impossible to cover them all, and (3) acoustical properties are often very complex. Thorough discussions of all the possibilities are beyond the scope of this book.

One way of organizing these three categories is by separating instruments into those that are pitched (e.g., xylophones and marimbas) from those that are unpitched (e.g., maracas and rainsticks). Body percussion is almost entirely unpitched, with limited exceptions such as patting an open mouth and modifying the oral cavity. Drums with an indefinite pitch may have one head (e.g., djembé) or two heads attached at either end of a cylindrical body (e.g., snare drum, bass drum, Japanese *taiko*). Vibratory rates are more complex than pitched drums, as the two drumheads may move in opposite directions at higher modes. In unpitched instruments, the vibration rates and patterns change rapidly over time such that the waves are aperiodic and as a result the pitch is indefinite (Fig. 5.22).

Actually, one of the aforementioned complexities is a fuzziness in the distinction between pitched and unpitched instruments. There are many different types of gongs or tam-tams around the world and some of them are pitched; many, however, have an indefinite pitch. Cymbals, gongs, and tam-tams produce many different frequencies. Although the size of the vibrating plate may result in higher or lower qualities, pitches are indefinite. Percussionists talk about "tuning" a bass drum; changing the tension on the drumhead raises and lowers the pitch, although, again, it is still somewhat indefinite.

Pitched idiophones and membranophones, here classified as percussion instruments, include an enormous variety of instruments around the world. In the interests of space, we will discuss only two types: xylophones and timpani.

Xylophones and marimbas generally have a series of bars made of wood, metal, or synthetic material laid from lowest to highest sounding pitches. The width of the bar has no effect on the pitch, but length and thickness do (Suits, 2001). In Western instruments, the bars are arched on the underside (i.e., the center is thinner than the ends) as a means of tuning the

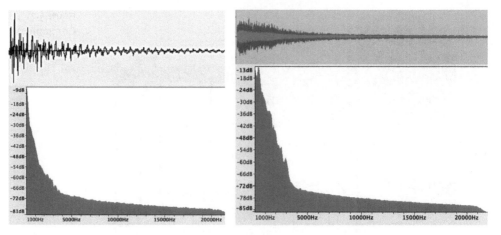

FIGURE 5.22 | Bass Drums (Left Panels) and Gongs (Right Panels) Vibrate with Many Frequencies but There Is an Immediate and Rapid Drop-Off. Notice with the gong there is a slight build up to the peak energy; this is because it takes a fraction of a second to put the mass of the gong into full vibration. That is why in the orchestra, the player normally "warms up" the gong by stroking it or striking it softly and silently to set the gong into vibratory motion without producing an audible sound. This is done a few seconds before the actual entrance of the gong in the music so that it will produce the desired sound immediately.

overtones (Fig. 5.23). Researchers tested the acoustical properties of 59 different species of wood bars (Aramaki, Baillères, Brancheriau, Kronland-Martinet, & Ystad, 2007). One conclusion was that an instrument maker cannot judge the suitability of the wood independent from the bar dimensions.

In drums with a fixed pitch such as timpani or the Indian tabla, a membrane is stretched over a circular frame and held under adjustable tension. Drumheads vibrate in many different patterns, with each pattern representing different frequencies and amplitudes. Radial patterns divide the membrane into halves, fourths, sixths, eighths, and tenths (Hall, 2002). In each case, during each half of the frequency cycle a portion of the drumhead is above the equilibrium plane and its corresponding opposite portion is below the plane. There are also circular patterns and combinations of circular and radial patterns. The first ten vibratory modes with a fundamental of B^3 produce overtones as notated in Figure 5.24. This complexity of vibrations is at least a partial explanation for why even well-tuned timpani do not produce sharply defined pitches.

Electrophones

Electronic music instruments have proliferated in recent decades (Hartmann, 2013; Manning, 2013). Music controllers (e.g., MIDI keyboard) allow musicians to control input while music synthesizers generate the sounds. Software sequencers allow composers to record, edit, mix, and play back audio files. Drum machines provide control over percussion instrument sounds, as well as create new ones. Analog synthesizers produce music from a collection of electronic circuits, samplers utilize digital recordings, and digital synthesizers use digital signal processing (DSP). Mixers allow for the combination of two or more sounds. Most often, computers and computer software are used in electronic music composing, often at digital audio workstations. The internet allows for global networking, meaning that musicians can work or perform together even though they are separated by thousands of miles.

FIGURE 5.23 | Xylophone and Marimba Bars Are Tuned by Thinning the Underside in an Arch.

FIGURE 5.24 | Overtones Produced on a Timpani Tuned to B³. Open noteheads are pitches that do not correspond well to equal temperament

Howard and Angus (2006) list several elements of electronic music from an acoustics point of view:

- Filtering removes unwanted components from a sound source such as background noise.
- Equalization is a process of increasing/decreasing aspects of an audio signal to achieve a desired balance. This could include correcting deficiencies accrued in the recording process (e.g., caused by microphone placement), modifying timbres for artistic purposes, or altering the balance of sounds in the mix.
- Adding artificial reverberation. An interesting application of this technology is in creating virtual acoustic spaces such as music practice rooms or small rehearsal rooms where the acoustics can be made to resemble a much larger and more desirable space (Lokki, Pätynen, Peltonen, & Salmensaari, 2009; Pätynen, 2007).
- Chorus, automatic double tracking (ADT), phasing, and flanging are special effects related to artificial reverberation. These effects include creating the illusion of a large group from a single source (chorus), and so on.
- Pitch processing and time modification allow for the manipulation of the signal by shifting pitches up or down, speeding up or slowing down, and so on.
- Sound morphing and vocoding. Sound morphing allows for the creation of new sounds by combing sound sources. An interesting example can be heard in the movie *Farinelli* where the sounds of a soprano and counter tenor were combined to give the effect of a castrato singer. Vocoding is a process of turning sounds into speech, so that a waterfall or a violin might talk.
- Spatial processing refers to creating stereo, surround effects, binaural stereo for headphones, and other spatial effects.
- Loudness processing refers to the manipulation of various components of an audio signal to make them softer or louder.

New possibilities for electronic music are becoming available at increasingly rapid rates and the landscape of music is changing drastically. For example, the sound tracks for many television shows are produced at a digital audio workstation in one location with the final product sent via the internet to a studio production facility on the other side of the country (Holman, 2010).

ROOM ACOUSTICS

What makes a great concert hall acoustically? Beranek (2004) interviewed over 100 famous conductors and music critics about their acoustical preferences as a partial means of determining the best concert halls. Three of the most highly rated halls were the Musikverein in Vienna (Fig. 5.25), Boston Symphony Hall, and Carnegie Hall in New York City. Reverberation time (RT) was one of the first things that most conductors mentioned. Six conductors from the pre-1962 era—George Szell, Bruno Walter, Herbert von Karajan, Dimitri Mitropoulos, Eugene Ormandy, and Pierre Monteux—said that the Musikverein was the liveliest and that Carnegie Hall was somewhat drier. This was born out in acoustical studies; when the halls were occupied, the Musikverein had a reverberation time of 2 seconds and Carnegie Hall was 1.8 seconds (Beranek, 2008). Thus, a reverberation time of around 1.9 seconds is best suited to symphonic repertoire. Concert halls judged to be dry had RTs between 1 and 1.4 seconds. Of course, there are many other factors to be considered, such as size of the hall, seating capacity, type of music being performed, and many other factors, as well as personal preferences.

Hall (2002) listed seven important standards for judging acoustics of a concert hall:

- clarity—all sounds should be heard clearly and distinctly.
- uniformity—the sound should be even across the hall, with no dead spots
- envelopment—audience members should not feel separate from the sound, though it should clearly emanate from the stage.
- smoothness—reflections should blend and not be perceived as separate sounds. The initial time-delay gap (ITDG) is the length of the gap between when the direct sound is heard and the first reflection. In Boston Symphony Hall, the ITDG is about 15 milliseconds, which is considered ideal (Beranek, 2008).
- Reverberation—as indicated previously, the ideal RT is around 1.9 seconds.
- Performer satisfaction—performers on the stage should be able to hear each other well and have a good sense of the overall sound being heard by the audience.
- Freedom from noise—performers on stage and audience members should not be distracted by extraneous noises (e.g., ventilators fans, backstage or street noises, etc.). Ambient noise with no audience present should not be much above 40 dB.

FIGURE 5.25 | The Golden Hall of Musikverein Vienna. Photo taken on the 147th anniversary of the building, which was inaugurated January 6, 1870.

Obviously, designing and building successful concert halls requires a blend of architectural and acoustical engineering, along with artistic input. Often, after a hall is built, modifications are necessary to "tune" the hall. For example, after the Toyo Opera City concert hall was built, a tuning concert was held with Seiji Ozawa conducting the New Japan Philharmonic Orchestra (Hidaka, Beranek, Masuda, Nishihara, & Okano, 2000). On the basis of acoustical measures taken during the concert and post-concert responses by performers and audience members, further adjustments were made. As a means of creating a more desirable acoustical profile or changing the acoustics for different types of performances, tunable (i.e., adjustable) surface diffusers can be placed in various parts of the hall, such as the ceiling and walls (Cox & D'Antonio, 2003; Jaffe, 2005).

CONCLUSION

Investigating human perception of sound is a highly complex study, but this study can be aided by a basic understanding of how sound works outside the human organism—measurable, physical acoustics as opposed to perceptual psychoacoustics. While by no means exhaustive, this chapter has presented an overview of some well-established basic principles related to physical acoustics in an attempt to build such a framework for a deeper investigation of how sound and music affect us all. Practical applications of acoustics principals are found in tuning systems, musical instruments, and room acoustics.

DISCUSSION QUESTIONS

When Einstein developed his theory of relativity, he engaged in several "thought experiments" to help him conceptualize the universe. He later applied mathematics as a way of confirming his ideas. In a similar way, the first seven questions are thought experiments. As you have read in this chapter, you can also use mathematics to confirm and explain these ideas. As a basis for the first five questions, you are a participant in a science fiction experiment and have been made weightless and small enough to sit on a single molecule of air.

1. Pick a single molecule of air inside a concert hall that you will ride on. Describe the motion you would experience in two conditions: (1) when the hall is empty (i.e., no people in the seats; no activity going on) and (2) when an audience files in prior to a concert.
2. Imagine that someone on stage is sounding a tuning fork, which emits a pure tone. Describe the motion of your molecule of air as the sound wave reaches it.
3. What will happen to your molecule of air if a small tuning fork is set into motion with very little energy and then after the sound stops a much larger tuning fork is sounded with a great deal of energy?
4. Imagine a tuning fork being sounded and then when the sound stops a single note on a trumpet (or any other musical instrument) is played? Further, imagine that the tuning fork and the trumpet are vibrating at the same frequency, amplitude, and length of time. What would the difference be in the motion of your molecule of air to these two sounds?
5. Imagine you are sitting on your molecule of air in a completely silent concert hall. Describe how the motion of your molecule would change if a cello on stage left and flute on stage right being playing at the same time.
   For the next two questions, you are no longer sitting on a single molecule of air but are riding on a sound wave at it travels across the space of the concert hall.

6. Once again, small and large tuning forks are sounded one after the other. Which of the waves you are riding on would be shorter (i.e., as measured from peak to peak)? Why? If one was sounded with little energy and the other sounded with much more energy, would that change the lengths of the sound waves they produce?

7. Imagine you are perched on a violin string and are suddenly cast into the auditorium when the violin begins to play. What are the possible things that might happen to the sound wave you are riding on as you travel across the room?

8. Do you think all musicians should understand the basic principles of music acoustics? Why or why not?

9. Apply what you have learned about acoustics to your own musical situation (e.g., as a performer, conductor, teacher, composer, etc.).

10. Discuss tuning systems as they apply to your principal instrument/voice both individually and as a member of a larger ensemble.

Chapter 6

Musical Hearing[MT6]

HEARING is considered by some to be the most important sense in humans (Carey, 2008). Whether it is or not, a thorough understanding of the physiology of the hearing mechanism is essential to understanding many aspects of musical behavior, because it is primarily the sense of hearing that makes music possible. Three elements are needed for the perception of sound to take place—a source of vibrations, a medium of transmission, and a perceiver. The first two elements were discussed in the previous chapter; this chapter includes a discussion of the third element—the perception of sound. In the following pages, a sound wave will be traced from outside the ear to the brain and the perception of psychological attributes of sound will be discussed.

Throughout this discussion, the reader is urged to keep in mind the incredible sensitivity of the hearing mechanism and its extreme miniaturization. For instance, one can perceive sound when the eardrum has been deformed as little as one-tenth the diameter of a hydrogen molecule (Everest, 1986). The softest sounds we can hear result from air pressure changes of two ten-billionths of atmospheric pressure (Watson, 2009), and the ratio of the loudest sound we can hear to the softest is more than a trillion to one (Schroeder, 1993). Kunchur (2008) found that listeners could discern temporal alterations on a time scale of five microseconds. One of the bones of the middle ear, the stirrup, is the smallest in the human body at "about half the size of a grain of rice" (Stevens & Warshofsky, 1965, p. 35) (see Fig. 6.1) and Reissner's membrane in the cochlea is only two cells thick (Gulick, Gesheider, & Frisina, 1989). This marvelous engineering should give musicians and all others who enjoy the sounds they hear a feeling of awe and appreciation.

THE HEARING MECHANISM

Outer Ear

The outer ear consists of the visible ear on the outside of the head (the auricle or pinna), ear canal, and eardrum. The hearing process begins as sound pressure waves, traveling through the atmosphere, strike the ears. Ears, as one can readily observe, vary considerably in size and shape from person to person. Some animals have muscular control over their ears and can tilt or rotate them in different directions, an aid to the localization of sound. Humans do not possess this ability and, instead, turn their heads toward a sound to aid in localization[MT6.2].

A commonly supposed function of the outer ear (pinna) is that it catches sound waves. "The sound waves coming towards us from all sides, however, have wave lengths measured

FIGURE **6.1** | The Stirrup (Stapes) Is the Smallest Bone in the Human Body.

in many inches, feet, or even yards, whereas the diameter of the pinna and especially of the inner conch [the ear canal] is not much more than one inch. The sound is, therefore, scattered rather than collected and focused" (Lowenstein, 1966, p. 126). Man's outer ears do help to make sounds originating from in front of the head slightly more intense than those originating from behind and this aids in sound localization. Cupping a hand behind an ear demonstrates how the outer ear makes sounds louder and easier to hear.

Another aid to sound localization is the inner contour of the ear shell. As sound waves reflect off the ridges and folds of the outer ear, they provide localization cues to the brain (Blauert, 1997). Using a dummy head equipped with artificial ears, researchers demonstrated that by gradually smoothing out the inner surface of the outer ears they were able to reduce the ability to localize sounds (Everest, 1986; Moore, 1987). Localization of sounds is also greatly aided by timing cues. Sounds arrive at the two ears a microsecond apart (e.g., a sound coming from your left side must go around the head to reach the right ear) and the brain uses these minute discrepancies in arrival time to locate the direction of the sound.

Another portion of the outer ear is the *ear canal* (external auditory meatus). This air-filled cavity has two protective devices to keep unwanted dust particles or other foreign bodies from entering the ear; the outermost edge is lined with hairs and the surface of the ear canal is lubricated with a sticky wax. The primary function of the ear canal is to channel air pressure waves to the eardrum. It also acts as a resonator and amplifies sounds in the range of 2,000–4,000 Hz as much as 15 dB, precisely the frequencies most important for music and speech (Handel, 1989). Finally, the ear canal has the function of controlling the temperature and humidity of the eardrum (tympanum), which lies at the far end of the canal.

The *eardrum* receives air pressure waves from the atmosphere via the ear canal and vibrates in accordance with the frequency and intensity of the waves. It is an extremely sensitive membrane. Responding to the movement of molecules of air, the eardrum transmits a wide variety of vibrations, from the faintest whisper to the loudest explosion. Evidence of the eardrum's sensitivity is the fact that its thinnest portion is only 0.055 mm thick (Donaldson & Duckert, 1991).

Middle Ear

Between the eardrum and the cochlea in the inner ear is the air-filled cavity called the middle ear. This cavity is not completely closed, but has an opening into the oral cavity, the Eustachian tube. The eardrum connects with the inner ear by means of three small bones. Known collectively as the *ossicles*, and separately as the hammer (malleus), anvil (incus), and stirrup (stapes), these bones are among the smallest in the human body. The ossicles serve as a link between the outer ear and inner ear. At one end, the hammer is attached to the eardrum, and, at the other end, the stirrup is connected to the cochlea at the oval window (see Figure. 6.2).

A sound wave traveling in the atmosphere reaches the ear and is channeled through the ear canal to the eardrum[MT6.3]. The eardrum, in sympathetic vibration with the sound wave, vibrates back and forth, moving the hammer, anvil, and stirrup. These bones not only transfer the vibration to the oval window, but, due to their specific motions and the disparity in size between the eardrum and oval window, also amplify the vibrations. As they travel through the air, sound waves meet with very little resistance, especially when compared to the resistance found in the dense fluid (perilymph) of the cochlea. In fact, the impedance of cochlear fluid is approximately 3,750 times greater than that of air (Everest, 1986). If a sound wave traveling through the air struck the oval window directly, without receiving amplification from the auditory canal, the eardrum and the ossicles, less than one percent of the energy would be transmitted to the fluid-filled cochlea (Watson, 2009). Actually, the motions of the middle ear are quite complex, but the important fact is this increase in energy from the eardrum to the oval window.

The increase in energy from that found at the eardrum to that necessary at the oval window as it pushes against the perilymph is created in three ways. First, the eardrum is much larger than the oval window, which causes an increase in pressure of 35 times. Second, the eardrum buckles in the middle, which doubles the pressure at the oval window. Third, the

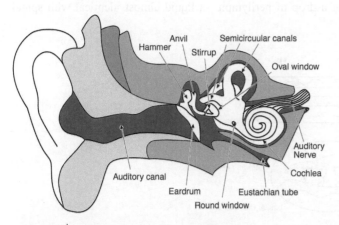

FIGURE **6.2** | Detail of the Hearing Mechanism.

ossicles, acting as levers, increase the pressure by a factor of 1.15. Taking these three factors into account gives an overall increase of pressure at the oval window of 80.5 times (35 × 2 × 1.15 = 80.5) (Handel, 1989).

Three muscle actions, combining to form the acoustic (or stapedius) reflex, play an important role in protecting the ear against loud noises. First, the muscles that control the eardrum can contract and draw the drum into a conical shape. This stiffens the membrane so that it cannot vibrate so much. Second, the muscles of the ossicles can twist the bones so that they are somewhat rotated and lose a little of their amplifying efficiency. Third, an attached muscle can alter the stirrup in relation to the oval window, again causing a loss of amplification. Also, the Eustachian tube, normally closed, can be opened by opening the mouth or swallowing. This allows air pressure to be equalized on both sides of the eardrum. Unfortunately, even with all these protective devices, the ear has no way of protecting itself against sudden, loud noises. Each of the muscle actions can take place only after a realization that a sound is too loud and even though the reaction is very quick—about 10–20 ms—it is not quick enough to protect against a sudden, unexpected, loud noise (Hall, 2002).

Inner Ear

The oval window separates the air-filled middle ear cavity from the fluid-filled inner ear. The inner ear consists of the semicircular canals and the cochlea. The semicircular canals serve an important function in determining body position but they are not involved in the process of hearing. The cochlea has another surface membrane besides the oval window. This is the round window, which serves to release pressure built up in the cochlea (see Figure 6.3).

The *cochlea* is a spiral-shaped body of two and one half turns (Howard & Angus, 2006; see Fig. 6.4), "no bigger than the tip of the little finger" (Stevens & Warshofsky, 1965, p. 43). "It is about 1⅓ inches long and perhaps 1/8 inch wide at its broadest point" (Pierce & David, 1958, p. 136). Along most of its length, it is divided by the cochlear duct into two parts: the vestibular canal (scala vestibuli) and the tympanic canal (scala tympani) (see Figure. 6.3). These two canals are connected at the tip of the cochlear spiral by the helicotrema and are filled with perilymph. The cochlear duct is filled with endolymph and is bound on one side by Reissner's membrane (next to the scala vestibuli) and on the other side by the basilar membrane (next to the scala tympani).

The system of vestibular and tympanic canals, with the cochlear duct, is so tiny that it takes only a fraction of a drop of perilymph—a liquid almost identical with spinal

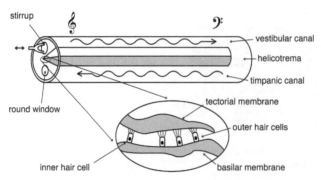

FIGURE **6.3** | Diagram of the Cochlea as if it Were Unrolled.

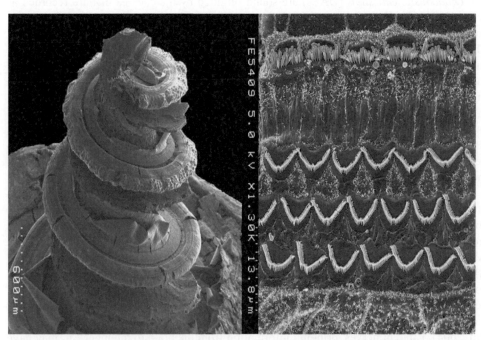

FIGURE **6.4** | The Cochlea and Auditory Hair Cells. On the left is a cast of the cochlea, which is a hollowed canal in the temporal bone. On the right are auditory hair cells, with one row of inner hair cells at the top and three rows of outer hair cells at the bottom in their characteristic V or W shape.

fluid—to fill the canals, and even less endolymph—similar to the fluid within cells—to fill the duct.

(Stevens & Warshofsky, 1965, p. 43)

Reissner's membrane, only two cells thick, is the thinnest in the human body. The *basilar membrane* is made of relatively stiff fibers and, from the oval window to the apex, widens to six times its original size (Gulick et al., 1989). One side of the basilar membrane is attached to a bony shelf; the other side is attached to ligaments and is free to vibrate.

Resting on the basilar membrane is the *organ of Corti*. The organ of Corti contains the arches of Corti, which support one inner and three (four or five near the apex) outer rows of sensory hair cells (see Figure 6.4). There are about 3,500 *inner hair cells* and 20,000 *outer hair cells* (Donaldson & Duckert, 1991). Approximately 30,000 auditory neurons synapse onto the inner hair cells (Stainsby & Cross, 2009). Outer hair cells can shorten their length up to two microns as many as 30,000 times per second. This is 100 times faster than anything else in biology (Miller, 1993). The conjecture is that this rapid length change may enhance the auditory signal, improving sensitivity and fine-tuning. Overlapping the organ of Corti is the tectorial membrane (see Figure 6.3). About 100 microscopic, threadlike filaments, called stereocilia, emerge from each outer hair cell and are embedded in the tectorial membrane. About 50 stereocilia emerge from each inner hair cell but these are not embedded in the tectorial membrane. "At the threshold of hearing, the faintest sound we can hear, tiny filaments associated with the stereocilia move about 0.04 nm—about the radius of a hydrogen atom" (Everest & Pholmann, 2009, p. 46).

Otoacoustic emissions (OAEs) are sounds emitted by the cochlea that are recorded as acoustic vibrations in the ear canal (Probst, Lonsbury-Martin, & Martin, 1990). These sounds are created by a reverse electrical-to-mechanical transduction process in the outer hair cells. Their presence may explain the role of outer hair cells in sharpening pitch perception. Measuring OAEs provides a noninvasive means of studying the mechanics of the cochlea and forms an important part of clinical hearing tests. OAEs can be suppressed through activation of the efferent system (i.e., from brain to ear) (Hood, 2001). There is a relationship between the suppression of OAE and pitch matching and pitch discrimination in trained musicians, as trained musicians have better OAE suppression than musically untrained individuals (Brashears, Morlet, Berlin, & Hood, 2003). Untrained individuals did not show a relationship between OAE suppression and pitch skills (Moore, Estis, Zhang, Watts, & Marble, 2007); therefore, musical training appears to have a positive effect on OAE suppression.

Linking the inner ear to the brain is the *auditory nerve*, which allows for two-way communication. For each cochlea, there are about 50,000 fibers that carry information from the cochlea to the brain along ascending (afferent) pathways and 1,800 fibers that carry signals from the brain to the cochlea along descending (efferent) pathways (Gulick et al., 1989). About 93% of the fibers of the auditory nerve supply the inner hair cells (Hackney, 1987), which represent only 20% of the total number of hair cells. While many outer hair cells may converge on a single auditory nerve, each inner hair cell may stimulate up to 20 auditory nerve fibers, most of which are afferent (Plack, 2005). Because of this arrangement, inner hair cells provide more acoustic information (Frolenkov, Belyantseva, Friedman, & Griffith, 2004). Efferent nerves, bringing information from the brain to the inner ear, may have to do with increasing the frequency resolution of the inner hair cells (Handel, 1989; Wallin, 1991).

As the stirrup pushes on the oval window, causing it to move in and out, waves are propagated through the perilymph and passed along the vestibular canal to the *helicotrema*, making the return trip through the tympanic canal. At the end of this two-way trip through the spirals of the cochlea, the waves push against the round window. When the oval window is pushed in by the action of the stirrup, the round window is pushed out by the pressure of the waves traveling through the perilymph. The energy transmitted by the movements of the round window is released into the air cavity of the middle ear, where it returns to the atmosphere via the Eustachian tube.

On its journey through the vestibular and tympanic canals, the pressure wave transmits some of its energy to the membranes of the cochlear duct and the endolymph contained in it. As the membranes and the endolymph vibrate, the arches of Corti are also vibrated. "When the basilar membrane is deformed in vibration, the reticular lamina, tectorial membrane and organ of Corti slide with respect to each other, bending the hairs" (Pierce & David, 1958, p. 140).

It is this shearing action—caused by the membranes traveling in opposite directions—that excites the hair cells. Hair cells can be stimulated when they are deformed as little as 100 picometers, or one-trillionth of a meter (Hudspeth, 1983). An analogous experience can be felt if the hairs on the arm are lightly stimulated; as the hairs are bent, they propagate signals to the brain transmitting information about the touch sensation, such as whether the touch was closer to the wrist or the elbow. The hair cells act as transducers, and it is at this point that the mechanical energy of the waves in the cochlear fluid is converted to electrochemical energy.

The hair cells are arranged along the length of the basilar membrane in such a way that those nearest the oval window respond to higher frequencies and those nearest the helicotrema at the far end respond to lower frequencies. It is interesting to note that, "the musically most important range of frequencies (approximately 20–4,000 Hz) covers roughly two-thirds of the extension of the basilar membrane (12–35 mm from the base)" (Roederer, 1975, p. 21). MMT 6.1, Ear Anatomy, provides additional details and visualizations.

From Ear to Brain

Auditory information does not travel from the inner ear to the primary *auditory cortex* along a simple, straight-line route. Rather, information is transmitted along a very diffuse and intricate pathway (Beament, 2003). Since even the brief overview that follows is fairly complicated, it may be more important to remember these general points: (1) Analysis of auditory information takes place in many localized processing centers scattered along a diffuse pathway between the inner ear and the auditory cortex; (2) each of these processing centers analyzes the auditory information for a particular feature, such as location of the source of the sound; and (3) all these bits and pieces of information are put back together to create a coherent sound experience with meaning (e.g., music) in the primary auditory cortex and the surrounding association areas.

Frequency representation of the basilar membrane is retained along the auditory nerve. Fibers in the center of the auditory nerve carry information about low frequencies, and fibers on the outside carry higher frequencies (Plack, 2005). Maintenance of frequency information in a spatial representation or map is called tonotopicity or *tonotopical organization*. The first portion of the auditory nerve is sometimes referred to as the bottle neck of auditory sensation because at this point all the information relayed between the ear and the brain is carried in a single bundle of fibers, unlike the more diffuse pathways higher in the brain.

The auditory nerve, as part of the eighth cranial nerve, divides as it enters the brainstem and sends fibers to both the upper (dorsal) and lower (ventral) cochlear nuclei (see Figure. 6.5). More fibers go to the larger ventral cochlear nucleus than to the smaller dorsal cochlear nucleus. Beginning at this level, the auditory pathway rapidly increases in diversity and complexity. Tonotopic organization is retained, with higher frequencies represented in the dorsal cochlear nucleus and lower frequencies in the ventral cochlear nucleus. Different neurons in the cochlear nuclei respond to different aspects of the acoustic information, such as stimulus onset or offset (Handel, 1989). The cochlear nuclei not only relay information, but also sort, enhance, and encode information to be sent to higher auditory nuclei (Gulick et al., 1989).

As fibers leave the cochlear nuclei, the first crossovers (*decussations*) in the auditory pathway occur and some fibers are sent to the superior olivary complex and inferior colliculus on the opposite (contralateral) side. This is the beginning of bilateral representation of sound. Other fibers that leave the cochlear nuclei extend to the superior olivary complex and inferior colliculus on the same (ipsilateral) side, and to the reticular formation (Plack, 2005).

The superior olivary complex is tonotopically organized in some portions. The portions not so organized are believed to be involved in processing binaural time and intensity disparity cues for sound localization (Plack, 2005). Also, at the superior olivary complex there are already individual cells that receive incoming signals from both ears, as well as from the eyes (Shepherd, 1994).

Some of the fibers from the ventral cochlear nucleus extend to the reticular formation. The reticular formation communicates with virtually all areas of the brain, including the cortex and spinal cord. There is a parallel pathway in the reticular formation (not shown in Figure. 6.5) that connects with descending tracts in the spinal cord to allow for reflex-type responses to sound stimuli. The descending or efferent pathway emanating from the reticular formation also serves to inhibit lower auditory centers and elevate thresholds of hearing. The ascending pathway from the reticular formation serves to alert the cortex of important upcoming signals (Silverstein, Silverstein, & Nunn, 2001). Animals whose classical auditory

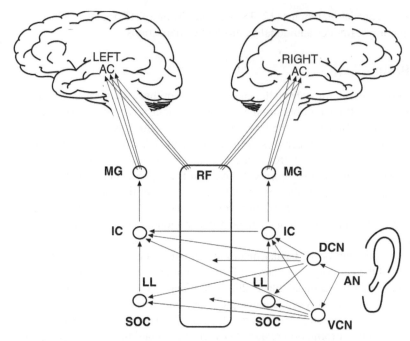

FIGURE **6.5** | Schematic Drawing of the Ascending Auditory Pathway.

Notes: AN = Auditory Nerve (Cochlea), VCN = Ventral Cochlear Nucleus (Brainstem), DCN = Dorsal Cochlear Nucleus (Brainstem), SOC = Superior Olivary Complex (Midbrain), IC = Inferior Colliculus (Midbrain), LL = Lateral Lemniscus (Midbrain), RF = Reticular Formation (Midbrain), MG = Medial Geniculate (Thalamus), AC = Auditory Cortex (Cerebral Cortex).

pathways have been cut regain their ability to respond to sounds using this alternate auditory pathway through the reticular formation.

Cells in the medial olivary complex respond to temporal delays and are tuned to specific tonal frequencies. Because there are more cells tuned to lower frequencies, these nuclei may have a significant role in locating the source of lower frequencies (Hackney, 1987). Cells in the lateral superior olive specialize in detecting intensity differences in the two ears and provide localization of higher frequency tones (Gulick et al., 1989). As sound waves travel through the air, the head casts a "shadow" such that there is a slight time differential in the arrival of the sound wave at the two ears. Since lower frequencies have longer waves, this shadow effect has more consequences for higher frequency tones. One role of the olivary complex, then, is to create a spatial map (Handel, 1989).

The last point for fibers from one ear to cross over to the opposite side is at the inferior colliculus, which receives its fibers from the superior olivary complex via the lateral lemniscus and from the cochlear nuclei. These crossing fibers, which extend to the contralateral inferior colliculus, are probably responsible for certain forms of sound integration, since up to 80% of the cells can be stimulated binaurally (Handel, 1989; Moore, 1987). There is considerable tonotopical organization with low frequencies at the sides and higher frequencies in the center.

The final relay station before the auditory pathway reaches the cortex is the medial geniculate body, located in the thalamus. Frequency-specific fibers leaving the medial geniculate body fan out in ascending auditory radiations and provide frequency information to the auditory cortex. For a detailed examination of all the auditory way stations between the inner ear and the auditory cortex, see Altschuler, Bobbin, Clopton, & Hoffman, 1991; Brugge, 1991; Gulick et al., 1989; Hackney, 1987; Handel, 1989; Wallin, 1991.

The ratio of contralateral to ipsilateral fibers is approximately 5 to 1 (Musiek & Baran, 2018). As a result, conduction is faster and stronger for the crossed pathway (Handel, 1989). Thus, while both ears send all information to both sides, each hemisphere listens more carefully to the ear on the opposite side and will suppress information from the ipsilateral side if there is any conflict (Calder, 1970).

THE AUDITORY CORTEX

The final connection for the auditory pathway is in the temporal region of the cerebral cortex (see Figure. 6.6). The primary auditory projection areas lie in the superior temporal gyrus and occupy a surface only one-half to one-third the size of the optic cortex. This represents 0.3 to 1.0% of the surface of the entire cerebral cortex (Blinkov & Glezer, 1968). According to Weinberger (1999), "the primary auditory cortex lies in Heschl's gyrus which is within the Sylvian fissure. The surface of the primary auditory cortex thus extends more or less perpendicular to the surface of the temporal bone, in depth within the fissure" (pp. 63–64). That is, the auditory cortex is not only on the outer surface of the cortex, but also folds inward into the recesses of the brain.

There are about 100 million auditory cells in each auditory cortex (Handel, 1989), and various neural units within the auditory cortex respond to different types of sound stimuli. For instance, some neurons respond to pure tones and others to complex tones (Bendor &

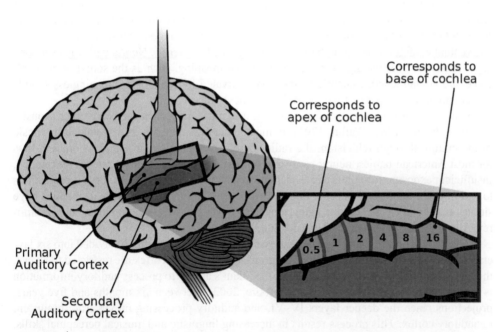

FIGURE **6.6** | Lateral View of the Human Brain, with the Auditory Cortex Exposed. The Sylvian fissure is the dividing line between the primary and secondary auditory cortices. The primary auditory cortex contains a topographic map of the cochlear frequency spectrum (shown in kilohertz). The base of the cochlea is near the oval window and the apex is at the end of the spiral.

Wang, 2005). Other neural units respond to stimulus onset, termination of a stimulus, or to on-off (Pickles, 1988). The primary auditory cortex is further organized in that tonotopicity is retained and, for pure tones, cells are systematically arranged according to their characteristic frequencies (that is, the frequencies to which they best respond). Some cells respond not only to pure tones, but to complex tones, as well (Bendor & Wang, 2005). Also, cells are arranged so that those excited by one ear are separated from those inhibited by the other ear. In other words, ear dominance is anatomically represented (Gulick et al., 1989).

As shown in Fig. 6.6, the secondary auditory cortex is adjacent to the primary auditory cortex, where additional sound processing takes place in the *planum temporale,* planum polare, belt, and parabelt areas. Contralateral processing (i.e., listening preferentially to sounds coming from the opposite ear) and tonotopical organization (i.e., retaining a frequency map) are stronger in primary than secondary areas (Langers, Backes, & van Dijk, 2007). Reponses to sound occur in primary sooner than secondary and primary areas only respond to the perception of sound whereas the secondary areas can also respond during sound imagery. Differences in primary and secondary auditory cortex may represent the transition from processing physical characteristics of sound to processing information about the sound object in context (see discussion of auditory scene analysis in Chapter 8).

In the womb, the auditory cortex develops sufficiently such that the fetus can respond to sounds during the last three months of pregnancy (Lecanuet, 1996; Moore et al., 2001; Staley, Iragui, & Spitz,1990). Assuming a lack of conscious awareness, prenatal listening experiences can hardly be called musical (Parncutt, 2009). Nevertheless, there are indications that the fetus can register and remember musical sounds that will affect behavior after birth (Lecanuet, 1996; Olds, 1985). However, since the brain does not know what particular sounds the baby must attend to (i.e., what languages, music, or environmental sounds), the infant brain has up to 150% more synaptic connections in the auditory cortex than it will have as an adult (Johnson, 1998). Learning experiences throughout childhood will shape the brain into its eventual configuration through neural pruning (see Chapter 9). Neural pathways supporting sounds heard repeatedly or that have particular meaning, such as the sound of mother's voice, are strengthened. Synaptic connections activated by random or meaningless sounds wither and may disappear altogether if they are never heard again.

Once we learn the sounds of our culture, it is more difficult to perceive other acoustic patterns (Handel, 1989; Wallin, 1991). In most situations, the baby is surrounded by music of the culture through television, the radio, family members singing, and so on, and thus for most American babies, neural pathways supporting Western, tonal music are developed. Insufficient exposure to sounds causes deficits in neural development and cortical projections to and from the auditory cortex are diminished. Thus, although congenitally deaf adults have similar auditory areas as hearing adults, they have fewer pathways leading in and out (Emmorey, Allen, Bruss, Schenker, & Damasio, 2003).

The auditory cortex, like the rest of the cerebral cortex, is commonly divided into six layers. Until about four months, functional neurons in the auditory cortex are restricted to layer I, the top, outer portion of gray matter. Thus, the infant's ability to process auditory information is mostly limited to brainstem analysis (Moore, 2002). Between six months and five years, projections reach the deeper layers IV–VI, and auditory processing moves from brainstem to auditory cortex. This process results in increasing linguistic and musical perceptual skills. Over the next five or six years, mature axons in layers II and III appear and the auditory cortex is more strongly connected throughout all six layers, between hemispheres, and to the surrounding auditory association areas. These association areas provide an interpretive function. They place information gleaned from brainstem and primary auditory cortex into a broader context. Eventually, this information is sent on to convergence zones that combine auditory information with input from the other senses.

Progressive development of the auditory cortex is demonstrated in infant studies. At age of two weeks, the detection threshold for changes in pure tone frequency is 50 dB p/ than adults; this gap narrows to 15–30 dB at three months, and 10–15 dB from 6–12 months (Aslin, Jusczyk, & Pisoni, 1998). Similar developmental progression is seen for intensity discrimination. Another critical aspect of auditory perception is auditory stream segregation, that allows the baby to parse sounds from mother's voice and the television into separate sources. Amazingly, two- to five-day-old newborns are as adept at this task as 18- to 23-year-olds (Winkler et al., 2003). In addition, two-month-old babies can discriminate between target and altered sound patterns, but 31% at three months, 58% at four months, and nearly all at six months perform with more adult-like responses (Trainor et al., 2003).

It appears that there are inherent auditory mechanisms for the perception of both language and music (Aslin et al., 1998) and that a developmental trajectory in the auditory cortex can be demonstrated for perceptual aspects of both. Brain images of one- to three-day-old newborns in response to normal and altered versions of Western tonal music indicated that neural networks for music processing are present at birth (Perani et al., 2010). Infants respond to music at very early ages (Fassbender, 1996; Panneton, 1985; H. Papousek, 1996). They prefer consonance over dissonance (Trainor, Tsang, & Cheung, 2002) and they can detect melodic changes in terms of pitch, rhythm, tempo, and contour (Trehub, 2001, 2003, 2004, 2006, 2009). Zentner and Eerola (2010) demonstrated that 5- to 24-month-old infants engage in more rhythmic activity to music than to speech, they exhibit some degree of tempo flexibility, and the extent to which they entrain with musical rhythms is related to positive affect (i.e., smiling). Infant preverbal and premusical vocalizations also demonstrate modulation of timbre, melodic contour, rhythmicity, and so on, at very early ages (Fridman, 1973; M. Papousek, 1996). The fact that these behaviors appear so early is an indication that these skills are more due to inherited neural wiring than to learning (Imberty, 2000; Trehub, 2000).

Another aspect of auditory cortex development is *hemispheric asymmetry*; that is, differences between the left and right sides. In two-thirds of hearing adults and in congenitally deaf adults, the auditory association area is larger on the left than on the right (Johnson, 1998). Although asymmetries may be affected by learning (see Chapter 9), they are already present at birth (Emmorey et al., 2003). At 29 weeks gestation, the left side is already larger than the right. The right hemisphere is more specialized for spectral processing and the left for temporal resolution, though again, this may be more true of primary than secondary auditory cortex. For example, speech sounds are often lateralized to the left and music to the right hemisphere. However, such lateralization is often affected by sex, age, and training (Purves et al., 2018).

As indicated previously, over 80% of the fibers cross over from the inner ear on one side to the auditory cortex on the other side (Musiek & Baran, 2018). Left-ear (LE)/right hemisphere (RH) preferences for music timbre discrimination were demonstrated in four-day-old newborns (Bertoncini et al., 1989), and also in two-, three-, and four-month-old infants (Best, Hoffman, & Glanville, 1982). More sophisticated processing in 8.5-month-old babies indicated LE/RH preferences for melodic contour changes and RE/LH preferences for preservation of melodic contours (Balaban, Anderson, & Wisniewski, 1998). Hemispheric preferences persist as five-to-seven-year-olds showed an increase in left auditory cortex activations for rhythmic processing and right auditory cortex activations for melodic processing (Overy et al., 2004). These left-right differences are smaller than those found in adults, indicating a continuation of this developmental arc (Samson, Ehrle, & Baulac, 2001; Zatorre, 2001).

As early as two days after birth, neonates can detect the sound of their mothers' voices (DeCasper & Fifer, 1980). Limited musical timbre judgments can be made at the end of the first week (O'Connell, 2003). By eight months, infants can discriminate timbral changes important in both speech and music (Tsang & Trainor, 2002). In terms of timing, electrical activity responses to durational changes in the brains of two- to six-day-old newborns are similar to those in older children and adults (Cheour, Kushnerenko, Ceponiene, Fellman, & Näätänen, 2002). Electrical activity in the brains of three-, six-, nine-, and twelve-month-olds showed an overall increase in power while listening to music (Schmidt, Trainor, & Santesso, 2002). By seven months, infants can remember music they previously heard (Saffran, Loman, & Robertson, 2001).

The receptive fields of certain individual auditory cortex neurons are capable of being retuned to respond more favorably to a different frequency (Weinberger, Ashe, & Edeline, 1994). Retuning neurons indicates that learning can cause modifications in sensory processing. Another idea is that place information (tonotopic organization) in the auditory cortex is based on frequency for pure tones and pitch for complex tones (Pantev, Hoke, Lutkenhoner, & Lehnertz, 1989). This indicates that considerable frequency analysis has taken place at the subcortical way stations (for more on pitch perception, see Chapter 7). Using a superconducting quantum interference device (SQUID), researchers documented that there is a common mapping in the primary auditory cortex, with the pitch for complex tones superimposed onto the same areas as frequency for pure tones. Thus, one group of cells responds to middle C, another to C-sharp, and so on (Berger, 1992; Lu, Williamson, & Kaufman, 1992). "This kind of tone map shows that each octave (factor of two in frequency) of the frequency scale spans equal distance across the cortex, much like the arrangement of keys on a piano keyboard" (Williamson & Kaufman, 1988, pp. 503–504). Higher tones are mapped deeper in the fold and lower tones are nearer the surface (Hari, 1990).

There are a number of auditory cortical maps and these are plastic, responding to learning experiences (Schreiner & Winer, 2007). One research group identified five areas in the human auditory cortex that contain at least six tonotopic organizations that systematically increase in frequency sensitivity, and additional areas that are not tonotopically organized (Talavage et al., 2004). In relation to music processing, the auditory cortex responds differentially depending on the musical elements involved and the musical context. Although different cells in the auditory cortex respond best to specific frequencies, their response sensitivity can be altered by experience or training. For example, melodic patterns make a difference to individual cells, as they respond differently to a tone depending on placement in the melody, whether the melody is ascending, descending, or has a more complex contour (Weinberger, 2006). Training can significantly improve auditory perception. For example, compared to untrained controls in auditory perception tasks, trained musicians were much more accurate—requiring a difference of only 0.67% of a base tone compared to 2.95% to distinguish between two pitches—and much faster—33.7 ms compared to 76.7 ms (Hodges, Hairston, & Burdette, 2005). Melody, harmony, rhythm, and timbre can be processed preferentially in either the left or right auditory cortex, depending on levels of training and other variables; for more information see Chapter 9.

There may be significant anatomical variations in different portions of the auditory cortex between hemispheres. For instance, some areas (Heschl's gyrus and the planum temporale) are frequently larger in the left hemisphere (Dorsaint-Pierre, et al., 2006; Schlaug, Jancke, Huang, & Steinmetz, 1995), while another portion (the frontal area of the *superior temporal* region), is usually larger in the right hemisphere. Wide variability also exists between subjects, some of whom have a larger middle, basal, or superior temporal subregion. "Evidently this type of variability is associated with individual differences in the development of certain auditory functions (for example, those connected with music)" (Blinkov & Glezer, 1968, p. 233).

The primary auditory zone is surrounded by association areas. These areas serve interpretive functions. Damage to these or other portions may cause amusia (loss of musical skills). For instance, damage to one area produces an inability to understand or interpret sounds, while primary sensory discriminations are not impaired (Grossman, 1967). Other areas are concerned with frequency or temporal aspects, with the association of sound and past experiences, or with the retention of aural memories.

The roles of the subcortical areas, the primary auditory cortex, and the association areas are not completely understood. Research with animals indicates, for instance, that the auditory cortex may not be necessary for certain aspects of hearing and that many auditory discriminations may be mediated at subcortical levels (Moore, 1987; Pickles, 1988). In general, however, it appears that the subcortical levels provide basic auditory discriminations, the auditory cortex makes more sophisticated discriminations, and the association areas provide integration, interpretation, and understanding. Also, a sound stimulus perceived in one ear is better processed by the hemisphere on the opposite side. Finally, there are anatomical variations in various areas of the auditory cortex and surrounding association areas that may account for some of the variations in the abilities shown by individuals.

CONCLUSION

Of all our senses, hearing is the most pervasive. Although the other senses can be regulated somewhat, we can never escape from sound. With our eyes closed, we cannot see; with our nose held shut, we cannot smell. As long as we do not touch anything with our skin or tongue, there is no sensation of touch or taste. However, no amount of putting our hands over our ears will shut out the world of sound. Even during sleep, the body responds to sounds that are not consciously perceived (Raloff, 1983). Hearing has other advantages in that we can detect information emanating from considerable distances. We can hear sound even when the source of it is not visible; sound travels through a forest, across a valley, and from within hiding places. In addition, we can understand emotional content encoded in sound.

At the outset, much was made of the delicate engineering of the hearing mechanism. Unfortunately, we live in much louder environments than the ears were designed for; thus, we are at considerable risk of noise-induced hearing loss[MT6.4]. This topic and the implications it has for musicians are explored in Chapter 15: Music and Health.

Our sense of hearing has had important consequences for human beings and the music we produce. We may have invented music, in part, because we were surrounded by a sound world from which we could not escape. Musical sound results, at least in part, from the human need to organize and elaborate sensory input.

Knowledge about the way the hearing mechanism works influences our understanding of general musical behavior. Beyond simply knowing about the hearing process, understanding musical behavior requires comprehension of the relationships among the physical (frequency, amplitude, signal shape, and time), and perceptual (pitch, loudness, timbre, and duration) attributes of sound,

DISCUSSION QUESTIONS

1. Based on the first paragraph of this chapter, discuss this long-standing conundrum: If a tree falls in the forest and there is no one there to hear it, is there any sound?

2. Although Carey (2008) stated that hearing is our most important sense, it may be pointless to debate which sense is more important (more important for what? to whom? in which circumstances?). Rather than argue about which sense is most important, discuss the unique contributions hearing makes to your inner and outer worlds.

3. What would happen if the eardrum were situated on the surface of the head instead of being buried in the bony skull?

4. What advantages does having two ears give us?

5. Being left- or right-handed is an easy concept to grasp for most of us. You can demonstrate eye dominance with this simple exercise: Lay your hands out flat in front of you. Slide them toward each other until they overlap slightly. Make a small triangle in the webbing between your thumbs and forefingers. Now stretch out your arms and focus on an object at some distance away from you that you can see within the triangle with both eyes open. Without moving your arms, close one eye. If the object remains within the triangle, the open eye is your dominant eye. With regard to ear dominance, in most situations sounds are presented to both ears. However, there are circumstances, such as cell phone usage, when the sound comes more strongly to one ear. Do you have an ear preference when talking on the phone? What is this preference based on—keeping your dominant hand free to write, for example? If you switch the phone to the other ear, does the sound change or your ability to focus on it?

6. Recall the discussion from Chapter 3 about the importance of hearing to our nighttime foraging ancestors. Describe situations when hearing has been your only or primary source of information.

7. One of the advantages of hearing is that sounds travel long distances and can go around objects. One example of a musical situation is the sounds of an enemy's military music coming from a long way away. Can you think of other examples?

8. Our ears are very sensitive. What would happen if they were even more sensitive?

9. How important is excellent hearing to good musicianship?

10. Do you think your musical training has been dominated more by the culture of the eye (e.g., a focus on music reading) or the ear?

Chapter 7

Psychoacoustics and the Perception of Music^{MT7}

M ILDRED is listening to her daughter practice the piano in the next room as she reviews a patient's file for upcoming surgery tomorrow. Based on what we learned in Chapter 5, we know that the music comes to her in a series of compressions and rarefactions or waves that travel through the air from the piano to her ears. We know that these waves reflect off various surfaces in the house and are absorbed by others. We learned how she can still hear the music, even though it is coming from another room, because the sound diffracts or bends around corners. In Chapter 6, we learned that once the sound pressure waves enter her ear canals, they set the eardrums in motion, which in turn activate the hammer, anvil, and stirrup. As the stirrup pushes against the oval window of the cochlea, the fluid inside is set in motion which causes the basilar membrane to rise and fall in waves. As a result, hair cells inside the cochlea are stimulated to fire and send signals through the auditory nerve to the brain.

Now we turn our attention to how these sounds become music inside the listener's mind. We will do this in two steps. First, we will learn about psychoacoustics, the study of how we perceive sounds subjectively. Sensory psychologists and those working in psychoacoustics have generally thought of receiving and understanding sensory information as consisting of sensation→perception→cognition. Sensation deals with the basic processing of raw sensory information and it is strongly recommended that readers review this material in Chapters 5 and 6 before reading this chapter. A basic understanding of acoustics and the hearing process will make it much easier to understand how we perceive music. Second, we will cover music cognition in Chapter 8, which deals with ways the mind interprets and responds to sensory information or, of more relevance, how we derive musical understanding from the basic perceptual elements.

Perception, then, represents a midpoint between raw sensory input and full, cognitive apprehension of sounds. In terms of music, we might say that sensation occurs when we first become aware of sounds and process those sounds in pre-musical ways, for example, paying attention to certain sounds within the environment, determining location, and so on. Perception of music occurs when we process musical elements, such as pitch and timbre. Music cognition is a higher order of musical awareness, apprehending and responding to melody, rhythm, harmony, form, and so on.

An important concept to remember is that our sensations and perceptions can be highly influenced by cognition. That is, past experiences, motivations, and so forth, can affect what we hear and how we interpret what we hear. As a simple, nonmusical example, consider the circumstance of hearing your own name over the loudspeaker at a busy airport. Airports are noisy places and you can selectively ignore sounds that have no particular meaning. However, in the midst of all these irrelevant sounds, the sound of your own name announced over

TABLE 7.1 | Seashore's Model of Musical Perception.

Physical	Psychological	Musical
Frequency	Pitch	Tonal
Amplitude	Loudness	Dynamic
Signal Shape	Timbre	Qualitative
Time	Duration	Temporal

In keeping with more current word usage, a few of the words have been altered. Seashore's original terms were: Physical: frequency, amplitude, form, and duration; Psychological: pitch, loudness, timbre, and time; Musical words are the same.

the loudspeaker tends to stand out. In a similar fashion, when we hear music we do not just collect raw sensations from our ears that deliver true and factual information to our brains. Think of the difference, for example, between hearing a piece of music for the first time versus hearing a very familiar piece.

Seashore (1938) created a model of musical perception that organizes these processes from physical to perceptual to musical (see Table 7.1). Physical attributes of music are those qualities of sound that can be measured objectively by an instrument—frequency, amplitude, signal shape, and time. Psychological perceptions are based on physical attributes of sound, but frequency, amplitude, signal shape, and time are not synonymous with pitch, loudness, timbre, and duration, respectively. Human perception of sound involves subjective interpretations that can be influenced by factors such as past experiences or present circumstances. Some authors also include volume and density as psychological variables. When an individual or culture has determined that perceived sounds are musical, physical and perceptual attributes lead to such aspects of music as melody, harmony, rhythm, form, and expression. The focus of this chapter will be on the middle column of Table 7.1. Topics in the Musical column are discussed in Chapter 8.

Before leaving Table 7.1, it is important to note one additional feature. Physical variables have a primary relationship with a corresponding perceptual variable, but the other physical variables may also have an effect. For instance, our perception of pitch is determined primarily by frequency, but amplitude, signal shape, and time variables may also influence the pitch we perceive. In general, these secondary relationships hold for all the perceptual variables and will be discussed in more detail subsequently in this chapter.

THE CRITICAL BAND

The concept of the *critical band* is crucial to understanding musical perception. In Figure 7.1, you see a photograph of the cochlea showing the basilar membrane lined with hair cells (for more on auditory hair cells, see Chapter 6). These hair cells respond to a particular frequency by setting up a resonance region whose width along the basilar membrane is determined by the amplitude. Higher frequencies create resonance regions nearer the oval window, the base of the cochlea. Sounds with more energy spread along the basilar membrane, creating a wider resonance region (Roederer, 1975).

Two pure tones (sine waves) with different frequencies create two distinct resonance regions. If the frequencies of the tones are far enough apart, the resonance regions do not overlap and the perceiver will hear two different pitches. For example, we perceive

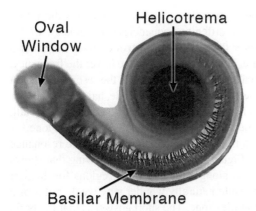

Oval
Window

Helicotrema

Basilar Membrane

FIGURE 7.1 | The Inside of a Cochlea, Showing the Basilar Membrane Lined with Hair Cells. The oval window is at the base of the cochlea, the helicotrema is at the apex.

the frequencies of 440 Hz and 880 Hz as A4 and A5, an octave apart. However, if the frequencies are so close together that the resonance regions overlap, the perceiver only hears one pitch accompanied by a sense of roughness or beating. Suppose we use two tone generators; with both of them set to 440 Hz, we would only perceive a single pitch. However, if we hold one of them constant and change the other one to 441 Hz, a single tone would still be heard along with a pulse or beat occurring once per second. Two tones with frequencies of 440 and 442 Hz would produce a single tone with two beats per second, and so on. Beats occur when the two sound waves come into phase and the number of beats per second corresponds to the difference between the two frequencies. As the frequencies move farther apart, increasing roughness will gradually give way to a perception of two distinct pitches. This marks the boundary of the critical band. Hall (2002) stated that,

> critical bandwidths for frequencies above 500 Hz are about 15–20% of the center frequency, or about 2½–3 semitones, or about 1–1.5 mm along the basilar membrane, enough to include some 1000–1500 receptors out of a total of 20,000 or 30,000. Lest there be any misunderstanding, we do *not* mean that there are any fixed boundaries; rather, you can pick *any* point on the basilar membrane (and corresponding frequency) and consider a critical band to be centered there.
>
> (p. 392)

THE PERCEPTION OF PITCH

Pitch is the psychological variable most closely related to the physical variable of frequency, although other physical variables can also have an effect. Pitch is the place we perceive a tone to occupy from low to high. In general, the higher the frequency, the higher the perceived pitch. Human beings can hear at best from 20 Hz to 20,000 Hz (Backus, 1977). As we get older, the top range decreases as a natural function of aging in a process called *presbycousis*. In music, the most useful pitch range is based on frequencies from approximately 27.5 Hz to 4,186 Hz, the range of the piano.

Several theories are used to explain pitch perception. The *place theory* is simply the notion that points along the basilar membrane respond to different frequencies (von Békésy, 1960). Higher frequencies stimulate the hair cells nearer the oval window, while lower frequencies stimulate those nearer the helicotrema. In Figure 7.2, you can see that the lower the frequency, the farther along the basilar membrane is the peak of the wave. Although the resonance region spreads along the basilar membrane, its width determined by the amplitude, hair cells on either side of the point of maximum excitation are inhibited, thus sharpening the perception (Hall, 2002). The name *spectral pitch* is given to the perceived pitch of a sine wave or pure tone.

The foregoing discussion applies to pure tones. For complex tones, multiple resonance regions are set up along the basilar membrane. Figure 7.3 is a schematic drawing that shows a resonance region for a fundamental of 110 Hz, along with resonance regions for the first seven overtones. In looking at this figure, one might naturally wonder why we do not hear a series of separate pure tones rather than one complex tone. The short answer is that the brain fuses these components of a complex tone into one perceived pitch. A more detailed answer is provided subsequently in the discussion of the missing fundamental.

Returning to the place theory, it provides a reasonable explanation of pitch perception, but it cannot account for pitches below 200 Hz. This is because at 100 Hz and below, the basilar membrane vibrates as a whole (von Békésy, 1960). A second explanation involves the

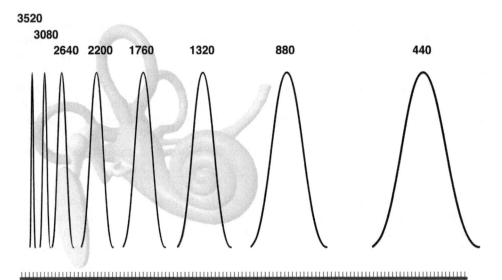

Oval Window   **Helicotrema**

FIGURE 7.2 | Resonance Regions. As the stirrup pushes against the oval window, resonance regions are generated along the length of the basilar membrane. higher frequencies create peaks nearer the oval window, while lower frequencies have peaks nearer the helicotrema.

Oval Window   **Helicotrema**

←etc. 880 770 660 550 440 330 220 110

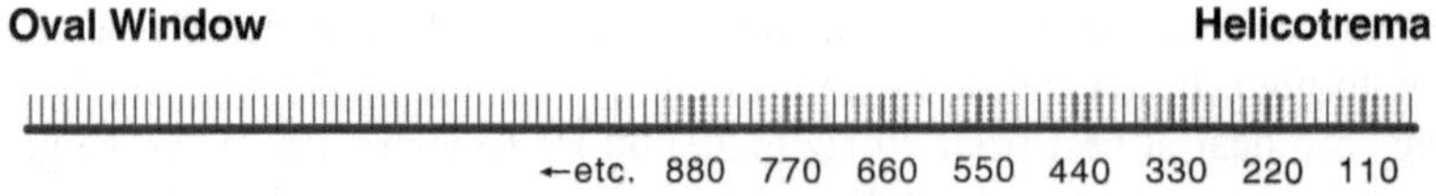

FIGURE 7.3 | Complex Tones Create Multiple Resonance Regions Spaced Along the Length of the Basilar Membrane.

periodicity of the incoming sound wave (Dowling & Harwood, 1986). The *periodicity* (Butler, 1992) or *temporal* (Howard & Angus, 2006) *theory* of pitch perception is that the upper partials of a complex tone are grouped perceptually into an apparent pitch, called variously the residue, subjective, virtual, or periodicity pitch (Pierce, 1999; Rasch & Plomp, 1999; Roederer, 1975).

According to the periodicity theory, the repetition rate of the upper partials of a complex tone provides the information necessary for the brain to compute the pitch of the fundamental, whether it is actually present or not. The firing rate of hair cells along the basilar membrane matches the frequency of a tone. The higher the frequency, the faster the neurons fire, resulting in the perception of a higher pitch. The primary limitation of the periodicity theory is that the upper limit for the firing rate of a hair cell is approximately 1,000 times per second. To allow for pitch perception above 1,000 Hz, the firing rates of groups of hair cells are combined. This has been called the *volley theory*.

Previously, the question was raised why we do not hear a series of separate pure tones rather than one complex tone. Through experience, the brain registers the pattern of overtones generated by the fundamental frequency and later perceives the pitch as the fundamental frequency based on this pattern. In fact, you can demonstrate this for yourself with the missing fundamental experiment. Using the Wave Form Generator[MT7.3], create a complex tone and listen to it. Then, remove all the energy of the lowest frequency and listen to the result. You will perceive the same pitch, but the timbre will be different.

The upper panel of Figure 7.4 shows the Wave Form Generator with the fundamental of A3, followed by the first eight overtones. The lower panel shows a similar wave, but notice that there is no energy in the fundamental. Note, too, the lowest A is notated on the staff in the upper but not in the lower panel, indicating that there is zero amplitude in A3 in the lower panel. Log onto the Wave Form Generator, then create and listen to these two signal shapes. You will notice a timbre change but the perceived pitch will be the same. This is because the ear—brain has stored a template for the overtones in fixed relationships. When you hear a complex wave made of second octave, fifth, third octave, third, fifth, and so on, the brain recognizes these as the partials of a tone whose fundamental is the first octave. In the case of our example in Figure 7.4, the partials are for a tone whose fundamental is A3. The missing fundamental actually has quite a few musical applications. For example, organ pipes can be built using this principle. Also, when we listen to music over inexpensive speakers or headphones, we can still hear low tones (e.g., from a double bass) even though a spectral analysis will show no energy present for those frequencies (Butler, 1992; Dowling & Harwood, 1986).

Combining the place, periodicity, and volley theories together, we see that there are two important factors: the particular location of the resonance region being stimulated, as well as the fact that within each resonance region, hair cells are firing individually or in groups at specific rates. In other words, where the hair cells are located and how fast they are firing combine to provide a sense of pitch. As it stands now, none of the three theories, nor all of them combined, adequately explain how we perceive pitch. For the time being, the place theory is the best explanation for pitches based on frequencies from 200–20,000 Hz, while the periodicity theory is the best explanation for pitches based on frequencies from 20–2,000 Hz. Where they overlap, 200–2,000 Hz, is where we are able to discriminate pitches most accurately (Dowling & Harwood, 1986).

Pitch Discrimination

A related area of interest is pitch discrimination. The *just noticeable difference* (JND), or *difference limen* (DL), is the smallest change in frequency a person is able to detect.

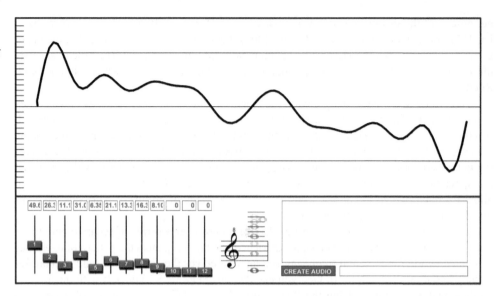

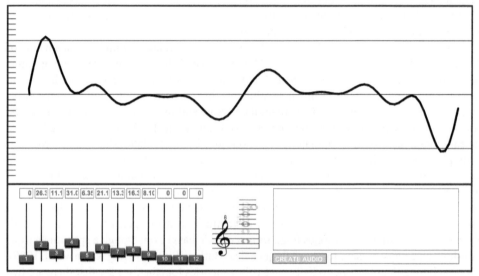

FIGURE 7.4 | Demonstration of the Missing Fundamental. Two signal shapes with (top) and without (bottom) energy in the fundamental and with identical amplitude in the first eight overtones. Listeners will perceive different timbres but the same pitch[MT7.3].

Handel (1989) states that the JND can be from 0.5–4 Hz at frequencies below 3,000 Hz. Above 6,000 Hz, pitch perception is very poor. Testing conditions can make a significant difference in the size of the JND. Three techniques have been used—judging successive tones (one tone sounded after another), judging two simultaneously sounding tones, or judging a single tone that is fluctuating up and down. The smallest differences can usually be detecting with the single, fluctuating tone, especially if the fluctuations are sudden rather than continuous.

Hedden (1980) lists other factors that influence pitch discrimination: (a) More refined discriminations can be made with complex tones than pure tones, at least below 4,000 Hz.

(b) Presenting stimuli under standardized free field conditions (i.e., subjects sit in the same place in a room) lead to smaller JNDs than group testing in a free field or using headphones. (c) More refined discriminations can be made at an optimum loudness level. (d) More refined discriminations can be made in the 500–1,000 Hz range than above or below. (e) Smaller JNDs are obtained with binaural presentation of stimuli than with monaural.

Pitch Matching

Pitch matching—asking a subject to match one tone exactly to another—is a different task altogether. Although pitch matching is an often-used skill in the real musical world (e.g., when instruments in an ensemble must play in tune with each other), it has not been thoroughly studied experimentally. One such study, however, indicates the degree of refinement capable by accomplished musicians. During a concert in 1963, 106 musicians of the Boston Symphony Orchestra were performing Britten's *War Requiem* in the outdoor Shed at Tanglewood (Pottle, 1970). With a high temperature that was raised further by television cameras and lights, the orchestra was faced with the prospect of trying to play in tune with a pipe organ tuned at A-447.5, a portative organ at A-446.5, pre-tuned percussion instruments such as chimes at A-444, and a piano at A-442. The orchestra started right in the middle at A-444.6, and, although the pitch center changed throughout the performance, in fifteen measurements the maximum discrepancy recorded within the orchestra was an incredibly minimal 19 cents (there are 100 cents in a half step).

Pitch Height and Pitch Chroma

Most listeners probably have a conception that pitch is on a unidimensional scale from low to high, referred to as *pitch height*. However, in terms of mental representation of pitch, music psychologists recognize another category called variously *pitch chroma* or *pitch class* (Justus & Bharuca, 2002). Pitch chroma refers to octave equivalence, or that feature shared by all Cs, all C♯s, all Ds, and so on. Thus, when females and males sing the same melody an octave apart, we say they are singing in unison. One way to test this out is through the use of Shepard tones (Shepard, 1964). A Shepard tone is a complex tone constructed by spacing ten pure tone frequencies each an octave apart, with the peak amplitude at the middle component. When scales are created using Shepard tones, they seem to rise or fall continuously; the auditory illusion is similar to the visual illusion of watching a spinning barberpole. Experiments using Shepard tones (e.g., Deutsch, 1986) demonstrate that pitch height and pitch chroma are related, but independent, phenomena.

Absolute Pitch

Fewer than one person in 10,000 can immediately and accurately name or produce a pitch without external reference (Deutsch, Henthorn, & Dolson, 2004). *Absolute pitch* (AP), as this ability is known, appears to have both a genetic and a learned component. The role of genetic instructions is studied by dividing populations into those with and without AP. Evidence for the importance of genes comes from an unequal distribution among populations (there is a higher incidence among Asians), differences in brain morphology (a more exaggerated leftward asymmetry of the auditory association cortex), and higher prevalence among siblings and identical twins, with a corresponding deficit for melodic processing among those with congenital amusia (Zatorre, 2003). Even though there appears to be a clear distinction between those who have AP and those who do not, there is, in fact, wide variability among those who either self-report or are tested as AP possessors (Bermudez & Zatorre, 2009).

Investigating the influence of genetic instructions, researchers studied a cohort of 981 individuals with AP and determined that it is likely that AP could result from the inheritance of only one or a few genes that are influenced by early exposure to music (Athos et al., 2007). Baharloo and colleagues (1998, 2000) studied more than 600 musicians and found that AP tended to cluster in families, providing support for inheritance. However, the greater preponderance of those with AP started their musical training before the age of four, supporting the notion that both genes and experience play a role in the acquisition of AP. Brain imaging studies indicate that AP possessors do not access working memory, as do those with relative pitch (identifying a pitch in relation to a known pitch); rather they activate distinctive areas involved in associative learning. This supports the known importance of early music learning experiences. Without early training, development of AP is highly unlikely.

Early childhood musical training, particularly with the use of *fixed do*, enhances the probability of AP in genetically susceptible individuals, but is not an absolute requirement. Factoring out different ethnicities (e.g., Chinese, Korean, Japanese) and early onset of music instruction, researchers believe that persons of Asian descent still have a higher incidence of musical AP (i.e., not AP for tonal languages) than those of other backgrounds; why this is so is not known (Gregersen, Kowalsky, Kohn, & Marvin, 2001). In a study of identical and fraternal twins, Drayna and colleagues (Drayna, Manichaikul, deLange, Snieder, & Spector, 2001) estimated heritability of AP at 0.71–0.80 based upon performances on a distorted tunes test; however, they, too, acknowledge the important role of learning.

Deutsch et al. (2004) studied speakers of Mandarin and Vietnamese, both tonal languages. These individuals were highly consistent and accurate in the intonation of their speech. Based on several experiments, the researchers proposed a model positing that everyone is born with absolute pitch. Those who learn tonal languages may have an unusually long critical period such that it encompasses the time when they would also have music lessons. Children then learn to associate pitches with labels during the period they are learning a tone language. In contrast, Schellenberg and Trehub (2008) found no support for the contribution of genetics or tone language usage for tonal memory.

Researchers have demonstrated the learning component of AP in numerous experiments. One of the key findings is that AP possessors are faster and more accurate at identifying diatonic than non-diatonic tones or white key tones better than black key tones (Bermudez & Zatorre, 2009; Miyazaki, 1990, 1993). AP possessors performed worse on F$_\sharp$ than the most common tones, C and G. This supports the contention that AP possessors acquire their abilities through frequency of exposure, sometimes called a distributional approach. Quite simply, they hear diatonic tones more frequently than non-diatonic tones. This notion of statistical learning and its application to other areas of music learning is explored in Chapter 8.

Although the importance of learning has been recognized in those who possess AP, another question arises. Can a person without AP acquire it through a training regimen? Ward (1999) reviewed a number of published studies and reported mixed results with adults learning AP. In some studies, subjects showed improvement, but no study was able to demonstrate that individuals without AP can acquire it with training and practice. Huron (2006) concurred with this assessment. However, more recently, Miyazaki and Ogawa (2006) trained 4- to 10-year-old Japanese students to have AP. Most students improved, learning the white keys first, then the black keys. Older children had more difficulty, suggesting that the optimal time to develop these skills is before the age of seven. In fact, Sakakibara (2014) worked with children who were two to six years old and did not have absolute pitch. Using a "Chord Identification Method," all the children were successful in acquiring AP.

Relative pitch (RP), the ability to identify pitches from a consistent reference point, can improve with training and practice, however. In many musical situations, RP may be more advantageous than AP. Miyazaki found that participants with AP fared no better (1992), and sometimes worse (Miyazaki, 1993) than those with RP when pitch tasks were couched in a musical context where RP would be more useful. In fact, he contends that AP can get in the way when AP possessors persist with AP tactics instead of switching to RP strategies when to do so would be advantageous. Temperley and Marvin (2008) obtained similar results and concluded that while a distributional view is important, structural aspects (such as when and where pitches occur) are also important. Thus, while AP may provide advantages for certain tasks, there are many musical tasks in which RP is equally valuable or superior. We discuss the role of pitch and tonality in Chapter 8, including the role of structural and distribution strategies in key finding.

THE PERCEPTION OF LOUDNESS

Loudness is the psychological variable most closely related to the physical variable of amplitude, although other variables can also have an effect. Amplitude is expressed as sound pressure level (SPL), most often measured in decibels. In general, the greater the decibel level, the louder the perceived sound. The decibel scale is logarithmic, which means that 20 dB has an intensity level 10 times greater than 10 dB, 30 dB has an intensity level 100 times greater than 10 dB, and so on. However, this does not mean that we perceive a ten dB increase as ten times louder.

The range of loudness we can perceive varies with the frequency, but at best it starts at 0 dB, the threshold of hearing, and ends with a sensation of pain somewhere around 120 dB. Thus, from the softest to the loudest sound we can perceive is a ratio of a trillion to one (Roederer, 1975). The threshold of hearing, or the softest sound we can hear, requires approximately 10^{-12} watts per square meter (W/m^2) at a distance of approximately three feet (Backus, 1977). The loudest sound, or what musicians might call *fff*, is 10^{-2} W/m^2.

In musical performance, loudness ranges from pianissimo somewhere around 40 dB to brief bursts of full-orchestra fortissimo at more than 95 dB (Howard & Angus, 2006). This is still a difference of about a million to one. Five classically trained female singers performed *messa di voce*, a crescendo-decrescendo on one note, on a variety of pitches throughout their ranges and produced a range of dynamics of 19.6–24.8 dB from softest to loudest sounds (Collyer, Davis, Thorpe, & Callaghan, 2007). Backus (1977) reports the following figures for instruments playing *pp* to *ff* measured at a distance of approximately ten meters: strings 45–60 dB, woodwinds 50–60 dB, and brass 60–75 dB (p. 94). Measuring the loudest sounds various instruments could produce, the bass drum produced a 25-watt burst of energy, while a clarinet could only muster 0.05 watts (p. 52). Hall (2002) measured sound levels throughout a professional orchestra concert and found that they rarely fell outside a range of 60–85 dB. Of course, all of these values are approximations, since in real-world situations the room acoustics would have a significant influence. For example, Winckel (1962) measured the Cleveland Orchestra in 15 different concert halls and found that the ambient or background noise level varied from 33 to 50 dB.

To recapitulate briefly material from Chapter 5, Fletcher and Munson (1933) published a landmark article entitled "Loudness, Its Definition, Measurement and Calculation" that included a figure of Loudness Level Contours, often referred to as equal loudness contours. Subjects adjusted pure tones at varying frequencies to a reference tone of 1,000 Hz of varying loudness levels so that the adjusted tones were judged to be equal in loudness to the reference

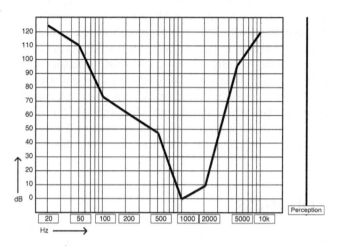

Equal Loudness Contours

FIGURE 7.5 | Demonstration of the Fletcher-Munson Loudness Level Contours (Equal Loudness Contours). This graph illustrates how one person judged varying frequencies in comparison to the reference tone of 1,000 Hz. Notice how much more energy is required at the lower and higher frequencies to match the reference tone[MT7.6].

tone. The results clearly demonstrate that the ear requires more energy at the lowest and highest ends of the frequency spectrum than in the middle for tones to sound equal in loudness. To test your own hearing, you can use the online multimedia program entitled Equal Loudness Contours[MT7.6]. Figure 7.5 illustrates one possibility using this program. Try it out for yourself and compare your results with the contours of fellow students.

Although it is not completely clear how amplitude is coded in the nervous system, in general it has to do with the total number of signals fired within a resonance region. This is a combination of the firing rates of individual hair cells, and the number of hair cells firing within the resonance region. As intensity increases, hair cells quickly reach their maximum firing rate and more hair cells are recruited, with the result that the resonance region spreads along the basilar membrane (Roederer, 1975).

THE PERCEPTION OF TIMBRE

Timbre, the psychological quality that allows us to distinguish one instrument from another, is most dependent on signal shape, although it can be affected by other physical variables as well. Suppose we were to listen to two complex tones. If both tones have exactly the same frequency and amplitude and sound for the same length of time, but have a different tone quality, the physical difference between them would be the signal shape.

A pure tone has a simple signal shape; there is only one component. Though some organ stops and a flute or piccolo in the upper register come closest, no musical instrument produces a pure tone. Rather, musical instruments produce tones with complex signal shapes consisting of many components. The vibrating medium—for example, the vocal cords of a singer, the lips of a brass player, or a violin string—vibrates not only as a whole, but also in parts. The result is a complex signal shape that consists of a fundamental and several overtones. We can notate the components of a complex tone as seen in Figure 7.6.

As indicated in Figure 7.6, some of the overtones are not in tune with the equivalent pitch in equal temperament. This is because of the compromises necessary in equal tempered tuning. Each component sets up its own resonance region along the basilar membrane. At the highest end, overtones may be so close together that they fall within a critical band. Three factors affecting overtones influence our perception of timbre (Hedden, 1980):

- First, the number of overtones can vary from instrument to instrument, or from pitch to pitch played by the same instrument.
- Second, the frequencies of the overtones present are important.
- Third, the amplitude of the overtones can vary.

In sum, all three factors—how many overtones, which particular ones, and the strengths of each overtone—create a signal shape for a complex tone.

Although many additional factors influence timbre perception—such as the dynamic level—one important factor is that each instrument, or individual in the case of singers, has one or more formant regions. These are areas that are amplified due to characteristics in the instrument itself; overtones that fall within a formant region are amplified. In singers, for example, the size and shape of the oral cavity create unique resonating characteristics.

When we look at the fundamental and overtones as a whole, we can see the envelope of the signal shape (Figure 7.7). As described in Chapter 5, there are four aspects to an envelope: an attack or onset, the decay, the sustain, and the release. The attack is the amount of time it takes for a reed, lip, string, or vocal cord (i.e., the vibrating medium) to be set in motion. After an initial burst of energy to initiate the sound, the energy decays slightly into the sustain

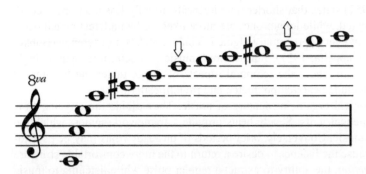

FIGURE 7.6 | The First 13 Partials in the Overtone Series. The down arrow indicates the pitch is flat relative to equal temperament and the up arrow indicates sharpness.

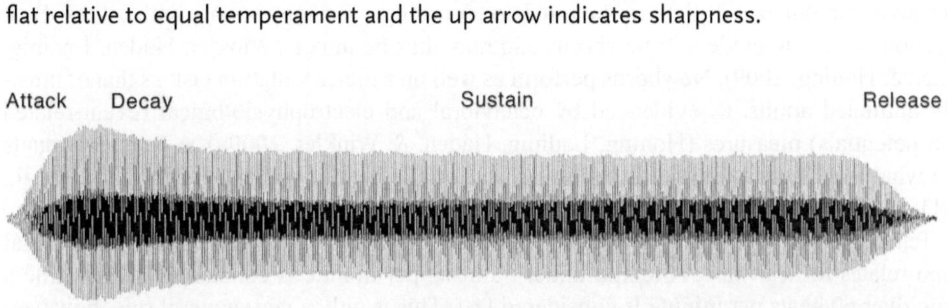

Attack   Decay   Sustain   Release

FIGURE 7.7 | An Envelope of a Signal Shape, with Four Aspects Identified.

portion. The sustain represents the length of the tone and the release occurs when the singer runs out of air, the bow stops moving across the string, and so on. In musical applications, these features will vary considerably depending on such aspects as articulation, length of note, and other stylistic features.

Several researchers have reported that the attack portion of the envelope is critically important in the identification of instrumental timbres (e.g., Elliott, 1975; Risset & Wessel, 1999; Saldanha & Corso, 1964). When researchers removed the attacks from single tones of various instruments, the timbres were difficult to identify. However, listeners were more easily able to identify instruments when Kendall (1986) used similarly altered tones in a musical context by creating a melody with them.

THE PERCEPTION OF DURATION

Duration is the psychological variable most closely related to the physical variable of time. Time is an obvious element of music as one musical event follows another in what seems to be an even flow. However, there can be differences between the psychological perception of duration as we experience it subjectively ("felt" time) and time as measured objectively by a clock. In general, pleasurable or interesting experiences seem to be over more quickly than unpleasant or dull experiences that may be the same length in terms of minutes and seconds. In music, composers can vary the temporal aspects of the music so that some compositions (usually with faster tempos) seem to move time ahead quickly and others appear to last for an inordinately long time (Dowling & Harwood, 1986). Time can also appear to be suspended or transcended, that is, time seems to stop or the listener seems to be "outside of time."

Psychologists have measured subjects' ability to estimate the length of single tones. *Vierordt's Law* (Woodrow, 1951) states that shorter time intervals, usually less than one second, are commonly over-estimated, while longer ones are more likely to be underestimated (Colman, 2001). As with nearly every perceptual judgment, context makes a difference (Bobko, Schiffman, Castino, & Chiappetta, 1977). Furthermore, music is much more than a single tone. Musicians normally talk about the temporal aspects of music under the heading of rhythm. Major concepts include beat, tempo, meter, and rhythm pattern.

Beats are a psychological organizing feature of music. They divide the ongoing flow of music into equal or unequal units. Steady beats provide a framework against which the listener can organize the music. Conversely, brief periods of unsteady beats may be psychologically unsettling and cause the listener to desire a return to the more comfortable structure of steady beat. *Beat induction*, the ability to extract a regular pulse while listening to music is nearly universal in humans (Honing, 2002). This allows us to entrain the beat so that we can clap or tap our feet in time to the music or coordinate our movements with others. Beat induction is already evident in newborns and may thus be innate (Winkler, Háden, Ladinig, Sziller, & Honing, 2009). Newborns perform as well on a meter violation task as that of musically untrained adults, as evidenced by behavioral and electrophysiological (event-related brain potentials) measures (Honing, Ladinig, Háden, & Winkler, 2009a). A few individuals have what is called beat deafness, an ability to find the beat in music (Phillips-Silver et al., 2011).

Tempo simply refers to how quickly the beats occur. Some psychologists contend that tempo relates to heart rate. A tempo under 60 beats per minute is considered slow, while a tempo over 60 beats per minute is considered fast. This is only a very general rule, however, and different individuals may have different experiences with the same piece of music. We can hear beats in a range from 30 beats per minute (BPM) to 300 BPM, although tempos slower than 42 BPM or faster than 168 BPM are rarely used in music (London, 2004). Decreases in tempo were easier to detect than increases by professional musicians (Kuhn, 1974), college students (Madsen, 1979), and high school students (Moore in Kuhn, 1974). However, even musically untrained listeners can make accurate tempo judgments (Honing & Ladinig, 2009). They do this on the basis of exposure, an indication that active listening to music is more important than formal training in this regard.

Meter is another extremely important organizing principle. It is determined by the arrangement of strong and weak beats. In Western music, listeners most often expect duple or triple meter. When presented with a series of steady taps that have no strong or weak beats, listeners tend to organize the taps into twos or threes (Handel, 1989). This is called subjective rhythmization. Reviewing a number of studies, London (2004) concluded that 100 ms is the lower limit for both the perception and production of metrical rhythm. That is, 100 ms or one-tenth of a second is the shortest interval between beats that we can organize metrically. This equates to a tempo of 600 BPM and anything over 200 BPM is considered too fast for musical purposes. At the other end of the scale, when beats are as far apart as 1800 ms (nearly two seconds), the tempo is too slow for us to organize the beats into a meter. You can check this out for yourself in the online multimedia program[MT7.8].

Windsor (1993) conducted a series of experiments demonstrating that meter perception is categorical; that is, listeners identify meter as duple or triple, for example, on the basis of discrimination of metrical versus non-metrical patterns. Perception of meter is robust, and regularly placed accents create a predictive pattern that causes listeners to disregard non-regular accents. Listeners without advanced musical training can reliably extract meter (Honing, Ladinig, Háden, & Winkler, 2009b). This process, in fact, happens preattentively, that is, without conscious awareness. Researchers confirmed this when brain wave readings were the same under attentive, unattentive (i.e., performing a concurrent task), and passive (i.e., participants were instructed to ignore all sounds and to watch a muted movie) listening conditions. In other words, meter perception is a mental representation that does not require formal training. Meter induction and rhythmic perception are closely related, as discriminating rhythmic patterns is much easier within a metrical context (Desain & Honing, 2003). Other features, such as tempo and articulation patterns, also influence rhythm perception.

Long and short tones organized within a given meter and tempo make up rhythm patterns. Rhythm patterns are so important in the perception of music that it is sometimes possible to identify a melody from just the rhythm pattern alone (White, 1960). While meters in Western music are relatively more simple than those in many non-Western musics (Dowling & Harwood, 1986), there is considerable rhythmic complexity within those meters. Earlier, it was stated that the lower and upper boundaries for organizing meter are 100 ms to 1800 ms. For rhythmic organization, that is temporal organization of pitches within a metrical structure, the limits appear to range from 50 ms to nearly two seconds (Handel, 1989).

In the lab, Hirsch (1959) found that listeners could identify which of two tones appeared first, a higher or lower one, when as little as 20 ms separated them; this is a difference of only two-hundredths of a second. To make this discussion more musically relevant, think how often musicians work during rehearsals to make attacks and releases precise. A cymbal player who does not place an entrance precisely is immediately noticed. One of the defining attributes of a superior string quartet is the sense of ensemble, that feeling that the four players are breathing and reacting as one. Clearly, music requires us to utilize our perceptual capacities to a maximum.

SECONDARY RELATIONSHIPS

So far, discussions have focused on the primary relationships between psychological and physical attributes. That is, pitch is most strongly determined by frequency, loudness by amplitude, timbre by signal shape, and duration by time. However, there are secondary relationships such that other physical variables may also have an effect (see Fig. 7.8). For example, as the previous discussion of equal loudness contours indicated, amplitude affects pitch perception and Haack (1975) found that changes in amplitude also had a significant effect on rhythm, duration, loudness, and timbre discriminations. Subjects were best able to make discriminations at optimum loudness levels, with less intensity enhancing timbre discriminations and louder presentation levels enhancing loudness discriminations. The purpose of this section is to identify how physical attributes other than the primary one can also influence perception by means of secondary relationships.

Pitch

Although we primarily identify a given pitch based on its frequency, our perceptions can also be influenced by amplitude, signal shape, and time. Altering the amplitude of a pure tone may cause a change in the perception of pitch. Frequencies at 3,000 Hz and above tend to be perceived as going sharp with increasing amplitude, while frequencies from 2,000 Hz and below tend to sound flatter as they get louder, as shown in Figure 7.9.

Although results similar to this are widely reported in the literature (e.g., Lundin, 1967), they are frequently based on the results of a study conducted by Stevens in 1935 (Stevens, 1935). Stevens used only three subjects to produce these data and the graph most often seen

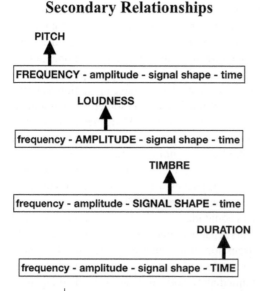

Secondary Relationships

PITCH

FREQUENCY - amplitude - signal shape - time

LOUDNESS

frequency - AMPLITUDE - signal shape - time

TIMBRE

frequency - amplitude - SIGNAL SHAPE - time

DURATION

frequency - amplitude - signal shape - TIME

FIGURE 7.8 | Primary and Secondary Relationships. Capitalized words in each box indicate a physical variable that has a primary relationship with the psychological variable indicated. Lowercase words in each box indicate a secondary relationship; secondary variables have a weaker effect on the primary psychological variable.

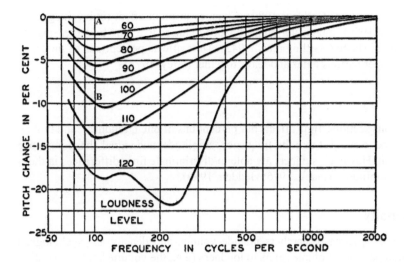

FIGURE 7.9 | The Influence of Amplitude on Pitch Perception. Changes in amplitude influence our perception of pitch. *"For example, a 100-Hz tone will be perceived ten per cent downward in pitch if raised from an amplitude of 40 dB (A) to 100 dB (B)."*

in the literature reflects the perceptions of a single subject. This hardly meets the standard for generalizing to the overall population, as Hedden (1980) rightly pointed out.

Iverson and Krumhansl (1989) found that pitch and timbre interact such that changes in timbre affected pitch judgments. The length of time a tone sounds can also change the perceived pitch. We perceive tones less than 10–15 ms long as a click (Roederer, 1975). As the tone gets longer, the pitch gradually becomes more apparent until it stabilizes; the amount of time needed varies with the frequency. Pitch discrimination is impaired when the time lengths of stimuli are reduced (Turnbull, 1944). The lower the frequency the longer the stimulus needs to be for accurate discrimination.

Loudness

The influence of frequency on loudness perception has already been mentioned in the discussion on equal loudness contours. To reiterate, frequencies at the lower and upper end of the spectrum require more energy to be perceived at the same loudness as tones in the mid-range. Signal shape also affects loudness perception, as a complex tone sounds louder than a pure tone (Bartholomew, 1942). Time has an effect on loudness perception in that the shorter the stimulus the softer the sound up to about one-half second; after that loudness stabilizes (Plomp & Bouman, 1959). Fabiani and Friberg (2011) investigated perceptions of loudness in instruments such as flute, clarinet, trumpet, violin, and piano. Their data confirmed that loudness perception depends on frequency and timbre, as well as amplitude.

Timbre

The perception of timbre can be influenced by frequency, amplitude, and time, as well as the primary physical variable of signal shape. Frequency affects perception of timbre in that the upper registers of an instrumentalist's or singer's range are generally judged less rich than the middle and lower registers (Hedden, 1980). Changes in pitch affect timbre judgments (Iverson & Krumhansl, 1989). Increasing intensity adds richness to a tone by increasing the complexity of the signal shape (Bartholomew, 1942). Time affects perceptions of timbre in the degree to which upper partials enter and leave together (Grey, 1977).

Duration

As indicated in previous sections, time affects our perceptions of pitch, loudness, and timbre. There is scant evidence to suggest that the frequency, amplitude, and signal shape influence perceptions of duration. However, subjects are able to discriminate finer differences in duration with increasing amplitude (Haack, 1975; Hedden, 1980).

Volume and Density

As mentioned previously, some researchers include volume and density as psychological attributes. In common parlance, volume refers to loudness (e.g., the volume knob on a radio). However, in psychoacoustics, volume is the amount of space we perceive a sound to occupy, while density refers to the compactness of a sound. Thus, we would likely perceive a tuba playing in the low register as occupying a large space with a diffuse (i.e., less dense) sound, while we would perceive a piccolo playing in the upper register as occupying a smaller space with a more compact, dense sound. These attributes cannot be measured objectively, so they are considered psychological rather than physical variables. Frequency and amplitude influence volume and density. Increasing frequency leads to a decrease in perception of volume and an increase in density (Lundin, 1967). Increasing amplitude leads to a perception of increasing volume and density.

CONCLUSION

A focus of this chapter has been relationships among physical and psychological variables. We do not derive our perceptions directly from the physical characteristics of the sound. If that were true, all of us would hear the same things from a given sound stimulus. Duerksen (1972) had 500 college students listen to recordings of a Beethoven piano sonata. Participants were told they would hear two recordings of the same piece and that they were to rate the performances on such aspects as rhythmic and pitch accuracy, appropriateness of tempo and accent, dynamic contrast, tone quality, interpretation, and overall quality of performance. They were told that a professional pianist made one recording and a student seeking admission to graduate school made the other recording. Half the subjects were told that they would hear the professional performance first and the other half were told that the student performance was first. In effect, however, they heard the same performance of the professional both times. In spite of hearing the exact same performance twice, subjects consistently gave higher ratings to the performance they were told was the professional.

This experiment provides support for a notion expressed at the outset of the chapter: past experiences, expectations, motivations, training, and so on can highly influence our perceptions. More details and specific musical applications are given in Chapter 8: Music Cognition. In the meantime, the primary message of the current chapter is that the psychological variables of frequency, amplitude, signal shape, and time are the basis for our psychological perceptions of pitch, loudness, timbre, and duration. There are strong primary relationships and weaker secondary relationships.

DISCUSSION QUESTIONS

1. Imagine you are in a concert hall listening to a live performance. Further, imagine that you can slow time down considerably. Can you step through the sensation→perception→cognition sequence and describe in a chronological fashion the musical sounds you hear coming from the stage?

2. Describe some of the ways your past experiences and your current thoughts influence your musical sensations and perceptions. For example, if you are in the audience waiting for your favorite artist to come on stage, how would your past experiences of hearing him/her perform or your current anticipation influence what you actually hear when the concert begins?

3. How could you use two trombonists or two string players to demonstrate the critical band?

4. How would you explain the concept of the missing fundamental to someone who has not taken acoustics?

5. Besides the missing fundamental, what other concepts can you demonstrate using the online Wave Form Generator?

6. If you sing or perform on a tunable instrument, what adjustments do you make while performing in order to stay in tune?

7. What advantages or disadvantages are there for a musician to have absolute pitch? Do you think someone without absolute pitch can acquire it through training and practice?

8. Equal loudness contours demonstrate that we need more energy in the upper and lower frequencies in order to hear them at the same loudness level as middle frequencies. What effects does this have on your everyday music listening experiences (e.g., on a car radio, an iPod, etc.)?

9. Discuss *felt* time as opposed to *clock* time in terms of musical experiences.

10. When you listen to music in live settings, do you experience *volume* and *density* as described in Chapter 7?

Chapter 8

⊳ Music Cognition^MT8

IMAGINE sitting in a darkened concert hall listening to a recital. The central question we address in this chapter is: How do we make sense of musical sounds as we encounter them in real time? Previous chapters dealt with basic acoustical properties of sound (Chapter 5), with our ears and how we hear sound (Chapter 6), and psychoacoustics and the perception of music (Chapter 7). Readers are encouraged to review these chapters before continuing with this chapter, as the information is cumulative. With an understanding of acoustics, hearing, and perception, it is time now to consider how the mind organizes music on a higher level.

Sloboda (1985) describes the cognitive processing of music by comparing it with the telling of a joke. Imagine that you are listening to a friend tell a joke. You must perceive and understand individual words, you must connect the words into longer units such as phrases and sentences. You must retain information being presented, even if some of it does not make immediate sense. As you follow the logic and store relevant information (often based on repetition), you create expectancies or a hunch about where the joke is heading. At the punch line, ideally, there is a pay-off and the joke "makes sense." Notice that your reaction is both cognitive and emotional; that is, you have a psychological sense of understanding and completion, along with a reaction ranging from a tepid smile to a belly laugh.

Music cognition is concerned with how we make sense of music (Justus & Bharucha, 2002). As music unfolds over time, we must perceive and understand individual notes and phrases as they connect to even longer units. We must retain important information (main themes, rhythmic patterns, etc.) and as the music progresses, form expectations about what is happening in the music. If we do all these things successfully, we are likely to have both a sense of psychological coherence and an emotional response. Of course, as is true of most analogies, there are considerable differences between listening to someone tell joke and listening to a piece of music. It is the purpose of this chapter to present a more detailed and nuanced discussion of the processes involved in music cognition.

Another way to grasp the idea of music cognition is to think about how it is to listen to music from an unfamiliar style. Individual notes and phrases are not necessarily understandable and it is not clear how they connect to larger units. It is difficult to retain important information—or even to decide what is important—and this makes it difficult to form expectations. Finally, although we may have a feelingful experience, our emotional responses may not be based on a psychological understanding. Indeed, it likely that we will overlay expectations based on our past music listening experiences on a musical system that is not structured in the same ways.

One further point must be made before continuing this discussion. Of necessity the chapter will proceed section-by-section in a linear fashion. But, the mind does not necessarily operate in a similar way. Many processes may be ongoing in parallel, overlapping, or kaleidoscopic fashion. Music cognition is an extremely complicated phenomenon and many variables are integrated into the holistic experience we seem to be having. These variables include such things as age, gender, ethnicity, training, experience, personality, existing mood, social circumstances, and so on. Thus, while the discussion proceeds sequentially, the reader should constantly consider that these are artificial abstractions from a more holistic process.

GESTALT LAWS OF COGNITIVE ORGANIZATION

The brain is an extremely efficient pattern or feature detector. We want to make sense of things and to organize our surroundings. In this chapter, we will consider how the mind organizes musical information and *Gestalt psychology* provides a good starting point. Early in the 20th century, German psychologists such as Max Wertheimer (1880–1943), Kurt Koffka (1886–1941), and Wolfgang Köhler (1887–1967) developed ideas related to organizational principles (Hochberg, 2004). Here are some of the primary features of Gestalt theory applied to Western tonal music:

- *Gestalt = whole.* The word *gestalt* means whole, shape, form, or configuration; Gestalt theory is concerned with the "big picture" and how we organize smaller units into a coherent whole. A familiar phrase is "the whole is different from the sum of its parts" (Goldstein, 1996) or its variant: "the whole is greater than the sum of its parts." A pianist might rehearse individual passages in the practice room, but a subsequent performance on stage is different from all the constituent parts.
- *Figure-ground relationships.* When we perceive something, certain features stand out—the figure, while others recede into the background. Imagine sitting at a piano recital. Most likely, the pianist is the figure (i.e., the primary focus of your visual attention) and not the backs of the heads of those sitting in front of you or the walls and floor of the stage. However, you can shift your attention to other features at will and focus, for example, on a friend sitting several rows away (see the Spotlight of Attention in the subsequent section).
- Figure-ground relationships hold for auditory stimuli, as well as for visual and other sensory stimuli. In many musical experiences, the melody serves as the figure and the harmony or accompaniment as the ground. As before, however, you can shift your attention to focus on various features at will, particularly if you have the training and experience to do so. Listen to the musical examples in Gestalt Principles of Musical Organization[MT8.1] and try out the effect of shifting your attention.
- *The Law of Prägnanz* says that stimulus patterns are organized in the simplest way possible (Ryan, 1997). Stated another way, whenever you encounter a perceptual field (e.g., unfamiliar music), you will tend to impose order on it in a predictable manner, according to the following corollaries that help to explain how the figure is extracted from the ground (Taetle & Cutietta, 2002; see Fig. 8.1).
- *Proximity:* notes closer together are more likely to be grouped together. In most tonal music, intervals of a third or smaller predominate in the melody, as is shown in Figure 8.2. Radocy (1980) examined classical and popular melodies and found that two thirds of the intervals were a major second or smaller and nearly 95% were a fourth or smaller. Examine some of the music you are currently studying to see if this holds true.

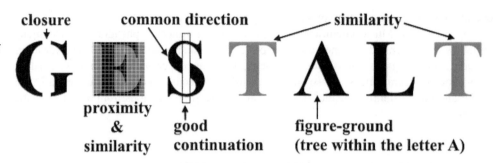

FIGURE **8.1** | Gestalt Principles. Illustration of the gestalt principles of closure, proximity, similarity, common direction, good continuation, and figure-ground relationships. Simplicity is also demonstrated in that the word *gestalt* is the simplest way to make sense of everything in the image.

FIGURE **8.2** | Proximity. Notation of the familiar theme known as "Ode to Joy" from Beethoven's Ninth Symphony, showing the proximity of the notes[MT8.1].

- *Similarity*: musical phrases that are similar are more likely to be grouped together than dissimilar phrases. This is why we continue to recognize the theme in a theme and variations, the return of the main theme in rondo form, or the subject in a fugue. The principle of similarity also applies to timbres, rhythms, and all other aspects of music. Notice in Figure 8.3 how the voices of the choir are grouped by similarities in text, rhythm, register, dynamics, and phrasing, while the soprano soloist becomes the figure by virtue of a contrast in text, in register, rhythm, and timbre.
- *Common direction*: another unit of perceptual organization is that music moving in a common direction is more likely to be grouped as a unit. Figure 8.4 is a passage from the fourth movement of Beethoven's Piano Sonata, Op. 2, No. 3. Notice that the upper voices are heard as descending, while the lower voices move in an opposite direction. A related concept is *good continuation*; objects that appear to continue in a direction already established are more easily perceived than those that do not continue in the same direction. Melodic contour provides an example of good continuation, as melodies with smooth contours are easier to understand and remember than melodies with a disjunctive contour.
- *Simplicity*: perceptually we organize things into their most simple units. At a slow tempo, a time signature of 6/8 leads to six beats per measure. However, at faster tempos, we most often perform 6/8 meter with two primary beats per measure, as illustrated in Figure 8.5.
- *Closure*: tonal music's penchant for cadences provides a clear example. Closure other than a full cadence (e.g., a deceptive cadence) is psychologically unsettling or leads to a feeling of incompleteness. Perceptually we look for and find pleasure in complete closure (e.g., a full cadence in tonal music) as represented in Figure 8.6. Several additional aural examples are included in Gestalt Principles of Musical Organization[MT8.1].

Although Gestalt theory does not completely account for musical perception, it provides a strong foundation from which to proceed. The application of these principles to music learning is covered in Chapter 14. The following discussions of auditory scene analysis, musical

FIGURE 8.3 | The First Four Measures of *Prayer* by Joe Stuessy[MT8.1].

FIGURE 8.4 | Common Direction. A passage from Beethoven Piano Sonata, Op. 2, No. 3, fourth movement, illustrating the principle of common direction[MT8.1].

FIGURE 8.5 | Simplicity. Brahms Symphony No. 1, 3rd Mov., mm 71–75, demonstrating simplicity. With a meter signature of 6/8 and a tempo marking of *Un poco Allegretto e grazioso*, the passage is conducted and heard in two beats per measure.

FIGURE 8.6 | Deceptive and Full Cadences. Left panel: A deceptive cadence, leading to an incomplete feeling of closure. Right panel: A full cadence, giving a feeling of complete closure[MT8.1].

memory, statistical learning in music, expectancy theory, tonality, cognition of musical elements, cognition of larger musical forms, cross-cultural comparative research in music, and music and language are nearly all built on the building blocks of Gestalt theory.

AUDITORY SCENE ANALYSIS

Bregman (1990, 1993) and others used Gestalt principles as a basis for explaining auditory scene analysis or how we make sense of complex auditory environments. Simplistically, sounds that arise from the same source or same environmental event are perceptually grouped as a unit and we are able to parse out different streams of auditory information (Bregman, 1990). Suppose you are in an environment where there is sound coming from a television set, sound coming from a child playing, and sound coming from a person talking. You are able to separate these sounds into recognizable streams; they do not blend together as one sound conglomerate. Even newborns come into the world already able to focus attention selectively on such tasks as separating the sound of their mothers' voices from background noise (Winkler et al., 2003). Major features of auditory scene analysis include schemata, the spotlight of attention, and the cocktail party phenomenon, and auditory stream segregation.

Schemata

Schemata are knowledge structures that may change as we learn and gain experience. A *schema* is a mental representation of something we have learned that has regularity in our experience (Bregman, 1990). Our name and Social Security number are simple examples of unchanging schemata. Musically we might think of a familiar melody such as *Happy Birthday*; although the tune itself does not change, we are likely to hear many different renditions throughout our lives that we recognize as all having something in common. Other schemata alter to fit new experiences or levels of understanding. As we engage in more sophisticated musical experiences, regularities in the timbres of instruments—a trumpet sounds different from a clarinet because of "trumpet-like" consistencies in the signal shape—or regularities in meters, and so on, also help us to organize our musical experiences. Schemata, or internal mental representations, are what enable us to make sense of the immense complexity inherent in music (Dowling & Harwood, 1986).

Gjerdingen (2007) provided illuminating commentary on musical schemata in music of the galant period (18th c.). In the introduction to his book, he describes how musical patterns were used to train European court musicians, with an illustration from figure skating. Throughout many years of training, a young figure skater spends thousands of hours learning very specific figures such as a double axel or a sit spin. Later, when constructing a program for a competition, the skater weaves any number of these figures (some compulsory and some freely chosen) together in a unique and individualized performance choreographed to music. Judges are able to assess the quality of the performance at least in large part based on the execution of these figures.

In a similar fashion, musicians in the 18th century spent hours at the keyboard learning hundreds of stock musical phrases notated in collections called *zibaldone*. Students learned these "prototypes" or "exemplars" by rote in a variety of major and minor keys, and as harmonic skills in the left hand increased, decorations and embellishments in the right hand assumed priority. Later, as accomplished musicians, they were able to combine and recombine these schemata in a seemingly endless variety. As Gjerdingen (2007) states, "a *zibaldone* of figured and unfigured basses (*partimenti*), along with examples of graceful melodies paired with unfigured basses *(solfeggi)*, provided an important repository of stock musical business from which a young composer could later draw" (p. 10). Fortunately, Gjerdingen has made a treasure trove of partimenti available online (http://faculty-web.at.northwestern.edu/music/gjerdingen/partimenti/index.htm) in both notated and recorded formats.

The Spotlight of Attention

From the perspective of behavioral psychology (see Chapter 14), the environment imposes itself on the perceiver. Insights from cognitive psychology, however, have helped us to understand that this is only partially true. While the environment can impose itself on your perceptions (e.g., a loud noise is likely to cause you to look in that direction), you can also actively seek out features of the environment on which to focus your attention.

Imagine that you are at an orchestra concert. The music coming from the stage certainly imposes itself on your awareness. However, you can selectively listen to the flutes, then switch your focus to violins. You can also attend to different features such as melody or harmony. In other words, you can direct the spotlight of attention onto certain aspects of the environment. The likeliest targets for your attentional spotlight are schemata. That is, you will most often focus your attention on knowledge structures learned from past experiences.

The Cocktail Party Phenomenon and Auditory Stream Segregation

The *cocktail party phenomenon* refers to a circumstance in which we are trying to focus on the sound of one person's voice in the midst of several people talking, such as we might experience at a cocktail party (Cherry, 1953). Most of us have also had an experience when we have seemingly followed more than one conversation at a time. Focusing our attention on a sound stream aids in perceptual grouping and using selective attention, we can move very rapidly move back and forth between stimuli (Cusack, Deeks, Aikman, & Carlyon, 2004). If you are at a party talking with someone in front of you and yet following a conversation taking place behind you (she did *what?*), you are actually switching your attention back and forth between the two conversations. Experiments have shown that you can actually follow speech four times faster than the normal rate (Foulke & Sticht, 1969). This means that the brain has time to leave one conversation to pick up part of another one and return. Most likely you don't pick up every word of both conversations, but enough of each that you can place what you do pick up into context. Of course, this kind of multitask monitoring can lead to errors of understanding when you fail to pick up a critical word or phrase.

Although the "cocktail party" phenomenon traditionally refers to language, the concept can also be applied to music. *Auditory stream segregation*[MT8.2] describes how the listener is able to segregate two or more streams of sound. Dowling (1973) studied this process, using interleaved melodies. He alternated the pitches of two familiar melodies—*Mary Had a Little Lamb* and *Yankee Doodle*. When the pitches overlapped, the tunes were difficult to recognize, but when they did not—for example if they appeared in different octaves—they were much easier to recognize. Many composers have created the effect of two lines coming from one instrument by alternating pitches in this manner. Figure 8.7 illustrates how Bach did it in an unaccompanied suite for cello. *Melodic fission*[MT8.3] occurs when one line appears to diverge into two and *melodic fusion* occurs when two lines appear to converge into one. Auditory stream segregation describes how we are able perceptually to track independent musical lines.

There are many examples of compositions in which auditory stream segregation is required to perceive two or more overlapping musical ideas. The Bach chorale prelude for organ illustrated in Figure 8.8[MT8.2] provides a clear illustration. At the outset, Bach establishes

FIGURE **8.7** | Bach Suite No. 1 for Unaccompanied Cello; Prelude, Measures 37–39[MT8.3]. An illustration of musical fission as two independent lines appear to emerge from one instrument.

FIGURE **8.8** | Bach: Choral Prelude "Wachet auf, ruft uns die Stimme," BWV 645, Measures 13–15[MT8.2]. An example of auditory stream segregation in which the Gestalt principles of proximity, similarity, and common direction help the listener separate the chorale tune in the middle voice from the two outer voices.

the moving figure in the top voice. In the 13th measure, he introduces a chorale tune in the middle voice. Perceptually, the listener is aided in segregating these into streams in several ways: (a) the top voice has been firmly established in the ear for 12 measures, (b) the chorale tune has much longer note values, (c) although there is some note overlapping, the chorale tune primarily occupies a middle ground between the top and bottom voices, and (d) it is often played with a different registration (i.e., timbre), one that stands out from the upper and lower voices. Additionally, in Bach's day, most listeners would have recognized the chorale tune; for them, chorale tunes would be represented as schemata. Notice how the top voice changes from figure to ground, as the chorale tune becomes the figure. The Gestalt principles of proximity, similarity, and common direction also help this auditory scene analysis.

A final example illustrates the strong influence that Gestalt principles exert on auditory scene analysis. In the fourth movement of Tchaikovsky's Sixth Symphony, the first and second violins have what appear to be nonsensical lines, as indicated in A of Figure 8.9. However, primarily based on the principles of proximity and good continuation, what is perceived are the smoother lines in B of Figure 8.9. Notice that the first violin is perceived to be starting with the F♯ that is actually notated in the second violin part (A), then alternates every other note to create the stepwise, descending line as notated in B. This holds true for the second violin and the same effect is obtained in the viola and cello parts, as illustrated in the multimedia module MT8.4. Striking as this example is, it is an anomaly and similar examples are difficult to identify.

MUSICAL MEMORY

Almost every facet of musical experience is impacted by memory, including how we mentally organize music (Snyder, 2009). Imagine trying to understand a piece of music in ABA form

FIGURE **8.9** | Tchaikovsky: Symphony No. 6, Fourth Movement[MT8.4]. (A) The first and second violin parts as notated. (B) The first and second violin parts as perceived.

if you don't recognize the A section when it returns. Most theorists posit a two-stage memory process: short-term memory (STM) and long-term memory (LTM) (Rose, 2004). Short-term or working memory persists for only brief periods of a minute or less (Brown, 2004). In the brain, STM is electrical in nature and remains available for immediate use. For example, when you look up an unfamiliar phone number, it is usually gone from your memory as soon as you dial. Long-term memory is encoded in the brain for permanent storage (Deutsch, 2004). Important information such as your social security number, your birthdate, and so on, is available over long periods of time.

Musicians utilize many different kinds of memory. *Declarative memory* involves remembering facts or specific information, such as how many sharps there are in the key of D Major or how many symphonies Beethoven wrote. *Procedural memory* is remembering how to do something, like how to create vibrato or the proper fingering for a g minor scale on the piano, and so on. Auditory, visual and *kinesthetic* memory strategies have been identified in the memorization of music (Aiello & Williamon, 2002). The internal recall of musical pitches, rhythms, timbres, and so on, is another kind of memory. Gordon (2007) uses the term *audiation* to refer to inner hearing that involves a deeper comprehension of musical sounds than simple recall (see Chapter 14 for more details).

An interesting (but perhaps impossible, or at least extremely difficult) experiment to conduct would be to try to determine how much music one has stored in long-term memory. Just think of all the children's songs, church music, music from commercials and television shows, movie themes, popular music, classical music, and so on that you can remember or recognize. That this ability is rather common and surprisingly powerful was demonstrated in the aforementioned television show called *Name That Tune* where contestants tried to identify a tune in the fewest number of notes. How is this possible? Here are some key ideas in music memory:

■ Repeating information numerous times is an obvious strategy to place it into long-term storage. Musicians, of course, use repetition not only to memorize information, but also to create muscle memory (Aiello & Williamon, 2002).

- Information that has particular meaning is much easier to remember than unimportant trivia. Practicing scales without knowing how they relate to real music may be less effective than identifying scalar passages in repertoire and making the connection between scales in isolation and scales in music.

- Events that interrupt rehearsal can disrupt transfer of information from short to long-term storage. Imagine, for example, that you were rehearsing for an important recital and the phone kept ringing.

- *Chunking* information, that is, organizing it into smaller, more manageable units or chunks, makes remembering easier. Notice how you say strings of numbers like your phone number or social security number. They are written in chunks as an aid to memory: (919) 458-5317; 552-34-2314. Miller (1956) established seven units of information, plus or minus two, as normal limits for the number items or chunks one can store for immediate recall.

- Tonal music, scales, intervals, and harmonic progressions provide invaluable cues. In a sense, tonality provides a skeleton or structure on which the music is hung. Scales, intervals, and harmonic progressions are like scaffolding. They are structural features that provide an organizational framework for the mind.

- Researchers have investigated whole versus part learning. In general, shorter pieces are more easily learned as a whole, while longer pieces need to be learned in parts (Bartlett, 1996b). Experts may begin with an overall artistic vision of a new piece before filling in the details (Chaffin & Imreh, 2003).

- *Mental rehearsal* or silent practice is an effective technique for learning music. Neuro-musical research indicates that mental rehearsal stimulates the brain much as does actual practice (Halpern, Zatorre, Bouffard, & Johnson, 2004). There are three other advantages: (1) mental rehearsal can be done anywhere at any time; (2) while physical practice is tiring and may lead to muscular fatigue or even injury, mental rehearsal does not; (3) with enough concentration, perfect trials are possible in mental rehearsal, but rarely in physical practice. Mental rehearsal combined with physical practice has been demonstrated to be effective (Barry & Hallam, 2002; Coffman, 1990; Ross, 1985) and mental rehearsal combined with listening is also more effective than mental rehearsal alone (Lim & Lippman, 1991). (See Chapter 13: Music Performance for more details.)

Perhaps all these ideas can be collapsed into three main attributes of effective memorization: (1) knowledge, (2) strategy, and (3) effort (Chaffin, 2007). Accomplished musicians may analyze the music to understand the underlying structure and encode information in ready-made chunks, such as scales and chords. They also have a plan for learning music; practice sessions are not mere periods of repetitiously playing through the music. Rather, they employ conscious strategies that utilize the knowledge base gained from study and analysis. Finally, experienced musicians work hard. Sustained practice sessions focus on establishing performance cues that will aid in memory retrieval. These cues facilitate motor and auditory memories needed for fluid performances.

STATISTICAL LEARNING IN MUSIC

The concept of *statistical learning* is relatively easy to explain, yet very far-reaching in providing insights into how we make sense of the world. Infants are bombarded by a vast array of new sensory inputs. Over time some of the same sights, sounds, smells, tastes, and touch sensations are repeated frequently, while others seldom occur. The more frequently a given stimulus occurs, the stronger the neural networks supporting its perception. Statistical learning is a powerful means of explaining how we gradually come to understand such complex systems as language and music (Saffran, 2003).

Saffran and colleagues (1999) demonstrated that eight-month-old infants performed as well as adults on a statistical learning task with nonverbal auditory stimuli. Listeners heard a seven-minute-long tone stream, such as DFDFCF♯CC♯EDGDD♯EDGG♯ABFB♭EDG. . ., which contained target tone sequences. Following three repetitions of this tone stream, they were asked to identify the targets, which were discoverable only by means of statistical learning, that is, by their frequency of occurrence. For example, if the pattern EDG, from the pattern above, appears frequently but the pattern DFC occurs only rarely, listeners will gradually come to identify EDG as a recognizable unit, but not DFC.

From a more musical perspective, numerous experiments (e.g., Bigand & Poulin-Charronnat, 2006) show that listeners learn musical styles through mere exposure (e.g., from hearing music in the environment such as on television and in the movies). A major reason for this is the perception of statistical regularities. For example, Jonaitis and Saffran (2009) demonstrated that listeners "take advantage of the statistical patterning of chords to acquire new musical structures" (p. 951).

EXPECTANCY THEORY

In language, a single, isolated word may have meaning; consider words such as *stop* or *ouch*. Likewise, there are many environmental sounds that have meaning, such as the honk of a car horn or a doorbell ring. But in music, a single note or chord rarely has meaning by itself. Rather, every musical event causes the listener to expect another event, as long as the listener is familiar with the style. For example, if you hear I-IV-V^7 you naturally expect I to be the next chord. However, if you hear a short passage of unfamiliar Chinese music, you will be much less likely to form an expectation for what will follow. In the two examples below (Fig. 8.10), fragments from Mozart and Berg are truncated in the middle of a passage; how well can you imagine what will happen next?

Although this sounds very simple, *expectancy theory* actually provides the basis for a deep understanding of how we derive meaning from music. Composers find numerous ways to play off listener's expectations. Simple examples include the use of a deceptive cadence, a Picardy third, or a trill on the last note before a cadence. Brahms' use of hemiola and other rhythmic devices provides more complex illustrations. What examples can you think of?

Meyer (1956) provided the first, detailed exposition of expectancy theory as related to music. Many of our expectations are built on the Gestalt organizational principles. For example, if we hear a series of pitches in an unfamiliar melody we are more likely to expect the next pitch on the basis of (a) proximity; that is, we would predict a neighboring pitch rather than a large leap, (b) simplicity; we expect a note that fits the established harmonic and metrical structure in the simplest or "most predictable" way, (c) good continuation; we would expect the next pitch to be one that extends the established musical line, (d) closure; at the appropriate time we would expect a pitch that moves us toward a conclusion rather than extending the phrase.

The foregoing should not be taken to imply that we are consciously making predictions from note-to-note throughout a piece of music. Rather, expectancy theory recognizes that unconsciously we are constantly making sense of our surroundings and because music flows in time, making sense of what we are hearing occurs in real-time streaming (Koelsch, Vuust, & Friston, 2018). Every aspect of the music, and our knowledge of these aspects,

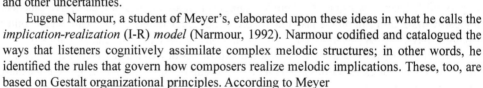

FIGURE **8.10** | Incomplete Passages from Mozart and Berg. How well can you predict what will happen in the music next? Top panel: Mozart Piano Sonata in C, K545, 3rd mvt., measures 1–3. Bottom panel: Berg *Lament Melody* from Violin Concerto.

helps to channel the flow of music along a path of understanding. The overall form, tonality, metrical organization, dynamics, timbres, and so on, are key ingredients in our ability to make sense of music as it comes to us in a moving, stream of sound.

Much of our ability to make sense of the music we hear comes simply from hearing music of similar styles repeatedly. Music in popular culture—for example the music in movies, television shows, commercial advertising, music on the radio across a broad spectrum of genres such as rock, country-western, gospel, and so on—is immediately understandable to most people even if they have not had specific musical training. More complicated musical genres, such as classical music or jazz, may require additional training and experience to be more fully understood.

In classical music, and to a lesser extent in nearly all types of music, composers use a variety of strategies to create uncertainty (Meyer, 2001). They employ surprise, delay, suspense, ambiguity, and a host of other techniques to create and maintain interest. Listen to the Beethoven examples in Expectancy Theory[MT8.6] to hear how he creates ambiguity in the meter and other uncertainties.

Eugene Narmour, a student of Meyer's, elaborated upon these ideas in what he calls the *implication-realization* (I-R) *model* (Narmour, 1992). Narmour codified and catalogued the ways that listeners cognitively assimilate complex melodic structures; in other words, he identified the rules that govern how composers realize melodic implications. These, too, are based on Gestalt organizational principles. According to Meyer

> An implicative relationship is one in which an event—be it a motive, a phrase, and so on—is patterned in such a way that reasonable inferences can be made both about its connections with preceding events and about how the event itself might be continued and perhaps reach closure and stability.
>
> (1973, p. 110)

Narmour identified both implicative melodies—listeners can reasonably predict where the tune is going—and non-implicative melodies—where there is greater uncertainty. An implicative interval is unclosed and implies that certain tones are more likely to come next than others are. A realized interval is the last note of an implicated interval and the next note.

Narmour developed five predispositions that describe how implicative intervals imply realized intervals. Schellenberg (1997) felt that I-R was unnecessarily complicated and through a series of experiments he and others conducted, he was able to reduce the model to two principal ideas. His two-factor model of melodic expectancy consists of *pitch proximity*—the notion that listeners expect the next pitch in a tonal sequence to be nearby, a small interval, and *pitch reversal*—when pitch proximity has been disregarded because the following tone was farther away, listeners expect the next pitch to reverse and fill in the gap. In other words, it is more common for melodies to move in stepwise direction and when larger leaps do occur, the melody tends to reverse itself and move back in stepwise fashion.

Figures 8.2 through 8.5 are good examples of pitch proximity. These figures are also examples of implicative passages. If any of these examples were paused on a given note, it would be fairly easy to predict what note should follow. An excellent example of a non-implicative passage can be seen/heard in the opening to Verdi's overture to his opera *La Forza del Destino* (The Force of Destiny). In Figure 8.11 you see that the orchestra sounds three loud octave Es and then stops. After a brief pause, this pattern is repeated. Although this sets up the expectation that something is to follow, it is not at all clear what will come next. You can hear how Verdi follows these three tones in the multimedia module[MT11.9].

Figure 8.12 in an example of pitch reversal, or a *gap-fill melody*[MT8.7]. Some organizational patterns are used frequently enough that they form a largely unconscious basis for making sense of melodies. Bigand (1993) calls these a "lexicon of schemas". Nearly always, when a large leap occurs in a melody, the tendency is for this "gap" to be filled in with stepwise motion. This happens so often in music that listeners unconsciously come to expect that to be the case.

Another schema, called a *changing-note pattern*[MT8.8], is illustrated in Figure 8.13 in its simplest form. Here, the pattern revolves around the tonic, going (a) below and above it or (b) above and below and returning to tonic. Often composers elaborate this underlying scheme, as Mozart does in Figure 8.14.

The importance of schema and organizational principles such as those described in the subsequent sections on tonal and event hierarchies is heightened when they are absent. Early

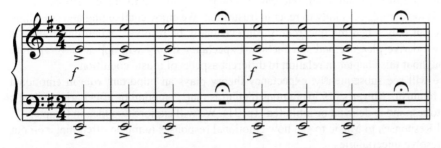

FIGURE **8.11** | The Opening Chords to Verdi's Overture to *La Forza del Destino*. This is an example of a non-implicative passage. Listen to MT11.9 to hear how Verdi continues.

FIGURE **8.12** | This Passage from Beethoven Symphony No. 1 Illustrates a Gap-Fill Melody. Each time a leap occurs, the following notes fill in the gap with stepwise motion[MT8.7].

FIGURE **8.13** | A Changing-Note Pattern, with Pitches Revolving Around the Tonic. In (a) the notes go below and above tonic, while in (b) the pattern is reversed[MT8.8].

FIGURE **8.14** | A Changing-Note Pattern from Mozart: Sonata in Eb Major, K. 282, Second Movement, mm. 1–4[MT8.8].

in the 20th century composers like Schoenberg, Berg, and Webern wrote music that did not follow Gestalt principles of organization. Listen to the examples in the Schoenberg multimedia module[MT11.6] to hear how expectations are more difficult to make. This does not mean that one cannot find beauty and meaning in such music; it simply illustrates that most of our musical experiences are based on general principles of cognitive organization.

Meyer (2001) encapsulated all these ideas with his use of the term "uncertainty." The human mind dislikes uncertainty. We strive to make sense of our world. If the world is too predictable we find it boring. If it is too unpredictable, we find it confusing and unbearable. Between those two extremes, we often challenge our minds to find patterns. This is why many people derive pleasure from solving crossword puzzles, jigsaw puzzles, mazes, Sudoku, Where's Waldo, and so on. A ten-piece jigsaw puzzle designed for a child is likely to be too simple to afford much pleasure to an adult, unless the adult is helping a child do the puzzle. At the other end of the continuum, one who is completely unable to solve a Rubik's Cube because it is too complex is likely to react in frustration. We enjoy challenging and stretching our minds, but only when the uncertainty can eventually be resolved; when uncertainty is resolved, we derive pleasure and satisfaction. Expectancy theory will appear several more times throughout this chapter in relation to different aspects of music cognition.

As we will see subsequently, expectancy theory plays an important role in emotional responses to music. Meyer's (1956) famous dictum is that, "emotion or affect arises when a tendency to respond is delayed or inhibited" (p. 31). We will explore this idea in Chapter 11: Emotional Responses to Music to see how emotional responses to music often hinge on our ability to resolve uncertainties.

TONALITY

Tonality is a central organizing factor in the greater preponderance of Western musical genres, such as classical, jazz, and popular music. Tonal hierarchy refers to the relative importance of pitches and chords within a given key, following the order of tonic (1st scale degree or I chord), dominant (5th scale degree or V chord), mediant (3rd scale degree or iii chord), subdominant (4th scale degree or IV chord), and so on.

Krumhansl (1990) used a probe-tone technique to establish tonal hierarchies experimentally. In one experiment, ascending and descending C major scales were played with the final tonic missing. Listeners rated a following probe tone, one of the 12 chromatic pitches, in terms of how well it completed the scale. In a second experiment, listeners heard complete scales, tonic triads, and chord sequences that created a musical context. They then rated the following 12 chromatic pitches used as probe tones in terms of the "goodness of fit" of these separate tones with the musical context. Further, Krumhansl investigated relationships between various keys. Every major key is related most closely to its parallel and relative minor keys and to the dominant and subdominant keys, next to the parallel and relative minors of the dominant and subdominant keys, and least to the non-diatonic keys. Krumhansl (1990) stated that,

> These experiments suggest that what is special about the human musical capacity is the ability to relate the sounded events dynamically to one another, and to comprehend the multiplicity of structural functions of the events at many different levels simultaneously. This process evolves continuously as the events unfold in time.
>
> (p. 284)

Based on these and many other experiments, two models of tonal hierarchy have emerged as the most explanatory. In tonal pitch space theory (TPST), Lerdahl (2001) conceived of music as a multidimensional space. He gathered "empirical evidence that listeners of varying degrees of training and of different cultures hear pitches (and pitch classes), chords, and regions as relatively close or distant from a given tonic and in an orderly way" (p. v). TPST represents related keys with short distances across a space, while unrelated keys are more distant from each other. Tonal hierarchies are organized in three levels. The first two specify relationships within a given key: the pitch class level is concerned with specific pitches and the chordal level maps chord relationships across a diatonic space. The third level, the regional level, maps relationships among various keys. "Lerdahl suggests that listening to music corresponds to a journey through pitch space" (Bigand & Poulin-Charronnat, 2009, p. 65).

Building on a *neural network* model, Bharucha (1987) developed a tri-level system that linked tones, chords, and keys in a hierarchical order. At the first level, tones, or individual pitches, link to all the second level chords in which they appear; for example, in C Major, the note C occurs in the following triads: C Major, F Major, and A Minor. The third level is keys. Some keys, such as C Major and G Major, share several chords and tones. Other keys share only one pitch, for example, C Major and F♯ Major share only the pitch B. A pattern of activation spreads from level one to levels two and three. This hierarchical network is self-organizing and even untrained listeners learn to make sense of the music in their environment through mere exposure (Tillmann, Bharucha, & Bigand, 2000). One way of explaining this implicit learning of tonal hierarchies is through the previously discussed concept of statistical learning.

Bigand and Poulin-Charronnat (2009) reviewed the influence of tonal hierarchies on music perception. One example is tuning, as string players adjust individual pitches up or down according to the role of the pitch in the tonal hierarchy. Tonal hierarchies also influence perception of melodic contour, memorization of melody, musical stability, expectancy in musical contexts, and emotional responses to music. Finally, tonal hierarchies are intimately related to event hierarchies, that is, how we perceive certain structural features as more important than others.

One of the most intriguing things about tonality is its ability to convey feelings so powerfully. A seventh scale degree moving to tonic is called a leading tone, because it actually does seem to lead us onward toward a goal. Final chords at the end of a long movement guide the listener toward closure, either directly or through a tortuous, winding path. In common practice music (roughly the music of Baroque, Classical and Romantic periods or music from 1600–1900), we even refer to it as *functional harmony*, because a series of chords implies movement or motion or serves some particular purpose. Tonality operates similarly in the vast majority of music heard in the Western tradition, including popular music, music in advertising, church music, and so on. For the remainder of this section, we will assume that the discussion refers to any musical style that uses common practice tonality.

Huron (2006) provided an explanation for at least some of tonality's expressive qualities. What follows is a brief outline of his account:

- First, he asked ten experienced musicians to describe the distinctive quality of each scale degree of a major scale. For example, they described tonic as stable and satisfying, the mediant (3rd scale degree) as bright and lifted, and the leading tone as unstable and restless. These descriptors, or *qualia* as Huron called them, were given for each tone in isolation, that is in the absence of a musical context.

- Next, based on the work of Aarden, Krumhansl, and others, he reviewed data on event frequencies for scale degrees. When we listen to music, we do not hear all the tones with the same degree of frequency. (From now on, for clarity, all pitches will be transposed and presented in C Major.) By analyzing thousands of pieces of music, analysts have determined that in major keys, the tones of a tonic triad are the most commonly heard tones, in the order of G, E, and C. Far more rarely heard are C♯, E♭, F♯, A♭, and B♭. These reflect stable patterns in Western music, and listeners are able to predict pitch movement faster and more accurately based on how frequently these tones appear. This is another example of statistical learning.

- Initially this frequency distribution of tones did not match exactly the key profiles developed by Krumhansl (1990) with her probe-tone technique as described at the outset of this section. A student of Huron, Brett Aarden (2003) resolved the discrepancy in his dissertation when he realized that the probe-tone technique led listeners to hear the tones as if they were at the ends of phrases. When he adjusted the task to reflect mid-melody contexts, the distribution was much more in alignment with the event frequencies for scale degrees and the role of statistical learning was supported even more strongly.

- The next step was to examine tendencies in terms of pitch movement. Are there regularities in what pitch follows each scale degree? The quick answer is "yes." Analyzing more than a quarter of a million tone pairs in several thousand German folk songs in major keys, Huron constructed probability tables. Thus, E moving to D, G repeating itself, and D moving to C are the most probable pitch movements. Conversely, there were no instances of C♯–C, G♯–C, A♭–A, or other unlikely successions.

- By pairing the qualia of scale degrees with their likelihood of moving from one to another, one can begin to see how tonality conveys different feelings. For example, recall that the leading tone was described as unstable and restless and that tonic was characterized as stable and satisfying. If we hear B–C, we move from unstable to stable, from restless to satisfying. Is it not difficult to see, then, why closure in tonal music brings about a psychological feeling of completion, as if we are finally home and at rest. To the degree that the "way home" has been routine, delayed, or has taken a circuitous or surprising route, to that degree we may feel more or less psychological relief.

While other scale tone qualia and pitch movements dealing with such feelings as uncertainty or surprise have yet to be fully explicated, one can sense that this explanation, partial though it may be at the moment, has enormous potential to reveal tonality's powerful evocative effects. The fact that these experiences are based on statistical learning means that anyone in the culture, having heard thousands of examples, can respond meaningfully to a movie soundtrack, music on the radio, or other everyday listening experiences. One does not have to have formal music training to be swayed by tonal sequences. In fact, though these data are based on Western tonal music, Huron presented information suggesting that statistical learning is in operation for other musical systems. It is reasonable to suppose that listeners everywhere learn the music of their culture through exposure and that frequency maps revealing underlying regularities could be developed for their musical traditions as well as our own.

COGNITION OF MUSICAL ELEMENTS

Melody and Harmony

For many listeners, melody may be the most obvious feature of music. If asked to sing a familiar composition, the tune or melody is what nearly all of us would present. In a review of melody research, Schmuckler (2009) identified tonality and contour as the two most important aspects of melody cognition.

Tonality in Melody Cognition. Here, we consider tonality in melody cognition in the sense of key finding. That is, how do listeners determine the key of the music they are hearing? Essentially, there are two approaches. Structural-functional models posit that the frequent occurrence of specific pitches, say the notes of the tonic triad, provides clues to the key. Yoshino and Abe (2004) asked trained musicians to identify the key as they listened to 30 Bach fugue subjects. They did so primarily on the interpretation of melodic tones as members of a given diatonic scale.

The second approach relies on event-distribution strategies. Schmuckler and Tomovski (2005) tested a key-finding algorithm that matched the 12 chromatic tones with tonal hierarchy values. The algorithm successfully predicted listeners' abilities to determine key in passages by Bach and Chopin. Given the success of these two approaches, is it possible that the two might work together in some combination? Based on a review of relevant comparison studies, Schmuckler (2009) contends that, "the two types of information support each other in tonal perception" (p. 95).

Melodic Contour. Melodic contour is the overall up and down shape of a melody. Early on, we learn melodies by the overall contour (Dowling & Harwood, 1986). This feature-detecting capability allows us to recognize a familiar tune such as *Happy Birthday* in different keys (Thompson & Schellenberg, 2002). In fact, it is also what allows us to recognize a melody even when one or more pitches have been altered. Some researchers concentrate on how individual intervals contribute to the contour (e.g., Marvin & Laprade, 1987). Others (e.g., Dowling, 1978) have demonstrated that the shape of the melody is remembered independently from the exact pitches. Likely, the two work together, especially for longer or more complex melodies, as contour plays a significant role in melody cognition (Schmuckler, 2009).

Consonance-Dissonance. Consonance-dissonance is related to perceptions of pleasantness-unpleasantness of two or more simultaneously sounding tones. Sensory dissonance occurs independently of a musical context (Thompson, 2009). When two sounding tones have small integer ratios (e.g., 2:1 = octave, 3:2 = perfect fifth, etc.), listeners are likely to rate them as consonant. These tones have overtones that are aligned with each other or that fall outside critical bands. When ratios are more complex (e.g., 32:45 = tritone), listeners are more likely to rate them as dissonant. These tone combinations have overtones that fall within a critical band, creating a beating or rough sensation.

Judgments of musical consonance—dissonance are highly influenced by the musical context, by learning, and by cultural convention. Thus, listeners might judge a two-tone combination presented in a lab in isolation as dissonant, while they might judge the same interval as consonant when presented in a musical context. There are numerous examples throughout music history of intervals once thought to be dissonant that were later considered quite pleasant. "Since the early 20th century many composers have accepted the Schoenbergian concept of the 'emancipated' dissonance, in which traditionally dissonant intervals and chords could be treated as relatively stable harmonic entities, functioning in effect as 'higher' or more remote consonances" (Whittall, 2010).

Rhythm

Metrical and rhythmic organization provide their own kind of structure. In fact, temporal aspects may predominate over tonal aspects in some recognition tasks (Carterette, Monahan, Holman, Bell, & Fiske, 1982). Of course, rhythm and pitch integrate to create a more holistic sense of melody (Thompson & Schellenberg, 2002). Musical rhythm includes such concepts as tempo, beat, and meter. In experimental studies of rhythmic perception, a central concern has been *interonset interval* (IOI). IOI is the time interval between the starting points of two successive tones. Lower and upper limits for IOI are from around 100 ms to five or six seconds (London, 2004).

Dynamic attending theory (DAT) attempts to explain how listeners keep track of varying time-scale events, such as rhythm patterns, while maintaining a stable time structure (Large & Jones, 1999). As discussed in Chapter 3, there are numerous biological oscillators in the human body keeping track of such things as heart rate, awake—sleep cycles, and so on. According to DAT, internal oscillators are self-sustaining and stable, however, they can adapt to external rhythmic changes, including multiple oscillators attending to multiple time levels. Jones (2009) built on DAT by proposing a metric binding hypothesis. "It adds learning principles to address training and enculturation that contribute to listeners' familiarity with metric categories" (p. 84).

To coordinate one's perceptions with ongoing musical events, listener expectations must match hierarchically structured, time-based patterns. Through mere exposure, nearly everyone can entrain to the rhythmic structure of familiar music. According to London's (2004) *Many Meters Hypothesis*,

> A listener's competence resides in her or his knowledge of a very large number of context-specific metrical timing patterns. The number and degree of individuation among these patterns increases with age, training, and degree of musical enculturation.
>
> (p. 153)

Timbre

Timbre plays an important role in the cognition of musical patterns, as it particularly affects perceptual grouping (Wessel, 1989). Timbre also affects perceptions of musical tension—relaxation (Paraskeva & McAdams, 1997). Researchers have been interested in quantifying differences in musical timbre through multidimensional scaling techniques in which listeners provide similarity ratings for pairs of sounds (McAdams & Giordano, 2009). These ratings are mapped onto a distance model, with similar timbres closer together and dissimilar sounds farther apart. In one experiment (McAdams, Winsberg, Donnadieu, De Soete, & Krimphoff,

1995), listeners made similarity-dissimilarity judgments of 18 synthesized timbres of brass, woodwind, string, and keyboard instruments. The results led to the mapping of these timbres into five classes. There was no significant difference between musically trained and untrained listeners, however, musicians tended to make more precise judgments than controls.

COGNITION OF LARGER MUSICAL FORMS

As musical performances progress across time, not all events are equally important. In order to make sense of the music, the mind must be able to distinguish salient moments from less important ones. Thus, a main theme normally has greater importance than a transitional passage. A primary means of making sense of musical sounds across time is to create hierarchies. Generally, research has focused on two types—tonal hierarchies, how pitches are organized and arranged in importance as previously discussed, and event hierarchies, how occurrences are organized by motives or phrases or into higher level large forms, such as sonata or rondo form.

Event hierarchy refers to a logical organization of structurally important events. Some musical events have structural importance, while others are more ornamental. Ornamental passages give character or flavor to the music, but if removed, the musical idea would still be relatively intact. Heinrich Schenker developed a means of analyzing music into a hierarchically ordered series of structural levels (Burkhart & Schenker, 1978). At the lowest level— lowest in the sense of least reduced, not least important—was the actual surface of the music or the music as it was notated and heard. Each level above was a reduction of the level below until at the highest level the music was reduced to its essential elements, the *Ursatz* (fundamental structure); see Figure 8.15.

In Schenker's view, the *Ursatz* was the beginning, not the end; that is, he started with the composition reduced to its essence, the background, and then gradually expanded the view to include more and more details in the foreground. According to Sadie (1988),

> the *Ursatz* represents the large-scale *Auskomponierung* ('composing out') of the fundamental harmony, the tonic triad. The concept of structural levels provides for a

FIGURE **8.15** | Final Three Measures from Schubert, *Wandrers Nachtlied*, Op. 4, No. 3., D. 224. In the lower score you see the *Ursatz* indicating a I-V-I chord progression with a 3–2–1 melodic line.

hierarchical differentiation of musical components, which establishes a basis for describing and interpreting relations among the elements of any composition.

(p. 667)

Jackendoff and Lerdahl disagree with Schenker's notion of Ursatz (Lerdahl, 2009) and also reverse Schenker's order, while taking a similar reductionist approach. They refer to the uppermost layer of musical structure as the *musical surface*, which includes pitches and note lengths, along with timbre and expression, as heard by the listener (Jackendoff & Lerdahl, 2006). Below the surface, pitch and rhythm combine to create several layers of structure that are seen as event hierarchies. At the lowest level is the deep structure of the composition.

Lerdahl and Jackendoff (1983) developed their generative theory of tonal music (GTTM) as a means of identifying rules of musical grammar. These rules describe how experienced listeners organize the music they hear. GTTM is based on four types of hierarchical structure: (1) Grouping structure shows how listeners segment music into motives, phrases, and sections. Phrases marked by a fermata in a typical Bach chorale provide a clear example. (2) Metrical structure is based on a hierarchy of strong and weak beats. Meter signatures, bar lines, and so on, guide the performer, whose emphasis on first beats of measures, for example, aids the listener in organizing the temporal flow of the music. (3) Time-span reduction is the primary link between pitch and rhythm and establishes the structural importance of rhythmic events. Time-span segmentation helps the listener organize music from smaller units such as motives and phrases to ever-longer units such as periods, theme groups, and sections. (4) Prolongational reduction creates a hierarchy of tension-release patterns (Fig. 8.16). Simpler patterns of tension—release are superimposed to create more complex patterns. GTTM, then, is a means of organizing music hierarchically from the top or surface level to the deep, underlying structures.

Another goal of GTTM is to delineate how listeners make choices about the musical structures they hear. Well-formedness rules define the structures that are possible and preference rules identify analytic choices from among all the possible structures. The Gestalt principles of organization provide a basis for many preference rules. For example, Grouping Preference Rule 2 concerns the principal of proximity. With all the possible ways one can hear pitches in a given passage, strong preference is given to organizing those pitches that are closer together as a unit. Figure 8.9 and the relevant discussion concerning a passage from the fourth movement of Tchaikovsky's Sixth Symphony is a clear example.

Lerdahl (2001) identifies four assumptions on which GTTM is based. (1) GTTM ignores the processes by which the musical surface is constructed from the acoustical signal. Furthermore, it is assumed that the musical score represents the musical surface. (2) GTTM is based on the notion of an experienced listener. (3) Event hierarchies as specified in GTTM represent the final state of a listener's understanding. It does not describe how the listener understands the music as it unfolds in time. (4) GTTM is hierarchical, not associational. That is, each layer nests into deeper layers.

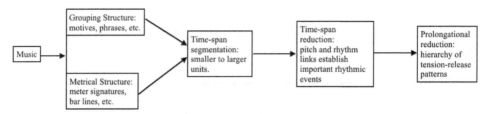

FIGURE **8.16** | Major Components of Generative Theory of Tonal Music.

Although GTTM has received the lion's share of attention, other theories are worth noting. For example, Temperley (2001) based his approach on computer models. He saw his work as "an attempt to quantify and implement Lerdahl and Jackendoff's initial conception, and to expand it to other musical domains" (p. 13). In particular, he utilized a *dynamic programming* procedure borrowed from computer science. Dynamic programming keeps track of the preferred analysis from the beginning throughout the score, and also allows for revisions of previous analyses based on what occurs later in the music. In this it moves closer to a real-time analytic process, representing how listeners make musical judgments from the outset of a performance, rather than after the performance is completed.

Deliège and Mélen (1997) created a *cue abstraction theory* to account for attentional listening processes, that is, how a listener actively engages with musical structures with maximum cognitive resources. As a listener attends to a musical performance, the musical surface is segmented into different lengths. Utilizing principles of sameness and difference, a listener abstracts cues, or distinctive features, that allow for segmentation of the music in the flow of time. These prominent surface markers create memory units that serve to integrate features of the musical style.

Deliège (2001a) underscored the underpinnings of Gestalt theory in her introduction to a special issue of *Music Perception* devoted to similarity perception and its relationship to categorization and cue abstraction. Likewise, *cues* are related to the concept of figure-ground relationships. The remainder of the special issue was devoted to such related topics as music analysis, segmentation, computational techniques, motivic structure, memorization, categorization principles, and prototypicality. Consideration of the latter topic, prototypicality, led to the concept of imprint formation (Deliège, 2001b). When the same cue or its variants are consistently abstracted throughout a composition due to frequent usage (i.e., through statistical learning), an imprint is formed and stored in memory. For more on the preference for prototypes theory, see Chapter 12.

While there are many details left unexplored in these brief overviews, it is clear that there is considerable progress in understanding how the mind makes sense of music as it sounds across time. A question that naturally occurs to some is whether these organizing principles are universal. Do listeners from other cultures track musical processes in ways similar to Western listeners?

CROSS-CULTURAL COMPARATIVE RESEARCH IN MUSIC

Recall from Chapter 4 that ethnomusicologists are hesitant to talk about music universals. Psychologists, too, qualify the term when they speak of universal aspects of music processing. They recognize that the immense variety of musical behaviors across the globe makes the concept of universality a difficult one. In addition, there is simply not enough research on music cognition in non-Western musical cultures to have a rich enough database to make claims of universality. In light of this, when they use the term, they refer to the fact that while the majority of individuals and cultures may process music in a similar way, there is always the possibility of outliers.

Stevens and Byron (2009) identify some likely candidates for universal cognitive music processes. Pending further experimentation and confirmation across many varied cultures, these remain potential candidates at best.

■ Perceptual principles of grouping and segmentation. Because infants and animals demonstrate the Gestalt laws of perceptual organization, it is possible these principles represent processes inherent in mammalian behavior. Recall, too, from previous discussions that infants are nearly as adept at auditory streaming and segmentation tasks as adults.

- Features of musical environments and perceptual and cognitive constraints. These include such things as discrete pitch levels, musical scales with different sized intervals from note to note, pitches and melodies at different octaves recognized as similar, inter-onset intervals (IOI) between 100 ms and 1500 ms, and steady beat.
- Higher-order processes in music cognition. Many musical styles contain tonal, temporal, and event hierarchies.

Remember that even if a majority of cultures is found to understand their music with similar processes, there may be exceptions to any or all of these organizing principles.

Krumhansl (1995) reported on an experiment in which she investigated whether listeners used the principles of Narmour's implication-realization (I-R) model for processing British folksongs, atonal music by Webern, and Chinese folksongs. The results confirmed the I-R model and furthermore, that the application of psychological principles of melodic expectancy was not influenced by training or enculturation, as Chinese and Western listeners provided similar responses. These findings were confirmed by Schellenberg (1996) and also in a study of North Sami yoiks (Krumhansl et al., 2000). The Sami (Fig. 8.17) live in an area that overlaps Norway, Sweden, Finland, and Russia. Yoiks are folksongs with a spontaneous, improvisatory character, containing short, repetitive motives.

Researchers have investigated the cognition of rhythmic aspects of music as well as pitch. Speaking of studies of Ghanaian and German drummers and their perceptions of performances from both cultures (Kopiez, Langner, & Steinhagen, 1999), Lehmann, Sloboda, and Woody (2007) comment, "These experiments provide evidence for the existence of perceptual universals in the evaluation of rhythm performances, which imply common standards of regularity regarding timing and dynamics" (p. 214).

Demorest and Morrison (2016) developed the concept of cultural distance as a means of understanding cognitive processing of culturally familiar and unfamiliar music. The closer the statistical patterns of pitch and rhythm of a particular music are to familiar music, the more efficient the processing will be. Using a computational model, they were able to determine how closely related music from different cultures were to each other.

FIGURE **8.17** | Sami People in Karesuando (Gárasavvon), Lappland, Sweden.

In these few experiments, we see Gestalt organizational principles, a music theory model, psychological research, neural network models, and cross-cultural comparisons converging to point toward universal cognitive strategies. One additional note concerning cross-cultural comparative research in music concerns a note of urgency. So little of this work has been done to date, and Western styles are pervading more and more cultures. Already many listeners are more familiar with Western musical styles than with music from their own cultures. Soon, it may be difficult to find groups who have not been exposed to non-indigenous music.

MUSIC AND LANGUAGE

Language has long been a topic of interest to psychologists, and particularly to cognitive psychologists. The ninth edition of *Cognition* (Matlin & Farmer, 2015), for example, includes two chapters devoted to language, along with discussions of speech and language sprinkled throughout the book. It is no wonder, then, that music psychologists are interested in relationships between music and language. Evidence of a burgeoning interest in this topic is seen in *Music, Language, and the Brain* (Patel, 2008) and in a special issue of the journal *Music Perception* on music and language (Bigand, Lalitte, & Dowling, 2009).

Infants acquire both language and music via statistical learning (Saffran, 2003), however, infants focus their attention longer on infant-direct singing than on infant-directed speech (Nakata & Trehub, 2005). Songs enhance language learning because of the emotional attraction of song and redundant structural components (Schön et al., 2008). In turn, the language infants learn influences the melodic contour of their vocalizations (Mampe et al., 2009).

A sense of pitch is important in both music and speech. Monotone speech is highly unusual and natural speech includes many inflections of rising and falling tones. More than half the world's languages are described as tone languages, meaning that a change of pitch can change the meaning of a word (Patel, 2008). Consider the five examples presented in Table 8.1. The syllable *ma* has five different intonations in Mandarin Chinese, leading to five different meanings (Wei Jiao, personal communication; Xu, 1997). Musical training facilitates processing of lexical stress (Kolinsky, Cuvelier, Goetry, Peretz, & Morais, 2009).

Rhythm also plays a crucial role in language acquisition (Hauser & McDermott, 2003). Newborns move their limbs in rhythm to the speech they hear around them (Bohannan, 1983; Malloch & Trevarthen, 2009b). If they hear a different language, their rhythms will change subtly. Patel (2008) found connections between the rhythm of a given language and musical

TABLE 8.1 | The Syllable *ma* in Mandarin Chinese.

Tone	Pinyin*	Chinese	English Meaning
First tone	mā	妈	Mother
Second tone	má	麻	Hemp or torpid
Third tone	mǎ	马	Horse
Fourth tone	mà	骂	Scold (verb)
Neutral tone	ma	吗	Question particle, usually added at the end of a sentence, along with a question mark. 你好吗? How are you?

*Pinyin is the romanization of Mandarin Chinese.

rhythms of that culture. Rhythmic activities in the acquisition of language are so important that they form the basis for acquiring cognitive expectancies and for interrelating cognition and affect (Stern, 1982).

Patel and Daniele (2003) demonstrated that speech rhythms in French and English were similar to rhythmic patterns in French and English music. Hannon (2009) found that listeners could classify instrumental music on the basis of whether they were French or English folk-songs. They were able to do this primarily on the basis of rhythmic structure, as when in a follow-up experiment they were successful in classifying instrumental music with a rhythm soundtrack only (i.e., no pitches). According to Campbell (1986), the ability to interpret micro-timed intervals in sound exists only for speech and music, and nowhere else.

In organizing these and other findings, Patel (2009) identified three links between language and music:

- Sensory encoding of sound. Considerable evidence is mounting to support the notion that musical training affects the processing of language sounds.
- Processing of melodic contours. Tracking melodic contour is important in both music and language.
- Syntactic processing. The processing of both music and language relies on awareness of hierarchical structures, however, there are significant differences in the syntactical aspects of the two.

Based on these findings, Patel (2011) developed the OPERA hypothesis to elucidate connections between music and language and to support the notion that musical training can benefit language learning.

- **O**verlap: Music and language overlap in the brain.
- **P**recision: Music places more precise demands on neural systems than language.
- **E**motion: Music elicits strong emotions, which reinforces learning.
- **R**epetition: Musical experiences involve a great deal of repetition, which reinforces learning.
- **A**ttention: Music demands focused attention.

According to Patel's work, "When these higher demands are combined with the emotional rewards of music, the frequent repetition that musical training engenders, and the focused attention that it requires, neural plasticity is activated and makes lasting changes in brain structure and function which impact speech processing" (2014, p. 98).

Jackendoff (2009) identified four general capacities shared by music and language—nonhumans do not have music and language in the human sense, both involve sound production, every culture has local variants of both, and the two are combined in song in every culture. Jackendoff also outlined fundamental differences between language and music, for example, music enhances affect while language conveys propositional thought. He also discussed similarities and differences in structural elements such as rhythm, pitch, words, and syntax. Finally, he identified seven capacities shared by music and language with other domains. Thus, in his view, they are not as closely related as others believe. Data presented in Chapter 9 indicate that language and music are processed in shared, parallel, and distinct neural networks (Brown, Martinez, & Parsons, 2006). Both Patel and Jackendoff agree that considerably more research is needed to reach a more complete understanding of the linkage between music and language.

CONCLUSION

In this chapter, we have considered how we make sense of the music we hear as it comes to us in real-time streaming. The Gestalt laws of cognitive organization provide a foundation for music cognition and form the basis for how we structure sensory stimuli. The concept of auditory scene analysis helps us understand how we organize complex auditory environments. Through experience, we create schema or mental representations of basic musical elements. Continued learning allows us to shine the spotlight of our attention onto different schema within a complex auditory scene and to parse different strands from the whole through auditory stream segregation.

Over time, we build up music memory strategies by repeating information and chunking it into manageable units. Those musical experiences that we encounter most frequently are the ones we learn best. Statistical learning explains how we can learn the music of our culture without formal training. Thus, nearly everyone can enjoy the music s/he hears on television or in the movies. However, with the additional information gained through formal training, we have the possibility of understanding more complicated and nuanced musical experiences. One way we do this is by making stronger predictions about what is happening in the music. Each musical idea leads us to expect what will follow. To have few expectations, say in listening to unfamiliar music, generally means less engagement with the musical process.

Tonality is a primary building block of the vast majority of music we hear in Western culture. Other building blocks include such things as melodic contour, consonance and dissonance, and perception of rhythm and timbre. GTTM is a model for how all these building blocks come together in the perception of music as a whole. At the musical surface are the pitches, rhythms, and so on, as we hear them. Below the surface are deeper layers structured as event hierarchies. Thus, how experienced listeners sort out what they hear is not random; rather, GTTM and other theories such as dynamic programming and cue abstraction attempt to arrange cognitive strategies into a logical, coherent order.

Nearly all the work from Gestalt laws to cue abstraction has utilized Western listeners encountering Western music. Logically one might wonder whether these ideas explain how non-Westerners experience music. The small amount of extant research suggests that there are some universal cognitive strategies. However, it must be remembered that *universal* is understood to mean *more common than not* and that there is always the likelihood of cultural outliers who organize their musical listening experiences in very different ways. Finally, music psychologists have had a strong interest in relationships between music and language. These two cognitive domains share many features and yet have many distinctive features. Music psychologists need to conduct considerably more research before they achieve a more complete understanding.

As a means of knitting all this together, consider a scenario in which a husband and wife attend an opera performance. Jane has a moderate background in opera, having taken voice lessons for some time and performed minor roles in several college productions. Mike has almost no musical training and prefers the "classic" rock of his youth, along with country music. She instigated the excursion, buying tickets online, and has eagerly anticipated the event for weeks. He has good-naturedly agreed to attend, but with some reluctance and, truth-be-told, some trepidation. Dressed in their finery, they meet another couple at an expensive restaurant and will meet up with them again at the Opera House (Fig. 8.18). They have plans for drinks, coffee, and dessert following the performance.

In chapters 9, 10, and 11, we will consider what transpires in Mike and Jane's brains, and how they respond bodily and emotionally as they experience the performance. Please keep in

FIGURE **8.18** | Somewhere in This Audience Mike and Jane Are Sitting with Their Friends in Anticipation of an Opera Performance.

mind that thoughts, bodily reactions, and emotions are not discrete responses but integrated into a coherent whole. Furthermore, a host of socio-cultural influences colors their experiences, as well. For the moment, however, we will focus on the cognitive process in play as they listen to the music.

One thing we have learned from our review of music cognition is that even though Mike is not formally trained, mere exposure to the music he has heard throughout his lifetime enables him to understand and make sense of much of what he will hear in the opera. Let us assume that he is actually concentrating and attempting to make sense of the music. Much of what he understands is unconscious, but he can find and respond to the beat. Often, he can identify the melody and follow it. He can segment much of the music into manageable units. He may even occasionally recognize when the soprano repeats a melody that just sounded in the orchestra. He has some expectations of closure as the music builds to a climax or fades into nothingness.

Jane's musical training gives her the ability to process much beyond what Mike can. For one thing, Mike's attention is severely tested and although at the beginning of each act he follows along, after a while his focus wanes and he becomes distracted. Jane is able to attend throughout the opera. Her library of musical schemata is much larger and this allows her to apprehend many more nuances and subtleties and to process more of the complexities. For example, in a *da capo* aria, she not only recognizes the return of the melody in the repeated A section, but also correctly expects that the melody will be highly ornamented in the return. Furthermore, she can recall a melody from the opening act that is restated in the orchestra near the end of the opera, only this time slower and in a minor key to reflect the tragic ending. Her command of the "spotlight of attention" allows her to switch rapidly from one voice to another in a scene in which all four main characters are singing at the same time. Thus, Mike and Jane share certain abilities to understand the music they are hearing. However, because of her training and experience, Jane has enhanced capabilities.

Music psychologists have much to learn about how we process music. However, they have made considerable progress in recent years. Over time, we will know even more about the complex and elusive processes involved in music cognition. One area of necessary exploration is the integration of music cognition with bodily and emotional responses, covered in Chapters 10 and 11. First, however, we will explore the role of the brain in Chapter 9.

DISCUSSION QUESTIONS

1. Sloboda says that listening to music is like listening to someone tell a joke. Can you think of a joke and make a comparison between listening to it and a specific piece of music?
2. Choose a piece of music you are currently rehearsing. How do the Gestalt laws of cognitive organization apply to this piece?
3. What other common, simple schemata can you name besides phone numbers and social security numbers? What more complex and changing musical schemata, like partimenti or chorale tunes, can you think of? Can you identify schemata in music you are currently performing or studying?
4. When you listen to music (either live or recorded), are you able to switch your attention between difference voices (e.g., SATB in a chorus, left or right hand in a solo piano performance, different instrument sections in a band, orchestra, or jazz ensemble)? Is there a difference between consciously directing your attention to different voices and having your attention drawn to different voices because of what is happening in the music?
5. Describe the strategies you use when you memorize music. Do you rely more on auditory memory, visual memory, kinesthetic memory, or some other strategy? What are some "chunking" strategies you use when learning music?
6. Choose a particular piece of music and, starting from the beginning, describe how the composer sets up musical expectations. Can you connect the way these expectations are met or not met with your emotional responses?
7. Can you find examples of gap-fill melodies and changing-note patterns in music you are currently studying or performing?
8. Many modern compositions do not follow the Gestalt laws or tonality as closely as music from the 17th to 19th centuries. Do you think this is related to the difficultly some listeners have in understanding modern music? What other factors account for the lack of popularity of modern music for some listeners?
9. Do event hierarchy theories resonant with you as a musician? That is, do you think they help you as a listener, performer, or teacher? If so, how? If not, why not?
10. As a person with both musical and linguistic skills, do you see these two as related, overlapping, or distinctly different? What if you only had one skill and not the other; what differences would that make in your daily life?

Chapter 9

Music and the Brain

W E just left Mike and Jane at the opera at the end of the previous chapter. What is going on in their brains as they listen to the music? What would we learn if we could "lift the lid" and peer inside? Perhaps no other area of music psychology has seen such rapid advancement as the neuroscience of music. Evidence of this is seen in several recent books, such as *The Oxford Handbook of Music and the Brain* (Thaut & Hodges, 2019) and *Music and Brain* (Koelsch, 2012). Further examples come in the form of a series of books from the New York Academy of Sciences:

- *The Neurosciences and Music VI: Music, Sound, and Health* (2018).
- *The Neurosciences and Music V: Cognitive Stimulation and Rehabilitation* (Bigand et al., 2015).
- *The Neurosciences and Music IV: Learning and Memory* (Overy, Peretz, Zatorre, Lopez, & Majno, 2012).
- *The Neurosciences and Music III: Disorders and Plasticity* (Dalla Bella et al., 2009).
- *The Neurosciences and Music II: From Perception to Performance* (Avanzini, Lopez, Koelsch, & Majno, 2005).
- *The Neurosciences and Music: Mutual Interactions and Implications on Developmental Function* (Avanzini, Faienza, Minciacchi, Lopez, & Majno, 2003).
- *The Biological Foundations of Music* (Zatorre & Peretz, 2001).

Books in the popular press have also dealt with the topic, such as *Musicophilia: Tales of Music and the Brain* (Sacks, 2007) and *This is Your Brain on Music* (Levitin, 2006). By 2007 well over 2,000 articles had been published (Edwards & Hodges, 2007), with more appearing constantly. One reason for this surge of interest may be that technology now allows scientists to peer inside the brain to monitor inner workings in detail never before possible.

The sheer volume of relevant research literature is such that an exhaustive treatment is beyond the scope of a single chapter. Rather, the purpose of this chapter is to review and synthesize the research to provide an overview of the field as well as a general understanding of specific topics. The chapter is divided into two main sections. The first is devoted to an explanation of how the brain works and the second, to important findings concerning music and the brain.

BRIEF INTRODUCTION TO THE BRAIN

Ideally, this section will help make it possible for readers to understand better the ensuing reviews of neuromusical research. Because the brain is incredibly complex, and because thorough explanations of neuroanatomy and neurophysiology are beyond the scope of this chapter, what follows is only a grossly simplified and greatly generalized introduction. Readers wishing to acquire more detailed knowledge are encouraged to consult the sources that are cited. Another point to consider before we begin is that is impossible to separate biology from culture (Hodges, 2019). The brain does not live in a jar on a shelf in a lab. It resides in a person with a unique personality, with numerous interactions with other humans and the environment, and so on. Thus, we cannot pretend to understand the brain in isolation from the totality of human experience.

The human central nervous system consists of the brain, brainstem, and spinal cord, as well as the peripheral nerves and the autonomic nervous system. The *cerebral cortex*—the center for most of the special attributes that separate human beings from other animals—is identified by the thin layer of *gray matter* that covers the outer surface of the brain. In contrast to other animals that have no cortex at all (e.g., birds) or that possess a smooth one (e.g., rats), the human cerebral cortex is a sheet of neurons that is the thickness of two to three dimes, which is thinner than an orange peel (Calvin, 2014; Cohen, 1996). This is a surface area of about two square feet or approximately the surface area of an unfolded daily newspaper.

The surface of the brain is wrinkled in appearance. This is because as the brain develops it folds in upon itself in a process called *gyrification* (White, Su, Schmidt, Kao, & Sapiro, 2010). Gyrification, or cortical folding, can be demonstrated by cupping the hands facing each other with fingertips touching. Notice the distance from the first knuckle on each finger to the first knuckle on the finger opposite. Roll the fingers inward so that the first knuckles on all fingers are touching. This can be repeated so that the second knuckle on each finger is touching the second knuckle on the finger opposite. Rolling the fingers inward to make the total hand area smaller roughly approximates how the brain folded in upon itself as it tripled in size over the millennia from roughly 450 cubic centimeters (cm^3) to about 1350 cm^3 and three pounds in weight in modern *homo sapiens* (Lee & Wolpoff, 2003; Roth & Dicke, 2005; Vandervert, 2016). Gyrification also creates shorter distances for messages to travel across the brain.

Seen from above, the cortex looks to be bilaterally symmetrical; that is, the left and right hemispheres appear to be identical. Actually, there can be substantial anatomical variations between the two halves (Toga & Thompson, 2003); but while there is general agreement that the hemispheres may process information in various ways, these differences are not so simple or contrasting as was once thought. Each hemisphere is divided into four lobes based on general functions (see Figure 9.1) (Carter, 2009): the occipital lobe (vision), parietal lobe (sensory processing), temporal lobe (auditory perception, language, and visual processing), and frontal lobe (long-term planning, movement control, and speech production). Within each lobe are sensory, motor, and association zones. Sensory zones receive information from the senses, motor zones are concerned with control and coordination of muscle movements, and association zones, making up nearly 80% of the cerebral cortex, deal with the more cognitive aspects of human behavior, such as interpretation and understanding (Mark & Ulmer, 2005). Other important brain sites include the sensory cortex (that provides a map of the body surface), the motor cortex (that initializes movement), the *limbic system* (site of complex chemical processes and emotions; see Fig. 9.10), the brainstem (that controls such automatic body functions as breathing), and the *cerebellum* (that governs muscle coordination and the learning of rote movements).

The adult brain weighs about three pounds and consists of more than 100 billion neurons or brain cells (Carey, 2008). Neurons are so small that 100 million of them can fit into one cubic inch. They are so richly interconnected that one neuron may connect with as many as

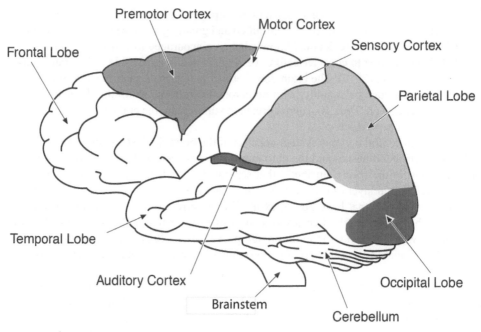

FIGURE 9.1 | Diagram of Major Areas of the Brain.

a thousand other neurons and there may be as many as a thousand trillion connections in the average human brain (Zull, 2002). This close proximity between neurons and the vast number of interconnections are important in the rapid transfer of information. In the first few years of life, neurons grow in size and in the number of connections. It is believed that a rich sensory environment stimulates these connections, while an impoverished one inhibits cognitive growth (Huttenlocher, 2002).

The cortex or *gray matter* wraps around an inner core called *white matter*. It is so called because the neuronal axons are coated with a white, fatty sheath in a process called myelination. This improves message transmission in terms of both speed—messages travel up to 100 times faster in myelinated axons (Zull, 2002; see Fig. 9.2)—and accuracy and is related to cognitive functioning (Webb, Monk, & Nelson, 2001). White matter, with its billions of fibers, occupies nearly half the brain and is responsible for connecting different regions of gray matter into neural networks (Filley, 2005).

Although there are four different types (see Fig. 9.3), neurons generally possess four distinctive features: a cell body, an *axon*, multiple *dendrites*, and *synapses* (Andreassi, 2007). Dendrites bring messages to the cell body and the axon carries messages away from it. Synapses are connecting points between the axon of one neuron and the dendrites of another neuron. Axons and dendrites do not actually touch each other at a synapse. Rather, there is a tiny gap only 200 nanometers wide, called the synaptic cleft that separates the two (Ho, Lee, & Martin, 2011). A single neuron can receive as many as 100,000 signals on a dendritic tree (Zull, 2002). Synapses are modified by becoming larger, by adding new synapses, or by regressing and these modifications are very important to the understanding of learning and memory. The concepts of plasticity, pruning, critical periods, and neural networks are also vitally important.

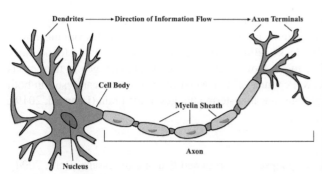
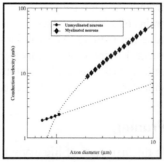

FIGURE 9.2 | Myelinated Neurons. Left panel: Multiple dendrites bring information into the cell body. Axons (one per neuron) send information on to other neurons. Right panel: Myelinated axons send information much more rapidly than unmyelinated ones.

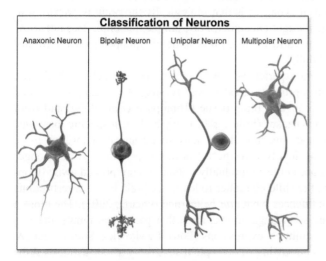

FIGURE 9.3 | Four Types of Neurons. In an anaxonic neuron, the axon cannot be distinguished from the dendrites. Bipolar neurons have one axon and one dendrite. Unipolar neurons have one process attached to the cell body. Multipolar neurons have one axon and multiple dendrites.

Plasticity

The brain has a marvelous ability to change itself (Doidge, 2007). *Neural plasticity* means that brain structures can be modified under certain conditions, either as a result of injury or through learning experiences (Gottesman & Hanson, 2005). In some circumstances, healthy parts of the brain can assume functions once performed by diseased or injured portions (Dalla Bella, 2016). Although this is more likely to occur in young children, it is also the underlying rationale for many therapies used to retrain the brains of those who suffer from stroke, Parkinson's disease, or brain trauma.

Plasticity is also a central feature of learning experiences (Stiles, 2000). A common axiom in neuroscience is that *neurons that wire together fire together* and correspondingly, *neurons that fire apart, wire apart* (Doidge, 2007). This means that learning experiences cause the brain to re-wire itself into neural networks. Musicians are good models for plasticity, as the brains of adults who have received significant musical training are different from those who have not (Münte, Altenmüller, & Jäncke, 2002). For example, neuroscientists found early musical training, especially before the age of 7, leads to significant changes in the corpus callosum (Steele, Bailey, Zatorre, & Penhune, 2013). Musical experiences can result in both short-term (i.e., lasting for several hours) or long-term changes in the brain (Lennard, 2019).

Pruning

In the first years of life many more synapses are produced than are necessary (Berk, 2004). The number of synapses peaks at different times in different places in the brain (Johnson, 2001) and overproduction is as high as 50% (Stiles, 2000). This large number of redundant synapses, along with the energy expended in myelinating the axons, doubles glucose metabolism in the frontal cortex from ages two to four (Thompson et al., 2000) and reaches 190% to 226% of adult values between ages three and eight (Chugani, Phelps, & Mazziotta, 1993). The reason for the overproduction of synapses is that biologically the brain is preparing to meet any environmental challenge it might encounter. For example, the brain does not know what language the individual will need to learn, so it is initially equipped to learn all languages (Kuhl & Rivera-Gaxiola, 2008).

Genetic instructions and learning experiences work together to sculpt a child's brain into its eventual adult configuration in a process called *neural pruning*. For example, between the ages of seven and eleven up to 50% of brain tissue (Thompson et al., 2000) and from 20 to 80% of cortical neurons and synapses (Stiles, 2000) may be lost in specific locations. A child is constantly engaged in learning, initially in daily living and later through more formal schooling. Synapses that are involved in these learning experiences grow stronger through repetition, and those that are not used gradually wither and are pruned away (Gopnik, Meltznoff, & Kuhl, 2001). As the child continues to learn, the brain imposes restrictions on itself so that what *is* learned influences what *can be* learned (Quartz, 2003). The more a child learns about her own culture's language, music, and other perceptual inputs, the less sensitive she becomes to the other cultures' expressions (Pons, Lewkowicz, Soto-Faraco, & Sebastián-Gallés, 2009). There is a narrowing of perceptual sensitivity as one acquires skills and knowledge embedded in the native culture.

Genetic and environmental influences on neural pruning can be seen in music learning. Initially, the child is prepared to learn any musical system s/he encounters. As music learning progresses, however—and this includes both informal learning (as in hearing music on television) and formal music learning—the microtunings and polyrhythms inherent in non-Western music may be difficult, if not impossible, to apprehend or produce for an adolescent who has been exposed only to Western music (Patel, Meltznoff, & Kuhl, 2004). In one experiment, six-month-old American infants perceived rhythmic violations in both Western and non-Western music, but adults responded better to Western than non-Western musical violations (Hannon & Trehub, 2005).

Critical Periods

For normal brain development, it is vital that brain regions undergoing a growth spurt receive appropriate stimulation (Berk, 2004). Enriched environments improve brain development (Carey, 2008). If children are raised in impoverished or sterile environments, the neural networks necessary for optimal functioning will not develop properly. For example, one child who lived a severely deprived existence until the age of 13 was thereafter extremely limited in her use of language, even after years of concentrated efforts on the part of therapists (Curtiss, 1977; Rymer, 1993).

In adults who suffered childhood trauma, certain parts of the brain may be up to 18% smaller (Doidge, 2007). Physical, social, and emotional growth can be severely stunted if children do not receive adequate stimulation at the appropriate times. For example, a large number of children born in Romania in the late 1980s when that country was experiencing social and economic problems were placed in orphanages and did not receive adequate care and attention. The result was that many children experienced mild neurocognitive impairment, impulsivity, and attention and social deficits (Chugani et al., 2001). However, the window of opportunity for learning many things may never be permanently shut (Braun & Bock, 2007) and Bruer (1999) cautions against an over-reliance on critical periods as rigid determinants of human learning.

In contrast to critical periods, optimal or sensitive periods are growth phases during which learning may come more easily and more quickly. If appropriate experiences do not occur during optimal periods, learning may still occur at a later time, though it may be more difficult. (See Flohr & Hodges, 2006, for a discussion of this concept in a musical context.) An examination of professional musicians supports the common perception that an early start is essential to eventual success as a concert artist (Moore, Burland, & Davidson, 2003). Conversely, *It's Never Too Late* (Holt, 1978) documented the author's experiences in learning to play the cello as an adult. It can be done, but as with learning a language, it is more easily accomplished in earlier years (Raufschecker, 2001). In *Tone Deaf and All Thumbs? An Invitation to Music-Making for Late Bloomers and Non-Prodigies*, Wilson (1986b) presented a neurological explanation of music learning, with implications for adult beginners.

Neural Networks

Many of the properties and processes of the brain, such as perception, attention, and memory, are best understood through the concept of neural networks (Fig. 9.4) (Rolls, 1989).

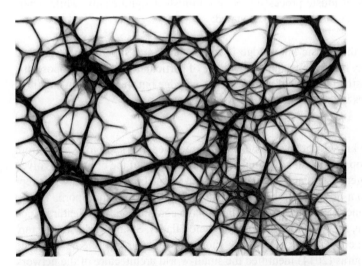

FIGURE 9.4 | Neural Network. Individual neurons organize themselves into networks so that complex processes such as language and music are represented in collections of millions of neurons.

Harkening back to the statement that "neurons that fire together, wire together," neural networks represent groups of neurons that act as collectives. Information storage is distributed so that any particular item is represented throughout a network rather than in a specific place; furthermore, processing proceeds in parallel rather than in serial fashion (Matlin & Farmer, 2015). Another key fact about networks is that they learn and self-organize.

At a more global level, language and music, for example, represent neural networks or perhaps more accurately, multiple neural networks. A significant body of literature is concerned with whether language and music activate some of the same neural networks (e.g., Patel, 2008). Brown et al. (2006) provided brain imaging data to support a notion of shared, parallel, and distinctive neural networks. Shared: language and music activate some of the same areas in auditory and motor cortices. Parallel: speaking and singing arise from nearby sensory and motor areas. Distinct: semantic and syntactic aspects of language and music activate domain-specific areas of the brain.

Considering music specifically, Janata (2005) reported on two experiments that identified brain networks involved in tracking musical structure. These networks changed subtly as the nature of the tasks changed. Tillman, Bharucha, and Bigand (2000) demonstrated that learning tonal regularities through mere exposure was represented in self-organizing neural maps. In another experiment, researchers scanned experienced musicians as they heard a melody that systematically modulated through all 24 major and minor keys (Janata et al., 2002). Different tonal centers activated different portions of a neural network in prefrontal areas known to be a central site for cognitive, affective, and memory processing. In other words, this dynamic network changed in response to different musical keys.

As more work such as the foregoing continues, a picture gradually emerges of music as a widely diffuse system comprised of numerous self-organizing musical networks. While varying aspects of music are processed in different parts of the brain, they come together in such a way that our experience is whole and coherent. Researchers confirmed this by examining two expert musicians, one with semantic dementia and the other with Alzheimer's disease (Omar, Hailstone, Warren, Crutch, & Warren, 2010). Their performances on a battery of music assessments were compared to scores of healthy musicians. For the two impaired musicians, certain aspects of music processing were diminished significantly, while others were well preserved. In conclusion, researchers stated:

> The findings suggest that music knowledge is fractionated, and superordinate musical knowledge is relatively more robust than knowledge of particular music. We propose that music constitutes a distinct domain of non-verbal knowledge but shares certain cognitive organizational features with other brain knowledge systems.
>
> (p. 1)

The idea of superordinate knowledge systems has led some researchers to move away from reductionism, that is, to stop looking at how smaller, particular areas of the brain are involved in specific aspects of a larger system and to begin looking at whole brain responses. This represents a shift in focus from microstructure to macrostructure. Bullmore and Sporns (2009) posit that structural and functional systems of the brain have complex network features such as small-world architecture, highly connected hubs, and modularity. Small-world architecture means that there is a local clustering of nodes with short paths that link all the nodes in the network. Koelsch and Skouras (2014) identified the small-world architecture of the network supporting joy as a response to music. Hubs provide a central site for nodal connections and connector hubs link different modules. Wilkins, Hodges, Laurienti, and Steen (2012) found that the hub location and connectivity patterns in the auditory cortex varied according to different genres of music (e.g., classical, country, rock, rap, and Chinese opera). High clustering improves specialized processing at the local level and short paths increase the transfer of distributed information. Global efficiency (i.e., shorter path lengths) was greater for preferred music than for music that was disliked (Wilkins et al., 2014). Complex brain network analysis provides a means of looking at the whole brain rather than at smaller, localized units.

MUSIC IN THE BRAIN

With the modicum of background provided in the previous section, we now turn our attention to findings from neuromusical research. Although the primary focus in this section is on direct evidence from studying the brain, much supporting evidence comes from ancillary disciplines and from indirect evidence. Thus, the first subsection includes brief acknowledgements of contributions from anthropology and ethnomusicology, ethology, and music psychology. The second subsection presents input from indirect approaches to studying the brain, including fetal and infant research and studies of special musicians. Finally, findings from neuroimaging research are organized under the following topics: techniques for studying the music in the brain, imaging music perception and cognition, imaging affective responses to music, imaging musical performance, and imaging the effects of music learning.

Support from Ancillary Disciplines

As we learned in Chapter 4, all societies, always and everywhere, are musical. This supports the notion that all people inherit a brain predisposed to be musical. In Chapter 8, we raised the issue that too little research has been conducted with non-Western listeners. With regard to how music perception and cognition relate to brain function in non-Western listeners, Morrison and Demorest (2009) reviewed the available evidence (e.g., Demorest et al., 2009; Morrison, Demorest, Alyward, Cramer, & Maravilla, 2003; Nehaus, 2003). They suggested that though this line of investigation is in its early stages, preliminary evidence suggests that there is support for common processing strategies, expressed in varying cultural idioms. Confirming this notion, one group revised the Montreal Battery of Evaluation of Amusias (see subsequent discussion of amusia, loss of musical skills due to brain damage) to fit musical specifics of Eastern Greek music (Paraskevopoulos, Tsapkini, & Peretz, 2010). Although the revised battery tested the same musical elements, participants performed better on the version that best fits their cultural background. Regardless of cultural familiarity, music appears to recruit similar brain regions, though strength and extent of activation may vary according to specifics (Morrison & Demorest, 2019).

Other ancillary evidence comes from ethology, including the study of sound-making among all living creatures (e.g., Merker, 2019). Regardless of one's stance on whether animals are creating music, the evolutionary basis of human musicality is linked to our understanding of the brain. Finally, this entire book is filled with evidence from music psychology experiments that provide insights into how music is represented in the brain. Collectively, results from ethnomusicology, ethology, and music psychology experiments provide a strong foundation for neuroscientific investigations.

Support from Indirect Approaches

As reviewed in Chapter 6, there is abundant evidence showing that neonates are aware of and responsive to musical sounds. That newborns possess music processing skills supports the notion that we are born with a brain predisposed to be musical. Sometimes, however, the brain is damaged and neuroscientists find it very revealing to study such individuals as a means of understanding cognitive functioning.

The Effects of Brain Damage on Musical Behaviors. Topics covered in this section include musical prodigies and savants, amusia, Williams Syndrome, and Alzheimer's disease. Readers interested in the effects of brain damage on musical behaviors will also find a wide variety of special cases in three books by Oliver Sacks (1983, 1987, 2007). Neuroimaging studies have been conducted with some of these populations, however, much of the research is behavioral and is thus included in this section on indirect approaches.

Of course, prodigies are not brain damaged, but there are some striking similarities with savantism and often discussions of one include the other (e.g., Gardner, 2006; Hermelin, 2001; McPherson, 2016). Throughout music history, there have been a number of child prodigies, such as Mozart, Schubert, and Mendelssohn. Revesz (1925) studied a musical prodigy by the name of Erwin Nyiregyhazy from the age of six to twelve. While Revesz thoroughly documented the child's musical skills, he was unable to account for these gifts (see also Feldman, 2016). Although learning is obviously present—each prodigy learned the music of his culture—it is difficult to account for such rapid acquisition of skills unless one posits highly receptive brain mechanisms. How was it possible for Mozart to compose and perform at such an astonishingly high level at a young age unless he possessed a brain capable of learning these skills at a rate and to a degree far beyond the ordinary? McPherson (2016) has edited a comprehensive examination of prodigies.

A *musical savant* is similar to a prodigy in that both possess highly advanced skills; however, the savant usually is advanced in only one or two areas and is otherwise cognitively limited. Many examples of savants with musical abilities have been cited (e.g., Howle, 1993). Musical savantism frequently, though not always, appears in combination with blindness and autism (Hermelin, 2001). One blind, cognitively impaired girl was reportedly able to play a piano composition perfectly after hearing it only once. Another young man, though blind as well as cognitively impaired, gave piano recitals to high critical acclaim. A young lady, known as Harriet, was studied extensively by a psychologist. She was extremely advanced in a wide variety of musical skills, yet she was diagnosed as both cognitively impaired and psychotic. Miller (1989) provided a detailed look at a particular musical savant and at musical savant syndrome in general. Ockelford (2016, 2019) has created an ecological model of auditory development in partial explanation of how musicians with autism can sometimes be extraordinary. Continued study of prodigies and musical savants with more sophisticated techniques and cognitive theories will be important in understanding music-brain relationships.

A significant body of research concerns *amusia,* or the loss of musical skills due to brain damage (Slevc, Rosenberg, & Patel, 2009). Amusia is parallel to *aphasia,* the loss of language skills, about which much more is known. Aphasia, which deals with loss of language skills due to selective destruction of neural tissue, consists of many particularized deficits (e.g., Broca's aphasia, loss of ability to speak coherently; Wernicke's aphasia, loss of speech comprehension; alexia, loss of ability to read; agraphia, loss of ability to write; etc.). In both amusia and aphasia, losses may be global or specific. Amusia is divided into receptive amusia—loss of the ability to perceive or understand music (Di Pietro, Laganaro, Leemann, & Schnider, 2004); the person may no longer be able to track rhythms or follow pitch direction—and expressive amusia—loss of the ability to express oneself musically; the person may no longer be able to sing or play an instrument (Brust, 2001). For example, Terao and colleagues (2006) studied a professional singer who suffered brain damage in the right superior temporal cortex. Although she could recognize familiar music and discriminate melodic contours, she was no longer able to sing in tune (expressive amusia). Peretz, Champod, and Hyde (2003) developed an assessment tool called the Montreal Battery of Evaluation of Amusia (MBEA) to determine whether there are auditory processing deficits.

The term *congenital amusia* is a class of learning disabilities that refers to persons who are born with severe music processing deficits (Ayotte, Peretz, & Hyde, 2002). Although it may be known anecdotally as tone deafness, it can also affect other musical aspects such as timing, recognition of familiar tunes, and so on. For example, "beat deafness" refers to an inability to find the beat in music (Loui, 2016). Often, such individuals can enjoy music in spite of their inability to perform certain tasks. Congenital amusia is domain specific, in that amusical persons often show no other cognitive deficits (Mosing & Ullén, 2016). They may, for example, be able to accurately process pitch inflections in spoken language, recognize friends by the sound of their voices, and accurately interpret nonmusical sounds in the environment. Structural and processing deficiencies in white matter pathways connecting frontal and temporal regions have been implicated in amusia.

Williams Syndrome (WS) is caused by a genetic defect that leaves individuals cognitively impaired (Bellugi, Lichtenberger, Jones, Lai, & St. George, 2000). Although the average IQ is 55, it is more appropriate to think of WS individuals as mentally asymmetric. That is, they often have peaks and valleys in different cognitive domains. Most WS individuals have relatively stronger abilities in language, music, social drive, and face processing and very poor abilities in spatial and mathematical skills (Levitin & Bellugi, 1998). This relatively stronger performance in music suggests a genetic influence (Di Rosa, Cieri, Antonucci, Stuppia, & Gatta, 2015).

Individuals with WS are more likely to take music lessons, play an instrument, and have higher ratings of musical skills than those with other forms of cognitive impairment (Dykens, Rosner, Ly, & Sagun, 2005). Only a few research reports have been published, and the subjects were often attendees at a music camp, possibly introducing a selection bias. More clearly, WS individuals experience hyperacusis or extreme sensitivity to sound (Bellugi et al., 2000). Although they may or may not be accomplished performing musicians, generally speaking they spend an inordinate amount of time listening to music and have strong emotional reactions to music (Don, Schellenberg, & Rourke, 1999). Brain activation patterns while listening to music and noise were considerably different among WS individuals compared to control participants and there were stronger activations in the amygdala (dealing with emotions) and the cerebellum (Levitin et al., 2003). Likewise, in WS individuals there is a leftward asymmetry to a portion of the auditory cortex called the planum temporale that is comparable to professional musicians (Don et al., 1999).

The study of musical behaviors in Alzheimer's patients is revealing. Persons with previously learned musical skills often demonstrate resilient procedural memories (e.g., singing or playing the piano) even in the presence of severe cognitive impairment. One 82-year-old male showed a preserved ability to play the piano from memory, even though he could not identify the composer or the title (Crystal, Grober, & Masur, 1989). It was felt that this type of procedural memory was stored in the neostriatum, an area of the brain spared until the final stages of Alzheimer's disease. Johnson and Ulatowska (1995) studied an Alzheimer's patient for two years, documenting the progress of deterioration in music and language. In this case, song text persisted after speech was severely disturbed and song production was possible even when the patient could no longer sing the words.

There is some support for music as a means of reducing the risk for developing Alzheimer's or other forms of dementia. For example, older adults who engage in leisure activities such as playing board games, reading, dancing, and playing music, were less likely to develop dementia (Verghese et al., 2003). More specific to music, musical twins were less likely to develop dementia than their nonmusical co-twins (Balbag, Pedersen, & Gatz, 2014). Early musical instruction is associated with reduced levels of mild cognitive impairment and slower rates of cognitive decline in older age (Wilson, Boyle, Yang, James, & Bennett, 2015). Note, however, that this was also true for early instruction in foreign language and that both populations had a higher initial level of cognitive function. Collectively, there is a note of caution in interpreting these results, as there may be other mitigating factors, such as the fact that those who are engaged in musical activities are often more socially engaged and questions of nature/nurture are not fully resolved (Ferreri, Moussard, Bigand, & Tillmann, 2019). These caveats notwithstanding, however, music does seem to provide positive benefits in ameliorating or delaying cognitive decline. By studying musical behaviors in prodigies and those with amusia, Williams Syndrome, or Alzheimer's disease, we can learn much about how music is processed in the brain.

Taken together, support from ancillary disciplines and indirect evidence strengthens findings from neuroimaging studies. If all people, always and everywhere, are musical, that must be because we possess a brain that predisposes us to be so. Creating a plausible explanation for how we came to be musical, from an evolutionary standpoint, underscores the genetic basis for musicality (Järvelä, 2019). The many studies conducted by music psychologists provide abundant behavioral observations of music processing in the brain. The critical importance of fetal and infant research is that their musical behaviors are likely to represent inborn mechanisms rather than learned actions. Finally, the fact that musical behaviors persist in those who suffer from cognitive impairments indicates that there are intact neural structures that allow for musical possibilities in spite of their deficits.

The information gleaned from ancillary disciplines and indirect approaches is critical for creating theories about music in the brain that can be tested using modern imaging technologies. Each of these approaches has strengths and weaknesses and it is always important to pool findings from different approaches for a more complete picture.

Imaging Techniques for Studying Music

Modern neuroscientists have at their disposal technologies that allow them to peer inside the living brain. A detailed examination of these technologies is beyond the scope of this book, and so what follows are very brief descriptions followed by at least one example of a musical application. The musical examples were chosen to illustrate the imaging technique rather than to provide a coherent overview. Relevant studies are organized more logically in subsequent sections.

Electroencephalography. *Electroencephalography* (EEG) is a means of monitoring the ever-changing electrical activity of the brain (Andreassi, 2007). Electrodes placed strategically on the skull (Figure 9.5) measure the summed electrical activity of millions of neurons directly beneath in terms of frequency, amplitude, form, and distribution (Olejniczak, 2006). Using EEG, researchers investigated brain responses of musically trained and untrained participants as they listened to different kinds of music and to text being read (Bhattacharya, Petsche, & Pereda, 2001). They computed a similarity index (SI) that indicated interdependencies of different brain regions; in other words, this was a measure of how different cortical areas communicated among themselves during specific listening tasks. Musically trained listeners had higher degrees of interdependencies than untrained controls for music but not for text. Thus, musical training led to greater dynamic cooperation between different regions of the brain while listening to music.

EEG signals are normally divided into frequency bands: delta (2–4 Hz), theta (4–8 Hz), alpha (8–13 Hz), beta (13–30 Hz), and gamma (30–49 Hz) (Hadjidimitriou & Hadjileontiadis, 2012). Beta band activity is involved in the translation of timing information in auditory-motor coordination (Fujioka, Ross, & Trainor, 2015). Listening to pleasant music elicited a stronger response in theta band activity in frontal areas, associated with subjective assessment

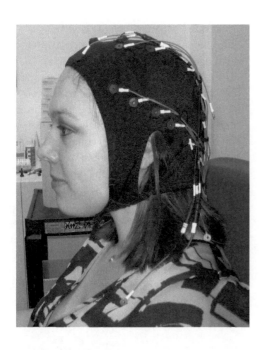

FIGURE **9.5** | A Participant Wearing an EEG Cap with Electrodes Sewn into Fixed Positions Over the Scalp. These electrodes are connected to a computer that can monitor and record the electrical activity of millions of brain cells directly underneath each contact point. The number of electrodes determines the number of channels of electrical activity. many applications use 19 electrodes, but as many as 256 can be used.

of pleasantness, and in the alpha band over parietal and occipital areas, indicating suppression of distracting external stimuli (Nemati, Akrami, Salehi, Esteky, & Moghimi, 2019). Gamma band waves are associated with attention, expectation, memory retrieval, and integrating multisensory experiences; adult musicians respond to music with larger gamma-band waves than nonmusicians, an indication of executive function processing that might enhance learning and cognitive performance (Trainor, Shahin, & Roberts, 2009).

Event-Related Potentials. An *event-related potential* (ERP) is a transient aspect of the EEG that occurs immediately after an internal or external event (Sur & Sinha, 2009). The ERP has three characteristics: (1) there is a positive or negative change in the direction of the wave pattern, (2) there is an intensity level or amplitude to the wave, and (3) there is a delay in response from roughly 50 to 600 milliseconds; this is the time the brain takes to process information (Fig. 9.6). Early waves, within the first 100 milliseconds, reflect sensory processing; later waves pertain to cognitive processing. ERPs are time-locked to a stimulus and provide a means for studying the timing of different mental processes. For example, Honing, Bouwer, and Háden (2014) discuss the role of ERPs in the study of beat perception.

Predictions (*what*) and expectations (*when*) are critically important in music listening and mismatch negativity (MMN) is a means of measuring brain responses via ERP during these processes (Trainor & Zatorre, 2016). MMN refers to the difference in brain response between a standard and a deviant stimulus. For example, suppose we repeatedly present a brief single pitch played on the oboe (standard stimulus). At random times in the sequence we insert a flute tone (deviant stimulus), where everything is the same (i.e., pitch, loudness, and length of tone) except the timbre. We can compute the difference in ERP responses between the oboe and flute tones. Differences can be in speed of response (latency) and strength of response (amplitude). MMN is generally computed by subtracting the average responses to the standard stimulus from the average responses on the deviant stimulus. These so-called "oddball" sequences could be a series of standard pitches with a deviant pitch, a series of major chords with a deviant minor chord, and so on.

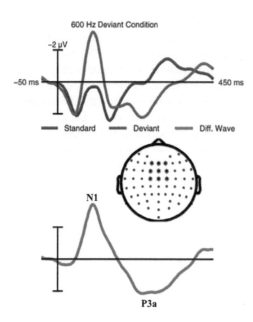

FIGURE **9.6** | Mismatch Negativity. An example of a mismatch negativity (MMN) response of the event-related potential (ERP). Two tones were presented in an odd-ball paradigm, with a standard tone of 500 hz and a deviant tone of 600 hz both lasting 100 ms. There were 1,000 trials with 85% standard tones and 15% deviant. The dark black line indicates average ERP responses to the standard tone from the nine black electrodes indicated in the brain map. The gray line indicates a much stronger response to the deviant tone. The line below represents an average of the difference between standard and deviant responses, with a negative peak at N1 (around 200 milliseconds after the presentation of the deviant tone) and a positive peak between 200–300 ms (labeled P3a).

Jazz musicians had larger MMN-amplitude than classical or rock/pop musicians to six different sound features (pitch, timbre, intensity, rhythm, location—stereo location moved to left of center slightly, and slide—pitch approached from two semitones below) (Vuust, Brattico, Seppänen, Näätänen, & Tervaniemi, 2012). Musicians' brains are shaped by the type of training received, as well as the style/genre of the music and listening experiences. Furthermore, musicians from different backgrounds (i.e., classical, jazz, and rock/pop) respond differentially in neural processing to various musical features.

Magnetoencephalography. The brain's electrical activity produces a magnetic field in the space surrounding the head, and measurements of these magnetic fields by means of *magnetoencephalography* (MEG) can be used to locate neural activity with highly refined temporal precision (Kuhl & Rivera-Gaxiola, 2008). Compared to nonmusicians, musicians showed a left-hemisphere MEG lateralization for pattern mismatch negativity, that is for recognition of violations in sequential pitch patterns (Herholz, Lappe, & Pantev, 2009). In another comparison of musicians and nonmusicians, stimulating the lips of trumpet players elicited a peak response in the corresponding somatosensory cortex at 33 ms as measured by MEG, compared to 60–80 ms for nonmusicians (Schulz, Ross, & Pantev, 2003).

Positron Emission Tomography. *Positron emission tomography* (PET) identifies metabolic activity or blood flow in a living brain by tracking a radioactive tracer (Carey, 2008). Paired-image subtraction is a commonly used technique in which the PET image of a control task is subtracted from an experimental task. This procedure allows the identification of areas of the brain that are most active during the experimental task. In one experiment, professional pianists underwent PET scans while performing a portion of the Bach *Italian Concerto* and a control task of playing scales (see Fig. 9.7) (Parsons, Sergent, Hodges, & Fox, 2005). Performance of the Bach, minus activations from the rest condition, resulted in widely distributed activations in both hemispheres, most strongly in motor and auditory areas. In addition, frontal areas of the brain were strongly deactivated, indicating a high degree of focused attention.

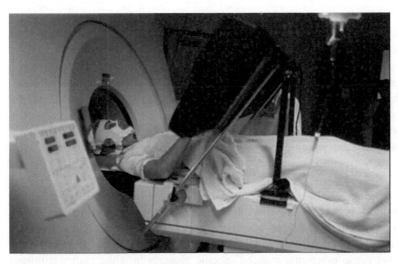

FIGURE **9.7** | A Pianist in the PET Scanner. Note the IV bag at the top right, delivering a small amount of radiated water. During the actual experiment, the eyes were covered to eliminate activations in the visual cortex.

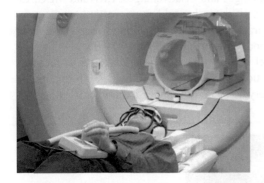

FIGURE **9.8** | A Participant is Just About to Go into the MRI Scanner. The bed he is lying on will be raised and positioned so that his head will be inside the circular cage at the top. He is wearing goggles through which he will receive a visual stimulus and headphones through which he will receive an auditory stimulus. His hand is on a joystick, through which he will deliver his responses to the tasks.

Magnetic Resonance Imaging. *Magnetic Resonance Imaging* (MRI) is an imaging technique in which the subject is placed inside a large magnet (Liang & Lautebur, 2000). MRI distinguishes structures with precise detail, but cannot provide information about functions (but see next section). Researchers used MRI data to document that a portion of the left auditory cortex, the planum temporale, and corpus callosum of musicians was larger than those of nonmusicians (Schlaug, Jancke, Huang, & Steinmetz, 1994). This difference was exaggerated for those musicians who started their training before age seven. Researchers concluded that these results gave evidence of early musical training affecting brain organization. A subsequent study of 30 musicians and 30 nonmusicians, matched for age, sex, and handedness (all right-handed), revealed that a portion of the auditory cortex was more strongly lateralized (i.e., larger) in the left hemisphere for musicians than nonmusicians. Those musicians who possessed absolute pitch (AP) were more strongly lateralized to the left than musicians without AP (Schlaug et al., 1995).

Functional Magnetic Resonance Imaging. *Functional Magnetic Resonance Imaging* (fMRI) combines the best of MRI and PET in that it provides information on both structure and function (see Figure 9.8) (Buxton, 2009). For example, researchers used fMRI to investigate brain responses of pianists and nonmusicians who participated in music-related tasks (Bangert et al., 2006). Results indicated a distinct musicianship-specific network in the pianists not seen in the controls that involved audio-sensorimotor integration.

Transcranial Magnetic Stimulation. *Transcranial Magnetic Stimulation* (TMS) is a means of temporarily inhibiting or exciting neural transmissions (Hallett, 2000). This allows for functional mapping of cortical regions. Using TMS, neuroscientists mapped the reorganization of sensorimotor and association areas in adults learning a stringed instrument (Kim et al., 2004). Evidence indicated that learning to play the violin caused a reorganization of the right hemisphere motor maps used in left hand fingering.

Diffusion Tensor Imaging. *Diffusion Tensor Imaging* (DTI) is a type of MRI imaging that maps white matter pathways, that is, the ways different regions of the brain connect to each other (Fig. 9.9) (Filley, 2005). DTI reveals underlying neural infrastructures and is useful for analyzing white matter networks (Mark & Ullmer, 2005). Using DTI, researchers demonstrated that extensive piano practicing induced specific changes in white matter pathways (Bengtsson et al., 2005). Comparing white matter in adult, adolescent, and younger pianists, they found positive correlations between amount of practice and fiber tract organization in specific regions, thus supporting the notion of plasticity.

Each of the imaging techniques has advantages and disadvantages. ERP and MEG, for example, are very good at measuring the brain's extremely rapid responses in increments of less than one second. PET, on the other hand, tracks regional cerebral blood flow (rCBF) over a period of a minute or more. While PET is good for determining function, it does not provide minute anatomical details about location. MRI is very good for determining precise location, but does not provide information about function. Functional MRI provides information on both function and location, but because it is very noisy in the scanner, experiments with music

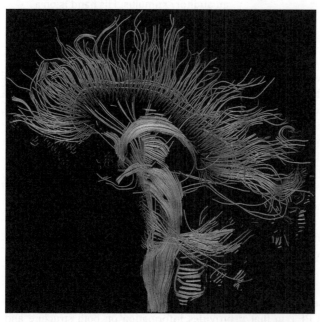

FIGURE **9.9** | White Matter Fiber Tracts as Measured by Diffusion Tensor Imaging.

are compromised unless special precautions are used (e.g., MRI-compatible headphones). PET is totally silent.

Thus, even without reviewing all the pros and cons for each methodology, it is clear that no one approach can provide all the information one might want. Ideally, one might wish to conduct the same experiment with several technologies. Unfortunately, this is not so easily done for reasons of time, money, and expertise—that is, repeating a study several times would require an inordinate commitment from researchers and participants and extend the time line to publication; it is difficult to find funding for one study, let alone several; although some large facilities support a variety of methodologies, researchers tend to concentrate on a particular approach. Finally, each methodology imposes restrictions on what participants can do while being imaged, such that it would be difficult or impossible to replicate the same experiment using different technologies. Periodic reviews of neuroimaging findings that synthesize results from all approaches are currently the best way of developing a complete understanding of music in the brain.

Imaging Music Perception and Cognition

In order to lay the groundwork for the eventual goal of understanding musical behaviors from a more holistic perspective, the bulk of neuromusical research to date has been focused on discrete components, such as pitch, rhythm, or timbre. Some evidence supports the notion that pitch perception is more strongly monitored in the right hemisphere (Peretz & Zatorre, 2005), while rhythm is processed in the left hemisphere (Bengtsson & Ullen, 2006). However, such findings do not tell the whole story.

Brain imaging studies that require musicians to perform more generalized tasks revealed widespread activity with many sites involved on both sides of the brain (Bunzeck, Wuestenberg, Lutz, Heinze, & Jancke, 2005). For example, when violinists performed or simply imagined performing a musical sequence, similar areas on both sides of the brain were activated during both conditions (Kristeva, Chakarova, Schulte-Mönting, & Spreer, 2003). Combining evidence from discrete and holistic tasks led to the conclusion that music processing involves widely distributed, but locally specialized neural networks (Sergent, 1993).

Musical neural networks are somewhat more fluid than fixed. That is, changing the kind of musical stimuli—say, from Mozart to electronic tones—or changing the tasks with the same music—say, from listening to the entire piece to focusing only on the rhythm—may change activation sites (Janata, 2005). Learning and experience alters brain activity, as trained and untrained listeners often respond differently. Numerous experiments have demonstrated that musicians with extensive training use their brains differently than those with less training (Peretz & Zatorre, 2003; Zatorre & McGill, 2005).

Imaging Affective Responses to Music

Very little work had been done on the neurobiology of musical emotions until Blood, Zatorre, Bermudez, and Evans published one of the earliest neuroimaging studies on this topic in 1999. Since then, attention to this central aspect of musical experiences has received much greater attention. One line of investigation involves monitoring the release of neurotransmitters (chemicals that relay messages from one neuron to another) in response to musical experiences. Music affects levels of serotonin (associated with feelings of satisfaction; Evers & Suhr, 2000) and dopamine (associated with feelings of pleasure) (Menon & Levitin, 2005; Salimpoor, Benovoy, Larcher, Dagher, & Zatorre, 2011; Salimpoor et al., 2013), as well as activating areas of the brain responsible for mediating reward, and autonomic and cognitive processes. (See Chapter 10: Bodily Responses to Music for more details.) Dopamine plays a particularly important role in modulating musical pleasure (Ferreri, Mas-Herrero et al., 2019).

In an approach similar to the organization of this chapter, Peretz (2010) incorporated cross-cultural ethnomusicological work as a prelude to neuroscientific investigation. Recall that in Chapter 4 we presented information that listeners discerned some basic emotions in culturally unfamiliar music (e.g., Adachi et al., 2004; Balkwill & Thompson, 1999; Balkwill et al., 2004; Fritz et al., 2009). Research on infant auditory perception (reviewed in Chapter 6 and briefly in this chapter) supports the notion of inherent networks for music processing. With specific regard to emotional processing, nine-month-old infants can discriminate happy and sad musical excerpts (Flom, Gentile, & Pick, 2008). Furthermore, Masataka found that two-day-old hearing infants of deaf parents preferred consonant over dissonant music (2006) and preferred infant-directed singing over adult-directed singing (1999). Learning is unlikely to account for these preferences to any great extent.

Building on this foundation, Peretz (2010) provided evidence for a neural pathway for music emotions that engages the brainstem and both subcortical and cortical structures that may be distinct or shared with other behaviors. The auditory brainstem response, also called acoustic startle reflex or auditory startle response, is an extremely rapid response mechanism to sudden, unexpected sounds (Hall, 2007). Musical events, such as a cymbal crash or an unexpected loud chord (as in the Haydn *Surprise* Symphony) can elicit initial reactions in as little as 5–6 ms.

Subcortical structures lie above the brainstem and below the cerebral cortex. Evidence from a number of studies (e.g., Blood & Zatorre, 2001; Brown, Martinez, & Parsons, 2004) demonstrated that subcortical structures play a significant role in music emotions. The limbic system plays a primary role in emotions (Fig. 9.10). The limbic system contains the hypothalamus, amygdala, hippocampus, thalamus, cingulate gyrus, and ventral striatum, which contains the nucleus accumbens. Koelsch, Siebel, and Fritz (2010; also see Koelsch, 2014) provide a review of research on:

- the *amygdala*, involved in processing both pleasant and unpleasant stimuli. Music can alter activity in the amygdala (Blood & Zatorre, 2001).

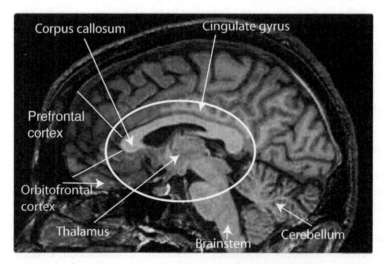

FIGURE 9.10 | Interior of the Brain. The limbic system generally falls inside the white circle. Many of the limbic structures (e.g., hypothalamus, hippocampus, amygdala, and ventral striatum; see fig. 11.3) are not clearly shown.

- the *hippocampus*, involved in learning and memory, as well as emotional processing. Pleasant music, in contrast to a rest condition activated the hippocampus (Brown et al., 2004).
- parahippocampal gyrus, involved in the storage of emotional memories. This region was activated in response to unpleasant music (Blood et al., 1999).
- the *nucleus accumbens*, involved in intensely pleasurable experiences. This area was activated in response to pleasant music (Menon & Levitin, 2005).
- a network consisting of amygdala, hippocampus, parahippocampal gyrus, and temporal poles. These structures were activated in response to unpleasant music contrasted with pleasant music (Koelsch, Fritz, Cramon, Müller, & Friederici, 2006).

This is not an exhaustive list, but it should suffice to provide evidence that the limbic system is involved in processing the emotional aspects of music.

Finally, cortical areas are also involved in processing music emotions. These include the orbitofrontal cortex, ventromedial prefrontal cortex, along with the superior temporal cortex and the anterior cingulate cortex (Skov, 2010; Vuust & Kringelbach, 2010). One study reported findings that

> suggest that an emotion processing network in response to music integrates the ventral and dorsal striatum, areas involved in reward experience and movement; the anterior cingulate, which is important for targeting attention; and medial temporal areas, traditionally found in the appraisal and processing of emotions.
>
> (Mitterschiffthaler, Fu, Dalton, Andrew, & Williams, 2007, p. 1150)

Because appraisal is also involved, it is not always easy to separate emotional processing from non-emotional cognitive activity. Much work remains to be done in order to achieve a complete understanding of the neurobiology of music emotions, but the rapid progress being made is both exciting and promising (Juslin & Sakka, 2019; Vuust & Kringlebach, 2010).

Imaging Musical Performance

The act of making music is so intensely physical that one neuroscientist referred to musicians as small-muscle athletes (Wilson, 1986). The sensorimotor cortex is responsible for interpreting incoming sensory information and controlling the muscles throughout the body. In conjunction, the basal ganglia control large groups of muscles in cooperative functions, and the cerebellum regulates intricate muscle movements and stores habituated motor patterns. The brain is highly adaptable and with repetitive training, the brain's map of the body is reorganized accordingly (Medina & Coslett, 2010). For example, long-term musical training has been found to increase the area of the motor cortex responsible for controlling the fingers of violinists (Elbert, Pantev, Wienbruch, Rockstroh, & Taub, 1995) and pianists (Meister et al., 2005). For additional details, see Chapter 13: Music Performance. See also Altenmüller, Furuya, Scholz, & Ioannou, 2019; Brown, Penhune, & Zatorre, 2015.

Brain imaging studies of musicians in the act of performing are difficult, but the following provide a few examples:

- Pianists. Imagining a piano performance activated the brain much as did a real performance (Pascual-Leone et al., 1995). Musicians showed significant differences in brain structures compared to nonmusician controls, and those who practiced piano/organ more intensively than those who practiced keyboard to a lesser degree (Gärtner et al., 2013).

- Violinists. Studies with violinists echoed that of pianists. That is, motor and auditory areas on both sides were activated, and imagined and actual performances were similar (Kim et al., 2004; Kristeva et al., 2003).
- Singers. Auditory cortices, motor cortex, and frontal operculum were activated during singing (Brown, Martinez, Hodges, Fox, & Parsons, 2004).
- Guitarists. Entrainment occurred in EEG rhythms when eight pairs of guitarists performed together, demonstrating synchronized cortical activity (Lindenberger, Li, Gruber, & Muller, 2009).
- Musical Improvisation. Musical improvisation activated a neural network that involved the dorsal premotor cortex, dealing with movement coordination, the rostral cingulate zone, having to do with voluntary selection, and the inferior frontal gyrus, concerned with sequence generation and additional areas across a wide network (Berkowitz & Ansari, 2008).

Motor maps increase during training, but eventually neurons get more efficient and fewer neurons are required to perform the task (Doidge, 2007). For example, a child learning to play scales on the piano uses the whole body—arms, wrist, shoulder, even facial muscles— for each note. Later, there is much more efficient use of the motor system, requiring fewer neurons.

Imaging Music Learning

While every brain has the same basic anatomy, complex interactions of nature and nurture combine to produce the unique neural organization of each human brain. Thus, the representation of music in the brain is a product of both genetic instructions and of learning and experience. Researchers are only now beginning to examine the genetic basis of musicality. In time, it is likely that scientists will identify hundreds of genes in various combinations that provide the foundation for human musicality (Järvelä, 2019). These genes are expressed within particular environmental circumstances, resulting in individual musicianship.

As models of neuroplasticity, musicians show evidence of numerous modifications in brain structures. Normally such changes are more substantial when individuals started studying music seriously before the age of seven. Researchers have observed alterations in the following brain structures in relation to musical experiences:

- *Auditory cortex.* Bermudez and Zatorre (2005) collected brain images of 43 musicians and 51 nonmusicians. Gray matter concentration in the right auditory cortex, in an area known to be important for pitch processing, was significantly larger among the musicians, with no difference between those with ($N = 22$) and without absolute pitch.
- The *corpus callosum* is the bundle of fibers providing primary communication between the two hemispheres. Lee, Chen, and Schlaug (2003) examined the brains of 56 professional musicians and 56 nonmusicians. They found that male musicians had a larger corpus callosum than controls, but that female musicians did not. Most likely the increase in corpus callosum fibers is due to early, extensive training requiring the coordination of both hands. The authors speculated that the gender result might be due to the fact that females have a tendency for more symmetric brain organization and that there were more absolute pitch processors among the females.
- The *cerebellum* is involved in motor learning, cognitive functioning, and sensory integration in preparation for motor output. Hutchinson, Lee, Gaab, and Schlaug (2003) imaged the brains 60 professional pianists (23 of whom also played violin) and 60 matched

controls. Male musicians had a significantly greater cerebellar volume than controls, but females did not.

■ *Gray matter* is the cortex, or outer covering of the brain. Gaser and Schlaug (2003) compared 20 male professional pianists and 20 male amateur pianists with 40 male nonmusicians. The professional musicians had a greater volume of gray matter in widely diffuse areas related to musical performance, primarily in motor, auditory, and visuospatial brain areas.

■ *White Matter*, found in the core of the brain, contains fibers that serve a variety of cognitive and motor functions, primarily communication between and among various regions of the brain. Researchers investigated white matter structure in eight concert pianists and eight nonmusicians (Bengtsson et al., 2005). They found positive correlations between the amount of time practiced during childhood, adolescence, and adulthood and white matter organization.

■ *Sensorimotor cortex.* Bangert and Schlaug (2006) asked trained neuroanatomists to perform visual examinations of brain images of 32 musicians and 32 nonmusicians, without knowing which images belonged to which group. These experts were able to tell the difference between the two groups and could even further distinguish the musician group into string players and pianists. The primary distinguishing characteristic was the precentral gyrus associated with hand movements. String players had stronger identifying markers in the right hemisphere (associated with refined left-hand movements) and pianists had stronger markers in the left hemisphere. Unusual confirmation of this finding came in an examination of Albert Einstein's brain (Falk, 2009). As an accomplished amateur violinist, he, too, had a larger area in the right hemisphere motor cortex.

■ *Multimodal integration areas*, sometimes called convergence zones, are where sensory information from eyes, ears, and so on, are integrated into a coherent whole. Earlier it was mentioned that compared to controls, conductors were faster and more accurate in making distinctions between two tones that were very close together in both pitch and time (Hodges et al., 2005). Furthermore, they were faster and more accurate in locating tones in space and received an additional boost when auditory and visual information were combined. Subsequently, fMRI scans indicated that the conductors had increased activity in brain regions involved in multisensory processing, while the controls did not (see Figure 9.11). In a follow-up experiment, it was shown that the controls had to turn-off visual processing centers of the brain in order to concentrate on auditory tasks, even though they still did not perform as well as the conductors (Hodges, Hairston, Maldjian, & Burdette, 2010).

One of the central issues with these examples of brain plasticity is whether musicians were born with these differences or whether their brains changed in response to musical experiences. Hyde et al. (2009) examined the brains of 15 children who took weekly piano lessons for 15 months (average age at start = 6.32 years) and 16 children who did not did not take weekly piano lessons, but who did have a weekly 40-minute group music class where they sang and played bells and drums. There were no differences in brain structures at the beginning of the study. At the end of 15 months, the music lesson group showed relatively enlarged areas compared to controls in motor-hand areas, corpus callosum, right primary auditory cortex, and cingulate gyrus. These structural brain changes in motor and auditory areas correlated with improved performances on motor and auditory-musical tasks and appear to be a result of intensive musical training. Norton et al. (2005) and Schlaug, Norton, Overy, and Winner (2005) arrived at similar conclusions. Thus, although genetic advantages for music processing cannot be ruled out, there do appear to be significant changes in brain organization

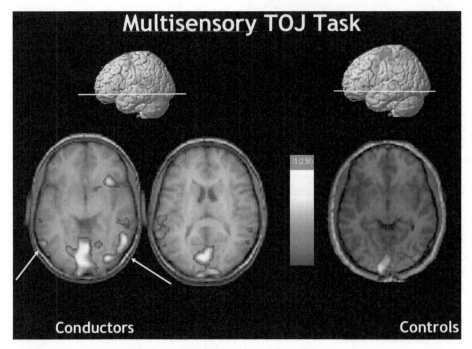

FIGURE 9.11 | The arrows point to increased activity in areas of conductors' brains that are involved in multisensory processing. These areas are not so strongly activated in control participants' brains. TOJ stands for temporal-order judgment.

and structure because of musical training and experiences. For an expanded discussion of cognitive neuroscience and music learning, see Chapter 14: The Psychology of Music Learning.

CONCLUSION

The oldest brain map on record was drawn on papyrus in Egypt almost 5,000 years ago (Minagar, Ragheb, & Kelley, 2003) and soon after that, the ancient Greeks were speculating about the nature of music. From that time to the present, much progress has been made. Here are some general conclusions that one can make based on current evidence:

- A brain predisposed for music is the birthright of all human beings.
- Music processing in the human brain is different from sound processing in animal brains.
- The brain processes and responds to musical sounds before birth and throughout life.
- Music in the brain is highly resilient and may persist to some degree even in individuals who are afflicted with physical, cognitive, or emotional impairment.
- Genetic instructions and life experiences work together to shape how music is processed in the brain.
- Early and ongoing musical training affects the organization of music in the brain.
- Music is represented in extensive neural systems, involving widely distributed, but locally specialized regions of the brain.
- Although some locally specific neural sites have been identified for music processing in the brain, activation sites may change in response to changes in subject, stimuli, or task variables.

- Some of the neural networks for music are distinct and not shared with other cognitive processes, while others may be shared with language and other cognitive domains.
- Music processing involves auditory, visual, motor, cognitive, affective, and memory components in the brain.
- The vast majority of neuromusical studies have been conducted with subjects familiar with Western music. Considerably more research is needed with those engaged in non-Western musical experiences. Short of multi-cultural investigations, universal explanations of the musical processing in the brain are not possible.

How does all this relate to Mike and Jane, the couple we met at the opera at the end of the previous chapter (see Fig. 8.18)? Imagine that we observed them again, only this time we were able to monitor their brains as they listened to the music. First, we would notice that their brains are activated in the front and back, on the left and the right, and from top to bottom in widely distributed patterns. Each of the local nodes represents some particular aspect, and the aggregate represents the neural networks involved in music processing. Motor, cognitive, affective, and memory networks are all activated in a grand interplay.

We would observe that even though Mike does not have formal training in music, many areas of his brain are activated in patterns similar to those in Jane's brain. Because of her training, some of the areas in Jane's brain are more strongly activated than in Mike's brain and there are some additional areas of activation representing processing that he is not able to do. In addition to specific locations, suppose we could also track functions. We might observe that both of them process some sounds such as a cymbal crash very rapidly. We might also observe longer time courses, as blood flowing to a specific area during a particularly emotional aria or when a twist in the plot is revealed. We would see the patterns of activation shift and change throughout the evening as Mike and Jane individually pay attention to various aspects of the performance. All in all, we would have dramatic evidence that Mike and Jane, along with everyone else in the audience, have brains that are well suited to process music. In addition, we would see the effects of musical training, life experiences, and other variables on the configuration and functioning of their brains.

As much as has been discovered, there are still many mysteries yet to be explored. In time, researchers will make many important discoveries and we will gain increasingly more sophisticated understandings. In the meantime, we can simply enjoy the fact that our brains make it possible for us to derive infinite delight and pleasure from the music we love best, whether we are listening to it, performing it, or creating it. Now we turn from the brain to the body in the next chapter.

DISCUSSION QUESTIONS

1. What amazes you the most about the human brain?
2. Does the material in this chapter strengthen or weaken the notion of an evolutionary basis for musicality as presented in Chapter 3?
3. How convinced are you that we come into the world with a musical brain?
4. Discuss plasticity and pruning in terms of music.
5. What implications does the statement that "neurons that fire together wire together" have for musical behaviors?
6. Discuss the concepts of critical periods and optimal periods in terms of your experiences with music learning.
7. In what ways does information about music in the brain from ancillary disciplines and indirect approaches complement information from neuroimaging studies?

8. Some have criticized neuroimaging studies of music as being too atomistic (i.e., focusing on such narrow aspects) and providing not much more than "this part of the brain lights up for this part of music and that part lights up for another part." Do you think the time and expense of conducting brain imaging studies of musicians is warranted? Are the results encouraging and moving us forward in reasonable ways?

9. What does neuromusical research have to offer you in your particular musical endeavors?

10. What type of information would most useful to you in the future? If current limitations in brain imaging could be overcome, what experiments would you most like to see conducted?

Chapter 10

Bodily Responses to Music

THINK for a moment about a truly memorable musical experience you have had and try to catalogue how your body responded. Did your heart rate speed up? Did you feel goosebumps or did the back of your neck feel prickly? Did you cry or laugh? Ever since David played the harp to help Saul with his insomnia, and probably long before that, the influence of music on the body has been a topic of interest. For our purposes, we have divided bodily responses into two categories: physiological, those bodily process that happen internally, and physical, external events that we can observe. Sometimes researchers refer to these collectively as psychophysiological responses (Hodges, 2009). As you read this chapter, it is important to remember that normal musical experiences are holistic; that is, the different kinds of bodily responses meld into one integrated experience.

PHYSIOLOGICAL RESPONSES TO MUSIC

Physiological responses include internal bodily processes, such as heart/pulse rate, blood pressure, respiration, skin conductivity, biochemical responses, skin/finger/body temperature, and miscellaneous responses such as blood volume, blood oxygen saturation, and gastric motility. Although occasionally these internal processes are observable, for the most part detection requires some sort of monitoring device such as a heart rate monitor (see Fig. 10.1).

Musical experiences can have profound effects on our bodies. To make what can be extremely complicated internal processes more understandable, we can say simplistically that three things can happen when we listen to music: physiological systems can speed up, slow down, or remain unchanged. Although there have been many attempts to define the connections between music and these responses in order to control the changes intentionally, it has turned out to be a more complicated process than first thought.

A generally consistent feature of the research reviewed in this chapter is the comparison of the relative effects of stimulative and sedative music. As defined by Gaston (1951), *stimulative* music emphasizes rhythm rather than melody or harmony and is characterized by loud, *staccato* passages with wide pitch ranges and abrupt, unpredictable changes. Conversely, *sedative* music emphasizes melody and harmony more than rhythm and is characterized by soft, *legato* passages with narrow pitch ranges and gradual, predictable changes.

A hypothesis often tested is that stimulative music increases physiological responses, while sedative music decreases them. As the following reviews will show, research findings do not unanimously support such a direct relationship between stimulative and sedative music and physiological responses. A simple anecdote illustrates why this may be so.

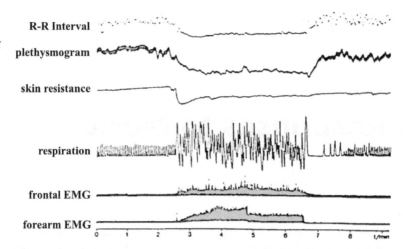

FIGURE 10.1 | In This Image We See the Coordination of Several Different Physiological Measurements in Response to Music. R-R Interval refers to the time between heart beats. The plethysmogram is a recording of blood pressure changes. Skin resistance indicates the electrical conductivity of the skin. Respiration indicates changes in breathing (inhalation and exhalation). Frontal and forearm EMG (electromyography) indicates muscular tension in forehead and forearm. The time scale across the horizontal axis is in minutes.

While working on his review of physiological responses (Bartlett, 1996a), Bartlett conducted an informal experiment with his students (personal communication). During a discussion of stimulative and sedative music, he asked twelve students in a graduate music glass to rate the Barber *Adagio for Strings* on a scale from 1 (highly sedative) to 5 (highly stimulative). Eleven students gave the piece a 1 or 2 rating; one person gave it a 5. When asked why the outlier found such a slow piece so highly stimulating, she responded by saying: "I am a cellist and this is one of my favorite pieces to play. I get very excited every time I hear it." Thus, what is calming to one may be exciting to someone else. Each of us has a personalized listening history, along with many other variables, that determines how we will respond.

The following reviews of literature are intentionally brief and designed to focus on broad conclusions (see Hodges, 2016a, 2010b, for more extensive reviews). For the most part, brain response measurements, such as EEG, are not included in this chapter (see Chapter 9). The first thing one is likely to notice while reading the following sections is the bewildering array of contradictions. There are at least ten reasons why this may be so: (1) There are no standard protocols. (2) The type of music varies from study to study. (3) Definitions of stimulative and sedative music may be too general and not allow for a clear enough distinction between the two kinds of music; furthermore, such a division may be too simplistic. (4) Frequently, researchers select happy or sad music (or other emotions), which are also somewhat vague and arbitrary designations. (5) Unreliable and inaccurate measurements of various physiological responses may render some of the data invalid. (6) Listener variables, such as age, gender, socioeconomic status, training, and experience vary considerably among different studies. (7) What researchers ask listeners to listen for or to do in response to the music varies. (8) It is extremely difficult to control confounding variables, such as the testing situation itself, movement on the part of the subject, or extraneous sights and sounds. (9) It is also important to note that bodily responses do not occur in a vacuum. They are highly influenced by personal, social, and cultural factors. (10) Of course, it is also possible that even if all these variables were carefully controlled, listeners' bodily responses might simply vary as a result of individual responsiveness. Perhaps musical responses are more idiosyncratic than homogeneous (Chamorro-Premuzic & Furnham, 2007; Rentfrow, Goldberg, & Levitin, 2011).

Heart Rate and Pulse Rate

Measuring the effects of music on the heart rate and pulse rate is one of the easier physiological measurements to make. An electrocardiogram records beats per minute (Andreassi, 2007); sometimes researchers are interested in other variables such as inter-beat interval or cardiac output (Krumhansl, 1997; Nyklíček, Thayer, & Van Doornen, 1997). While the measurement may not be so difficult, obtaining a clear picture from the reported literature certainly is.

Researchers have drawn contradictory conclusions from their investigations of the effects of music on heart rate. First, some found that stimulative music tended to increase heart rate, while sedative music tended to cause a decrease (Bernardi, Porta, & Sleight, 2006; Etzel, Johnson, Dickerson, Tranel, & Adolphs, 2006; Guhn, Hamm, & Zentner, 2007). In a smaller number of studies, both stimulative and sedative music tended to increase heart rate (Krumhansl, 1997; Rickard, 2004). In two older studies, stimulative and sedative music caused changes in heart rate, but these changes were not predictable (Bierbaum, 1958; Sears, 1954). In one study, stimulative music did not change heart rate, but sedative music caused a decrease (Iwanaga, Ikeda, & Iwagki, 1996). Finally, some researchers found that music had no effect on heart rate (Gomez & Danuser, 2004; Gendolla & Krüsken, 2001; Gupta & Gupta, 2005).

Studying musicians' heart rates while they perform is difficult, although it has been done a few times. Heart rate increased during choral singing (Olsson, von Schéele, & Theorell, 2013) but can vary according to song structure (Vichoff et al., 2013). The conductor Herbert von Karajan had higher heart rates during more emotional passages than during more physically demanding passages (Harrer & Harrer, 1977). His heart rate was sometimes higher during certain conducting situations than it was when he was piloting his jet plane. Heart rates of 24 members of the Vienna Symphony were monitored during rehearsals and performances (Haider & Groll-Knapp, 1981). With peaks up to 151 beats per minute, heart rate was higher during performances than during rehearsals. The tempo of the music being performed was more influential on heart rate than other musical attributes. Interestingly, for one horn player, heart rate increased in the moments prior to an entrance (possibly an indication of anticipatory anxiety), decreased immediately at the moment of entrance, then gradually increased again throughout the passage. Support for the notion of anticipatory anxiety was found in recordings of brain waves (EEG) that clearly showed an expectancy wave, characterized as "intention-induced anticipatory stress" (Haider & Groll-Knapp, 1981, p. 30). High school and university musicians also experienced increased heart rate, likely again reflecting performance anxiety, before or during performances in front of audiences or judges (Abel & Larkin, 1990; Brotons, 1994; Hunsaker, 1994; LeBlanc, Jin, Obert, & Siivola, 1997).

Blood Pressure

Blood pressure is measured by a sphygmomanometer (Andreassi, 2007). Systolic blood pressure reflects maximal pressure in the blood vessels, and diastolic blood pressure reflects minimal pressure. Blood pressure varies in music listening situations (Bernardi et al., 2006; Savan, 1999). Teng, Wong, and Zhang (2007) found that self-selected music was effective in lowering blood pressure. Some researchers, however, found that blood pressure did not change in music listening conditions (Gupta & Gupta, 2005; Strauser, 1997).

Respiration

A respiratory inductive plethysmograph is used to measure respiration or breathing rate (Sackner et al., 1989). The effects of music on respiration, both rate and amplitude, have been measured in a number of studies, leading to the following conclusions. Stimulative music tends to increase respiration and sedative music tends to decrease it (Blood & Zatorre, 2001; Gomez & Danuser, 2004, 2007; Thayer & Faith, 2001). In two very early studies, researchers found that any music, whether stimulative or sedative, tended to increase respiration (Binet & Courtier, 1895; Dogiel, 1880). Enjoyable music tends to increase respiration (DeJong, van Mourik, & Schellekens, 1973; Ries, 1969). Listening to music did not cause a change in respiration (Davis, 1992). Stimulative music did not cause an increase in respiration, but sedative music caused a decrease (Iwanaga et al., 1996).

Berger (1965) measured the intraoral air pressure of trumpet players (i.e., the amount of pressure inside the oral cavity) and found that loud tones required greater air pressure than soft tones, and high tones somewhat more than low tones. Trumpet playing requires greater intraoral air pressure than other wind instruments. Bouhuys (1964) examined pulmonary function in 42 professional players on 15 different wind instruments. Vital capacity was larger than expected in brass players and lung function was equal to or superior to control subjects.

Skin Conductance Responses

Skin conductance response (SC), also known as electrodermal response or previously as galvanic skin response (GSR), is a temporary fluctuation in the electrical resistance of the skin. Measured by a psychogalvanometer, usually attached to the fingers and/or palm of the hand, SC is a result of mental activity, most often of an affective nature (Venables, 1987). An increase in SC indicates a decrease in resistance, which in turn indicates an increase in arousal. The results of studies concerning the effects of music on SC are highly inconclusive.

Listening to music caused changes in SC readings (Gomez & Danuser, 2004, 2007; Grewe, Nagel, Kopiez, & Altenmüller, 2007b; Guhn et al., 2007; Khalfa, Peretz, Blondin, & Manon, 2002; Lundqvist, Carlsson, & Hilmersson, 2000; Rickard, 2004). Stimulative and sedative music produced different effects on GSR reading; in two studies, stimulative music produced greater GSR deflections than sedative music (Michel, 1952; Shrift, 1955), while in three other studies, GSR readings decreased during stimulative music (Weidenfeller & Zimny, 1962; Zimny & Weidenfeller, 1962, 1963). Music listening produced no meaningful changes in skin conductance for Blood and Zatorre (2001). There is a significant relationship between verbal reports of like/dislike and SC readings (Peretti & Swenson, 1974). Ries (1969) reached the opposite conclusion. Various elements of music, such as pitch range, melody, and rhythm, affected SC readings for Wilson and Aiken (1977). Skin conductance changes were pronounced during transitional passages of piano improvisations, likely indicating mental concentration (Dean & Bailes, 2015).

Biochemical Responses

One of the modern advances in studying bodily responses has been an increasing ability to measure changes in biochemicals as a result of listening to music (Koshimori, 2019). A variety of different chemicals have been measured and the results are highly complex, contradictory, and confusing (see Table 10.1). Nevertheless, it is readily apparent that music listening can exert a strong influence on body chemistry. Although there are already direct applications of the effects of music on biochemicals in music medicine (Pratt & Spintge, 1995; Spintge, 2012; see Chapter 15), this line of investigation is still in its infancy. This is particularly true when it comes to the role of hormones in emotional responses to music.

TABLE 10.1 | Biochemical Responses to Music.

Increased	Decreased	No change
Adrenocorticotropic hormone (ACTH) Gerra et al., 1998	Keeler et al., 2015 Möckel et al., 1994 Oyama et al., 1987	Evers & Suhr, 2000
Arginine vasopressin receptor (AVPR1A) Ukkola-Vuoti et al., 2011		
Beta-endorphins Gerra et al., 1998 Goldstein, 1980	McKinney et al., 1997b	
Blood glucose		
	Decreased—initially blood glucose increased due to pre-surgical stress, then decreased while listening to music: Miluk-Kolasa, Matejek, & Stupnicki, 1996	
Cortisol Beck, Cesario, Yousefi, & Enamoto, 2000 Gerra et al., 1998 Pilger et al., 2014	Beck et al., 2000 Enk et al., 2008 Kreutz, Bongard, Rohrmann, Hodapp, & Grebe, 2004 Leardi et al., 2007	Clark, Iversen, & Goodwin, 2001 Rickard, 2004 Stefano, Zhu, Cadet, Salamon, & Monatione, 2004 Yamamoto, Naga, & Shimizu, 2007

Increased in music majors but decreased in nonmusic majors (VanderArk & Ely, 1992, 1993). Participants were given a psychological stressor that caused a sharp increase in salivary cortisol. Listeners who heard relaxing music had a sharper decrease in salivary cortisol than those who recovered in silence (Khalfa, Dalla Bella, Roy, Peretz, & Lupien, 2003). In another experiment, salivary cortisol did not increase during music listening with a stressor (Knight & Rickard, 2001). Increased in orchestral musicians during performance (Pilger et al., 2014).

Dehydroepiandrosterone		Conrad et al., 2007
Dopamine Pleasurable music listening experiences elicit a release of dopamine. This was detected by activations in brain structures involved in reward processing (Blood & Zatorre, 2001; Brown et al., 2004; Ferreri et al., 2019; Mavridis, 2015; Menon & Levitin, 2005; Salimpoor et al., 2011).	Hirokawa & Ohira, 2003	
Epinephrine Kumar et al., 1999	Conrad et al., 2007	Hirokawa & Ohira, 2003
Genetic stress hormone markers		

Participants in a recreational music-making program experienced reversal in 19 of 45 genetic stress hormone markers (Bittman et al., 2005).

Growth hormone
Conrad et al., 2007

(Continued)

TABLE 10.1 | (Continued)

Increased	Decreased	No change
Interleukin-1 Bartlett et al., 1993		
Interleukin-6	Conrad, 2007	
Interleukin-10	Wachi et al., 2007	
Melatonin Kumar et al.,1999		
Mu opiate receptor expression Stefano et al., 2004		
Natural killer cells Increased after one hour of recreational music making: Wachi et al., 2007		Hirokawa & Ohira, 2003
Neutrophils and lymphocytes	Rider & Achterberg, 1989	
Norepinephrine Kumar et al., 1999		Hirokawa & Ohira, 2003
Oxytocin Grape, Sandgren, Hansson, Ericson, & Theorell, 2002 Nilsson, 2009		
Prolactin		Evers & Suhr, 2000
Secretory Immunoglobulin A (SIgA) Beck et al., 2000 Charnetski & Brennan, 1998 Enk et al., 2008 Knight & Rickard, 2001 Kreutz et al., 2004	Miluk-Kolasa, Obminski, Stupnicki, & Golec, 1994	Hirokawa & Ohira, 2003
Serotonin Increased to pleasant music and decreased to unpleasant music: Evers & Suhr, 2000		Kumar et al., 1999
Testosterone Increased in females; decreased in males: Fukui, 2001		
T lymphocytes (CD4+, CD8+, CD16+)		Hirokawa & Ohira, 2003

In spite of the lack of consensus on some details, several reviews of the pertinent literature have found that the positive benefits of music experiences are associated with neurochemicals related to reward, motivation, and pleasure (Chanda & Levitin, 2013; Kreutz, Murcia, & Bongard, 2012).

Skin, Finger, or Body Temperature

A plethysmograph is used to measure skin temperature, related to blood flow in skin tissue (Andreassi, 2007). Several studies report data indicating that skin temperature changed in response to music listening (Baumgartner, Esslen, & Jäncke, 2006; Lundqvist, Carlsson, Hilmersson, & Juslin, 2009; Rickard, 2004). However, there was very little consistency in results. Temperature increased in response to sedative music (Kibler & Rider, 1983; Peach, 1984), to stimulative music (Lundqvist et al., 2009), or to any music (Rickard, 2004), but decreased in other cases (Krumhansl, 1997; Savan, 1999) or experienced no change (Blood & Zatorre, 2001, Craig, 2005).

Miscellaneous Responses

Blood volume is the amount of blood in a specific area, such as the hands, and is measured by a plethysmograph (Andreassi, 2007). Significant changes in blood volume were found by Davis and Thaut (1989) and Krumhansl (1997); however, no changes were found by Nater, Krebs, and Ehlert (2005) or Pignatiello, Camp, Elder, and Rasar (1989).

The amount of oxygen present in the blood is measured by an oximeter (Hill & Stoneham, 2000) and is known as blood oxygen saturation. Music has significant effects on blood-oxygen saturation levels that vary according to changes in the stimulus (Cassidy & Standley, 1995).

Gastric motility, or peristalsis, refers to stomach contractions that move food along the alimentary canal. It is measured by electrogastrography (Rothstein, Alavi, & Reynolds, 1993). Chen, Xu, Wang, and Chen (2005, 2008) found supporting evidence that music affected gastric motility. However, they were not able to determine specific relationships between type of music and type of effect (i.e., increasing or decreasing peristalsis).

The bewildering contradictions in the results of these studies must make one wonder whether we know anything at all about the effects of music on physiological responses. Because physiological responses are often combined with physical responses into a larger category of psychophysical responses, these findings will be discussed after the following section.

PHYSICAL RESPONSES TO MUSIC

Physical responses are external, readily observable, reflexive motor movements such as facial gestures, foot tapping, head nodding, or body swaying. These responses occur naturally, without specific training. Physical responses that require training, such as learned performance skills, are discussed in Chapter 13: Music and Performance. In some circumstances, physical responses may be amenable to objective measurement, such as when muscular tension is measured by electromyography (EMG). Other times, physical responses are monitored by observation, as when facial gestures are observed and coded.

Muscular and Motor Responses

EMG readings indicate that muscular tension changes in response to music listening (Blood & Zatorre, 2001). Others reported no significant changes in muscle tension during music listening (Davis & Thaut, 1989; Scartelli, 1984). When musical tension increased, participants squeezed harder on a pair of tongs (Nielsen, 1983, 1987). Tension decreased in response to sedative music more quickly than it increased in response to stimulative music (Sears, 1958). Harrer and Harrer (1977) and Wilson and Davey (2002) monitored foot tapping to music. Postural stability increased during music listening (Carrick, Oggero, & Pagnacco, 2007).

Research on the neuromotor aspects of music making offers potential benefits in several areas (see Chapter 13). Research is also important in the area of performing arts medicine, not only for treating those performers with motor problems, but also for educating performers in ways to avoid problems. In addition, the use of music as a rhythmic organizer of motor behaviors is important for stroke and Parkinson's patients. Researchers are using music, particularly its rhythmic and tempo aspects, in a neurologic rehabilitation program to facilitate walking in stroke and Parkinson's patients (McIntosh, Thaut, & Rice, 1996). Additional information on performer's motor problems and neurologic rehabilitation using music can be found in Chapter 15: Music and Health.

Sacks (1983) eloquently described the power of music to activate motor systems. In this case, he used it to awaken a catatonic patient.

> This power of music to integrate and cure, to liberate the Parkinsonian and give him freedom while it lasts ("You are the music/while the music lasts," T. S. Eliot), is quite fundamental, and seen in every patient. This was shown beautifully, and discussed with great insight, by Edith T., a former music teacher. She said that she had become "graceless" with the onset of Parkinsonism, that her movements had become "wooden, mechanical— like a robot or doll," that she had lost her former "naturalness" and "musicalness" of movement, that—in a word—she had been "unmusicked." Fortunately, she added, the disease was "accompanied by its own cure." We raised an eyebrow: "Music," she said, "as I am unmusicked, I must be remusicked." Often, she said, she would find herself "frozen," utterly motionless, deprived of the power, the impulse, the *thought*, of any motion; she felt at such times "like a still photo, a frozen frame"—a mere optical flat, without substance or life. In this state, this statelessness, this timeless irreality, she would remain, motionless-helpless, *until music came*: "Songs, tunes I knew from years ago, catchy tunes, rhythmic tunes the sort I loved to dance to."
>
> With this sudden imagining of music, this coming of spontaneous inner music, the power of motion, action, would suddenly return, and the sense of substance and restored personality and reality; now, as she put it, she could "dance out of the frame," the flat frozen visualness in which she was trapped, and move freely and gracefully: "It was like suddenly remembering myself, my own living tune." But then, just as suddenly, the inner music would cease, and with this all motion and actuality would vanish, and she would fall instantly, once more, into a Parkinsonian abyss.
>
> (pp. 294–295)

Chills

Many music listeners experience responses to music that have been characterized by what have been called *chills* or *thrills*. The label *frisson* has also been used (Huron, 2006). Chills commonly include such things as crying, lump in the throat, shivering, a prickly feeling on the back of the neck, tingling along the spine or in the extremities, and goosebumps (pilomotor reflex; see Fig. 10.2) (Konečni, 2005). Chills appear to be a fairly common experience, as 75–96% of those interviewed reported having had chills in response to music (Goldstein,

FIGURE 10.2 | Musical Chills May Elicit Goosebumps on the Arm, Along With Other Physical Responses Such As Crying, Prickling on the Back of the Neck, or Having a Lump in the Throat.

1980; Nusbaum, Silvia, Burgin, Hodges, & Kwapil, 2014; Sloboda, 1991) and doing so reliably (Konečni, Wanic & Brown, 2007; Waterman, 1996; though see Grewe, Nagel, Kopiez, & Altenmüller, 2007a for a contradiction).

It would seem logical that chills would be linked to physiological responses, but that is not always the case. In one experiment, musical passages that elicited the greatest number of chills also elicited the greatest increase in heart rate and skin conductance. Skin conductance was also higher for those who experienced chills than for those who did not (Guhn et al., 2007); however, there was no difference in heart rate (even though both groups did experience an increase in heart rate). These results confirmed previous findings (Baltes, Avram, Miclea, & Miu, 2011; Craig, 2005; Grewe et al., 2007b; Grewe, Kopiez, & Altenmüller, 2009; Panksepp, 1995; Rickard, 2004). Blood and Zatorre (2001) did not find an increase in skin conductance, but did find increases and decreases in blood flow to different areas of the brain, along with increases in heart rate, respiration, and forearm muscular tension. Activity was elevated in brain areas known to be involved in attention. Chills appear to be related to distinct musical structures (e.g., phrases) or events (e.g., a sudden change in dynamics) (Grewe et al., 2007b; Sloboda, 1991). Chills are also connected to emotional and aesthetic responses to music (see Chapter 11).

Facial Gestures

Researchers have attempted to monitor facial gestures in response to music by taping electrodes on the "smile" muscle (*zygomaticus*), the brow muscles (*corrugator*), and muscles under the eye (*orbicularis oculi*). Facial EMG indicated that happy, positive-arousing music caused an increase in smiling more so than sad, negative-arousing music (Grewe et al., 2007a; Lundqvist et al., 2000; Witvliet & Vrana, 2007) and that facial gestures in response to music display the discrete emotions of happiness, sadness, agitation, and serenity (Thayer & Faith, 2001). Although coding systems have been developed to place observations of facial gestures into discrete categories (Cohn, Ambadar & Ekman, 2007; Levenson, 2007), they have not yet been used with music listening. Slaughter (1954) did observe listeners' eyes to determine that pupils dilated during stimulative music and constricted during sedative music. Thompson

FIGURE 10.3 | Dancing, and Many Other Body Movements, Are a Natural Reaction to Music.

and Russo (2007) used video-based motion tracking to monitor movements of the head, eyebrows, and lips of singers. It was found that these facial gestures carried information about size of intervals being sung, when rated in the absence of sound.

Body Movements

Natural responses to music include body movements such as head nodding, body swaying, finger snapping, and foot tapping (Figure 10.3) (Koepchen et al., 1992) and music often causes a desire to move (Grewe et al., 2007a). Entraining body movements with the rhythm of music is pleasurable (Levitin, 2006). An audio-visual-motor mechanism connects auditory and visual representations of rhythm to the body's motor systems (Baumann et al., 2007; Brown et al., 2006; Mandell, Schulze, & Schlaug, 2007; Thaut, 2003; Zatorre, Chen, & Penhune, 2007). Representations of body movements are linked by the cerebellum into sensory-guided actions. Even if the body is not physically moving, there may be a sensation of movement based on auditory or visual patterns. Thus, music with strong dance-like rhythms, for example, may lead to vicarious or mental dancing rather than to physical dancing.

DISCUSSION OF PSYCHOPHYSIOLOGICAL VARIABLES

After reading these brief reviews, the contradictory nature of these research findings is surely evident. It may be tempting even to disregard the entire body of literature. However, there are definite applications in medical-clinical settings that are explored in Chapter 15. In the meantime, it is worth considering the nature of *psychophysiological responses* to music further to determine what useful conclusions might be drawn.

Some researchers have been able to link psychophysiological variables to emotional responses (e.g., Khalfa et al., 2008). For example, advanced pianists demonstrated that performing elicited stronger emotion-related heart rate and heart rate variability than musical perception (Nakahara, Furuya, Obata, Masuko, & Kinoshita, 2009). However, in general, the search for an emotion-specific physiology has been elusive (Grewe, 2007a). Thus, when a particular piece of music causes the heart rates of listeners to increase, what does this mean? Often, it is not known whether the heart rates increased because the subjects enjoyed the music, were excited by it, or were made anxious by it or the testing situation, because of a particular emotional response such happiness or fear, or because of any other unknown reason.

In a previous study (Hodges, 2010b), I reviewed 158 published articles, finding that only 50 of those attempted to link psychophysiological variables with emotional responses. Of those, 17 had to do with stress and anxiety, either during musical performances or in medical situations. This left only 39 articles connecting psychophysiological variables and emotions. This is not to suggest that this type of research is futile and therefore unnecessary or irrelevant, but rather that conclusions must be viewed with some caution and without overly generalizing to other situations. For example, Konečni (2013) raised a note of caution in interpreting findings from these studies because he felt researchers had not always distinguished adequately between the perception of emotions expressed in music and the actual experience of those emotions (see Chapter 11 for further discussion of this point). In time, however, newer research techniques and enhanced technology may allow for a better understanding of this core aspect of the musical experience.

One strategy to improve our understanding of the connections between psychophysiological responses and music is to look for patterns among different responses, in contrast to single variables as presented in the previous review sections (Nyklíček et al., 1997). A first step is to determine whether there are emotion-specific patterns of psychophysiological activity. Larsen and colleagues (2008) identified three major theories: (1) that different psychophysiological patterns produce different emotions, (2) the reverse, that different emotions produce different patterns of psychophysiological activity, and (3) that relationships between psychophysiological activity and emotions depend on the given situation.

A simpler way of thinking about it is to polarize two opposite views: every emotion is psychophysiologically unique or every emotion is psychophysiologically the same (Levenson, 2003). Research supports neither extreme view. Some researchers found data to support the notion of emotion-specific bodily responses (Ekman, Levenson, & Friesen, 1983; Levenson, 1992), while others did not (Zajonc & McIntosh, 1992). Cacioppo, Berntson, Larsen, Poehlmann, and Ito (2000) conducted a meta-analysis and determined that negative emotions are associated with stronger bodily responses, but that no emotions can be fully identified by bodily responses alone.

Several researchers have taken a multivariate approach (i.e., studying more than one variable at a time) in obtaining data in support of emotion-specific patterns for music. For example, Krumhansl (1997) monitored 11 physiological variables and found that sad music elicited the largest changes in heart rate, blood pressure, skin conductance, and temperature, while respiration changed more for happy music. Nyklíček and colleagues (1997) found evidence for psychophysiological differentiation of emotions, while monitoring 16 cardiorespiratory variables during music listening. Similar results have been obtained by Gomez and Danuser (2007), Guhn et al. (2007), Khalfa et al. (2008), Lundqvist et al. (2009), and Witvliet and Vrana (2007). In a pioneering effort, Pilger and colleagues (2014) obtained blood and salivary samples from 48 orchestral musicians during rehearsal and a performance. Increased levels of pro-inflammatory markers (e.g., Interleukin 6) and salivary cortisol were found in the performance situation. Emotional valence played a significant role. The role of multivariate psychophysiological processes in emotional responses to music needs continued investigation.

As researchers continue to make progress on this issue, they will need to address several important issues. First, most of the studies cited utilize brief musical excerpts ranging from less than 30 seconds (e.g., Witvliet & Vrana, 2007) to about three minutes (e.g., Krumhansl, 1997). While this gives greater internal validity, or control over independent variables, it has lower ecological or external validity, that is, generalizability to real-world situations. A second issue concerns the use of unimodal excerpts. Often, researchers carefully choose stimuli to reflect a single emotion. Beside the fact that these are somewhat arbitrary choices, as has been noted, it does not reflect a great deal of the music that people listen to, in which there are contrasting or even overlapping emotions. A third, related issue concerns experiments done in laboratory settings as opposed to more naturalistic listening circumstances (see Chapter 11).

Vaitl, Vehrs, and Sternagel (1993) conducted an experiment that addressed all three of these issues. They monitored listeners for skin conductance, respiration, and emotional arousal continuously throughout a performance of Wagner's opera *Die Meistersinger von Nürnberg*. They found that physiological responses did vary with leitmotivs, although there was only a weak correspondence between these readings and emotional arousal ratings. Progress in *ambulatory assessment*, monitoring physiological responses in unconstrained settings, allows researchers to monitor physiological responses in naturalistic, real-world circumstances (Fahrenberg, 2001). Ideally, more studies of this type will appear in the literature in the coming years. Especially needed are studies of everyday listening experiences.

Researchers also need to address two additional areas of concern. They have seldom investigated the influence of musical structures on psychophysiological variables. Sloboda (1991) asked 83 participants to identify specific points in the music when they had a physical response. Only 57, all but two of whom were performers, could point to a specific motive, theme, chord, or specific moment in the music. This may indicate that considerable musical experience is necessary before one can make specific linkages. Gomez and Danuser (2007), Guhn and colleagues (2007), and Rickard (2004) have also investigated this topic, but much more is required before we have a more complete understanding.

Researchers also need to conduct more research into relationships between personal variables, such as age, gender, and training, and psychophysiological responses. Some researchers found gender differences (McFarland & Kadish, 1991; McNamara & Ballard, 1999; Nater et al., 2006), but Lundqvist et al. (2009) did not. Rickard (2004) positively correlated heart rate with extraversion and skin conductance with agreeableness, among other relationships, but this is an area in need of considerably more attention.

CONCLUSION

Recall from the two previous chapters that we considered Mike and Jane's cognitive and neural processes as they attended the opera (Fig. 8.18). Now imagine the swirling thoughts, feelings, emotions, and bodily responses of Jane and Mike as the curtain rises and the performance begins. Even as we focus on bodily responses, we must surely recognize that these bodily responses occur within a social context that exerts its own influence on expectations and existing moods. Did they have a delightful time with their friends? Was the restaurant meal too expensive or a culinary delight? Was there difficulty in finding parking or did they get a prime spot? Does Mike feel out of place, assuming that others in the audience are wealthier or more knowledgeable? Even seemingly trivial things, such as temperature in the hall or a patron nearby with a noisy cough, can impact the experience Jane and Mike are going to have.

Suppose we were magically able to monitor every one of the psychophysiological responses detailed in this chapter throughout the entire evening. What an impossibly rich assortment of data that would provide, in a constantly shifting kaleidoscope of patterns. If we could also have a clear view of all their physical responses, what gestures would we observe and could we accurately interpret their meanings? Would we know from watching whether Jane and Mike were enjoying the performance? Could we detect subtleties, such as a circumstance in which Jane is thrilled with the costumes and staging and is particularly taken with the tenor, but somewhat disappointed with the soprano? What if Mike was generally bored but (perhaps secretly) enjoyed the comic basso? Finally, if we could observe them with their friends and eavesdrop on their conversation on the ride home what behaviors would they exhibit? Would Jane gush enthusiastically, complete with animated hand gestures? Would Mike pretend enjoyment to placate his wife or would he roll his eyes? Would Jane follow up by reading a review in the paper the next day, while Mike regaled his next-door neighbor with a parody of the ridiculous plot? This fictitious scenario illustrates how bodily responses are situated within richly complicated, multi-dimensional, personal-social-cultural matrices.

In the next chapter, we will conclude our review of this fictitious scenario by considering Mike and Jane's emotional responses. In the meantime, however, the central message of this chapter is relatively clear, even if the specific details are not. Music listening experiences have wide-ranging and significant influences on bodily responses. Reversing the sentence, we might say that bodily processes are a central part of musical experiences.

DISCUSSION QUESTIONS

1. Discuss your bodily responses to the most powerful, meaningful musical experiences you have had.
2. What psychophysical responses can you observe when you watch others listen to music? What, if anything, can you deduce about their reactions from these observations?
3. Try a simple experiment: Take your pulse to establish a baseline. Then listen to different pieces of music and note how your pulse responds. What musical factors (e.g., tempo, dynamics, etc.) seem to affect your pulse rate most strongly? What nonmusical factors (e.g., familiarity, like-dislike, etc.) appear to affect your pulse rate the most? Are there times when your pulse rate changed in an opposite direction to what you would have predicted?
4. Instead of the informal experiment in question 3, suppose you were asked to conduct a more formal study of heart rate responses to music. How would you design a study to control for all the extraneous variables that could confound the results?
5. When you listen to music, do you commonly find yourself engaging in involuntary physical responses, such as toe-tapping or head nodding?
6. What do you think of the following notion? Patrons at a classical music concert may burst into exuberant applause or yell *bravo!* at the end partly because they have constrained their physical reactions during the performance.
7. Much of the literature on bodily responses is contradictory. Conduct a poll among members of the class to determine whether there is a consensus or disagreement on bodily responses to a specific musical experience.

8. Why do you think researchers have had such a difficult time making strong connections between bodily and emotional responses?

9. What activities do you engage in while listening to music (e.g., car washing or jogging)? Why do you listen to music during those times? What do you think music contributes to the activity?

10. Are there times when hearing music in the background is a distraction rather than an enhancement? What activities do you prefer to do without music?

Chapter 11

Musical Emotions^{MT11}

IN Chapters 8, 9, and 10, we imagined Mike and Jane at the opera as we considered their cognitive and neural processing, along with bodily responses. Now we consider the same couple in terms of their emotional responses. Jane, as you remember, had considerably more training than Mike. Likely, there are subtleties and nuances in the music that she detected and that he did not notice. Suppose, too, that she was in a happy mood and that he was in a foul temper as they arrived at the concert. These aspects, along with many, many others, influenced the emotions each felt during and after the concert. Without enumerating all of these potential issues at this point, let us proceed, understanding that there are many complex variables at work.

The topic of emotions, in general, and musical emotions, in particular, is exceedingly complex. Until recently, this was a neglected subject in psychology and in music psychology. A landmark publication, *Music and Emotion* (Juslin & Sloboda, 2001), spurred new interest and brought this topic to the fore. A revision of this book (Juslin & Sloboda, 2010) expanded the original from 540 to 975 pages. More recently, Juslin has published his comprehensive survey entitled *Musical Emotions Explained* (2019). These, and other publications are indications that music psychologists are paying more attention to this central, core aspect of musical experiences.

Perhaps one place to begin our study of this topic is with the notion that each person has an individual capacity for the perception and cognition of, and responsiveness to complex aural stimuli such as music. This personalized profile is made up of an amalgam of biological, psychological, and socio-cultural aspects, some of which may be relatively stable (e.g., aural acuity) and others of which are highly modifiable (e.g., those aspects that are influenced by training and experience).

The next step in untangling all the intertwining complexities of this topic is to make note of two viewpoints that have arisen: the cognitivist and the emotivist positions (Kivy, 1989, 1990). Those who subscribe to a *cognitivist* viewpoint believe that listeners can perceive an emotion being expressed in the music without necessarily experiencing that emotion. It may be that the listener has no particular emotional reaction to a piece of music, although recognizing that the music is expressing joy, for example, or it may be that the listener experiences high arousal without being able to identify a specific underlying emotion. *Emotivists*, on the other hand, believe that listeners can and do actually experience specific emotions induced by the music. A shorthand way of speaking about these two positions is the perception and induction of musical emotions.

FIGURE 11.1 | Each of Us Has a Personal Capacity to Respond to Music.

Sloboda and Juslin (2010) make the point that perception and induction of emotions are separate processes. Wager and colleagues (2008) reviewed 163 neuroimaging studies and came to the conclusion that there is a "striking dissociation" (p. 259) between perception and induction of emotions. Although these two positions will be discussed sequentially in subsequent sections, it seems reasonable to assume that a listener could experience both viewpoints in shifting, kaleidoscopic patterns. Thus, while some researchers take a polarized view, readers should integrate the two in a coherent conception that matches their own experiences. Before examining these positions in more detail, along with a third alternative that follows, let us take a broad look at emotions.

INTRODUCTION TO THE STUDY OF EMOTIONS

As a first step, we must clarify exactly what an emotion is. Juslin and Västfjäll (2008) defined emotions as involving cognitive appraisal and further added that emotions are:

> Relatively intense affective responses that usually involve a number of subcomponents—subjective feeling, physiological arousal, expression, action tendency, and regulation—which are more or less synchronized. Emotions focus on specific objects, and last minutes to a few hours.
>
> (p. 561)

Thus, emotions are to be distinguished from such terms as *mood* or *affect*, which may be longer lasting and more general in nature.

In the following paragraphs, we build on information from previous chapters to present a brief review of the major components involved in emotion (Bloom, Lazerson, & Hofstadter, 1985; LeDoux, 1986, 1994; Panksepp & Bernatzky, 2002).

■ The *autonomic nervous system* (ANS) contains both the *sympathetic* division (prepares the body for fight or flight) and the *parasympathetic* division (works to conserve energy).

The sympathetic division energizes the body by speeding up the heart rate, stimulating the secretion of adrenalin and a variety of neurotransmitters, and stimulating the conversion of glycogen for energy. The parasympathetic division slows down the heart rate and stimulates peristalsis (digestion) and the secretion of saliva. Although the two divisions seem to be contradictory, they work in tandem as the ANS regulates a complicated series of chemical reactions. The historical view of the ANS was one of mass discharge; however, recent evidence indicates that the ANS can respond with a wide variety of patterns of integrated peripheral activity.

■ The *reticular activating system* (RAS), located in the brainstem, consists of ascending fibers in the reticular formation that communicate with many different regions in the brain (see Fig. 11.2). The RAS monitors incoming signals from all the sensory organs and acts as a filtering device. Signals that are weak or unchanging are ignored; for example, a person who wears glasses constantly may be unaware of them unless they begin to rub uncomfortably. Strong or changing signals are sent on to other parts of the brain for further analysis and/or action. The RAS is also an alerting mechanism, fast-tracking important or critical information. The RAS has fibers that connect with the cortex, the limbic system, and motor systems. Within the reticular formation, the locus coeruleus regulates the secretion of the neurotransmitter norepinephrine, triggering emotional arousal, and the substantia nigra regulates the secretion of dopamine, facilitating pleasurable sensations.

■ The *limbic system* is that portion of the brain most closely involved in feelingful responses (Fig. 11.3; see also Fig. 9.10). Primary components of the limbic system include the:
– *thalamus*—a major relay between sensory input and the cortex; it is also involved in the arousal and activation of the association areas of the cortex
– *hypothalamus*—regulates the autonomic nervous system
– pituitary—the master gland that controls the release of hormones into the bloodstream)
– *amygdala*—involved with aggressive behaviors and fear reactions
– *hippocampus*—integrates incoming sensory information and is involved in memory storage)
– additional subcortical structures such as the basal ganglia are not shown in Figs. 9.10 or 11.3

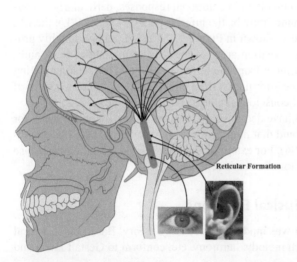

Reticular Formation

FIGURE 11.2 | The Reticular Activating Formation. Sensory information (from all the sensory organs, not just ears and eyes) is brought into the reticular formation. Ascending fibers filter out unnecessary or irrelevant signals and alert the brain to important upcoming information. Descending fibers modulate musculoskeletal activity via the spinal cord.

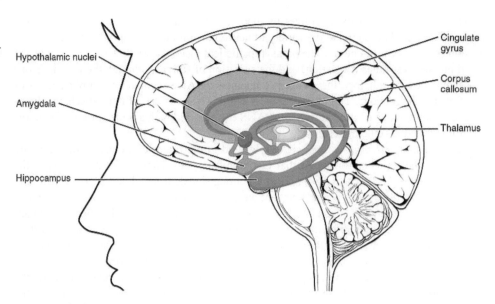

FIGURE 11.3 | The Limbic System Regulates Emotions, Among Other Functions. Only a few of its many components are illustrated here.

There are rich interconnections among the various components of the limbic system and between the limbic system and other parts of the brain. The limbic system receives messages about external events directly from sensory organs and from the primary and association cortices.

Because many hormonal reactions take place here, the limbic system is highly involved in emotional experiences. The limbic system contains a large number of opiate receptors, or nerve endings that are highly sensitive to the presence of such chemicals as endorphins. Music listening may stimulate an increase in the release of biochemicals that, in turn, elicit emotional responses in the limbic system. While many relationships between music and biochemicals are not yet clear, this is obviously a fruitful area of research. (See the previous chapter for more details on biochemical responses to music.)

Various parts of the cortex are also involved in emotional responses, particularly in cognitive assessment. Of particular importance may be the inferior parietal lobule (IPL); the IPL is the lower portion of the parietal lobe as shown in Figure 9.1. The IPL receives highly processed information directly from the association areas of the sensory modalities (e.g., auditory association area) as well as direct input from the limbic system and reticular activating system. The IPL, thus, serves to integrate information from all these inputs. "Such a pattern of inputs seems ideal for the mediation of conscious feelings" (LeDoux, 1986, p. 352).

Interestingly enough, experiments have demonstrated that the cortex is not necessary for certain types of emotional experience and that many emotional experiences take place without conscious awareness (LeDoux, 1994). For example, auditory fear conditioning can cause a fear reaction in a rat, even if the auditory cortex is removed.

The Role of Expectations in Musical Emotions

In Chapter 8: Music Cognition, much was made of expectancy theory. Based on structural characteristics of music (ways in which melody, harmony, etc. conform to Gestalt laws) and a person's previous experiences with the particular style of music, a listener interacts with incoming information by forming expectations. The ways in which and degrees to which expectations are or are not fulfilled results in affective responses. Generally, emotion or affect arises when a tendency to respond is delayed or inhibited (Meyer, 1956).

One musical event causes the listener to expect another musical event. The tension created by expectations is (or can be) resolved by a following musical event. It might happen something like the following. (Note: this explanation is a little cumbersome, but be patient. It will make more sense when applied to music.)

We have a fast path and slow path in responding to novel stimuli$^{MT11.1}$ (see Fig. 11.4). The fast path (biological arousal) stems from our earliest days as a species. Living in nature, it would not do us much good if we had to stop and think about a sudden auditory or visual threat. Thus, built into us is a rapid response mechanism. Even though we no longer use it to avoid saber-tooth tigers, it comes in handy when we have stepped off a curb without first noticing the bus heading right for us. As described previously, the sympathetic division of the

FIGURE 11.4 | Fast and Slow Path Processing. In the upper panel, a man is surprised by a barking dog and has an instantaneous "fast-path" reaction. In the lower panel, a microsecond later, "slow path processing" allows the man to realize that the dog is behind a fence and he is safe. See the complete description in MM11.1.

ANS speeds up breathing and heart rate, shunts blood to the large body muscles, and heightens alertness. All this happens without our having to think about it.

Imagine we are hearing Haydn's *Surprise Symphony*[MT11.5] for the first time. Recall from Chapter 9 that when the loud chord in the second movement comes crashing in, it activates an auditory brainstem response that can cause us to react as quickly as 5–6 ms (Hall, 2007). Motor responses such as a head turn or facial grimace occur soon after, within 14–22 ms of an auditory stimulus (Kofler et al., 2001). This pathway runs from the inner ear via the brainstem to the auditory thalamus. There it divides, with the fast pathway running directly to the amygdala, adding an emotional component to the reaction.

The slow path runs through the medial geniculate nucleus in the thalamus to the auditory cortex, from there to auditory association cortex, then back to the amygdala. The fast and slow pathways converge in the lateral amygdala, with information via the slow path arriving approximately 20 ms after the fast path information. The slow path adds additional information. In one experiment, it took approximately 43 ms for a stimulus to reach the auditory cortex (Howard et al., 2000), while in another experiment, information that combined multisensory information of sound and touch into a more coherent gestalt registered in 50 ms (Murray et al., 2005). Thus, this "slower pathway" is still extremely rapid.

What follows is an attempt at a step-by-step explanation of how cognition works in this regard.

- We constantly generate expectations about upcoming events and about future actions.
- These expectancies are largely unconscious.
- These expectancies are usually in the form of schemata, which themselves are based on Gestalt principles of organization.
- Any disruption to our ongoing expectancies causes biological arousal via the fast path (ANS).
- Biological arousal, in turn, causes a search for an explanation. What happened? What is that? What's going on?
- Biological arousal and the search for cognitive meaning combine to create an emotional response.

Return to the *Surprise Symphony* momentarily. Assuming our first-time listener is familiar with Western tonal music, certain expectations are almost immediately set up. This is done through the use of meter, tonality, and so on. By repeating the opening melody, Haydn confirms these expectations and by making it softer the second time, he draws the listener in with more focused attention. Although you can consciously attend to these expected schemata, in the typical listening experience, they would be largely unconscious.

It is not always the case that the biological fast path occurs prior to the cognitive slow path. The expectations we have, which are based on prior experience, often moderate what we experience. For example, in the case of the *Surprise Symphony*, if you have heard it before, you expect the loud chord to occur. Thus, you are not startled in the same way as you were the first time. However, the anticipation of the surprise may still make it a pleasurable experience.

Huron (2006) elaborated upon this fast-path-slow-path model with his ITPRA theory of expectation. ITPRA stands for Imagination Response, Tension Response, Prediction Response, Reaction Response, and Appraisal Response. Two types of responses occur before an event occurs:

- Imagination responses occur when we anticipate an outcome. Not all of our predictions come true, but forecasting the short-term future allows us to operate with some degree of structure in our lives.

■ Tension responses allow us to mentally and bodily prepare for an anticipated event. Recall a time when you had to stop rather suddenly while driving in a car. Even though an accident may not have occurred, you were prepared for that possibility.

Three additional responses occur during or after an event has taken place:

■ Prediction responses are concerned with expectation-related emotions. That is, we respond positively and more efficiently when the outcome of an event matches our Imagination Response. Likewise, when we incorrectly imagined the outcome, the response is likely to be negative and less appropriate.
■ Reaction responses are similar to the fast-path reactions described previously. This is not a thoughtful response, but rather an immediate, knee-jerk reaction.
■ Appraisal responses are akin to the slow-path response. Immediately following the Reaction Response, we engage in conscious processing that places the event into some kind of context.

Suppose we have just inserted ear buds in preparation for listening to a new song. Imagination and tension responses allow us to anticipate what we are about to hear and to prepare ourselves cognitively and bodily to hear the music. We might be curious if it is completely unknown or eager if we have heard from a friend that this is a wonderful song. Once the music starts, imagine our feelings if we were really looking forward to hearing this song (imagination response) only to be very disappointed when we actually heard it (prediction response). We might have an immediate negative response to the introduction (reaction response). However, once we listened to the song several times, we may eventually come to like it (appraisal response). Huron provided many more details in his book *Sweet Anticipation* about how the ITPRA Theory applies to musical expectations.

Measuring Musical Emotions

Examining emotional responses to music presents some challenging difficulties. The development of ways to capture emotional responses is an ongoing process. A major concern is to make a more determined effort to make a cleaner delineation between perceived and induced emotions. That is, the instructions to participants must make it clear whether they are to report the emotions they perceive or the emotions that are actually induced and experienced. Konečni (2008) contended that there are often problems in research design, such as imprecise wording in instructions to the participants, along with conceptual, methodological, and measurement problems, so that often it is not clear what is being reported—perceived or induced emotions.

Generally, psychologists have studied emotion via three approaches—self-report, expressive behavior, and bodily responses (Juslin, 2019; Sloboda & Juslin, 2010). Gabrielsson (2009) lists six specific ways that music psychologists have measured responses: free descriptions, adjective checklists, a combination of free descriptions and checklists, a rating of how well selected terms match the music, nonverbal methods, and continuous measurement devices. Free descriptions allow participants wide latitude in how they characterize their emotional responses to music. Gabrielsson (2001, 2010) used free descriptions in several projects that will be described subsequently. Essentially, he asked participants to write extended essays detailing their emotional experiences with music. These essays are analyzed by means of content analysis to determine whether major themes might emerge.

Kate Hevner was a pioneer in music emotion research (1936). She developed an adjective checklist, arranging 66 adjectives (e.g., soaring, dreamy, mournful, etc.) into eight clusters

(Fig. 11.5). Listeners checked each adjective they found appropriate for describing the music. Hevner found relatively consistent and uniform patterns of response. Thus, for example, listeners characterized the Scherzo from Mendelssohn's *Midsummer Night's Dream* as exciting, impetuous, and soaring, while the first movement of Tchaikovsky's *Symphony No. 6 in B Minor*, was described as dignified, solemn, and serious (Fig. 11.6). Numerous variants of the Hevner adjective checklist have been developed and used since her first efforts. Unfortunately, this approach is limited in that respondents are restricted to the descriptive words provided, and each person may have a personal interpretation of what a word like "soaring" means.

Neuroscientist and musician Manfred Clynes (1977) invented a nonverbal means of measuring emotional responses, called a *sentograph*. Participants pushed numerous times on a button (actually a strain gauge linked to a computer) to express a particular emotion (see Fig. 11.7). A computer averaged all these button pushes (expressions) into an overall shape called an *essentic form*. Different shapes or essentic forms were found for hate, anger, love, sex, grief, joy, and reverence. No significant differences were found based on gender, race, or training. Next, when world-class musicians Pablo Casals, Rudolf Serkin, and Murray Perahia pushed on the button to express the music of particular composers, distinctive shapes were found for Bach, Mozart, Beethoven, and many other composers. Clynes believed that music has the emotional effect it does, in part, because the shapes generated by music match emotional shapes wired into every human being.

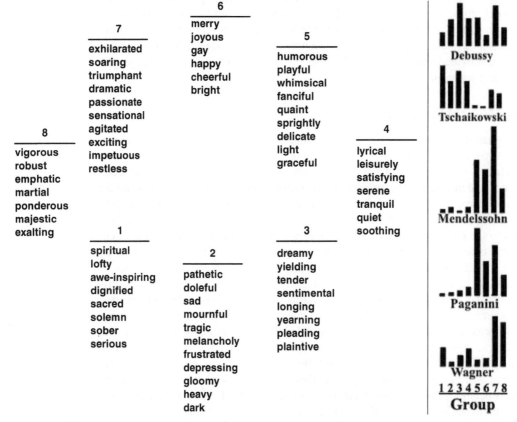

FIGURE 11.5 | Hevner Checklist. FIGURE 11.6 | Hevner Data From 1936. Group Numbers Refer to the Adjective Categories in Figure 11.5.

FIGURE 11.7 | Clynes's Sentograph. Here, a participant listens to music and presses on the button to indicate the emotion felt.

Unfortunately, there have been few replications of Clynes's work. However, at least two investigations obtained supporting results. De Vries (1991), for example, constructed a sentograph according to Clynes's description. Thirty participants produced sentograms while listening to 11 pieces of music. An analysis indicated that the sentograms for the same pieces of music were similar among listeners. The shapes of the sentograms were not dependent upon the subjects' appreciation of or familiarity with the music, and the sentograms produced resembled those that Clynes found for various emotions. Gabrielsson and Lindström (1995) likewise constructed a sentograph and asked four performers to play two pieces on a synthesizer and express them on a sentograph. Each piece was played five times to express happiness, solemnity, anger, softness/tenderness, and indifference. Data were treated to allow comparisons between the two performances in terms of tempo, sound level/pressure, timing, and articulation. Performances on the two devices were similar in most respects, confirming that emotions were expressed through the sentograph in much the same way as they were through the synthesizer.

Another means of measuring emotional responses that has been influential in the literature is a two-dimensional model based on pleasure and arousal (see Fig. 11.8). Russell (1980) aligned pleasure-displeasure along the horizontal axis and degree of arousal along the vertical axis. While they listen to the music, participants indicate pleasure on a left and right scale and arousal up and down. Several researchers have used this model, often replacing pleasure-displeasure with the term *valence*, to study emotional responses to music (e.g.,

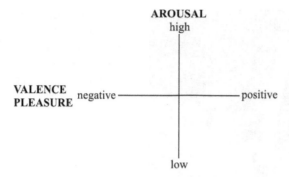

FIGURE 11.8 | Two-Dimensional Model of Pleasure and Arousal. While listening to music, participants indicate their degree of arousal from low to high and their degree of pleasure/ valence from negative to positive.

Gomez & Danuser, 2004; Witvliet & Vrana, 2007). Zentner and Eerola (2010b) note the limitations of this approach and propose an alternative. According to them, a two-dimensional model fails to account for all the variances apparent in music emotions. Their suggested three-dimensional model employs valence, energy arousal, and tension arousal dimensions. However, this model has yet to be fully investigated with regard to music emotions.

In a series of studies, researchers have combined a dimensional approach with a continuous response digital interface (CRDI). While listening to music, listeners move a computer mouse across a continuum to indicate responses. Madsen (1997) asked participants to use a two-dimensional CRDI to rate a 20-minute excerpt from Act I of Puccini's *La Bohème* along two dimensions—exciting and beautiful. He found a low, positive degree of relationship (correlation of 0.398) between the two dimensions. Although some degree of arousal seems necessary for an affective response, the relationship between the two was highly complex, with some moments of beauty characterized by high arousal and others low. Madsen (1998) repeated the experiment with the first movement of Haydn's Symphony No. 104. In this composition, there was nearly a mirror image between the two dimensions (correlation = −0.58).

From these brief descriptions, one can see that although a variety of strategies have been employed, there is no perfect or best way to capture how listeners respond emotionally to music. A further confound relates to the setting. Rating emotional responses while sitting in a lab or in any artificial listening situation is likely to compromise authentic feelings. One way to get around this problem is through experience sampling method (ESM); researchers contact participants randomly throughout the day via a pager or cell phone and ask them to record their activities and feelings. As we will see later in several examples, this does create a more naturalistic setting. However, participants are not always engaged in musical activities when contacted and it would be more difficult to use this technique in formal music settings such as a concert or recital. With the struggles to record emotional responses in mind, and recognizing that different views can be integrated, we begin with a look at the perception of musical emotions.

PERCEIVED EMOTIONS: THE COGNITIVIST POSITION

Cognitivists believe that listeners can perceive emotions expressed in the music without necessarily feeling those emotions (Figure 11.9). Thus, a listener might recognize that a certain piece

FIGURE 11.9 | The Cognitivist Position: Listeners Can Perceive Emotions in the Music Without Necessarily Experiencing Those Same Emotions.

of music is expressing happiness without herself feeling happy at that moment. What is there in the music that leads to such perceptions? Obviously, music varies tremendously in complexity and in other attributes that might influence awareness of emotional expressivity. Consider something as simple as length of time. Many popular songs are less than five minutes long, while a Wagner opera might take more than four hours. Even if everything else were magically held constant, the time factor alone would likely result in different feelingful expressions. Suffice it to say that instrumentation (simple guitar accompaniment to a solo voice or a grand pipe organ); melodic (easily singable tune versus a pyrotechnical, virtuosic display), rhythmic (duple time versus mixed meters) and harmonic complexity (degree of chromaticism, atonality); and formal structure (ABA versus a multi-voice fugue) are only a few of the variables that are influential. Media Tutorials provide numerous musical examples[MT11.2–11.9].

Several reports provide extensive reviews of studies investigating musical variables and perceived emotions (e.g., Gabrielsson & Juslin, 2003; Gabrielsson & Lindström, 2001; Juslin & Laukka, 2004). In one example, Collier (2007) conducted a series of five investigations of emotional responses to music. He found that listeners could identify expressed emotions reliably along the dimensions of valence and arousal. Subtle emotions required descriptors other than valence and arousal and they were less reliably identified.

Thompson and Robitaille (1992) asked five composers to incorporate six emotion terms—joy, sorrow, excitement, dullness, anger, and peace—into six compositions, one emotion word per composition. Subsequently, 14 listeners with a moderate degree of musical training rated the extent to which each composition reflected a particular emotion. In general, there was a good match between the perceived and intended emotion. For example, melodies intended to express joy were characterized by movement through rhythmic variation, while sorrowful melodies were slow and in a minor key or used chromatic harmony. Ratings for joy were higher for joyful melodies than for any of the others; ratings for sorrow were higher for sorrowful melodies than for the others, and so on.

In contrast to the results of Thompson and Robitaille (1992), Gerling and dos Santos (2007) did not find such a close correspondence between intended and perceived emotions. In their study, six pianists performed the same piece in a manner to convey an intended emotion of their choosing, which included anger, rudeness, astuteness, sadness, transience, and intolerance. Eight listeners indicated their perceptions of the emotions expressed in the performances by free response. Listeners' responses were mapped onto Russell's (1980) two-dimensional model. The match between intended and perceived emotions was somewhat closer for discrete emotions such as anger and sadness, but overall there was only moderate correspondence.

Taking these three examples as representatives of a much larger body of literature, it is apparent that listeners can perceive emotions expressed in the music. Even in the case of Gerling and dos Santos (2007), listeners did perceive emotions expressed in the music, although they did not always match the intended ones.

An additional component that may be a part of many musical experiences is neglected frequently in the literature (though see Dutton, 2009; Huron, 2006). This additional element is one of admiration for specific elements of an outstanding performance. We may be highly impressed with the vocal quality of a singer, the extreme high register of a jazz trumpeter, or the fast guitar licks of a rock star. We may eagerly look forward to hearing some such aspect of a favorite performer, or be highly attracted to an artist heard for the first time on the basis of some amazing skill. Virtuosity may bring admiration, even envy, and with it, feelings of pleasure or excitement. Other, nonmusical aspects such as the costumes and scenery in an opera, the dancing and on-stage antics that accompany a rock performance, and so on, may also heighten the effect.

INDUCED MUSICAL EMOTIONS: THE EMOTIVIST POSITION

Nearly everyone agrees with cognitivists that listeners can perceive emotions expressed in the music without necessarily feeling those emotions. Emotivists, however, contend that listeners actually feel real emotions (henceforth referred to as musical emotions) that are induced by the music being heard (Juslin, 2009b; Figure 11.10). This position is somewhat more controversial, as not everyone agrees that listeners actually experience musical emotions.

FIGURE 11.10 | The Emotivist Position: Listeners Sometimes Actually Feel the Emotions that Are Induced by the Music They Are Hearing.

Juslin and colleagues reviewed the literature and concluded that sufficient data exist to support the notion of musical emotions (Juslin, Liljeström, Västfjäll, Barradas, & Silva, 2008). They then employed ESM to investigate emotional responses in everyday listening. College students ($N = 32$) carried a small device that emitted a signal seven times a day at random intervals.

On each beep, participants were asked to stop what they were doing and to answer 16 questions concerning three broad aspects: (1) the experienced emotion (emotion category; valence; intensity; stress), (2) the situation (physical location; activity; other persons present; occurrence of music), and—depending on whether music was indeed present and influenced the participants' emotions—(3) the characteristics of musical-emotion episodes (music type; source of music; liking, familiarity, and choice over music; importance of music for activity; possible cause of the emotion; and listening motive).

(p. 670)

Music was present in 886 of 2,424 (37%) randomly sampled episodes, and participants reported musical emotions in 64% of those.

Based on his work with colleagues over several years, Juslin (2013) created the BRECVEMA model as way to account for *how* music induces emotions:

- **B**rainstem reflexes are very rapid reactions that have an evaluative component. Ashley (2008) found that listeners could assign a happy-sad valence at 50 ms that corresponded well with similar judgments made at longer time courses.
- **R**hythmic entrainment occurs when bodily responses (e.g., head nodding or heart rate) synchronize with the rhythmic elements of the music. Clayton et al. (2005) review numerous examples of musical entrainment occurring in many places in the world.
- **E**valuative conditioning refers to the pairing of a piece of music repeatedly with a specific event that has an emotional component (e.g., *Happy Birthday to You*). When Blair and Shimp (1992) exposed listeners to music in an unpleasant context, they later found that the listeners had more negative attitudes toward a product associated with that music.
- emotional **C**ontagion occurs when a listener internally mimics the perceived emotion expressed in the music. Psychophysiological measurements supported self-reports and confirmed that listeners felt the emotions that were expressed in the music (Lundqvist, Carlsson, Hilmersson, & Juslin, 2009).
- **V**isual imagery plays a role in musical emotions when the listener imagines an internal scene that bears a close relationship to the music. Burns (2001) found that cancer patients who used a Guided Imagery and Music approach scored higher on a Profile of Mood States questionnaire.
- **E**pisodic memory occurs when music evokes a past experience and its attendant emotions. Listeners were asked to identify an autobiographical episode when music was associated with a particular experience, such that every time the same music is heard it invokes both a remembrance of the experience and the accompanying emotion (Baumgartner, 1992). Only 3 of 73 participants were not able to do so.
- **M**usic expectancy is based on Meyer's (1956) idea that emotion arises when a tendency to respond is delayed or inhibited. Listeners heard three versions of a Bach chorale which differed only by an expected, unexpected, or very unexpected final chord (Steinbeis, Koelsch, & Sloboda, 2008). Psychophysiological and neural responses confirmed emotional responses to unexpected violations.

- **A**esthetic judgments are influenced by perceptual, cognitive, and emotional inputs of such aspects as beauty, skill, novelty, style, message, expression, and emotion. Trost et al. (2012) were able to map aesthetic emotions in the brain using fMRI.

At this point, we can add six more points of refinement to our discussion.

1. Dowling and Harwood (1986) use the analogy of driving a car. If you are driving a familiar route (say from home to work), you decide where to go and then mostly unconscious and automatic processes take over. Consciously, you may be thinking about your day, listening to the radio, or talking with a passenger. Subconsciously, there are numerous schemata that occur (flipping a turn signal, stopping at a red light, etc.). The sudden interruption of your plan (say by a car pulling out in front of you) causes a disruption in your conscious activities and forces you to pay attention to your driving. Moreover, such a disruption is likely to cause an emotional reaction.

   In listening to music, a number of largely unconscious schemata are at work in your mind creating expectancies for upcoming musical events. Creative composers continuously interrupt these ongoing plans, causing emotional responses (see subsequent point 3 for more details).

2. Recall from Chapter 8 that Sloboda (1985) illustrated how cognition and affect are related in the musical experience by the analogy of hearing a joke. When you hear a joke, you must follow along by understanding the propositions being asserted, remembering details, and determining the incongruity, double meaning, or whatever makes the joke. If you "get" the joke, you may have an emotional reaction of laughter. It's also possible to get the joke without having an emotional reaction. However, the reverse is less likely— to have an emotional reaction without understanding the joke. More correctly, you may have a reaction of frustration, bewilderment, or boredom, but not laughter.

   So it is with music. A person may understand a piece of music without being moved by it (cognitivist position). Contrarily, being moved by music normally means some level of cognitive understanding, even if it is largely unconscious. The music has to make sense, at least to some degree. Finally, it is possible to have an emotional reaction that does not match the emotion expressed in the music.

3. As we learned in Chapter 8, Meyer (1973) wrote that patterns of music are implicative in that they may lead to a number of alternative realizations. Narmour (1990) further developed these ideas into the implication-realization model.

   In general, human beings dislike uncertainty; making sense of the world brings satisfaction. However, we have created many experiences (e.g., sports, games, puzzles, etc.) that allow us to experience uncertainty in safe, constrained situations. The outcome is mentally pleasurable. Music can be seen in the same way. Composers set up largely unconscious musical implications that can be realized in any number of ways. How creative the composer is in creating these implication-realization patterns (through subtle variations, unexpected surprises, etc.) may say something about his or her greatness and is the *stuff* of musical pleasure. In music, "the arousal and resolution of uncertainty is an essential basis for aesthetic-emotional experience" (Meyer, 2001, p. 353).

4. Patterns of tension/release or expectations/fulfillments do not fall along a simple continuum: less information ⇔ more information, fewer expectations ⇔ more expectations, weaker tension/release ⇔ greater tension/release. Rather, research from experimental aesthetics (Berlyne, 1971) gives us the model seen in Figure 11.11.

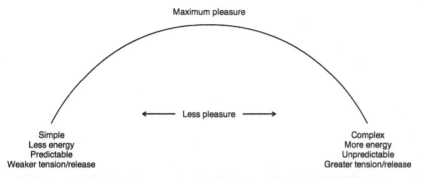

FIGURE 11.11 | Model of Musical Pleasure. Pleasure tends to increase as musical elements increase, up to an optimal point. If the element continues to increase beyond the maximal point, pleasure will begin to decrease.

As any musical element changes (for example, as the music moves from simplicity to complexity), there will be a point of maximum pleasure. When a piece of music is perceived to be either too simple or too complex, it will be less pleasurable to the listener. The point of maximum pleasure will vary for each individual and may vary for the individual on different hearings. A wide variety of factors influences how one responds to a given piece of music, including training and experience, age, gender, race, socioeconomic status, personality, mood at the time of hearing, and so on. Consider, for example, a performance of *Twinkle, Twinkle* and a performance of Mozart's "Twelve Variations on 'Ah vous dirai-je, Maman,' K. 265/300e" based on the same tune. Whether you find pleasure in the music depends: an adult may find little pleasure in the child's tune, unless he is hearing his daughter play it in her first piano recital. Likewise, a child may find little pleasure in the complexity and sophistication of the Mozart variations until such time as she has had more formal music training.

5. McMullen (1996) further developed this concept as illustrated in Figure 11.12. Our acceptance is high when activation (based on structure and energy) is at a mid-point. When activation is too high or too low we will reject a musical experience (or tend to value it less).

    Taking the activation element of energy as an example, when a musical experience is perceived to be lacking in excitement and intensity, the experience is evaluated less positively or nearer the rejection end. As energy increases, an optimum level will be reached, and the musical experience will achieve greatest acceptance. If the intensity is increased beyond the optimum level, the musical experience moves back toward the rejection end of the continuum.

6. Fridja (1988) posited a number of laws of emotion. Although he did not apply these to music specifically, most of them fit quite well. Here are selected laws, followed by a brief musical example.

    ■ The Law of Situational Meaning. Emotions arise in response to the meaning structures of a given situation; different emotions arise in response to different meaning structures. Music at a funeral is likely to aid in the expression of grief, while music at a wedding expresses joy.

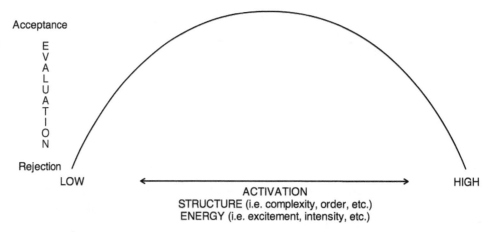

FIGURE 11.12 | A Two-Dimensional Framework of Affective/Aesthetic Responses.

- The Law of Concern. Emotions arise in response to events that are important to the individual's goals, motives, or concerns. Music at the funeral of a loved one is likely to have stronger emotional impact than music at the funeral of a stranger.
- The Law of Apparent Reality. Emotions are elicited by events appraised as real, and their intensity corresponds to the degree to which this is the case. Hearing one's favorite musician perform live is a more powerful experience than listening to a recorded performance.
- The Law of Change. Emotions are elicited not so much by the presence of favorable or unfavorable conditions but by actual or expected changes in favorable or unfavorable conditions. Music is full of changes, both gradual and sudden.
- The Law of Habituation. Continued pleasures wear off; continued hardships lose their poignancy. Popular songs are often listened to with a high degree of frequency for relatively brief periods of time. After a few weeks, the novelty of the latest "hit" tune has worn off to be replaced by a new one.
- The Law of Comparative Feeling. The intensity of emotion depends on the relationship between an event and some frame of reference against which the event is evaluated. When we hear a piece of music, frequently we compare it favorably or unfavorably to previous hearings; often, favorite pieces of music are stored in memory along with benchmark performances.
- The Law of Conservation of Emotional Momentum. Emotional events retain their power to elicit emotions indefinitely, unless counteracted by repetitive exposures that permit extinction or habituation, to the extent that these are possible. Favorite pieces of music may continue to be enjoyable over long periods of time.
- The Law of Closure. Emotions tend to be closed to judgments of relativity of impact and to the requirements of goals other than their own. A person who is passionate about a certain piece or certain type of music does not need to justify that feeling; for example, parents or teachers are not likely to convince a teenager that his or her style of music is not good.

Gabrielsson (2001, 2010, 2011; Gabrielsson & Wik, 2003) provided compelling evidence that listeners do, in fact, experience real emotions based on the music. In a project entitled *Strong Experiences with Music* (SEM), he asked hundreds of people to "describe in your own words the strongest (most intense, most profound) experience of music you have ever had" (2011, p. 7). Gabrielsson performed a content analysis of more than 1,300 written responses that revealed conclusively that listeners experienced strong emotional reactions to the music. Although many of their experiences were beyond verbal description, many intense reactions were recorded, including weeping, overwhelming waves of feelings, exhilaration, joyful intoxication, and total ecstasy. Classical music accounted for more than half the total examples mentioned, but other styles such as folk, jazz, rock, and popular music were also represented (Gabrielsson, 2011). While feelings or emotions are the most frequently mentioned reaction, some reports do not mention them at all. Other categories include physical, quasi-physical, perceptual, cognitive, existential, transcendental, and religious reactions that have important personal and social ramifications.

SEM reports suggest that relationships between expressed and induced emotions are complicated. As one group of researchers stated, "Whether a piece of music that express a particular emotion will induce the same emotion, a different emotion, or no emotion at all is not a simple issue" (Juslin et al., 2010, p. 632). They estimate that music induces emotions in 55–65% of reported listening experiences.

A THIRD VIEWPOINT: AESTHETIC TRINITY THEORY

The previous discussions of cognitivist and emotivist positions may leave the reader polarized and perhaps confused or unsatisfied. One reason is that, as demonstrated in the SEM project, both positions are possible. That is, it is entirely reasonable to assume that musical experiences both express and induce emotions. Another reason may be that neither position adequately captures the true feeling one has with intensely personal and deeply meaningful musical experiences. Konečni (2005) posited the *aesthetic trinity theory* (ATT) as a third alternative.

According to ATT, profound responses to music involve *awe, being moved*, and *thrills*. Konečni began with the notion of the sublime. Objects considered sublime are extremely rare, possess exceptional beauty, and often, though not always, have an element of physical grandeur. The notion of the sublime first occurred in response to natural wonders such as the Grand Canyon, the Alps, and Niagara Falls. Later, these feelings transferred to human artifacts such as the Great Wall of China or the Egyptian Pyramids, and eventually to artworks.

Awe is a feeling of profound reverence in the presence of the sublime. Aesthetic awe occurs with artistic expressions and represents the most pronounced, ultimate aesthetic response. In aesthetic awe, one may feel overwhelmed or overcome. Aesthetic and religious feelings can often combine in sublime spaces, such as great cathedrals like St. Peter's in Rome. One can switch off aesthetic awe simply by changing focus.

Two concomitants of aesthetic awe are being moved or touched and experiencing thrills or chills. Non-artistic events, such as observing selfless acts of generosity or kindness, may also lead to being moved. However, being moved is a particular aspect of aesthetic awe requiring a personal associative context. Konečni (2005) described thrills/chills as consisting of bodily responses such as crying, lump in the throat, shivering, a prickly feeling on the back of the neck, tingling along the spine or in the extremities, and goosebumps. (See Chapter 10 for more details.) He further specified that thrills are connected to feelings of joy and chills to fear. Being moved and experiencing thrills/chills can be reliably reported and measured (Konečni, 2005).

Konečni (2008) reviewed major published studies on whether music can induce emotions and concluded that there was weak evidence in support of the emotivist position. First, relatively few studies specifically measure the causal effects of music on personal, felt emotions. Second, imprecision in wording and conceptual, methodological, and measurement problems lead to questionable results. For example, fuzziness in written instructions to participants had a substantive effect on how they rated emotional responses to music. Finally, it is not clear whether listeners were judging the emotional expressiveness of the music or their own emotional response. In addition to analyzing published research, Konečni and colleagues conducted their own studies (Konečni, 2005; Konečni, Brown, & Wanic, 2008; Konečni et al., 2007) and determined that music may sometimes engender mild emotional responses. Music may have effects on mood, motor behavior, facial expression, and physiological responses that may in turn give rise to memories and associations that result in genuine emotions. Based on his analysis of other studies and his own research, Konečni proposed the substitution of "aesthetic awe," "being moved," and "thrills/chills" as replacements for musical emotions.

Zentner, Grandjean, and Scherer (2008) provided support for the notion that emotional response to music often go beyond "mere" emotions. In four related studies, they found that most affective responses to music could be grouped in the following categories: wonder, transcendence, tenderness, nostalgia, peacefulness, power, joyful activation, tension, and sadness. The authors concluded that, "Although there is some overlap between these terms and the terms used in categorical and dimensional models, these aesthetic emotions also differ substantially from everyday emotions" (pp. 133–134). On the basis of these findings, they developed the Geneva Emotional Music Scale (GEMS) as a means of measuring musical emotions.

Another aspect of the musical experience may lend support to Konečni's position. Consider that many musical events may last for many minutes or even hours. During that time, the music may express many different moods or emotions. There may be abrupt switches, rapid alternations, or even parallel and overlapping emotions. It is hardly likely that a listener will go through these same changes in emotion in real time.

Finally, nearly all the literature on this topic focuses on the listener. What about performers and composers? Some performers may claim that like method actors, they actually feel the emotions they are trying to express. Others might counter that if one were experiencing true grief, for example, it would be extremely difficult to play an instrument or sing. As in the previous paragraph, how could members of an orchestra playing a Mahler symphony, for example, continue to experience true emotions in such dizzying profusion in a sustained manner for nearly an hour or more all the while having complete control over their instruments?

Anecdotally, we have heard of a composer sitting down to write a popular song in the heat of inspiration, finishing it all at one sitting. Dolly Parton (1995), for example, recorded that she wrote her hit song *Coat of Many Colors* on the back of a dry-cleaning receipt while riding on a tour bus. However, emotions, as defined at the outset of this chapter, are relatively transitory and most longer compositions take some time to complete, even days, weeks, or months. A composer may write a short piece during an emotional outburst, but it is doubtful that a given emotion could be sustained long enough to complete a major work. As just one example of the possible disconnect between the compositional process and the emotional expression inherent in a work, consider that Tchaikovsky's Sixth Symphony in b minor, subtitled *Pathétique*, is dark and gloomy throughout much of its length. However, in the throes of composing it he wrote a letter to his nephew Vladimir Davidov, in which he stated, "I must tell you how happy I am about my work" (Tchaikovsky, 1906, p. 702). By numerous accounts (e.g., www.kennedy-center.org/artist/composition/2138), the period of composing this melancholy work was generally a pleasant, happy time for the composer.

Konečni's aesthetic trinity theory shares some features with three other influential ideas—*peak experiences* developed by Maslow (1968a), *flow* as described by Csikszentmihalyi (1990, 2014), and research on *Strong Experiences in Music* conducted by Gabrielsson (2001). Peak experiences, covered more fully in Chapter 14, are mountaintop experiences. Words like bliss, rapture, and transcendent ecstasy, are used to describe moments that stay in the memory for a lifetime and help to shape the person in profound ways. Music is one of the most common ways that people have peak experiences (Maslow, 1968a).

Flow deals with exhilaration, creativity, and total involvement and it occurs when the individual is completely engaged in an optimal experience. During flow, it is as if nothing else exists or matters. "The best moments usually occur when a person's body or mind is stretched to its limits in a voluntary effort to accomplish something difficult and worthwhile" (Csikszentmihalyi, 1990, p. 3). An optimal experience is achieved when the level of challenge is met with an equal level of skill. An expert engaged in a simple task is likely to be bored, while a novice faced with a challenge beyond her skill level is likely to be frustrated. Csikszentmihalyi frequently refers to music and musicians when describing flow, and, in a subsequent book (1993), he quotes a pianist (p. 181) and a composer (p. 183), who give descriptions of flow experiences in music.

Previously, we discussed Gabrielsson's (2001) research on Strong Experiences in Music (SEM). Recall that he asked participants to describe the strongest, most intense experience of music they had ever had. Although specific emotion words were used, "many respondents frankly stated that their SEM was impossible to describe by words . . . the experience seemed ineffable" (p. 447). This, along with rich descriptions quoted in his review of SEM and the connections Gabrielsson himself makes to both flow and peak experiences, appear to hint at an overarching experience that goes beyond a specific emotion.

MUSICAL EMOTIONS IN EVERYDAY EXPERIENCES

The bulk of the research conducted on musical emotions has utilized music or experiences that are not common occurrences. Thus, the music itself is mostly art music and when it is not, the context of the study is frequently in laboratory settings or other special circumstances. The question naturally arises: does the music we encounter in everyday living elicit different emotions than special musical experiences like a concert or music we choose to focus our attention on at a given moment? Although there is no clear dividing line between everyday and non-everyday events, everyday music listening generally occurs while we are occupied in some other activity such as washing dishes, walking the dog, exercising, and so on.

Sloboda (2010) developed ten propositions based on an extensive review of research on emotions in everyday musical experiences. Compared to non-everyday musical experiences, everyday emotions to music tend to:

1. be of low intensity. By definition, everyday experiences are routine, mundane, and happen more frequently (i.e., every day) than special, extraordinary events. Thus, emotional responses are likely to be more low-key during music listening experiences that occur more commonly.
2. be unmemorable on average. Important events, accompanied by powerful emotions, are the ones we are most likely to remember. It is not surprising that we would not remember the music we listened to while we washed the dishes or read the newspaper last week.

3. be short-lived and multiple. For most people, the daily routine includes a series of brief, fragmented music listening experiences as they drive to work, shop in a store, watch television, have the radio on while getting ready for bed, and so on.

4. include more negative emotions. This proposition may seem counter-intuitive. However, it refers to circumstances that we may find ourselves in when we are forced to listen to music we did not choose. This could happen while on telephone hold, waiting in a dentist's office, or hearing the next-door neighbor kids' garage band rehearsal. As is seen in the next proposition, positive emotions predominate, but everyday listening has the potential to include some negative listening experiences.

5. be more self-referring. People who describe their everyday listening experiences list emotions that refer to how they feel (happy, relaxed, and calm are most often cited) much more than they name emotions that refer to others (e.g., admiration). This is likely to be so because a great deal of everyday music is anonymous in the sense that the listener often does not know the names of the composer, the performers, or the piece. Contrarily, if one attends a concert by a popular artist, the reverse is true.

6. reflect and be influenced by personal emotional meanings of a nonmusical context. If a couple in love are eating in a restaurant where music is playing in the background, their focus is likely to be more on themselves than on the music. This does not mean that the music has no effect. It means that the emotional experience is colored strongly by the nonmusical context. If I am working on my taxes or sitting in the waiting room of the car repair shop with music playing in the background, my emotional state is likely to be more determined by how much I owe in taxes or how large the repair bill will be than by the music.

7. prioritize basic rather than complex emotions. As stated in proposition 3, everyday listening experiences tend to come in snatches here and there throughout the day. Thus, the circumstances are not ideal for an exploration of subtle or complex emotions. Rather, these brief listening events are likely to elicit basic emotions that lay on the surface.

8. be elicited by retrospective self-report. The bulk of the research literature on everyday musical emotions comes from participants who describe their experiences after the fact. An alternative is the previously described ESM, in which participants are cued at random intervals by pager or cell phone to describe what they are doing at that moment and how they are feeling. Although this shortens the time lag, ESM still relies on self-report. Some progress is being made in ambulatory assessment of physiological responses, as described in Chapter 10, but the connection between heart rate and other psychophysiological variables to emotions is not a linear one. Thus, researchers must still rely on a participant's ability to describe accurately their emotional responses to music.

9. be listener focused. At a special music listening event, say while attending an opera, a primary focus is likely to be on the music. In everyday listening experiences, the music is most often secondary. When participants describe their everyday listening experiences, they talk much more about themselves (e.g., what they were doing, how they felt, etc.) than about the music. If we listened in on two patrons talking immediately after the opera performance, we would probably hear them talk about the music, the singers, and other aspects about the performance. If we followed the same two people after they had been shopping in a grocery store for some time, it is unlikely we would overhear them talking about the music they had just heard while buying groceries.

10. arise from task demands rather than musical attributes. In a previous review, Sloboda, Lamont, & Greasley, 2009) identified four functions of everyday listening when the listener made a choice of what music to hear. Music was either distracting (diverting attention from a boring task), energizing (focusing attention on a task), entraining (coordinating movements with the music), or enhancing meaning (adding significance to a task).

On the basis of these ten propositions, it is safe to say that in general musical emotions in everyday listening experiences are somewhat different from those we experience in special music listening circumstances. This does not mean they are unimportant; rather, it shows that music can play a number of roles in our lives. The results of one study of everyday listening using ESM were discussed previously in support of the emotivist position (Juslin et al., 2008). In another ESM study designed to investigate the prevalence of chills during everyday music listening, researchers surveyed 106 undergraduate students ten times per day for a week via their cell phones (Nusbaum, Silvia, Beaty, Burgin, Hodges, & Kwapil, 2014). Participants were listening to music during 22% of the completed surveys, and 14% of their music listening experiences included chills. From the total group of participants, 79 (81%) experienced chills, with the average number being 3.73 chill episodes. Factors that increased the likelihood of a chill episode included self-selected music, closely attentive listening, music that had personal meaning, and feeling happy or sad but not worried. Even though it may seem as if we are not paying particular attention to much of the music in our environment, we would surely notice its absence if it were suddenly removed and undoubtedly the quality of our daily experiences would change significantly.

CONCLUSION

Although the cognitivist and emotivist positions have been presented separately, most scholars would recognize the validity of both viewpoints. There are many excellent reviews that consider both perception and induction of musical emotions (e.g., Juslin, 2009, 2019; Juslin & Laukka, 2004; Juslin et al., 2010; Sloboda & Juslin, 2001, 2009). Furthermore, according to Konečni, whose ideas share similarities with Maslow, Csikszentmihalyi, and Gabrielsson, the experiences of aesthetic awe, being moved, and thrills/chills may represent the deepest and most profound musical experiences. We discuss how musicians express emotions in performance in Chapter 13.

To musical variables involved in musical emotions, such as tempo, tonality, and so on, we must add a host of personal attributes (e.g., age gender, training, etc.), and these must then be placed in a socio-cultural situation. Many musical experiences occur within social structures that are understood by those who have been indoctrinated into that musical culture. For example, in a classical violin recital it is considered inappropriate to clap between movements of a multi-movement piece. At a jazz ensemble concert, however, applause is expected following an improvised solo. Someone naïve about both traditions would be confused by the differences in acceptable behavior. Beyond this simple example, however, there are complex behavioral expectations that relate more directly to the perception and experience of musical emotions. Audiences at a rock concert are free to express themselves quite actively during the performance while patrons at a symphony concert must restrain emotional responses until the ends of pieces. Even these cursory descriptions of personal, musical, and social variables are enough to suggest the incredible complexity attending perceptions of emotion in music. Philosophers and psychologists have written voluminously in an attempt to account for how it is that music conveys emotions.

Consider Jane and Mike at the opera a final time (Fig. 8.18). Or, substitute any musical experience you like—a student alone in a music practice room, thousands of people at a stadium rock concert, and on and on through the limitless possibilities of musical interactions. In each case, one can easily imagine that some emotional aspects of the experience might be perceptual only. Mike, for example, might perceive that the tenor is expressing terror at being found out by the Duke, but he, himself, might feel nothing of the sort. Other aspects of the experience might, indeed, induce emotional responses as Jane finds herself weeping when the heroine sings that she would rather die than live without her husband. Finally, while Jane might be able to identify specific emotions that occurred during the opera, her overarching feelings may be those of awe and wonder; she may have been moved in a profound way that superseded particular, transitory emotions. If it was a particularly powerful and meaningful experience, in later years she may remember the feeling of aesthetic awe more so than any individual emotions.

Scholars and researchers will likely continue to debate and study emotional responses to music for the foreseeable future. In the meantime, even if we do not fully understand it, the rest of us can enjoy the music, each with our own personalized emotional experiences.

DISCUSSION QUESTIONS

1. Why do you think the topic of emotions has been so neglected in psychology, generally, and music psychology, specifically?
2. Describe a time when your fight or flight response mechanisms were activated by a non-musical experience (e.g., with elevated heart rate, sweaty palms, etc.). Can you think of musical experiences that led to similar bodily reactions?
3. Provide a musical example for each of Huron's six response types from the ITPRA theory of expectation.
4. What are strengths and weaknesses of each of the approaches for measuring emotional responses: self-report, behavioral, and bodily reactions?
5. Suppose you were asked to head up a research team charged with studying emotional responses to music. Which measures would you use? How would you design your study?
6. Do you agree with the cognitivist position? Do you agree with emotivists? Does the aesthetic trinity theory seem like a reasonable alternative? How reasonable is it that all three may be part of the same musical experience?
7. If you were asked to perform a simple melody such as *Mary Had a Little Lamb* to express different emotions such as joy, grief, anger, and sadness, how would you perform differently each time?
8. Some researchers have found a good correspondence between intended and perceived emotions, while others have not. Can you describe musical situations that support both positions? That is, have you experienced a close correspondence between what you think the composer intended and how you felt? Have you experienced different emotions from what you think the composer intended?
9. Do you think the emotivist position is reasonable for performers? That is, can performers experience the emotions they are expressing and still have enough control to perform?
10. Which of the three positions described in this chapter resonate most closely with your own musical experiences, or do you subscribe to some combination of all three?

Part III

Being Musical

WHAT does it mean to be musical? What are musicians like? In Chapter 12: The Musical Person, we examine five related issues. The first of these is the extent to which our musicality is inherited or acquired. There is evidence to support both positions and the general conclusion is that musicality is a combination of genetic traits expressed within particular environmental circumstances, such as learning opportunities. Anecdotally, many people may attribute certain personality traits to musicians, even ascribing different characteristics to singers, violinists, rock guitarists, and so on. We look at the data on these issues and describe the prevailing views on musicians' personalities. We will also consider what connections there may be between music and religious or spiritual experiences. Another important topic is the role music plays in shaping one's self-identity. Finally, we discuss the preferences we have for singing or playing a particular instrument and for the music we enjoy the most.

Making music is at the core of being a musician. In Chapter 13: Musical Performance, we examine motor, cognitive, and expressive skills. In motor skills, we discuss neuromotor and motor aspects of music making, the acquisition of motor skills, audio-motor systems, and quantity of practice. In cognitive skills, the topics are quality of practice, mental rehearsal, music reading, and metacognition, self-regulation, motivation, and self-efficacy. Under expressive skills, we consider body movement and musical cues for expressiveness, along with creativity.

How we acquire musical skills is critically important. In Chapter 14: Music Teaching and Learning, we discuss Freudian psychotherapy, and contributions from behavioral, humanistic, Gestalt, developmental, cognitive, and social psychology. None of these viewpoints has a final or complete answer, but each contributes to a deeper understanding of how we learn music. Once we have a better grasp on how people learn music, we can then design better instructional approaches as we endeavor to teach music.

Music plays a central and critical role in health. Chapter 15: Music and Health is organized into three sections. Music therapy, music medicine, and performing arts medicine are distinct approaches with overlapping aspects. Music therapists use music to accomplish personalized goals in a therapeutic setting. Physicians and other health care professionals use music to aid patients who are dealing with pain and anxiety associated with illness. Other physicians specialize in treating performing musicians with profession-related problems such as hearing, vocal, bodily, or psychosocial health issues.

Although musicians may spend time alone while practicing or composing, music is an intensely social activity. In Chapter 16: Music in Social Contexts, we take a broad look at music in society, such as in the home, in the workplace, and in politics, religion, the media, and so on. Next, we examine reflections of society in music in terms of the social behaviors among performing musicians and among music listeners. Finally, we investigate the influence music has on social behaviors and how it influences thoughts and attitudes among members of a society.

Chapter 12

The Musical Person

WHAT do a rock singer/guitarist, a jazz drummer, an erhu player, and an organist have in common (Fig. 12.1)? The obvious answer, of course, is that they are all musicians. The purpose of this chapter is to investigate five important issues related to being a musical person. The first of these issues has to do with whether some people are born musicians or whether it is a learned skill. Do we inherit musical talent or do we develop it? The second issue concerns musical personality. Do musicians have a distinctive personality, different from those less musical? Do all musicians share certain personality traits or do these vary among, say, singers and instrumentalists? The third issue involves religious and spiritual aspects. What connections are there between music and religious or spiritual experiences? Are musicians more religious or spiritual than nonmusicians? The fourth issue concerns musical identity. What does it mean to think of oneself as a *musician*? Are there relationships between one's self-identity and group identity, such as being a member of a band or choir? The final issue is one of musical preferences. What influences cause people to choose certain musical experiences over others? As is nearly self-evident, these five issues overlap somewhat, so that although they are considered separately, the reader is encouraged to meld each successive topic into an overall conception of the musical person.

IS MUSICALITY INHERITED OR ACQUIRED?

Chapter 3: How We Came to be Musical provided arguments for an evolutionary basis for human musicality. If, indeed, there is an evolutionary basis for musicality, obviously some aspects are genetically influenced. The discussion in Chapter 2 on the nature of human musicality indicated that we are not controlled by instincts, so just as obviously, certain aspects of musicality are not genetically dictated, but must be learned. The extent to which human musicality is inherited or acquired has been and continues to be a subject of interest.

Genetic Factors in Musicality

To what extent do genes predispose us to be musical? The issue of nature versus nurture is always a difficult one because musicality consists of physical, physiological, cognitive, and dispositional traits in a complex series of interactions. That some aspects are genetic, others dependent on environment, and many on genetic-environmental interactions is assumed. Recall the discussions of absolute pitch in Chapter 7 and of prodigies in Chapter 9. In both cases, it is apparent that genetic predispositions must be expressed in nurturing experiences

FIGURE 12.1 | What Do a Rock Singer/Guitarist, a Jazz Drummer, an Organist, and an Erhu Player Have in Common?

in order for full development to take place. In other words, both genes and life experiences are necessary. No accomplished musician was simply born that way and did not need learning experiences. Conversely, hard work can improve almost anyone's musical skills, however, there may be limitations on what one can achieve. In contrast to studying those with special musical abilities, one can also study the absence of such traits. Recall from chapter 9 the term congenital amusia, used to refer to the fact that some persons are born with deficits in musical processing (Peretz, 2001). An examination of this and other cognitive impairments based on known genetic defects, such as savant or Williams Syndrome, provides insights into the heritability of musicality.

A brief look at the fundamentals of genetics may help to explain the inheritance of factors that influence musicality. Each normal human cell contains 46 chromosomes arranged into 23 pairs (Dixon-Salazar & Gleeson, 2010); see Figure 12.2. Approximately 20,000 genes encode the information that determines the presence or absence of specific traits in any individual. The human genome, our complete set of DNA, includes approximately 3 million DNA base pairs.

Genetic instructions are stored in chemical compounds known as deoxyribonucleic acid (DNA) that are "read" by messenger ribonucleic acid (RNA) (Watson, 1968). The genetic influence on any given trait may be determined by the specific chemical content of a given gene pair, in many instances by the interaction of a number of gene pairs, by the order of the gene pairs, and by the environmental (i.e., lived) circumstances in which the gene was expressed. If one person's gene pairs were passed under an electron microscope at the rate of one per second, it would take 200 years to identify the order in which they are lined up for that individual (Fincher, 1976).

Given even this limited information about genetics, one may quickly see the enormous complexity of a question such as the inheritance of musical attributes. The Human Genome Project (2017), begun in the 1970s, was completed in 2003. Although researchers have successfully identified all the genes and chemical base pairs in human DNA, analysis will continue for many years. In spite of the rapid progress in genetics, scientists know the function of only about 20% of the genes (Järvelä, 2019). They have traced single-base DNA differences to diseases such as diabetes or arthritis and are working on more complex diseases such as cystic fibrosis, but linking genetic instructions to sophisticated behaviors such as language or music is still a work in progress.

Early work relied on correlational studies to determine relationships between family backgrounds and incidences of musicality (e.g., Heymans & Wiersma, 1954; Shuter, 1966; Shuter-Dyson & Gabriel, 1981). Some studies involved twin pairs (Coon & Cavey, 1989). More recently, however, genomics research is providing more direct evidence of genetic

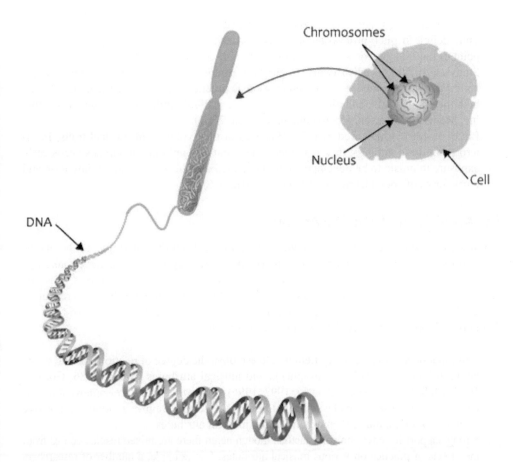

Chromosomes

Nucleus

Cell

DNA

FIGURE 12.2 | Inside the Nucleus of Each Cell Are 46 Chromosomes Arranged in 23 Pairs. A gene is a sequence along the strand of dna that encodes specific genetic information.

influences. In a comprehensive review, Järvelä (2019) cited numerous studies to support the contention that musical abilities are a combination of both genes and environment. Genes affecting inner-ear development, biochemical systems, learning, and memory influence music aptitude, listening, performing, perception, and practice. However, genes are only expressed in lived experiences. Here are a few examples of individual studies:

- Finnish researchers tested 234 members of 15 different family groups for musical aptitude. They found that heritability averaged 48% for three combined music aptitude tests (Pulli et al., 2008). Ukkola-Vuoti et al. (2011, 2013) obtained similar results using music aptitude tests and indicators of musical creativity.
- Another group of researchers found genetic associations with musical ability when they tested 1,008 individuals from 73 family units in Mongolia (Park et al., 2012).
- Oikkonen et al. (2015) tested 767 individuals in 76 family units for music perception abilities and determined that genes play an important role in the development of auditory pathways important in music perception.
- Oikkonen, Onkamo, Järvelä, and Kanduri (2016) conducted a meta-analysis of 105 published studies and identified candidate genes for musical traits. Genetic factors important to learning and memory are also fundamental to musical abilities.

■ Peretz, Cummings, and Dubé (2007) found that 39% of first-degree relatives had the same deficit in pitch processing skills as a proband (the person serving as the starting point of familial genetic studies) compared to only 3% in control families.

■ Studying 10,500 Swedish twins, researchers examined associations between musical ability and music practice and found that music practice was 40–70% heritable. That is, both the ability and inclination to practice music is highly influenced by genetics (Mosing, Madison, Pedersen, Kuja-Halkola, & Ullén, 2014).

■ Liu et al. (2016) identified genetic influences in the evolution of musical traits. In interpreting these findings, they concluded that, "musical aptitude in humans needs early exposure to music to be developed and that is mediated through teaching, imitation and other forms of social learning" (Liu et al., 2016, p. 6).

The Acquisition of Musical Attributes

If a musical person is found to have come from a musical family, could this not be due as much to the musical home environment in which he grew up as to his genetic make-up? For example, several of J. S. Bach's children grew up to be successful musicians. Was this because musical genes were passed down from father to son, because the children grew up in household filled with music, or both? One can use the following conclusions drawn from the literature in support of the acquisition of musical attributes.

■ A number of researchers have attempted to establish the degree of relationship that exists between home and social environments and musical attributes (Brand, 1986; Gordon, 1967, 1968; Parker, 1961; Zdzinski, 1992, 1996). While the results are somewhat inconclusive, a generalized conclusion might be that the results support a moderate, positive influence of home musical environments on musical attributes.

■ Strong support for environmental factors, though again there are mixed results, comes from the effects of practice on various musical attributes. For example, a number of researchers have provided data in support of the hypothesis that pitch discrimination can be improved with training (Andrews & Diehl, 1970; Lundin, 1963; Lundin & Allen, 1962; Pflederer, 1964).

■ Thousands of private and classroom music teachers believe that performance skills do improve with training. Fortunately, there are data to support such a hypothesis (Ericsson, Krampe, & Tesch-Römer, 1993; Howe, Davidson, & Sloboda, 1998; Sloboda, Davidson, Howe, & Moore, 1996; also see Chapter 13).

In an interesting counterpart to the foregoing studies, however, Ullén, Hambrick, and Mosing (2016) found that deliberate practice was insufficient to account for performance progress (see Chapter 13 for more details on deliberate practice). They developed the multifactorial gene-environment interaction model (MGIM) to indicate that expert music performers are developed through genetic instructions, deliberate practice, and gene-environment interactions. In a supporting study involving 10,500 twins, researchers found that genetic influences accounted for 69% of practice time in males and 41% in females (Mosing et al., 2014).

■ Less conclusive are the results of studies in which researchers measured the effects of training on the scores of standardized music tests. In general, the results from these studies indicate minimal effects of training on test scores (Gordon, 1961, 1968; Heller, 1962; Tarrell, 1965). One reason for such a conclusion may be the lack of specific training geared toward specific tasks of the test at hand. Another reason may be the relatively brief time lapse between multiple administrations of a given test. Most persons would probably show greater musical gains because of training over a period of years than over a period of months. Furthermore, the effects of training will be different for aptitude than for achievement tests. *Aptitude tests* measure one's potential for learning; *achievement tests* measure what one has actually learned.

Summary of the Inheritance/Acquisition of Musical Attributes

As stated previously, a commonly accepted solution to the discrepancy between data in support of inheritance or acquisition of musical attributes is the premise that behavior is a function of the organism and the situation (Fig. 12.3). Thus, behavioral traits are subject to modification by genetic as well as environmental factors. No less an authority than the former president of the Human Genome Project, Walter Bodmer, stated that "musical aptitude . . . is inextricably bound up both with environmental influences and a person's genetic heritage" (Bodmer & McKie, 1994, p. 5). Several excellent reviews support Bodmer's contention (Järvelä, 2019; Mosing, Peretz, & Ullén, 2018; Yi, McPherson, Peretz, Berkovic, & Wilson, 2014; Yi, McPherson, & Wilson, 2018).

An analogy may help to illustrate the premise: Corn seeds cannot produce wheat plants. However, environmental factors, such as soil acidity, amounts of rainfall and sunlight, or presence of disease, will determine whether a corn seed produces a tall, healthy plant or a weak, spindly one. Likewise, to take the position that either inheritance or the environment is solely responsible for musical attributes does not seem tenable. It is difficult to imagine that a brilliant performer, composer, music therapist, or music educator could simply emerge without years of study and practice. Conversely, it is equally as difficult to accept the notion that a musician needs only more practice to become great. Quite clearly, most, if not all, musical attributes are a result of inherited characteristics, realized in a particular set of environmental circumstances.

The Relationship of Musical Attributes to Other Human Attributes

Several studies have been conducted to determine whether there are any significant and meaningful relationships between musical attributes and other human attributes. Examples of

FIGURE 12.3 | This Saxophonist's Musical Abilities Are a Combination of What She Inherited and What She Has Learned. (Incidentally, you may notice the small device on her right shoulder. This is a dosebadge used to collect sound levels she is experiencing in the practice room. For more information on music-related hearing loss, see Chapter 15.)

the latter are aural acuity, intelligence, sex, race, and abilities in the other arts. Regardless of the criterion, the results are mixed and therefore inconclusive. It should be emphasized that research results are as much a function of the test used as they are of the criterion. Thus, the results may be due to the relative inadequacy of the music tests. Nevertheless, one could reasonably assume, without a specific research base, that persons who are better auditory learners can be successful in learning music, at least as a sophisticated listener. It is also reasonable to assume that persons who achieve well academically will probably achieve well in music. Any differences found between sexes and among races likely can be attributed primarily to cultural and social phenomena. Generalized conclusions are as follows.

- Farnsworth (1941) concluded that aural acuity is related to musical ability, while Sherbon (1975) reached the opposite conclusion.
- Phillips (1976) found a relatively high degree of relationship between musical ability and intelligence, while Gordon (1968) found only moderate or low correlations between the same two factors. See Robinson, 1983, for a review of additional studies.
- Butzlaff (2000) conducted a meta-analysis of 24 correlational studies and found a range of correlations ranging from $r = -0.19$ to $r = 0.65$, with a median of $r = 0.17$ between music instruction and standardized measures of reading ability. Douglas and Willatts (1994) obtained results showing an association between musical ability and literacy skills. Slevc and Miyake (2006) found that musical ability was a positive aid in acquiring a second language.
- Vaughn (2000) reviewed 20 studies and found a small, positive relationship between engagement in music studies and mathematical achievement. Note that such a relationship does not mean that one caused the other, only that they are related to a small degree.
- Those who have studied the problem agree that the major differences between males and females, beyond early childhood developmental differences such as found by Petzold (1963) and Shuter-Dyson (1979) in terms of musical attributes are the result of socio-cultural influences (Abeles & Porter, 1978; Bentley, 1966).
- A similar conclusion has been reached in terms of racial differences in musical attributes: while some differences have been identified, they have, for the most part, been ascribed to differences in cultural backgrounds (Drake, 1957; Woods & Martin, 1943).
- Only one researcher found a significant relationship between musical ability and other artistic abilities (Alexander, 1954); others found little or no relationship between the two (Strong, 1959; Williams, Winter, & Wood, 1938).

Thus, data support the notion that both genetic inheritance and learning experiences help to shape eventual musicianship. Furthermore, there are only moderate relationships between musicality and other attributes. Finally, the dates on many of the studies in this section indicate that this topic has not received much attention in recent years.

THE MUSICAL PERSONALITY

For many years, psychologists have engaged in the study of personality. Personality encompasses all of human behavior and includes such personal traits as one's abilities, character, opinions and beliefs, attitudes, emotional responses, temperament, and cognitive style. Personality is that which gives a person identity, wholeness, and uniqueness (Caprara & Cervone, 2000). Some aspects of personality may be inherited and others acquired (*APA Dictionary of Psychology*, 2007; Sutin, McCrae, & Costa, 2011). Often psychologists use adjectival descriptors in paired antonyms to identify specific traits, such as introverted/extroverted, relaxed/tense, and practical/imaginative.

Psychologists have developed numerous assessment tools to determine a person's personality characteristics. *The Twentieth Mental Measurement Yearbook* (Carlson, Geisinger, & Jonson, 2017) lists dozens of such tests, including the *California Test of Personality, (Cattell) 16 Personality Factor Questionnaire, Early School Personality Inventory, Gordon Personal Profile-Inventory, Minnesota Multiphasic Personality Inventory-2*, and *Myers-Briggs Type Indicator*. A commonly used approach is the five-factor model (FFM) consisting of broad dimensions of Neuroticism, Extraversion, Openness to Experience, Agreeableness, and Conscientiousness (Sutin et al., 2011). Persons with relatively stable personality traits are said to be of a certain personality type. However, with something as complicated as human personality, it is understandable that there are limitations inherent in a pencil-and-paper test. Personality traits may change over time and often depend on subtle interactions with other human beings. For example, a person may be quite shy and retiring in one social setting and very outgoing and garrulous in another.

These difficulties, the complexity and diversity of musical behaviors, and the paucity of research on musical personalities are perhaps the main reasons there is no clear profile of what personality traits might characterize musicians. So many different personality traits have been identified in musicians that many have said that musicians have a heterogeneous or varied personality. Schleuter (1971) and Thayer (1972) found that personality factors were not systematically related to either musical achievement or aptitude. Kemp (1982), however, felt that these studies were in error and that musicians have instead a polymorphous or many-faceted personality. He contended that all musicians share a common core of traits that he considered musicianship-linked. The core of traits Kemp (1996) identified in musicians included introversion, independence, sensitivity, anxiety, and psychological androgyny.

By introversion, Kemp did not mean timid withdrawal, but inner strength, resourcefulness, self-sufficiency, and richly diversified thought processes; he characterized musicians as bold introverts, able to spend time alone in practice and in creating a vivid internal sound world, yet able to muster the strength to perform in public. He obtained data (1982) indicating that all types of musicians (e.g., student musicians, adult amateurs, professionals) commonly shared these traits.

Another important personality trait of musicians is independence. Exemplifying the boldness aspect of the bold introvert, musicians possess characteristics of originality, imagination, and a preference for complex ideas. Unlike the consistency of introversion found across the age span, younger students are more likely to be dependent and somewhat submissive. However, as they make their way toward higher levels of musical achievement, they become more dominant and independent.

Kemp (1996) presented considerable data of his own and others to support the contention that sensitivity is a core trait of musicians. Sensitivity refers to imagination, outgoingness, and intuition. In the context of introversion, musicians may conceal these traits from others, yet they serve as important motivating factors in seeking out rich possibilities in aesthetic experiences.

Anxiety is a core trait that all musicians must confront. Of all the common traits, perhaps anxiety has received the most attention. Commonly, it is divided further into two types. *Trait anxiety* is a long-term personality characteristic, while *state anxiety* has to do with nervousness in an immediate situation. Stage fright or the stress of performing publicly is perhaps the major form of state anxiety among musicians. It is reasonable to assume that a certain amount of stage fright "comes with the territory" and that many musicians are able to overcome it. Performance anxiety is dealt with in Chapter 14, but at this point, it is perhaps sufficient to remark that anxiety can either enhance or disrupt musical performances. Beginning with first

228

encounters with teachers or conductors, through seemingly endless auditions and juried/refereed performances, to the life of a concertizing artist, musicians must learn how to handle this critical aspect of the profession.

According to Kemp (1985), the final core personality trait of musicians is psychological androgyny. This term refers to the fact that male musicians are more sensitive than nonmusician males, often assumed to be a feminine trait, and that female musicians are more aloof and self-sufficient than female nonmusicians, a trait more often found in males. Having a successful career as a musician demands that males and females alike must be strong and independent, yet sensitive and intuitive.

Although musicians appear to share core personality traits of introversion, independence, sensitivity, anxiety, and psychological androgyny, researchers have also investigated differences among various types of musicians. In one study, Kemp (1981) obtained data about the personality traits of members of 16 major symphony orchestras. Often string players were at opposite ends of a continuum from brass players. String players tended to perceive themselves and to be perceived by others as unathletic, insecure, and introverted while brass players had more of an athletic, self-confident, and extroverted image and self-image. The remaining orchestra members were in the middle, with woodwind players nearer to string players in personality and percussionists nearer to brass players (Figure 12.4). Davies (1978)

FIGURE 12.4 | What Role Does a Chosen Instrument Play in Shaping the Personalities of String, Woodwind, Brass, and Percussion Performers? (Note that the bassoonist is playing in front of a sound shield. See chapter 15 for a discussion of sound shields and hearing protection.)

reported similar findings. Lipton (1987) asked 227 professional musicians from 16 orchestras in the United States and Canada to rate themselves and members of the other sections in the orchestra. He found that strings and brass were consistently at polar opposites and, in general, his results corroborated those of Davies and Kemp.

One issue that has not been explored adequately is whether different personality types are drawn to certain instruments or musical styles, or whether playing an instrument or in a particular group for a long time influences the personality. With regard to the latter, consider the culture or social structure surrounding being a classical guitarist or a rock guitarist. As a young musician struggling to fit in and to find acceptance, perhaps either consciously or unconsciously one adopts a persona that resonates with the surrounding group. Dyce and O'Connor (1994) found that rock and country musicians were more arrogant, dominant, extraverted, open to experience, and neurotic than university males. Similarly, Gillespie and Myors (2000) found that rock and popular musicians tended toward a profile of high Neuroticism and Openness to Experience, average Extraversion, and low Agreeableness and Conscientiousness.

Builione and Lipton (1983) found that singers were found to be more extroverted than instrumentalists, perhaps because they are required to project themselves more directly rather than through an instrument. Keyboard musicians were characterized by extroversion and paradoxically by conservatism and submissiveness. One possible explanation, though one of pure speculation, is that the former trait might be more pronounced in solo performers, while the latter two are more appropriate for accompanists and chamber musicians. Music educators tend to be intelligent, assertive, less interested in social approval, and somewhat defensive. It must be remembered that these differences are all within the relative constraints of the overall polymorphous profile of introversion, independence, sensitivity, anxiety, and psychological androgyny.

MacLellan (2011) administered the Myers-Briggs Type Indicator (MBTI) to 355 members of a high school choir, band, or orchestra. Differences were found among the ensemble members and between them and MBTI norms for high school students. For example, choir members were more Extraverted than orchestra members and all the musicians were more likely to be Intuitive and Feeling. Regarding a previous discussion, it would be interesting to determine whether singers were more extraverted prior to being in choir or being in choir enhanced the extraverted part of their personality.

In a dissenting view, Woody (1999a) felt that there was very little empirical support for the notion that musicians have unique personality characteristics. In a critique of the existing literature, he suggested that rather than comparing musicians to the general population, they should be compared with highly accomplished persons in other disciplines. Likewise, researchers have neglected the different styles of music and the social contexts in which they occur. For example, social and economic reinforcers are different for symphony musicians and rock band members. A third omission is the lack of consideration for degree of success in the musicians studied. Those who have reached a high level of success are in a much different situation than those who are still struggling to achieve and Woody contended that this has a bearing on personality. Cultural differences among musicians from different countries have not been explored. As a result of these limitations, Woody's conclusion was that current conceptions of musicians' personalities are based on inadequate and unpersuasive research. He called for a much more sophisticated line of investigation.

RELIGIOUS AND SPIRITUAL ASPECTS

Religious and spiritual aspects of a musical person are related to but not the same as musical personality and musical identity. Therefore, this discussion is placed between the two in an autonomous section. The topic of music in connection with religion and spirituality has spawned an enormous literature. Some of this literature deals with the music itself in a musicological (e.g., Bohlman, 2005, 2006) or ethnomusicological (Becker, 2001, 2004; Penman & Becker, 2009) sense. Much of it is represented in the religious (e.g., Brown, 2008) and philosophical literature (e.g., Foley, 2005). There are more specialized concentrations, for example on music education (Boyce-Tillman, 2014; McCarthy, 2009; Palmer, 1995, 2006, 2010) or music therapy (Bonny, 2001; Magill, 2002). A general consensus of this literature is that music and musicians have strong connections with religion and spirituality. Avoiding a lengthy discursive on distinctions between the two, for shorthand we will say that religion involves a belief in and worship of a higher power. Interactions with the divine are frequently in the form of codified or ritualized worship, such as in Judaism, Christianity, Islam, Hinduism, or Buddhism. Spirituality is a concern for non-material aspects of life such as the soul or human spirit. Discussions of spirituality often include such terms as transcendence, ecstasy, and supernatural.

In contrast to the voluminous literature alluded to in the previous paragraph, references to religion and spirituality are considerably more limited in music psychology. In this book, scattered references to religion and/or spirituality are made in Chapters 2, 4, 11, and 16. Here, our focus in this brief section will be on what music psychologists have to offer in terms of research findings related to connections between music and religion or spirituality.

Sloboda (2000, 2005) acknowledged that music "affords" worship, that is, music provides a structural context that facilitates worship. The next step, he contended, is for music psychologists to demonstrate how. As a way of promoting investigation into music's role in worship, he outlined these possibilities:

- *Music as unattended background.* Music in worship may guide or constrain behavior (e.g., encourage stillness) even if one is not focused specifically on the music.
- *Music as a source of personal associations.* In worship, music may elicit the recall of strong memories and feelings appropriate to the circumstance.
- *Music as a vehicle for the exercise of judgment.* Recall the discussion of statistical learning from Chapter 8. Simply by hearing music over a period of time we gain the ability to make musical judgments even if we are unable to verbalize them.
- *Ineffability and judgment.* Many musical judgments, as well as much that happens in worship, are incapable of being expressed in words; they are ineffable. Borrowing heavily from Raffman (1993), Sloboda identifies three aspects of ineffability related to music and worship:

  – structural ineffability. We may be able to say many things *about* the structure of a piece of music (e.g., the time signature, the formal structure—rondo or sonata form, etc.) but verbalizing the piece as a whole—its "rightness", its nature as a complete expression, the sense of the music beyond the large structural details, and so on—is extremely difficult or impossible. Similarly, we may speak of different parts of a worship service but the service as a whole may have a meaning that alludes our verbal capacity to describe.

  – feeling ineffability. Describing a moving musical experience, like describing any intense or meaningful sensory experience—such as a wonderful meal or a beautiful scene in nature—is difficult. Again, we may say many things about a performance, we may recognize that the music expressed or that we felt certain emotions, but still feel that these descriptions are inadequate in expressing the profundity or sublimity of the music. In worship, one of music's roles may be to draw attentiveness to feelings that cannot be verbalized and thus afford us the opportunity to be open to worshipful feelings that likewise cannot be put into words.

– nuance ineffability. At the opposite end from structural ineffability, both music and worship may have fine-grained details, nuances, that we have no words to describe. "Where worship seems to be afforded a particularly strong foothold is precisely at the boundaries of what can be said. Music brings us particularly effectively into an awareness of the ineffable and thus into a core attribute of worship" (2005, p. 355).

■ *Music as a vehicle for non-judgmental contemplation.* Much processing of familiar musical styles continues without conscious awareness. Rarely would one listen to music, except perhaps in an academic setting, with a running, internal dialogue (e.g., "we have just now finished the development section and are moving on to the recapitulation"). Yet, in following the music we may, in fact, be very aware of the imminent reappearance of the main theme, even in the absence of a verbalized account. So, it may be that worship music serves, in part, to free the mind for contemplation.

■ *Music as a vehicle for experiencing personal relationships.* It should take no extended discussion to recognize the ways in which music forms connections among performers, among listeners, and among performers and listeners. Likewise, a central idea of worship is the corporate experience; music may facilitate a feeling of oneness among the congregants and between congregants and the divine being worshipped.

Having laid out a number of areas ripe for investigation, Sloboda concludes that much of the careful experimentation necessary to confirm these ideas remains to be done. Atkins and Schubert (2014) took an important step when they obtained data to confirm Sloboda's central thesis. Their findings from a survey of 117 individuals indicated that spiritual experiences through music are neither intrinsic (i.e., not inherent in the music itself) nor extrinsic (i.e., not arising explicitly from external sources) but are rather profound and transcendent experiences that "come to life" within the music itself. One might say that the music afforded spiritual experiences.

Gabrielsson's Strong Experiences with Music project (2011) was previously discussed (see Chapter 11); here, we focus on that part of his work related to religion and spirituality. Recall that 1,300 respondents were asked to "describe in your own words the strongest (most intense, most profound) experience of music you have ever had" (2011, p. 7). In his organization of respondents' reports, he included three subcategories under the heading "Existential and Transcendental Aspects":

■ **Existence**
Meaning of human life/existence
Meaning of one's own life/existence
Intense feeling of life/living
Pure being
Feeling of unsurpassable/optimal/ultimate/holy moments in life
Changed view of life/existence

■ **Transcendence**
Magical/mysterious/supernatural/ heavenly/spiritual experiences
Trance, ecstasy
Out-of-body experience
Experience of totality (e.g., the experience includes "everything")
Cosmic experience, merge with something greater/endlessness/eternity
Experience of other worlds, other existences

■ **Religious experience**
General religious experience

Vision of heaven/life after this/paradise
Spiritual peace/harmony/fellowship
Holy/devout atmosphere/mood
Be addressed by religious/Christian message
Seeking/getting in contact with God in prayer, songs of praise
Contact/meeting with the divine/sacred, religious confirmation (pp. 466–467)

Sprinkled throughout his book, Gabrielsson includes many statements from respondents illuminating how music is related to these descriptors.

A national sample of over 1,500 Americans revealed that listening to music was the strongest trigger of mystical experiences when respondents were asked whether they had ever felt very close to a powerful, spiritual force that seemed to lift one out of one's self (Greeley, 1995). Lamont investigated strong experiences of music among university students, finding that spiritual or religious aspects were among the multiple routes to happiness and well-being in both listening (2011) and performing (2012). Schäfer, Smukalla, and Oelker (2014) also found confirmation of this notion when they conducted in-depth interviews of individuals and their intense musical experiences. Clearly, there is strong evidence of music's role in religious and spiritual aspects of life.

Hills and Argyle (1998) asked 230 adults to fill out scales measuring their happiness, and the strength of their personal feelings about religious experiences and music. Many of the respondents were members of musical groups, churches, or both. Findings indicated that being a member of a musical group or a church intensified feelings of the respective organization compared to non-participants. Scores on the musical scale and religious scale were compared for the 54 individuals who were members of both a musical group and a church. There were significant differences on six of the 11 items, indicating that there were contrasts in the two experiences. Primarily, musical experiences were more intense than religious experiences. Factor analysis revealed a transcendental factor for religious experiences and challenge and performance factors for musical experiences. Social aspects of both religious and musical experiences generate well-being.

Shuter-Dyson (2000) asked 350 music students to complete attitude and personality assessments; both male and female musicians were more extraverted than the general population of males and females. Also, both male and female musicians were more religious than non-music students, but the differences in female scores were not statistically significant. Bourke and Francis (2000) investigated religiosity within personality dimensions among 422 university music students. With personality profiles significantly different from published norms, researchers confirmed that significantly lower scores on the psychoticism scale were related to personality traits fundamental to religiosity. Previous studies indicated that persons who score low on psychoticism are more likely to pray, attend church, and hold positive attitudes toward religion.

MUSICAL IDENTITY

Hargreaves, Miell, and MacDonald (2002), believed that musical personality and musical identity are linked closely. They adopted Kemp's (1996) contentions of core, music personality traits, as described in the previous section. From these core personality traits, they recognized *Identities in Music* and *Music in Identities*. Identities in Music, again relying on the work of Kemp, refers to the notion that musicians often gain identity in terms of a performance medium, that is, as a singer, an oboist (Figure 12.5), conductor, and so on. They may

FIGURE 12.5 | Identity in Musical performance. To what extent might this oboist find his identity in the instrument he plays, the repertoire he performs (i.e., classical instead of country western), and the particular ensembles in which he participates (e.g., band, orchestra, chamber music groups)?

also identify themselves with a particular genre, such that they find their identity in classical, jazz, popular, or other styles. Thus, one musician might think of himself as a jazz guitarist, while another thinks of herself as an opera singer.

Music in identity is concerned with how musicians use music in developing such aspects of identity as gender or nationality. Faulkner and Davidson (2006) found that singing in an all-male chorus provided both self and gender identity for the members. Dibben (2002) made the point that although music can play a significant role in gender identity, it also intersects with other aspects of identity formation, such as generation, socio-economic status, ethnicity, and so on.

According to *social identity theory*, people develop a sense of social identity as well as personal identity. Being a member of an Irish band is an example of national identity through music. The role of music in creating a sense of national identity has been discussed for German (Applegate & Potter, 2002), Israeli (Gilboa & Bodner, 2009) and Russian (Daughtry, 2003) citizens, for example. In the latter case, Russian President Vladimir Putin caused a "national anthem crisis" when he abruptly switched the national anthem to a previously used melody, with new lyrics. Folkestad (2002) recognizes both an inclusive and exclusive role for music in national identity in what he calls "inside-looking-in" and "outside-looking-in." In the former situation, group members use music as a way of strengthening bonds; in the latter case, music enables outsiders to recognize a particular group as belonging together.

Music is such a ubiquitous aspect of modern living that many use it increasingly as a means of constructing personal identity. For many, music serves as an ever-present means of moving through the day, from waking up to an alarm clock, to driving to work or school listening to music, to falling asleep to music. (For more on these ideas, see Chapter 16: Music in Social Contexts). The music of one's life often defines one's sense of self-identity. In contrast to earlier personal identity theories, social constructivists believe that each of us may have many identities and that these can change depending on social circumstances (Hargreaves et al., 2002). For example, a concert pianist may have an identity as a performing artist when on stage, an identity as a teacher when working with a pupil, and identity as a mother when with her children.

One of the earliest identity constructions regarding music is the notion of musician—not musician (Lamont, 2002). Adults, who were told as children that they could not sing, often carry the shame and embarrassment throughout their lives (Welch, 2006). Most often, however, classification of musician or nonmusician is based on whether the child plays a musical instrument and has had formal training. Children who do not play an instrument or who have not had formal lessons, tend to think of themselves as nonmusicians, even if they did participate in classroom music activities. Nearly half the children of a very large sample ($N = 1,800$) classified themselves as nonmusicians. In another study, Lamont (1998) placed 408 children between the ages of 6 and 16 into one of three categories—trained musicians, for those children who indicated they had music lessons; playing musicians, for those children who did play an instrument but did not have lessons; and nonmusicians, if they did not play an instrument or have lessons. However, these designations did not adequately represent the range of the children's perceptual abilities.

Researchers have demonstrated the significant role of the family on a child's developing sense of identity (Creech, 2009). Budding musicians were included in a five-year longitudinal study of over 200 talented teenagers (Csikszentmihaly, Rathunde, & Whalen, 1997). Musically successful adolescents usually had a strong family support system. Intensive interviews with 12 families showed how parents and children developed a family musical identity (Borthwick & Davidson, 2002). Parents served as role models and created expectations of musicianship. Often, parent and child bonded over shared musical interests. Siblings, too, had an influence. "Therefore, the child's musical identity is shaped primarily by the responses and values given by his/her immediate family" (p. 76). It is important to note, however, that having musical parents is not necessary for the child to develop musicality. Howe and Sloboda (1991) found that only one-tenth of a group of exceptional music students had parents who were active musicians. Although the parents' musical skills were not critical, the level of their involvement was (Isbell, 2008; McClellan, 2007). Parents of successful music students were nearly always highly involved in monitoring the students' practice times, interacting with the music teacher, and so on.

Music consumes an excessive amount of time, energy, and money on the part of teenagers (Zillman & Gan, 1997), and it continues to be an important contributor to identity (North & Hargreaves, 1999). For example, 90% of 1,687 adolescents listened to music on MP3 players (Vogel, Verschuure, van der Ploeg, Burg, & Raat, 2009). College students rated music, along with hobbies, as more important lifestyle and leisure activities than movies, TV, books, clothes, and food (Rentfrow & Gosling, 2003). Mehl and Pennebaker (2003) found that college students listened to music 14% of their waking hours. Music acts as a badge of identity that relates to other aspects of lifestyle, such as speech, dress, and attitude. In addition, teens favor those who like the same kind of music. In a similar fashion to national inclusion and exclusion, music plays an important role in determining "ingroup" and "outgroup" identification (Tarrant et al., 2001). Popular music is a major force in generational identity (Roe, 1999); that is, adolescents use it as a means of creating an identity different from parents and teachers. Overall, it is clear that music plays a critical role in identity construction throughout the life span (MacDonald, Hargreaves, & Miell, 2002, 2009).

MUSICAL PREFERENCES

Nearly everyone makes musical choices. Those who decide to become a musician must decide what instrument(s) to play or whether to sing. Those who choose not to perform still make choices about the music they prefer, such as what concerts they attend and what music is loaded on their listening devices. Many things influence musical preferences, including inherited and acquired attributes, personality traits, and musical identity (Rentfrow & Gosling, 2003). The literature generally falls into two categories: preferences for instruments and preferences for musical genres.

Preferences for Instruments

Abeles and Porter (1978) conducted four studies to examine gender associations with musical instruments, with each study demonstrating a gender-instrument association (Figure 12.6). In the first experiment, adults indicated music instrument preferences for children that were clearly gender-biased. Adults preferred that girls play clarinet, flute, or violin and that boys play drums, trombone, or trumpet. In the second experiment, university students completed a paired-comparison ranking of 32 pairs of instruments, indicating the most masculine instrument of each pair. Results were similar to the adults' ratings, with flute, violin, and clarinet rated the most feminine and drums, trombone, and trumpet the most masculine. In the third experiment, 598 elementary school children indicated their instrument preferences, following visual and aural presentations of eight instruments. Gender bias was weak for kindergarten through second grade students, but was more pronounced for students in grades three through five. Boys consistently chose more traditionally masculine instruments and girls gradually moved toward more traditionally feminine instruments. In study four, 47 children ages three to five learned about musical instruments in three different modes of presentation. Results were similar to the previous study in that boys chose masculine instruments and girls indicated a wider variety of preferences.

Nineteen years later, O'Neill (1997) reported a considerable amount of research that supported the findings of Abeles and Porter (1978). In reviewing the literature that might explain gender preferences for musical instruments, O'Neill found that boys tend to avoid activities that they perceive as feminine. Girls do the opposite, but at a somewhat later age. In addition, both boys and girls felt that peers would bully, tease, and like them less if they played a gender "inappropriate" musical instrument. Zervoudakes and Tanur (1994) examined 590 concert programs from 1959–76, 1977–86, and 1987–90 from 200 elementary schools, 200 high schools, and 200 universities in all 50 states. Analyses of ensemble rosters indicated that little had changed at the high school and university levels across these time periods; females still tended to perform on traditionally female instruments. Subsequently, Abeles (2009) conducted two follow-up studies that essentially confirmed earlier findings.

FIGURE 12.6 | Gender Bias in Musical Instrument Selection. While numerous studies have demonstrated that there is a gender bias for certain instruments, identifying the tuba as a "male" instrument, there is no reason a female cannot be an excellent tubist as well.

Gender-based instrument choices can also affect ensemble participation. McKeage (2004) surveyed 628 college students participating in bands. Principle instrument choices were strongly aligned with traditional gender assignments, but secondary instrument choices were less so. Fewer females participated in jazz ensembles, in part because females more often played instruments not commonly found in such groups. Eighty percent of the men had participated in high school jazz ensembles, compared to 52% of the women; figures for college jazz ensemble participation were 50% and 14%, respectively.

Singing involves more obviously gender-related issues. Based on data from 542 third through sixth grade students, Mizener (1993) found that girls had more positive attitudes about singing than boys, and fewer boys than girls wanted to continue with choral singing. In fact, many boys choose not to sing in chorus during secondary school years (Demorest, 2000). Although issues with the changing voice can be a factor, the overwhelming reason boys give for not continuing to sing has to do with male identity (Kennedy, 1999). Male participation in choral singing has long been a problem in the United States (Koza, 1993) and has declined steadily since the 1930s (Gates, 1989). In the 1930s, 28.3% of high school boys and 29.9% of high school girls participated in chorus. By 1984, these figures were 9.1% (males) and 24.9% (females).

Preferences for Musical Genres

One of the most amazing things about making musical choices is that listeners can make certain judgments in fractions of a second. In three separate studies, listeners were able to determine positive or negative valence in as little as one-eighth of a second (Ashley, 2008; Bigand, Filipic, & Lalitte, 2005; Peretz, Gagnon, & Bouchard, 1998). Mace, Wagoner, Teachout, and Hodges (2012) extended these findings and found that more than 350 listeners were able to identify the correct musical genre with 76% accuracy from among five possibilities—classical, jazz, country, metal, and rap/hip-hop—in excerpts that were 125 ms, 250 ms, 500 ms, or 1,000 ms in length. Gender, musical training, and musical preferences exerted moderate influences on listeners' abilities to make correct identifications.

Although we are capable of making extremely rapid categorical judgments, most musical preferences are based on longer exposures. Abeles and Chung (1996) organized their literature review of responses to music along a time continuum. At the shortest end are mood-emotional responses to music that occur at the moment of listening. Preference responses to music are moderately stable and represent choices listeners make during certain periods, for example, while in high school or college. Musical taste represents more stable valuing of certain styles of music that reflect a long-term commitment. Thus, one adult may be a heavy metal fan, while a neighbor is a jazz aficionado.

Table 12.1 presents those listener characteristics affecting music preferences that have been investigated. As indicated, certain characteristics such as gender, personality, and training affect all three types of response. Short-term characteristics of existing mood and familiarity only affect mood-emotional responses. In reality, there are mutual influences among the three response types, such that taste can affect preferences, mood-emotional responses can affect taste, and so on (Hargreaves, North, & Tarrant, 2006).

Hargreaves et al. (2006) provided a different organizational scheme. They placed issues of preference and taste in the context of three primary variables: the listener (e.g., age, gender, personality), the music (e.g., the style, familiarity, complexity), and the listening situations and context (e.g., formal concert, leisure, at work). Each of these variables can influence the other two. Thus, a teenage girl might prefer popular music while at a party with her friends, but prefer classical music while playing violin in her school orchestra. Naturalistic research,

TABLE 12.1 | Characteristics Affecting Responses to Music.

	short-term characteristics	long-term characteristics
mood-emotional responses	mood familiarity	gender personality training socio-economic class
preferences		gender personality short-term training long-term training repetition
taste		gender personality training age general aptitude race social factors political orientation mass media and peer group influences

based on everyday musical experiences rather than laboratory experiments, supports the contention that people choose specific music for specific situations (Lamont, 2009).

The Listener. Listener variables that influence music preferences include such things as gender, age, and training. Abeles and Chung (1996) concluded that in general there were little or no differences in music preference due to gender. However, North and Hargreaves (2008) review newer studies suggesting that adolescent boys may prefer more aggressive musical styles, such as rap and metal. In contrast, the influence of age on music preference has been confirmed in numerous research studies (Russell, 2007), as in one study that polled listeners from ages 9 to 78 (North & Hargreaves, 1995). By casual observation, one could pair infants to lullabies, children to nursery songs, preteens to popular music, teenagers to proliferating styles of music including metal, rap/hip-hop, and so on. Evidence suggests that, in general, musical training leads to a preference for more complex music (North & Hargreaves, 2008). Overall, listener variables are important determinants of musical preference.

The Music. Hargreaves et al. (2006) contended that two theories, which were initially in opposition, could be used to explain how different aspects of the music itself influence preference. The first theory comes from the work of Berlyne (1971; also see Chapter 11). He plotted *arousal potential* on an inverted U-curve to indicate that the music that is most preferred has an intermediate level of properties such as complexity or familiarity. Too little or too much complexity, for example, results in lower preference. Chmiel and Schubert (2017) reviewed 57 investigations of musical preference and found that the inverted-U model is a viable explanation for the findings in the majority of these studies. The second theory comes from Martindale and Moore (1988). They argued that preference is based on the degree to which a given composition is typical of its class, or what is called prototypicality. Thus, for a classical music lover, Mozart may be more prototypical (i.e., better represent the salient features of classical music) than Schoenberg, and thus be more preferred. Both theories provide important insights into ways in which preference is based on musical variables.

The preference for prototypes theory (PPT) is one of the strongest ways to account for why we like the music we do. PPT has a base in cognitive psychology (e.g., Martindale, 1984; Posner & Keele, 1968) and is compatible with Berlyne's ideas (Hekkert & Snelders, 1995; Martindale, Moore, & West, 1988; North & Hargreaves, 2000; Whitfield, 1983, 2000, 2009). First presented by Whitfield and Slatter (1979) and later developed by Martindale and Moore (1988), PPT is based on the notion that listeners classify the music they hear by matching it to previously formed schema or prototypes. Early in our listening history, we place different aspects of the music we hear into categories that gradually become recognizable prototypes. Over time, we form well-defined, discrete prototypes for the music we like the best. Thus, if we grow up listening to and liking popular music, the timbres, rhythms, and so on of that style of music become associated with a prototype called popular music.

The faster and more easily we can process features of the music we listen to, the more positive our aesthetic response will be (Smith & Melara, 1990; Repp, 1997). Suppose a person who favors country music hears some opera. Musical and nonmusical features of opera do not fit so readily into her preformed schema. Because she has to work harder to process these features, she is less likely to have a positive reaction. When she later hears some country music, she processes the incoming information much more fluently because it fits her preferred prototype and thus she is more likely to have a positive, aesthetic response.

Situations and Contexts. As described previously, social identity theory (SIT) is concerned with the notion that individuals seek positive social identity; that is, they tend to think of their social relationships in a positive light. SIT can be used to explain music preferences (Hargreaves et al., 2006). For example, in one study (Tarrant, North, & Hargreaves, 2001), male adolescents showed in-group favoritism on both musical preference and evaluative dimensions (in-group members were seen as more masculine, more fun, etc.) compared to the out-group.

CONCLUSION

The interrelationships of the major topics of this chapter are readily apparent. However, as a means of drawing major themes of this chapter together, consider the following connections. Using the Short Test of Music Preferences (STOMP), which they developed, Rentfrow and Gosling (2003) discovered that college students believe that music, second only to hobbies and activities, can reveal more about their own personalities and the personalities of others than such things as movies, TV, books, clothes, and food preferences. In a series of six studies involving over 3,500 participants, they demonstrated that *personality*, along with self-views (i.e., *identity*) and cognitive abilities—all of which are both *inherited* and *acquired*, has an impact on music *preferences*. They identified four music-preference dimensions—Reflective and Complex, Intense and Rebellious, Upbeat and Conventional, and Energetic and Rhythmic—that were related to various personality dimensions, such as openness. Colley (2008) found similar links between personality traits and music genre preferences. However, she also found gender differences such as males preferring heavy metal and females preferring pop music.

In a follow-up study (Rentfrow & Gosling, 2006), found that music was the most common topic of conversation among strangers who were getting acquainted. Music revealed aspects of personality that were consistent, accurate, valid, and different from that obtained from other conversational topics such as books, clothing, movies, television, and sports. Zweigenhaft (2008) obtained general support for the findings of Rentfrow and Gosling, but provided a more detailed examination of relationships between personality traits and music genres. He found that certain music preferences (e.g., for folk or rap/hip-hop) were more revealing of personality than others (e.g., classical or rock). In other studies (Rentfrow & Gosling, 2007; Rentfrow, McDonald & Oldmeadow, 2009; see Rentfrow & McDonald, 2010), they obtained support for stereotypes concerning music listener's personalities, personal qualities, values, and alcohol and drug choices.

Rentfrow et al. (2011) developed a five-factor model called MUSIC:

- **M**ellow factor found in smooth and relaxing styles,
- **U**rban factor prominent in rhythmic and percussive music such as rap, funk, and acid rock,
- **S**ophisticated factor associated with classical, opera, world, and jazz styles,
- **I**ntense factor found in forceful and energetic music, and
- **C**ampestral factor of direct, rootsy music as a common component of country and singer-songwriter styles. (p. 1139)

In a subsequent study, they renamed the five factors to: **M**ellow, **U**npretentious, **S**ophisticated, **I**ntense, and **C**ontemporary (Rentfrow, Goldberg, Stillwell, Kosinski, Gosling, & Levitin, 2012). An analysis of the genre preferences of over 3,000 individuals for entertainment (music, books and magazines, film, and television) led to five-entertainment genre preferences (Rentfrow et al., 2011). These included Communal, Aesthetic, Dark, Thrilling, and Cerebral aspects that were related to personality traits.

In the largest such study to date, North (2009) asked 36,518 people from around the world to rate how much they liked 104 musical styles and to complete a personality test. The results clearly indicate that personality is linked to a wide range of musical styles. For example, both jazz and classical music lovers tend to be creative and have good self-esteem, but the former are more outgoing and the latter more shy. Country fans are hardworking and shy, indie fans are creative and lack self-esteem, and heavy metal fans are gentle and at ease with themselves.

A musical person inherits some attributes and acquires others. A musical person has a distinct personality, finds his or her identity in music, and expresses musical preferences. All persons are musical to some degree, though some engage more actively in performing. Musical persons live in societies and in broader cultural groups. The musical person in cultural and social context is examined more thoroughly in the final chapter.

DISCUSSION QUESTIONS

1. How would you define the term *musician*? Thinking of it the opposite way, who is not a musician? Would you consider someone a musician if she does not play an instrument, sing, or read music, but listens to music very attentively and with great responsiveness?
2. What portion of your own musicianship skills, if any, do you attribute to inheritance and what portion to learning? What roles did inheritance and learning play in the nonmusical skills you possess that influence your musical skills, such as tenacity or patience?
3. Thinking about musicians you know, do you feel that there are enough common traits among them that musicians could be distinguished from other groups, such as engineers, doctors, lawyers, and so on? If so, what are those traits?

4. Discuss the traits that Kemp identified in terms of yourself and other musicians you know: introversion, independence, sensitivity, anxiety, and psychological androgyny. Would you agree that these are core traits of musicians?

5. Do you think personality traits commonly used to describe different musician groups such as singers and instrumentalists, different instrumentalist groups (e.g., woodwinds, brass, strings, percussion, keyboard), or different kinds of musicians (e.g., classical, jazz, country-western, or pop musicians), have a basis in reality or are these artificial descriptions?

6. What connections can you draw between your own musical experiences, as performer or listener, and religious or spiritual responses?

7. Discuss your own musical identity (identity in music) and what role music plays in your self and group identities (music in identity).

8. Discuss the role music plays in creating *ingroup* and *outgroup* identities among you and your friends.

9. What influenced your choice of musical participation (i.e., to become a singer, violist, composer, etc.)? Do you see evidence of gender stereotyping among the musical choices made by your friends?

10. What are the major influences on your musical preferences? In terms of your personal preferences, what are the relationships among your personality traits, variables in the music itself, and social contexts?

Chapter 13

Music Performance

O N July 28, 1986, the front page of the *New York Times* carried this headline: "Girl, 14, Conquers Tanglewood with 3 Violins" (Rockwell, 1986). The article describes a performance by Midori of Bernstein's *Serenade*, under the baton of the composer. In the fifth movement, she broke a string, quickly exchanged her violin for that of the concertmaster and continued playing. Amazingly, it happened again—she broke a string on the second violin, quickly exchanged it for the associate concertmaster's violin and continued playing, finishing on the third violin. To add to the impressive feat, Midori's own instrument was slightly smaller than the other two. So, on stage with the Boston Symphony, a world-renowned conductor, and in front of a large audience, she performed an extremely difficult piece on three different violins in what was described as a technically near-perfect performance, all at the age of 14 (see a video of this performance at: www.youtube.com/watch?v=Rkp8YSuePPM).

The legendary conductor Arturo Toscanini was renowned for his amazing memory. His eyesight was so poor that he memorized scores; according to one source (Marek, 1975), this included about 250 symphonic works and nearly 100 operas, besides chamber music and solo literature. His memory was so accurate that upon one occasion a second bassoonist rushed up to Toscanini just before a concert, having just discovered that the key for the lowest note on his instrument was broken. Toscanini pondered for a moment and then calmed the bassoonist by saying, "That's all right—that note does not occur in tonight's concert" (Marek, 1975, p. 414). On other occasions, while conducting Wagner operas from memory at Bayreuth and at the Metropolitan Opera, he corrected mistakes in orchestral parts that had gone uncorrected for decades (Sachs, 1978).

Clynes and Walker (1982) examined three recordings of the Brahms *Variations on a Theme by Haydn*, Op. 56 made by Toscanini and the NBC Symphony Orchestra in 1935, 1938, and 1948. Although conceptions of a composition can change over time, a remarkable stability is evident in these performances. This piece, with a theme and nine variations, includes many changes of tempo yet the overall timings of the three performances are very similar: 16'44" (1935), 16'50.6" (1938), and 16'50.3" (1948). These minute differences in timing are scarcely noticeable between 1935 and the other two, and probably almost impossible to detect between the 1938 and 1948 recordings. Making this stability even more astonishing are the facts that (a) Toscanini himself aged 13 years during this time span, (b) those musicians who were in the orchestra for all three recordings also aged 13 years, (c) it is likely that membership in the orchestra changed somewhat for the three recordings, though this was not noted in the paper, and (d) the social-cultural climate was considerably different before and after World War II.

Finally, Portuguese pianist, Maria João Pires, was on stage preparing to play a Mozart piano concerto. Instantly, with the first notes of the orchestral introduction, she realized they were playing a different concerto from the one she was prepared to perform (Keegan, 2013). In despair, she looked at the conductor and mouthed the words, "I can't play it." The conductor, Riccardo Chailly, kept conducting and calmly leaned over to assure her that she knew this concerto; they had done it together in the past. She calmed herself, closing her eyes during the rest of the long introduction. By the time of her first entrance, she had resurrected the entire piece in her mind and proceeded to play it flawlessly. You can watch the performance at www.youtube.com/watch?v=fS64pb0XnbI.

Such astonishing feats seem apocryphal. Can music psychologists offer any insights to help understand such extraordinary accomplishments? Although Seashore (1932, 1936a, 1936b, 1938) and others conducted numerous experiments on topics such as vibrato, violin phrasing, and singing in the early decades of the 20th century, musical performance was a neglected topic for many years in music psychology (Gabrielsson, 2003). For example, Jørgensen (2004) estimated that two-thirds of the empirical research on musical practice in the last century occurred after 1990. Such recent work has brought this topic to the fore again and new studies are shedding light on the act of performing music.

This chapter is organized along lines similar to Bloom's Taxonomy of Educational Objectives (Bloom, 1956; Krathwohl, Bloom, & Masia, 1964; Simpson, 1966). The original terminology—cognitive, psychomotor, and affective domains (see Chapter 14)—has been paraphrased and re-ordered to be Motor Skills, Cognitive Skills, and Expressive Skills. Although of necessity these topics are considered in linear fashion, a key concept to remember is the reality of total integration into a coherent whole. That is, the most effective musical performances are likely a fluid balance among the three. Another key concept relates to the deliberate choice of the word *skills*. This implies that one can learn motor behaviors, cognitive strategies, and expressive gestures.

MOTOR SKILLS

Listening to virtuoso performers is awe-inspiring, not the least because of their amazing physical prowess. For example, Midori played the 1,242 notes of Paganini's *24 Caprices*, Op. 1, No. 1 in 105 seconds or 11.8 notes per second in a recording in 1989 made when she was still a teenager. Smith (1953) contended that high-level piano playing, which involves memory, complex integration, and muscular coordination, surpasses any other known intricate and perfectly controlled voluntary movements in the entire animal kingdom (p. 205). He gave examples of a pianist who performed the Mendelssohn *Perpetuum mobile*, Op. 119—5,995 notes in 4m 3s, or 24 notes per second. Another pianist performed the Schumann *C Major Toccata*, Op. 7—6,266 notes, in 4m 20s, which is 24.1 notes per second (p. 208). Amazingly, Münte, Altenmüller, and Jäncke (2002) top that. Their analysis indicates that a performance of the 11th variation from the *6th Paganini-Etude* by Liszt required 1,800 notes per minute or 30 notes per second. This would involve as many as 600 separate motor actions per second in just the fingers alone, not counting wrist, forearm, shoulder, trunk, foot pedaling, and other body movements. For the Liszt, this would require a minimum of 3,759,600 muscle movements. Beyond the sheer mechanical finger actions is the recognition that this must happen live, on stage in real time, often under considerable stress as to standards of accuracy and musicality, and so on.

The primacy of motor movements in music performance is such that anything a performer wants to share with an audience must be expressed in action. The actual notes, along with expressions of beauty, emotion, or other profound thoughts can only be shared with the audience if the performer engages in a body movement of some type, such as increasing air pressure or bow speed, modifying a vowel sound, striking the keys with more force, and so on. The incredible complexity of motor movements necessary for virtuoso music making, which are among the most demanding tasks encountered by the human central nervous system (Altenmüller, Ioannou, & Lee, 2015; Altenmüller & McPherson, 2007; Jabusch, 2006), naturally begs the question: How is this possible?

Neuromotor Aspects of Music Making

The act of making music is so connected with physical actions that one neurologist calls musicians small-muscle athletes (Wilson, 1986; see Fig. 13.1). Throughout years of training, musicians train the fine-motor musculature of the lips, tongue, larynx, fingers, and hands primarily, and extensive, repetitive training strongly activates multiple brain regions that must be highly coordinated. One example of this is the extensive increase of fibers in the corpus callosum in adult musicians (Schlaug, Jancke, Huang, Staiger, & Steinmetz, 1995). The corpus callosum is the primary highway of interconnectivity between the two hemispheres and when young musicians (most often pianists or string players) begin to practice seriously, they are requiring the brain to coordinate movements of the two hands.

Various parts of the central nervous system play active roles in motor movements. Although many different areas are involved, the principal components include the following (Altenmüller & McPherson, 2007; Altenmüller, Wiesendanger, & Kesslring, 2006; Chusid, 1985; Freund & Hefter, 1990; Thaut, 2005a; Wilson, 1986, 1988, 1998):

- Each hemisphere has *sensory-motor areas*. The body is represented in the sensory-motor cortex as a map, known as the homunculus (see Fig. 13.2). Those parts over which we have more control are given more space in the cortex. The hands, lips, and tongue—

FIGURE 13.1 | Musicians Are Small-Muscle Athletes. Musical performance relies on the acquisition of many motor programs that are stored in the brain. The moment of execution is not the time to think about how to do something like finger a specific passage.

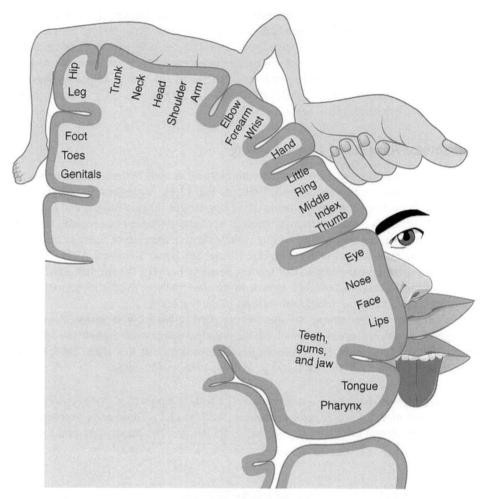

FIGURE 13.2 | Sensorimotor Homunculus. In this depiction, you see the parts most commonly involved in musicing—the hands and fingers, lips, and tongue—occupying more territory.

precisely those muscle groups most used in musical performance—require almost two-thirds of the neurons in the primary motor cortex (Altenmüller & McPherson, 2007). Sensory and motor areas are arranged topographically as mirror images. The left side of the body is represented in the right hemisphere and vice versa.

The motor cortex is involved in conscious decisions to contract specific muscles. If you wanted to crook your left index finger, the right motor cortex would give the command that the finger obeys. Because considerably more space in the motor cortex is devoted to the hand, lips, and tongue than to other parts of the body, we have much greater control over these muscle groups than we do over our toes or back muscles. It is no accident, then, that our music making involves primarily the hands, mouth, and throat.

An interesting feature of sensory and motor maps is that they can be reorganized based on experience (Kaas, 1991). The more a body part (e.g., a finger) is stimulated or used, the more extensively it is represented in the brain's map. Extensive training, such as that undertaken by musicians, causes the maps to be redrawn.

- In front of the motor cortex is the *premotor cortex*, an area involved in preparing and planning some of the programs run by the motor cortex. It is particularly involved in processing visual aspects of motor behavior and in learning, executing, and recognizing limb movements.
- The *supplementary motor cortex* plays a major role in the coordination of the two hands, in sequencing complex movements, and executing sequential motor movements that depend on internal cues, such as memorized performances.
- The *basal ganglia* are large clusters of cells that facilitate the cooperative efforts of groups of muscles. They send messages to the spinal cord and muscles through the neurons in the motor cortex. The basal ganglia are involved in coordinating muscle actions so that the commands sent by the motor cortex will be carried out most effectively.
- The *corpus callosum* has already been mentioned as the primary pathway of communication between the two hemispheres, allowing the two halves of the body to operate as an integrated unit.
- The *cerebellum* carries out a number of important roles in motor control. Some of these important roles are maintaining balance, coordinating the timing of intricate movements, monitoring feedback on how well the actions are being carried out, learning and storing habituated motor patterns, integrating sensory input in preparation for motor output, and optimizing complex motor functions.

Motor Aspects of Music Making

Musicians frequently rely on the rapid execution of intricate patterns. According to Wilson (1986), the motor cortex acting alone is far too slow to allow for the necessary speed of these movements to be carried out in the tempo required. Accomplishing this feat demands the cooperation of the cerebellum. When a particular sequence of muscle movements is repeated frequently, the pattern of those movements is stored as a unit or program. Thus, when an adult signs his signature, the motor cortex is not directing each of the required muscle movements individually. Rather, the cerebellum has stored a "signature signing" program. Likewise, musicians may store patterns for nearly everything they do that is repetitive—how to hold an instrument, the finger pattern for a three-octave d minor scale, and so on.

At the time the cerebellum is learning the sequence of movements to a given program, it accepts information whether right or wrong. This is why it is important to practice early attempts at new motor patterns slowly and correctly. Once a program is learned, the cerebellum allows for speed of movement because it has figured out all the required movements in advance. When the command is given to run a specific program, the entire sequence of movements is run automatically. Speed is also attained through ballistic movements. Just as a bullet runs its course with no more force applied after the initial explosion, so a muscle completes its specified range of movement following an initial burst of energy. The motor cortex, basal ganglia, and cerebellum work in concert to provide for smooth, facile, musical performances.

Motor maps change as a result of experience. In one experiment, five subjects in a control group pushed buttons in random order in response to numbers flashed on a computer screen (Pascual-Leone, Grafman, & Hallett, 1994). Their reaction times and cortical motor output maps did not change. Five subjects in an experimental group pushed buttons without knowing that there was an embedded pattern. As they gradually became aware that a pattern existed, their reaction times decreased and their cortical output maps became progressively larger. When they had learned the sequence, indicated by a shift in strategy from one of reaction to one of anticipation, the cortical maps returned to baseline conditions. This experiment demonstrated the rapid plasticity of motor cortex associated with learning. Also, the return of the motor cortex to baseline measurements may indicate that the motor cortex was operating more efficiently once the task was learned.

In another study, pianists and nonmusicians learned a complex finger-tapping task (Hund-Georgiadis & von Cramon, 1999). In the pianists, there was increased activation in the primary motor cortex throughout learning, but activity in supplementary and premotor cortices and cerebellum decreased compared to the controls. In the controls, primary and secondary motor areas showed increased activity initially, followed by a rapid decline. These results can be explained by recognizing that the pianists rapidly learned the required finger movements. This is supported by the findings of Jäncke, Shah, and Peters (2000), who showed that primary and secondary motor areas were activated in professional pianists to a much less degree than control subjects on one- and two-handed tapping tasks. The researchers concluded that long-term training on the part of the pianists led to greater efficiency, requiring fewer neurons to perform specific finger movements.

Results of another study (Elbert et al., 1995) indicated that early musical training has long-term effects on brain organization. Cortical representation of left-hand fingers was larger in the right primary somatosensory cortex of string players than it was for non-string players. Also, the total neuronal activity in this area was greater for string players than for controls. There was a correlation ($r = 0.79$) between the age string players began studying and the magnitude of neuronal activity. The earlier the subjects started playing a stringed instrument, the greater the effect. Those who started playing between five and seven years of age showed the greatest changes; those who started as teenagers showed little change over controls. Thus, it is apparent that playing a stringed instrument beginning at an early age causes long-term changes in the organization of the brain.

Obviously, advanced music performances require enormously complicated timing sequences and muscle movements. While one can ponder how the brain and body make these intricate movements possible, researchers are only at the beginning stages of unraveling these mysteries. Some researchers have been concerned about the location of music-related timing mechanisms in the brain (Freund & Hefter, 1990; Miller, Thaut, & Aunon, 1995; Moore, 1992; Thaut, Brown, Benjamin, & Cooke, 1996; Wilson, 1991, 1998). They recorded muscle movements via electromyography (EMG) by using transducers to convert movements into electrical signals and, more recently, by using MIDI devices (Musical Instrument Digital Interface) to record precise details of muscle movements. A variety of experiments have been conducted with cellists to monitor arm movements in bowing and vibrato and finger movements in trills (Moore, 1988; Moore, Hary, & Naill, 1988; Winhold, 1988; Winhold & Thelen, 1988). Other studies have involved pianists (Moore, 1984, 1992; Wilson, 1989, 1993).

Most measurements of brain activity, such as EEG, cannot be used while a musician is performing, because physical movements on the part of the subject disturb the readings. Mazziotta (1988) used PET scans to study movements that were similar to, but were not specifically musical motions; these involved a novel task, tapping the fingers in a prescribed sequence, and an overlearned task, signing one's name. In both tasks, primary and premotor cortices were activated. The basal ganglia were activated only during the overlearned task, not during the novel task. Mazziotta hypothesized that this was because the motor cortex had to take on more of the burden for the novel task, but that the basal ganglia took over some of this burden for the overlearned task.

When pianists performed with the right hand, PET data indicated activation in the left premotor cortex, left motor cortex, and right cerebellum, corresponding to motor representation of the right hand (Sergent, Zuck, Tenial, & MacDonall, 1992). PET data for pianists performing scales and Bach with both hands indicated bilateral activation of primary motor cortex and cerebellum, left lateralized activation of supplementary motor cortex for scales, and right lateral activation of supplementary motor cortex for Bach (Parsons et al., 2005). Activation in motor areas predominated over other cortical areas; one could hypothesize that other aspects of musical performance, such as associated thoughts or feelings, were encoded in muscle movements.

The Acquisition of Motor Skills

Motor learning, and indeed all learning, involves changes in behavior that result from physical changes in the brain (Wolpert, Ghahramani, & Flanagan, 2001). These physical changes, whether changes in existing synapses or recruitment of new synapses (Brashers-Krug, Shadmehr, & Bizzi, 1996), give rise to the notion of plasticity in the brain. To reiterate, a number of brain regions are involved, including the sensory-motor cortex, basal ganglia, and cerebellum. Motor programs, sometimes called motor memory traces, allow for rapid execution of complex movements. Recent work has significantly increased our understanding of how musicians learn these motor programs.

At least five stages have been posited (Doyon & Benali, 2005): (1) A *fast* or *early stage* signals an initial boost in performance that may occur within 5–30 minutes after training begins (Gaab, Paetzold, Becker, Walker, & Schlaug, 2004). Bangert and Altenmüller (2003) found co-activity in auditory and motor areas occurring within 20 minutes of beginning piano instruction. (2) A *slow* or *later stage* shows further gains with repetition or practice. (3) Motor skills continue to evolve during rest following practice in a *consolidation stage* (Albert, Robertson, & Miall, 2009; Brashers-Krug et al., 1996). Gaab and colleagues (2004) demonstrated that sleep plays a critical role in consolidation. An equivalent amount of wakeful rest did not produce the same level of improvement as did sleep. (4) During the *automatic stage*, a newly learned motor skill requires minimal cognitive resources and is more resistant to interference in the form of competing motor tasks. Over the course of five days of practicing a one-handed piano exercise, cortical maps for the fingers enlarged but their activation threshold decreased (Pascual-Leone, Dang, Cohen, Brasil-Neto, Cammarota, & Hallett, 1995; see also Krings et al., 2000). (5) In the *retention stage*, the motor skill can be executed without the need for further practice. Palmer and Meyer (2000) demonstrated that for advanced pianists, mental plans for motor sequencing become independent of actual movements and transferable.

As indicated previously, rest and sleep play important roles in consolidation of motor skills. Overnight sleep provides a maximum benefit to motor skills that are the most difficult to learn (Kuriyama, Stickgold, & Walker, 2004). Simmons and Duke (2006) found that sleep improved performance on a 12-note keyboard melody, but 12-hours of wakeful rest did not, a finding that supported the results of Gaab and colleagues (2004). However, others have found support for two discrete motor-learning processes, wakeful rest and sleep (Robertson, Press, & Pascual-Leone, 2005; Shadmehr & Brashers-Krug, 1997; Walker et al., 2003). Obviously rest and sleep are only useful in the context of actual physical practice.

Audio-Motor and Mirror Neuron Systems

Musical performance is among the most demanding tasks humans undertake, placing extraordinary demands on both auditory and motor systems and, in particular, on information sharing between the two (Zatorre et al., 2007). Playing or singing requires motor control of timing (rhythm), sequencing, and spatial organization of movement (pitch). Rapid communication between auditory and motor areas of the brain is supported by feedforward and feedback loops (Baumann, Koeneke, Schmidt, Meyer, Lutz, & Jäncke, 2007). What a performer hears influences what she does and what she does influences what she hears.

Co-activations in auditory and motor areas have been shown for singers (Hickok, Buchsbaum, Humphries, & Muftuler, 2003), pianists (Bangert et al., 2006; Baumann, et al., 2007; Haslinger, Erhard, Altenmüller, Schroeder, Boecker, & Ceballos-Baumann, 2005; Haueisen & Knösche, 2001), violinists (Lotze, Scheler, Tan, Braun, & Birnbaumer, 2003), and cellists (Chen, Woollacott, & Pologe, 2006; Chen, Woollacott, Pologe, & Moore, 2008). Genetic differences in white matter audio-motor pathways may influence the speed with which one can learn new motor patterns at the keyboard (Engel et al., 2014).

Mirror neurons may be activated not only by observed actions but also by the sounds that accompany those actions (Zatorre et al., 2007). For example, compared to controls, professional pianists had increased brain activations in fronto-parietal-temporal and auditory networks while observing videotapes of silent piano playing. Additionally, listening to piano sounds activated sensorimotor networks (see also Bangert, 2006).

Mirror neurons, along with audio-motor interactions may also play a role in emotional experiences that performers experience (Zatorre et al., 2007). Wantanabe, Savion-Lemiux, and Penhune (2007) found evidence to support a sensitive period in sensorimotor integration. Those with extensive training before the age of seven performed better on a timed motor sequence task than those who trained after seven, but who had an equivalent amount of training.

Quantity of Practice

Old Vaudeville joke—Question: "How do you get to Carnegie Hall?" Answer: "Practice, practice, practice." Similarly, another hoary maxim is: "If I don't practice for one day, I notice it. If I don't practice for two days, the critics notice it. If I don't practice for three days, the public notices it" (variously ascribed to Heifetz, Paderewski, and others). Obviously, practicing or rehearsing is central to the concept of musical performance. Simplistically, there are two aspects—quantity and quality, how much one practices and how one practices. Here, quantity of practice is included in the Motor Skills section and quality of practice is placed in the following Cognitive Skills section.

Amount of practice is a good predictor of eventual level of musical performance excellence (Howe et al., 1998; Sloboda et al., 1996). This is a general rule that applies to many different domains. Gladwell (2008) provided details on the enormous amounts of time Bill Joy, cofounder of Sun Microsystems, Bill Gates, founder of Microsoft, and the Beatles spent in their childhoods working to develop skills. In his autobiography, Pete Sampras, holder of 14 Grand Slam singles titles in tennis, described hitting a million balls to burn in muscle memory so that he could hit his shots automatically (Sampras & Bodo, 2008).

Sosniak (1985) provided data for the notion that it takes at least ten years of sustained effort to achieve an international level of performance excellence. She interviewed 21 pianists, each of whom had been a finalist in an international piano competition. As a group, they averaged 17 years of piano study at the time of their first international recognition.

Ericsson et al. (1993) further clarified the requirements necessary to achieve the highest levels of peak performance by stating that it takes approximately 10,000 hours of deliberate practice over a decade. They studied ten best, ten good, and ten lower achieving violinists who had been studying for at least ten years. By the age of 20, the best violinists had accumulated 10,000 hours of practice, the good violinists had amassed 7,500 hours, and the least accomplished a little over 4,000 hours of practice. They followed this up with a study of pianists and found that by age 20, expert pianists had averaged more than 10,000 hours of practice, while amateurs had aggregated less than 2,000 hours. In addition, the average starting age for violinists and pianists who achieved the highest levels of performance was between five and six years of age. Thus, there appear to be four related criteria for advancement to an elite level: (1) practice begins at an early age, (2) at least 10,000 hours of practice are accumulated over (3) a ten-year period, and (4) rehearsals are characterized as deliberate practice.

Interestingly, neither Wagner (1975) nor Madsen (2004) found strong relationships between amounts of time practiced and improvement or success. Wagner (1975) found that the use of practice records was not helpful for music students, and Madsen (2004) found that adults' recollection of how much they practiced, when compared to actual records kept 30 years earlier, were not accurate. Furthermore, it is important to reiterate some information from the previous chapter. Mosing et al. (2014) obtained data from 10,500 twins indicating that factors influencing how much and how well one practices is 40–70% heritable. Heritable factors accounted for 41% of practice time in females and 69% in males. Ullén et al. (2016) confirmed that deliberate practice cannot account for all the improvements made in performance. Their multifactorial gene-environment interaction model (MGIM) posits that genetic instructions, deliberate practice, and gene-environment interactions combine to influence the development of musical expertise.

It would be inappropriate to end a section on the importance of accumulating hours of practice time without mentioning a potential concern of overuse. Focal dystonia is the name given to a task-specific movement disorder that can affect musicians. Sometimes known as musician's cramp, focal dystonia is a painless, loss of muscular control for complex, over-learned movements. Most often it affects the hands, for example of keyboard and string players, but it can also affect a brass player's embouchure. Although the exact causes of focal dystonia can vary, workload, stress, and complexity of movements are major culprits. For further information, see Chapter 15 and the following sources: Altenmüller (2006), Byl and Priori (2006), Jabusch and Altenmüller (2006), Rosenkranz (2006).

COGNITIVE SKILLS

The motoric aspects of musical performance are clearly important, but perhaps they sometimes receive an inordinate amount of attention. Thoughtful, reflective aspects of music learning are just as critical to the development of musicianship. Though motor and cognitive skills are discussed in separate sections, the notion of a Cartesian schism between the two is outdated. Mental and physical aspects occur in an integrated fashion; one might wish to speak of a thinking musician and a musical thinker. Thus, the discussions in this section should be integrated into the previous discussions as a coherent whole.

Quality of Practice

The use of the phrase *deliberate practice* indicates that more is required than simply putting in time. Deliberate practice occurs when individuals are: "1) given a task with a well-defined goal, 2) motivated to improve, 3) provided with feedback, and 4) provided with ample opportunities for repetition and gradual refinements of their performance" (Ericsson, 2008, p. 991). Ericsson (1997) contended that large amounts of deliberate practice are even more important to eventual success than being a child prodigy or having a great deal of talent.

Chaffin and Imreh (2001) and Miklaszewski (1989) observed how highly accomplished pianists learned new music for performances. In both cases, practice sessions were highly structured and confirmed the importance of deliberate practice (Figure 13.3). In contrast, Lisboa (2008) monitored the practice sessions of three beginning cellists. These young students mainly used repetitive practice strategies that actually embedded pitch and rhythm errors. Williamon and Valentine (2000) followed 22 pianists placed into one of four skill levels as they learned and memorized a composition by Bach for performance. The amount of practice time increased systematically with each level of performance; those in the highest level practiced the most. However, further analysis indicated that quantity alone was not significantly related to quality of performance. The crucial role of deliberate practice was confirmed in this study, as it was in Duke, Simmons, and Cash (2009), who found that the practice strategies employed were more influential in level of performance attained than how much or how long pianists practiced. Those who used the widest variety of strategies improved the most. Jabusch and colleagues (2009) found that quantity but not quality of practice was related to performance skill in expert pianists. However, assessment was made only of motor skills in temporal evenness while playing scales. In expert pianists, amount of practice time was most highly related to maintenance of these selected motor skills.

Studying the biographies of student and accomplished performers has confirmed the necessity of large amounts of deliberate practice. Sosniak (1985) interviewed 21 emerging concert pianists. Their practice habits started early and consumed more time than any other childhood activity. Their parents were also highly involved in supervising practice to ensure that the sessions were structured and productive. Sloboda et al. (1996) interviewed 257 young musicians divided into levels of musical competence. A subset also kept practice diaries for 42 weeks. Although there was considerable variance in amounts of practice time, there was an 800% difference between the top and bottom groups, with the top group practicing the most. Interestingly, the highest achieving group did a much higher percentage of their practicing in the

FIGURE 13.3 | It Takes Many Hours of Deliberate Practice to Become an Accomplished Performer.

morning than the lower groups, a finding that was similar to the violinists in a previous study (Ericsson et al., 1993). Finally, parents assumed a much more prominent role in the musical life of the high achieving group than the lower groups (Davidson, Howe, Moore, & Sloboda, 1996).

O'Neill (1997b) asked 44 beginning instrumentalists to keep a practice diary for two weeks. Performances were evaluated at the end of the period and the highest rated group had practiced significantly more than the lowest rated group. High levels of parental involvement in the student's musical progress were also associated with higher levels of performance. Practice sessions of child prodigies are often supervised, as an informal study of biographies confirmed for Yo-Yo Ma, Cecilia Bartoli, Evgeny Kissin, and Sarah Chang (Lehmann & Ericsson, 1997). McPherson and Davidson (2002) conducted 157 mother and child interviews, where the children were beginning instrumentalists. There were considerable differences between the mothers' and the children's reports of practicing. Sloboda and Howe (1991) did not find a difference in parental involvement between higher and lower achieving music students, however, the fact that all these students were enrolled in a special school for musically gifted children may account for this finding. Overall, the critical role of parental involvement is confirmed in the literature.

Barry (1992) determined that a highly organized and systematic approach to practice sessions led to more accuracy and increased musicality in instrumentalists, grades seven to ten. Rohwer and Polk (2006) found that eighth-grade instrumental students who utilized analytic techniques in their practice sessions, such as stopping to remediate or fix specific errors, made significantly more gains than those who spent more time playing through their pieces, whether they stopped to correct errors or not. Miksza (2007) found similar results for high school wind players. Significant relationships were found between performance achievement and deliberate practice. Byo and Cassidy (2008) found a discrepancy between how students said they practiced in terms of specific techniques and their actual practice. Geringer and Kostka (1984) also found discrepancies between what students said they practiced on and what they actually did.

Mental Rehearsal

Musicians have long used *mental rehearsal* as an effective learning strategy. In his marvelous autobiography, Arthur Rubinstein (1973) tells how he learned Falla's *Nights in the Gardens of Spain* by reading the score on trains, and then played the first rehearsal from memory. Mental rehearsal is thus an imaginary rehearsal of musical performance without overt muscular movement (Connolly & Williamon, 2004).

Significant work has been done in athletics to demonstrate that motor systems in the brain receive training through mental rehearsal; while the applications should transfer to music making, less research has been done. However, in one intriguing experiment, researchers (Pascual-Leone et al. 1995) divided subjects who had never previously played the piano into three groups. One group learned and practiced a specific five-finger pattern on the piano. Cortical motor mapping for finger control was revealed by transcranial magnetic stimulation. The area of the motor cortex controlling the fingers tripled in size, as indicated by a significant increase in peak amplitude and in size of scalp positions from which signals were received. Another group played random finger patterns on the piano for the same length of time; the size of the motor cortex representing their fingers did not change. Finally, a third group mentally rehearsed the same five-finger pattern as the first group, but did not physically play on the piano. The area in the motor cortex representing the fingers tripled in size, just as it had for those who physically practiced the pattern. Apparently, mental rehearsal had the same effect as actual physical rehearsal.

Pascual-Leone (2003) asked a group of non-pianists to rehearse a five-finger pattern at the keyboard without physically moving hands or fingers. They mentally rehearsed an equivalent amount of time as a group that practiced physically. Motor maps controlling finger movements were reorganized in both groups and performance improved, as well. Mental practice stimulated many of the same areas of the brain as did physical practice, including prefrontal and supplementary motor areas, basal ganglia, and cerebellum (see also Bangert, 2006).

Seven violinists executed or imagined a musical excerpt while being imaged with high-resolution EEG (Kristeva et al., 2003). Many similar brain regions were activated for both conditions. In particular, the bilateral frontal opercular regions were crucial for both executing and imagining the musical passage. The authors posit the possibility of *mirror neurons* in these regions that are involved in the observation or imagining of one's own performance.

Coffman (1990) monitored college pianists and found that physical practice alternating with mental practice was just as effective as physical practice alone, and that both methods were superior to mental practice alone. Ross (1985) also found for college trombonists that combining physical and mental practice was as effective as physical practice alone. Lim and Lippman (1991) asked piano performance majors to learn a short piece from memory by one of three methods: physical practice, mental practice, or mental practice with listening. Physical practice led to the best performance; mental practice and listening were superior to mental practice alone. In a study with vocalists and guitarists, Theiler and Lippman (1995) found that mental practice and listening was effective for both groups and mental practice alone and physical practice alone were effective strategies for the guitarists. Connolly and Williamon (2004) provided numerous exercises designed to improve mental rehearsal techniques.

Music Reading

Many of the world's musical practices do not require music reading skills. However, for many musicians, particularly those trained in the Western classical musical tradition, music reading is a core requirement. Space is too limited to present a full review of music reading research literature, however, more complete details can be found in Hodges and Nolker (2011).

Brain imaging studies of musicians support the notion that music and language are represented in distinct, shared, and parallel neural networks (Brown et al., 2006); furthermore, music reading specifically is monitored in different areas of the brain than reading words or numerals (Peretz & Zatorre, 2005). Researchers have identified specific brain regions involved in music reading, including the superior parietal cortex and fusiform gyrus (Nakada, Fujii, Suzuki, & Kwee, 1998; Stewart, 2005; Stewart et al., 2003). They have also made further refinements in mapping specific music reading functions, such as pitch or rhythm reading (Fasanaro, Spitaleri, Valiani, & Grossi, 1990; Kawamura, Midorikawa, & Kezuka, 2000).

Another group of researchers has been interested in the eye movements involved in music reading. Music reading involves eye movements, called saccades, and sudden stops, called fixations (Rayner, 1998). Progressive saccades are left-to-right movements and regressive movements are the reverse (for reading English and music). Fixations, lasting from less than 100 ms to 500 ms, are when movements stop and the eye is focused on a circular area about one inch in diameter (Goolsby, 1989). Eye movements of experienced music readers are different from inexperienced readers (Kinsler & Carpenter, 1995; Polanka, 1995; Waters & Underwood, 1998). Experienced music readers use more efficient strategies, such as looking ahead more frequently, looking farther ahead, and adjusting eye movements to suit the music, with more horizontal eye movements for contrapuntal music and more vertical movements for choral music (Goolsby, 1994a, 1994b; Kopiez & Galley, 2002; Polanka, 1995). Eye movements of proficient music readers also focus on important structural markers such as phrase boundaries (Sloboda, 1974, 1977) and on the recognition of patterns such as scales or arpeggios (Fine, Berry, & Rosner, 2006; Salis, 1980; Thompson, 1987). Poor music readers tend to move from note-to-note and engage in many needless shifts from the music to the keyboard, in the case of pianists.

Many researchers have investigated particular approaches to the teaching of music reading, however, there are few examples of a sustained line of research leading sequentially to a greater understanding. Topics of interest have been solmization, body movement, pattern instruction, notational variables, and choral sight-reading. Using solfège syllables or other mnemonic devices has been effective frequently (Bebeau, 1982; Cassidy, 1993; Colley, 1987; Palmer, 1976; Shehan, 1987), though it is not clear whether fixed or moveable *do* is most effective (Demorest & May, 1995; Henry & Demorest, 1994). Results have been mixed in evaluating the effectiveness of body movement (e.g., foot tapping, clapping rhythms, etc.); some have found body movement useful (Boyle, 1970; Skornicka, 1972), while others have not (Klemish, 1970; Martin, 1991; Salzburg & Wang, 1989).

Research on pattern recognition has confirmed the basic research studies mentioned previously, in that better readers utilize structural elements such as phrases to their advantage (Azzara, 1992; Gruzmacher, 1987; Henry, 2004; MacKnight, 1975; Richardson, 1972). Manipulating a variety of notational variables has met with mixed success. Beamed notation helped high school band students (Sheldon, 1996); colored notation led to improvements in rhythm reading, but did not transfer to traditional notation (Rogers, 1996). Byo (1988, 1992) and Gregory (1972) did not find unique notational schemes to be useful. Cutietta (1979) designed a manual for middle school choral singers that improved sight singing. High school choral members used strategies such as singing aloud, practicing with hand signs, and employing body movements with positive results (Henry, 2008; Killian & Henry, 2005).

Metacognition, Self-Regulation, Motivation, and Self-Efficacy

A number of personal/cognitive variables have been found to influence the quality of musical practice, including metacognition, self-regulation, motivation, and self-efficacy. *Metacognition* is thinking about one's own thoughts. Hallam (2001) interviewed 22 professional musicians and 55 novices from beginners to college students, asking them to examine a piece of music and to describe how they would go about learning that composition. Professional musicians displayed extensive use of metacognition; they were very self-aware of strengths and weaknesses and of strategies that would be effective in learning the piece. With a few exceptions among more advanced students, novices were far less able to plan effective practice strategies (see also Pitts, Davidson, & McPherson, 2000).

Self-regulation has to do with the individual learner setting personal goals and then monitoring progress toward those goals. Self-regulation involves adjusting one's own learning strategies (behavioral self-regulation), adjusting environmental circumstances such as finding a good place to practice (environmental self-regulation), and monitoring cognitive and affective states (covert self-regulation) (McPherson & Zimmerman, 2002).

McPherson and Renwick (2001) examined self-regulation in young beginning music students. They found very low levels of self-regulatory behavior. Most students simply played through their assigned pieces once or twice. Repetition was also the most frequently used strategy among band students (Leon-Guerrero, 2008) and pianists (Gruson, 1988). McPherson and Renwick (2001) found wide variations among different students and McPherson (2005) also found many differences among 157 beginning instrumentalists aged seven to nine. Those who experienced difficulties early on in note reading and ear-to-hand coordination were the most likely to drop out. Accumulated practice time was important in performing rehearsed music successfully, but mental strategies employed were more important in predicting ability to sight read, play from memory, and play by ear. The best performers overall utilized the most sophisticated mental strategies.

Austin and Berg (2006) completed a factor analysis of practice inventory responses from 224 sixth-grade instrumentalists. Motivation and self-regulation were distinct elements of practice sessions. *Motivation* is an integral aspect of learning to be a musician. Without motivation, it is unlikely that beginners will persist in developing the myriad skills, behaviors, and attitudes necessary to be successful. Sources of motivation can be intrinsic (e.g., personal enjoyment and satisfaction) or extrinsic (e.g., parents, teachers, peers, etc.) (Lehmann et al., 2007). O'Neill and McPherson (2002) described expectancy-value theory, a means of explicating motivation, as including four components: *attainment value*—how important it is to do well on a task such as playing a recital, *intrinsic motivation*—personal enjoyment in performing, *extrinsic utility*—how useful learning music is to future goals, and *perceived cost*—aspects such as practicing.

Davidson (2002) linked motivation to self-belief. Those musicians who have a strong, positive self-belief are likely to be more motivated to persist in developing performance skills. Contrarily, those plagued with self-doubt and negative self-appraisal are more apt to become unmotivated. Persson (2001) lists hedonic, social, and achievement motives as being important reasons musicians give for their career choice. The hedonic motive, personal satisfaction derived from positive emotional experiences, was the most common reason. Social identification, related to belonging to particular groups or having reinforcing affiliations, was also important. Although rated lowest in priority, achievement motives include exhibitionism, independence, dependence, aesthetics, and support from parents and teachers.

Self-efficacy for musicians is the belief that one can perform at a competent level in particular situations, such as public or adjudicated performances. McCormick and McPherson (2003) surveyed 332 college instrumentalists and found that self-efficacy was the best predictor of actual performance. They followed their previous work with an even larger sample, investigating the performances of 686 student musicians (McPherson & McCormick, 2006). Their results confirmed the critical role of self-efficacy. Whether a student thought she could or could not perform well was the strongest predictor of actual performance. According to Nielsen (2004), college music students high in self-efficacy were more likely to employ cognitive and metacognitive strategies than those low in self-efficacy.

Furthermore, students who are highly motivated and had a strong sense of self-efficacy are more likely to experience flow. *Flow* is a state of being that occurs when a person is fully engaged in a task and feeling energized and perhaps even transported. Flow theory, according to Csikszentmihályi (1990) is an optimal balance between task challenges and ability to meet those challenges. O'Neill (1999) found support for this theory when she compared practice amounts for moderate- and higher-achieving music students. The lower achieving students had fewer flow experiences. In contrast, Wait and Diaz (2012) found that flow was not dependent upon skill level. The groundwork for a flow experience is laid during the many thousands of hours of intense, concentrated practice when the budding musician is fully engaged and completely absorbed (Chaffin & Lemieux, 2004). Experiencing flow may contribute toward engaging in daily practice among advanced musicians (Araújo & Hein, 2018). In fact, flow may be the largest predictor of music practice (Butkovic, Ullén, & Mosing, 2015). Although Marin and Bhattacharya (2013) also found that flow was associated with daily practice, they did not find a strong association between flow and high achievement (e.g., winning a prize in a competition). Flow and performance anxiety have an inverse relationship; that is, when flow is high, performance anxiety is low (Fullagar, Knight, & Sovern,

2013). Mik=

2013). Mik# Miksza, Tan, and Dye (2016) found flow was related to mastery goal orientation in band rehearsals.

Barry and McArthur (1994) developed a *Music Practice Instruction Inventory* that was administered to college and pre-college music teachers. Although nearly all teachers regularly stress the importance of practice, there were differences in the practice strategies endorsed by the two groups of teachers. Clearly, music teachers need to focus more strongly on how students learn on their own and Jørgensen (2004) has presented many helpful strategies for effective practice. Sinnamon, Moran, & O'Connell (2012) found that the Dispositional Flow Scale-2 (DFS-2) was applicable for measuring flow experiences among musicians, with some concerns about the validity of particular subscales. They found that flow experiences were common among music students.

EXPRESSIVE SKILLS

Many teachers and audiences have described some performers as "mechanical." That is, they may play the notes and rhythms correctly, but musical expression is missing. The first two sections have dealt with physical and mental aspects and the discussion now turns to the affective domain. As before, the goal is to connect the three into an integrated conception of musical performance.

Body Movement

Casual observation confirms the notion that body movements are an important aspect of musical performances. Because audience members may take in an ordinate amount of information visually, up to 75% according to McPherson and Schubert (2004), this topic warrants careful consideration. Indeed, some performers engage in excessive body movements, facial grimaces, and other gesticulations that detract from their performances (Vickers, 1995). However, successful performances involve a certain amount of movement (Davidson, 2005). Appropriate and effective gestures include such things as nodding to reinforce an accent or suspending a hand in the air at the end of a long, quiet cadence. A jazz trumpeter might raise the bell of the instrument and lean back with bended knees during an extremely high passage. Popular singers often lean back as well, and this has the function in vocal production of enhancing acoustic output (Turner & Kenny, 2010). Such movements as swaying in pianists are not meaningless, but in fact essential to expressiveness. For example, pianists who were physically restrained did not perform as expressively as when they were given freedom of movement (Davidson, 2005).

There are many other circumstances when body movements and gestures become necessary in musical performance. Singers have an added responsibility to communicate the lyrics in a song in addition to the music (Welch, 2005). This is even more pronounced in opera and musicals (Figure 13.4). Unquestionably, chamber music requires a great deal of nonverbal communication in order to maintain group coherence. Rasch (1988) investigated "ensemble," or how well ensemble members coordinate their entrances. He found an ensemble of two performers had an onset gap of 18 ms; that is 18 ms separated the two performers when they attempted to enter together. As ensembles increased in size, onset times likewise increased so that an ensemble of nine players had a gap of 24 ms between the first and last performers to enter on a downbeat. Ensembles larger than nine players more often use a conductor, although there are certainly exceptions such as the Orpheus Chamber Ensemble.

Being Musical

FIGURE **13.4** | Singers Use Many Facial Expressions and Body Gestures to Communicate Expressive Intent.

FIGURE **13.5** | Jascha Heifetz and B.B. King. Heifetz (Top) was criticized for his impassive facial look and limited body movements, while King (Bottom) enhanced the expressiveness of his performances with facial gestures and body movements.

Davidson (1993) asked four violinists and a pianist to perform in three different ways: deadpan, with a minimal amount of expressiveness; exaggerated, where all the expressive elements were overstated; and projected, as if performing in a recital. She videotaped performers in front of a black curtain, wearing tight-fitting black outfits with reflector tape at head, wrist, elbow, shoulder, hip, knees, and ankles. Subsequently, she altered the recordings so that observers saw a visual image only, an aural image only, or an aural-visual image. Observers rated expressivity on a 7-point scale from deadpan to exaggerated. For the violinists, rated by 21 undergraduate music majors, the highest ratings of expressivity were in visual only, next in aural-visual, and least in aural only. Thirty-four undergraduate music students rated the piano performances with the same results. The author concluded that physical gestures communicate important information about the expressive intent of a performance.

In a following study, Davidson (1994) found that body movements became larger as musical expressiveness increased. Head movements projected more information about expressive intentions than collar or hand movements. Juchniewicz (2008) asked 112 participants to rate a professional pianist performing with three conditions: no movement, head and facial movement, and full body movement. Pianists' movements significantly increased ratings of phrasing, dynamics, rubato, and overall musical performance. There are, of course, exceptions. Jascha Heifetz, considered one of the greatest violinists of the 20th century was severely criticized for his impassive, "deadpan" facial expressions and limited body movements while playing (Fig. 13.5) (McLellan, 1987).

Tsay (2013) conducted seven experiments concerning the relative roles of visual and auditory information in making judgments of music performances. Contrary to people's reports of what is important, "findings demonstrate that people actually depend primarily on visual information when making judgments about music performance" (p. 14580). In fact, both novices and professional musicians could reliably identify competition winners from silent video recordings alone, but could not do so from audio recordings alone.

Researchers have examined other performance styles than classical music. Several trained musicians reviewed filmed performances by B.B. King (Fig. 13.5) and Judy Garland to identify intentional movements and gestures that communicated emotionality (Thompson, Graham, & Russo, 2005). Both performers used a variety of facial expressions and body gestures that served to emphasize or clarify expressive aspects. In a series of five subsequent experiments, researchers confirmed that visual aspects of performances reliably influenced perceptions and interpretations of the music made by listeners/observers. Singers' facial expressions and head movements also conveyed information about interval size (Thompson & Russo, 2007).

Aho (2009) mapped the gestural content of a recording made by a popular Finnish singer, Olavi Virta. Virta used a wide variety of facial and vocal gestures (including glissando, variations in vibrato, timings of phrasing breaths, etc.) to convey meanings of the lyrics. Micro-level analysis of fleeting nuances underscored the amazing complexity of the performance. Davidson (2009) reviewed her previous work with popular, jazz, and Cantonese opera singers. As detailed in a series of studies, Annie Lennox used provocative sexual body postures; the Corrs, a popular Irish band, communicated with each other and the audience through body movements; Robbie Williams, a popular singer, engaged his audience through familiar, stylized gestures; and Amy Wu, a Cantonese opera singer, embodied elements of the text in body movements and dramatic postures.

Several studies have reinforced connections among cognitive, motor, and affective skills. Woody (1999b) obtained evidence that supported connections between planning and execution. Twenty-four pianists listened to expressive excerpts that contained both musically appropriate and inappropriate features. Pianists reported their observations of dynamic variations and then attempted to imitate the model in their own performances. Results buttressed the contention that explicit planning strongly influenced dynamic expressivity.

In another nod toward the triumvirate that forms the basis of this chapter, Davidson and Malloch (2009) contended that performance goals, including both technical and expressive aims, and self-monitoring during a performance, which includes conceptual understanding and motor execution, influence the degree of bodily engagement of the performer. Of course, audience-performer interactions occur in a socio-cultural context, adding more layers of complexity. Davidson (1997), for example, found that performers' body movements enhanced audience members' understanding of the music. Further connections between body movements and expressivity are explored in the next section.

Musical Cues for Expressiveness

Another body of literature more directly connects body movements to music expressiveness. For example, Juslin, Friberg, Schoonderwaldt, and Karlsson (2004) provided an informative discussion of musical expressivity. In particular, they emphasized earlier work of Juslin (2003) in developing the *GERMS model*, which outlines the sources of musical expressivity:

- **G**enerative rules mark structural boundaries that performers emphasize, such as slowing down at cadence points.
- **E**motional expression comes from the manipulation of performance features such as tempo, timbre, dynamics, and so on.
- **R**andom fluctuations are limitations in human motor precision. Unlike quantized computer performances, unevenness in even the most expert performers is what gives music its human character.
- **M**otion principles relate tempo changes to natural body movements.
- **S**tylistic unexpectedness adds unpredictability or uncertainty to a performance.

Juslin developed the GERMS model on the basis of research studies, such as the following, that examined ways that performers alter musical parameters as a means of communicating emotions. Behrens and Green (1993) asked 58 undergraduate students, placed into high- and low-musicianship categories, to rate 24 solo improvisations created by performers on voice, trumpet, violin, and timpani. Performers improvised to express sad, angry, and scared emotions. Listeners were relatively accurate in assessing the emotional content. In a related experiment (Gabrielsson & Juslin, 1996), nine professional musicians performed short melodies on violin, electric guitar, flute, and voice to communicate various emotions. As before, listeners were generally successful in decoding intended expression. There were both similarities and differences in expressive gestures among the performers, and some emotions were easier to communicate than others.

Dahl and Friberg (2007) invited 20 participants with various musical backgrounds to rate silent video clips of marimba (Figure 13.6), bassoon, and saxophone performances of excerpts intended to express happy, sad, angry, and fearful emotions. The first three were well recognized, but fear was not. Emotional ratings correlated with specific musical characteristics; for example, happy excerpts were fast, loud, staccato, and strongly articulated, while sad excerpts were slow, soft, and legato. Body movements also corresponded to musical characteristics; tempo was related to gesture rate, loudness to gesture size, articulation to fast or slow gestures, and tone attack to gesture speed.

Chaffin, Lemieux, and Chen (2007) videotaped a pianist's practice sessions as she prepared for a professional recording of Bach's *Italian Concerto*. They analyzed seven uninterrupted performances for tempo, mean dynamic level, and dynamic variability as they related to musical

FIGURE 13.6 | Performers Can Enhance the Expression of Musical Emotions Through Body Gestures and Facial Expressions.

features such as large leaps, scales, changes of key, starts of phrases, and expressive intensity reported by the pianist. Variations in tempo and dynamic level were minimal. Mean tempo within performances varied by no more than three percent. Mean dynamic level varied by only one percent. Thus, the pianist balanced stability and accuracy with variety and spontaneity.

In a similar study, Sloboda and Lehmann (2001) tracked performance correlates of changes in perceived intensity of emotion during different interpretations of a Chopin piano prelude. Ten expert pianists recorded Chopin's Prelude, Op. 28, No. 4. Twenty-eight musicians evaluated these performances by rating expressivity both in moment-to-moment continuous responses and in post-performance ratings. The correlation between the two ratings was moderate ($r = 0.50$). The authors found systematic relationships between emotion ratings and deviations in such performance characteristics as timing, loudness, and phrasing. These deviations were intentional, as evidenced from interviews with the performers.

Timmers and Ashley (2007) examined the effects of ornamentation on emotional affect in violin and flute performances of a Handel sonata. Performers added ornamentation to three melodies to express happiness, sadness, love, and anger. Ornamentation involved variations in duration, timing, density, complexity, and loudness. Listeners were generally able to identify the portrayed emotion at well above chance levels, although they identified happiness less often than the other emotions.

As mentioned previously, singers have to express emotions inherent in both music and text. Researchers have used a variety of strategies to understand mechanisms and processes involved in vocal expressivity. One strategy has been to conduct acoustical analyses of live performances (Jansens, Bloothooft, & de Krom, 1997; Kotlyar & Morozov, 1976; Salgado, 2006; Sundberg, Iwarsson & Hagegård, 1994) or recordings (Rapoport, 1996; Siegwart & Scherer, 1995). In general, these researchers found systematic correlations among specific acoustical parameters and expressed emotions. For example, Jansens et al. (1997) found that joy was characterized by a shallow spectral slope (a measure of intensity) and fear with a steep spectral slope. Changes in timbral colors as reflected in variations in fundamental frequency and singer's formant/higher frequency bands were associated with emotional expressions in several studies (Kotlyar & Morozov, 1976; Rapoport, 1996; Siegwart & Scherer, 1995; Sundberg et al., 1994).

Another general strategy has been to link listeners' evaluations of emotional expression to such vocal characteristics as vibrato, tonal durations, tempo, and loudness. In one study (Jansens et al., 1997), 14 professional singers sang a phrase from Schubert's *Der Erlkönig* in five different ways, expressing anger, joy, fear, sadness, and a neutral expression. Although there was considerable variety in responses, in general listeners did successfully identify different emotions. They rated the performances such that anger was most associated with the presence of vibrato; joy with vibrato and short, final durations; and sadness with the absence of vibrato, long durations, and low intensity. Salgado (2006) asked an expert singer to prepare "Die Post" from Schubert's song cycle *Die Winterreise*. Fifteen participants observed a live performance while seated in front of a computer and provided real-time feedback on musically conveyed emotional content. The singer reviewed these responses and performed a second time. Ratings for emotional content improved the second time, as participants' ratings more closely matched the performer's intended expressions.

Juslin (2009a) provided two tables that help to organize the bewildering number of variables involved in music performance, one for the primary acoustic cues in musical performance and the other a summary of cues correlated with specific musical emotions. The first table explains how the following acoustic cues are defined and measured: pitch—fundamental frequency (F0), F0 contour, and vibrato; intensity—intensity and attack; temporal features—tempo, articulation, and timing; timbre—high-frequency energy and the singer's formant. The second table pairs specific emotions with acoustic and musical cues. For example, Juslin linked *happiness* to fast tempo, small tempo variability, major mode, and so on. He indicated cues that the performer can modulate (e.g., pitch, timing variability, etc.), as well as those that the performer does not control directly (e.g., specific pitch intervals, rhythm patterns, etc.).

Some researchers have investigated the extent to which performers can learn expressivity. Woody (2000) asked 46 college music students about how they learned and continued to develop expressivity in their performances. Their private instructors primarily used verbal-based instruction, but those teachers who modeled expressivity had a strong impact on the amount of time students spent practicing felt emotions. Woody (2002) also found that performers' prior conceptions of expressive aspects of a particular composition influenced perceptions of performances of that piece. Although music conservatory students felt that expressivity was the most important characteristic of performance, they also felt that it needed much more attention in their lessons (Lindström, Juslin, Bresin, & Williamon, 2003).

Marchand (1975) investigated two approaches to developing expressive performance. He placed 89 non-music major college students into one control and two treatment groups. Strategies in the Discovery Group focused on developing intrinsic learning motivation and self-initiated problem solving, while the approach in the Expository Group was more teacher-driven. Based on evaluations of musical performances, it was determined that both experimental methods were effective in teaching expressive performance skills. Furthermore, improving expressivity enhanced technical skills as well. McPhee (2011) investigated the teaching of musical expressiveness in one-to-one teaching of instrumental music. She found that although a variety of strategies were used, it may be more important to ensure that students have a solid grasp of the teachers' approach and that they develop a sense of personal meaning in their musical performances.

MUSICAL CREATIVITY

As has been the case with several topics in music psychology (e.g., musical emotions, religious and spiritual aspects, etc.), creativity was long neglected (e.g., Sloboda, 1985) but has more recently received a resurgence of interest (e.g., Hargreaves et al., 2012). Also, in keeping with many other topics, there is now such a body of literature that there is space here for only a cursory overview. A first difficulty in investigating musical creativity is an agreed-upon definition. In fact, there is none, although Runco and Jaeger (2012) discuss the pros and cons of what they call *the standard definition of creativity*: "Creativity requires both originality and effectiveness" (p. 92). Also, there is a general consensus that creativity normally involves such components as memory, divergent and convergent thinking, and flow (Gute & Gute, 2015), which will be discussed subsequently.

Frequently, one encounters the terms Big-C creativity and little-c creativity (Merrotsky, 2013). The first refers to the creative outputs of recognized experts, which is illustrated in the subtitle of Gardner's (2011) book, *Creating Minds: An Anatomy of Creativity Seen Through the Lives of Freud, Einstein, Picasso, Stravinsky, Eliot, Graham, and Gandhi*. Restricted to musical composition, we might include composers like Bach, Duke Ellington, and Paul McCartney. In contrast, little-c creativity refers to the fact that creativity is a hallmark of humanity and all of us possess it to one degree or another. Following brief descriptions of Big-C and little-c creativity, we will look at the more generic constructs of the aforementioned memory, divergent and convergent thinking, and flow, as well as the particular case of creativity during improvisation.

In studying Big-C creativity, musicologists and psychologists often use autobiographical and other historical writings (e.g., Abell, 1987; Fisk, 1997; Morgenstern, 1956). They also study manuscripts and sketches, such as those by Beethoven (Johnson, Tyson, & Winter, 1985) and Stravinsky (Stravinsky, 1969). Music psychologist John Sloboda, an avid amateur musician, described his compositional process through a protocol, in which he tried to describe his thoughts about various musical problems and solutions (Sloboda, 1985).

For all who are not recognized geniuses, little-c creativity is often investigated through an investigation of the four Ps: process, products, persons, and press (relationships between the person and the environment; Rhodes, 1961).

- Researchers may study the *process* and *products* through student compositions (e.g., Webster, 1990, 2012). In one instance, for example, Riley (2008) compared songs composed by Mexican children to traditional Mexican songs.
- Creativity in *persons* may be studied by such assessments as the *Guilford Test for Creativity* (Guilford, 1951), which tests for the ability to generate multiple uses for common objects) or the *Torrance Tests of Creative Thinking* (Frey, 2018), which tests for fluency, flexibility, originality, and elaboration. Webster (1994) developed *Measures of Creative Thinking in Music*, which measures four factors: musical extensiveness (the amount of time involved in creative tasks), musical flexibility (how the musical parameters of pitch, tempo, and dynamics are manipulated), musical originality (uniqueness in musical responses), and musical syntax (the extent to which the musical response is logical or makes sense).
- *Press* is represented in Csikzentimihályi's notion that "creativity depends on social context" (2014, p. 165). Gardner echoed that thought when he wrote, "because nearly all of Stravinsky's work was collaborative, an examination of his creative activity casts light on the political factors that permeate the planning, staging, and critical review of artistic performances" (2011, p. 11). In a study of children's composition, nine- and ten-year-old

Spanish students worked as a group to create a joint music composition (Viladot, Gómez, & Malagarriga, 2010).

Memory and Creativity

Memory plays a number of significant roles in creativity. Aspects of long-term memory are evident, first in the mechanics of composition, as codified by Berlioz (Macdonald, 2004), Rimsky-Korsakov (1922/1964), Schoenberg (1999), and many other composers. Perhaps more important, in terms of creativity, is the inspiration that comes from musical remembrances—folk music, other composers' music, one's own musical ideas, and so on. Brahms, for example, was highly inspired by the music of Bach, Mozart, and especially Beethoven. Nonmusical memories can also be inspirational, as Brahms was able to quote long passages of scripture from memory (Abell, 1987).

Short-term memory, or what is more frequently referred to as working memory, is the linkage between perception, long-term memory, and action (Baddeley, 2003). Information coming in from the senses or retrieved from memory storage is held in consciousness until it can be acted upon. Such a buffering mechanism also allows us to imagine this information as something new or utilized in a different way (Baddeley, 2012). After a series of experiments, one research group confirmed the connection between working memory capacity (WMC) and creativity (De Dreu, Nijstad, Baas, Wolsink, & Roskes, 2012). Among a group of cellists, for example, those with high WMC performed more creative improvisations than those with low WMC. Roden, Grube, Bongard, and Kreutz (2013) found that music training improved working memory.

Divergent and Convergent Thinking

Divergent thinking (DT) is a cognitive process in which many different ideas may be explored as possible solutions to a problem. Convergent thinking (CT) is the cognitive process of determining a correct or conventional solution (Runco, 2010). Although DT is more frequently linked to creativity, in actuality both are important (Sawyer, 2006). Webster (2002) developed a model in which creativity in music is seen as a result of interactions involving both DT and CT (see Fig. 13.7). Barbot and Lubart (2012) developed and tested an assessment tool for creative thinking in music called the Musical Expression Test (MET). MET was designed to test both divergent and convergent thinking skills in four subtests: free exploration, alternative-uses, composition, and improvisation. The first two tasks are behavioral and the last two "product-based." Compositions and improvisations produced by students were evaluated by eight judges and linkages were found between the behavioral and product-based measures. In other words, the importance of exploratory behaviors to creativity was confirmed by the musical products.

Flow

Flow is a state of complete absorption in a task in which nothing else seems to matter, time is suspended, and the individual in a flow state experiences joy and fulfillment (Csikzentmihályi, 2008). Flow is strongly connected to creativity, as exemplified in this quote from a composer trying to describe his experience of writing music:

> You yourself are in an ecstatic state to such a point that you feel as though you almost don't exist. I've experienced this time and time again. My hand seems devoid of myself,

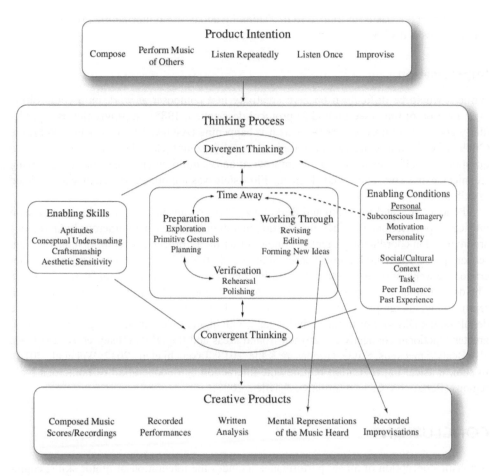

FIGURE 13.7 | Model of Creative Thinking Process in Music.

and I have nothing to do with what is happening. I just sit there watching it in a state of awe and wonderment. And it just flows out by itself.

(Csikzentmihályi, 2014, p. 142)

Flow is highly dependent upon a match between the task at hand and the skill level of the individual. A beginning violin student may become frustrated, angry, or want to quit if given a piece that is far beyond her ability to perform. Conversely, an advanced performer may be bored or unmotivated if asked to play literature that is too easy. When individuals at any level of development are intently engaged in activities that are well suited to their abilities, they may enter a flow state.

Flow involves a high degree of concentration. Limb and Braun (2008) asked jazz pianists to improvise while undergoing brain scans. One result was deactivation in frontal areas associated with self-monitoring and conscious control of ongoing behaviors. A similar deactivation was also seen in pianists performing Bach (Parsons et al., 2005). Clearly, whether performing a learned piece or improvising, the "mind" must get out of the way and let the "body" do what it has been trained to do. Thinking about or monitoring the process while it is in progress is disruptive.

Improvisation

While it would be difficult to observe creativity in a composer at work on a composition over a period of time (see Sloboda's protocol description, 1985), improvisation is a particularly good way to observe creativity as it is happening (Ashley, 2016). Biasutti and Frezza (2009) asked 76 musicians to improvise in classical, jazz, or rock styles, and to complete two questionnaires. Results indicated that improvisation is a multidimensional concept, involving technical, expressive, and social elements. Flow state was important, particularly as it related to skill level.

Beaty (2015) and Erkkinen and Berkowitz (2019) reviewed neuroscientific literature on musical improvisation. Together, the existing literature indicates that numerous brain regions are involved in coordinating attention, higher-order motor processing, emotional processing, sensory processing, and linguistic processing (e.g., in freestyle rap). A central theme is cooperation between brain networks involved in cognitive control and in spontaneous thought. The default mode network (DMN), implicated in autobiographical introspection, emotional reprocessing, and empathy for others, is also involved in creativity (see Chapter 9 for more details on the DMN). For instance, individuals with higher divergent thinking scores showed greater functional connectivity between frontal areas and the DMN (Beaty et al., 2014; see also Beaty, Smeekens, Silvia, Hodges, & Kane, 2013; Takeuchi et al., 2012; Wei et al., 2014). In sum, musical improvisation requires the interaction and cooperation of numerous brain regions (Bengtsson, Csikzentmihályi, & Ullén, 2007).

CONCLUSION

A holistic conception of music performance includes the integration of motor skills, cognitive skills, and expressive skills. If a performer expresses something in the music, she must do it by a physical gesture. Getting louder, changing timbral colors, or accenting a note are all performed by doing something—bowing faster, changing the shape of the oral cavity, or striking a key with more force. Furthermore, although in the moment of execution these gestures are likely to be more or less automatic, during the learning process they are more often thoughtful choices made in the planning of a performance. Within this broad outline, there are many additional subtopics. Wonderful resources that provide information beyond that which could be contained in this chapter include Altenmüller et al. (2006), Barry and Hallam (2002), Davidson (2005, 2009), Davidson and Correia (2002), Davidson, Howe, and Sloboda (1997), Gabrielsson (1992, 2003), Hallam (1997), Jørgensen (1997), Juslin and Persson (2002), Lehmann and Davidson (2002), Palmer (1997), and Sloboda (1982, 1985).

DISCUSSION QUESTIONS

1. Why are musicians called *small-muscle athletes*? What does this imply?
2. Have you ever experienced an improvement in your musical motor skills after sleeping? Do you regularly use sleep and rest as a strategy to improve motor learning skills?
3. 10,000 hours of deliberate practice over a period of ten years is an approximate benchmark for high-level music performance. Can you estimate how many hours you practiced up to the age of 20? At what age did you start studying music?

4. To what extent were your parents involved in your early music studies? Did they supervise or monitor your practice sessions? What other kinds of support did they provide (e.g., driving you to lessons or rehearsals, purchasing instruments, music, or supplies, etc.)? What are some possible effects of parents who provide too little support or who apply too much pressure to succeed?

5. Have you ever used mental rehearsal as a strategy for learning music? How did it work? What are some advantages and disadvantages of such an approach?

6. Discuss the role of music reading in developing musicianship skills. Is sight-reading an important skill for you to develop for your musical career? For what musical practices is music reading less important or not important at all? Is ability to read music related to level of musicianship?

7. Comment on the relevance of the following terms to your own musical growth and development: metacognition, self-regulation, motivation, and self-efficacy.

8. Describe the role of body movement in musical performance. How much is too much and how much is too little? How much do you consciously attend to body movement in your own performances?

9. Choose a simple melody and play it a number of times, each time expressing a different emotion. What musical changes did you make to express happiness, sadness, anger, and so on? What body movement changes did you have to make? In a related experiment, select a solo piece you are working on and try to perform it expressively, while restraining physical movement. How did that feel? How did it affect the performance?

10. What suggestions have your teachers given you to improve musical expressiveness? Have they modeled expressiveness for you?

Chapter 14

The Psychology of Music Learning

EXACTLY how human beings learn has puzzled and challenged psychologists for decades. The general term for their conclusions is called *learning theories*, although that phrase is no longer in vogue. One cannot automatically assume that a general theory of learning is relevant to music learning, however, a number of researchers have applied selected theories to musical teaching/learning situations. Thus, psychologists have much to offer in the way of understanding music learning.

One way to approach this topic is to imagine that the same behavior is being examined from different perspectives. As indicated in Figure 14.1, psychologists from each viewpoint can consider the same musical behavior and provide unique insights. Often the ideas of one theorist are antithetical to those of another. It is important to remember that none of the current perspectives has the ultimate answer so far. One viewpoint may be more useful in a given setting than another, but none is the correct, true, or only one. This is a vast topic, and the present chapter can only provide a brief overview of selected theories. Many resources are provided for those who wish to delve deeper into these matters.

Because of the complicated nature of human learning, there is no agreed-upon organizational scheme. For simplicity, many authors (e.g., Bigge & Shermis, 2004; Olson & Hergenhahn, 2008; Pritchard, 2009) group various theories primarily into two camps: behaviorist and cognitivist. The central focus of behaviorism is on observable human behavior. All of the varying viewpoints grouped under cognitivism share a common notion that there are internal or mindful processes at work as well.

In contrast to a two-part scheme, this chapter is organized into four sections (Table 14.1). We begin with psychoanalysis because even though it is not, strictly speaking, a learning theory, it does have the potential to provide insights into musical behavior. Behavioral psychology is discussed next because although it is no longer as prevalent or dominant as it once was, it still has much to offer in practical applications to music teaching and learning. Cognitive approaches to learning receive the lion's share of attention because of their currency and prominence in explaining how we learn. Finally, a brief section on music teaching and learning provides one example of a research-based approach.

PSYCHOANALYSIS

Sigmund Freud was so dominating as a theorist of the mind that an entire viewpoint has been developed around his ideas. Even today, many of the disagreements among his followers center on whether to maintain a strict adherence to his writings or whether to admit modifications

**Psychoanalysis
Behavioral Psychology**

**Cognitive Approaches:
Humanistic Psychology
Gestalt Psychology
Developmental Psychology
Social Psychology
Cognitive Psychology
Cognitive Neuroscience**

FIGURE 14.1 | Varying Psychological Viewpoints, Each Considering the Same Musical Behavior From a Unique Perspective.

TABLE 14.1 | Psychological Approaches Applied to Music Learning.

PSYCHOANALYSIS

BEHAVIORAL PSYCHOLOGY

COGNITIVE APPROACHES
  Humanistic psychology
  Gestalt psychology
  Developmental psychology
  Social psychology
  Cognitive psychology
    Bruner
    Taxonomies
    Music intelligence
    Music cognition, music learning, and reflective thinking
Cognitive neuroscience

MUSIC TEACHING AND LEARNING

(Gardner, 2007). As noted, psychoanalysis is not a learning theory (Hilgard & Bower, 1966), although some see a connection to cognitive psychology (Getzels, 1964). Freud has many detractors as well as apologists (Marinelli & Mayer, 2006; Western, 1999). Nevertheless, some of the central ideas are worth examining as they appear to offer important insights into musical behavior.

One of Freud's central beliefs was that human beings store repressed memories in the unconscious mind (Freud, 1910/1957). *Psychoanalysis* is a technique Freud developed to gain access to the unconscious mind through free associations, along with the interpretation of dreams and hypnosis, for the purpose of curing neuroses (Davis, 2004; Zangwill, 2004). In *free association*, the therapist invites the patient to say anything that comes to mind, without filtering. Through intuition, the therapist links ideas together and facilitates the patient's journey of self-discovery. Ideally, the patient will allow unresolved conflicts to surface for conscious examination and resolution. In 1910, Gustav Mahler consulted with Freud for four hours, possibly concerning his relationship with his wife, Alma (Fig. 14.2) (Kuehn, 1965–

FIGURE 14.2 | Sigmund Freud (1856–1939), Gustav Mahler (1860–1911), and Alma Mahler (1879–1964).

66). Whether or not these sessions helped, Gustav and Alma seemed to be happier in their last few months together before he died.

In spite of the session with Mahler, music played a minor role in Freud's writings and teachings. Because of its ineffable nature, he thought music was obscure and unreachable (Gilman, 2019). However, Freud did refer more often to art in general, viewing art as a disguised expression for unconscious, unfulfilled wishes. Although art is similar to imagination, dreams, and other forms of fantasy, it has the distinction of having value for more than the artist. Other persons may also learn from or find symbolic meanings in art's reflection of reality. Oddly enough, in spite of music's symbolic nature and its power to elicit strong and associative responses, psychoanalysts have largely ignored music as a therapeutic tool. In a corresponding vein, music therapists have also tended to avoid a connection with Freudian theory, in spite of an extensive review of psychoanalytic theory and the meaning of music in a series of articles in the *Journal of Music Therapy* (Noy, 1966–67).

The lack of strong connections between psychoanalytic theories and music notwithstanding, it is possible to find examples of psychoanalysts who use music and music therapists who base their treatments on psychoanalytic techniques. An example of the former is Theodore Reik (1888–1969), who was a student and close follower of Freud. He wrote a book, *The Haunting Melody*, about "the significance of musical recollections within the flow of our thoughts" (Reik, 1953, p. 8). As a psychoanalyst, he was interested in learning what remembered melodies (that is, melodies that might come to mind during free association) might reveal about unconscious thought. In this book, he recounted many examples of how melodies recalled during psychoanalytic sessions provided keys to the understanding of a problem. Pfeifer proposed a theory that might account for Reik's experiences. Pfeifer theorized that, "music preoccupies the conscious mind, allowing unconscious fantasies and repressed memories to be released" (cited in Ingeber, Broudy, & Pearson, 1982, p. 78).

A noted music therapist, Helen Bonny, used music more directly in therapeutic settings. In a co-authored book (Bonny & Savary, 1973), she described a technique of using music in combination with relaxation-concentration exercises to explore imagery in altered states of consciousness. Guided Imagery and Music (GIM), as the technique is called, involves an exploration of conflicted areas of the self. It may be used in private psychiatric practice to help release blocked areas of the personality, to bring about insight into why the problems have arisen, and to suggest modes of action to correct and sustain growth (Bonny, 1980, p. 230).

Thus, a Freudian view of human nature appears to be rich with possibilities for applications to musical behavior (Feder, Karmel, & Pollock, 1993). However, psychoanalytic theory has not been brought to bear on music to the degree that other psychological viewpoints have. Perhaps this is so because few musicians have the requisite training to be competent in applying psychoanalytic techniques to musical situations.

BEHAVIORAL PSYCHOLOGY

A number of psychologists, notably including Ivan Pavlov and B.F. Skinner (see Fig. 14.3), have been concerned primarily with observable behavior and ways of modifying those behaviors. Pavlov (1927/2003) was the first to establish the basic principles of *classical conditioning*. By pairing the sound of a tone with food presented to a hungry dog, he created a connection between the stimulus (the tone) and the response (salivation), even in the absence of food. A number of important behaviorists, who came between Pavlov and Skinner, made important additions, including Edward Thorndike (1874–1949), John Watson (1878–1958), Clark Hull (1884–1952), and Edwin Guthrie (1886–1959). See Buttram (1996) for more details on their contributions.

Skinner (1953) further developed behavioral approaches into what he called *operant conditioning*, in which he emphasized the consequences of an action. Key concepts include:

- *Positive reinforcement*: the addition of something pleasant following a behavior.
- *Negative reinforcement*: the removal of something unpleasant following a behavior.
- *Punishment*: the removal of something pleasant or the presentation of something unpleasant following a behavior.
- *Extinction*: the lack of any reinforcement following a behavior.

FIGURE 14.3 | Ivan Pavlov (1849–1936) and B.F. Skinner (1904–1990).

The first three are ways of increasing the likelihood of a behavior reoccurring, with positive reinforcement being the most effective. Often, these are referred to globally as *feedback* (Duke, 2005). Extinction can be a very powerful way of eliminating undesired behaviors because a behavior is unlikely to persist in the absence of reinforcement or feedback.

One can modify complex behaviors through behavioral conditioning. To do so, the operation of interest, say playing the violin, is first analyzed and then divided into a series of less complicated behaviors, a procedure called *task analysis*. As the first step in the series is accomplished, it is immediately followed by a pleasurable reward, which makes it more likely that the desired behavior will occur again in similar circumstances. *Modeling* the appropriate or desired behavior is also an effective technique. Behaviors are *shaped* toward the desired outcome in a process called *successive approximation*. As each step in the series is learned, it is linked to previously acquired steps to form a larger unit of the complex behavior in a process called *chaining*. In these ways, behavior is shaped toward the desired outcome.

In its simplest format, applying *behaviorism* to music teaching can be stated in three steps: "(1) teacher presentation of a task, (2) student response, and (3) teacher reinforcement" (Yarbrough & Price, 1981, p. 212). The results of numerous experiments indicate that students are likely to be more on-task academically and socially, have better attitudes, and demonstrate better achievement when the learning environment is positive. Madsen and Yarbrough (1980, p. 39) outlined five techniques for establishing a positive approach to music teaching/learning based on research. According to the data, the most effective teachers:

1. *Establish classroom rules and contingencies for both social and academic behavior.* Classroom rules should be stated explicitly and students should know what benefits there are to following the rules and what penalties there are for not following them.
2. *Act in an approving way toward appropriate student behavior for about 80% of the total reinforcement frequency.* Positive feedback can be verbal or nonverbal and should be age and ability appropriate. Notice that it does not say to act approving 80% of the time, but for 80% of the total reinforcements given. Younger students need much more feedback for their behavior. As students get older they may need less feedback, but 80% of it should still be positive. We never outgrow our need for people to approve of our behavior.
3. *Act in a negative or disapproving way toward inappropriate student behavior for only 20% of the total reinforcement frequency.* A teacher may think, "There is so much misbehavior in my classroom, how can I be disapproving for only 20% of my reinforcements?" Ignore the inappropriate behaviors (extinction) and approve the appropriate ones. Catch someone in the class behaving correctly and reinforce that instead of paying attention to and thus reinforcing the inappropriate behavior. Often a teacher ignores those in the class who are on task and instead focuses her attention on the students who are off-task. Research indicates that disapproving or ignoring inappropriate behavior in the absence of approving appropriate behavior actually increases the undesired behaviors. When 80% of the feedback is approval of appropriate behavior, 20% is disapproval of inappropriate behavior, and the remaining inappropriate behaviors are ignored, students show the highest percentage of on-task behavior. Because music and music making are so reinforcing, music classrooms and rehearsals with a lower rate of positive feedback can still be perceived as a positive environment.
4. *Never make errors of reinforcement;* that is, the most effective teachers strive not to approve inappropriate behavior or disapprove appropriate behavior. Approval errors teach students two things: when I'm bad, good things happen to me and when I'm good, bad things happen to me. Obviously, we want the reverse.

5. *Use dramatic elements such as high intensity, rapid change of pace, and exaggeration in their teaching.* Teachers are more effective when they maintain eye contact, use frequent physical proximity as a reinforcer, vary vocal inflections and loudness, use extensive gestures and animated facial expressions, and keep a fast pace with less talking and more performing or other student activities.

Duke (2005) made the point that expert teachers do not simply wait until the student acts and then provide appropriate feedback. Rather, they structure tasks in such a way that the outcome is likely known. They intentionalize student success; after all, why plan to have a student fail? He stated that, "purposeful feedback is the planned consequence of a sequence of events that is highly structured and whose outcome is predictable" (Duke, 2005, p. 136).

Music performing and music listening activities have been used successfully as reinforcers for learning in traditional school subjects such as mathematics or language arts. For example, it has been demonstrated that music listening activities of both a group and individualized nature serve as effective rewards in significantly increasing correct responses to mathematical problems (Madsen & Forsythe, 1973). Similar results have been obtained in numerous studies with other academic subjects.

Closely allied to the use of music in the learning of academic material is the use of music in the modification of social behaviors. For example, in a classic behavior modification experiment, researchers wished to decrease the amount of fighting and out-of-seat behaviors engaged in by emotionally disturbed children as they rode on a school bus (McCarty, McElfresh, Rice, & Wilson, 1978). Popular music was played on the bus as long as appropriate behaviors were observed; the music was turned off at the incidence of inappropriate behavior. The use of music was effective in reducing inappropriate behaviors.

In contrast to the lack of application of a Freudian view, many applications of a behavioral view have been made to music (Greer, 1981). A major strength of this research strategy has been the accumulation of many techniques that are useful in improving musical behaviors or in modifying nonmusical behaviors using music as a reinforcer. Although these principles are based on published research, Sink (2002) found that some research did not support all these claims. For example, Yarbrough (1975) observed four mixed choruses who were rehearsed by their regular conductor, a high magnitude conductor, and a low magnitude conductor. Yarbrough found that different conductor behaviors had no significant effect on student performances, student attentiveness, or student attitudes. In a similar vein, Kuhn (1975) investigated the effects of teacher approval and disapproval on attentiveness, musical achievement, and attitude. He randomly assigned 99 fifth-grade students to one of four treatment groups. Three groups received six taped instructional lessons covering content assessed in a pretest and posttest. For Group 1, the teacher approval rate was 80%, for Group 2 it was only 20%, and for Group 3 there was no teacher feedback. Students in Group 4 received music lessons unrelated to the pretest-posttest content. Students in Group 1, receiving teacher approval, followed class rules better than the other students, but there were no significant differences in music achievement or in attitude among the four groups.

Behaviorism is no longer a prevailing view in psychology because it fails to account for mediating cognitive processes. Behaviorists worked hard to dispel the notion of a mental life. J.B. Watson, one of the most influential behaviorists, wrote these statements in 1924: "You know he [a behaviorist] recognizes no such thing as mental traits, dispositions or tendencies" (p. 78). "Talking and thinking which, when rightly understood, go far in breaking down the fiction that there is any such thing as a 'mental life'" (p. 180). Perhaps Watson's position is understandable given the lack of knowledge at the time, but exactly 50 years later, well after the cognitive revolution was underway, B. F. Skinner made these comments: "The present argument is this: mental life and the world in which it is lived are inventions" (1974, p. 104). "The objection to the inner workings of the mind is not that they are not open to inspection but that they have stood in the way of the inspection of more important things" (1974, p. 165). That behaviorism is no longer a dominant view was confirmed by Robins, Gosling, and Craik (1999) when they conducted an empirical review of schools of psychology based on an extensive analysis of publications. They found that behavioral psychology had declined since the 1970s and that cognitive psychology was the most prominent school. Nevertheless, behavioral principles still have a great deal to offer teachers and therapists.

COGNITIVE APPROACHES

Uttal (2000) framed the contrast between behaviorism and cognitivism (or mentalism as he called it) in the ways the two groups responded to these questions: "Can the mind be observed, measured, and then analyzed into its parts? In other words, is it accessible to scientific examinations?" (p. 1). We have already seen that the behaviorists answered "no" to these questions. With a variety of approaches, psychologists who have taken a cognitive approach have said, "yes." In turn, we will see how humanistic psychologists, Gestalt psychologists, developmental psychologists, social psychologists, cognitive psychologists, and cognitive neuroscientists have framed their own positions on this matter.

Humanistic Psychology

Abraham Maslow (1908–1970) and Carl Rogers (1902–1987) are two of the foremost names in *humanistic psychology*. Maslow (1968c) referred to his approach as *third force psychology* because he viewed it as an alternative view to Freudianism and behaviorism. The primary focus of humanistic psychologists is on *self-actualization*, the natural, healthy development of a person to become fully who he or she has the potential to become. Maslow (1943) created a *hierarchy of human needs*, which can be visualized as a pyramid with a number of steps leading to self-actualization at the top (see Fig. 14.4). Each step represents a category of needs that must be satisfied before one proceeds to the next step.

These needs, in order from lowest to highest, are the following:

- Physical needs, such as the need for food, water, and air. Everyone must satisfy physical needs just to survive. Beyond that, however, those who are living at a subsistence level are not free to develop themselves to the fullest. Their concentration is on simply staying alive.

FIGURE 14.4 | Maslow's Hierarchy of Human Needs.

- Safety and security needs. It is a basic human need to feel safe and secure. We need to live in an orderly, predictable, and nonthreatening environment. Music teachers can provide a safe haven or they can create a very threatening environment.
- The need for love and belongingness. We need to feel loved and as if we belong. Music teachers have the opportunity to provide a loving environment where students have a sense of belonging to a larger unit.
- Esteem needs. It is normal and healthy for a person to feel good about herself and to want others to feel good about her as well. Stunted personal growth comes when the individual becomes paranoid about what others think of her or when she has a deep and abiding lack of self-esteem; we might characterize this as having an inferiority complex. Contrarily, someone with a superiority complex may think too highly of herself. Music teachers can promote or destroy healthy self-esteem, often by the most casual of comments or actions.
- The need for knowledge and understanding. An important higher order need is to satisfy the thirst human beings have to acquire knowledge. This natural inquisitiveness goes beyond the acquisition of mere facts and extends to an understanding of the meaning of facts, the underlying principles or theories, and the relationships among parts that create "the big picture." Music learning provides unlimited growth potential, not only in developing technique, but also in musical expressivity, and in understanding and responding to subtleties and nuances in music.
- Growth needs. It is at this point in a person's self-actualization process that he is free to search for truth and beauty. Satisfying aesthetic needs is an important growth process. No longer bound by a need to establish oneself or a need to worry about one's reputation, this type of individual is about the business of becoming the most complete version of who one can be. Music learning at this point moves beyond technique and into artistry.
- Self-Actualization. People who are self-actualized have a high-level of maturity, psychological/emotional health, and self-fulfillment (Maslow, 1968b). A self-actualized person is "more truly himself, more perfectly actualizing his potentialities, closer to the core of his Being, more fully human" (1968b, p. 97). Speaking of the need for self-actualization, Maslow wrote, "A musician must make music, an artist must paint, a poet must write, if he is to be ultimately happy. What a man *can* be, he *must* be. This need we may call self-actualization." (1943, p. 382). Rowan (1998) contends that the use of a pyramid to represent growth toward self-actualization is misleading. He feels that it indicates that there is an end to personal growth; rather, it should be open-ended because the process is ongoing.

Every learning experience has both extrinsic and intrinsic aspects. *Extrinsic learning* experiences are those that are common to a group and that can be shared among members of the group. Furthermore, extrinsic learning experiences do not fundamentally change a person's self-identity. For example, when Jill learns, along with her classmates, how to finger G on the recorder, she is learning shared knowledge.

Intrinsic learning experiences are individualized, internal experiences that cannot be shared with someone else, in the sense that another person will feel or experience the same thing. Even though Jill and her classmates have learned how to finger G on the recorder in the same way, how Jill interprets this new knowledge is personal. Suppose her best friend Emily missed that lesson. Jill could show Emily how to finger G on the recorder, and she could share how she feels about it, but she cannot enable or cause Emily to have the same internal experience. Consider such experiences as playing a first solo in public, hearing a great concert artist in person, or listening to a favorite recording. One could share extrinsic aspects (e.g., the date of the recital or concert, the pieces performed, etc.). Personal, intrinsic aspects—the fear of performing in public, the elation at hearing a great artist, and so on—can be shared in only a limited way.

Intrinsic learning experiences help shape and mold us as human beings. Maslow does not denigrate extrinsic learning experiences; in fact, they may in some circumstances serve to enhance intrinsic learning experiences. However, he does believe that too many individuals seem unaware of the critical importance of intrinsic learning experiences. Special intrinsic experiences called *peak experiences* are particularly crucial (Maslow, 1971, 1976). These are mountain-top experiences that transport the individual beyond immediate circumstances. Peak experiences are difficult to verbalize, but characteristic descriptions are of moments of bliss, rapture, or great joy, moments of transcendence, moments when an individual feels at his or her very best—strong, whole, and in control. Peak experiences often leave vibrant, emotionally charged memories; they frequently serve as milestones to mark the progress of one's life.

Music is one of the most common ways of having a peak experience (Maslow, 1968a). In fact, Maslow stated that, "the two easiest ways of getting peak experiences (in terms of simple statistics in empirical reports) are through music and through sex" (1970, p. 169). Music, then, is one of the major avenues toward the full development of a person, toward the discovery of self-identity. Musical experiences, particularly those classified as peak experiences, have important consequences and are to be valued for the role they can play in the self-actualizing process. Musical peak experiences may lead to startling discoveries or enlightening insights that may leave a person profoundly changed. Recall from Chapter 11 that Gabrielsson (2001, 2010) found strong connections between peak experiences and the reports his participants wrote on Strong Experiences with Music.

Carl Rogers developed a person-centered approach to therapy and learning. "Individuals have within themselves vast resources for self-understanding and for altering their self-concepts, basic attitudes, and self-directed behavior; these resources can be tapped if a definable climate of facilitative psychological attitudes can be provided" (Rogers, 1980, p. 115). These psychological attitudes included genuineness, acceptance, and empathetic understanding on the part of the therapist.

1. The nonevaluative and acceptant quality of the empathetic climate enables persons . . . to take a prizing, caring attitude toward themselves.
2. Being listened to by someone who understands makes it possible for persons to listen more accurately to themselves, with greater empathy toward their own visceral experiencing, their own vaguely felt meanings.
3. The individuals' greater understanding of and prizing of themselves opens to them new facets of experience that become part of a more accurately based self-concept.

(1980, p. 159)

There should be a place for learning by the whole person, with feelings and ideas merged.

Rogers (1951, 1961, 1969) applied humanistic principles to teaching and learning situations and to therapy. Some of the main features are a focus on individual growth and development rather than group comparisons, a nonthreatening learning environment, the teacher or therapist as facilitator, and learning that involves the whole person, both intellect and emotions. Music programs can provide a positive atmosphere within which to achieve each of these goals. Each individual has the opportunity for a personal experience in music, even as a member of an ensemble. Music classes can provide the opportunity for everyone to succeed at his or her own level; even the last chair player can be "successful" if the musical experience is a positive and rewarding one.

As can be seen, there is much in humanistic psychology that can be applied to music. Although most of the applications have not yet been validated through experimental research, the potential for significant transfer is apparent.

Gestalt Psychology

Recall from Chapter 7 that Gestalt psychology, as developed by Wertheimer (1880–1943), Köhler (1887–1967), and Koffka (1886–1941), primarily deals with the organization of perceptions. The term *Gestalt* means "whole" and thus a main concern was for the overall structure or total viewpoint of a given situation. This is aptly summarized in the statement: "The whole is different from the sum of its parts," which indicates that analyzing an experience for its constituent parts will not necessarily lead to a complete understanding. Other key concepts include figure-ground relationships and the Law of Prägnanz, with its corollaries.

Because we covered Gestalt principles so thoroughly in Chapter 7, we only need to make a few additional points. Two aspects of Gestalt psychology have particular application for learning. The first is that people often learn through *insight* rather than trial and error (Wertheimer, 1959). This is sometimes known as *Aha!* learning. The second is a rejection of reductionism and instead an emphasis on a holistic view of learning. Cognitive psychologists have built on these ideas and a more complete discussion is found in that section of this chapter.

Developmental Psychology

Developmental psychologists are particularly concerned with human growth and development. Their work has been highly influenced by the Swiss scholar Jean Piaget (1896–1980). One of Piaget's major contributions was to identify the stages of development through which all children go (Piaget, 1947/2001; Piaget & Inhelder, 1969/2000). These include the sensorimotor stage (from birth to age two), the pre-operational stage (from two to seven years of age), the concrete operational stage (from age 7 to 11), and the formal operational stage (from age 11 to adulthood). These ranges represent approximate periods of development. Throughout these stages of development, children adapt to the environment by developing schemas or patterns of response. New experiences that call for previously established responses are said to be *assimilated*; experiences that require a change in response cause a modification in the schema called *accommodation*.

During the *sensorimotor stage* a child learns primarily by direct sensory experiences and through physical involvement with the environment. Objects are "real" only when they are physically present to be touched, tasted, heard, seen, or smelled. A vocabulary is developed during the *pre-operational stage* that allows the child to refer to objects symbolically. Thus, the word "ball" refers not just to the particular object a child is holding, but to a class of objects, which might have a variety of sizes, shapes, colors, and functions.

The *concrete operational stage* is characterized by increasing language skills and a growing sense of the relationship between and among objects and events. A noteworthy watershed occurs when a child is able to retain a sense of the whole, even though the parts or relationships among parts of the whole are changed. *Conservation*, as Piaget called this skill, is demonstrated, for example, by the illustration of a lump of clay retaining the same weight and volume of space, while being manipulated into different shapes or by a beaker of water poured into two smaller glasses (Fig. 14.5). The *formal operational stage* is characterized by advancing skills in logical and abstract thought processes. At this stage a person attains adult problem-solving skills.

Using the foregoing brief descriptions, parallels can be made between Piagetian stages of development and stages of musical development. Thus, the sensorimotor stage would be

FIGURE 14.5 | Illustration of Piaget's Concept of Conservation. The amount of water in the two glasses matches the amount in the beaker. Even though the water changes shape, it retains the same volume.

characterized by immediate aural and physical experiences with a child's sonic environment. Cooing and babbling, followed by increasingly sophisticated vocalizations, shaking a rattle, listening to a crib mobile or mother's singing would be common infant experiences with sounds. During the pre-operational stage, increasingly musical experiences occur, with the child able to sing and recognize an ever-wider repertoire of songs. Conservation, attained during the concrete operational stage, allows for the retention of melodic contour in spite of transpositions and the maintenance of steady tempo despite the occurrence of fast or slow note values. Finally, during formal operations, dealing with more sophisticated musical analyses becomes possible, as does dealing with abstract musical concepts.

Most of the research that would substantiate the application of Piaget's theories to musical development has centered on the concept of conservation. Following a series of studies, involving melodic and rhythmic conservation, Pflederer (1964) concluded that Piaget's concept of conservation could be applied to musical thought. Children were much better at such tasks as conserving a melody under deformation of pitch at age 8 than at age 5. This conclusion is supported by other research findings as well. The acquisition of conservation may not, however, be impervious to the effects of training. Botvin (1974) influenced melodic conservation by using reinforcement techniques and Foley (1975) increased second graders' conservation of tonal and rhythmic patterns through training.

Not all developmental psychologists adhere strictly to Piaget's stages. Looking at the development of musical skills from a broader, less categorized, perspective leads to the following profile (greatly reduced and simplified). (For more details see Andress, 1986; Davidson, McKernon, & Gardner, 1981; Dowling, 1999; Gembris, 2002; Gembris & Davidson, 2002; Imberty, 1996; McDonald & Simons, 1989; McPherson, 2014; H. Papousek, 1996; M. Papousek, 1996; Pouthas, 1996; Simons, 1986).

- Pre-natal: While more is being learned about fetal reactions to sound and music, very little is known about the impact of these experiences on later musical development. See Chapter 6 for information on fetal and infant auditory processing.

- Birth to 1: Newborns one to five days old demonstrate an ability to discriminate differences in frequency. The onset of cooing and purposeful vocal sounds is 15–16 weeks. Five-month old babies show a sensitivity to melodic contour and rhythmic changes. Some six-month old babies are successful in matching specific pitches. During the first year of life, most babies are alert and responsive to musical stimuli; through babbling and cooing they engage in considerable melodic and intonational experimentation.
- 1–1.5 years: Activation to music through rocking, marching, rolling, and attending intently is more pronounced. Experimentation with pitch variations continues; movement between tones is by glissando, not discrete pitches.
- 1.5–2.5 years: The glissando technique for sliding between ambiguous pitches changes into a capacity for producing discrete pitches. The child begins systematic drill of intervals in fragments, including seconds, minor thirds, and major thirds, gradually expanding to include fourths and fifths. This is a period of spontaneous song, that is, improvised song fragments consisting of selected intervals are practiced. These songs are not clearly organized, and contain little tonality or regularity of rhythms.
- 2.5–3 years: Spontaneous songs gradually give over to recognition and imitation of folk tunes in the environment, such as the *ABC Song*, *Old MacDonald*, and *Mary had a Little Lamb*. Often these take the form of multiple repetitions of learned fragments and/or variations. For Piagetian researchers, singing between 1.5 and 2.5 represents assimilation; fitting any song into a schema the child has already developed. During the next period, the child must accommodate to the limitations of culturally approved songs. By the end of the third year a rhythmic structure is learned.
- 3–4 years: By now the child is capable of reproducing an entire song in terms of the overall contour. However, accurate pitch representation, as opposed to contour, is not always possible.
- 5 years: An underlying pulse is extracted from surface rhythm so that a child is able to keep a steady beat. The child is now able to sing an entire song in the same key without modulating, with an increasing awareness of a set of pitches instead of contour only.

During the next five years, the child increasingly acquires a stable, internal pitch framework. This process has some temporary plateaus, but pitch and rhythm accuracy increase slowly, yet inexorably, in most children. Musical development continues to occur throughout a person's lifetime and encompasses the changing voice for boys, vocal maturation, music reading skills, listening skills, movement, the development of specific musical behaviors (such as learning to play a certain instrument), and increasing aesthetic sensibility.

Critical to musical development in the earliest years is the home environment. Opportunities, not just to hear music, but to interact in musical games and activities is critical to emotional and psychological development (Dissanayake, 2000; Gembris & Davidson, 2002). Developmental psychologists have made major strides in documenting the various stages of musical growth. However, what remains is for these data to be unified and placed in a theory that would be prescriptive as well as descriptive.

Social Psychology

Social psychology deals with how individuals grow, develop, learn, and interact in the societies in which they live (Fraser, 2004). As a whole, social psychology is concerned with three major themes: (1) the social nature of the individual; that is, how the biologically inheritable traits have been acted upon by the environment such that the person develops into a functioning adult; (2) social interactions; that is, how language and non-verbal forms of

Being Musical communication allow for the exchange of ideas, information, feelings, and group coopera-tion; (3) representations of the social world; that is, how the image we have in our minds of our surrounding environment impacts our behavior.

Because this discipline is far too broad for thorough coverage in this book, the focus in this chapter will be on social learning. (Additional aspects of music and sociology are covered in Chapter 16.) From this perspective, individuals learn a great deal from others within the immediate social circle, for example, parents, siblings, friends, teachers, and so on. Social learning involves concepts such as observational learning, imitation, and modeling (Ormond, 1999). Put more simply, "social learning involves the acquisition of those behavior patterns which society expects" (Lefrancois, 1979, p. 100). Social learning not only helps to bring about acceptable behaviors, it also discourages unacceptable behaviors.

Kurt Lewin (1890–1947) is considered by some to be the father of social psychology (Taetle & Cutietta, 2002). Lewin developed a *field theory* that involved a person's *life space* (Buttram, 1996). A person's life space is the immediate social environment in which he or she lives. The life space is like a map that contains goals that attract the individual (posi-tive valence) or factors that repel the individual (negative valence). Approach and avoidance behaviors are seen as attempts to move toward or away from these factors. Barriers may prevent one from approaching. There are many depictions of life space, but Figure 14.6 pro-vides a simple one. In it, one can see that learning should be understood within the context of the individual's social environment. Learning rarely, if ever, takes places place in a vacuum; rather, it occurs as the person engages with people and things in his or her surroundings.

Another early figure in social learning was Lev (Leo) Vygotsky (Fig. 14.7). In particular, his ideas influenced a social constructivist approach to learning. In this view, a child con-structs knowledge on the basis of interactions with the environment (Taetle & Cutietta, 2002). *Constructivism* is an educational approach that has roots in both cognitive and social psychol-ogy. The ideas of Bruner and Vygotsky are central and formative (Hanley & Montgomery,

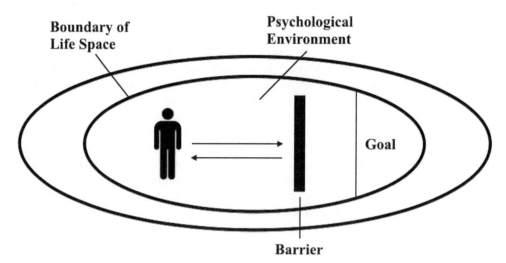

FIGURE 14.6 | A Simple Model of Lewin's Life Space. Persons may exhibit approach and avoidance behaviors as they encounter barriers blocking progress toward a desired goal. For example, in seeking to perform an excellent recital (i.e., the goal), music students may seek either to overcome (approach behavior) or succumb to (avoidance behavior) performance anxiety (a barrier).

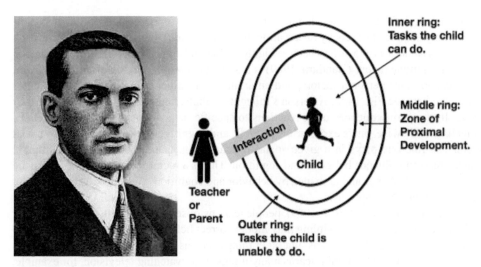

Inner ring:
Tasks the child
can do.

Middle ring:
Zone of
Proximal
Development.

Interaction

Child

Teacher
or
Parent

Outer ring:
Tasks the child is
unable to do.

FIGURE 14.7 │ Lev Vygotsky (1896–1934) and His Zone of Proximal Development (ZPD). The ZPD is an area between what the child can accomplish by himself and what he can do with assistance.

2002), along with those of Dewey and Piaget (Imig, 1997). Richardson (1997) characterizes the approach in this way:

> constructivism is a learning or meaning-making theory. It suggests that individuals create their own new understanding, based upon the interaction of what they already know and believe, and the phenomena or ideas with which they come into contact. Constructivism is a descriptive theory of learning (this is the way people learn or develop); it is not a prescriptive theory of learning (this is the way people *should* learn).
>
> (p. 3)

Constructivist teachers create an environment where children can explore, discover, and create their own knowledge. Constructivist teachers are guides for their students' learning and respond to children's interests and curiosity. Morford (2007), Scott (2006), and Wiggins (2004) are among those who have specifically applied a constructivist approach to the teaching of music.

While studying language development, Vygotsky became convinced that higher psychological processes have a social origin (Luria, 2004). A key idea was his notion of the *zone of proximal* (or *potential*) *development* (ZPD) that reflects the difference between a person's capacity to solve a problem on his own and the capacity to solve a problem with assistance (Fig. 14.7). Teachers, parents, or older children often help a child perform functions and activities beyond what the child can do alone. Gradually, the child learns to perform independently. Thus, an area of future development (ZPD) surrounds what a child can do independently.

Neil Miller (1909–2002) and John Dollard (1900–1980) wrote an influential book entitled *Social Learning and Imitation* (Miller & Dollard, 1941). As the title implies, they believed that the behavior of others served as a cue for an individual's behavior. Children naturally imitate the behaviors of those around them who are more capable. As just one example, consider that children's toys are often miniatures of the adult versions. Playing with a toy hammer, truck, doll, stove, baseball, and bat allows the child to mimic adult behaviors. Children not only acquire skill sets by observation, but also attitudes, beliefs, and feelings as well.

Albert Bandura (1925–) has been a highly influential figure in social learning theory. His social cognitive theory (Bandura, 1989) is based on a three-part model wherein behavior, cognition and other personal factors, and environmental influences interact with and influence each other (see Fig. 14.8). A person's thoughts, beliefs, and feelings influence how they behave. In turn, consequences of or reactions to specific behaviors shape thoughts, beliefs, and feelings. Likewise, one's expectations, beliefs, and cognitive skills are modified by social factors. The role one plays in a given social structure (e.g., parent, child, authority figure, student, etc.) can influence behavior and cognition. This is a reciprocal interaction, where the environment both shapes and is shaped by behavior and cognition. We shape the environment and the environment shapes us.

According to Bandura (1977, 1989), people learn by observing and imitating the behavior of others. A parent, teacher, or sibling may model correct behavior before the child begins to imitate. People provide live models, but other things such as books, photographs, and videos provide symbolic models. A child learns many things from watching television, for example.

To put social learning into a music-learning context, think of two fourth-graders learning to play the recorder. Suppose that one is a boy, the other a girl. One comes from an affluent, two-parent home, the other from a disadvantaged, single-parent home. One is physically coordinated, with facile motor skills while the other is somewhat awkward and clumsy. One is bright and successful academically, while the other struggles. Each of the three variables—behavior, cognition and other personal factors, and the environment—interact with the other two in unique combinations. Learning to play the recorder for each child, then, is a result of individual personal characteristics, including both biological and learned factors, resulting in behaviors that take place within a social context.

Nearly all the concepts discussed in this section can be seen in the learning situation of playing the recorder. The music classroom can be viewed as a life space (Lewin) with playing a recorder as a goal. One student may approach the goal eagerly, while another one avoids it. It is even possible to imagine approach-avoidance conflicts in a child who wants to play the recorder but shies away from it for fear of failure. Vygotsky's zone of proximal development

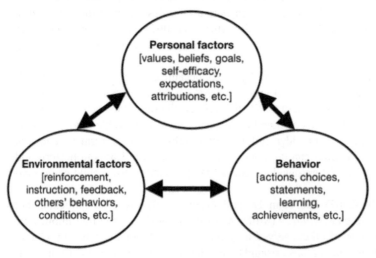

FIGURE 14.8 | Bandura's Model of Triadic Reciprocality.

is illustrated by what the children can play on the recorder independently and what they are capable of doing with assistance. Although the recorder certainly has a valid musical existence of its own, it can also be viewed as a precursor to learning to play a wind instrument in the school band. That is, children may mimic adult music making (Miller & Dollard, 1941) by playing a child's version of a band instrument.

More specifically, Byrne (2005) presented a four-stage model of interaction in music teaching and learning which was also based on prior work of Vygotsky, as well as DeCorte (1990) and Williams and Sternberg (1993).

- In stage one, *Modeling*, the teacher engages in active teaching as she models (sets tasks, demonstrates, provides examples, etc.) for the students who are in a more passive learning mode (e.g., listening, observing). Passive learning does not mean passive as in inactive or not engaged; rather it is defined as teacher directed with student participation (Byrne, 2005, p. 313). In our example of learning to play the recorder, the teacher may model correct hand position and embouchure on the recorder and may play a tune before the children attempt to play it. Children may observe and imitate the teacher as a live model, or may also listen to a recording or watch a video as forms of symbolic modeling. For modeling to be successful, the children must pay attention to the model, must remember the observed behavior, must translate symbolic concepts into appropriate actions, and must be motivated to learn.

- During stage two, *Scaffolding*, the teacher is still in active mode by asking questions, defining goals, and providing further exemplars. Students are also in active learning mode as they answer the teacher's questions and attempt the task. The teacher may ask students questions such as how to control the breath, what is the proper angle to hold the recorder and so on. She may also provide feedback as students answer questions and make their first efforts to play the recorder. In scaffolding, the teacher breaks a complex task into more manageable units or chunks and guides the students step-by-step through the learning process. This is very akin to Vygotsky's ZPD; bridging the gap between what the learner can do on his own and what he can do with the teacher's help.

- Over time, the scaffold declines as the student gains more skill and confidence in playing the recorder. Gradually, the student becomes more independent and together teacher and student move into the *Coaching* phase. Here, teacher and learners are all in active mode as the students conduct independent trials and the teacher provides encouragement or hints for progressing to the next level. Students ask and answer their own questions, seek out help or additional information, and so on.

- Finally, in stage four, *Fading*, the teacher moves into a more passive role (available for guidance, support, and practical involvement) and the student is actively engaged in self-regulated learning. Students may want to learn a song on their own, they may want to improvise, or to create a duet with one student harmonizing to the learned melody of another. Peer teaching also becomes a possibility, as successful students can work with their fellow classmates.

Modeling, Scaffolding, Coaching, and Fading are elements in what Byrne calls a powerful learning environment.

Beyond these brief descriptions of major concepts in social learning theory, lies the richness and complexity of personal relationships and interactions that fill every home and classroom. Music learning cannot be understood fully without considering the social context in which children grow and develop. Students engaged in music learning do not do so in isolation. Even when they are making music alone, there are motivations and internal dialogues that are shaped and influenced by social conditions and circumstances. Froehlich (2007) and Hargreaves and North (1997) provide elaborations of these and many other ideas.

Cognitive Psychology

Cognitive psychologists, as the name implies, are primarily concerned with cognitive functioning and higher mental processes. They investigate such topics as memory, attention, mental representation, language, thinking, problem solving, decision-making, imagining, and creativity (Lefrançois, 2006; Matlin & Farmer, 2015). *Cognitive psychology* has roots in both Gestalt and developmental psychology. Recognition is given to the idea that human beings are active seekers of knowledge. Cognitive psychologists are interested in understanding what strategies individuals use to explore the environment in the acquisition of information and in how we order and use that information.

According to this viewpoint, people choose much of what they know and how they respond to what they learn. Because there is generally more to see or hear than we can look at or listen to, we make choices. Factors that influence our choices include such things as past experiences, anticipation or readiness, selective attention, the application of particular cognitive skills, and environmental factors. Likewise, we have some influence over how we respond to given experiences based on a perception of how our own well-being will be affected. A person's cognitive appraisal of events can affect the intensity and quality of an emotional response.

Jerome Bruner. One of the pioneers of cognitive psychology was Jerome Bruner (1915–2016), who made many contributions that have applications for music teaching and learning (1963, 1966; Bruner, Goodnow, & Austin, 1956). In a chapter entitled "Notes on a Theory of Instruction," Bruner (1966) turned from learning theory, which is descriptive, to a theory of instruction, which is prescriptive. He stated that a theory of instruction:

1. *"Should specify the experiences which most effectively implant in the individual a predisposition toward learning—learning in general or a particular type of learning"* (pp. 40–41). Music teachers should be concerned with motivating students and nurturing in their pupils a desire to learn.
2. *"Must specify the ways in which a body of knowledge should be structured so that it can most readily be grasped by the learner"* (p. 41). Music content can be represented in *enactive* mode through action, in *iconic* mode through visual or other sensory images, and in *symbolic* mode through language.
3. *"Should specify the most effective sequences in which to present the materials to be learned"* (p. 41). This concern for sequences led to the notion of the spiral curriculum. In a spiral curriculum, concepts taught at the most elemental level are revisited in sequential fashion at ever-increasing levels of sophistication. The Manhattanville Curriculum, based on the spiral curriculum model, was a sequential music-learning program developed for early childhood through high school (Thomas, 1970).
4. *"Should specify the nature and pacing of rewards and punishments in the process of learning and teaching"* (p. 41). Here, music teachers should strive to move from immediate to delayed gratification and from external to internal rewards.

Two additional ideas of importance contributed by Bruner were intuitive thinking and discovery learning. Sometimes we arrive at solutions to problems by playing a hunch or by arriving at an answer without having fully explicated the means for deriving it. Bruner felt that this type of learning, akin to the Gestaltists' Aha! learning, was an important way of discovering.

Exploring, figuring it out for oneself, in short discovering answers to questions is a powerful and rewarding experience. *Discovery learning* promotes process over product, it is intrinsically rewarding to students, and allows students to be creative. Although Bruner claimed to have support for the effectiveness of discovery learning, psychologist David Ausubel (1918–2008) disagreed. Orton (2004) described the debate that occurred between the two. Ausubel countered that expository teaching could be just as exciting and motivational as discovery learning. Furthermore, discovery learning takes more time, if nothing was discovered students could become discouraged, and there was no evidence that students were creative in this process. In fact, there was little evidence to support the notion that discovery learning was superior to expository teaching in terms of long-term learning. A general consensus now is that discovery learning is important for younger children and for those who have sufficient knowledge to provide self-guidance, but it is not so well suited for the bulk of school learning experiences (Kirschner, Sweller, & Clark, 2006).

Taxonomies. Another way to think about learning experiences is to divide them into cognitive (what one knows), psychomotor (what one can do), and affective (how one feels) domains. Bloom and his colleagues created a *Taxonomy of Educational Objectives* with hierarchical arrangements within each of the domains (Bloom, 1956; Krathwohl et al., 1964; Simpson, 1966). A brief musical example is given for each item.

I. Cognitive Learning
    1. Knowledge: the ability to recall specific items of information without regard to the understanding of it; for example, naming notes on the bass clef.
    2. Comprehension: the ability to grasp the meaning of the material, including interpretation, translation, and prediction; for example, understanding the function of the tonic chord in tonal music.
    3. Application: the ability to use material in new situations; for example, finding the tonic chord in a number of different pieces of music.
    4. Analysis: the ability to divide material into component parts so that the underlying structure is understood; for example, describing the factors in a piece of music that characterize it as Romantic in style.
    5. Synthesis: the ability to put parts together to form a new understanding through new structures or patterns; for example, creating a description of the effect of chromaticism in Wagner's music.
    6. Evaluation: the ability to judge the value of material for a given purpose; for example, the ranking of Wagner's music dramas in terms of their presentation of the characteristics of romanticism.
II. Psychomotor Learning
    1. Perception: the awareness of the object and relationships through the use of the sense organs; for example, hearing and feeling different intervals in trombone slide positions.
    2. Set: the readiness for an action; for example, learning the correct position for playing the cello.
    3. Guided Response: the ability to execute an overt action under the guidance of a teacher; for example, playing major scales on the saxophone during a lesson.

4. Mechanism: the development of an automatic learned response; for example, when playing the piano, maintaining an Alberti bass pattern in the left hand while concentrating on the melody in the right hand.

5. Complex Overt Response: the ability to execute a complex set of actions smoothly and efficiently; for example, playing a Beethoven violin sonata well.

6. Adaptation: the ability to change the execution of actions to make them more suitable; for example, while playing in a jazz trio, adjusting one's performance to match the other two players.

7. Origination: the ability to develop new skills; for example, Franz Liszt's adaptation of techniques he heard in Paganini's violin playing to piano compositions.

III. Affective Learning

1. Receiving: willingness to pay attention; for example, being willing to listen to a musical work.

2. Responding: willingness to participate in an activity; for example, taking part in the singing of a song.

3. Valuing: placing value on an object or activity; for example, buying a recording of a piece of music or checking it out of the library.

4. Organization: bringing together different values and resolving conflicts between them, and building a consistent value system; for example, a concern for preserving the music of other cultures, even though one does not fully understand or appreciate all other cultures.

5. Characterization by a Value: maintenance of a system of values over a long period of time so that it is consistent, pervasive, and predictable; for example, consistently supporting music through attending music programs, buying recordings or sheet music, and giving financial support to the local symphony orchestra.

Anderson and Krathwohl (2001) revised the cognitive domain to include four categories: factual knowledge, conceptual knowledge, procedural knowledge, and metacognitive knowledge. They labeled six cognitive processes as remember, understand, apply, analyze, evaluate, and create. Marazano and Kendall (2007) also revised the cognitive domain; they included the knowledge domains of information, mental procedures, and psychomotor procedures. They created a six-tiered organization as follows: retrieval, comprehension, analysis, knowledge utilization, metacognitive system, and self-system. Table 14.2 places the three versions side-by-side.

TABLE 14.2 | Taxonomies in the Cognitive Domain.

Bloom	Anderson & Krathwohl	Marazano & Kendall
Cognitive Domain	Factual, Conceptual, Procedural, and Metacognitive Knowledge	Information, Mental Procedures, and Psychomotor Procedures
Knowledge	Remember	Retrieval
Comprehension	Understand	Comprehension
Application	Apply	Analysis
Analysis	Analyze	Knowledge Utilization
Synthesis	Evaluate	Metacognitive System
Evaluation	Create	Self-System

Regardless of which particular version one prefers, all three provide a hierarchical arrangement of cognition. Generally, speaking, the first tier is considered the lowest level; that is, remembering or retrieving factual knowledge is less advanced than evaluating that knowledge, creating knowledge, or identifying to oneself why this particular knowledge has meaning (self-system). Music teachers can apply any of these structures to music learning. Colwell and Wing (2004) provided some general applications of these taxonomies to music education and Hanna (2007) applied them to the National Standards in Music Education. Although the other domains have received less attention, they, too, have been revised: psychomotor domain (Simpson, 1972), and affective domain (Hauenstein, 1998).

Music Intelligence. In studying human behavior, one of the topics psychologists inevitably deal with is intelligence. At a superficial level, it is easy to understand that human beings are intelligent creatures and that some human beings are more intelligent than others. However, specifying exactly what intelligence is or in what ways one person is more intelligent than another is quite a different matter. For example, one might ask whether a nuclear physicist is necessarily more intelligent than a poet. When a baseball player at bat adjusts his swing to the rotation and movement of a ball moving toward him at 90 miles per hour so that the bat and ball intersect at a precise moment in time and space—is that a form of intelligence? More to the point of this book, are composing a song, conducting a band, or improvising on a guitar, intelligent behaviors?

Traditional definitions of intelligence normally involve such various mental abilities as the ability to think and reason, to learn, or to solve problems (Cancro, 1971). The most prevalent means of evaluating a person's intelligence is through the use of a test that yields an *intelligence quotient* (IQ). Although there are more than 200 different IQ tests available, the average IQ is commonly around 100, with persons scoring above 130 considered to be of superior intelligence and persons scoring below 70 considered to be mentally deficient (Butcher, 1968; Fincher, 1976). Closely related, and even more frequently used in academic settings, are standardized tests of academic achievement, such as the *Scholastic Aptitude Test* (SAT), the *Iowa Tests of Basic Skills* (ITBS), or the *Graduate Records Examinations* (GRE). There is such a high correlation between IQ tests and academic achievement tests that they are often considered nearly synonymous measures of intelligence. For example, there is a 95% overlap between the *Otis Quick-Scoring Test of Mental Ability, Beta* and the *Stanford Achievement Tests* (Gage & Berliner, 1975).

Quite understandably, the connection between a person's IQ score and his or her value as a person has been unavoidable. This is particularly true in school, where many gifted and talented programs use specific cut-off scores on mental ability tests as the primary criterion for selection. Likewise, in school, recognition is given to those with high SAT scores. The notion that a person's worth should be determined by a score on a test is anathema to many, of course, and they have found many faults with the usage of IQ tests. In addition to the philosophical disagreements, critics have contended that IQ tests are culture bound, discriminating against minorities, and that they are not good predictors of adult success (Goleman, 1986). In fact, the data show only a moderate correlation between IQ and success in later adult life.

One of the major criticisms of these tests is that they are too narrow in their concept of intelligence (Eisner, 1982). Skills exhibited by the poet, baseball player, and oboist are clearly excluded by most of these tests. Because the direction of intelligence testing was highly influenced by the original interest in predicting success in school and the obvious intent of academic achievement testing, these tests do not measure human intelligence in a broad sense. Other societies in other times and places would not place as high a premium on linguistic and mathematic skills as we do. Even in our own society, social skills, artistic gifts, and many other types of intelligence are not measured by these tests.

Since the early 1900s, the notion of a general factor of intelligence or *g* has dominated psychology (Sternberg, 2000). Recent brain imagining evidence supports the notion of general intelligence (e.g., Duncan et al., 2000). Network Neuroscience Theory proposes that general intelligence depends upon an ability to transition rapidly between network states subserving crystallized intelligence, based on prior knowledge and experience, and those subserving fluid intelligence, adaptive reasoning in novel situations (Barbey, 2018). In contrast to *g*, domain intelligences focus on specific areas, such as a triarchic theory involving analytical, creative, and practical intelligence. Guilford (1968) created a three-factor structure of intellect containing 120 vectors of the mind. Deary (2001) contended that the most viable is a three-layer model with *g* accounting for roughly half of individual differences, group factors of narrower abilities, and very specific abilities.

One of the more recent domain theories of multiple intelligences (MI) is that proposed by Gardner (2006). Although not well-accepted by scientific psychology, it has gained considerable popularity in education. Gardner suggested the following eight and a half* types of intellectual competence:

1. Linguistic intelligence
2. Musical intelligence
3. Logical-mathematical intelligence
4. Spatial intelligence
5. Bodily-kinesthetic intelligence
6. Interpersonal intelligence
7. Intrapersonal intelligence
8. Naturalist intelligence
9. Existential intelligence (*this form of intelligence only partially qualifies)

Gardner stressed the idea that each of these forms of intelligence is an equally valuable, independent, and important way of knowing. His book, *Creating Minds* (2011) presents Stravinsky as an exemplar of musical intelligence, along with the following: T.S. Eliot (language), Einstein (logical-mathematical), Picasso (spatial), Martha Graham (bodily-kinesthetic intelligence), Freud (intrapersonal), and Gandhi (interpersonal); naturalist and existential intelligence were not part of the list at that point. Of course, each of us has skills in more than one type of intelligence, as Stravinsky wrote a book, Einstein was an accomplished violinist, and so on.

In support of his theory of multiple intelligences, Gardner lists eight criteria of an intelligence, or signs by which a type of intelligence might be identified. We have discussed many of these ideas in previous chapters.

1. Potential isolation by brain damage.
2. The existence of savant syndrome, prodigies, and other exceptional individuals.
3. An identifiable core operation or set of operations.
4. A distinctive developmental history, along with a definable set of expert "end-state" performances.
5. An evolutionary history and evolutionary plausibility.
6. Support from experimental psychological tasks.
7. Support from psychometric findings.
8. Susceptibility to encoding in a symbol system.

Through these eight criteria Gardner makes a strong case for considering musical intelligence as an autonomous form of human intelligence.

Clearly, human beings are just as equipped to function musically as they are linguistically, mathematically, or in any other way. Each form of intelligence provides us with a unique way of knowing. To the extent that we fully engage in exploring all the possibilities of each mode of knowing, we realize our fullest human potential. To the extent that we devalue or delimit our use of any particular form of intelligence, we are less than we have been created to be. Gardner's theory has strong connections to cognitive psychology in that he was co-director of Project Zero. This project was founded by Nelson Goodman, who was instrumental in applying cognitive development to arts education (Mark, 1996).

In spite of wide acceptance of Gardner's theory, particularly on the part of educators, others have argued against it in favor of general intelligence (Deary, 2001). Visser, Ashton, and Vernon (2006) investigated MI and found strong support for general intelligence. They did, however, find that bodily-kinesthetic and musical intelligence were less strongly associated with general intelligence. Perhaps general intelligence and multiple intelligences are not mutually exclusive. Ruthsatz, Detterman, Griscom, and Cirullo (2008) found that higher levels of musical achievement were due to a combination of three factors: general intelligence, domain-specific skills, and amount of deliberate practice.

Three additional concepts are related to intelligence;

- Brain size matters. Total volume correlates with general intelligence and additional gray and white matter in specific brain regions is related to higher intelligence (Haier, Jung, Yeo, Head, & Alkire, 2004). As indicated in Chapter 9, musical training increases both gray and white matter in specific brain regions (e.g., Gaser & Schlaug, 2003).
- Mental processing speed is related to performance on measures of high-order cognition (Kail & Salthouse, 1994). As related previously, trained musicians performed auditory discrimination tasks faster and more accurately than controls (Hodges et al., 2005).
- Processing efficiency is related to intelligence, as more intelligent people expend less energy while performing mental tasks (Eliot, 2000). In addition, once a person has learned a task, fewer resources are required to complete the task. Music students who received extensive training in harmonic discrimination had a decrease in overall cortical activation compared to those who did not receive equivalent training (Altenmüller, Gruhn, Parlitz, & Liebert, 2000).

Music Cognition, Music Learning, and Reflective Thinking. Many of the previous chapters have had a decided cognitive orientation. In Chapter 7, relevant topics included the Gestalt laws of cognitive organization, auditory scene analysis, schemata, and the spotlight of attention, musical memory, statistical learning, expectancy theory, cognition of musical elements, cognition of larger musical forms, cross-cultural comparative research in music, and music and language. In Chapter 12, we explored the role of music in identity construction. Chapter 13 includes a section entitled Cognitive Skills, with discussions of mental rehearsal, deliberate practice, metacognition, self-regulation, motivation, and self-efficacy.

With specific regard to the topics in Chapter 13, the notion of *reflective* thinking is especially pertinent. John Dewey (1959–1952) wrote that, "Thought or reflection . . . is the discernment of the relation between what we try to do and what happens in consequence" (1916, p. 169). Reflective thinking has become an increasingly important aspect of education.

Reflective thinking is also an important component of music education, as evidenced by a recent search (December, 2018) of the archives of the *Journal of Music Teacher Education* that turned up 291 relevant articles. Asking students to think reflectively about their personal learning skills and their own learning is an important opportunity for growth. A wide variety of strategies gives teachers many options. For example, studio teachers can audio or video-tape lessons and ask students to write a reflection of the recording. Rather, than writing an open reflection, teachers could highlight specific topics, such as intonation, vowel placement, articulation, and so on.

Ensemble directors can give students brief islands of time, even as little as 30 seconds, to reflect on just-rehearsed passages. Ensemble members could also keep a journal in their music folders and jot down thoughts as they occur. Portfolios are a staple of many under-graduate and graduate music programs. The notion is not only to collect a variety of exhibits that document the student's progress (e.g., term papers, projects, recordings, etc.), but also to accumulate thoughtful reflections of personal growth and learning.

Cognitive psychologists have accumulated a considerable amount of data concerned with the perception of music. Although much of the early research dealt with brief, isolated pitch or rhythm patterns that could hardly be called musical, a new phase of research, one more concerned with "real" music in "real world" situations is underway. Certainly, many of the most exciting advances in our understanding of musical behaviors are taking place in the arena of cognitive psychology. An example of this is the number of books with both music and cognition or cognitive in the title, including

- *Musical Structure and Cognition* (Howell, Cross, & West, 1985)
- *The Musical Mind: The Cognitive Psychology of Music* (Sloboda, 1985),
- *Music Cognition* (Dowling & Harwood, 1986)
- *Music as Cognition* (Serafine, 1988)
- *Cognitive Foundations of Musical Pitch* (Krumhansl, 1990)
- *Music, Gestalt, and Computing: Studies in Cognitive and Systematic Musicology* (Leman, 1997)
- *Music, Cognition, and Computerized Sound* (Cook, 2001)
- *Conceptualizing Music: Cognitive Structure, Theory, and Analysis* (Zbikowski, 2002)
- *The Cognitive Neuroscience of Music* (Peretz & Zatorre, 2003)
- *The Cognition of Basic Musical Structures* (Temperley, 2004)
- *MENC Handbook of Musical Cognition and Development* (Colwell, 2006)
- *Music Cognition and Emotions* (Aiello, 2007)
- *Embodied Music Cognition and Mediation Technology* (Leman, 2007)
- *Musical Cognition: A Science of Listening* (Honing, 2014)
- *The Routledge Companion to Music Cognition* (Ashley & Timmers, 2017).

Unfortunately, most general textbooks on cognitive psychology do not include music as one of the relevant topics. However, Levitin (2002) did include the subject of music psychology in *Foundations of Cognitive Psychology: Core Readings*.

Taken collectively, the writers of these and similarly oriented publications approach an understanding of musical behavior through the mental processes involved. Musical behaviors are learned and cognitive psychologists are interested in the mental strategies involved in this learning process. They are also interested in explaining the boundaries of musical memory, in discovering how we organize and process the music we hear, and in accounting for the pleasures we derive from musical activities and our emotional responses to music. All of this inquiry naturally leads to the question, "what is going on in the brain"?

Cognitive Neuroscience

Although cognitive psychologists obviously recognize the role of the mind in learning, many of them do not conduct research involving direct brain imaging. *Cognitive neuroscientists* combine tenets of cognitive psychology with findings from neuroscientific investigations (Ochsner & Kosslyn, 2013). A goal is to account for higher order mental skills in the structures and functions of the brain. We have already reviewed neuromusical research findings in Chapter 9 (see also Janata, 2013; Thaut & Hodges, 2019; Tervaniemi, Tao, & Huotilainen, 2018). Here, we combine that information with the previously presented information on cognitive psychology in an attempt to shed light on music teaching—learning processes (see Hodges, 2010a for extended discussion of these ideas).

Consider first, a simplified learning model as presented in Figure 14.9. Basing this model on brain imaging studies, Zull (2002) explains that learning often begins with concrete experiences. Say, for example, that Johnny hears his father playing the guitar. Johnny reflects on this experience, identifying it as "music," as he recognizes that this is similar to hearing his mother sing or his sister practicing the piano. Generating abstract hypotheses, he thinks that he would like to learn how to play the guitar. He wonders how difficult it might be; it does not look as if it would be that hard. Finally, to test out his ideas, he needs to do something requiring action. He asks his father to show him how to hold the guitar and begins to strum the strings hesitantly.

Several factors have been discussed previously and will only be mentioned briefly.

- Active learning is more effective than passive learning. Similar to Bruner's notion of enactive learning, teachers should strive to keep students actively engaged. Johnny can learn to play the guitar by actually holding it and strumming on it much more effectively than if he merely observes his father.
- Learning activates reward centers. Successful learning elicits hormones such as serotonin and dopamine (Braun & Brock, 2007) as the brain rewards itself for accomplishing

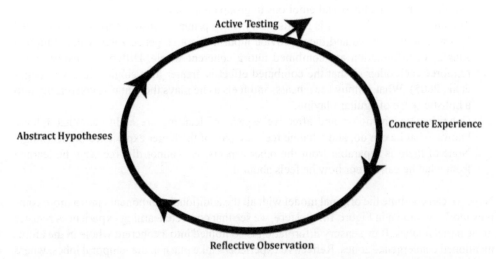

FIGURE 14.9 Diagram of a Learning Cycle. To this simplistic model we must add additional components.

something. Students can, of course, learn through fear and intimidation, but they learn best when they find pleasure and joy in the acquisition of new knowledge and skills. As Johnny begins to learn how to play the guitar, his brain rewards himself for his efforts.

- All learning is emotionally colored and we learn best that which we most enjoy. Recall Figure 9.10 and the attendant discussion of brain structures devoted to emotional processing. Teachers should not be afraid to make learning pleasurable; in so doing they are taking advantage of natural brain responses. Whether Johnny's father is a harsh and demanding teacher or loving and nurturing will have a profound effect on the quality of Johnny's learning experience.
- Plasticity, neural pruning, genetic influences and learning experiences, critical and optimal periods, and memory—concepts discussed in previous chapters—are important additions to the model. The age at which Johnny starts to play guitar, his biological potentialities and proclivities, the effort he puts into it, and so on, will all play a determining role in his eventual success.
- The brain is especially good at pattern detecting. Statistical learning, as discussed in Chapter 7, helps us to identify schema that occur most frequently in the music we hear. Johnny's father can help by showing him a I and V chord that he can use to accompany several different songs.
- We learn through imitation and through social reinforcement. Mirror neurons in Johnny's brain fire when he observes his father and they continue to fire when Johnny attempts to mimic his father's actions (Schlaug, 2006). Presumably, Johnny could learn to play the guitar to some degree by reading a method book, but interactions with his father make learning more effective.
- Group learning is also an effective strategy. After Johnny has learned a few chords, he can join his sister on piano, with his mother singing, and his father playing on another guitar. These family sessions activate shared attention mechanisms (Meltzoff, Kuhl, Movellan, & Sejnowski, 2009).
- Social learning activates specialized neural networks for empathizing with others (Hein & Singer, 2008). As Johnny plays his guitar with his family and later with his friends, he is learning to regulate his social emotions in group cooperation.
- The most effective learning is multisensory. Each primary sensory cortex is surrounded by association cortices and these provide input into convergence zones where multiple sources of information are combined into a coherent whole. Different sensory inputs reinforce each other so that the combined effect is greater than single sources (Hodges et al., 2005). What Johnny sees, hears, and feels as he plays the guitar is converging into a holistic sense of "guitar playing."
- Cognitive, psychomotor, and affective aspects of learning are additive. What Johnny knows, what he can do, and what he feels are part of the larger experience of "learning." None of them is separable from the other aspects. He cannot divorce what he learned from what he can do nor how he feels about it.

Now, we can combine the original model with all the additional components into a more complex model as shown in Figure 14.10. Here, we see that concrete learning experiences register in the parietal lobes. Raw sensory information is combined into a coherent whole in the aforementioned convergence zones. Reflective experiences take place in the temporal lobes, where memory, language, and object identification systems are activated. Abstract hypotheses are formed in the frontal lobes where problems are solved and new action plans are developed. Finally, active testing engages motor systems as abstract hypotheses are acted upon. Note,

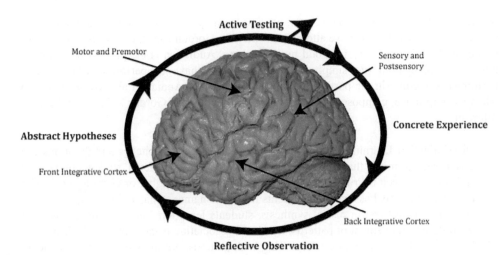

Active Testing

Motor and Premotor

Sensory and
Postsensory

Concrete Experience

Abstract Hypotheses

Front Integrative Cortex

Back Integrative Cortex

Reflective Observation

FIGURE 14.10 | Learning Cycle Overlaid on the Brain Showing How the Learning Cycle Matches the Structure of the Brain.

too, that an extra arrow has been added, indicating that active testing continues the cycle by creating new sensory inputs, and so on.

Our current level of understanding is such that neuroscientific findings are more likely to support best practices than to establish radically new approaches. Eventually, further developments may eventually lead to new paradigms. In the meantime, another issue of concern is whether the changes indicated in this review that occur as a result of music learning transfer to other domains. In an excellent review of the subject, Forgeard, Winner, Norton, and Schlaug (2008) discussed near transfer (from music learning to music-related skills) and far transfer (from music learning to other domains). A review of published research leads to mixed results in the degree of relationship between music learning and general IQ and spatial, verbal, and mathematical skills. Data from their own experiment demonstrated that children who received at least three years of instrumental music training performed better on near transfer tasks closely related to musical performance—auditory discrimination and fine motor skills—and on two far-transfer tasks—vocabulary and nonverbal reasoning skills. Music students did not outperform controls on far transfer tasks of heightened spatial skills, phonemic awareness, or mathematical abilities. They found support for domain-specific transfer effects, that is, from music to related domains. They also found support for domain-general transfer effects on general IQ. Although the music students did not outperform the controls on all tasks, they did have higher mean scores on all tasks.

MUSIC TEACHING AND LEARNING

There is so much contemporary literature on music teaching and learning (e.g., Barrett & Webster, 2014; McPherson & Welch, 2012) that a discussion of the numerous methodologies and approaches is far beyond the scope of this book. From a music psychology standpoint, however, perhaps one music teaching-learning approach can stand as an exemplar. Edwin Gordon (1928–2015) spent decades developing his music learning theory, which is based on dozens of published research studies. The fundamental basis of this theory is related to how we learn language. As preverbal infants, we first learn by listening. We hear and internalize a great deal of speech before we attempt to imitate it. Gordon uses the term *audiate* to refer to the aural skills necessary for good musicianship. "Audiation is the process of assimilating and comprehending (not simply rehearing) music we have just performed or have heard performed sometime in the past" (Gordon, 2007, pp. 3–4). Audiation also comes into play when we improvise, compose, or read music. Key features of Gordon's theory include the following:

- Discrimination Learning involves identifying differences in pitches and durations in a given piece of music that is learned by rote. At the aural/oral level, students move back and forth between hearing tonal or rhythm patterns and singing or chanting back what they hear. In verbal association, students use letter names, tonal and rhythmic syllables and other identifiers. In partial synthesis, students learn tonal and rhythmic syntax, or the orderly arrangement of patterns. Symbolic association is the stage in which students learn to read and write music, beginning with patterns, not individual notes. Musically intelligent listening, reading, and writing take place in the composite synthesis stage; partial and symbolic association levels are synthesized as students gain simultaneous awareness of tonality and meter.
- Inference Learning is conceptual learning where students learn to transfer and manipulate patterns with unfamiliar music. At the generalization-aural/oral level, students learn to discriminate differences in familiar and unfamiliar tonal and rhythm patterns. Creativity/improvisation involves manipulation of acquired patterns in new musical expressions. In theoretical understanding, students use previously acquired knowledge to structure deeper understandings of music.

Most importantly, music learning theory fosters the culture of the ear, rather than the eye. Fundamental musicianship is based upon the development of keen aural perception and understanding.

CONCLUSION

Human learning is a vast, complicated, challenging, and endlessly fascinating topic. Over the past century, psychologists from a variety of orientations have made immense strides in understanding more about how we acquire and use knowledge as well as how we learn music. Psychoanalysts, for example, seek to access repressed memories in order to bring about resolution of hidden conflicts. From a psychoanalytic perspective, music has symbolic meanings and it may be a means of expressing unconscious desires. Music therapists have used music as a means of resolving repressed conflicts. Psychoanalysis probably has more to offer our understanding of music learning than has yet been realized.

In contrast to psychoanalysis, and most of the other psychological approaches for that matter, behavioral psychologists have made numerous applications to music teaching and learning. The use of positive feedback is generally effective for shaping both academic and social behaviors. Music, itself, provides reinforcement for many learning activities. However, behavioral psychology fails to account for the cognitive processing that many assume to be apparent in human learning.

Those who espouse a cognitive approach take many different paths to understanding the role of the mind/brain in learning. Humanistic psychologists seek to facilitate each individual's growth toward his or her fullest potential. Music is a common way for people to have peak experiences and often plays a significant role in a person's progress toward self-actualization.

Gestalt psychologists focus on the whole experience rather than on the constituent parts. They see lawful relationships in the way people organize their perceptual experiences. Gestalt principles such as figure-ground relationships and the law of Prägnanz form the bedrock of modern theories of music perception. Developmental psychologists recognize that learning has a growth trajectory. People learn differently at different ages. Musical growth parallels intellectual growth in that one can trace musical development from infancy and childhood through adolescence and adulthood. Social psychologists contend that considering how humans learn without considering the role of social context is limiting and even misleading. While musicians often practice alone, most people engage in musical activities along with others as a shared experience. Human learning is highly dependent upon interactions with others.

Cognitive psychology includes contributions from Gestalt, developmental, and social psychology and dominates the landscape today, though the lines between it and cognitive neuroscience are blurring considerably. Cognitive psychologists want to understand the mental operations involved in learning. Current understandings of memory, attention, mental representation, and thinking in music rely heavily on cognitive psychology. As a forerunner, Bruner delineated many of the basic principles of cognitive psychology as applied to teaching, including the spiral curriculum, intuitive thinking, and discovery learning. Others organized learning into cognitive, psychomotor, and affective domains, or similar structural groups. Learning is connected intimately with the notion of intelligence. While many traditional IQ tests do not include music, Gardner's theory of multiple intelligences recognizes that music is a viable way of knowing. Through his music learning theory, Gordon contends that the best way to learn music is by training our ears. Exploration of these topics leads naturally to investigations of how music is represented in the brain. Cognitive neuroscientists are actively probing these issues with ever-increasing power and sophistication.

Musical behavior can be studied from any psychological perspective. Because music is a form of human behavior, psychologists can study it much as they do any other form of behavior, such as language or mathematics. Older viewpoints still have much to offer and many new discoveries and developing theories provide optimism for increased insights into music teaching and learning processes.

DISCUSSION QUESTIONS

1. Even though you presumably lack the training to be a psychoanalyst, can you see how such an approach might provide insights into your own musical behaviors, or that of other musicians? Can you give examples of pieces of music (e.g., the late string quartets of Beethoven, *Strange Fruit* as sung by Billie Holiday, or Alan Jackson's *Where Were You (When the World Stopped Turning)?*) that might have symbolic meanings?
2. Can you think of times when a teacher used behavioral reinforcement techniques to shape your learning or behavior? How did you respond to that? Have you used such techniques yourself in a teaching situation? How successful were you in helping students achieve their desired goals? Have you ever tried extinction? With what results?
3. Suppose you were on a debate team arguing against the use of behavioral techniques. What would be some of your strongest points? If you now switch sides, what would be your strongest arguments in support of behaviorism?
4. What are you on your personal journey toward self-actualization? What things are keeping you from moving ahead to the next level(s)? What role does music play in this

process for you? Describe some nonmusical and musical peak experiences you have had. How have these shaped you to be the person you are now?

5. Have you had experiences with younger children such that you can recall their progress through the Piagetian stages of development? Suppose you were asked to demonstrate the principle of conservation in music; how would you do that?

6. Draw a picture of your own life space. Can you identify any barriers that stand in the way between you and your goals? What approach-avoidance behaviors do you recognize in yourself? Do you think it would help you achieve your goals to identify them, potential barriers, and approach-avoidance behaviors intentionally and explicitly?

7. In what ways do you construct your own reality? What internal and external influences are there on this construction process? Although we might think of the ZPD as referring to younger students, do you have ZPDs of your own? How do the concepts of social learning apply to your own progress toward mastery?

9. Cognitive psychology and cognitive neuroscience are the current, dominating viewpoints on human learning. If you could wave a magic wand, what music learning issues would you want them to tackle next? What are the big questions still waiting to be answered?

10. As you think about your own journey to musicianship, do you think you began with the "culture of the eye" or the "culture of the ear?" Do the basic principles behind music learning theory resonate with you? If you were to teach beginners at any age, would you use MLT? Why or why not?

Chapter 15

Music and Health

SUZANNE delivered a premature baby who was placed in the neonatal intensive care unit (NICU). A music therapist provided music that helped to lower the baby's heart rate, increase oxygen intake, and shortened her stay in the NICU (Fig. 15.1). Ace was a rock drummer with an ulnar neuropathy, a compressed nerve in the elbow. He went to a physician who specialized in performance-related injuries who was able to help him heal so that he could resume his career. Maria was extremely anxious about her upcoming surgical procedure. Fortunately, her physician used music to help calm her nerves, and as a consequence she needed fewer drugs during the procedure.

These vignettes represent three interrelated disciplines that deal with music and health—music therapy, music medicine, and performing arts medicine. Each of the disciplines shares certain commonalities, yet they remain distinctive. Triangular relationships among music therapy, music medicine, and performing arts medicine are in a process of being established. Definitions, distinctions, research strategies, and persons involved (both as healers and as clients/patients) are evolving. Although the following descriptions are not universally agreed upon, there is a strong sense among those interested that while much growth is necessary, there is enormous potential for using music effectively as a healing agent. Table 15.1 indicates the primary similarities and differences in the three disciplines. Further details are provided in subsequent sections.

MUSIC THERAPY

According to the American Music Therapy Association (2018),

> Music therapy is the clinical and evidence-based use of music interventions to accomplish individualized goals within a therapeutic relationship by a credentialed professional who has completed an approved music therapy program.

Music therapy has also been characterized as, "the scientific application of music or music activities to attain therapeutic goals. Music therapy can also be defined as the structured use of music to bring about desired changes in behavior" (Carter, 1982, p. 5). Thus, "music therapy is a systematic process of intervention wherein the therapist helps the client to promote health, using musical experiences and the relationships that develop through them as dynamic forces of change" (Bruscia, 1998, p. 20). It is a broad field, encompassing psychotherapeutic, educational, instructional, behavioral, pastoral, supervisory, healing, recreational, activity, and interrelated arts applications of music. Many of the treatment protocols are supported by research (Wheeler, 2016).

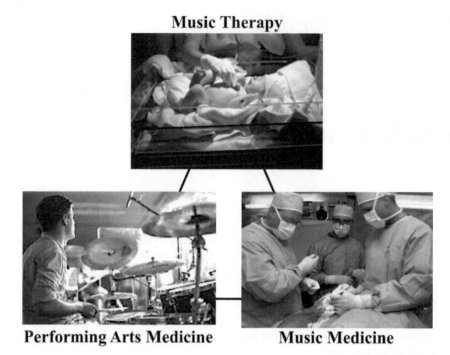

FIGURE 15.1 | Music Therapy, Performing Arts Medicine, and Music Medicine are Related Fields of Music and Health.

TABLE 15.1 | Overview of Practitioners and Clients/Patients.

	Music Therapy	**Music Medicine**	**Performing Arts Medicine**
Practitioners	Specially trained musicians	Primarily physician-driven, can also involve nurses and music therapists	Physicians, audiologists, speech therapists, counselors, and other health care professionals
Clients/Patients	Persons of all ages with a wide variety of physical and mental health needs	Primarily surgical and pain patients	Performing musicians* experiencing hearing, vocal, bodily, or psychosocial health issues related to musical activities

*Performing arts medicine encompasses dancers, actors, and other performing artists in addition to musicians. In this chapter, however, we will only deal with musicians.

Client populations for music therapists are extremely broad and diverse, including persons of all ages who have mental health needs, developmental and learning disabilities, Alzheimer's and other age-related conditions, substance abuse problems, brain injuries, physical disabilities, and acute or chronic pain (Fig. 15.2). Some music therapists work in "wellness" clinics with non-disabled individuals. Equally as diverse as the client population are the facilities where music therapists work; these include psychiatric hospitals, rehabilitative facilities, medical hospitals, outpatient clinics, day care treatment centers, agencies serving developmentally disabled persons, community mental health centers, drug and alcohol programs, senior centers, nursing homes, hospice programs, correctional facilities, halfway houses, schools, and private practice (American Music Therapy Association, 2018).

FIGURE 15.2 | Music Therapists Trained in Neurologic Music Therapy Work with Wounded Warriors to Help Improve Motor Skills and Memory Retention and Relieve Stress.

Music therapists are professionally trained musicians who take music theory, history, and performance courses along with other music majors. In addition, they take particular nonmusic courses (e.g., abnormal psychology) and courses in music therapy (e.g., clinical practicum). Rather than the recital for performance majors or student teaching for certification students, they complete an internship of approximately 1000 hours, wherein they work in a clinical setting under the supervision of a music therapist. Those who successfully pass the requisite coursework and national board examinations receive the designation of MT-BC (Music Therapist-Board Certified).

The roots of music therapy go back thousands of years as almost all known societies have used music in connection with healing, often within a religious context (Horden, 2017; Thaut, 2015). The shaman, witch doctor, or medicine man/woman was a spiritual healer who frequently used music as a mode of treatment. These practices are still continued in some parts of the world today (e.g., see Häussermann, 2006; Jankowsky, 2006). From the perspective of music therapy as defined at the outset of the chapter, the beginnings are found in treatments given to veterans who returned from World War II with serious injuries. Here are a few salient dates (Pratt, 1996):

- 1944. The first curriculum designed to train music therapists was established at Michigan State University.
- 1946. The first didactic and laboratory courses were taught at the University of Kansas.
- 1950. The National Association for Music Therapy (NAMT) was established and headquartered in Lawrence, Kansas.
- 1961. By this date, 500 registered music therapists were certified.
- 1964. The *Journal of Music Therapy* began publication with editorial offices in Lawrence, Kansas.
- 1971. The American Association for Music Therapy (AAMT) was established.
- 1998. The American Music Therapy Association (AMTA) was formed by the unification of NAMT and AAMT.
- 2003. The Academy of Neurologic Music Therapy was established.

TABLE 15.2 | Processes in Music Therapy.

Experience within Structure
1. Music demands time-ordered behavior.
   a. Music demands reality-ordered behavior.
   b. Music demands immediately and continuously objectified behavior.
2. Music permits ability-ordered behavior.
   a. Music permits ordering of behavior according to physical response levels.
   b. Music permits ordering of behavior according to psychological response levels.
3. Music evokes affectively-ordered behavior.
4. Music provokes sensory-elaborated behavior.
   a. Music demands increased sensory usage and discrimination.
   b. Music may elicit extramusical ideas and associations.

Experience in Self-organization
1. Music provides for self-expression.
2. Music provides compensatory endeavors for the handicapped individual.
3. Music provides opportunities for socially acceptable reward and non-reward.
4. Music provides for the enhancement of pride in self.
   a. Music provides for successful experiences.
   b. Music provides for feeling needed by others.
   c. Music provides for enhancement of esteem by others.

Experience in Relating to Others
1. Music provides means by which self-expression is socially acceptable.
2. Music provides opportunity for individual choice of response in groups.
3. Music provides opportunities for acceptance of responsibility to self and others.
   a. Music provides for developing self-directed behavior.
   b. Music provides for developing other-directed behavior.
4. Music enhances verbal and nonverbal social interaction and communication.
5. Music provides for experiencing cooperation and competition in socially acceptable forms.
6. Music provides entertainment and recreation necessary to the general therapeutic environment.
7. Music provides for learning realistic social skills and personal behavior patterns acceptable in institutional and community peer groups.

In the foreword to his landmark text *Music in Therapy*, Gaston (1968) stated three principles of music therapy: (1) The establishment or reestablishment of interpersonal relationships. (2) The bringing about of self-esteem through self-actualization. (3) The utilization of the unique potential of rhythm to energize and bring order. William Sears (1968), one of Gaston's students and later his colleague at the University of Kansas, created an outline of processes in music therapy as shown in Table 15.2. Some of these processes are determined by the music itself, as shown in Experience within Structure. For example, because of music's time-based nature, individuals must coordinate their movements moment-to-moment with the music. Experience in Self-Organization refers to internal attitudes and interests that have personal meanings. Personal expression through music is an important process of music therapy. Finally, Experience in Relating to Others takes advantage of the social nature of the musical experience. Personal expressions may find social acceptance through participation in group musical activities.

Among the most important areas in the treatment of persons with disabilities are communication, academic, motor, and social skills (Eagle, 1982). Music therapists are not primarily interested in the development of musicianship *per se*. Music is a means, not an end, and nonmusical behaviors take precedence over musical skills. However, it is important to realize that all persons, those with disabilities and those without, have a need for aesthetic experiences, and moments of musical beauty and truth are important ingredients in the healing process.

Perhaps the greatest power of music as a healing agent comes from the fact that it is a form of nonverbal communication. For those who are unable to communicate via language or for those for whom verbal communication is threatening, music provides a vehicle for interchange. Too, the nonverbal aspect of music often allows a music therapist to establish a personal relationship with a client who resists personal contacts. In this way, music therapy can be used to establish bonds of communication so that other therapists can become involved in the healing process. Another important aspect of music as nonverbal communication is the ambiguity of that communication. While words are often discrete and delimiting, music can express the ineffable and can support personal feelings. Trying to describe what music therapists do and the results they achieve is somewhat difficult because of the wide diversity of clinical situations in which they operate. The following examples are meant to serve as illustrations of just a few of the possibilities.

Alzheimer's Disease

Music therapy has been shown to be an effective treatment for patients with Alzheimer's Disease (AD) and other forms of dementia (Bruscia, 2011; Cevasco & Grant, 2003; Koger, Chapin, & Brotons, 1999; Särkämö, Laitinen, Tervaniemi, Nummien, Kurki, & Rantanen, 2012; Sherratt, Thornton, & Hatton, 2004). For example, patients with AD improved on a battery of standardized tests concerning social and emotional behaviors following music therapy sessions involving music listening, singing, playing instruments, and movement/dance (Brotons & Marti, 2003). Likewise, patients with AD who received four weeks of music therapy intervention showed significant increases of melatonin, norepinephrine, and epinephrine; melatonin levels remained elevated six weeks after the music therapy sessions ended, while norepinephrine, and epinephrine returned to baseline (Kumar et al., 1999). These hormonal changes are related to enhanced well-being. Prolactin and platelet serotonin levels remained unchanged throughout. Individual music sessions decreased agitation in home-dwelling patients with dementia (Park, 2013). Simmons-Stern, Budson, and Ally (2010) suggest that music may achieve its positive results with AD patients because (a) music processing networks may be preserved longer as the dementia progresses and (b) music heightens arousal, which improves focus and memory.

Autism

Music is a special interest for 40% of individuals with autism (Heaton, 2003), suggesting that music therapy may be a viable aid to learning (Bakan, 2018; Berger, 2002, 2016; Hammel & Hourigan, 2013; Kern & Humpal, 2012; Ockelford, 2013a, 2019). For example, eight young adults diagnosed with severe autism took part in weekly 60-minute music therapy sessions (Boso, Emanuele, Minazzi, Abbamonte, & Politi, 2007). Musical activities included singing, piano playing, and drumming. At the end of one year, the participants' scores on clinical rating scales improved significantly, along with their musical skills. Katagiri (2009) investigated the efficacy of using background music as a means of improving emotional understanding of children with autism. Compared to three additional conditions—no contact control, teaching selected emotions using verbal instruction alone, and singing songs about selected emotions—background music representing selected emotions was most effective in improving understanding. Children with autism who received violin instruction improved social and communicative adaptive behaviors (Chinn Cannon, 2018) (Fig. 15.3). Significant changes in cortical activation of brain sites associated with social and language learning were found in those children involved in violin lessons.

Being Musical

FIGURE 15.3 | Michelle Chinn Cannon with One of Her Violin Students.

Cerebral Palsy

Researchers divided 60 children with cerebral palsy into two groups, one treated with acupuncture and the other with acupuncture plus music (30 minutes of listening to music during acupuncture treatment and 30 minutes of participating in music activities). Although both groups improved, the music group had significantly better improvement in creeping, kneeling, standing, and walking (Yu, Liu, & Wu, 2009). Kwak (2007) used rhythmic auditory stimulation (see the subsequent section on Parkinson's Disease and Stroke) to improve gait performance in children with spastic cerebral palsy. Enhanced balance, trajectory, and kinematic stability helped to improve stride-length, velocity, and symmetry without increasing cadence. Krakouer, Houghton, Douglas, and West (2001) engaged young adults with cerebral palsy in music therapy activities to enhance positive emotional responses. Participants engaged in music making with specialized instruments chosen to meet their individual needs. All participants demonstrated consistent, positive improvement in emotional responses.

Dyslexia

Dyslexia may have as much to do with sound as sight, as children with dyslexia often have rhythmic/timing difficulties. Magnetoencephalography (MEG) responses from the auditory cortex of poor readers were weaker and slower than those from good readers, indicating difficulties in ability to process brief and rapidly successive auditory inputs (Nagarajan, Mahncke, Salz, Tallall, Roberts, & Merzenich, 1999). Following this line of work, Karma (2003) developed a computerized method of presenting auditory patterns in a gaming format that has been used successfully to identify and train children with auditory dyslexia. In another study, music lessons improved language and literacy skills of dyslexic children, but not reading skills (Overy, 2003). Another group developed and tested a specially designed method called Cognitive-Musical Training (CMT) that is

> based upon three principles: (1) music-language analogies: training dyslexics with music could contribute to improve brain circuits which are common to music and language processes; (2) the temporal and rhythmic features of music, which could exert a positive

effect on the multiple dimensions of the "temporal deficit" characteristic of some types of dyslexia; and (3) cross-modal integration, based on converging evidence of impaired connectivity between brain regions in dyslexia and related disorders.

(Habib, Lardy, Desiles, Commeiras, Chobert, & Besson, 2016, p. 1)

Results of two studies confirmed the efficacy of CMT for aiding reading and related disorders.

Parkinson's Disease and Stroke

The efficacy of *Neurologic Music Therapy* (NMT) in improving motor movements among Parkinsonian and stroke patients has been well documented (McIntosh, Brown, Rice, & Thaut, 1997; Miller, Thaut, McIntosh, & Rice, 1996; Thaut, McIntosh, Rice, Rathbun, & Brault, 1996). In fact, NMT, which involves rhythmic entrainment, has been listed as one of five research-supported treatments for motor rehabilitation (Hummelsheim, 1999; Mauritz, 2002). In one study, ten hemispheric stroke patients were provided with rhythmic cueing in which the beat was matched to the step rate (Prassas, Thaut, McIntosh, & Rice, 1997; Thaut, Kenyon, Schauer, & McIntosh, 1999; Thaut, McIntosh, Rice, & Prassas, 1993). Movement parameters were assessed with EMG (electromyography), three-dimensional motion analysis, and computerized foot sensors. The results indicated that participants experienced significant improvement as a result of rhythmic auditory stimulation. A similar study with 20 stroke patients demonstrated that improvements in gait were sustained and were significantly greater than gains from conventional physical therapy (Thaut, Rice, & McIntosh, 1997). Specialized training is available at the Academy for Neurologic Music Therapy (https://nmtacademy.co). Originally developed for improving gait mobility with stroke and Parkinsonian patients, NMT is now also used to treat difficulties with memory, attention, motor control, emotions, perception, executive function, and language.

Premature and Newborn Infants

Music has a positive effect on premature infants, including lowered heart rate, higher oxygen saturation, shorter stays in the NICU (neonatal intensive care unit), reduced distress behaviors, higher caloric intake and weight gain, and reduction of fear and anxiety perception in parents (Chou, Wang, Chen, & Pai, 2003; Coleman, Pratt, Stoddard, Gerstmann, & Abel, 1997; Loewy, Stewart, Dassler, Telsey, & Homel, 2013; Standley, 1999). Standley (2003) found that music significantly improved feeding rates for premature infants. She also conducted a meta-analysis of ten studies and found that researchers have consistently demonstrated the efficacy of using music in the neonatal intensive care unit, providing clinically important benefits (Standley, 2002). Live music therapy is more effective than recorded music or no music therapy for stable preterm infants (Amon et al., 2006).

Psychiatric Disorders

Silverman (2009) contrasted a group music therapy *psychoeducation session* with a group psychoeducation session for acute psychiatric inpatients. Psychoeducation refers to the attempt to increase psychiatric patients' knowledge and illness management skills. Although he did not find significant differences, music therapy groups had slightly higher mean scores in measures of helpfulness, enjoyment, satisfaction with life, or psychoeducational knowledge. Similarly, though not significantly different, there were nearly 20 more participant verbalizations during music therapy sessions than during psychoeducation. On the basis of these results, Silverman concluded that clinical psychoeducational music therapy was at least as effective as a strong and active psychosocial intervention (i.e., psychoeducation). Mössler, Chen, Heldal, and Gold (2011) conducted a review of eight studies (483 participants) on the effects of music therapy with patients with schizophrenia and schizophrenia-like disorders. Their conclusions were that, "Music therapy as an addition to standard care helps people with schizophrenia to improve their global state, mental state (including negative symptoms) and social functioning if a sufficient number of music therapy sessions are provided by qualified music therapists" (p. 2).

These examples indicate just a few of the activities and results of music therapy treatment sessions. Singing, playing instruments, listening, creating or improvising, and moving to music are all a regular part of the program. Sometimes these activities are couched within a particular therapeutic framework, such as behavior modification. Sometimes particular approaches are characterized by certain activities, such as in guided imagery sessions or psychodrama. Often, however, the therapeutic approach is eclectic and based on a careful, ongoing assessment of the individual client's needs. Whatever the approach, music therapists are proving more and more to be accepted as valuable members of treatment teams.

MUSIC MEDICINE

It is not possible, nor even preferable, to make sharp distinctions between music therapy and music medicine, as there are many interrelationships. In general, however, *music medicine* refers to the use of music to affect health directly, normally as administered by a doctor, nurse, or other health care practitioner. It is primarily physician-driven as they make up the largest segment of membership in the two major organizations—the International Society for Music in Medicine and the International Arts Medicine Association (Spintge & Droh, 1992b). Music therapists are sometimes involved in the practice of music medicine, especially as a team member with other health care professionals.

Spintge (1999) provided the following formal definition of music medicine:

> MusicMedicine is defined through multidisciplinary scientific evaluation, including mathematical, physical, physiological, medical, psychological, musicological, and music therapeutic means, as well as through preventative, curative, and rehabilitative application of musical stimuli in healthcare settings, in order to complement usual medical procedures, while regarding specific pending or actual existing health disorders and their ordinary treatment on an individual basis.
>
> (p. 9)

Figure 15.4 shows anesthesiologist Ralph Spintge in the operating theater. Notice that the patient is wearing headphones. These are connected to a music delivery system that allows the patient to choose the type of music and control the loudness level. Based on a number of studies, "we currently know that musical pieces chosen by the patient are commonly, but not always, more effective than pieces chosen by another person" (Bernatzky, Presch, Anderson, & Panksepp, 2011, p. 1989).

Examples of music medicine include the use of music to control pain (*anxiolytic music*), to reduce blood pressure, heart rate, or muscle tension; or to effect changes in the endocrine system. Music has been used in perioperative stress, surgery, anesthesia, acute and chronic pain therapy, palliative and intensive care, obstetrics, pediatrics, geriatrics, gastroenterology,

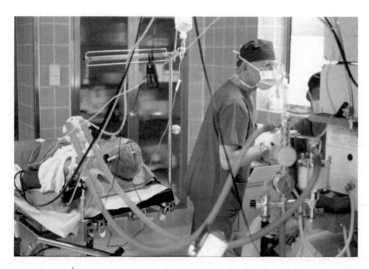

FIGURE 15.4 | A Patient in the Operating Theater Wearing Headphones.

behavioral disorders, motor dysfunction, cancer care, ophthalmology, neurology, and dentistry, to name a few clinical applications. Spintge, Executive Director of the International Society for Music in Medicine, has collected data on over 160,000 surgical and pain patients, documenting the efficacy of music in reducing pain, anxiety, and length of hospital stay (Spintge, 2012). In doing so, he and his colleagues have utilized a multi-modal approach involving psychological tests, behavioral observations, self-reports, and monitoring of neurovegetative systems (e.g., pulse rate, blood pressure, beat-to-beat EKG, heart rate variability, respiratory rate and rhythmicity, skin temperature, finger-plethysmography, oxygen consumption, CO_2 production, and blood levels of neurohormones such as beta-endorphin, ACTH, cortisol, etc.; see Koshimori, 2019) (Spintge & Droh, 1992c). In a series of controlled studies over many years, he has used music to reduce dosages of sedatives, analgesics, and anesthetics by as much as 50% in certain prescribed clinical situations.

Use of music also has the benign advantage of avoiding toxic reactions and speeding up recovery time. As just one example, researchers examined the effects of music listening on 75 patients who were randomly assigned to hear music during surgery, after surgery, or no music (Nilsson, Unosson, & Rawal, 2005). Results indicated that music during surgery may decrease postoperative pain and that postoperative music may reduce pain, anxiety, and the amount of morphine consumed. Interestingly, Health care professionals also use music in their work for their own benefit. In one survey, 63% of physicians and nurses listened to music in the operating room (OR) and 78.9% of them felt that music in the OR helped them to be calmer and more efficient (Ullmann, Fodor, Schwarzberg, Carmi, Ullmann, & Ramon, 2008).

Stress, Pain, Anxiety, and the Immune System

Psychoneuroimmunology (PNI) is the study of interactions among the brain, behavior, and the immune system (Maier, Watkins, & Fleshner, 1994). The notion of PNI is that the brain and the immune system communicate with each other bidirectionally, both in physical pathways (sympathetic nervous system) and by means of hormones. PNI research suggests that

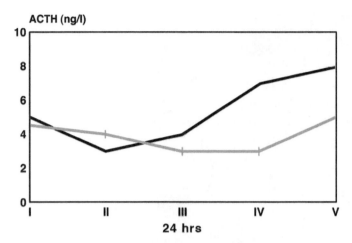

FIGURE 15.5 | This Graph Shows the Level of Adrenocorticotropic Hormone (ACTH) in the Bloodstreams of Women During 24 Hours of Labor. ACTH, measured in nanograms per liter (ng/l), is secreted in response to stress, which in turn stimulates the adrenal cortex to secrete cortisol. This helps in stress management. The gray line is for women who listened to music and the black line is for those who did not. Music reduced the body's response to stress experienced during childbirth.

behavioral experiences (e.g., music) affect the mind/brain, which in turn can alter the immune function (Conti, 2000; Maranto & Scartelli, 1992; Scartelli, 1992).

Music has been found to reduce stress (measured in decreased cortisol levels) in patients awaiting surgery (Miluk-Kolasa et al., 1994), in those undergoing surgery (Reilly, 1999), in those who experienced psychological stress (Fukui & Yamashita, 2003; Khalfa, Dalla Bella, Roy, Peretz, & Lupien, 2003), and women in labor (see Figure 15.5). Music has also been found to be effective in ameliorating pain in a variety of clinical settings, for example, with elders suffering from chronic osteoarthritis pain (McCaffrey & Freeman, 2003), with patients undergoing bone marrow transplantation (Sahler, Hunter, & Liesveld, 2003), and with women undergoing colposcopy (Chan, Lee, Ng, Ngan, & Wong, 2003). Music is not uniformly effective: music listening reduced pain medication and anxiety among patients awaiting surgery (Pratt, 1999; Reilly, 1996), but caused no significant reduction of pain or anxiety among burn patients (Ferguson & Voll, 2004) or in patients undergoing coronary angiography (Bally, Campbell, Chesnick, & Tranmer, 2003).

Fancourt, Ockelford, and Belai (2014) reviewed 64 studies on the psychoneuroimmunology of music, including the effects of music on neurotransmitters, hormones, cytokines, lymphocytes, vital signs, and immunoglobulins, as well as psychological assessments. Although strong linkages between music and immune system responses are noted, weaknesses in methodologies elicited a new model. The model calls for more specific details concerning variables such as the music and the stress experienced by participant and a broader view of interactions among various components of the nervous, endocrine, and immune systems as they react to music.

Aphasia

Melodic-Intonation Therapy (MIT) is recognized by the American Academy of Neurology as an effective treatment for aphasia (Albert, 1998). In MIT, patients are taught to intone speech with exaggerated rhythmic and pitch stress. Working with stroke patients who suffered from severe nonfluent aphasia, researchers found that patients receiving MIT showed significant improvement in verbal communication over those who did not. Furthermore, MIT intervention at the soonest possible time following the stroke may lead to greater improvements.

The notion is that since Broca's aphasia involves a left-sided lesion, prosodic (i.e., quasi-musical) processes are still available in the intact right side. Confirmation of this notion has come from several studies. CT scans showed that aphasic patients with good response to MIT had left-sided lesions (primarily in Broca's area), while patients with poor response to MIT had bilateral lesions or right-sided lesions (Naeser & Helm-Estabrooks, 1985). Subjects with unilateral, left-hemisphere (LH) lesions and who exhibited nonfluency and expressive speech difficulties were not impaired on pitch perception or production but were grossly impaired on rhythm production and perception (Alcock, Wade, Anslow, & Passingham, 2000). Subjects with right-hemisphere (RH) lesions were impaired on measures of pitch perception and production. Nonfluent aphasic patients who were successfully treated with MIT underwent PET scans to determine brain changes (Belin et al., 1996). Without MIT, LH brain areas normally associated with speaking were deactivated while homologous RH areas were activated. Following MIT and repeating words with MIT, Broca's area and left prefrontal cortex were activated, while deactivating the counterpart of Wernicke's area in the LH. Finally, speaking the words to *Happy Birthday* activated the left hemisphere (monitored by PET) in traditional language areas, while singing the words to the same song activated widely ranging areas in the right hemisphere (Jeffries, Fritz, & Braun, 2003). Stahl and Kotz (2014) uphold the efficacy of MIT but discuss some issues related to future research and clinical applications.

Music is not widely used in medical practice, at least not as widely used as perhaps it could be. Understandably, most physicians do not receive training in the use of music as a medical intervention. As research findings continue to mount over the coming years, perhaps music will occupy a more prominent niche in additional medical specialties.

PERFORMING ARTS MEDICINE

A new medical specialty devoted to treating the medical problems of performing artists is developing and there are a growing number of specialists and clinics scattered around the country (Brandfonbrener & Lederman, 2002). Physicians, nurses, orthopedic surgeons, neurologists, psychiatrists, psychologists, audiologists, otolaryngologists, speech pathologists, and other health care professionals are engaged in dealing with medical issues related to musical performance. Others, such as those practicing *Alexander Technique*, Feldenkrais Method, Rolfing Structural Integration, acupressure, acupuncture, chiropractic, massotherapy, therapeutic touch, herbal medicine, homeopathy, biofeedback, or desensitization training may also be involved. Generally speaking, medical problems of musicians can be divided into four categories: hearing health, vocal health, bodily health, and psychosocial health. For excellent review articles on performing arts medicine and each of these four topics, see the *Music Educators Journal: Special Focus Issue on Musicians' Health and Wellness* (Chesky, 2008; see also Horvath, 2008; Kageyama, 2019; Klickstein, 2009; LaPine, 2008; Palac, 2008; Sternbach, 2008).

Hearing Health^{MT6.4}

Musicians spend an inordinate amount of time in environments where loud sounds are present, such as ensemble rehearsal rooms, teaching studios, practice rooms, and concert halls. Professional musicians have a four times greater risk of hearing loss than the general public and a 57% greater chance of developing tinnitus (Schink, Kreutz, Busch, Pigeot, & Ahrens, 2014). In a survey of 693 professional musicians, 40% had hearing loss or related issues (Greasley, Fulford, Pickard, & Hamilton, 2018). As discussed in Chapter 6 on hearing, exposure to loud

TABLE 15.3 | National Institute for Occupational Safety and Health Standards.

dB level	Time
85	8 hours
88	4 hours
91	2 hours
94	1 hour
97	30 minutes
100	15 minutes
103	7.5 minutes
106	3.25 minutes
109	1.6 minutes

Note: NIOSH standards for safe exposure to loud sounds. Generally, it is considered safe to be exposed to 85 dB of sound for up to eight hours per day. With each 3-dB increase, the amount of time is reduced by half. Thus, it may take less than two minutes per day of repeated exposures to 109 dB for damage to occur.

sounds can lead to Noise-Induced Hearing Loss (NIHL). According to the National Institute for Occupational Safety and Health (NIOSH) exposure to loudness levels more than 85 dB during an eight-hour period may be deleterious to hearing acuity (2018; Table 15.3). Each three-decibel increase reduces by half the amount of time one can safely be exposed. Thus, 88 dB for four hours, 91 dB for two hours, and so on, are considered safe levels.

Walter, Mace, and Phillips (2008) monitored university musicians for noise exposure in a variety of settings. All students exceeded 85 dB and some reached a level of 94 dB, which would only give them one hour of safe exposure. Students in three different bands wore dose-badges (Figure 15.6), personal dosimeters that record the average sound level of exposure over a given period of time and report a daily sound dose percentage (Walter, 2009). Anything over 100% places wearers at risk of NIHL if they experience continued exposure at that level. Across the three bands, which met for different amounts of time during the week, students experienced from 26–296% noise doses. Alto saxophone, trumpet, horn, trombone, and tuba sections experienced the highest dosages.

Walter, Mace, and Phillips (2008) monitored students in a high school marching band. Fifteen of 16 students experienced noise doses in excess of 500% on the first day of collection and in excess of 300% on the second day. One snare drummer reached 3,925% and 1,866% on the two days. In a drum and bugle corps, four snare drummers experienced doses of 5,320%, 8,222%, 9,155%, and 9,455% in one 12-hour day of rehearsals (Presley, 2007). On a more positive note, Presley demonstrated that these students could have reduced their exposure to a safe limit (i.e., under 100%) if they had worn adequate hearing protection. The least expensive foam earplugs (Fig. 15.6) would have sufficed.

Nearly half of university music students rehearsing in music practice rooms experienced loudness levels that put them at risk of permanent hearing damage (Phillips & Mace, 2008). Brass players experienced significantly higher doses than other instrument groups. In ensemble

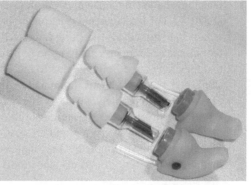

FIGURE 15.6 | Dosebadge and Earplugs. In the left panel is a dosebadge. This is a personal dosimeter, worn on the shoulder (see figure 12.3) or on a cap to be near the ear. It is used to record the sound levels experienced for a given time, which are then calculated into dose percentages. Anything over 100% dose potentially puts the wearer at risk of permanent hearing loss with repeated exposures at that level. In the right panel are three earplugs. In the upper left corner are the least expensive foam earplugs, which are useful for reducing loud sounds but are not so useful during sensitive musical performances. In the middle are mid-range earplugs that attenuate the sound more evenly and that are more useful for music than foam earplugs. In the lower right corner are custom-made musicians' earplugs. They are the most satisfactory for sensitive musical performances.

settings, sound shields are plastic barriers that can be placed behind the heads of performers (see bassoonist in Figure 12.4) and Libera and Mace (2010) found that in some circumstances they reduced sound levels. However, the reduction they provided was insufficient and the recommendation is that they be used along with other reduction strategies such as earplugs. Based on three years of data collection, more than half of undergraduate music majors experienced declines in aural acuity (Phillips, Shoemaker, Mace, & Hodges, 2008). Mace (2005) studied university music teachers as they carried out their normal teaching, practicing, and performing routines during two normal days of teaching. Daily noise doses ranged from 2% to 727%, with brass and percussion teachers and accompanists in the highest risk categories.

Prevention is key to the preservation of hearing. Hearing loss is deceptive, in that once one becomes aware of deficits in hearing it is too late to restore those losses. Following hearing health protocols, however, may stave off NIHL or at least keep it from getting worse. Preservation strategies include:

- Having an audiometric test to establish a hearing baseline. For example, the School of Music at the University of North Carolina at Greensboro has a Hearing Conservation Policy, mandating that all undergraduate students have their hearing tested once per year.
- Maintaining the greatest distance possible from a sound source. Voice teachers, for example, sometimes sit at the keyboard while a student stands very close. Having the student stand farther away will reduce the loudness level.
- Scheduling quiet times or rest periods as frequently as possible will allow the hair cells in the inner ear time to recover.
- Using sound-absorbing panels in teaching studios, rehearsal spaces, and practice rooms. Carpets, drapes, and other sound absorbing materials are also useful.
- Keeping hard reflective surfaces such as mirrors or framed photographs to a minimum.

Being Musical

- Obtaining and using musicians' earplugs on a regular basis (Toppila, Koskinen, & Pyyk-kö, 2011). The least expensive earplugs (from 15–25 cents) are foam inserts and they can reduce loudness levels by approximately 29 dB (see Figure 15.6). Unfortunately, they alter timbres and reduce sensitivity to refined pitch and timing judgments to such a degree that they may have limited value to musicians. However, they may be useful to percussionists in marching bands, drum and bugle corps, and jazz and rock groups. Mid-range earplugs (approximately $12.00) offer a 20-dB reduction. These earplugs attenuate the sound more evenly and are more useful in musical situations than the foam plugs. Best of all are musician's earplugs that are custom fit for each individual. Typically, these earplugs cost around $120.00, but they may well be worth the investment. Filters that reduce loudness levels by 9 dB, 15 dB, and 25 dB are available (Niquette, 2009; Owens, 2007).

Perhaps the most important strategy is information. Musicians should be educated about risks to hearing health in order to preserve that which is critical to their success and enjoyment (see Chasin, 2009).

Vocal Health

Singers are at risk of damage to the vocal mechanism. Culprits can be such things as inordinate tension while singing or improper technique, overuse, yelling, speaking at a low fundamental pitch level, smoking, alcohol or drug usage, dehydration, allergies, gastroesophageal reflux disease (GERD), laryngitis, and so on (David, 1996). The result can be a wide range of acute or chronic problems, including hoarseness, fatigue, volume disturbance, growth on the vocal folds, nodules or calluses, polyps (Fig. 15.7), cysts, granulomas, singers (overuse) nodes, hemorrhage of a vocal fold (rupture of blood vessel), and so on (Heman-Ackah, Sataloff, & Hawkshaw, 2013; Sataloff, 1998b). Although anyone who uses the voice—teachers, conductors, and so on—may experience difficulties, the focus in performing arts medicine is primarily on singers.

Depending on the type or severity of vocal problems, singers may need to consult a speech-language pathologist, an otolaryngologist, or singing voice specialist. Ideally, the focus should be on education and prevention to avoid more serious problems. Treatments include (Levine & Finnegan, 1987; Sataloff, 1998b):

- Vocal rest; limiting singing, yelling, excessive talking, and whispering
- Dinking enough water to be fully hydrated

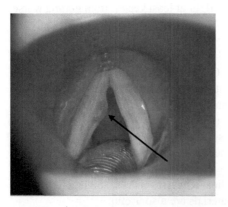

FIGURE 15.7 | An Arrow Points to a Vocal Fold Polyp as Seen Through Endoscopic Examination.

- Exercising to strengthen musculature that supports singing (e.g., back and abdominal muscles) and to improve breath support
- Taking medications such as antihistamines
- Surgery

Sataloff (1998a) provides concise discussions of a wide variety of ailments and treatment procedures. Much more extensive is the three-volume set (Sataloff, 2005) that contains 106 chapters and over 1,700 pages. This invaluable compendium is not limited to the singing voice, as it also includes actors and other speakers, but it is difficult to imagine a more comprehensive resource for musicians concerned about vocal health.

Vaughn (2007) surveyed middle and high school choral singers and found that a large percentage of them engaged in at least some harmful activities, such as yelling (75%), constantly clearing their throats (70%), or experiencing stress (50%). In addition, these adolescent singers performed in classical choral, gospel, and musical theater styles. Videostroboscopy, filming the vocal cords in action in simulated slow motion, revealed that laryngeal tension was greatest in musical theater style, followed by gospel, with classical choral style exhibiting the least tension. One major conclusion is that prevention efforts must begin with young children.

Bodily Health

Instrumental musicians, in particular, are prone to neuromusculoskeletal health risks (Lederman, 2003; Ginsborg, Spahn, & Williamon, 2012). More than three-fourths (76%) of 2,212 professional symphony musicians reported at least one health problem that affected performance (Fishbein & Middlestadt, 1988). Of the 59 medical problems listed on the survey, 34 were physical locations for muscular or skeletal problems. Flute players may have right shoulder problems; clarinet, oboe, and bassoon players may have joint pain in the thumb and index fingers; upper string players may have shoulder, neck, elbow, or wrist joint pain; and many instrumentalists may experience lower back and neck pain, along with eyestrain (Abréu-Ramos & Micheo, 2007; Dawson, 2007; Kochan, 2003; Lee, Park, et al., 2013).

More formally, neuromusculoskeletal problems include musculoskeletal or muscle-tendon pain (experienced by 64% of 1,353 patients at a Medical Center for Performing Artists); focal entrapment neuropathies (20%), and focal dystonias (8%) (Lederman, 2003). Musculoskeletal problems include shoulder impingement or rotator cuff disruption, ligament sprain (including tendonitis) and regional pain often characterized as overuse syndrome. The highest risk factors for these problems are gender (females are more susceptible), years of playing experience, type of instrument played (pianists are at highest risk), playing-related physical (e.g., long hours, over practicing) or psychological stressors (e.g., auditions), lack of preventative measures (e.g., not taking breaks), and previous trauma (Wu, 2007).

Focal entrapment neuropathies or nerve entrapments include carpal tunnel syndrome, cubital tunnel or ulnar (elbow) neuropathy, and thoracic outlet syndrome; these occur when a nerve is compressed or stretched, often as a result of the posture and position required for playing an instrument or from overuse. For example, one violinist developed difficulties with the left index finger while practicing up to ten hours a day for a competition (Lederman, 2006). In his case, there was a painless tendency for the index finger to collapse, but he was able to continue with his orchestral career. Another violinist was not so fortunate as he was forced to retire from his orchestral position when he was unable to hold the bow as a result of a neuropathy. Three university student pianists out of 19 examined were found to have evidence of neuropathy (Gohl, Clayton, Strickland, Bufford, Halle, & Greathouse, 2006). Of the 311 instrumentalists who presented with a neuropathy in Lederman's (2003) clinic review, 143 were string players, 101 were pianists, 61 were wind/brass players, and only six were percussionists.

Nonsurgical treatments may include rest, nonsteroidal anti-inflammatories, occasionally steroids, and splinting for absolute rest (Brandfonbrener & Kjelland, 2002). Carpal tunnel is the most common nerve entrapment and involves the median nerve where it passes from the palm of the hand to the wrist. Cubital tunnel syndrome involves a compression of the ulnar nerve at or slightly above the elbow. Thoracic outlet syndrome (TOS) involves nerves and blood vessels that come from inside the upper chest to supply the arms. While there can be physical restrictions, TOS can also be intermittent based on posture.

Focal dystonia, sometimes called musician's cramp, came to public attention when internationally acclaimed pianists Gary Graffman and Leon Fleischer suffered major blows to their careers as a result of the loss of functioning in their right hands (Sataloff & Hawkshaw, 1998). *Focal* indicates that the problem is localized, most often to the hands of pianists and string players, but also to the embouchures of wind and brass players (Brandfonbrener, 1995). *Dystonia* refers to an involuntary and generally painless loss of muscle control in the affected hand (or other body part), even though the hand may work perfectly well when engaged in nonmusical tasks; that is, the problem tends to be task-specific. An exception is that pianists may also have difficulty with other keyboarding (e.g., computer) tasks.

Approximately one percent of all professional musicians experience focal dystonia (Altenmüller, 2010). This disorder seems to be most related to overuse, although incorrect hand or body position and stress may also play roles; there may even be a genetic predisposition. Physical and neurological examinations do not normally lead to abnormal findings, although musicians affected may have more perfectionist tendencies and more anxiety. Due to the difficulties in diagnosis, Spector and Brandfonbrener (2005) developed an objective and quantitative method for clinical evaluation. Called the Frequency of Abnormal Movements Scale, objective observers use it to identify the number of abnormal movements per second during instrumental performance. This scale is not useful for dystonias that do not involve the hand. Dystonias are extremely difficult to treat (Lederman, 2003), although interventions such as treatment with botulinum toxin or other drugs, behavioral therapies, or sensory motor retraining may have some effect (de Lisle, Speedy, Thompson, & Maurice, 2006; Peterson & Altenmüller, 2019; Spector & Brandfonbrener, 2005).

As with other medical problems of musicians, education and prevention are paramount in dealing with neuromusculoskeletal problems (Dawson, 2008). Positive steps toward prevention include proper warm up, stretching exercises, physical exercise, proper nutrition, taking frequent breaks, and correct posture. Instrumentalists may also choose to use devices such as neck straps for clarinetists or other ergonomically designed instruments that consider the biomechanics of musical performance (Manchester, 2006; Norris & Dommerholt, 1998; Wilson & Roehmann, 1992). Treatment of performance injuries can include physical therapy, ultrasound, steroids, massage, Pilates, Feldenkrais, Alexander Technique, yoga, acupuncture, acupressure, herbs, and hot and cold packs (Batson, 1996; Conable, 1995; Conable & Conable, 2000; Horvath, 2010; Lieberman, 1997; Spire, 1989). In some extreme cases, surgery may be necessary.

Psychosocial Health

Some aspects of psychosocial health issues among musicians are connected with hearing, vocal, or bodily problems as previously discussed. That is, along with a physical ailment, there is considerable stress and success in music studies, auditions, or professional performances may be compromised (Brandfonbrener & Kjelland, 2002). Furthermore, emotional stress may be reflected in increased muscular tension (Brandfonbrener & Lederman, 2002). Thus, psychological and physical aspects of musical performance are intertwined in a symbiotic relationship.

Mental health issues include performance anxiety or stage fright, memorization problems, teacher-student relationships, and other forms of stress. While there is considerable research on memorization strategies (e.g., Aiello & Williamson, 2002), little is directed toward the specific effects of memorization difficulties on mental health.

Performance Anxiety. The most frequently mentioned severe health problem among symphony musicians in one study was stage fright (Fishbein & Middlestadt, 1988). Kenny, Driscoll, and Ackermann (2014) surveyed 377 orchestral musicians, finding that female musicians had higher rates of anxiety (trait, music performance, and social anxiety) than males. Levy, Rosen, and Sataloff (2005) identified three aspects of performance anxiety: (a) *stressors*, both external (e.g., an important audition) and internal (e.g., worrisome thoughts, anxious feelings); (b) *distress*, such as internal feelings of tension or anxiety caused by stressors; and (c) *biological responses*, such as fight or flight responses.

Lehrer (1978) likewise divided performance anxiety into three components: (1) physiological responses, (2) cognitive activity, and (3) behavioral responses. Physiological responses to performance anxiety may include increases in heart rate, perspiration, and blood-pressure, "weak knees," "butterflies in the stomach," sweaty palms, dry mouth, and general muscle tension. The primary cognitive activity in connection with performance anxiety is worrying. Some individuals may report a general feeling of disorientation or inability to think clearly, and withdrawal symptoms such as lethargy or avoidance behaviors. Behavioral responses might include nervous mannerisms and superstitious or ritual behaviors. Each individual has a different tolerance level for these symptoms and may find them only mildly annoying or completely debilitating. Musicians who are placed in chronic, stressful situations may suffer more harmful effects, such as ulcers, high blood pressure, or nervous breakdowns.

In a study of stress among symphony musicians, Haider & Groll-Knapp (1981), monitored representative members of the Vienna Symphony during rehearsals and public performances for heart rate and brain wave activity. Maximum pulse rate averages ranged from 110–120 beats per minute. However, certain individuals peaked at over 150 beats per minute for short periods. The mean pulse rate was 85.2 during rehearsals and 93.5 during concerts. Even more critical was the difference between resting pulse rate and maximum pulse rate, or the exertional rate. The mean exertional rate was 27.3, with individuals peaking as high as 83 beats over their resting rate. This is surely one significant indicator of stress.

Electroencephalogram (EEG) readings of brainwave activity are more difficult to interpret. However, one indicator of stress is the overriding predominance of beta wave activity over long periods of time. Alpha waves (8–12 cycles per second) are present during periods of relaxed awareness. These are replaced by beta waves (13–30 cycles per second) during periods of concentration or intense mental activity. In normal circumstances, beta waves are produced for only short periods of time, interrupted frequently by alpha waves. However, in the previously mentioned study of the Vienna Symphony (Haider & Groll-Knapp, 1981), EEG readings of the musicians during rehearsals and performances showed a significant preponderance of beta wave activity over relatively long periods of time. Particularly during concerts, interruptions by alpha waves were very rare.

These findings were corroborated by another report of these same symphony musicians (Piperek, 1981). A psychologist who interviewed these musicians remarked on the fact that most psychologists say that intense concentration cannot be maintained for more than 20–30 minutes (Schulz, 1981). However, concerts typically last for as much as two hours, during which time each individual must be integrated with the whole ensemble at intervals as small as 1/100th of a second, intonation and note accuracy is extremely high, and so on. The result, of course, is considerable stress. When this pattern is repeated several times a week throughout many years of a performing career, it is not difficult to imagine what some of the long-term effects might be. Other sources of strain in the orchestra included consistent loudness levels over 100 decibels, eyestrain due to poor lighting, general working conditions, and various social frictions between and among the musicians and management.

Another method of measuring performance anxiety is self-report. Salewski (1981) used three techniques: a behavioral checklist, an Anxiety Scale Questionnaire, and a structured interview. She found that performance anxiety could be measured with these devices and that their use could be useful to both teachers and students. LeBlanc et al. (1997) developed a self-report scale, *The Personal Performance Anxiety Report*, that they gave to high school band members following three conditions. Anxiety rose from performing alone, in front of one other person, and in front of a small audience of adults and peers. Ryan and Andrews (2009) found that moderate performance anxiety was common for semiprofessional choral singers. They also found that solo singing produced greater anxiety than ensemble singing and that conductors were a significant factor in the anxiety singers experienced.

Some research indicates that anxiety may actually enhance performance for certain individuals (Yerkes & Dodson, 1908; Fig. 15.8). This is especially true for those who have achieved a high level of task mastery. In several studies, anxiety increased in the period prior to a performance, but the performance was actually judged significantly better (Hamann, 1982, 1983; Hamann & Sobaje 1983; Weisblatt, 1986). This may indicate that worrying about a performance is more stressful than the actual performance. Salmon, Schrodt, and Wright (1989) found that anxiety increased as performance time approached and that those whose anxiety peaked before the performance had lower levels of anxiety and performed better than those whose anxiety peaked during performance.

In spite of the evidence that some performances are enhanced by anxiety (Wolfe, 1989), many performers would like to find a way to reduce their nervousness. Unfortunately, many do not avail themselves of appropriate coping strategies (Wolfe, 1990b). Psychological anti-dotes to performance anxiety include deep-breathing exercises, progressive muscle relaxation, relaxation training, cognitive therapy, systematic desensitization, meditation, visualization techniques, neuro-linguistic programming, hypnosis, and biofeedback (Andrews, 1997; Chesky, Kondraske, Henoch, Hipple, & Rubin, 2002; Kenny, 2011; Kirchner, 2004–2005; Lehmann et al., 2007; Nagel, 2017; Sataloff, Rosen, & Levy, 1999; Wilson & Roland, 2002; Wolfe, 1990a). Two newer treatments include eye movement desensitization and reprocessing (EMDR) and thought-field therapy (TFT) (Levy, Rosen, & Sataloff, 2005). *Alexander Technique* was not designed specifically to combat music performance anxiety; rather, it is a means of ridding the body of excess muscular tension (Alexander, 1990; Kleinman &

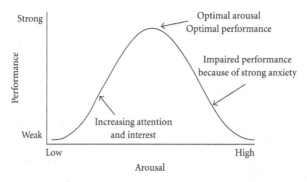

FIGURE 15.8 | Yerkes-Dodson Law. According to the Yerkes-Dodson Law, performance improves as anxiety increases until it reaches an optimal level. Past this point, increasing anxiety causes a decrease in performance.

Buckoke, 2013. However, as a form of relaxation therapy, it may be useful in dealing with performance anxiety (Brandfonbrenner, 1986; Kenny, 2006). This approach is based on three stages: inhibition (cessation of one's habitual responses), direction (conscious direction of certain muscle or motor patterns), and activity (allowing an activity to occur without interfering with the directions). Many musicians have found this technique to be helpful.

Aaron Williamon and his group at the Royal College of Music in London developed a performance simulator as a means of assisting musicians with performance anxiety, along with other performance-related issues (Williamon, Aufegger, & Eiholzer, 2014). This allowed musicians to perform in a virtual, simulated performance environment. As shown in Fig. 15.9, the performance simulator has backstage and on-stage areas. While waiting backstage, performers can view a video screen (CCTV footage) that shows an audience entering the hall. At the

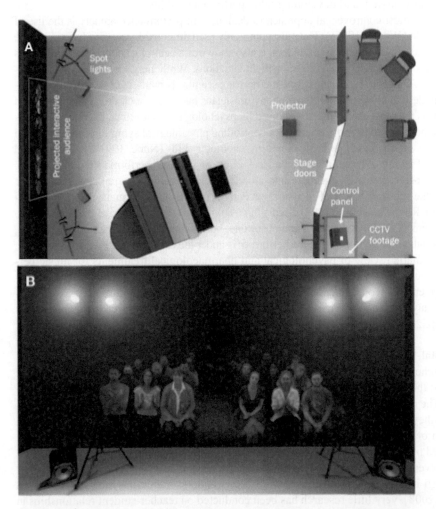

FIGURE 15.9 | Performance Simulator. (A) A diagram showing backstage and on-stage areas. (B) A virtual audience is projected on a screen. Spotlights and speakers playing audience noises add to the sense of a real, life-like experience. In an audition simulation, a panel of three judges is projected on the screen. Audience and judges' behaviors can be manipulated to be positive, neutral, or disapproving.

appropriate time, a backstage manager opens the door and ushers the performer onto the stage where s/he is greeted by spot lights and a video screen with the seated audience. During the performance, common audience noises (e.g., coughing, etc.) are played through loud speakers and audience responses can be manipulated to respond enthusiastically, politely, or visibly disapproving. Alternatively, the video screens can display a panel of three "expert" virtual judges, who likewise can respond positively, negatively, or by abruptly stopping an audition.

Advanced violin students performed a solo recital in front of the virtual audience and an audition in front of the virtual judges. A subset of the violinists also performed an actual audition for live judges; state anxiety and heart rate variability were measured in both circumstances. Levels of anxiety and heart rate data were comparable for both live and simulated performances. Taken as a whole, both the simulated recital performance and audition were described as realistic and convincing by the violinists and were found to be helpful in dealing with performance anxiety and developing other performance skills.

Perhaps the most controversial approach to dealing with performance anxiety is the use of drugs (Nies, 1986; Wilson, 1986a). The most commonly used drug in this regard is Inderal, whose generic chemical name is propranolol. Inderal is also known as a beta-blocker because it interferes with the body's natural response to fight-or-flight situations. While nervous symptoms are controlled, ability to concentrate, alertness, and memory are seemingly unaffected. According to Fishbein and Middlestadt (1988), 27% of symphony musicians have used such drugs and prescribed medication was the most used remedy, followed by psychological counseling, exercise, and hypnosis. Beta-blockers are generally effective in controlling physiological symptoms, but may have negative effects on cognitive, perceptual, and psychomotor skills (Nubé, 1991). In a controlled study, a dose of 20 mg of propranolol had a weak effect on pianistic performance (Nubé, 1994). No drug is risk-free, however. As more and more musicians seemingly are using Inderal, the debate about the appropriateness of such an approach to conquering performance fears is intensifying. Sataloff, Rosen, and Levy (1999) discuss other anxiolytics, including benzodiazepines (e.g., Valium, Librium, Xanax, Ativan, etc.) and buspirone, but in general do not support their usage, except in special circumstances when the performer is under the care of a qualified physician.

In a systematic review of psychological and pharmacological treatments for music performance anxiety, Kenny (2005) concluded that "the literature on treatment approaches for MPA is fragmented, inconsistent, and methodologically weak. These limitations make it difficult to reach any firm conclusions about the effectiveness of the various treatment approaches reviewed" (p. 206).

Other Mental Health Issues. In a survey of 429 opera and concert orchestra musicians, Voltmer, Fischer, Richter, and Spahn (2012) compared the physical and mental health of these musicians to the general population and to other professions (physicians and aircraft manufacturers). The musicians had better physical health but poorer mental health than the general population; they did not differ from the other professional groups in mental health scores. An examination of 40 eminent jazz musicians (Wills, 2003) revealed that while mental health (i.e., elevated psychopathology) was similar to other creative groups, there was significantly greater involvement with drugs (e.g., heroin and cocaine) and alcohol.

Although it is clear that musicians at all levels undergo numerous stressful situations (Sternbach, 2008), very little research has been conducted on teacher-student relationships in connection with health issues (Brandfonbrener & Lederman, 2002), counseling with musicians (Chesky et al., 2002), or conflict resolution (e.g., conductor-performer or among members of a conductorless chamber group). This is an area that needs much more attention.

Piperek (1981) conducted a landmark study of musicians in the Vienna Symphony. The title of the book indicates the breadth of the study—*Stress and Music: Medical, Psychological,*

Sociological, and Legal Strain Factors in a Symphony Orchestra Musician's Profession. Stress factors included, (1) musical factors: everything having to do with making music (e.g., difficulty of the work to be performed, difficulties in working with different conductors, etc.); (2) time spent: hours on the job, lack of leisure time, and so on; (3) stress: health issues, increased tension prior to performance, and so on; (4) social atmosphere: discord in relationships with colleagues, intrigues in the orchestra, and so on; (5) working conditions: too hot or too cold, poor lighting, uncomfortable chairs, and so on (Schulz, 1981). Nearly two-thirds (60%) felt that envy was an integral part of a musician's experience and more than one-third (36%) had personal enemies in the orchestra.

Butler (1995) found that conservatory music students who experienced both external (i.e., due to circumstances) and internal (relationships) stress tended to fail, while successful students experienced only one or none of these kinds of stress. Failing students have lower self-esteem, view their colleagues as competitors, and suffer ill health to a greater degree. Successful students are more likely to seek counseling and that counseling is more effective. Elite string musicians and dancers in the New York area completed the Adult Personality Inventory (Hamilton, Kella, & Hamilton, 1995). Results indicated that males were less adjusted than females and had more unstable personal relationships; all performers experienced occupational stress.

Raeburn (1987a, 1987b, 1999, 2000) examined stress conditions among rock and popular musicians. In addition to drug and alcohol abuse, other issues concerned relevant aspects of emotional stress, working conditions, competitiveness, perfectionism, and so on. O'Connor and Dyce (1997) studied 206 musicians in 54 bar bands (45 rock and roll, 9 country) and found that those groups with complementary relationships (i.e., mutually rewarding, anxiety-reducing, social interaction facilitating, etc.) had greater positive regard and group interaction within the group.

Andrews (1997) discussed psychological issues such as personal relationships and burnout, and offered a number of practical suggestions for remediation. As psychiatrists, Ostwald, Avery, and Ostwald (1998) presented a much more clinical view. They discussed affective disorders such as depression, personality disorders, musical training in infancy and childhood, competitiveness, the adult performing artist, somatoform disorders, schizophrenic disorders, and other conditions necessitating psychiatric care (e.g., bulimia, anorexia, substance abuse, sexual orientation). As stated previously, the mental health of musicians is an area that needs a great deal more attention and research.

One of the positive developments in recent years has been an increasing number of resources dealing with musician's health and fitness. While being physically fit is not a guarantee of avoidance of performance-related injuries, it does serve as a preventative and, given the known link between physical fitness and mental health, may also have positive effects in ameliorating the effects of performance anxiety, perfectionism, and other performance-related issues. Here are just a few of the resources available:

- Allan, D. Peak Performance for Musicians: www.musicpeakperformance.com
- Dawson, W. (2008). *Fit as a Fiddle: The Musician's Guide to Playing Healthy.*
- Horvath, J. (2010). *Playing Less Hurt: An Injury Prevention Guide for Musicians.*
- Kageyama, N. *The Bulletproof Musician:* https://bulletproofmusician.com
- Klickstein, G. (2009). *The Musician's Way; A Guide to Practice, Performance, and Wellness.* New York: Oxford University Press.
- Papageorgi, I., & Welch, G. (2014). *Advanced Musical Performance.* Farnham, UK: Ashgate.
- Rosset i Lobet, J., & Odam, G. (2016). *The Musician's Body: A Maintenance Manual for Peak Performance*

316

- Watson, A. (2009). *The Biology of Musical Performance and Performance-related Injury*.
- Williamon, A. (Ed.). (2004). *Musical Excellence: Strategies and Techniques to Enhance Performance*. Oxford, UK: Oxford University Press.

Incorporating diet and nutrition, exercise, meditation, and other practices for healthy living need to become an important part of the regimen of every musician.

CONCLUSION

Music therapists are trained musicians who use their skills to help clients attain therapeutic goals and to promote health. They work with a wide range of clients using music to improve interpersonal relationships, enhance self-esteem, and energize and organize individual and group behaviors through rhythm. Some physicians and other health care professionals practice music medicine by utilizing music in the amelioration of pain and anxiety in patients, particularly those undergoing surgery and those experiencing chronic or temporary pain. In performing arts medicine, physicians and other health care professionals treat profession-related injuries or difficulties that musicians undergo. These issues are classified under the headings of vocal health, hearing health, bodily health, and psychosocial health.

Music therapy, music medicine, and performing arts medicine share many commonalities, while each maintains a unique identity. Music therapy has the longest and richest heritage, but both music medicine and performing arts medicine are engaging physicians and health care professionals in a way that brings many new possibilities. Collectively, these three disciplines demonstrate the power of music to influence health and wellness in everyone. Music itself may have such a strong and pervasive effect on health and well-being because it is ubiquitous, emotional, engaging, distracting, physical, ambiguous, social, communicative, and because it affects both behavior and identity (MacDonald et al., 2012, pp. 5–6).

DISCUSSION QUESTIONS

1. Discuss similarities and distinctions among music therapy, music medicine, and performing arts medicine.
2. Compare and contrast the goals of music therapy, music medicine, and performing arts medicine.
3. What kind of musical skills do effective music therapists possess?
4. Why do you think one would choose to become a music therapist?
5. What do you think would need to happen for more physicians to accept music as a form of treatment?
6. Have you been in musical situations that seemed too loud and that might have had an adverse effect on your hearing? Have you ever worn earplugs while performing music?
7. Whether you are a singer or a teacher involved in using your voice professionally, what can you do to protect your voice?
8. If you are an instrumentalist, are those who play your instrument prone to any particular neuromusculoskeletal problems? Have you experienced any of these?
9. What music situations are most likely to cause you mental stress?
10. If you were to map out a comprehensive *Musicians' Wellness Plan*, what would it look like?

Chapter 16

Music in Social Contexts

IMAGINE several married couples at a dance. Following one dance, the couples all exchange partners for the next one. This is perfectly fine, as long as the music is playing. It immediately becomes socially unacceptable, however, if the new partners stay intertwined in each other's arms after the music stops. Eighty thousand people in a soccer stadium rise as the band prepares to play the national anthem. Regardless of their socioeconomic status, religious preferences, or the team they are there to root for, fans are united, at least for the duration of the music. Schoolgirls on the playground chant in a sing-song fashion as some twirl the ropes and others wait in line for their turn to jump. The music coordinates the timing of their actions. These three situations exemplify how music influences social behaviors in powerful ways.

Human beings are social creatures. We gather together in informal and formal groups, ranging from two friends spending time together to global institutions such as the United Nations. While we can exist alone or sometimes have a need for solitude, it is clearly our nature to interact with other human beings. Those rare individuals who prefer to live apart from human society are usually considered exceptions to the nearly universal rule. Likewise, musical behaviors are primarily group behaviors. Musicians may spend many hours in isolation composing or practicing, but almost always these are means toward an end of sharing with others. The purpose of this chapter, then, is to examine the role music plays in social behaviors. Anthropological and sociological perspectives are far from discrete topics and Chapter 4 has already included much about the present topic. However, the emphasis here is on contemporary society.

MUSIC IN SOCIETY

Music is such a pervasive form of human experience that everyone in any society can have some sort of meaningful experience with music. One way of expressing how music touches us all is by means of three continua: from birth to death, from lowest to highest cognitive functioning, and from one person to thousands.

From Birth to Death

Age is not a criterion for a meaningful musical experience. In previous chapters, we discussed how newborns respond actively to sounds, especially to lullabies and the musical aspects of speech. At the other end of the continuum, elderly people find music to be one of the pleasures of life still available to them. No one is excluded from a musical experience by virtue of age.

Some might even extend this continuum to pre-birth (Parncutt, 2009) and post-death (some individuals reporting on a near-death experience indicate hearing music; Osis & Haraldsson, 1997; Schwaninger, Eisenberg, Schechtman, & Weiss, 2002).

From Lowest to Highest Cognitive Functioning

Likewise, the presence or absence of cognitive abilities does not preclude a meaningful musical experience. Though lack of mental skills may somewhat limit certain kinds of musical involvement, persons with severe cognitive deficits can benefit significantly from musical experiences (Pujol, 1994). At the upper end of the scale, Nobel Laureates are four times as likely to be musicians than are other scientists (Root-Bernstein & Root-Bernstein, 2009).

From One Person to Thousands

Musical pleasure is not limited by how many persons are involved. Each one of us can find pleasure by ourselves in such solitary musical activities as listening, playing an instrument (see Figure 16.1), or singing. At the other end, there are no clear limits on how many persons can participate at one time. Van Halen was paid $1.5 million to perform at US Festival '83 for nearly 400,000 people (Christe, 2007). In 1994 Rod Stewart performed for 3.5 million people at Copacabana Beach in Rio de Janeiro, a feat matched by Jean Michel Jarre in 1997 in Moscow (The Economic Times, 2015). Live Aid was performed for an audience of 1.9 billion people in 150 countries linked by satellite (Garofalo, 2010; Jones, 2005).

To these three continua, we may add other criteria such as gender, race, ethnic background, and socioeconomic status, none of which are barriers to meaningful musical experiences. Music may not be the only human behavior that can fit all of these circumstances, but it is surely one of the most common of human experiences. In fact, there is so much music in societies worldwide that to detail its every usage would be nearly impossible. What follows is an attempt to give some general sense of how often and in what ways music appears in our midst. Almost every item on this list will be familiar, but many of them have come to be such a common part of the environment that we hardly take notice of them. There are two items to note: (1) Facts and figures concerning music in society change rapidly and (2) some of the figures are updated only sporadically. Because of this, the information that follows should be taken more as indicators than as absolutes.

- **Music at Home.** Music can be heard in almost any home, whether it is a mother's lullaby or music coming from a radio, television, or other media device.
- **Music at School.** Music is generally a part of the educational scheme from pre-schools to universities. Many schools worldwide offer music instruction, but even in those that do not, it is likely that a school anthem or other music is heard.
- **Music in the Community.** Music plays a central role in community life, as every hamlet and large city has musical performing groups, ranging from tribal singing to church choirs, school groups, community bands, professional and amateur orchestras, rock and jazz groups, and opera companies (Hallam & MacDonald, 2009).
- **Music in the Marketplace.** Music and the business world have an enormous reciprocal impact. Buying and selling music and musical instruments, purchasing music to listen to and equipment to listen on, purchasing tickets for live events, earning a living in the music business (see Fig. 16.2), and so on are enormous economic generators worldwide. For example, revenue from the recording industry alone, in sales of physical and digital recordings, amounted to nearly $16 billion in 2016 (Global Music Report, 2017).

FIGURE 16.1 | We Can Enjoy Meaningful Musical Experiences Alone Or in Large Groups. Top Panel: Flutist in a Garden in China. Bottom Panel: Live Aid Concert in Rome.

FIGURE 16.2 | Alberts Music Shop on Chertsey Road in Guildford, England.

- **Music in Religion.** Although there may be a few religious sects that restrict the use of music, it is far more common for music to be an integral part of the worship experience.
- **Music for Special Occasions.** From the riotous Carnival of Brazil to a funeral in a small village in Siberia, the calendar is punctuated with wild, extravagant celebrations and with quieter, more intimate times. The removal of all music from festivities, celebrations, and gatherings such as these would vastly change their nature.
- **Music in Politics.** Music has the power to help rally a crowd behind a candidate at a political rally or to help dramatize the visit of an important foreign dignitary.
- **Music in the Military.** Music has always been an important part of the military, as soldiers and warriors march off to battle to the sounds of bagpipes, bands, and singing. Music also helps those who stay at home to symbolize their support for or opposition to a war effort and more importantly, their hope that eventually loved ones will return home safely. Music has also been used as means of torture.
- **Music in Health Care Systems.** As detailed in the previous chapter, music therapy, music medicine, and performing arts medicine are thriving areas of research and treatment.
- **Music and Physical Activities.** Music has always had a close association with physical activities. Although some sporting events (e.g., golf and tennis) have limited or no musical involvement, many others have strong musical engagement. In addition, many people exercise to music, as they jog with a smart phone or participate in aerobic dancing or jazzercise.
- **Music in Media.** There are hundreds of magazines and journals specifically related to music, ranging from *Accordion Weekly News* to *She Shreds* (a magazine highlighting female guitarists and bassists worldwide). Radio, television, and movies as we know them now would be unthinkable without music. In addition to music stations and channels outright, or the music that accompanies various programs, music plays a prominent role in advertising. Online streaming has increased music distribution enormously.
- **Music in Professional and Social Organizations.** From the Afghanistan Music Foundation to the National Arts Council of Zambia, thousands of music organizations exist worldwide.
- **Musical Occupations.** Similarly, from audio engineer to vocal coach, people all over the world find ways to make a living in music.
- **Music in Places We Go.** Nearly every place we go has music as part of the environment, including such places as grocery stores, restaurants (Fig. 16.3), and doctors' offices. People select music to listen to when they travel about 90% of the time (Sloboda et al., 2009). In another study (Heye & Lamont, 2010), 98.9% of traveling participants were listening to an MP3 device, and only 1.1% were not listening to music. Enjoyment was the most frequent reason given for listening, although it also helped to create an "auditory bubble" while traveling in public places.
- **Miscellaneous.** There are numerous ways we encounter music throughout the day. Some of the unexpected places we encounter music come from cell phone ringtones, from being placed on hold on the telephone, street vendors, and so on.

The foregoing list is not exhaustive, but it certainly should suffice to indicate the omnipresence of music in society. An interesting experiment to conduct would be to try to go through a 24-hour period without hearing any music, noting the disruptions from the normal routine. The radio alarm couldn't be used to get up by, in fact no radio or television could be turned on all day. The places one went and the activities one engaged in would all have to be monitored very carefully. Such an experiment would confirm the ubiquity of music in our midst.

FIGURE **16.3** | Music in Restaurants Is Often Used to Create a Certain Ambience to Enhance the Dining Experience.

REFLECTIONS OF SOCIETY IN MUSIC

While artists sometimes function as visionaries, trying to lead a society toward a loftier goal (e.g., Beethoven's vision of all humankind living in peace and harmony as expressed in the Ninth Symphony), they also serve by holding up a mirror to society, reflecting how people live, what they think, how they feel. Musical behaviors are social behaviors and as such they influence and reflect the mores of the surrounding social structure. Thus, music is at times a headlight; at other times a taillight. The musical world is a microcosm of the larger world, operating on similar social principles. By examining the sociality of musical behaviors, we can gain a greater understanding of the significance music has for our lives.

Social behaviors occur simultaneously on two levels: the social behaviors of performing musicians and the social behaviors of music listeners. Implied, of course, are the social interactions between performers and listeners (see Figure 16.4).

Social Behaviors Among Performing Musicians

One level of social behavior occurs among the performers themselves. If the musicians have rehearsed and performed together over some period, they will have developed relationships and particular social bonds with one another (North, Hargreaves, & Tarrant, 2002). A new member of the group will need some time to feel totally comfortable and to be accepted as a part of the group. In larger groups, smaller cliques may form, based on a variety of factors, such as age, gender, or membership in a particular section of the musical ensemble (e.g., altos in a choir or trombones in a band).

Often these social bonds are so strong that members of a musical group are like members of an extended family. This may be due, in part, to the amount of time spent together, and may be especially true of those groups such as a touring string quartet that travel frequently. Furthermore, their collaborative efforts involve an expression of feelings. This expression does not require that all members feel or experience the same emotion simultaneously, but it

FIGURE **16.4** | There Are Social Interactions Among These Buskers in Brussels During Both Rehearsals and Performances. Although we cannot see the audience in this view, we can imagine the social behaviors of those who are listening.

does require that the musical elements are coordinated in such a way as to convey the desired expression. This, in combination with the tremendous physical and mental energy required for public performance, makes for powerful social bonding forces.

A feeling of family does not mean, of course, that all the social interactions are pleasant. As with any family, there may be rivalries, arguments, or even long-term feuds—recall from Chapter 15 that nearly two-thirds (60%) of orchestral musicians felt that envy was an integral part of a musician's experience and more than one-third (36%) had personal enemies in the orchestra (Schulz, 1981). No matter how much internal strife there may be, however, something larger continues to hold the bonds in place.

The social network operating within a musical organization may evidence itself in dress, mannerisms, and speech. Often the performance attire serves not only to separate the group from the audience, but also to reinforce the social behaviors within the group. Standing, sitting, or moving about the stage are all controlled by the conventions suited to particular circumstances. A symphony orchestra in formal black rises as a unit to acknowledge applause. A robed choir processes to its station in an appropriately decorous manner. A marching band in uniform maneuvers on the field or street in an exaggerated form of controlled precision (Fig. 16.5). The jargon used by any group also acts as a means of unification and, at the same time, as a means of separating the group from the audience. The musical language spoken by performers at the Metropolitan Opera and the Grand Old Opry is likely to be quite different.

These group social behaviors can be applicable to individual performers as well. For example, at her first recital appearance a budding pianist may learn to bow in polite acknowledgement of applause. Even for those who appear as soloists within a larger performing context (e.g., a rock singer), there may be the added element of a stage personality that influences the performing deportment. Behaviors scarcely acceptable in normal social settings may be adopted as attention-getting devices. Sometimes the stage personality is completely different from the private persona; at other times it may take over and dominate a person's behavior both on and off stage.

FIGURE 16.5 │ A Marching Band in a Street Parade. Uniforms help provide a sociological structure for members of the group.

Within any group of performers, there is a social hierarchy. This is clearly in place in an opera house where a *prima donna* is accorded special privileges, in jazz where the name of the group is often the name of the leader (e.g., the Count Basie Orchestra), and in commercial music where acts are often built around an individual performer (e.g., Gwen Stefani with No Doubt, or Beyoncé with Destiny's Child). Even different instruments or ensembles have a social hierarchy. The accordion, for example, suffers from a social stigma in some circles, but would reign supreme in others. A string quartet is a recognized ensemble with a great deal of social prestige, while a tuba quartet might not rank so highly.

For members of an ensemble that requires a conductor, there is an extra social dynamic to consider. The conductor must create a unified whole out of many disparate individuals and this often causes tension (Atik, 1994; Service, 2010). No ensemble can perform successfully as a pluralistic society; imagine what would happen if each member of a 40-voice choir decided to sing at a different tempo. The manner in which a conductor bends individual wills to his or her own is what creates such an interesting and potentially charged social atmosphere. On the performers' part, there may be a love/hate relationship with the conductor.

In classical music, the Orpheus Chamber Orchestra is an exception. They are a conductorless group. Each of the 40-plus members has the opportunity and bears the responsibility for contributing to the eventual musical outcome. They have demonstrated how to deal successfully with the issue of social dynamics in this unique collaborative venture. In fact, in 2009 they won a worldwide award for a freedom-centered workplace indicating their success in establishing an organizational democracy (WorldBlu, 2018).

Even within smaller groups that do not require a conductor, such as a garage band or a folk music group, there may be a social hierarchy of leader and followers. Sometimes this may be abundantly clear, at other times there may be shifting leadership roles. Leadership may be a focal point for disagreement. Sometimes the music itself will designate who is to be the leader. Music making involves following a set of social guidelines and structure, just as in any human activity. Cooperation and teamwork are essential ingredients in nearly every music-making situation.

Performers need cooperation and support from their audiences, too. Although the composer Milton Babbitt (1958) took an extreme position when he wrote an article entitled "Who

Cares If You Listen?", the majority of musical experiences are aimed at eliciting some type of response from the listeners.

Social Behaviors Among Music Listeners

Just as the musicians in different performance settings exhibit a variety of social behaviors, so do the audiences. Compare the audiences at a classical concert and a heavy metal rock concert (Fig. 16.6). The variance in socioeconomic status, age, dress, speech patterns, and mode of physical movement is likely to be considerable. Even if the same person went to both types of performances on successive nights, the dress, speech, and mannerisms would vary in order to provide social acceptability.

For more formal performances, there is an extended social ritual that involves placing the event on a calendar long in advance, purchasing tickets, planning a meal before or after the concert, leaving early to obtain a good parking space, being seated by an usher, perusing the program, growing quiet as the houselights dim, and so on. Even during the performance, a social etiquette is in place, as patrons of classical concerts learn not to applaud between movements of a symphony, while audience members at a jazz concert routinely clap as a soloist finishes his segment during a set.

The type of music one listens to can often reveal a considerable amount of personal information. For example, imagine walking down the corridors of a large apartment building. Pausing briefly outside each door we can hear music coming from inside each apartment. Using only this musical information, what could we know about who was inside? Certainly, there would be limitations on what we could know. Yet, if we heard nursery songs outside one door, would we not suspect that a young child lived there? If we heard the music of Lawrence Welk emanating from inside, whom would we suspect was listening? As with the larger network of human families where races, nationalities, and tribes are identifiable through their music, so it is within a pluralistic society. There are a number of ways different sub-groups might be identifiable somewhat through their music, such as age, gender, race, and socioeconomic status. However, these are generalized stereotypes and there are always exceptions.

As much as music listening habits might be a means of identifying and thus potentially separating one group from another, music also has a powerful capacity to bring people together. Through their common participation in or enjoyment of a shared musical experience, people of varied and disparate backgrounds are brought together. Music can transcend barriers of age, gender, economic status, race, and nationality. The opening

FIGURE **16.6** | Classical Concert Venue on the Left, Rock Concert on the Right.

and award ceremonies at the Olympic Games are good representations of how music both unites participants from all the countries and also represents each nationality uniquely.

Gaston stated that "the potency of music is greatest in the group" (1968, p. 27). By that, he was referring to the social nature of the musical experience. "Music provides a gestalt of sensory, motor, emotional, and social components in which, for the most part, the participants concur. It unifies the group for common action, and it is this setting that elicits or changes many extramusical behaviors" (p. 27).

THE INFLUENCE OF MUSIC ON SOCIAL BEHAVIORS

"Argument Over Loud Music Leads to Death" screamed a newspaper headline (*San Antonio Light*, 1986). The article, which detailed how one man was shot and killed as a result of another man being kept awake by his loud music, provided an extreme illustration of how music can influence social, or in this case anti-social, behaviors. The purpose of this section is to examine some of the ways music shapes social behaviors.

Music as a Socializing Agent

Human behavior is not instinctive and thus we must learn how to behave as human beings. We learn these behaviors through a process of socialization and it is important to note that the behaviors we learn are those that are appropriate to the society in which we are raised. The agents of socialization are many, but may include at the very least: home, school, worship center, peers, and the media. A comprehensive review of the socialization process might appear to give music only a small role to play. Without exaggerating its contributions, however, there are some aspects about the role of music (and its constituent elements such as rhythm, pitch patterns, and timbre) that bear detailed examination.

The process begins at birth with the onset of rhythmic breathing and continues as the baby gradually adapts to the rhythmic cycles of the world into which he or she has been born (Trainor & Marsh-Rollo, 2019). Over the next months, the patterns of family life, particularly the parents' cycles of activity and rest, will condition and shape the baby's social rhythms. This is highly important, since nearly all social interactions are rhythmically based. Rhythmic aspects of music play an important role in the organization of information that unfolds over time.

Further musical influences occur during infancy with the singing of lullabies, the playing of musical games (e.g., pat-a-cake and peek-a-boo), and the presence of crib mobiles and musical toys (e.g., Jack-in-the-box). Many of these musical activities enable parents and babies to establish critical bonds of communication. Moreover, first lessons are being learned in the most important subject of all—how to love and to be loved. A good example of this is the "I'm gonna gitcha" game (Stern, 1982). The parent chants: "I'm gonna gitcha. . . . I'm gonna gitcha. . . . I'm gonna gitcha. . . . Gotcha!" At each repetition, the pitch and loudness increase, while the amount of time between each repetition progressively elongates. Activities such as this are so important because "repetition and rhythm are chief means by which the infant acquires cognitive expectancies and affective involvement; . . . within the structure that rhythm provides, aspects of both affect and cognition are simultaneously organized" (Beebe et al., 1982, pp. 93–94).

Music continues to play an important role throughout childhood. There are singing games to be played repeatedly, the alphabet is frequently learned via song, and nursery rhymes are chanted in a sing-song fashion. Children's television programming is full of music and the musical background to cartoons often eliminates or diminishes the need for dialogue. Singing and chanting characterize children at play. Early religious instruction is often highly musical. In many elementary schools, children have their first instruction in dance when music and physical education classes combine. For many, this may be their first experience in learning how to interact physically with members of the opposite sex. Certainly, children learn a great deal about how to act in socially appropriate ways through musical means.

Music may actually increase in importance during adolescence (Hallam, 2010). British teens ($N = 2,465$) rated listening to music more important than any other indoor activity, except that females said they would rather go shopping than listen to music (North, Hargreaves, & O'Neill, 2000). The average 8- to 18-year-old watches more than four hours (4h 29m) of media (television, videos, movies) and listens to more than two hours (2h 31m) of audio (radio, CDs, MP3s) per day (Rideout, Foehr, & Roberts, 2010). Adding other media sources, such as video games and computer programs, this is 7h 38m hours per day of media exposure, the vast majority of which contains music, either in the foreground or in the background. With multitasking, using more than one medium at a time, teenagers pack in a whopping 10h 45m hours per day, seven days a week. Thus, music is always on in the background for some adolescents (Nuttall, 2008). Estimations are that the average teenager spends about 10,500 hours listening to music between grades 7 and 12 (North & Hargreaves, 2008).

In an analysis of adolescent essays concerning the value of music education, Campbell, Connell, and Beegle (2007) quoted several students:

> "Music is awesome! That's what makes my world go round" (girl, age 13), "Music is an expression of the heart" (girl, age 15), and the shouted message, "I LOVE MUSIC. IT'S A WAY TO EXPRESS MYSELF" (boy, age 14). . . . . "When I am angry or everything seems like it's spinning out of control, I write a song. It calms me down and gets my feelings out" (girl, age 13).
>
> (p. 228)

Csikszentmihalyi and Hunter (2004) used an experience sampling method (ESM) to study happiness ratings among 828 adolescents. Each participant wore an electronic pager that randomly signaled the wearer up to eight times per day for a week. Each time the pager signaled, participants indicated what they were doing and whom they were with; they also completed assessments of their experiential states. Music was one of the top three rated happiest experiences.

Music is part of the socializing force that influences how teenagers talk, dress, and act, how they feel, and what they think. It even influences how they spend money. Music was a primary agent in the creation of a new economic and social demographic group in the mid-1950s (McNair & Powles, 2005). Music worked in tandem with movies, which incorporated the new musical style. Prior to the mid-1950s, the under-24 demographic group was almost entirely subordinate to the socioeconomic power of adults. Since 1955, the under-24 demographic group has come to be an increasingly powerful force in the marketplace. In the 1960s, this group further divided into two distinct groups: teenagers and the 18- to 24-year-old market. In the 1980s, another group was created, with pre-teens forming another powerful buying public. Nearly 60% of 16- to 24-year-old young adults subscribe to an audio streaming service (IFPI Releases, 2018 Music Consumer Insight Report, 2018).

Music continues to be important to college-age students (see Figure 16.7). A number of them participated in a survey in which they identified the most common stimulus that gave them a *thrill* (Goldstein, 1980). Music was in first place, with 96% of the subjects indicating it was their most common thrill-causing experience. Music also plays an important role in the courtship of young adults; it is a part of their environment whether they are in the car, at the movies, dancing, or spending a quiet evening together. Many couples have identified a song as *our song*, which represents an important moment in their courtship and which

often symbolizes their love in first bloom for the remainder of their lives. Music may be an important part of the ambiance at the time of a marriage proposal. Certainly, music is an important part of most wedding ceremonies.

Because the socialization process is more nearly complete during adulthood, music may not function in quite the same way for adults. However, social aspects are still important in that musical tastes can be a part of one's social identity. Whether singing hymns at an old-time revival or being seen at the opera, adult social lives are often marked by particular musical experiences. Moreover, each kind of musical experience is accompanied by the appropriate dress, appropriate behaviors, and appropriate expectations. Even the way one walks and talks may vary with different musical experiences. Furthermore, music plays an important, perhaps even critical role, in health and well-being among adults (Croom, 2012; Koelsch, 2013, 2014; Tarr, Launay, & Dunbar, 2014; Shäfer, Smulkalla, & Oelker, 2014).

Koelsch (2013) identified seven social functions of music:

1. Contact: Music brings people together.
2. Social cognition: Music automatically causes listeners to engage in thinking about others involved in the musical experience, especially the composer.
3. Co-pathy: This word refers to social empathy; that is, listeners respond to the emotion being expressed in the music and are aware that this was evoked by others (i.e., the musicians) and shared by others (e.g., the musicians, the audience, etc.).
4. Communication: Music is often a means of sharing among a group. It can be as intimate an interaction as a mother singing a lullaby to her baby (communicating love and affection) and as large as protest songs communicating shared messages among large groups of people.
5. Coordination: Music enables and facilitates coordinated actions, such as in work and play songs.
6. Cooperation: Music performed by a group involves cooperation (e.g., to sing or play at the same tempo, etc.).
7. Social cohesion: Music facilitates group membership.

Schäfer et al. (2014) investigated the long-term effects of intense musical experiences (IMEs) and developed a model based on interviews with music listeners. IMEs lead to altered states of consciousness characterized by a sense of harmony and self-realization. Following an intense musical experience and a return to daily living there is an experience of disharmony that brings about a desire to return to the harmonious state. IMEs have long-term consequences for people's personal values, their perceptions of the meaning of life, social relationships, engagement, activities, and personal development. In short, "results suggest that music can indeed change our lives—by making it more fulfilling, spiritual, and harmonious" (p. 525).

Croom (2012) identified five factors characteristic of well-being and related them to music: positive emotion, relationships, engagement, achievement, and meaning. After investigating the literature thoroughly, Croom concluded that there is "compelling evidence that musical engagement can positively contribute to one's living a flourishing life" (p. 11). One explanation for these findings is that endorphins and the endogenous opioid system (EOS), which are associated with social bonding, are engaged by musical experiences (Tarr et al., 2014). Further, neural responses to music, particularly in the hippocampus, are strongly associated with social functions (Koelsch, 2014).

The Influence of Music in the Workplace

We used to sing while we worked as cowboys, fishermen, railroaders, and field hands. Talking was forbidden to slaves working in the fields, so they sang. Singing not only made the labor seem more endurable, but also became a primary means of communication. We do not sing as often while we work today, but music still influences how we work (Lesiuk, 2005)—perhaps in some ways even more than it used to.

Music is a multi-billion dollar per year business. Music consumption in the US reached 637 million units in 2017 (Caufield, 2018). In 2016, the music industry added $143 billion to the US economy, which is about one-third of the global market of $430 billion (US Music Industry's Jobs & Benefits Report, 2018). This amounted to nearly two million American jobs. The Tanglewood summer music festival brings more than $103 million into local Berkshires coffers each year (Fox, 2017). Cities and countries around the world report similar statistics for music spending: Melbourne, Australia—AUD1 billion in spending and 116,000 full-time jobs; United Kingdom—GBP3.8 billion, 111,000 jobs; Bogotá, Columbia—*Rock al Parque* attracted 400,000 people to hear 87 bands perform (Terrill, 2015). In 2016, global sales of recorded music, including digital downloads, was nearly $16 billion; however, this represents a 40% decrease from the nearly $24 billion generated in 1999 (Global Music Report, 2017). A significant amount of the decline was due to piracy, illegal file sharing, and user content sharing (e.g., YouTube) (Bustinza, Vendrell-Herrero, Parry, & Myrthianos, 2013). Streaming represents the largest increase in recent years and now accounts for 75% of total expenditures on recorded music (Hernandez, 2018). More than 112 million users pay for streaming services worldwide. In 2015–2016 growth occurred in Asia and Australia (5.1%), Latin America (12%), Europe (4%), and North America (7.9%). Russia, Brazil, China, and Mexico are emerging markets, primarily due to streaming. Africa's recorded music industry, long plagued by piracy, is also beginning to improve through streaming services which increased by 334.2% in 2016.

According to the National Endowment for the Arts (2018), nearly 200 million people attended a music or music-related performance in 2017 (see Fig. 16.8). This included as many as one-fourth of US adults who attended an outdoor performing arts festival. None of these figures include dance or school performances.

Music used in commercial advertising is extremely influential (Coloma & Kleiner, 2005; North & Hargreaves, 2008, 2009; Roschk, Loureiro, & Breitsohl, 2017; Zander, 2006), influencing consumers on cognitive, emotional, and behavioral levels (Jain & Bagdare, 2011). For example, music piped into supermarkets (see Fig. 16.9) influenced both the amount of time and money shoppers spent (Duncan Herrington, 1996).

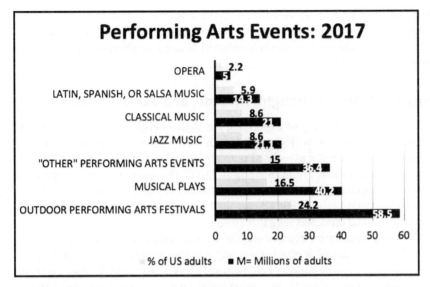

FIGURE **16.8** | Attendance at Performing Arts Events in 2017 in the United States.

FIGURE **16.9** | Music Piped into a Grocery Store May Influence Shoppers' Spending, However, the Type and Pace of the Music Is Important.

Music does not uniformly enhance sales, but its design and intentional application to achieve a "good fit" is crucial (Michel, Baumann, & Gayer, 2017). For example, fast, up-tempo music can ameliorate the effects of high-density, crowded stores (Knoeferle, Paus, & Vossen, 2017). When music fits the store, the product, and the salesperson's pitch, it enhances recall and recognition (Chebat, Chebsat, & Vaillant, 2001). Garlin and Owen (2006) conducted a meta-analysis of research on the effects of background music in retail settings. They concluded that there was small-to-moderate, yet robust support for positive effects on sales, time spent in store, and arousal and pleasure. After sampling 1,400 commercials, Young

(2008) found that advertisements with best-liked music had nearly twice the attention-getting appeal and doubled consumers' motivation to buy the brand as the commercials with worst-liked music. The positive valence of music is transferred to attitudes about a store or product (Morin, Dubé, & Chebat, 2007).

The Influence of Music on Thought, Attitude, and Social Behavior

Music is an extremely powerful way of expressing the shared beliefs, attitudes, mores, and values of a society or its sub-groups (Figure 16.10). In fact, a particular kind of music or a specific piece of music is normally associated with a group precisely because it communicates something important to that group. Singing *We Shall Overcome* was one of the most effective means of expressing what the Civil Rights Movement was about during the 1960s. People who shared in Martin Luther King's dream were brought together in a powerful, emotional way when they linked arms and sang that song.

Scholars have long been interested not only in the way music reflects how people feel but also in the way it influences what people think and how they behave. The ancient Chinese philosopher Confucius and Greek philosophers such as Damon, Plato, and Aristotle, were all proponents of the idea that music could, as Damon put it, "not only arouse or allay different emotions, but also inculcate all the virtues—courage, self-restraint, and even justice" (Strunk, 1965, p. xi). Music was highly prized for its ability to create model citizens for the ideal state.

Many scholars since the Greeks have advanced the same idea. Martin Luther included music in his formal educational scheme because of his belief that "music is one of the greatest gifts that God has given us; it is divine and therefore Satan is its enemy. For with its aid many dire temptations are overcome; the devil does not stay where music is" (Lewis, 1963, p. 15). Closer to home, Lowell Mason called upon similar ideas as part of his petition to include music in the public schools of Boston. After his first year of teaching music as part of the school curriculum, the Boston School Board reaffirmed this portion of his argument when they stated, "Of the great moral effect of vocal music, there can be no question" (Birge, 1928, p. 51).

FIGURE **16.10** | For Members of a Church Choir the Experience May Be Social at the Same Time as it is Musical and Spiritual.

In the 20th century, there were many examples of the connection between music and political or religious thought. Hitler used the music of Wagner for his own malevolent purposes (Moller, 1980). The Chamber of Culture, a committee of the Nazi Ministry of Propaganda, carefully screened and selected music appropriate for creating the desired emotional atmosphere at rallies, in factories, on radio broadcasts, and in all aspects of German life. Shostakovich was censured by the Russian government for writing music that was deemed inappropriate by the State (Volkov, 2004). In China during the Cultural Revolution, Western music was denounced as decadent and forbidden (Cheng, 1987). State-approved music was blasted over loud speakers as a massive propaganda device and much of this music was used for such mundane purposes as the dedication of a new hydroelectric facility. In Afghanistan, while the Taliban was in power, tight restrictions were placed on the types of music that could be heard (Rhythmless Nation, 2001).

In the United States, music has been connected with political movements from Colonial days until now (Garofalo, 2010). Preceding and during the Revolutionary War, groups such as the Freemasons and Sons of Liberty fanned the flames of rebellion through their songs. The Civil War, World Wars I and II, and all the other conflicts before and since have been fought to musical accompaniment. During the Vietnam War, protest songs by such folk singers as Bob Dylan and Joan Baez helped many express their feelings of revulsion toward America's involvement. Of course, music has been used as a means of influence for more than military campaigns. *Songs of Persuasion*, as Denisoff (1983) calls them, can be used in any social or political situation.

One of the most disturbing situations has been the use of music for torture (Service, 2015). Music that is offensive to prisoners, played at extremely loud levels and for long periods of time, is used in an attempt to break down their will. Military contracts have been drawn up to develop "acoustic weapons" (Cusick, 2006). Such misuse of music is not restricted to time or place, as it has occurred for centuries (Grant, 2014) and in numerous countries (e.g., Chornik, 2013).

Many have expressed concerns about the influence of rock, rap, and heavy metal music on adolescents. Stuessy and Lipscomb (2019) identified five basic themes of concern: drugs, sex, violent rebellion, Satanism, and suicide. The on- and off-stage behavior of many rock stars adds fuel to the flame of those who believe that heavy metal is anti-social. A review of the 100 most popular songs from 1958–1998 indicated that male artists increasingly used sex words, but that during 1976–1984, women referred to sex five times more often than men (Dukes, Bisel, Borega, Lobato, & Owens, 2003; see also Hall, West, & Hill, 2012; Vogel, van de Looij-Jansen, Mieloo, Burdorf, & de Waart, 2012). Listening to music with sexually degrading lyrics is linked to early sexual behavior among teens (Martino et al., 2006). In fact, music content affects a broad array of antisocial attitudes (e.g., concerning race, politics, etc.) (Timmerman et al., 2008).

Many teachers, ministers, youth workers, community leaders, and parents across the country have grown increasingly concerned about the possible negative effects of heavy metal music on teenagers and pre-teens. In a study of youth offenders, aged 13–18, Wass, Miller, and Redditt (1991) found that 91 of 120 (76%) were fans of rock music and more than half of those enjoyed music that advocated homicide, suicide, and satanic practices. Only 26% of adolescents have restrictions on the music they can listen to; this drops to 12% for 15- to 18-year-olds (Rideout et al., 2010)—and 20% of teens say they listen to music they know their parents wouldn't approve (Roberts, Foehr, & Rideout, 2005). Only 14% of parents read warning labels on music albums.

Styles of clothing, hair, makeup, jewelry, speech, dance, and mannerisms are all intertwined with musical styles. Buying habits are also influenced, as money is spent on smart phones and MP3 players, internet downloads and streaming services, albums, concert tickets, and tour T-shirts.

Rap/hip-hop is another category that has caused adults concern. Purchases of rap/hip-hop music increased from 3.8% to 11% from 1987 to 2008 (RIAA, 2009) and it is now the most popular music genre in the US (Caufield, 2018). Does this style of music influence teenagers' social behaviors?

Kubrin and Weitzer (2010) reviewed the literature on the effects of rap music's violent and misogynistic aspects on attitudes and behavior. There are both apologists who feel that rap plays a positive role and critics who decry the negative effects. However, they concluded that weaknesses in both the popular and scholarly literature are such that it is difficult to draw many strongly supported conclusions. "Indeed, there are a few superior studies that use empirical data to back up major assertions about the music's violent and misogynistic effects" (p. 126). "Media violence appears to lead some people under certain conditions to act violently, though most people exposed to violence in the media do not engage in aggressive behavior" (Kubrin & Weitzer, 2010, p. 135).

The extent of the influence of popular music on teenage behavior is shown in the fact that 80% of 14- to 25-year-olds feel that music has had a stronger influence in their lives than movies or sports, and 31% think it is more important than anything else (Pincus, 2005). North and Hargreaves (2008, 2010) reviewed pertinent research that demonstrated strong associations between preference for heavy metal and rap/hip-hop music and sensation seeking, disinhibition, high scores on psychoticism and aggression, assertiveness, indifference to others' feelings, disrespectfulness of society's rules, belief in Satanism, witchcraft, and the occult, and higher scores on delinquency and criminality. "Compared with adolescents who had less exposure to rap music videos, adolescents who had greater exposure to rap music videos were 3 times more likely to have hit a teacher; more than 2.5 times as likely to have been arrested; 2 times as likely to have had multiple sexual partners; and more than 1.5 times as likely to have acquired a new sexually transmitted disease, used drugs, and used alcohol over the 12-month follow-up period" (Wingood et al., 2003).

CONCLUSION

Sociological perspectives of musical behavior indicate that never before in the history of humankind have so many different kinds of music been available to so many different people. Of course, electronic media have played a major role in increasing this profusion of sounds. The amount and diversity of music, and the multiple roles it plays in society, give sociologists a very wide territory to cover.

So what important messages do sociologists have to give us about the significance of music? The first, and perhaps most important, message is that no member of a given society can be automatically kept from a meaningful experience by virtue of any generic criteria, such as age, intelligence, or race. Regardless of the diversity within a society, all can share in the experience of interacting with music. In fact, there is so much music in society, and it occurs in so many different settings, that it would be nearly impossible to avoid encountering music in some way. Music can be heard in the home, at school, at work, in worship, on holidays and special occasions, in politics, in the military, in health-care systems, in conjunction with physical activities, in the media, in professional and social organizations, in many occupations, in many of the places we go, and in numerous miscellaneous situations.

One of music's social functions is to reflect the society of which it is a part. One sociologist stated that "social structures crystallize in musical structures; that in various ways and with varying degrees of critical awareness, the musical microcosm replicates the social macrocosm" (Ballantine, 1984, p. 5). One way society is reflected in music is through the behaviors of the musicians themselves. Social rules and structures govern musicians' behaviors just as they do that of members of any group. In many ways, musical groups create their own social units, often with a unique set of strictures.

Society is reflected in the behaviors of music listeners. Music can either serve as a means of identifying certain groups, and thus potentially as a divisive force or as a unifier, bringing people of different backgrounds together. Listeners can sometimes be identified or categorized on the basis of age, race, or socioeconomic status. The type of music listened to can serve as a barrier to separate the listeners from the rest of society. On many other occasions, exactly the opposite occurs—barriers of age, race, and socioeconomic status are transcended by a common listening experience.

Music not only reflects the *way* a society lives, but also often influences *how* it lives. Music plays a significant role in the socialization process, for example. From cradle to grave we learn many important messages about what it means to be human and how to behave in certain situations through the music we hear. Music is one of the many factors that help shape each person into a unique individual. At each stage of development, we may gain important insights about who we are through reflection on our musical experiences and musical values.

Music influences us in many situations. There is ample reason to believe that it creates a pleasant ambience for diners at a restaurant, calms the nerves of patients waiting in doctors' and dentists' offices, and slows down or speeds up the walking pace of grocery shoppers, the better to maximize sales.

Historically, music has exerted a significant influence on people's thoughts, attitudes, and social behaviors. Songs of persuasion have been used as tools of propaganda for numerous social issues. Music always plays an important role during wartime; it is used to elicit support for a cause and to protest unwanted involvement. It can also be used as an instrument of torture. Music is particularly influential in the lives of teenagers. Many of their attitudes and behaviors are highly influenced by the music they listen to. Music exerts a powerful influence on our buying habits and is a major ingredient in radio and television advertising.

Though we are often unaware of the musical influences in our lives, its impact is highly significant. As Merriam (1964) has noted:

> The importance of music, as judged by the sheer ubiquity of its presence, is enormous. . . . There is probably no other human cultural activity which is so all-pervasive and which reaches into, shapes, and often controls so much of human behavior.
>
> (p. 218)

DISCUSSION QUESTIONS

1. Besides music, what other human experiences can you think of that fit all the criteria enumerated in this chapter such that all human beings have the possibility of a meaningful experience? Think of those relatively complex behaviors, like music, that go beyond simple reflexes such as breathing or blinking.
2. What are the advantages and disadvantages of the sheer amount of music and musical experiences that are available to Americans today?
3. Describe the social interactions you experience in different musical settings. Do you act, talk, think, or feel differently in jazz ensemble as compared to being in band? If you

sing in a choir and in a pop group, what are the similarities and differences in the social interactions of the two experiences?

4. What are the differences between being an audience member at a formal concert and listening to music at a club? Suppose on three successive nights you went to a piano recital, a jazz club, and a drum corps competition. How would you dress, talk, and act during the three occasions?

5. How would you characterize the role of music as a socializing agent in your own life history?

6. As you reflect on the places you work or shop, how aware are you generally of the music in those environments? Do you think trained musicians respond differently to music in the background than those who have less formal training? Likewise, how aware are you of the music soundtracks to movies and television shows? Do you think you are more or less easily swayed because of your musical training?

7. How many music soundtracks to commercial products can you recall? Can you think of purchases you have made that were influenced by music, say, in a commercial or in the store? Or, do you think you are immune from such influences?

8. Since the ancient Greeks and particularly for Americans since the birth of rock and roll, the debate has raged over whether listening to any kind of music can have positive or negative effects. What is your stance? Has any of the information in this book influenced your thinking one way or another? What do you think about the use of music as means of torture?

9. Do you think that Merriam's statement—that "there is no other human cultural activity which is so all-pervasive and which reaches into, shapes, and often controls so much of human behavior" than music—is an exaggeration? What other human cultural activities could you name that equal or surpass music's effects?

10. How do you account for the disparity between the important social role music plays, its strong economic impact, the personal connections people have with it, and so on, and its seeming unimportance in terms of lack of governmental funding, its status in education, its lack of prominence in the medical community, and so on?

Chronological Summary of Selected Books Published in Music Psychology.

Revised and expanded from a list initially compiled by Eagle (1996)

Year	Author(s)	Title of Book
1863	Helmholtz	*On the Sensations of Tone*
1880	Gurney	*The Power of Sound*
1883	Stumpf	*Tonpsychologie, Vol. 1*
1886	Wallaschek	*Aesthetics of Music*
1890	Stumpf	*Tonpsychologie, Vol. 2*
1892	Broadhouse	*Musical Acoustics or the Phenomena of Sound*
1893	Wallaschek	*Primitive Music*
1895	Billroth	*Who is Musical?*
1899	Bartholomew	*Relation of Psychology to Music*
1902	Bartholomew	*Relation of Psychology to Music*, 2d ed.
1905	Lipps	*Consonance and Dissonance in Music*
1919	Seashore	*The Psychology of Musical Talent*
1925	Révész	*The Psychology of a Musical Prodigy*
1926	Kries	*Wer ist musikalisch?*
1927	Howes	*The Borderland of Music and Psychology*
1927	Kwalwasser	*Tests and Measurements in Music*
1927	Schoen, ed.	*The Effects of Music*
1927	Swisher	*Psychology for the Music Teacher*
1929	Meyer	*The Musician's Arithmetic*
1930	Farnsworth, C.	*Short Studies in Musical Psychology*
1931	Mursell & Glenn	*The Psychology of School Music Teaching*

1931	Pratt, C.	*The Meaning of Music: A Study in Psychological Aesthetics*
1931	Vidor	*Was Ist Musikalität?*
1933	Hurd	*Musical Acoustics*
1937	Jeans	*Science and Music*
1937	Mursell	*The Psychology of Music*
1938	Seashore	*Psychology of Music*
1939	Diserens & Fine	*A Psychology of Music*
1940	Schoen	*The Psychology of Music*
1944	Buck	*Psychology for Musicians*
1946	Licht	*Music in Medicine*
1947	Seashore	*In Search of Beauty in Music*
1948	Schullian & Schoen, eds.	*Music and Medicine*
1948	Soibelman	*Therapeutic and Industrial Uses of Music*
1951	Barbour	*Tuning and Temperament*
1951	Culver	*Musical Acoustics, 3d ed.*
1952	Gutheil, ed.	*Music and Your Emotions*
1952	Olson	*Musical Engineering*
1953	Lundin	*An Objective Psychology of Music*
1954	Révész	*Introduction to the Psychology of Music*
1955	Kwalwasser	*Exploring the Musical Mind*
1956	Meyer	*Emotion and Meaning in Music*
1956	Zuckerkandl	*Sound and Symbol*
1957	Hall	*The Language of Musical Acoustics*
1958	Farnsworth, P.	*The Social Psychology of Music*
1958	Weber	*The Rational and Social Foundations of Music*
1959	Zuckerkandl	*The Sense of Music*
1960	Langdon	*Psychosomatic Music*
1960	Seashore	*Measures of Musical Talents*
1961	Murchie	*Music of the Spheres*
1962	Valentine	*The Experimental Psychology of Beauty*
1962	Whybrew	*Measurement and Evaluation of Music*
1963	Silbermann	*The Sociology of Music*
1964	Merriam	*The Anthropology of Music*
1964	Noble	*The Psychology of Cornet and Trumpet Playing*
1966	Bentley	*Musical Ability in Children and Its Measurement*
1966	Lowery	*A Guide to Musical Acoustics*
1966	Teplov	*Psychologie des Aptitudes Musicales*
1967	Lundin	*An Objective Psychology of Music, 2d ed.*
1967	Murchie	*Music of the Spheres* (revised)
1967	Olson	*Music, Physics and Engineering*
1968	Gaston, ed.	*Music in Therapy*
1968	Lehman	*Tests and Measurements in Music*

1968	Shuter	*The Psychology of Musical Ability*
1969	Culver	*Musical Acoustics, 4th ed.*
1969	Farnsworth, P.	*The Social Psychology of Music*, 2d ed.
1969	Phelps	*A Guide to Research in Music Education*
1969	Zuckerkandl	*Sound and Symbol, Vol. 1: Music and the External World*
1970	Colwell	*The Evaluation of Music Teaching and Learning*
1970	Madsen & Madsen	*Experimental Research in Music*
1970	McLaughlin	*Music and Communication*
1971	Gordon	*The Psychology of Music Teaching*
1971	Whybrew	*Measurement and Evaluation in Music*, 2d ed.
1972	Franklin	*Music Education: Psychology and Method*
1973	Bonny & Savary	*Music and Your Mind*
1973	Roederer	*Introduction to the Physics and Psychophysics of Music*
1973	Zuckerkandl	*Man the Musician, Vol. 2: Music and the External World*
1975	Madsen et al., eds.	*Research in Music Behavior*
1975	Roederer	*Introduction to the Physics and Psychophysics of Music*, 2d ed.
1976	Eagle	*Music Therapy Index, Vol. 1*
1976	Plomp	*Aspects of Tone Sensation*
1977	Benchmark papers in acoustics	*Musical Acoustics: Piano and Wind Instruments*
1977	Clynes	*Sentics: The Touch of Emotions*
1977	Critchley & Hensen, eds.	*Music and the Brain*
1977	Savage	*Problems for Musical Acoustics*
1977	Schafer	*The Tuning of the World*
1977	Shepherd et al., eds.	*Whose Music? A Sociology of Musical Languages*
1978	Davies	*The Psychology of Music*
1978	Eagle	*Music Psychology Index, Vol. 2*
1978	Grindea, C., ed.	*Tensions in the Performance of Music*
1979	Radocy & Boyle	*Psychological Foundations of Musical Behavior*
1980	Hodges, ed.	*Handbook of Music Psychology*
1980	Phelps	*A Guide to Research in Music Education*, 2d ed.
1981	Shuter-Dyson & Gabriel	*The Psychology of Musical Ability*, 2d ed.
1982	Clynes, ed.	*Music, Mind and Brain*
1982	Deutsch	*The Psychology Music*
1983	Droh & Spintge, eds.	*Angst, Schmerz, Musik in der Anästhesie*
1983	Lerdahl & Jackendoff	*A Generative Theory of Tonal Music*
1984	Cogan	*New Images of Musical Sound*
1984	Dasilva et al.	*The Sociology of Music*
1984	Eagle & Miniter	*Music Psychology Index, Vol. 3*
1985	De la Motte-Haber	*Handbuch der Musickpsychologie*
1985	Howell et al., eds.	*Musical Structure and Cognition*

1985	Lundin	*An Objective Psychology of Music*, 3d ed.
1985	Sloboda	*The Musical Mind*
1986	Dowling & Harwood	*Music Cognition*
1986	Evans & Clynes	*Rhythm in Psychological, Linguistic, and Musical Processes*
1986	Hargreaves	*The Developmental Psychology of Music*
1986	Wilson	*Tone Deaf and All Thumbs?*
1987	Boyle & Radocy	*Measurement and Evaluation of Musical Experiences*
1987	Madsen & Prickett	*Applications of Research in Music Behavior*
1987	McAdams, ed.	*Music and Psychology: A Mutual Regard*
1987	Rainbow & Froelich	*Research in Music Education*
1987	Spintge & Droh, eds.	*Music in Medicine*
1988	Frances	*The Perception of Music*
1988	Radocy & Boyle	*Psychological Foundations of Musical Behavior*, 2d ed.
1988	Roehmann & Wilson, eds.	*The Biology of Music Making*
1988	Serafine	*Music as Cognition*
1988	Sloboda	*Generative Processes in Music*
1988	Swanwick	*Music, Mind, and Education*
1989	Clarke & Emmerson, eds.	*Music, Mind and Structure*
1989	Handel	*Listening: An Introduction to the Perception of Auditory Events*
1989	Lee, ed.	*Rehabilitation, Music and Human Well-Being*
1989	McAdams & Deliège, eds.	*Music and the Cognitive Sciences*
1989	McDonald & Simons	*Musical Growth and Development*
1989	Parncutt	*Harmony: A Psychoacoustical Approach*
1990	Benade	*Fundamentals of Musical Acoustics*, 2d ed.
1990	Fiske	*Music and Mind*
1990	Krumhansl	*Cognitive Foundations of Musical Pitch*
1990	Narmour	*The Analysis and Cognition of Basic Melodic Structures*
1990	Walker	*Musical Beliefs*
1990	Wilson & Roehmann, eds.	*Music and Child Development*
1991	Bamberger	*The Mind Behind the Musical Ear*
1991	Geerdes	*Improving Acoustics for Music Teaching*
1991	Hauptfleisch	*Music Education: Why? What? How?*
1991	Howell et al., eds.	*Representing Musical Structure*
1991	Maranto, ed.	*Applications of Music in Medicine*
1991	Sataloff et al., eds.	*Textbook of Performing Arts Medicine*
1991	Shlain	*Art & Physics*
1991	Todd & Loy, eds.	*Music and Connectionism*
1991	Wallin	*Biomusicology*
1992	Balaban et al., eds.	*Understanding Music with AI: Perspectives on Music Cognition*

1992	Butler	*The Musician's Guide to Perception and Cognition*	*Appendix A*
1992	Colwell, ed.	*Handbook of Research on Music Teaching and Learning*	
1992	Meyers	*Ethnomusicology: An Introduction*	
1992	Spintge & Droh, eds.	*MusicMedicine*	
1993	Cross & Deliège, eds.	*Music and the Cognitive Sciences 1990*	
1993	Dowling & Tighe, eds.	*Psychology and Music*	
1993	James	*The Music of the Spheres: Music, Science, and the Natural Order of the Universe*	
1993	McAdams & Bigand, eds.	*Thinking in Sound: The Cognitive Psychology of Human Audition*	
1993	Raffman	*Language, Music, and Mind*	
1993	Storr	*Music and the Mind*	
1994	Aiello & Sloboda, eds.	*Musical Perceptions*	
1995	Fyk	*Melodic Intonation, Psychoacoustics, and the Violin*	
1995	Grindea, ed.	*Tensions in the Performance of Music, extended edition*	
1995	Spintge & Pratt, eds.	*MusicMedicine 2*	
1996	Cope	*Experiments in Musical Intelligence*	
1996	Deliège & Sloboda, eds.	*Musical Beginnings*	
1996	Hodges, ed.	*Handbook of Music Psychology*, 2d ed.	
1996	Kemp	*The Musical Temperament*	
1997	Brummett, ed.	*Music as Intelligence*	
1997	Deliège & Sloboda, eds.	*Perception and Cognition of Music*	
1997	Hargreaves & North, eds.	*The Social Psychology of Music*	
1997	Jørgensen & Lehmann, eds.	*Does Practice Make Perfect?*	
1997	Leman, ed.	*Music, Gestalt, and Computing: Studies in Cognitive and Systematic Musicology*	
1997	Radocy & Boyle	*Psychological Foundations of Musical Behavior*, 3d ed.	
1998	Gordon	*Introduction to Research and the Psychology of Music*	
1998	Price, ed.	*Music Education Research*	
1999	Addis	*Of Music and Mind*	
1999	Deutsch	*The Psychology of Music, 2d ed.*	
1999	Pratt & Grocke, eds.	*MusicMedicine 3*	
2000	Thaut	*A Scientific Model of Music in Therapy and Medicine*	
2000	Tubiana & Amadio, eds.	*Medical Problems of the Instrumentalist Musician*	
2000	Wallin et al., eds.	*The Origins of Music*	
2001	Benzon	*Beethoven's Anvil: Music in Mind and Culture*	
2001	Cook	*Music, Cognition, and Computerized Sound: An Introduction to Psychoacoustics*	

Appendix A	2001	Juslin & Sloboda, eds.	*Music and Emotion*
	2001	Lerdahl	*Tonal Pitch Space*
	2001	Snyder	*Music and Memory*
	2001	Zatorre & Peretz, eds.	*The Biological Foundations of Music*
	2002	Bunt & Hoskyns, eds.	*The Handbook of Music Therapy*
	2002	Colwell & Richardson, eds.	*The New Handbook of Research on Music Teaching and Learning*
	2002	Hall	*Musical Acoustics, 3d ed.*
	2002	Johnston	*Measured tones: The Interplay of Physics and Music*
	2002	MacDonald et al., eds.	*Musical Identities*
	2002	Parncutt & McPherson, eds.	*The Science and Psychology of Music Performance*
	2002	Zbikowski	*Conceptualizing Music*
	2003	Ashton	*Harmonograph: A Visual Guide to the Mathematics of Music*
	2003	Avanzini et al., eds.	*The Neurosciences and Music*
	2003	Beranek	*Concert Halls and Opera Houses: Music, Acoustics, and Architecture*
	2003	Peretz & Zatorre, eds.	*The Cognitive Neuroscience of Music*
	2003	Radocy & Boyle	*Psychological Foundations of Musical Behavior, 4th ed.*
	2004	Balaban et al.	*Understanding Music with AI: Perspectives on Music Cognition*
	2004	Clarke	*Empirical Musicology*
	2004	Davidson, ed.	*The Music Practitioner: Research for the Music Performer, Teacher and Listener*
	2004	London	*Hearing in Time: Psychological Aspects of Musical Meter*
	2004	Temperley	*The Cognition of Basic Musical Structures*
	2004	Williamon, ed.	*Musical Excellence: Strategies and Techniques to Enhance Performance*
	2005	Avanzini et al., eds.	*The Neurosciences and Music II*
	2005	Clarke	*Ways of Listening: An Ecological Approach to the Perception of Musical Meaning*
	2005	Fletcher & Rossing	*The Physics of Musical Instruments*
	2005	Miell, MacDonald & Hargreaves	*Musical Communication*
	2005	Cope	*Computer Models of Musical Creativity*
	2005	Sloboda	*Exploring the Musical Mind*
	2005b	Thaut	*Rhythm, Music, and the Brain*
	2005	Wheeler, ed.	*Music Therapy Research, 2nd ed.*
	2006	Altenmüller et al., eds.	*Music, Motor Control and the Brain*
	2006	Benson	*Music: A Mathematical Offering*
	2006	Colwell, ed.	*MENC Handbook of Musical Cognition and Development*
	2006	Deliège, & Wiggins	*Musical Creativity*

2006	Howard & Angus	*Acoustics and Psychoacoustics*
2006	Huron	*Sweet Anticipation: Music and the Psychology of Expectation*
2006	Levitin	*This is Your Brain on Music*
2006	McPherson, ed.	*The Child as Musician. A Handbook of Musical Development*
2006	Mithen	*The Singing Neanderthals: The Origins of Music, Language, Mind, and Body*
2006	Moravcsik	*Musical Sound: An Introduction to the Physics of Music*
2006	Rothstein	*Emblems of Mind: The Inner Life of Music and Mathematics*
2006	Schneck & Berger	*The Music Effect: Music Physiology and Clinical Applications*
2006	Simon	*Music and the Human Brain*
2007	Aiello	*Music: Cognition and Emotions*
2007	Gruhn & Rauscher, eds.	*Neurosciences in Music Pedagogy*
2007	Froelich	*Sociology for Music Teachers*
2007	Gordon	*Learning Sequences in Music*
2007	Lehman et al.	*Psychology for Musicians*
2007	Leman	*Embodied Music Cognition and Mediation Technology*
2007	Temperley	*Music and Probability*
2007	Sacks	*Musicophilia. Tales of Music and the Brain*
2008	Gilbertson & Aldridge	*Music Therapy and Traumatic Brain Injury*
2008	Koen	*Beyond the Roof of the Word*
2008	Koen, ed.	*Oxford Handbook of Medical Ethnomusicology*
2008	North & Hargreaves	*The Social and Applied Psychology of Music*
2008	Patel	*Music, Language, and the Brain*
2009	Clarke, Dibben, & Pitts	*Music and Mind in Everyday Life*
2009	Hallam et al., eds.	*The Oxford Handbook of Music Psychology*
2009	Kirnarskaya	*The Natural Musician*
2009	Klickstein	*The Musician's Way: A Guide to Practice, Performance, and Wellness*
2009	Malloch	*Communicative Musicality: Exploring the Basis of Human Companionship*
2009	Thompson	*Music, Thought, and Feeling*
2009	Watson	*The Biology of Musical Performance and Performance-Related Injury.*
2010	Ball	*The Music Instinct*
2010	Berkowitz	*The Improvising Mind*
2010	Juslin & Sloboda, eds.	*Handbook of Music and Emotion*
2011	Barrett, ed.	*A Cultural Psychology of Music Education*
2011	Clarke & Clarke, eds.	*Music and Consciousness*
2011	Deliege & Davidson, eds.	*Music and the Mind*
2011	Gabrielsson	*Strong Experiences with Music*

2011	Kenny	*The Psychology of Music Performance Anxiety*
2011	Ward-Steinman, ed.	*Advances in Social-psychology and Music Education Research*
2012	Bannan, ed.	*Music, Language, and Human Evolution*
2012	Berger & Turow	*Music, Science, and the Rhythmic Brain*
2012	Cornelius & Natvig	*Music: A Social Experience*
2012	Hargreaves, Miell, & MacDonald, eds.	*Musical Imaginations*
2012	Koelsch	*Brain and Music*
2012	London	*Hearing in Time, 2d ed.*
2012	MacDonald, Kreutz, & Mitchell, eds.	*Music, Health, and Wellbeing*
2012	McPherson, Davidson, & Faulkner, eds.	*Music in Our Lives*
2012	Radocy & Boyle	*Psychological Foundations of Musical Behavior, 5th ed.*
2012	Rebuschat et al., eds.	*Language and Music as Cognitive Systems*
2012	Stumpf	*The Origins of Music*
2013	Bader	*Nonlinearities and Synchronization in Musical Acoustics and Music Psychology*
2013	Bamberger	*Discovering the Musical Mind*
2013	Clayton, Dueck, & Leante	*Experience and Meaning in Music Performance*
2013	Cochrane, Fantini, & Scherer, eds.	*The Emotional Power of Music*
2013	Margulis	*On Repeat: How Music Plays the Mind*
2013	Morely	*The Prehistory of Music*
2013	Ockelford	*Applied Musicology*
2013	Tan, Cohen, Lipscomb, & Kendall, eds.	*The Psychology of Music in Multimedia*
2014	Fabian, Timmers, & Schubert, eds.	*Expressiveness in Music Performance*
2014	Honing	*Musical Cognition: A Science of Listening*
2014	James	*The Musical Brain*
2014	Rice	*Ethnomusicology: A Very Short Introduction*
2014	Thaut & Hoemberg	*Handbook of Neurologic Music Therapy*
2014	Thompson	*Music, Thought, and Feeling, 2d ed.*
2014	Williamson	*You Are the Music: How Music Reveals What It Means to be Human*
2015	Bigand et al., eds.	*The Neurosciences and Music V: Cognitive Stimulation*
2015	Nagari	*Music as Image: Analytical Psychology and Music in Film*
2016	Alexander	*The Jazz of Physics*
2016	Chaigne & Kergomard	*Acoustics of Musical Instruments*
2016	Fung & Lehmberg	*Music for Life*
2016	Hallam, Cross, & Thaut, eds.	*The Oxford Handbook of Music Psychology, 2d ed.*

2016	McPherson, ed.	*Musical Prodigies*
2016	McPherson, ed.	*The Child as Musician, 2d ed.*
2016	Powell	*Why You Love Music*
2016	Rosset i Lobet & Odam	*The Musician's Body*
2016	Wheeler & Murphy	*Music Therapy Research, 3rd ed.*
2017	Ashley & Timmers	*The Routledge Companion to Music Cognition*
2017	De Souza	*Music at Hand*
2017	Hodges	*A Concise Survey of Music Philosophy*
2017	Horden, ed.	*Music as Medicine*
2017	King & Waddington, eds.	*Music and Empathy*
2017	MacDonald et al., eds.	*Handbook of Musical Identities*
2017	Mantie & Smith, eds.	*The Oxford Handbook of Music Making and Leisure*
2017	Nagel	*Managing Stage Fright: A Guide for Musicians and Music Teachers*
2017	Tan, Pfordresher, & Harré	*Psychology of Music*
2018	Hallam	*Psychology of Music*
2018	McPherson & Welch, eds.	*Music and Music Education in People's Lives*
	[no eds.]	*Neurosciences and Music VI: Music, Sound and Health*
2019	Juslin	*Musical Emotions Explained*
2019	Kim & Gilman, eds.	*Oxford Handbook of Music and the Body*
2019	Margulis	*The Psychology of Music: A Very Short Introduction*
2019	Thaut & Hodges, eds.	*The Oxford Handbook on Music and the Brain*

Glossary

A

absolute expressionism A philosophical position in which the meaning and value of music is found in the music itself and in the expression of human feelings.

absolute formalism A philosophical position in which the meaning and value of music is found in the music itself; meaning is in musical relationships and is primarily intellectual.

absolutism, absolutists A philosophical position in which the meaning and value of music is found in the music itself.

absolute pitch The ability to identify or sing musical pitches without external references.

absorption In acoustics, absorption occurs when acoustical energy is dissipated as it is transmitted through a medium.

accommodation In Jean Piaget's **developmental psychology**, accommodation occurs when new learning causes a modification in a pre-existing schema.

achievement test (music) Measures how much a person has learned about music.

acoustic (stapedius) reflex Muscle actions in the middle ear protect the ear somewhat against loud noises.

acoustics The scientific study of sound; a branch of physics.

ADSR **Attack-Delay-Sustain-Release** are the four stages of a sound envelope.

adrenocorticotropic hormone (ACTH) (see under **biochemical**)

advance organizer David Ausubel's notion that presenting basic information on a topic to learners prior to in-depth study allows them to organize new material into a pre-existing cognitive structure that is hierarchically arranged.

aerophone A wind instrument such as a flute or trumpet.

aesthetics The branch of philosophy concerned with the nature and value of art, especially with beauty.

aesthetic trinity theory (ATT) According to Vladimir Konečni, profound responses to music lead to experiences of awe, being moved, and thrills.

Aha! learning A term used by Gestalt psychologists referring to insightful learning, or learning that occurs in a flash of inspiration rather than through trial and error.

Alexander Technique A program of body awareness developed by Frederick Alexander (1869–1955) to reduce physical stress and promote effortless posture and movement.

ambulatory assessment A portable means of gathering physiological data in naturalistic (i.e., non-laboratory) settings.

amusia (receptive; expressive) The loss of musical skills due to deficits in brain processing. Receptive amusia refers to an inability to perceive or understand certain aspects of music (i.e., pitch, timbre, rhythm, etc.). Expressive amusia is an inability to produce music accurately, such as sing in tune or clap the beat.

amygdala An almond-shaped neural structure in the **limbic** system involved in the processing of emotional responses, especially fear.

anterior cingulate cortex The frontal portion of the **cingulate gyrus**, involved in a wide variety of cognitive, emotional, and autonomic responses.

anthrophony Sounds created by human beings, such as engine noises.

anvil (incus) The second of three small bones (**ossicles**) in the middle ear that convey energy from the ear drum to the cochlea.

anxiolytic music Music used to ameliorate pain and anxiety.

aperiodic motion In acoustics, random molecular motion that creates noise.

aphasia The loss of language skills due to deficits in brain processing.

aptitude test (music) Measures a person's potential for learning music.

arousal In the context of measuring emotional responses, arousal refers to the degree of energy or excitement in a person's response to music.

Ashkenazi Jews from central or eastern Europe.

assimilation In Jean Piaget's **developmental psychology**, assimilation occurs when new information fits within a previously created schema.

association area A portion of the brain concerned with higher-level processing of raw sensory information.

asteroseismology The study of vibratory rates of stars.

attack In acoustics, the first portion or onset of a tone as the sound rises from nothing to its initial peak intensity (see **ADSR**).

audiate A term coined by Edwin Gordon referring to inner hearing; hearing music with comprehension in the absence of physical sound.

auditory cortex The primary seat of hearing in the brain, located in the temporal lobe.

auditory hair cells Hair cells in the inner ear that send acoustic information via the auditory nerve to the brain. Approximately 3,500 inner hair cells provide the bulk of the information and 20,000 outer hair cells sharpen frequency resolution.

auditory nerve The nerve that conveys information from the inner ear to the brain.

auditory scene analysis The process by which we organize incoming sounds into meaningful units.

auditory stream segregation The process by which we separate incoming sounds into different, coherent entities (i.e., in a noisy environment, identifying the sound of a person's voice as distinct from the sound coming from the television set).

audio-motor system (see **audio-visual motor system**)

audio-visual-motor system (audio-motor) Networks in the brain that connect what we hear, see, and feel into a coherent pattern; for example, when playing the piano hearing the notes we play, seeing the music and the keyboard, feeling the keys and the movements of our fingers and hands as one integrated experience.

Australopithecus africanus A precursor to modern humans that lived approximately two to three million years ago.

autonomic nervous system (ANS) The ANS regulates bodily responses to the environment. The sympathetic division prepares the body for "fight or flight," by increasing heart rate, muscle tension, aural acuity, and so on. The parasympathetic division calms the body. The two divisions work cooperatively to prepare the body to respond appropriately to ongoing circumstances.

axon The fiber extending from a neuron (brain cell) that carries nerve impulses away from the cell body (see **dendrite**).

B

ballistic movement   Muscle movement that once initiated continues on its own momentum.

basal ganglia   Neurons at the base of the brain involved in coordinated body movements.

basilar membrane   A membrane in the **cochea** that supports the **Organ of Corti** with its inner and outer hair cells.

beat induction   The ability to find and entrain the beat, or regular pulses, in music.

behaviorism   A psychological orientation that focuses on observable behavior.

beta-endorphin   (see under **biochemical**)

bilateral activation   Neural activity that occurs on both sides of the brain.

biochemical   Naturally occurring, or endogenous, chemicals in the human body.

adrenocorticotropic hormone (ACTH)   A hormone produced by the **pituitary** that is released under stress or injury and that stimulates the production of **cortisol** and other hormones.

Arginine vasopressin receptor (AVPR1A)   Modulates social cognition and behavior.

beta-endorphin   An **endorphin** produced by the pituitary that suppresses pain.

blood glucose   Blood sugar, or the amount of glucose in the blood.

cortisol   A hormone released by the adrenal gland under stress conditions.

dehydroepiandrosterone   A steroid produced by the adrenal gland.

dopamine   A **neurotransmitter** involved in reward-seeking behavior, pleasure, and motivation.

endorphin   **Biochemical** produced by the **pituitary** and **hypothalamus** in response to excitement and pain; natural pain killer, leads to sense of well being.

epinephrine   A **neurotransmitter** secreted under stress that stimulates the sympathetic nervous system.

genetic stress hormone markers   Inherited **biochemical** indicators of depression and other mood disorders.

growth hormone   A **biochemical** involved in regulating healthy growth and development.

interleukin-1, -6, -10   A group of **biochemical**s involved in the functioning of the immune system.

melatonin   A **biochemical** released by the pineal gland that regulates sleep and affects mood.

mu-opiate receptor   These receptors can be located on either side of a **synapse** (i.e., presynapse, postsynapse) and are involved in excitation of message transmission. They bind with natural pain killers or with various drugs.

natural killer cells   Innate cells that reject tumors and viruses.

neurotransmitter   Chemical messengers in the brain that activate or inhibit **axon** transmissions.

neutrophil and lymphocyte   White blood cells that form important parts of the immune system.

norepinephrine   A stress hormone involved in fight or flight responses, increasing body activation.

oxytocin   A hormone most often associated with childbirth; it plays a role in maternal—infant bonding.

prolactin   A hormone involved in lactation during pregnancy and childbirth, and in sexual satisfaction.

secretory immunoglobulin A (SIgA)   A protein that acts as an antibody in the immune system.

serotonin   A **neurotransmitter** that induces relaxation.

testosterone   A male hormone involved in sexual development.

T lymphocytes (CD4+, CD8+, CD16+)   A class of white blood cells that coordinates the immune system's response to malignant invaders.

BioMusic   The study of animal sound making and its relationship to music.

biophony   Animal sounds such as bird calls.

blood glucose   (see under **biochemical**)

blood oxygen saturation   The amount of oxygen in the blood

brainstem   The upper portion of the spinal cord that connects the lower brain to the **midbrain**.

Broca's area (Broca's aphasia)   The left, frontal part of the brain involved in speech. Persons who suffer from Broca's aphasia are unable to speak coherently.

Brodmann Areas 41, 42   (see **Heschl's gyrus**)

C

Cartesian   Relating to the ideas of French philosopher René Descartes (1596–1650). In Cartesian philosophy, there is one Truth and it is external to human perception.

cents   In acoustics there are 100 cents in a half step.

cerebellum   The "little brain" at the underneath portion of the back of the brain; involved in muscle coordination and movement, but also in the integration of sensory input in preparation for motor output, in cognition, and emotion.

cerebral cortex   The outer layer of the human brain.

chaining   In **behaviorism**, hooking together a series of small, discrete steps to form a complex behavioral act.

changing-note pattern   A musical **schema** or pattern in which notes move around the tonic, moving above or below and returning to tonic.

chills (thrills, frisson)   An emotional response to music that may include shivers, tingles down the spine, hair standing on the back of the neck, goosebumps, and so on.

chordophone   A stringed musical instrument, such as a violin.

chromosome   A unit of **DNA** that contains many genes. Humans have 23 pairs or 46 chromosomes in each cell.

chronobiology   The study of time in living organisms, both internal clocks and the effects of environmental periodicities (e.g., day-night, seasons) on behavior.

chunking   A means of organizing information into smaller, more manageable units, such as the way we parse phone numbers and social security numbers.

cingulate gyrus   A portion of the **limbic system** located just above the corpus callosum, it is involved in emotions, coordinates sensory input, responds to pain, and regulates aggressive behavior.

circadian rhythms   Day and night cycles, roughly 24 hours.

classical conditioning   Pairing a neutral stimulus with a meaningful stimulus. In Pavlov's famous experiment, he paired the sounding of a bell with the presentation of food to a dog. Eventually the ringing of the bell caused salivation in the absence of food.

closure   In Gestalt psychology, one of the corollaries of the **Law of Prägnanz** recognizing that psychologically we prefer to complete an incomplete pattern.

coaching   Third stage of Charles Byrne's four-stage model in which the teacher provides guidance and encouragement rather than direct instruction.

cochlea   The inner ear; houses the **basilar membrane** and **organ of Corti** with its inner and outer hair cells.

cochlear nucleus   Located in the **brainstem**, first way-station in the auditory system. Higher frequencies are represented **tonotpica**lly in the dorsal (back) cochlear nucleus and lower frequencies in the ventral (front) cochlear nucleus.

cocktail party phenomenon   The ability to track more than one auditory stream at a time, such as two conversations, by alternating rapidly back and forth between the two.

cognition   Mental activity such as thinking, knowing, remembering, sensing, and reasoning.

cognitive neuroscience   Bridging **cognitive psychology** and neuroscience, researchers in this field study mental processing in the brain.

cognitive psychology   Psychological viewpoint primarily concerned with cognitive functioning and higher mental processes.

cognitivist position   In music emotion studies, the position that listeners can perceive emotions being expressed in the music, but do not necessarily feel those emotions.

common direction   In **Gestalt psychology**, one of the corollaries of the **Law of Prägnanz** stipulating that objects (including musical sounds) moving in the same direction tend to be perceived as belonging together.

complex tone   In acoustics, any tone consisting of a fundamental and one or more overtones.

compression   In acoustics, compression occurs when molecules in the medium of transmission are squeezed together (see rarefaction).

concrete operational stage   In Jean Piaget's **developmental psychology**, the period from ages 7 to 11 characterized by increasing language skills and awareness of relationships among things. The end of concrete operations is marked by the acquisition of **conservation**.

congenital amusia   Innate deficits in processing music, such as the inability to recognize a familiar melody or to sing in tune.

conservation   In Jean Piaget's **developmental psychology**, the ability to conserve the whole even when it is modified into different configurations, such as recognizing *Twinkle, Twinkle Little Star* in different keys, tempos, or timbres.

constructivism   The view that each person constructs his or her own reality.

content analysis   A qualitative analysis of text or narratives for common themes or emergent ideas.

convergence zone   A region of the brain where input from different sensory inputs are integrated into a coherent whole.

corpophone   Body sounds such as hand clapping, finger snapping, or foot stomping.

corpus callosum   The bundle of fibers that forms the primary connection between the two hemispheres of the brain.

cortisol   (see under **biochemical**)

correlation coeficient   A statistic (often represented as *r*) that expresses the degree of relationship between two (or more) variables. A positive correlation indicates that as one variable increases, so does the other. A negative correlation indicates an inverse relationship; the higher one variable, the lower the other. The nearer the correlation coefficient is to +1.0 or −1.0, the stronger the relationship. As *r* approaches zero, the relationship weakens, until *r* = 0.0 indicates a complete lack of relationship. Note that correlation does not imply causation; that is, it indicates the degree to which two variables are related, but does not mean that one caused the other.

corrugator muscle   Eyebrow or frowning muscle.

critical band   A shifting region of the basilar membrane within which two different frequencies are not heard as distinct tones.

cue abstraction theory   Describes how listeners abstract cues or distinctive features of music through attentional listening processes to create memory units.

D

decay   In acoustics, the second portion of a tone; after the initial energy of the attack, the sound tends to settle into the sustain portion (see **ADSR**).

declarative memory   Memory for specific facts or events. Sometimes divided into semantic (impersonal knowledge such as famous composers in the Baroque era) and episodic (personal memories such as one's audition to enter a music school) memory.

decussation   In the auditory system, the crossing of auditory nerve fibers from one inner ear to the opposite hemisphere.

dehydroepiandrosterone   (see under **biochemical**)

deliberate practice   Structured musical practice with specific goals in mind.

dendrite   A nerve fiber that brings message impulses to the cell body (see **axon**). A neuron has only one axon, but may have many dendrites.

density   In **psychoacoustics**, the impression that some tones are more compact (i.e., a piccolo in the high register) than others (e.g., a tuba in the low register). This is a psychological or perceptual phenomenon, not a physical one.

developmental psychology   Psychological approach concerned with psychological growth over the lifespan.

difference limen (DL)   (see **just noticeable difference**)

diffraction   In acoustics, when a sound bends around an object or passes through a small opening.

diffusion tensor imaging (DTI)   A type of magnetic resonance imaging that maps white matter pathways showing how different regions of the brain connect to each other.

discovery learning   A teaching-learning process in which students explore and discover solutions to problems on their own.

distributional strategies   (see **event-distribution strategies**)

DNA deoxyribonucleicacid   DNA contains the instructions that govern the structure and function of all living things.

dopamine   (see under **biochemical**)

dorsal cochlear nucleus   (see **cochlear nucleus**)

dorsal premotor cortex   (see **premotor cortex**)

dorsal striatum   (see **neostriatum**)

dynamic attending theory   Stable, internal oscillators or time-keepers can adapt to external timing or rhythmic events

dynamic programming procedures   Applied to music, listeners keep track of musical events as they occur and revise previous understandings based on later occurrences in the music. Music listeners form impressions of the music as it unfolds.

dysrythmia   Lack of rhythmicity in social interactions. May be present in those with autism, manic-depression, or schizophrenia.

E

ear canal (external auditory meatus)   The auditory tube from the outside surface of the head to the **ear drum**.

350

eardrum (tympanum) The membrane at the end of the **ear canal** that vibrates in sympathy with sound waves present in the atmosphere

ecological validity (see **external validity**)

electrocardiogram (ECG or EKG) Electrical activity of the heart.

electrodermal response (see **skin conductance response**)

electroencephalography (EEG) Electrical activity of the brain.

electrogastrography Electrical activity of the stomach.

electromyography (EMG) Electrical activity of the muscles.

electrophone Mechanical or electronic music instrument such as a synthesizer.

emotional contagion Occurs when a listener internally mimics the perceived emotion expressed in music.

emotivist position In musical emotion studies, the position that listeners can experience emotions induced by the music.

enactive mode In Jerome Bruner's theory of instruction, knowledge as expressed in action; for example, when students clap strong and weak, duple and triple meter patterns.

entrainment Synchronizing one's actions to external rhythms, such as clapping along to the beat of a song.

envelope In acoustics, the overall shape of a sound wave.

epinephrine (see under **biochemical**)

episodic memory (see **memory, declarative memory**)

equal-temperament A scale system derived by dividing the octave into 12 equal intervals.

essentic form The shape created by a **sentograph** that expresses a perceived emotion expressed in music.

ethnography A field report or case study compiled by an anthropologist or ethnomusicologist based on observations, interviews, and so on.

ethnomusicology The study of social and cultural aspects of music around the world.

Eustachian tube A tube that allows air pressure to be the same on both sides of the eardrum.

event-distribution strategies A type of learning based on frequency of exposure or how often specific events occur.

event hierarchies The perception that some musical events are more important than others.

event-related potential (ERP) Measurement of the brain's immediate response to internal or external stimuli.

everyday music In contrast to special musical events such as a concert, everyday music listening experiences occur in such mundane activities as driving in the car, shopping in a store, or waiting in a doctor's office.

expectancy theory Each musical event leads the listener to expect a following event. Experienced listeners are more successful at making (largely unconscious) predictions of what will happen next in the music.

experience sampling method A technique of gathering data in naturalistic settings. Participants are contacted randomly via a pager or cell phone and asked to record their current activities and feelings.

experimental aesthetics Scientific investigation into aesthetic responses.

expressionism A philosophical position that finds the meaning and value of music to be in the expression of human feelings.

external validity (also **ecological validity**) The extent to which the results of an experiment can be generalized to a larger population based on control of independent variables.

extinction In behaviorism, the lack of feedback or reinforcement following a (usually unwanted) behavior.

extraversion   An aspect of personality relating to an outgoing, gregarious nature.

extrinsic learning   In **humanistic psychology**, learning that is independent of the person and can be shared from one person to another.

F

factor analysis   A statistical means of reducing a large number of variables or factors to a smaller number of variables that are highly related.

fading   Last stage of Charles Byrne's four-stage model in which the teacher recedes and allows the student to engage in self-directed learning.

feedback   In **behaviorism**, a term used in lieu of positive and negative reinforcement.

Feldenkrais   A method of somatic education that improves posture and movement.

Fibonacci series   A mathematical series—0, 1, 1, 2, 3, 5, 8, 13, etc.—derived from adding each succession of two numbers beginning with $0+1=1$, $1+1=2$, $1+2=3$, $2+3=5$, and so on. The ratio by dividing any two successive numbers gives the golden mean.

field theory   Kurt Lewin's conception of a person's life space, consisting of goals, barriers, approach—avoidance behaviors, and so on.

figure-ground relationship   In **Gestalt psychology**, some aspects of the environment are perceived as foreground (the figure) and other aspects as background.

fixation   In textual or music reading, a fixation is when the eye stops moving; the eye takes in information during a fixation (see **saccade**).

frequency   In acoustics, the number of times a sound wave repeats a full cycle in a given period, usually per second.

flow   Mihály Csíkszentmihályi's notion that when a person's level of skill matches the task at hand, s/he is operating at optimal capacity and may experience total absorption and exhilaration.

focal dystonia   An involuntary, painless loss of muscle control often associated with over-use syndrome. In musicians, it is most often found in the hands and fingers of pianists and string players, but may also occur in the embouchures of brass players.

focal entrapment neuropathy   A compressed peripheral nerve that comprises function, such as carpel tunnel syndrome.

formalism   A philosophical position in which the meaning and value of music is found in the intellectual appreciation of musical relationships.

formal operational stage   In Jean Piaget's **developmental psychology**, the period from approximately 11 years of age through adulthood that is characterized by a capacity for abstract thought.

formant region   In acoustics, a range of frequencies amplified by the acoustical characteristics of a musical instrument or the shape and size of the oral cavity in singers.

free association   In **psychoanalysis**, the patient says anything that comes to mind without editing.

frisson   (see **chills**)

frontal operculum   The most forward portion of the lower frontal cortex; implicated in higher-order musical processing.

fronto-parietal-temporal network   A neural network that links the frontal, parietal and temporal lobes.

Fourier theorem   The process of reducing a complex tone into its constituent parts (i.e., **sine waves**).

functional magnetic resonance imaging (fMRI)   An imaging technology that provides information on both brain structure and function.

fundamental   In acoustics, the lowest partial of a complex tone.

fusiform gyrus   A region of the temporal lobe implicated in face, body, word, number and color recognition.

G

galvanic skin response   (see **skin conductance response**)

gamelan orchestra   A musical ensemble from Indonesia consisting of primarily xylophones, gongs, and bells.

gap-fill melody (pitch reversal)   In Western music, a large intervallic leap is often followed by a stepwise return in the opposite direction.

gastric motility   Digestive activity in the stomach (peristalsis).

gastroesophageal reflux disease (GERD)   Chronic, abnormal reflux of stomach acid into the esophagus. Long-term GERD may do damage to the vocal folds.

general intelligence (*g*)   Intellectual capacity that influences performance across many cognitive domains in opposition to a specific type such as musical intelligence.

genetic stress hormone markers   (see under biochemical)

generative theory of tonal music (GTTM)   Rules of musical grammar developed by Fred Lerdahl and Ray Jackendoff that describe hierarchical structures in music.

geophany   Inanimate nature sounds such as waterfalls, thunder, and wind.

GERMS model   A model developed by Patrik Juslin and colleagues to identify the sources of musical expressivity.

Gestalt   The word *Gestalt* means whole, form, or shape and refers to the notion that we generally perceive entities as a coherent whole rather than its constituent parts.

Gestalt psychology   A psychological approach that emphasizes how various parts relate to the whole.

Geophony   The sounds of inanimate nature, such as wind, waterfalls, thunderstorms.

Golden mean   A ratio derived from the **Fibonacci series**. In music, a climax or other important events often occur at the golden mean, or roughly two-thirds of the way through a composition.

good continuation   In **Gestalt psychology**, objects (including musical sounds) that appear to continue in an established direction are more easily perceived as a unit than those that change direction.

gray matter   Neural cells with un**myelinate**d axons. A common term for the **cerebral cortex**.

growth hormone (ACTH)   (see under **biochemical**)

Guided Imagery and Music (GIM)   A music therapy technique developed by Helen Bonny to guide clients in introspection with music serving to facilitate access to repressed memories.

gyrification   Cortical folding in the brain, or how the brain folds in upon itself during development.

H

hammer (malleus)   The first of three small bones (**ossicles**) in the middle ear that convey energy from the ear drum to the cochlea. The hammer is attached to the inner surface of the **ear drum**.

harmonic   (see **partial**)

helicotrema   The far end of the coil of the **cochlea**.

helioseismology   The study of vibratory rates of the sun.

hemispheric asymmetry   Refers to differences in processing by the left and right hemi-spheres of the brain.

Heschl's gyrus   Located in the **superior temporal lobe**, the name given to Brodmann Areas 41 and 42. BA 41 is the primary **auditory cortex**. BA 42 is auditory association cortex.

hierarchy of human needs   Often represented by a pyramid, the concept in **humanistic psychology** that traces the natural progression from physical needs to self-actualization.

hippocampus   A neural structure in the **limbic** system involved in the formation of new memories and in spatial navigation.

homeostasis   The maintenance of stable internal states, such as body temperature, blood pressure, and so on. Psychological homeostasis refers to internal mental stability, in opposition to bipolar disorders, for example.

Homo erectus   A precursor of modern humans that lived approximately 1.3–1.8 million years ago.

Homo sapiens   modern humans.

homunculus   A mental representation of the body or body map in the sensory-motor cortex.

Humean   Relating to the ideas of Scottish philosopher David Hume (1711–1776). In Humean philosophy, there are many truths, as each person constructs his or her reality or truth.

humanistic psychology   Psychological viewpoint concerned with growth toward **self-actualization**.

hypnosis   A psychoanalytic technique designed to allow the therapist access to repressed memories.

hypothalamus   Located below the **thalamus** and above the brainstem, the hypothalamus links the nervous system to the endocrine system. It plays a role in homeostasis, regulating hunger, thirst, body temperature, and so on.

I

iconic mode   In Bruner's theory of instruction, knowledge as represented in some form of visual depiction such as musical notation or mathematical symbols; can also include pre-notation such as different shapes used to represent different note values, and so on.

idiophone   A musical instrument that is struck such as gongs, or shaken such as rattles.

implication-realization model   Eugene Narmour's extension of expectancy theory; specifies how listeners can reasonably predict where the tune is going in implicative melodies.

independent variable   In research, a variable that can influence the outcome of the (dependent) variable or what is being measured. For example years of musical training could be an independent variable that influences the outcome of how well the person performs.

infant-directed speech (IDS)   Exaggerated speech used by parents and care-takers with infants.

inferior colliculus   A principal way-station in the auditory pathway involved in sound integration; located in the **brainstem**.

inferior parietal lobule   Lower portion of the parietal lobe, important in sensory integration (see convergence zone).

infradian rhythms   Periodical cycle with a time span longer than 24 hours, such as seasonal rhythms.

inner hair cells   (see **auditory hair cells**)

insight (insightful learning)   (see **Aha! learning**)

intelligence quotient (IQ)   Intelligence dealing primarily with reasoning and problem solving as measured by a standardized test such as the Stanford-Binet or Wechsler Intelligence Scale.

interaction rhythms   Social rhythms between two or more people as they engage with each other.

interference   In acoustics, the complex wave patterns created when two or more sound waves interact as they travel through a medium. For example, the sound of the piano, violin, and cello in a trio combine to make complex interference patterns.

interleukin-1, -6, -10   (see under **biochemical**)

internal validity   In research, control over independent variables that might affect the outcome of an experiment.

interonset interval   The time gap between the starting points of successive two notes.

intrinsic learning   In **humanistic psychology**, learning that is internal and personal and cannot be shared from one person to another (see peak experience).

invariant   Aspects of human behavior that are universal, but whose particular realizations vary from culture to culture. All human societies have music in some form or fashion as part of their culture, but musical practices vary widely.

ITPRA theory of expectations   David Huron's theory of expectation-related responses, involving Imagination, Tension, Prediction, Reaction, and Appraisal responses.

J

Just intonation   A tuning system based on creating all intervals from whole number ratios.

just noticeable difference (JND)   In acoustics, the smallest difference one can perceive in frequency or amplitude, for example (also known as **difference limen**).

K

kinesthetic memory   Muscle memory; remembrance of body position and movements.

L

lateral lemniscus   A tract of fibers that carries acoustical information from the cochlear nucleus to the **superior olivary complex** in the brainstem.

Law of Prägnanz   In **Gestalt psychology**, the notion that we organize incoming stimuli in the simplest way possible.

learning theory   Psychological explanations for human learning.

life space   In Kurt Lewin's **field theory**, the life space represents a person's environment, the space within which one lives.

limbic system   Midbrain structures that form the inner border of the cortex. Involved in emotional responses and long-term memory.

lithophone   A musical instrument made of rocks that are struck to sound tones.

locus coeruleus   A brain structure in the **recticular formation** that triggers emotional arousal through release of the neurotransmitter **norepinephrine**.

longitundianal waves   In acoustics, sound waves that travel in the same direction as the vibratory disturbance, such as the waves that travel down the length of a trumpet (see **transverse wave**s).

luthier   A string instrument maker.

M

magnetic resonance imaging (MRI)   Brain imaging that provides minute details on brain structures.

magnetoencephalography (MEG)   Measurement of the brain's magnetic fields that allows location of neural structures as they respond over a very rapid time course of milliseconds.

Manhattanville Curriculum   A sequential music education program for early childhood through high school that included a spiral curriculum.

Many Meters Hypothesis   Through mere exposure, experience, and training, listeners can attend to a variety of metrical patterns in music.

meantone tuning   A tuning system in which fifths are slightly altered to create more acceptable thirds.

medial geniculate   Located in the **thalamus**, the final auditory relay station before acoustical information reaches the auditory cortex.

melatonin   (see under **biochemical**)

melodic fission   When one musical line appears to diverge into two lines.

melodic fusion   When two musical lines appear to converge into one line.

membranophone   A musical instrument with a membrane, such as a drum.

mental rehearsal   Practicing something like playing the violin in the mind, without physical motion.

meta-analysis   In research, analyzing the aggregated results of a group of similar experiments to yield more robust data sets than are obtainable through a single study.

metacognition   Thinking about one's own thinking, or knowledge about one's own knowledge.

meter induction   Determining the meter by listening to music.

midbrain   The upper portion of the brainstem involved in hearing, vision, and eye and body movement.

mirror neuron   A brain cell that fires when a person observes (sees or hears) someone else, as if the observer were performing the same action. For example, a piano teacher who listens to a student perform has neurons firing as if she were performing herself.

mnemonic   A memory or learning aid that relies on associations between an easily remembered cue and the thing to be remembered.

modeling   Used in many learning theories. In behaviorism, a teacher models the desired behavior and then reinforces the student's attempt to mimic. In Charles Byrne's four-state model, it is the first step when the teacher demonstrates and provides direct instruction.

monochord   A simple, one-stringed musical instrument used by Pythagoras to determine the harmonic ratios used in Western music.

motivation   In psychology, the desire to learn can come from intrinsic (e.g., personal enjoyment) or external (praise from parents or teachers) sources.

mu-opiate receptor expression   (see under **biochemical**)

multimodal integration areas   (see **convergence zones**)

multidimensional scaling techniques   Data analysis in which data are represented in geometrical space.

multiple intelligences theory   Howard Gardner's conception that we have linguistic, musical, logical-mathematical, spatial, bodily-kinesthetic, interpersonal, intrapersonal, naturalist, and existential intelligences.

music achievement test   Measures how much a person has learned about music.

music aptitude test   Measures one's potential for learning music.

music learning theory   Edwin Gordon's model for learning based on the development of aural skills.

music medicine   The use of music in medical—clinical applications by physicians and other health care professionals to ameliorate pain and anxiety and to promote health.

music psychology   A multidisciplinary and interdisciplinary study of music in the human experience

music therapy   The use of music interventions to accomplish individualized goals within a therapeutic relationship.

musical savant   An individual with highly advanced musical skills that stand in contrast to their other abilities.

myelination   The process of covering **axons** with a fatty sheath that enhances message transmission and gives portions of the brain the name **white matter**.

N

natural harmonic series   The name given to the way some entities naturally vibrate in integer-related **harmonics**.

natural killer cells   (see under **biochemical**)

natural selection   The evolutionary process by which certain characteristics increase the likelihood of reproduction and eventually become commonplace in a species.

Neanderthal   A precursor of modern humans that lived from approximately 30,000–130,000 years ago.

near-death experience   Describes the experience of being declared clinically dead or being apparently dead and then being revived.

negative reinforcement   In **behaviorism**, the removal of something unpleasant following a behavior.

neostriatum   A **subcortical** (i.e., lying beneath the cortex) structure that serves as a major input for the **basal ganglia**. "Dorsal" indicates the posterior part of this structure, "ventral" indicates the anterior portion.

neural network   Groups of brain cells that fire as a functionally coherent unit.

neural plasticity   The capacity for the brain to reshape itself following learning or injury.

neural pruning   The process of deleting unused synapses in the brain.

Neurologic Music Therapy   The therapeutic application of music to cognitive, sensory, and motor function in clients with neurologic disease.

neuromusical research   The study of music in the brain by means of neuroimaging techniques such **PET** or **fMRI**.

neurotransmitter   A **biochemical** that enhances message transmission among brain cells through excitation or inhibition.

neutrophils and lymphocytes   (see under **biochemical**)

niche hypothesis   An idea developed by Bernie Krause that each species occupies an acoustical niche in its habitat so that its sounds can be heard by other members of the species.

noise-induced hearing loss (NIHL)   Loss of hearing based on exposure to loud sounds (which can include music).

norepinephrine   (see under **biochemical**)
nucleus accumbens   A group of brain cells located in the **limbic system** that are involved in reward and pleasure.

O

operant conditioning   Skinnerian **behaviorism** in which the focus is on consequences to voluntary actions. A person "operates" on the environment and the consequences of that action make it more likely to occur or not.
opiate receptor   A type of protein in the brain that is activated in the presence of drugs.
orbicularis oculi   The muscle that closes the eyelids.
orbitofrontal cortex   A portion of the prefrontal cortex located just above the eyes that is involved in decision-making, emotion, and reward.
organ of Corti   A structure resting on the **basilar membrane** in the **cochlea** that houses **inner** and **outer hair cells**.
oscine songbird   A suborder of approximately 4,000 birds that includes all songbirds.
ossicles   The three small bones in the middle ear; the **hammer**, **anvil**, and **stirrup**.
otoacoustic emissions (OAE)   Sounds emitted by **outer hair cells** in the **cochlea** that are recorded as acoustic vibrations in the ear canal.
outer hair cells   (see **auditory hair cells**)
oval window   The membrane that transmits vibrations from the b to the fluid of the **cochlea**.
overtone   Beginning with the second **harmonic**, partials of a complex tone higher than the **fundamental**.
oximeter   Medical device the monitors the amount of oxygen in the blood.
oxytocin   (see under **biochemical**)

P

parasympatheic nervous system   (see **autonomic nervous system**)
partial (harmonic)   The components of a complex tone.
peak experience   In **Humanistic psychology**, a special intrinsic experience that is transcendent, blissful; such a mountain-top experience is especially memorable and plays a critical role in self-actualization.
perception   A midpoint between **sensation** and **cognition**; early stage processing of sensory information. In music, perception includes processing basic elements such as identifying the timbre of an instrument.
performing arts medicine   The treatment of performance-related injuries by specially trained physicians and health care professionals. Normally organized into hearing, vocal, bodily, and psychosocial health categories.
period   The time it takes to complete one waveform cycle.
periodic motion   In acoustics, regularity of molecular motion in sustained sound. Random, or aperiodic, motion creates noise.
periodicity theory (temporal theory)   Pitch perceived on the basis of perceptual grouping of upper partials of a complex tone.
person-centered approach   Therapeutic approach developed by Carl Rogers. Therapists show unconditional positive regard to their patients and use a non-directive approach to aid them in solving their own problems.

physiological response   Covert bodily responses such as heart rate or blood pressure.

pilomotor reflex   Goosebumps.

pinna   The outer ear shell.

pitch or pitch height   a psychological or subjective perception of the "highness" or "lowness" of sound, primarily based on frequency, but also on amplitude, waveform, and time.

pitch chroma (pitch class)   Octave equivalence; that quality shared by all Cs, all C♯s, and so on.

pitch proximity   In the **implication-realization model**, the notion that listeners expect the next pitch in a sequence to be nearby, a small interval.

pitch reversal   (see **gap-fill melody**)

pituitary   The master gland, located at the bottom of the **hypothalamus** in the base of the brain; secretes hormones necessary for **homeostasis**.

place theory   Perception of pitch is based on vibrating points along the **basilar membrane**.

planum temporale   The region of the brain just behind the **auditory cortex**, important in both language and music processing. In most individuals, the left planum temporale is significantly larger than the right planum temporale.

plethysmograph   Medical device used to measure the volume of blood or air (respiratory inductive plethysmograph) within the body.

positive reinforcement   In **behaviorism**, the addition of something pleasant following a behavior.

positron emission tomography (PET)   Identification of metabolic activity or blood flow in the brain. Provides good data on function, but is not so well suited for location.

precentral gyrus   The frontal lobe convolution in the brain that contains the primary motor cortex.

preference for prototype theory (PPT)   We tend to enjoy listening to music that matches schemas or prototypes previously developed.

premotor cortex   Lies in front of the motor cortex; involved in planning and execution of actions. "Dorsal" indicates the front part of the premotor cortex.

pre-operational stage   In Jean Piaget's **developmental psychology**, the period from ages two to seven characterized by rapidly increasing vocabulary.

presbycousis   The natural process of hearing loss due to aging.

prima donna   Literally "first lady"; honorific given to the leading female singer in an opera.

procedural memory   Memory for how to perform a specific skill, such as how to play a D Major scale on the piano.

probe-tone technique   A technique used by Carol Krumhansl and others to determine **tonal hierarchies**. In one version, ascending and descending major scales are played with the final tone missing. Listeners rate how well each of the twelve chromatic tones (the probe tones) complete the scale.

Project Zero   A research project at Harvard University devoted to understanding and promoting thinking and creativity in the arts.

prolactin   (see under **biochemical**)

prosody   Quasi-musical aspects of speech, such as the timbre of the voice, rhythmicity in speaking, vocal inflections, and so on.

proximity   In Gestalt psychology, one of the corollaries of the **Law of Prägnanz** recognizing that psychologically we tend to organize objects (including sounds) that are closer together as a unit.

psychoacoustics   The study of how we perceive sounds subjectively.

psychoanalysis   Technique developed by Freud for gaining access to the unconscious mind.

psychodrama   Therapeutic technique where persons can explore issues by acting out scenarios.

psychoeducation session   Learning experiences for persons with psychological disturbances that offer them insights into their illness.

psychogalvanometer   (see **skin conductance response**)

psychological androgyny   Male musicians are more sensitive than nonmusician males; a presumed female trait. Female musicians are more self-sufficient than nonmusician females; a presumed male trait. Successful male and female musicians are often strong and independent, yet sensitive and intuitive.

psychoneuroimmunology (PNI)   The study of interactions among the mind—brain—immune systems.

psychophysiological response   A combination of physiological (i.e., covert) and physical (i.e., overt) bodily responses.

punishment   In **behaviorism**, the removal of a pleasant consequence or the presentation of an unpleasant consequence following a behavior.

pure tone   see **sine wave**

Pythagorean scale   A musical scale based on 3:2 ratios (perfect fifths).

qualia   David Huron's term for subjective descriptors of scale degrees.

R

rarefaction   In acoustics, rarefaction occurs when molecules of the medium of transmission rebound from a compression and are pulled apart (see **compression**).

referentialism, referentialists   A philosophical position in which the meaning and value of music is found in things the music refers to outside itself.

reflection   In acoustics, when a sound wave encounters a barrier, energy that is not transmitted through the barrier or absorbed into it bounces off or is reflected.

reflective thinking   Learning activity in which the person engages in self-observation and introspection.

refraction   In acoustics, the direction and speed of a sound wave can change as it encounters a different medium.

relative pitch   Identification of a tone based on its relationship to a known reference tone.

release   In acoustics, the last portion of a tone as the sound ceases after the note is released (see **ADSR**).

repressed memory   In **psychoanalysis**, a significant memory that is unable to be consciously recalled.

residue pitch (also subjective or virtual pitch)   Apparent pitch perceived on the basis of perceptual grouping of upper partials of a complex tone even in the absence of a fundamental.

resonance region   The portion along the basilar membrane that is set into vibration by incoming energy.

respiratory inductive plethysmograph   (see **plethysomograph**)

reticular formation (reticular activating system)   A part of the brain located in the core of the **brainstem** that filters incoming sensory information.

rhythmic auditory stimulation   A major technique used in **neurologic music therapy** in which body movements are **entrained** to musical rhythms.

Rolfing Structural Integration   A form of bodywork that reorganizes connective tissues the body, enhancing and proving posture and movement.

round window   A membrane in the cochlea that releases pressure from the **cochlea** into the air cavity of the middle ear, eventually released into the atmosphere through the **Eustachian tube**.

S

saccade   In textual or music reading, a saccade describes eye movement; a progressive saccade is movement from left to right and a regressive saccade is from right to left (see **fixation**).

scaffolding   Second stage of Charles Byrne's four-stage model in which the teacher organizes a complex learning task and guides the student step-by-step through a series of smaller, more manageable units.

schema (pl. schemata)   A mental construct or knowledge structure that alters as we learn and gain experience.

secretory imunoglobulin (SIgA)   (see under **biochemical**)

sedative music   A type of music, often used in music therapy, characterized by slow, soft, *legato* passages with narrow pitch ranges and predictable changes (see **stimulative**).

self-actualization   In **humanistic psychology**, a state of being when a person become fully who he or she is meant to be; realization of full human potential.

self-efficacy   Belief concerning whether one can perform a task with competence.

self-regulation   The ability to determine and monitor progress toward self-determined, personal goals.

semicircular canals   Organ of balance located inside the ear; not involved in hearing.

sensation   First awareness of sensory input; precedes **perception** and **cognition**.

sensorimotor cortex   Parallel regions of the brain, one monitoring kinesthetic input, the other controlling motor output.

sensorimotor stage   In Piaget's developmental psychology, the period from birth to two years characterized by learning through direct sensory experiences and physical movement.

sentograph   Device invented by Manfred Clynes that allows for the expression of musical (or other) emotions through touch.

Sephardi   Jews primarily from the Iberian peninsula, also Persia and India.

serotonin   (see under **biochemical**)

shaping   In **behaviorism**, gradually modifying behavior toward a desired outcome.

Shepard Tone   Complex tone created by ten pure tones each spaced an octave apart, with the middle tone having the greatest amplitude.

similarity   In **Gestalt psychology**, one of the corollaries of the **Law of Prägnanz** recognizing that psychologically we tend to organize objects (including sounds) that are similar as a unit.

simplicity   In **Gestalt psychology**, one of the corollaries of the **Law of Prägnanz** recognizing that psychologically we tend to organize objects (including sounds) into their simplest form.

sine wave   In acoustics, a pure tone consisting of only one frequency.

skin conductance response (electrodermal response or galvanic skin response)   Temporary fluctuation of electrical resistance of the skin; measured by a psychogalvanometer.

social cognitive theory   Three-part model developed by Albert Bandura wherein behavior, cognition and other personal factors, and environmental influences interact with and influence each other.

social constructivism   The idea that individuals construct knowledge on the basis of interactions with the environment.

social identity theory (SIT)   People develop social identities as well as personal identities.

social psychology   A psychological viewpoint dealing with how people grow, develop, learn, and interact in the societies in which they live.

somatosensory cortex   The "sensori" portion of the **sensorimotor cortex**; monitors sense of touch, including sensitivity to pain, temperature, and body position.

sound wave   Propogation of acoustical energy through a medium such as air.

spectral pitch   The perceived pitch of a **sine wave** or pure tone.

spectrogram   In acoustics, a visual image of acoustical energy across time.

sphygmomanometer   A medical device used to measure blood pressure.

spiral curriculum   A concept developed by Jerome Bruner in which basic elements of a subject matter are taught in sequential fashion at ever-higher levels of sophistication.

standardized test   A test designed, administered, scored, and interpreted in a consistent manner. Normally, standardized tests are published and include reliability (i.e., consistency) and validity (i.e., well founded and appropriate) figures.

state anxiety   The degree of anxiousness experienced in a given situation (see **trait anxiety**).

statistical learning   The notion that we learn many things by the frequency of their occurrence.

stimulative music   A type of music, often used in music therapy, characterized by fast, rhythmic, loud, *staccato* passages with wide pitch ranges and abrupt, unpredictable changes (see **sedative music**).

stirrup (stapes)   The third of three small bones (**ossicles**) in the middle ear that convey energy from the ear drum to the **cochlea**. The footplate of the stirrup pushes on the **oval window** in the cochlea.

string theory   A core idea in quantum physics that the smallest particles in the universe are made of loops of vibrating strings.

Strong Experiences in Music   A research project by Alf Gabrielsson in which participants are asked to write about their strongest, most intense experience with music they have ever had.

structural-functional model   The idea that the frequent occurrence of specific pitches such as the notes of a tonic triad provides clues to the key.

subcortical   That portion of the brain lying underneath the **cerebral cortex**.

subjective pitch   (see **residue pitch**)

subjective rhythmization   When listeners organize a series of unstressed taps into duple or triple patterns.

substantia nigra   A structure in the **midbrain** that plays a role in reward and movement.

successive approximation   In **behaviorism**, moving toward the desired behavior in smaller steps or stages.

superconducting quantum interference device (SQUID)   A device that detects minute changes in magnetic fields in the brain.

superior olivary complex   Located in the **brainstem**, this small mass forms part of the **auditory cortex**; it is involved in sound localization. In addition, it receives information from both ears and eyes.

superior parietal cortex   Upper part of the **parietal lobe**; involved in sensory integration.

superior temporal gyrus   Upper part of the temporal lobe; location of primary and secondary **auditory cortices**.

supplementary motor area (SMA)   A part of the motor cortex involved in planning motor actions under internal control (i.e., memorized sequences such as musical performance).

survival of the fittest   (see **natural selection**)

362

sustain   In acoustics, the third portion of a tone; the relatively more constant middle portion of a tone (see **ADSR**).

Sylvian fissure   The cleft or groove dividing the temporal lobe (below) from the frontal lobe (above).

symbolic mode   In Jerome Bruner's theory of instruction, knowledge expressed abstractly, primarily through language.

sympathetic nervous system   (see **autonomic nervous system**)

synapse   The small-gap juncture of communicating neurons.

T

tabula rasa   Literally "blank slate;" the concept of the mind as empty prior to receiving information from the environment.

task analysis   In behavioral psychology, a complex task is divided into a series of simpler behaviors.

Taxonomy of Educational Objectives   Developed by Benjamin Bloom and colleagues, who created a hierarchical structure of knowledge divided into cognitive, psychomotor, and affective domains.

temporal theory   (see **periodicity theory**)

testosterone   (see under **biochemical**)

thalamus   Situated at the top of the **brainstem**, the thalamus relays sensory information to the **cerebral cortex**.

third force psychology   Abraham Maslow referred to **humanistic psychology** as a third alternative to Freudian psychotherapy and **behaviorism**.

thoracic outlet syndrome   Compression of nerves as they pass between the rib cage and the collar bone causes pain in the neck and shoulder, weakness or numbness in fingers.

thrills   (see **chills**)

timbre   In acoustics, the perceptual aspect of sound sometimes known as tone color, based primarily on waveform, but also on frequency, amplitude, and time.

T lymphocytes (CD4+, CD8+, CD16+)   (see under **biochemical**)

tonal hierarchies   How pitches and keys are arranged in hierarchical importance.

tonal pitch space theory   Fred Lerdahl's conception of music as occupying multidimensional space.

tone language   A language in which different meanings are given to the same syllable based on tonal inflection.

tonotopical organization   Maintenance of frequency representation or spatial arrangement throughout portions of the auditory pathway.

trait anxiety   Long-term or stable aspects of anxiety in the personality (see **state anxiety**).

transcranial magnetic stimulation (TMS)   Functional mapping of the brain by means of a temporary disruption of neural transmissions.

transmission   In acoustics, the propagation of a sound wave through a medium such as air.

transverse waves   In acoustics, sound waves that travel in a perpendicular direction to the vibratory disturbance, such as the waves transmitted by a violin string (see **longitudinal waves**).

U

ulnar neuropathy   Compression of the nerve in the elbow leading to tingling or numbness in the outside of the hand or little finger.

ultradian rhythm   Periodical cycle with a time span shorter than 24 hours, such as sleep cycles.

unconscious mind   Memories, thoughts, and feelings that are not available to the conscious mind.

V

valence   Positive or negative emotional value.

ventral cochlear nucleus   (see **cochlear nucleus**)

ventral striatum   (see **neostriatum**)

ventromedial prefrontal cortex   A portion of the prefrontal cortex involved in decision making.

Vierordt's Law   Karl von Vierordt's notion of time perception. We are likely to overestimate short intervals and underestimate long intervals.

volley theory   When **auditory hair cells** reach their maximum firing rates they combine their firing rates.

volume   In **psychoacoustics**, the impression that some tones appear to occupy more space (i.e., a tuba) than others (e.g., a piccolo). This is a psychological or perceptual phenomenon, not a physical one.

W

wavelength   In acoustics, the physical distance a sound wave travels in one cycle.

Wernicke's area   Area of the brain involved in understanding written and spoken language.

white matter   When axons are **myelinated** they turn white. White matter is the inner core of the brain where different regions of the cortex are connected in neural networks.

Williams Syndrome   A genetic disorder that leads to mental asymmetry; that is, individuals normally fare better with language and music than with mathematics and spatial tasks.

X

Y

Z

zone of proximal development (ZPD)   Lev Vygotsky's conception of the distance between a person's capacity to solve a problem independently and the capacity to solve it with assistance.

zygomaticus muscle   The "smile" muscle.

Illustration Credits

CHAPTER 1

Figure 1.1 CC BY-SA 4.0 /Flickr
Figure 1.2 Adapted from Eagle, 1996

CHAPTER 2

Figure 2.3a CC BY-SA 3.0 / Chris 73
Figure 2.3b CC BY-SA 3.0 / Alvesgaspar (derivative work: RDBury)
Figure 2.3c CC BY 2.0 / Steve Swayne

CHAPTER 3

Figure 3.1a NAS/NASA/CXC/M. Weiss.
Figure 3.3 Bernie Krause
Figure 3.5a CC BY 2.0 / anja_johnson

CHAPTER 4

Figure 4.3 CC BY-SA 2.5 / José-Manuel Benito Álvarez
Figure 4.7 Don Hodges
Figure 4.9 Powers, 1990

CHAPTER 5

Figure 5.1–5.5 David Sebald
Figure 5.6 CC BY-SA 3.0 / Oarih
Figure 5.7–5.17 David Sebald
Figure 5.18 CC BY-SA3.0 / Alexander Kershchofer (alias Multimann)
Figure 5.19 National Cancer Institute
Figure 5.22 Don Hodges

Figure 5.23 Don Hodges
Figure 5.24 Adapted from Hall, 2002
Figure 5.25 CC BY-SA 3.0 / Andreas Praefcke
Table 5.1 Lide, 2008, pp. 14–44

CHAPTER 6

Figure 6.1 CC BY-SA 3.0 / Welleschik
Figure 6.2 Don Hodges
Figure 6.3 Don Hodges
Figure 6.4 David Furness
Figure 6.5 Don Hodges
Figure 6.6 CC BY-SA 2.5 /Lars Chittka and Axel Brockmann

CHAPTER 7

Figure 7.1 David M. Lipscomb, University of Tennessee Department of Audiology
and Speech Pathology Noise Research Laboratory.
Figure 7.2–7.7 David Sebald
Figure 7.9 Olson, 1940, p. 322

CHAPTER 8

Figure 8.1 CC BY-SA 4.0 / Irenegarcia98
Figure 8.2 Don Hodges
Figure 8.3 Joe Stuessy
Figure 8.4–8.9 Don Hodges
Figure 8.11–8.14 Don Hodges
Figure 8.18 CC BY 2.0 public domain

CHAPTER 9

Figure 9.1 Don Hodges
Figure 9.2 CC BY-SA 3.0 / WillowW
Figure 9.3 CC BY-SA 4.0 / BruceBlaus
Figure 9.5 Leslie Johnson
Figure 9.6 CC BY-SA 4.0 / Alex Brandmeyer, Makiko Sadakata,
Loukianos Spyrou, James M. McQueen, and Peter Desain
Figure 9.7–9.8 Don Hodges
Figure 9.9 CC BY-SA 3.0 / Thomas Schultz
Figure 9.10–9.11 Don Hodges

CHAPTER 10

Figure 10.1 Ralph Spintge

CHAPTER 11

Figure 11.3 CC BY-SA 3.0 / OpenStax College
Figure 11.4 David Sebald
Figure 11.5 From *American Journal of Psychology*. Copyright 1936 by the Board
    of Trustees of the University of Illinois. Used with permission of the
    University of Illinois Press.
Figure 11.6 From *American Journal of Psychology*. Copyright 1936 by the Board
    of Trustees of the University of Illinois. Used with permission of the
    University of Illinois Press.
Figure 11.7–11.8 Don Hodges
Figure 11.9 Sandra Teglas
Figure 11.10 Brandy Santee
Figure 11.11–11.12 Don Hodges

CHAPTER 12

Figure 12.1c CC BY 2.0 / Paulo O
Figure 12.1d CC BY 2.0 / Tim Evanson
Figure 12.2 CC BY 2.0 / Genomics Education Programme
Figure 12.3–12.5 Sandra Teglas
Figure 12.6 CC BY 2.0 / The United States Army Band

CHAPTER 13

Figure 13.1 Don Hodges
Figure 13.2 CC BY 3.0 / OpenStax College
Figure 13.3 Sandra Teglas
Figure 13.4 Gladys Rolan-de-Moras
Figure 13.5b CC BY 2.0 / Heinrich Klaffs
Figure 13.6 Sandra Teglas
Figure 13.7 Peter Webster; used by permission

CHAPTER 14

Figure 14.1 Don Hodges
Figure 14.3b CC BY 3.0 / Silly Rabiit
Figure 14.4 Don Hodges
Figure 14.5 CC BY 3.0 / Waterlilly16
Figure 14.6 Don Hodges
Figure 14.7a CC BY-SA 3.0 / The Vygotsky Project
Figure 14.8–14.10 Don Hodges

CHAPTER 15

Figure 15.1 Newborn in NICU: CC by 2.0 / Topato
Figure 15.4 Ralph Spintge. Used by permission.
Figure 15.5 Ralph Spintge. Used by permission.
Figure 15.6 Sandra Teglas.
Figure 15.7 CC BY-SA 3.0 / Welleschik
Figure 15.9 Adapted from Williamon, Aufegger, & Eiholzer 2014; © Aaron
       Williamon, used by permission.

CHAPTER 16

Figure 16.1a Sandra Teglas
Figure 16.2 CC BY-SA 2.0 / Basher Eyre/Alberts Music Shop in Chersey Road
Figure 16.4 Don Hodges
Figure 16.7 David Sebald
Figure 16.8 Don Hodges
Figure 16.10 CC BY-SA 4.0 / Katiefelix2015

References

Aarden, B. (2003). *Dynamic melodic expectancy* (PhD dissertation). Ohio State University. Full text Retrieved from http://etd.ohiolink.edu/view.cgi?acc_num=osu1060969388

Abel, J., & Larkin, K. (1990). Anticipation of performance among musicians: Physiological arousal, confidence, and state anxiety. *Psychology of Music, 18*, 171–182.

Abeles, H. (2009). Are musical instrument gender associations changing? *Journal of Research in Music Education, 57*(2), 127–139.

Abeles, H., & Chung, J. (1996). Responses to music. In D. Hodges (Ed.), *Handbook of music psychology* (pp. 285–342). San Antonio, TX: IMR Press.

Abeles, H., & Porter, S. (1978). The sex-stereotyping of musical instruments. *Journal of Research in Music Education, 26*, 65–75.

Abell, A. (1987). *Talks with great composers*. New York, NY: Philosophical Library.

Abréu-Ramos, A., & Micheo, W. (2007). Lifetime prevalence of upper-body musculoskeletal problems in a professional-level symphony orchestra. *Medical Problems of Performing Artists, 22*(3), 97–104.

Ackerman, D. (1995). *A natural history of the history of the senses*. New York, NY: Vintage Books.

Adachi, M., Trehub, S., & Abe, J-I. (2004). Perceiving emotion in children's songs across age and culture. *Japanese Psychological Research, 46*(4), 322–336.

Addis, L. (1999). *Of music and mind*. Cornell, NY: Cornell University Press.

Ahmed, L. (2000). *A border passage: From Cairo to America—a woman's journey*. New York, NY: Penguin Books.

Aho, M. (2009). Gestures in vocal performance and the experience of the listener: A case study of extra-semantic meaning-making in the singing of Olavi Virta. *Popular Music, 28*(1), 33–51.

Aiello, R. (2007). *Music: Cognition and emotions*. New York, NY: Oxford University Press.

Aiello, R., & Sloboda, J. (Eds.). (1994). *Musical perceptions*. Oxford: Oxford University Press.

Aiello, R., & Williamon, A. (2002). Memory. In R. Parncutt & G. McPherson (Eds.), *The science and psychology of music performance* (pp. 167–181). New York, NY: Oxford University Press.

Albert, M. (1998). Treatment of aphasia. *Archives of Neurology, 55*(11), 1417–1420.

Albert, N., Robertson, E., & Miall, C. (2009). The resting human brain and motor learning. *Current Biology, 19*(12), 1023–1027.

Alcock, K., Wade, D., Anslow, P., & Pàssingham, R. (2000). Pitch and timing abilities in adult left-hemisphere-dysphasic and right-hemisphere-damaged subjects. *Brain and Language, 75*(1), 47–65.

Alexander, C. (1954). The longevity of scientists. *Journal of Social Psychology, 39*, 299–302.

Alexander, F. (1990). *The Alexander technique*. New York, NY: Carol Publishing.

Alexander, S. (2016). *The jazz of physics*. New York, NY: Basic Books.

Alexjander, S. (2007). *Our sound universe: The music of Susan Alexjander*. Retrieved September 1, 2009, from www.oursounduniverse.com/music_samples.html

Allan, D. *Peak performance for musicians*. Retrieved from www.musicpeakperformance.com

Allingham, R. (1999). South Africa—popular music: Nation of voice. In M. Ellingham, O. Duane, & V. Dowell (Eds.), *World music: The rough guide. Vol. 1: Africa, Europe and the middle east* (pp. 638–657). London: Rough Guides.

Allman, W. (1994). *The stone age present*. New York, NY: Simon & Schuster.

Altenmüller, E. (2006). The end of the song? Robert Schumann's focal dystonia. In E. Altenmüller, M. Wiesendanger, & J. Kesselring (Eds.), *Music, motor control, and the brain* (pp. 251–263). Oxford: Oxford University Press.

Altenmüller, E. (2010). Focal dystonia in musicians: Phenomenology, pathophysiology, triggering factors, and treatment. *Medical Problems of Performing Artists, 25*(1), 3–9.

Altenmüller, E., Furuya, S., Scholz, D., & Ioannou, C. (2019). Brain research in music performance. In M. Thaut & D. Hodges (Eds.), *The Oxford handbook on music and the brain* (pp. 459–486). Oxford: Oxford University Press.

Altenmüller, E., Gruhn, W., Parlitz, D., & Liebert, G. (2000). The impact of music education on brain networks: Evidence from EEG-studies. *International Journal of Music Education, 35*, 47–53.

Altenmüller, E., Ioannou, I., & Lee, A. (2015). Apollo's curse: Neurological causes of motor impairments in musicians. *Progress in Brain Research, 217*, 89–106.

Altenmüller, E., & McPherson, G. (2007). Motor learning and instrumental training. In W. Gruhn & F. Rauscher (Eds.), *Neurosciences and music pedagogy* (pp. 121–142). New York, NY: Nova Science Publishers.

Altenmüller, E., Wiesendanger, M., & Kesselring, J. (2006). *Music, motor control, and the brain*. Oxford: Oxford University Press.

Altschuler, R., Bobbin, R., Clopton, B., & Hoffman, D. (1991). *Neurobiology of hearing: The central auditory system*. New York, NY: Raven Press.

American Music Therapy Association. (2018). *What is music therapy?* Retrieved December 26, 2018, from www.musictherapy.org.

Amon, S., Shapsa, A., Forman, L., Regev, R., Bauer, S., Litmanovitz, I., & Dolfin, T. (2006). Live music is beneficial to preterm infants in the neonatal intensive care unit environment. *Birth, 33*(2), 131–136.

Anderson, L., & Krathwohl, D. (Eds.). (2001). *A taxonomy for learning, teaching, and assessing: A revision of Bloom's taxonomy of educational objectives, complete edition*. Upper Saddle River, NJ: Allyn & Bacon.

Andreassi, J. (2007). *Psychophysiology: Human behavior & physiological response* (5th ed.). Mahwah, NJ: Lawrence Erlbaum Associates.

Andress, B. (1986). Toward an integrated developmental theory for early childhood music. *Bulletin of the Council for Research in Music Education, 86*, 10–17.

Andrews, E. (1997). *Healthy practice for musicians*. London: Rheingold.

Andrews, F., & Diehl, N. (1970). Development of a technique for identifying elementary school children's musical concepts. *Journal of Research in Music Education, 18*, 214–222.

Annals of the New York Academy of Sciences. (2018). Neurosciences and music VI: Music, sound and health. *Annals of the New York Academy of Sciences, 1423*.

Applegate, C., & Potter, P. (2002). *Music and German national identity*. Chicago: University of Chicago Press.

Aramaki, M., Baillères, H., Brancheriau, L., Kronland-Martinet, R., & Ystad, S. (2007). Sound quality assessment of wood for xylophone bars. *The Journal of the Acoustical Society of America, 121*(4), 2407–2420.

Araújo, M. V., & Hein, C. F. (2018). A survey to investigate advanced musicians' flow disposition in individual music practice. *International Journal of Music Education*. doi.org/10.1177/0255761418814563

Ashley, R. (2008, August 25–29). *Affective and perceptual responses to very brief musical stimuli*. Paper presented at the International Conference on Music Perception and Cognition. Sapporo, Japan.

Ashley, R. (2016). Musical improvisation. In S. Hallam, I. Cross, & M. Thaut (Eds.), *The Oxford handbook of music psychology* (2nd ed., pp. 667–679). Oxford: Oxford University Press.

Ashley, R., & Timmers, R. (2017). *The Routledge companion to music cognition*. New York, NY: Routledge.

Ashton, A. (2003). *Harmonograph: A visual guide to the mathematics of music*. New York, NY: Walker.

Aslin, R., Jusczyk, P., & Pisoni, D. (1998). Speech and auditory processing during infancy: Constraints on and precursors to language. In E. Kuhn & S. Siegler (Eds.), *Handbook of child psychology* (Vol. 2, 5th ed., pp. 147–198). New York, NY: John Wiley & Sons.

References

Athos, E., Levinson, B., Kistler, A., Zemansky, J., Bostrorn, A., Freimer, N., & Gitschier, J. (2007). Dichotomy and perceptual distortions in absolute pitch ability. *PNAS (Proceedings of the National Academy of Sciences), 104*(37), 14795–14800.

Atik, Y. (1994). The conductor and the orchestra: Interactive aspects of the leadership process. *Leadership & Organization Development Journal, 15*(1), 22–28.

Atkins, P., & Schubert, E. (2014). Are spiritual experiences through music seen as intrinsic or extrinsic? *Religions, 5*(1), 76–89.

Aubert, M. (2012). A review of rock art dating in the Kimberley, Western Australia. *Journal of Archaeological Science, 39*(3), 573–577.

Aubert, M., Brumm, A., Ramli, M., Sutikna, T., Saptomo, E. W., Hakim, B., . . . Dosseto, A. (2014). Pleistocene cave art from Sulawesi, Indonesia. *Nature, 514*(7521), 223.

Aubry, T., Bradley, B., Almeida, M., Walter, B., Neves, M., Pelegrin, J., . . . Tiffagom, M. (2008). Solutrean laurel leaf production at Maitreaux: An experimental approach guided by techno-economic analysis. *World Archaeology, 40*(1), 48–66.

Austin, J., & Berg, M. (2006). Exploring music practice among sixth-grade band and orchestra students. *Psychology of Music, 34*(4), 535–558.

Ausubel, D. (1960). The use of advance organizers in the learning and retention of meaningful verbal material. *Journal of Educational Psychology, 51*(1), 267–272.

Avanzini, G., Faienza, C., Minciacchi, D., Lopez, L., & Majno, M. (Eds.). (2003). The neurosciences and music: Mutual interactions and implications on developmental function. *Annals of the New York Academy of Sciences, 999*.

Avanzini, G., Lopez, L., Koelsch, S., & Majno, M. (Eds.). (2005). The neurosciences and music II: From perception to performance. *Annals of the New York Academy of Sciences, 1060*.

Ayotte, J., Peretz, I., & Hyde, K. (2002). Congenital amusia. *Brain, 125*(2), 238–251.

Azzara, C. (1992). Audition-based improvisation techniques and elementary instrumental students' music achievement. *Journal of Research in Music Education, 41*(4), 328–342.

Babbitt, M. (1958). Who cares if you listen? *High Fidelity, 8*(2), 38–40, 126–127.

Backus, J. (1977). *The acoustical foundations of music* (2nd ed.). New York, NY: W. W. Norton.

Baddeley, A. (2003). Working memory: Looking back and looking forward. *Nature Reviews Neuroscience, 4*, 829–839.

Baddeley, A. (2012). Working memory: Theories, models, and controversies. *Annual Review of Psychology, 63*, 1–29.

Bader, R. (2013). *Nonlinearities and synchronization in musical acoustics and music psychology*. Heidelberg: Springer.

Bae, Y. (2001). *The distribution, construction, tuning, and performance technique of the African log xylophone* (Doctoral dissertation). The Ohio State University. Retrieved from https://etd.ohiolink.edu/!etd.send_file?accession=osu148639784122017&disposition=inline

Baharloo, S., Johnston, P., Service, S., Gitschier, J., & Freimer, N. (1998). Absolute pitch: An approach for identification of genetic and nongenetic components. *American Journal of Human Genetics, 62*, 224–231.

Baharloo, S., Service, S., & Risch, N. (2000). Familial aggregation of absolute pitch. *American Journal of Human Genetics, 67*(3), 755–758.

Bahat, A. (1980). The musical traditions of the oriental Jews. *The World of Music, 22*(2), 46–55.

Bakan, M. (2018). *Speaking for ourselves: Conversations on life, music, and autism*. Oxford: Oxford University Press.

Balaban, M., Anderson, L., & Wisniewski, A. (1998). Lateral asymmetries in infant melody perception. *Developmental Psychology, 34*(1), 39–48.

Balaban, M., Ebcioglu, K., & Laske, O. (2004). *Understanding music with AI: Perspectives on music cognition*. Menlo Park, CA: AAAI Press.

Balbag, M. A., Pedersen, N. L., & Gatz, M. (2014). Playing a musical instrument as a protective factor against dementia and cognitive impairment: A population-based twin study. *International Journal of Alzheimer's Disease, 2014*, 1–6.

Balkwill, L-L., & Thompson, W. (1999). A cross-cultural investigation of the perception of emotions in music: Psychophysical and cultural cues. *Music Perception, 17*, 43–64.

Balkwill, L-L., Thompson, W., & Matsunaga, R. (2004). Recognition of emotion in Japanese, Western, and Hindustani music by Japanese listeners. *Japanese Psychological Research, 46*(4), 337–349.

Ball, P. (2010). *The music instinct: How music works and why we can't do without it.* Oxford: Oxford University Press.

Ballantine, C. (1984). *Music and its social meanings.* New York, NY: Gordon and Breach.

Bally, K., Campbell, D., Chesnick, K., & Tranmer, J. (2003). Effects of patient-controlled music therapy during coronary angiography on procedural pain and anxiety distress syndrome. *Critical Care Nurse, 23*(2), 50–58.

Balter, M. (2004). Evolution of behavior: Seeking the key to music. *Science, 306*, 1120–1122.

Balter, M. (2009a). Early start for human art? Ochre may revise timeline. *Science, 323*, 569.

Balter, M. (2009b). On the origins of art and symbolism. *Science, 323*, 709–711.

Baltes, F., Avram, J., Miclea, M., & Miu, A. (2011). Emotions induced by operatic music: Psychophysiological effects of music, plot, and acting: A scientist's tribute to Maria Callas. *Brain and Cognition, 76*, 146–157.

Bamberger, J. (1991). *The mind behind the musical ear.* Cambridge, MA: Harvard University Press.

Bamberger, J. (2013). *Discovering the musical mind.* Oxford: Oxford University Press.

Bandura, A. (1977). *Social learning theory.* Englewood Cliffs, NJ: Prentice-Hall.

Bandura, A. (1989). Social cognitive theory. In R. Vasta (Ed.), *Annals of child development. Vol. 6. Six theories of child development* (pp. 1–60). Greenwich, CT: JAI Press.

Bangert, M. (2006). Brain activation during piano playing. In E. Altenmüller, M. Wiesendanger, & J. Kesselring (Eds.), *Music, motor control, and the brain* (pp. 173–188). Oxford: Oxford University Press.

Bangert, M., & Altenmüller, E. (2003). Mapping perception to action in piano practice: A longitudinal DC-EEG study. *BMC Neuroscience, 4*(26), 1–14.

Bangert, M., & Schlaug, G. (2006). Specialization of the specialized in features of external human brain morphology. *European Journal of Neuroscience, 24*, 1832–1834.

Bangert, M., Peschel, T., Schlaug, G., Rotte, M., Drescher, D., Hinrichs, H., . . . Altenmüller, E. (2006). Shared networks for auditory and motor processing in professional pianists: Evidence from fMRI conjunction. *NeuroImage, 30*, 917–926.

Bannan, N. (2012). *Music, language, and human evolution.* Oxford: Oxford University Press.

Baptiste, R. (2007). *William L. Dawson and the Negro folk symphony: Rediscovering the missing link from Africa to America.* Paper presented at the Annual Meeting of the Association for the Study of African American Life and History, Atlanta Hilton, Charlotte, NC. Retrieved September 1, 2009, from www.allacademic.com/meta/p207125_index.html

Barbero, F., Thomas, J., Bonelli, S., Balletto, E., & Schönrogge, K. (2009). Queen ants make distinctive sounds that are mimicked by a butterfly social parasite. *Science, 323*, 782–785.

Barbey, A. (2018). Network neuroscience theory of human intelligence. *Trends in Cognitive Sciences, 22*(1), 8–20.

Barbot, B., & Lubart, T. (2012). Creative thinking in music: Its nature and assessment through musical exploratory behaviors. *Psychology of Aesthetics, Creativity, and the Arts, 6*(3), 231.

Barbour, J. M. (1951). *Tuning and temperament: A historical survey.* East Lansing, MI: Michigan State College Press.

Barrett, J., & Webster, P. (2014). *The musical experience: Rethinking music teaching and learning.* New York, NY: Oxford University Press.

Barrett, M. (Ed.). (2011). *A cultural psychology of music education.* Oxford: Oxford University Press.

Barry, N. (1992). The effects of practice strategies, individual differences in cognitive style, and gender upon technical accuracy and musicality of student instrumental performance. *Psychology of Music, 20*(2), 112–123.

Barry, N., & Hallam, S. (2002). Practice. In R. Parncutt & G. McPherson (Eds.), *The science and psychology of music performance* (pp. 151–165). New York, NY: Oxford University Press.

Barry, N., & McArthur, V. (1994). Teaching practice strategies in the music studio: A survey of applied music teachers. *Psychology of Music, 22*(1), 44–55.

References

Bartholomew, E. F. (1899). *Relation of psychology to music*. Rock Island, RI: New Era Publishing.

Bartholomew, E. F. (1902). *Relation of psychology to music* (2nd ed.). Rock Island, RI: New Era Publishing.

Bartholomew, W. (1942). *Acoustics of music*. New York, NY: Prentice Hall.

Bartholomew, W. (1990). *Fundamentals of musical acoustics* (2nd Rev. ed.). New York, NY: Dover.

Bartlett, D. (1996a). Physiological responses to music and sound stimuli. In D. Hodges (Ed.), *Handbook of music psychology* (2nd ed., pp. 343–385). San Antonio, TX: IMR Press.

Bartlett, D. (1996b). Tonal and musical memory. In D. Hodges (Ed.), *Handbook of music psychology* (2nd ed., pp. 177–195). San Antonio, TX: IMR Press.

Bartlett, D., Kaufman, D., & Smeltekop, R. (1993). The effects of music listening and perceived sensory experiences on the immune system as measured by interleukin-1 and cortisol. *Journal of Music Therapy, 30*(4), 194–209.

Bassetti, C., & Bottazzi, E. (2015). Rhythm in social interaction: Introduction. *Etnografia e Ricerca Qualitativa, 8*(3), 1–14.

Batson, G. (1996). Conscious use of the human body in movement: The peripheral neuroanatomic basis of the Alexander Technique. *Medical Problems of Performing Artists, 11*, 3–11.

Baumann, S., Koeneke, S., Schmidt, C., Meyer, M., Lutz, K., & Jäncke, L. (2007). A network for audio-motor coordination in skilled pianists and non-musicians. *Brain Research, 1161*, 65–78.

Baumgartner, H. (1992). Remembrance of things past: Music, autobiographical memory, and emotion. *Advances in Consumer Research, 19*(1), 613–620.

Baumgartner, T., Esslen, M., & Jäncke, L. (2006). From emotion perception to emotion experience: Emotions evoked by pictures and classical music. *International Journal of Psychophysiology, 60*, 34–43.

Beament, J. (2003). *How we hear music: The relationship between music and the hearing mechanism*. Rochester, NY: Boydell Press.

Beaty, R. (2015). The neuroscience of musical improvisation. *Neuroscience and Biobehavioral Reviews, 51*, 108–117.

Beaty, R., Benedek, M., Wilkins, R., Jauk, E., Fink, A., Silvia, P., . . . Neubauer, A. (2014). Creativity and the default network: A functional connectivity analysis of the creative brain at rest. *Neuropsychologia, 64*, 92–98.

Beaty, R., Smeekens, B., Silvia, P., Hodges, D., & Kane, M. (2013). A first look at the role of domain-general cognitive and creative abilities in jazz improvisation. *Psychomusicology: Music, Mind, and Brain, 23*(4), 262–268.

Bebeau, M. (1982). Effects of traditional and simplified methods of rhythm-reading instruction. *Journal of Research in Music Education, 30*(2), 107–119.

Bebey, F. (1999). *African music: A people's art*. Chicago: Lawrence Hill Books.

Beck, R., Cesario, T., Yousefi, A., & Enamoto, H. (2000). Choral singing, performance perception, and immune system changes in salivary immunoglobulin a and cortisol. *Music Perception, 18*(1), 87–106.

Becker, J. (2001). Anthropological perspectives on music and emotion. In P. N. Juslin & J. A. Sloboda (Eds.), *Music and emotion: Theory and research* (pp. 135–160). Oxford: Oxford University Press.

Becker, J. (2004). *Deep listeners: Music, emotion, and trancing*. Bloomington, IN: Indiana University Press.

Becker, J. (2009). Ethnomusicology and empiricism in the twenty-first century. *Ethnomusicology, 53*(1), 478–501.

Bednarik, R. (2003). A figurine from the African Acheulian. *Current Anthropology, 44*(3), 405–413.

Beebe, B., Gerstman, L., Carson, B., Dolinas, M., Zigman, A., Rosensweig, H., . . . Korma, M. (1982). Rhythmic communication in the mother-infant dyad. In M. Davis (Ed.), *Interaction rhythms: Periodicity in communication behavior* (pp. 79–100). New York, NY: Human Sciences Press.

Behrens, G., & Green, S. (1993). The ability to identify emotional content of solo improvisations performed vocally and on three different instruments. *Psychology of Music, 21*(1), 20–33.

Békésy, G. von. (1960). *Experiments in hearing*. New York, NY: McGraw-Hill.

Belin, P., Van Eeckhout, P., Zilbovicius, M., Remy, P., François, C., Guillaume, S., . . . Samson, Y. (1996). Recovery from nonfluent aphasia after melodic intonation therapy: A PET study. *Neurology, 47*(6), 1504–1511.

Belkacem, K., Samadi, R., Goupil, M-J., Lefèvre, L., Baudin, F., Deheuvels, S., et al. (2009). Solar-like oscillations in a massive star. *Science, 324*, 1540–1542.

Bellugi, U., Lichtenberger, L., Jones, W., Lai, Z., & St. George, M. (2000). The neurocognitive profile of Williams syndrome: A complex pattern of strengths and weaknesses. *Journal of Cognitive Neuroscience*, 12(Suppl 1), 7–29.

Benade, A. (2012). *Fundamentals of musical acoustics* (2nd Rev. ed.). New York, NY: Dover.

Benchmark Papers in Acoustics. (1977). *Musical acoustics: Piano and wind instruments*. New York, NY: Dowden, Hutchinson & Ross.

Bendor, D., & Wang, X. (2005). The neuronal representation of pitch in primate auditory cortex. *Nature*, 436(7054), 1161–1165.

Bengtsson, S. L., Csikszentmihályi, M., And Ullén, F., (2007). Cortical regions involved in the generation of musical structures during improvisation in pianists. *Journal of Cognitive Neuroscience*, 19(5), 830–842.

Bengtsson, S. L., Nagy, Z., Skare, S., Forsman, L., Forssberg, H., & Ullen, F. (2005). Extensive piano practicing has regionally specific effects on white matter development. *Nature Neuroscience*, 8(9), 1148–1150.

Bengtsson, S. L., & Ullen, F. (2006). Dissociation between melodic and rhythmic processing during piano performance from musical scores. *Neuroimage*, 30(1), 272–284.

Benson, D. (2006). *Music: A mathematical offering*. New York, NY: Cambridge University Press.

Bentley, A. (1966). *Musical ability in children and its measurement*. London: Harappa.

Benzon, W. L. (2001). *Beethoven's anvil: Music in mind and culture*. New York, NY: Basic Books.

Beranek, L. L. (2003). Subjective rank-orderings and acoustical measurements for fifty-eight concert halls. *Acta Acustica United with Acustica*, 89(3), 494–508.

Beranek, L. L. (2004). *Concert halls and opera houses: Music, acoustics, and architecture* (2nd ed.). New York, NY: Springer.

Beranek, L. L. (2008). Concert hall acoustics—2008. *Journal of the Audio Engineering Society*, 56(7–8), 532–544.

Berg, R., & Stork, D. (2005). *The physics of sound*. Upper Saddle River, NJ: Pearson Prentice Hall.

Berger, B. (1992). Mapping the mindfields. *Omni*, 14(4), 56–58.

Berger, D. (2002). *Music therapy, sensory integration, and the autistic child*. Philadelphia: Jessica Kingsley Publishers.

Berger, D. (2016). *Kids, music 'n' autism: Bringing out the music in your child*. Philadelphia: Jessica Kingsley Publishers.

Berger, J., & Turow, G. (2012). *Music, science, and the rhythmic brain: Cultural and clinical implications*. London: Routledge.

Berger, K. (1965). Respiratory and articulatory factors in wind instrument performance. *Journal of Applied Physiology*, 20, 1217–1221.

Berk, L. (2004). *Development through the lifespan* (3rd ed.). New York, NY: Allyn & Bacon.

Berkowitz, A. (2010). *The improvising mind*. Oxford: Oxford University Press.

Berkowitz, A., & Ansari, D. (2008). Generation of novel motor sequences: The neural correlates of musical improvisation. *NeuroImage*, 41(2), 535–543.

Berlyne, D. (1971). *Aesthetics and psychobiology*. New York, NY: Appleton-Century-Crofts.

Berlyne, D. (1974). *Studies in the new experimental aesthetics: Steps toward an objective psychology of aesthetic appreciation*. New York, NY: John Wiley & Sons.

Bermudez, J., & Zatorre, R. (2005). Differences in gray matter between musicians and nonmusicans: The neurosciences and music II: From perception to performance. *Annals of the New York Academy of Sciences*, 1060, 395–399.

Bermudez, P., & Zatorre, R. (2009). A distribution of absolute pitch ability as revealed by computerized testing. *Music Perception*, 27(2), 89–101.

Bernardi, L., Porta, C., & Sleight, P. (2006). Cardiovascular, cerebrovascular, and respiratory changes induced by different types of music in musicians and non-musicians: The importance of silence. *Heart*, 92, 445–452.

Bernatzky, G., Presch, M., Anderson, M., & Panksepp, J. (2011). Emotional foundations of music as a non-pharmacological pain management tool in modern medicine. *Neuroscience & Biobehavioral Reviews*, 35(9), 1989–1999.

References

Bertoncini, J., Morais, J., Bijeljac-Babic, R., McAdams, S., Peretz, I., & Mehler, J. (1989). Dichotic perception and laterality in neonates. *Brain and Language, 37*, 591–605.

Besmer, F. (1983). *Horses, musicians, & gods: The Hausa cult of possession-trance*. Zarai, Nigeria: Ahmadu Bello University Press.

Best, C., Hoffman, H., & Glanville, B. (1982). Development of infant ear asymmetries in speech and music. *Perception and Psychophysics, 31*, 75–85.

Bharucha, J. (1987). Music cognition and perceptual facilitation: A connectionist framework. *Music Perception, 5*(1), 1–30.

Bhattacharya, J., Petsche, H., & Pereda, E. (2001). Interdependencies in the spontaneous EEG while listening to music. *International Journal of Psychophysiology, 42*, 287–301.

Biasutti, M., & Frezza, L. (2009). Dimensions of music improvisation. *Creativity Research Journal, 21*(2–3), 232–242.

Bierbaum, M. (1958). *Variations in heart action under the influence of musical stimuli* (Unpublished Master's thesis). University of Kansas.

Bigand, E. (1993). Contributions of music to research on human auditory cognition. In S. McAdams & E. Bigand (Eds.), *Thinking in sound: The cognitive psychology of human audition* (pp. 231–277). New York, NY: Oxford University Press.

Bigand, E., Filipic, S., & Lalitte, P. (2005). The time course of emotional responses to music. The neurosciences and music II: From perception to performance. *Annals of the New York Academy of Sciences, 1060*, 429–437.

Bigand, E., Lalitte, P., & Dowling, W. (2009). Special issue—music and language: 25 years after Ledahl and Jackendoff's GTTM. *Music Perception, 26*(3), 183–186.

Bigand, E., & Poulin-Charronnat, B. (2006). Are we "experienced listeners"? A review of the musical capacities that do not depend on formal musical training. *Cognition, 100*, 100–130.

Bigand, E., & Poulin-Charronnat, B. (2009). Tonal cognition. In S. Hallam, I. Cross, & M. Thaut (Eds.), *The Oxford handbook of music psychology* (pp. 59–71). Oxford: Oxford University Press.

Bigand, E., Tillmann, B., Peretz, I., Zarorre, R., Lopez, L., & Majno, M. (Eds.). (2015). The neurosciences and music V: Cognitive stimulation and rehabilitation. *Annals of the New York Academy of Sciences, 1337*.

Bigge, M., & Shermis, S. (2004). *Learning theories for teachers* (6th ed.). Upper Saddle River, NJ: Allyn & Bacon.

Bilbao, S. (2009). *Numerical sound synthesis*. Chichester, West Sussex: John Wiley & Sons.

Billroth, T. (1895). *Wer ist musikalisch? (Who is musical?)* Berlin: Gebruder Paetel.

Binet, A., & Courtier, J. (1895). Researches graphiques sur le musique. *Annee psychologigue, 2*, 201–222. Cited in Eagle, C. Jr., (1972). *A review of human physiological systems and their response to musical stimuli*. Paper presented at Southeastern Conference of National Association for Music Therapy, Tallahassee, Florida.

Birge, E. B. (1928). *History of public school music in the United States*. Washington, DC: Music Educators National Conference.

Bittman, B., Berk, L., Shannon, M., Sharaf, M., Westengard, J., Guegler, K., & Ruff, D. (2005). Recreational music making modulates the human stress response: A preliminary individualized gene expression strategy. *Medical Science Monitor, 11*(2), BR231–BR240.

Blacking, J. (1973). *How musical is man?* Seattle, WA: University of Washington Press.

Blacking, J. (1995a). *Music, culture, and experience*. Chicago: University of Chicago Press.

Blacking, J. (1995b). *Venda children's songs: A study in ethnomusicological analysis*. Chicago: University of Chicago Press.

Blair, M., & Shimp, T. (1992). Consequences of an unpleasant experience with music: A second-order negative conditioning perspective. *Journal of Advertising, 21*(1), 45–43.

Blake, E., & Cross, I. (2008). Flint tools as portable sound-producing objects in the upper palaeolithic context: An experimental study. In P. Cunningham, J. Heeb, & R. Paardekooper (Eds.), *Experiencing archaeology by experiment* (pp. 1–19). Oxford: Oxbow Books.

Blauert, J. (1997). *Spatial hearing: The psychophysics of human sound localization* (2nd ed.). Cambridge, MA: The MIT Press.

Blinkov, S. M., & Glezer, I. I. (1968). *The human brain in figures and tables: A quantitative handbook* (B. Haigh, Trans.). New York, NY: Basic Books.

Blood, A., & Zatorre, R. (2001). Intensely pleasurable responses to music correlate with activity in brain regions implicated in reward and emotion. *PNAS (Proceedings of the National Academy of Sciences)*, 98(20), 11818–11823.

Blood, A., Zatorre, R., Bermudez, P., & Evans, A. C. (1999). Emotional responses to pleasant and unpleasant music correlate with activity in paralimbic brain regions. *Nature Neuroscience*, 2(4), 382–387.

Bloom, B. (1956). *Taxonomy of educational objectives: Handbook I: Cognitive domain.* New York, NY: McKay.

Bloom, F., Lazerson, A., & Hofstadter, L. (1985). *Brain, mind, and behavior.* New York, NY: Freeman.

Boaretto, E., Wu, X., Yuan, J., Bar-Yosef, O., Chu, V., Pan, Y., . . . Weiner, S. (2009). Radiocarbon dating of charcoal and bone collagen associated with early pottery at Yuchanyan Cave, Hunan Province, China. *PNAS Early Edition (Proceedings of the National Academy of Sciences)*, 1–6. Retrieved June 19, 2009, from www.pnas.org/cgi/doi/10.1073/pnas.0900539106

Bobko, D., Schiffman, H., Castino, R., & Chiappetta, W. (1977). Contextual effects in duration experience. *American Journal of Psychology*, 90(4), 577–586.

Bodmer, W., & McKie, R. (1994). *The book of man.* New York: Scribner.

Bohannan, P. (1983). That sync'ing feeling. *Update: Applications of Research in Music Education*, 2(1), 23–24. First published in *Science*, 81(1981), 25–26.

Bohlman, P. (2005). Music. In M. Goodman (Ed.), *The Oxford handbook of Jewish studies* (pp. 852–869). Oxford: Oxford University Press.

Bohlman, P. (2006). Introduction: Music in American religious experience. In P. Bohlman, E. Blumhofer, & M. Chow (Eds.), *Music in American religious experience* (pp. 3–22). Oxford: Oxford University Press.

Boiles, C. (1984). Universals of musical behavior: A taxonomic approach. *The World of Music*, 26(2), 50–64.

Bond, K. (2009). The human nature of dance: Towards a theory of aesthetic community. In S. Malloch & C. Trevarthen (Eds.), *Communicative musicality* (pp. 401–422). Oxford: Oxford University Press.

Bonny, H. (1980). Music and sound in health. In A. Hasting, J. Fadiman, & J. Gordon (Eds.), *Health for the whole person.* Boulder, CO: Westview Press.

Bonny, H. (2001). Music and spirituality. *Music Therapy Perspectives*, 19(1), 59–62.

Bonny, H., & Savary, L. (1973). *Music and your mind: Listening with a new consciousness.* New York, NY: Harper & Row.

Borthwick, S., & Davidson, J. (2002). Developing a child's identity as a musician: A family "script" perspective. In R. MacDonald, D. Hargreaves, & D. Miell (Eds.), *Musical identities* (pp. 60–78). Oxford: Oxford University Press.

Boso, M., Emanuele, E., Minazzi, V., Abbamonte, M., & Politi, P. (2007). Effect of long-term interactive music therapy on behavior profile and musical skills in young adults with severe autism. *Journal of Alternative and Complementary Medicine*, 13(7), 709–712.

Bostwick, K. S., Riccio, M. L., & Humphries, J. M. (2012). Massive, solidified bone in the wing of a volant courting bird. *Biology Letters.* doi: 10.1098/rsbl.2012.0382

Botvin, G. (1974). Acquiring conservation of melody and cross-modal transfer through successive approximation. *Journal of Research in Music Education*, 22(3), 226–233.

Bouhuys, A. (1964). Lung volumes and breathing patterns in wind-instrument players. *Journal of Applied Physiology*, 19, 967–975.

Bourke, R., & Francis, L. (2000). Personality and religion among music students. *Pastoral Psychology*, 48(6), 437–444.

Bouzouggar, A., Barton, N., Vanhaeren, M., d'Errico, F., Collcutt, S., Higham, T., . . . Stambouli, A. (2007). 82,000-year—old shell beads from North Africa and implications for the origins of modern human behavior. *Proceedings of the National Academy of Sciences*, 104(104), 9964–9969.

Boyce-Tillman, J. (2014). Music and well-being. *The Journal for Transdisciplinary Research in Southern Africa*, 10(2), 12–33.

Boyle, J. (1970). The effect of prescribed rhythmical movements on the ability to read music at sight. *Journal of Research in Music Education*, 18(3), 307–318.

References

Boyle, J., & Radocy, R. (1987). *Measurement and evaluation of musical experiences*. New York, NY: Schirmer Books.

Brand, M. (1986). Relationship between home musical environment and selected musical attributes of second-grade children. *Journal of Research in Music Education, 34*(2), 111–120.

Brandfonbrener, A. (1986). Coping with stress. *Medical Problems of Performing Musicians, 1*(1), 12–16.

Brandfonbrener, A. (1995). Musicians with focal dystonia: A report of 58 cases seen during a ten-year period at a performing arts clinic. *Medical Problems of Performing Artists, 10,* 121–127.

Brandfonbrener, A., & Kjelland, J. (2002). Music medicine. In R. Parncutt & G. McPherson (Eds.), *The science and psychology of music performance* (pp. 83–96). Oxford: Oxford University Press.

Brandfonbrener, A., & Lederman, R. (2002). Performing arts medicine. In R. Colwell & C. Richardson (Eds.), *The new handbook of research on music teaching and learning* (pp. 1009–1022). Oxford: Oxford University Press.

Brandt, P. (2009). Music and how we became human—a view from cognitive semiotics. In S. Malloch & C. Trevarthen (Eds.), *Communicative musicality: Exploring the basis of human companionship* (pp. 31–59). Oxford: Oxford University Press.

Brashears, S., Morlet, T., Berlin, C., & Hood, L. (2003). Olivocochlear efferent suppression in classical musicians. *Journal of the American Academy of Audiology, 14*(6), 314–324.

Brashers-Krug, T., Shadmehr, R., & Bizzi, E. (1996). Consolidation in human motor memory. *Nature, 382,* 252–255.

Brattico, E. (2019). The neuroaesthetics of music: A research agenda coming of age. In M. Thaut & D. Hodges (Eds.), *The Oxford handbook of music and the brain* (pp. 364–390). Oxford: Oxford University Press.

Brattico, E., Bogert, B., & Jacobsen, T. (2013). Toward a neural chronometry for the aesthetic experience of music. *Frontiers in Psychology, 4*(206), 1–26.

Brattico, E., Brattico, P., & Jacobsen, T. (2009). The origins of the aesthetic enjoyment of music—a review of the literature. *Musicae Scientiae* (Special issue 2009–2010), *13,* 15–31.

Braun, A., & Bock, J. (2007). Born to learn: Early learning optimizes brain function. In W. Gruhn & F. Rauscher (Eds.), *Neurosciences in music pedagogy* (pp. 27–51). New York, NY: Nova Science Publishers.

Bregman, A. (1990). *Auditory scene analysis: The perceptual organization of sound*. Cambridge, MA: The MIT Press.

Bregman, A. (1993). Auditory scene analysis: Hearing in complex environments. In S. McAdams & E. Bigand (Eds.), *Thinking in sound: The cognitive psychology of human audition* (pp. 10–36). New York, NY: Oxford University Press.

Broadhouse, J. (1892). *Musical acoustics or the phenomena of sound* (3rd ed.). London: William Reeves.

Broadway Memorandum of Agreement, 2016–2019. Retrieved from https://www.local802afm.org/wp-content/uploads/2017/09/802-Broadway-MOA-2016-2019.pdf.

Bronowski, J. (1973). *The ascent of man*. Boston, MA: Little, Brown & Company.

Brotherson, S. (2005). *Understanding brain development in young children*. Retrieved from www.researchgate.net/publication/252178274_Understanding_Brain_Development_in_Young_Children

Brotons, M. (1994). Effects of performing conditions on music performance anxiety and performance quality. *Journal of Music Therapy, 31,* 63–81.

Brotons, M., & Marti, P. (2003). Music therapy with Alzheimer's patients and their family caregivers: A pilot project. *Journal of Music Therapy, 40*(2), 138–150.

Broudy, H. (1968). The case for aesthetic education. In R. Choate (Ed.), *Documentary report of the Tanglewood symposium* (pp. 9–13). Washington, DC: Music Educators National Conference.

Brown, F. (1982). Rhythmicity as an emerging variable for psychology. In F. Brown & R. Graeber (Eds.), *Rhythmic aspects of behavior* (pp. 3–38). Hillsdale, NJ: Lawrence Erlbaum Associates.

Brown, F. (2008). Music. In J. Corrigan (Ed.), *The Oxford handbook of religion and emotion* (pp. 200–222). Oxford: Oxford University Press.

Brown, J. (2004). Short-term memory. In R. Gregory (Ed.), *Oxford companion to the mind* (2nd ed., pp. 841–842). New York, NY: Oxford University Press.

Brown, R. M. (1981). Music and language. In R. Choate (Ed.), *Documentary report of the Ann Arbor symposium* (pp. 233–265). Reston, VA: Music Educators National Conference.

Brown, R. M., Zatorre, R. J., & Penhune, V. B. (2015). Expert music performance: Cognitive, neural, and developmental bases. In *Progress in Brain Research* (Vol. 217, pp. 57–86). Amsterdam: Elsevier.

Brown, S., Martinez, M., & Parsons, L. (2004). Passive music listening spontaneously engages limbic and paralimbic systems. *NeuroReport, 15*(13), 2033–2037.

Brown, S., Martinez, M., & Parsons, L. (2006). Music and language side by side in the brain: A PET study of the generation of melodies and sentences. *European Journal of Neuroscience, 23,* 2791–2803.

Brown, S., Martinez, M., Hodges, D., Fox, P., & Parsons, L. (2004). The song system of the human brain. *Cognitive Brain Research, 20,* 363–375.

Bruer, J. (1999). *The myth of the first three years.* New York, NY: The Free Press.

Brugge, J. (1991). Neurophysiology of the central auditory and vestibular systems. In M. Paparella, D. Shumrick, J. Gluckman, & W. Meyerhoff (Eds.), *Otolaryngology. Vol. 1 basic sciences and related principles* (3rd ed., pp. 281–314). Philadelphia: Saunders.

Brummett, V. (Ed.). (1997). *Music as intelligence.* Ithaca, NY: Ithaca College.

Bruner, J. (1963). *The process of education.* New York, NY: Vintage Books.

Bruner, J. (1966). *Toward a theory of instruction.* New York, NY: W. W. Norton & Co.

Bruner, J. (1969). *On knowing: Essays for the left hand.* New York, NY: Atheneum.

Bruner, J., Goodnow, J., & Austin, G. (1956). *A study of thinking.* New York, NY: John Wiley & Sons.

Bruscia, K. (1998). *Defining music therapy* (2nd ed.). Gilsum, NH: Barcelona Publishers.

Bruscia, K. (2011). *Case examples of music therapy for Alzheimer's disease.* Gilsum, NH: Barcelona Publishers.

Brust, J. (2001). Music and the neurologist: A historical perspective. In R. Zatorre & I. Peretz (Eds.), *The biological foundations of music. Annals of the New York Academy of Sciences, 930,* 143–152.

Buck, P. (1944). *Psychology for musicians.* Oxford: Oxford University Press.

Builione, R., & Lipton, J. (1983). Stereotypes and personality of classical musicians. *Psychomusicology, 3,* 36–43.

Bullmore, E., & Sporns, O. (2009). Complex brain networks: Graph theoretical analysis of structural and functional systems. *Nature Reviews Neuroscience, 10*(4), 186–198.

Bunt, L., & Hoskyns, S. (2002). *The handbook of music therapy.* New York, NY: Routledge.

Bunzeck, N., Wuestenberg, T., Lutz, K., Heinze, H. J., & Jäncke, L. (2005). Scanning silence: Mental imagery of complex sounds. *Neuroimage, 26*(4), 1119–1127.

Burkhart, C., & Schenker, H. (1978). Schenker's "motivic parallelisms". *Journal of Music Theory, 22*(2), 145–175.

Burns, D. (2001). The effect of the Bonny method of guided imagery and music on the mood and life quality of cancer patients. *Journal of Music Therapy, 38*(1), 51–65.

Bustinza, O. F., Vendrell-Herrero, F., Parry, G., & Myrthianos, V. (2013). Music business models and piracy. *Industrial Management & Data Systems, 113*(1), 4–22.

Butcher, H. (1968). *Human intelligence: Its nature and assessment.* New York, NY: Harper & Row.

Butkovic, A., Ullén, F., & Mosing, M. A. (2015). Personality related traits as predictors of music practice: Underlying environmental and genetic influences. *Personality and Individual Differences, 74,* 133–138.

Butler, C. (1995). Investigating the effects of stress on the success and failure of music conservatory students. *Medical Problems of Performing Artists, 10*(1), 24–31.

Butler, D. (1992). *The musician's guide to perception and cognition.* New York, NY: Schirmer Books.

Buttram, J. (1996). Learning theory and related developments: Overview and applications in music education and music therapy. In D. Hodges (Ed.), *Handbook of music psychology* (2nd ed., pp. 401–468). San Antonio, TX: IMR Press.

Butzlaff, R. (2000). Can music be used to teach reading? *Journal of Aesthetic Education, 34*(3–4), 167–178.

Buxton, R. B. (2009). *Introduction to functional magnetic resonance imaging: Principles and techniques.* Cambridge, MA: Cambridge University Press.

Byl, N., & Priori, A. (2006). The development of focal dystonia in musicians as a consequence of maladaptive plasticity: Implications for intervention. In E. Altenmüller, M. Wiesendanger, & J. Kesselring (Eds.), *Music, motor control, and the brain* (pp. 293–307). Oxford: Oxford University Press.

References

Byo, J. (1988). The effect of barlines in music notation on rhythm reading performance. *Contributions to Music Education, 15,* 7–14.

Byo, J. (1992). Effects of barlines, pitch, and meter on musicians' rhythm reading performance. *Journal of Band Research, 27*(2), 34–44.

Byo, J., & Cassidy, J. (2008). An exploratory study of time use in the practice of music majors: Self-report and observation analysis. *Update: Applications of Research in Music Education, 27*(1), 33–40.

Byrne, C. (2005). Pedagogical communication in the music classroom. In D. Miell, R. MacDonald, & D. Hargreaves (Eds.), *Musical communication* (pp. 301–319). Oxford: Oxford University Press.

Cacioppo, J., Berntson, G., Larsen, J., Poehlmann, K., & Ito, T. (2000). The psychophysiology of emotion. In R. Lewis & J. Haviland-Jones (Eds.), *The handbook of emotions* (2d ed., pp. 173–191). New York, NY: Guilford Press.

Calder, N. (1970). *The mind of man.* New York, NY: Viking.

Calvin, W. (2014). *How brains think: Evolving intelligence, then and now.* New York, NY: Basic Books.

Camera, L. (2015, April 8). Definition of 'core subjects' expanded under senate bipartisan NCLB rewrite. *Education Week.* Retrieved July 20, 2018, from http://blogs.edweek.org/edweek/campaign-k-12/2015/04/definition_of_core_subjects_ex.html

Campbell, D. (1926). *Arabian medicine and its influence on the middle ages* (2 Vols.). London: Kegan Paul, Trench, Trubner & Co.

Campbell, J. (1986). *Winston Churchill's afternoon nap.* New York, NY: Simon & Schuster.

Campbell, P., Connell, C., & Beegle, A. (2007). Adolescents' expressed meanings of music in and out of school. *Journal of Research in Music Education, 55*(3), 220–236.

Campbell, W., & Heller, J. (1980). An orientation for considering models of musical behavior. In D. Hodges (Ed.), *Handbook of music psychology* (pp. 29–36). Lawrence, KS: National Association for Music Therapy.

Cancro, R. (Ed.). (1971). *Intelligence: Genetic and environmental influences.* New York, NY: Grune & Stratton.

Caprara, G., & Cervone, D. (2000). *Personality: Determinants, dynamics, and potentials.* Cambridge, MA: Cambridge University Press.

Carey, J. (2008). *Brain facts.* Washington, DC: Society for Neuroscience.

Carlson, J., Geisinger, K., & Jonson, J. (2017). *The twentieth mental measurements yearbook.* Lincoln, NE: University of Nebraska Press.

Carrick, F., Oggero, E., & Pagnacco, G. (2007). Posturographic changes associated with music listening. *The Journal of Alternative and Complementary Medicine, 13*(5), 519–526.

Carter, R. (2009). *The human brain book.* London: Dorling Kindersley.

Carter, S. (1982). Mentally retarded. In W. Lathom & C. Eagle, Jr. (Eds.), *Music therapy for handicapped children.* Washington, DC: National Association for Music Therapy.

Carterette, E., Monahan, C., Holman, E., Bell, T., & Fiske, R. (1982). Rhythmic and melodic structures in perceptual space. *Journal of the Acoustical Society of America, 72,* S1–S11A.

Cassidy, J. (1993). Effects of various sightsinging strategies on nonmusic majors' pitch accuracy. *Journal of Research in Music Education, 41*(4), 293–302.

Cassidy, J., & Standley, J. (1995). The effect of music listening on physiological responses of premature infants in the NICU. *Journal of Music Therapy, 32*(4), 208–227.

Caufield, K. (2018). U.S. music consumption up 12.5% in 2017, R&B/Hip-Hop is year's most popular genre. *Billboard.* Retrieved from www.billboard.com/articles/columns/chart-beat/8085975/us-music-consumption-up-2017-rb-hip-hop-most-popular-genre

Cevasco, A., & Grant, R. (2003). Comparison of different methods for eliciting exercise-to-music for clients with Alzheimer's disease. *Journal of Music Therapy, 40*(1), 41–56.

Chaffin, R. (2007). Learning *Clair de Lune*: Retrieval practice and expert memorization. *Music Perception, 24*(4), 377–393.

Chaffin, R., & Imreh, G. (2001). A comparison of practice and self-report as sources of information about goals of expert practice. *Psychology of Music, 29*(1), 39–69.

Chaffin, R., & Imreh, G. (2003). "Seeing the big picture": Piano practice as expert problem solving. *Music Perception, 20*(4), 465–490.

Chaffin, R., & Lemieux, A. (2004). General perspectives on achieving musical excellence. In A. Williamon (Ed.), *Musical excellence* (pp. 19–39). Oxford: Oxford University Press.

Chaffin, R., Lemieux, A., & Chen, C. (2007). "It is different each time I play": Variability in highly prepared musical performance. *Music Perception, 24*(5), 455–472.

Chaigne, A., & Kergomard, J. (2016). *Acoustics of musical instruments.* New York, NY: Springer-Verlag.

Chamorro-Premuzic, T., & Furnham, A. (2007). Personality and music: Can traits explain how people use music in everyday life? *British Journal of Psychology, 98,* 175–185.

Chan, Y., Lee, P., Ng, T., Ngan, H., & Wong, L. (2003). The use of music to reduce anxiety for patients undergoing colposcopy: A randomized trial. *Gynecological Oncology, 9*(1), 213–217.

Chanda, M., & Levitin, D. (2013). The neurochemistry of music. *Trends in Cognitive Sciences, 17*(4), 179–192.

Chandra, M. (2003). *"Hears" a Black hole for the first time.* Retrieved April 21, 2007, from http://chandra.harvard.edu/press/03_releases/press_090903.html

Charnetski, C., & Brennan, F. Jr., (1998). Effect of music and auditory stimuli on secretory immunoglobulin A (IgA). *Perceptual and Motor Skills, 87,* 1163–1170.

Chasin, M. (Ed.). (2009). *Hearing loss in musicians: Prevention and management.* San Diego, CA: Plural Publishing.

Chebat, J-C., Chebat, C., & Vaillant, D. (2001). Environmental background music and in-store selling. *Journal of Business Research, 54,* 115–123.

Chen, D., Xu, X., Wang, Z., & Chen, J. (2005). Alteration of gastric myoelectrical and autonomic activities with audio stimulation in healthy humans. *Scandinavian Journal of Gastroenterology, 40*(7), 814–821.

Chen, D., Xu, X., Zhao, Q., Yin, J., Sallam, H., & Chen, J. (2008). Effects of audio stimulation on gastric myoelectrical activity and sympathovagal balance in healthy adolescents and adults. *Journal of Gastroenterology and Hepatology, 23,* 141–149.

Chen, J., Woollacott, M., & Pologe, S. (2006). Accuracy and underlying mechanisms of shifting movements in cellists. *Experimental Brain Research, 174*(3), 467–476.

Chen, J., Woollacott, M., Pologe, S., & Moore, G. (2008). Pitch and space maps of skilled cellists: Accuracy, variability, and error correction. *Experimental Brain Research, 188*(4), 492–503.

Cheng, N. (1987, June 8). Life and death in Shanghai. *Time Magazine,* 42–56.

Cheour, M., Kushnerenko, E., Ceponiene, R., Fellman, V., & Näätänen, R. (2002). Electric brain responses obtained from newborn infants to changes in duration in complex harmonic tones. *Developmental Neuropsychology, 22*(2), 471–479.

Cherry, E. (1953). Some experiments on the recognition of speech, with one and with two ears. *Journal of the Acoustical Society of America, 25*(5), 975–979.

Chesky, K. (2008). Preventing music-induced hearing loss. *Music Educators Journal, 94*(3), 36–41.

Chesky, K., Kondraske, G., Henoch, M., Hipple, J., & Rubin, B. (2002). Musicians' health. In R. Colwell & C. Richardson (Eds.), *The new handbook of research on music teaching and learning* (pp. 1023–1039. Oxford: Oxford University Press.

Chinn Cannon, M. (2018). *The effects of instrumental music instruction on the neurological responses and adaptive behaviors of children with autism spectrum disorder* (Doctoral dissertation). Retrieved from https://libres.uncg.edu/ir/uncg/f/Chinn%20Cannon_uncg_0154D_12444.pdf

Chmiel, A., & Schubert, E. (2017). Back to the inverted-U for music preference: A review of the literature. *Psychology of Music, 45*(6), 886–909.

Chornik, K. (2013). Music and torture in Chilean detention centers: Conversations with an Ex-Agent of Pinochet's secret police. *The World of Music,* 51–65.

Chou, L., Wang, R., Chen, S., & Pai, L. (2003). Effects of music therapy on oxygen saturation in premature infants receiving endotracheal suctioning. *Journal of Nursing Research, 11*(3), 209–216.

Christe, I. (2007). *Everybody wants some: The Van Halen Saga.* Hoboken, NJ: John Wiley & Sons.

Chugani, H., Behen, M., Muzik, O., Juhász, C., Nagy, F., & Chugani, D. (2001). Local brain functional activity following early deprivation: A study of postinstitutionalized Romanian orphans. *NeuroImage, 14,* 1290–1301.

References

Chugani, H., Phelps, M., & Mazziotta, J. (1993). Positron emission tomography study of human brain functional development. In M. Johnson (Ed.), *Brain development and cognition* (pp. 125–143). Cambridge, MA: Blackwell Publishers.

Chusid, J. (1985). *Correlative neuroanatomy and functional neurology* (19th ed.). Los Altos, CA: Lange Medical Publications.

Ciccone, A. (2015). Role of rhythmicity in infant development. *Encephale, 41*(Suppl 1–4), S15–S21.

Claiborne, R. (1974). *The birth of writing*. New York, NY: Time-Life Books.

Clark, L., Iversen, S., & Goodwin, G. (2001). The influence of positive and negative mood states on risk taking, verbal fluency, and salivary cortisol. *Journal of Affective Disorders, 63*, 179–187.

Clarke, D., & Clarke, E. (Eds.). (2011). *Music and consciousness*. Oxford: Oxford University Press.

Clarke, E. (2004). *Empirical musicology*. New York, NY: Oxford University Press.

Clarke, E. (2005). *Ways of listening: An ecological approach to the perception of musical meaning*. New York, NY: Oxford University Press.

Clarke, E., & Emmerson, S. (Eds.). (1989). *Music, mind and structure*. London: Harwood Academic Publishers.

Clarke, E., Dibben, N., & Pitts, S. (2009). *Music and mind in everyday life*. Oxford: Oxford University Press.

Clayton, M. (2009). The social and personal functions of music in cross-cultural perspective. In S. Hallam, I. Cross, & M. Thaut (Eds.), *The Oxford handbook of music psychology* (pp. 35–44). Oxford: Oxford University Press.

Clayton, M., Dueck, B., & Leante, L. (2013). *Experience and meaning in music performance*. Oxford: Oxford University Press.

Clayton, M., Herbert, T., & Middleton, R. (Eds.). (2003). *The cultural study of music: A critical introduction*. New York, NY: Routledge.

Clayton, M., Sager, R., & Will, U. (2005). In time with the music: The concept of entrainment and its significance for ethnomusicology. *ESEM Counterpoint, 1*, 1–82.

Clynes, M. (1977). *Sentics: The touch of emotions*. Garden City, NY: Anchor Press.

Clynes, M. (Ed.). (1982). *Music, mind, and brain: The neuropsychology of music*. New York, NY: Plenum Press.

Clynes, M., & Walker, J. (1982). Neurobiologic functions of rhythm, time, and pulse in music. In M. Clynes (Ed.), *Music, mind, and brain* (pp. 171–216). New York, NY: Plenum Press.

Cochrane, T., Fantini, B., & Scherer, K. (Eds.). (2013). *The emotional power of music*. Oxford: Oxford University Press.

Coffman, D. (1990). Effects of mental practice, physical practice, and knowledge of results on piano performance. *Journal of Research in Music Education, 38*(3), 187–196.

Cogan, R. (1984). *New images of musical sound*. Cambridge, MA: Harvard University Press.

Cohen, D. (1996). *The secret language of the mind*. San Francisco: Chronicle Books.

Cohn, J., Ambadar, Z., & Ekman, P. (2007). Observer-based measurement of facial expression with the facial action coding system. In J. Coan & J. Allen (Eds.), *Handbook of emotion elicitation and assessment* (pp. 203–221). New York, NY: Oxford University Press.

Coleman, J., Pratt, R., Stoddard, R., Gerstmann, D., & Abel, H. (1997). The effects of the male and female singing and speaking voices on selected physiological and behavioral measures of premature infants in the intensive care unit. *International Journal of Arts Medicine, 5*(2), 4–11.

Colley, A. (2008). Young people's musical taste: Relationship with gender and gender-related traits. *Journal of Applied Social Psychology, 38*(8), 2039–2055.

Colley, B. (1987). A comparison of syllabic methods for improving rhythm literacy. *Journal of Research in Music Education, 35*(4), 221–235.

Colman, A. (2001). *Oxford dictionary of psychology*. New York: Oxford University Press.

Collier, G. (2007). Beyond valence and activity in the emotional connotations of music. *Psychology of Music, 35*, 110–131.

Collyer, S., Davis, P., Thorpe, C., & Callaghan, J. (2007). Sound pressure level and spectral balance linearity and symmetry in the *Messa di voce* of female classical singers. *Journal of the Acoustical Society of America, 121*(3), 1728–1736.

Coloma, D., & Kleiner, B. (2005). How can music be used in business? *Management Research News*, *28*(11), 115–120.

Colwell, R. (1970). *The evaluation of music teaching and learning*. Englewood Cliffs, NJ: Prentice-Hall.

Colwell, R. (Ed.). (1992). *Handbook of research on music teaching and learning*. New York, NY: Schirmer Books.

Colwell, R. (Ed.). (2006). *MENC handbook of musical cognition and development*. New York, NY: Oxford University Press.

Colwell, R., Hewitt, M., & Fonder, M. (2017). *The teaching of instrumental music* (5th ed.). New York, NY: Routledge.

Colwell, R., & Richardson, C. (Eds.). (2002). *The new handbook on music teaching and learning*. New York, NY: Oxford University Press.

Colwell, R., & Webster, P. (2011). *MENC handbook of research on music learning*. Oxford: Oxford University Press.

Colwell, R., & Wing, L. (2004). *An orientation to music education: Structural knowledge for teaching music*. Upper Saddle River, NJ: Prentice-Hall.

Conable, B. (1995). *How to learn the Alexander technique* (3rd ed.). Portland, OR: Andover Press.

Conable, B., & Conable, B. (2000). *What every musician needs to know about the body*. Portland, OR: Andover Press.

Connolly, C., & Williamon, A. (2004). Mental skills training. In A. Williamon (Ed.), *Musical excellence* (pp. 222–245). Oxford: Oxford University Press.

Conrad, C., Niess, H., Jauch, K-W., Bruns, C., Hartl, W., & Welker, L. (2007). Overture for growth hormone: Requiem for interleukin-6? *Cricital care medicine*, *35*(12), 2709–2713.

Conrad, N. (2003). Paleolithic ivory sculptures from southwestern Germany and the origins of figurative art. *Nature*, *426*(6968), 830.

Conrad, N. (2009). A female figurine from the basal Aurignacian of Hohle Fels Cave in southwestern Germany. *Nature*, *459*, 248–252.

Conrad, N., Malina, M., & Münzel, S. (2009). New flutes document the earliest musical tradition in southwestern Germany. *Nature*, *460*, 737–740.

Constable, G. (1973). *The Neanderthals*. New York, NY: Time-Life Books.

Conti, A. (2000). Oncology in neuroimmunomodulation: What progress has been made? *Neuroimmunomodulation: Perspectives at the New Millennium. Annals of the New York Academy of Sciences*, *917*, 68–83.

Cook, P. (2001). *Music, cognition, and computerized sound: An introduction to psychoacoustics*. Cambridge, MA: The MIT Press.

Coon, H., & Cavey, G. (1989). Genetic and environmental determinants of musical ability in twins. *Behavior Genetics*, *19*(2), 183–193.

Cope, D. (1996). *Experiments in musical intelligence*. Middleton, WI: A-R Editions.

Cope, D. (2005). *Computer models of musical creativity*. Cambridge, MA: The MIT Press.

Cornelius, S., & Natvig, M. (2012). *Music: A social experience*. London: Routledge.

Cox, T. J., & D'Antonio, P. (2003). Engineering art: The science of concert hall acoustics. *Interdisciplinary Science Reviews*, *28*(2), 119–129.

Craig, D. (2005). An exploratory study of physiological changes during "chills" induced by music. *Musicæ Scientiæ: The Journal of the European Society for the Cognitive Sciences of Music*, *9*(2), 273–285.

Creech, A. (2009). The role of the family in supporting learning. In S. Hallam, I. Cross, & M. Thaut (Eds.), *The Oxford handbook of music psychology* (pp. 295–306). Oxford: Oxford University Press.

Critchley, M., & Hensen, R. (Eds.). (1977). *Music and the brain: Studies in the neurology of music*. Springfield, IL: Charles C. Thomas.

Cronshaw, A. (1999). Norway: Fjords and fiddles. In M. Ellingham, O. Duane, & V. Dowell, V. (Eds.). (Eds.). *World music: The rough guide. Vol. 1: Africa, Europe and the middle east* (pp. 211–218). London: Rough Guides.

Croom, A. M. (2012). Music, neuroscience, and the psychology of well-being: A précis. *Frontiers in Psychology*, *2*, 393.

Cross, I. (2009a). The evolutionary nature of musical meaning. *Musicae Scientiae*, Special Issue: Music and evolution, 179–200.

References

Cross, I. (2009b). The nature of music and its evolution. In S. Hallam, I. Cross, & M. Thaut (Eds.), *The Oxford handbook of music psychology* (pp. 3–13). Oxford: Oxford University Press.

Cross, I., & Deliège, I. (1993). Music and the cognitive sciences 1990. *Contemporary Music Review, 9*.

Cross, I., & Morley, I. (2009). The evolution of music: Theories, definitions and the nature of the evidence. In S. Malloch & C. Trevarthen (Eds.), *Communicative musicality* (pp. 61–81). Oxford: Oxford University Press.

Cross, I., Zubrow, E., & Cowan, F. (2002). Musical behaviours and the archaeological record: A preliminary study. In J. Mathieu (Ed.), *Experimental archaeology. British archaeological reports international series* (Vol. 1035, pp. 25–34). Also Retrieved from www.mus.cam.ac.uk/~ic108/lithacoustics/

Crow, C. (1897). *Maldon and Brunnanburh: Two old English songs of battle*. Boston, MA: Ginn & Co.

Crystal, H., Grober, E., & Masur, D. (1989). Preservation of musical memory in Alzheimer's disease. *Journal of Neurology, Neurosurgery, and Psychiatry, 52*, 1415–1416.

Csikszentmihályi, M. (1990/2008). *Flow: The psychology of optimal experience*. New York, NY: Harper & Row.

Csikszentmihályi, M. (1993). *The evolving self: A psychology for the third millennium*. New York, NY: HarperCollins.

Csikszentmihályi, M. (2014). *Flow and the foundations of positive psychology: The collected works of Mihaly Csikszentmihalyi*. London: Springer.

Csikszentmihályi, M., & Hunter, J. (2004). Happiness in everyday life: The uses of experience sampling. *Journal of Happiness Studies, 4*(2), 185–199.

Csikszentmihály, M., Rathunde, K., & Whalen, S. (1997). *Talented teenagers: The roots of success and failure*. Cambridge: Cambridge University Press.

Culver, C. (1951). *Musical acoustics* (3rd ed). New York, NY: McGraw-Hill Education.

Culver, C. (1969). *Musical acoustics* (4th ed.). New York, NY: McGraw-Hill Education.

Curtis, N. (1921). American Indian cradle-songs. *The Musical Quarterly, 7*(4), 549–558.

Curtiss, S. (1977). *Genie: A psycholinguistic study of a modern-day "wild child"*. New York, NY: Academic Press.

Cusick, S. (2006). Music as torture/Music as weapon. *Revista Trancultural de Música 10*. Retrieved from www.redalyc.org/articulo.oa?id=82201011

Cusack, R., Deeks, J., Aikman, G., & Carlyon, R. (2004). Effects of location, frequency region, and time course of selective attention on auditory scene analysis. *Journal of Experimental Psychology, 30*(4), 643–656.

Cutietta, R. (1979). The effects of including systemized sight-singing drill in the middle school choral rehearsal. *Contributions to Music Education, 7*, 12–20.

Dahl, S., & Friberg, A. (2007). Visual perception of expressiveness in musicians' body movements. *Music Perception, 24*(5), 433–454.

Daintith, J. (2010). *Oxford dictionary of physics* (6th ed.). Oxford: Oxford University Press.

Dalla Bella, S. (2016). Music and brain plasticity. In S. Hallam, I. Cross, & M. Thaut (Eds.), *The Oxford handbook of music psychology* (2nd ed., pp. 325–342). Oxford: Oxford University Press.

Dalla Bella, S., Kraus, N., Overy, K., Pantev, C., Snyder, J., Tervaniemi, M., Tillman, B., & Schlaug, G. (2009). The neurosciences of music III: Disorders and plasticity. *Annals of the New York Academy of Sciences, 1169*.

Dams, L. (1985). Palaeolithic lithophones: Descriptions and comparisons. *Oxford Journal of Archaeology, 4*, 31–46.

Dargie, D. (2007). "Umakhweyane": A musical bow and its contribution to Zulu music. *African Music, 8*(1), 60–81.

Darwin, C. (1897). *The descent of man*. New York, NY: Modern Edition.

Dasilva, F., Blasi, A., & Dees, D. (1984). *The sociology of music*. Notre Dame, IN: University of Notre Dame Press.

Daughtry, J. (2003). Russia's new anthem and the negotiation of national identity. *Ethnomusicology, 47*(1), 42–67.

David, M. (1996). Designing a program of vocal hygiene for singers. *Journal of Singing, 53*(1), 15–20.

Davidson, J. (1993). Visual perception of performance manner in the movements of solo musicians. *Psychology of Music, 21*, 103–113.

Davidson, J. (1994). Which areas of a pianist's body convey information about expressive intention to an audience? *Journal of Human Movement Studies, 26,* 279–301.

Davidson, J. (1997). The social in musical performance. In D. Hargreaves & A. North (Eds.), *The social psychology of music* (pp. 209–228). Oxford: Oxford University Press.

Davidson, J. (2002). The solo performer's identity. In R. MacDonald, D. Hargreaves, & D. Miell (Eds.), *Musical identities* (pp. 97–113). New York, NY: Oxford University Press.

Davidson, J. (Ed.). (2004). *The music practitioner: Research for the music performer, teacher, and listener.* Burlington, VT: Ashgate Publishing Co.

Davidson, J. (2005). Bodily communication in musical performance. In D. Miell, R. MacDonald, & D. Hargreaves (Eds.), *Musical communication* (pp. 215–237). Oxford: Oxford University Press.

Davidson, J. (2009). Movement and collaboration in musical performance. In S. Hallam, I. Cross, & M. Thaut (Eds.), *The Oxford handbook of music psychology* (pp. 364–376). Oxford: Oxford University Press.

Davidson, J., & Correia, J. (2002). Body movement. In R. Parncutt & G. McPherson (Eds.), *The science and psychology of music performance: Creative strategies for teaching and learning* (pp. 237–250). New York, NY: Oxford University Press.

Davidson, J., Howe, M., Moore, D., & Sloboda, J. (1996). The role of parental influences in the development of musical performance. *British Journal of Developmental Psychology, 14*(4), 399–412.

Davidson, J., Howe, M., & Sloboda, J. (1997). Environmental factors in the development of musical performance skill over the life span. In D. Hargreaves & A. North (Eds.), *The social psychology of music* (pp. 188–206). Oxford: Oxford University Press.

Davidson, J., & Malloch, S. (2009). Musical communication: The body movements of performance. In S. Malloch & C. Trevarthen (Eds.), *Communicative musicality* (pp. 565–583). Oxford: Oxford University Press.

Davidson, J., Sloboda, J., & Howe, M. (1995). The role of parents and teachers in the success and failure of instrumental learners. *Bulletin of the Council for Research in Music Education,* 40–44.

Davidson, L., McKernon, P., & Gardner, H. (1981). The acquisition of song: A developmental approach. *Documentary report of the Ann Arbor symposium* (pp. 301–315). Reston, VA: Music Educators National Conference.

Davies, J. B. (1978). *The psychology of music.* Stanford, CA: Stanford University Press.

Davies, S. (2010). Emotions expressed and aroused by music: Philosophical perspectives. In P. Juslin & J. Sloboda (Eds.), *Handbook of music and emotion: Theory, research, applications* (pp. 15–43). Oxford: Oxford University Press.

Davis, C. (1992). The effects of music and basic relaxation instruction on pain and anxiety of women undergoing in-office gynecological procedures. *Journal of Music Therapy, 29*(4), 202–216.

Davis, D. (2004). Psychoanalysis. In R. Gregory (Ed.), *The Oxford companion to the mind* (pp. 763–764). Oxford: Oxford University Press.

Davis, G., & Jones, R. (1988). *The sound reinforcement handbook.* Milwaukee, WI: Hal Leonard.

Davis, W., & Thaut, M. (1989). The influence of preferred relaxing music on measures of state anxiety, relaxation, and physiological responses. *Journal of Music Therapy, 26*(4), 168–187.

Dawson, W. (1964). *Negro Folk Symphony.* Recorded by Leopold Stowkowski and the American Symphony Orchestra. Decca, DL-710077.

Dawson, W. (2007). Trauma to the high-level instrumentalist's hand and upper extremity: An epidemiologic and outcome study. *Medical Problems of Performing Artists, 22*(3), 105–109.

Dawson, W. J. (2008). *Fit as a fiddle: The musician's guide to playing healthy.* Lanham, MD: Rowman & Littlefield Education.

Dean, R., & Bailes, F. (2015). Using time series analysis to evaluate skin conductance during movement in piano improvisation. *Psychology of Music, 43*(1), 3–23.

Deary, I. (2001). *Intelligence: A very short introduction.* Oxford: Oxford University Press.

DeCasper, A., & Fifer, W. (1980). Of human bonding: Newborns prefer their mothers' voices. *Science, 208*(4448), 1174–1176.

DeCorte, E. (1990). Towards powerful learning environments for the acquisition of problem solving skills. *European Journal of Psychology of Education, 5,* 5–19.

References

DeDreu, C. K., Nijstad, B. A., Baas, M., Wolsink, I., & Roskes, M. (2012). Working memory benefits creative insight, musical improvisation, and original ideation through maintained task-focused attention. *Personality and Social Psychology Bulletin, 38*(5), 656–669.

De la Motte-Haber, H. (1985). *Handbuch der musickpsychologie (Handbook of music psychology)*. Laaber, Germany: Laaber-Verlag.

de Lisle, R., Speedy, D., Thompson, J., & Maurice, D. (2006). Effects of pianism retraining on three pianists with focal dystonia. *Medical Problems of Performing Artists, 21*(3), 105–111.

d'Errico, F., Henishilwood, C., Lawson, G., Vanhaeren, M., Tillier, A-M., Soressi, M., . . . Julien, M. (2003). Archaeological evidence for the emergence of language, symbolism, and music—an alternative multidisciplinary perspective. *Journal of World Prehistory, 17*(1), 1–70.

De Souza, J. (2017). *Music at hand: Instruments, bodies, and cognition*. Oxford: Oxford University Press.

de Vries, B (1991). Assessment of the affective response to music with Clynes's sentograph. *Psychology of Music, 19*, 46–64.

DeJong, M., van Mourik, K., & Schellekens, H. (1973). A physiological approach to aesthetic preference-music. *Psychotherapy and Psychosomatics, 22*, 46–51.

Deliège, I. (2001a). Introduction: Similarity perception categorization cue abstraction. *Music Perception, 18*(3), 233–243.

Deliège, I. (2001b). Prototype effects in music listening: An empirical approach to the notion of imprint. *Music Perception, 18*(3), 371–407.

Deliège, I., & Davidson, J. (Eds.). (2011). *Music and the mind: Essays in honour of John Sloboda*. Oxford: Oxford University Press.

Deliège, I., & Mélen, M. (1997). Cue abstraction in the representation of musical form. In I. Deliège & J. Sloboda (Eds.), *Perception and cognition of music* (pp. 387–341). Hove East Sussex: Psychology Press.

Deliège, I., & Sloboda, J. (Eds.). (1996). *Musical beginnings: Origins and development of musical competence*. New York, NY: Oxford University Press.

Deliège, I., & Sloboda, J. (Eds.). (1997). *Perception and cognition of music*. New York, NY: Psychology Press.

Deliège, I., & Wiggins, G. (Eds.). (2006). *Musical creativity: Multidisciplinary research in theory and practice*. New York, NY: Psychology Press.

Demorest, S. (2000). Encouraging male participation in chorus. *Music Educators Journal, 86*(4), 38–41.

Demorest, S., & May, W. (1995). Sight-singing instruction in the choral ensemble: Factors related to individual performance. *Journal of Research in Music Education, 43*(2), 156–167.

Demorest, S., & Morrison, S. (2016). Quantifying culture: The cultural distance hypothesis of melodic expectancy. In J. Y. Chiao, S-C. Li, R. Seligman, & R. Turner (Eds.), *The Oxford handbook of cultural neuroscience* (pp. 183–194). Oxford: Oxford University Press.

Demorest, S., Morrison, S., Stambaugh, L., Beken, M., Richards, T., & Johnson, C. (2009). An fMRI investigation of the cultural specificity of music memory. *SCAN, 4*(4), 1–10.

Denisoff, R. (1983). *Sing a song of social significance*. Bowling Green, OH: Bowling Green State University Popular Press.

Desain, P., & Honing, H. (2003). The formation of rhythmic categories and metric priming. *Perception, 32*, 341–365.

Deshpande, V. (1973). *Indian musical traditions: An aesthetic study of the Gharanas in Hindustani music*. (S. Deshpande, Trans.). Bombay, India: R. G. Bhatkal.

Deutsch, D. (1986). A musical paradox. *Music Perception, 3*(3), 275–280.

Deutsch, D. (Ed.). (1982). *The psychology of music*. New York, NY: Academic Press.

Deutsch, D. (Ed.). (1999). *The psychology of music* (2nd ed.). New York, NY: Academic Press.

Deutsch, D., Henthorn, T., & Dolson, M. (2004). Absolute pitch, speech, and tone language: Some experiments and a proposed framework. *Music Perception, 21*(3), 339–356.

Deutsch, J. (2004). Memory: Experimental approaches. In R. Gregory (Ed.), *Oxford companion to the mind* (2nd ed., pp. 568–571). New York, NY: Oxford University Press.

Dewey, J. (1916). *Democracy and education: An introduction to the philosophy of education*. New York, NY: Palgrave Macmillan.

Di Pietro, M., Laganaro, M., Leemann, B., & Schnider, A. (2004). Receptive amusia: Temporal auditory processing deficit in a professional musician following a left temporo-parietal lesion. *Neuropsychologia*, 42(7), 868–877.

Di Rosa, C., Cieri, F., Antonucci, I., Stuppia, L., & Gatta, V. (2015). Music in DNA: From Williams syndrome to musical genes. *Open Journal of Genetics*, 5(1), 12–26.

Dibben, N. (2002). Gender identity and music. In R. MacDonald, D. Hargreaves, & D. Miell (Eds.), *Musical identities* (pp. 117–133). Oxford: Oxford University Press.

Diserens, C., & Fine, H. (1939). *A psychology of music*. Cincinnati, OH: Authors.

Dissanayake, E. (2000). Antecedents of the temporal arts in early mother-infant interaction. In N. Wallin, B. Merker, & S. Brown (Eds.), *The origins of music* (pp. 389–410). Cambridge, MA: The MIT Press.

Dissanayake, E. (2009a). Bodies swayed to music: The temporal arts as integral to ceremonial ritual. In S. Malloch & C. Trevarthen (Eds.), *Communicative musicality: Exploring the basis of human companionship* (pp. 533–544). Oxford: Oxford University Press.

Dissanayake, E. (2009b). Root, leaf, blossom, or bole: Concerning the origin and adaptive function of music. In S. Malloch & C. Trevarthen (Eds.) *Communicative musicality: Exploring the basis of human companionship* (pp. 17–30). Oxford: Oxford University Press.

Dixon-Salazar, T. J., & Gleeson, J. G. (2010). Genetic regulation of human brain development: Lessons from Mendelian diseases. *Annals of the New York Academy of Sciences*, 1214(1), 156–167.

Dogiel, J. (1880). Uver den einfluss der musik auf den blutkreislauf. *Archiv fur physiologie*, 416–428. Cited in Eagle, Jr., C. (1972). *A review of human physiological systems and their response to musical stimuli*. Paper presented at Southeastern Conference of National Association for Music Therapy, Tallahassee, FL.

Doidge, N. (2007). *The brain that changes itself*. New York, NY: Penguin Books.

Don, A., Schellenberg, E., & Rourke, B. (1999). Music and language skills of children with Williams syndrome. *Child Neuropsychology*, 5(3), 154–170.

Donahue, T. (2005). *A guide to musical temperament*. Lanham, MD: Scarecrow Press.

Donaldson, J., & Duckert, L. (1991). Anatomy of the ear. In M. Paparella, D. Shumrick, J. Gluckman, & W. Meyerhoff (Eds.), *Otolaryngology, Vol. 1. basic sciences and related principles* (3rd ed., pp. 23–58). Philadelphia: Saunders.

Dorsaint-Pierre, R., Penhune, V., Watkins, K., Neelin, P., Lerch, J., Bouffard, M., & Zatorre, R. (2006). Asymmetries of the planum temporale and Heschl's gyrus: Relationship to language lateralization. *Brain*, 129(5), 1164–1176.

Douglas, G. (2007). Myanmar's nation-building cultural policy: Traditional music and political legitimacy. In Y. Terada (Ed.), *Authenticity and Cultural Identity. Senri Ethnological Reports*, 65, 27–41.

Douglas, G. (2009). *Music in mainland Southeast Asia*. New York, NY: Oxford University Press.

Douglas, S., & Willatts, P. (1994). The relationship between musical ability and literacy skills. *Journal of Research in Reading*, 17(2), 99–107.

Dowling, W. (1973). The perception of interleaved melodies. *Cognitive Psychology*, 5(3), 322–337.

Dowling, W. (1978). Scale and contour: Two components of a theory of memory for melodies. *Psychological Review*, 85(4), 341–354.

Dowling, W. (1999). The development of music perception and cognition. In D. Deutsch (Ed.), *The psychology of music* (2d ed., pp. 603–627). San Diego, CA: Elsevier Academic Press.

Dowling, W., & Harwood, D. (1986). *Music cognition*. Orlando, FL: Academic Press.

Dowling, W., & Tighe, T. (1993). *Psychology and music: The understanding of melody and rhythm*. Hillsdale, NJ: Lawrence Erlbaum.

Doyon, J., & Benali, H. (2005). Reorganization and plasticity in the adult brain during learning of motor skills. *Current Opinion in Neurobiology*, 15, 161–167.

Drake, R. (1957). *Drake musical aptitude tests*. Chicago: Science Research Associates.

Drayna, D., Manichaikul, A., de Lange, M., Snieder, H., & Spector, T. (2001). Genetic correlates of musical pitch recognition in humans. *Science*, 291, 1969–1971.

Droh, R., & Spintge, R. (Eds.). (1983). *Angst, schmerz, musik in der anästhesie* (Fear, pain, music in anesthesia). Basel: Roche.

Dubos, R. (1974). *Beast or angel?* New York, NY: Scribner.

References

Dubos, R. (1981). *Celebrations of life*. New York, NY: McGraw-Hill.

Duerksen, G. (1972). Some effects of expectation on evaluation of recorded musical performance. *Journal of Research in Music Education, 20*(2), 268–272.

Duke, R. (2005). *Intelligent music teaching*. Austin, TX: Learning and Behavior Resources.

Duke, R., Simmons, A., & Cash, C. (2009). It's not how much; It's how. *Journal of Research in Music Education, 56*(4), 310–321.

Dukes, R., Bisel, T., Borega, K., Lobato, E., & Owens, M. (2003). Expressions of love, sex, and hurt in popular songs: A content analysis of all-time greatest hits. *The Social Science Journal, 40*(4), 643–650.

Duncan Herrington, J. (1996). Effects of music in service environments: A field study. *Journal of Services Marketing, 10*(2), 26–41.

Duncan, J., Seitz, R., Kolodny, J., Bor, D., Herzog, H., Ahmed, A., . . . Emslie, H. (2000). A neural basis for general intelligence. *Science, 289*, 457–459.

Dutton, D. (2009). *The art instinct*. Oxford: Oxford University Press.

Dyce, J. A., & O'Connor, B. P. (1994). The personalities of popular musicians. *Psychology of Music, 22*(2), 168–173.

Dykens, E. M., Rosner, B. A., Ly, T., & Sagun, J. (2005). Music and anxiety in Williams syndrome: A harmonious or discordant relationship? *American Journal on Mental Retardation, 110*(5), 346–358.

Eagle, C. Jr. (Ed.). (1976). *Music therapy index. An international interdisciplinary index to the literature of the psychology, psychophysiology, psychophysics and sociology of music* (Vol. 1). Lawrence, KS: National Association for Music Therapy.

Eagle, C. Jr., (Ed.). (1978). *Music psychology index: The international interdisciplinary index of the influence of music on behavior: References to the literature from the natural and behavioral sciences, and the fine and therapeutic arts for the years 1976–77* (Vol. 2). Denton, TX: Institute for Therapeutics Research.

Eagle, C. Jr. (1982). *Music therapy for handicapped individuals: An annotated and indexed bibliography*. Washington, DC: National Association for Music Therapy.

Eagle, C. Jr. (1996). An introductory perspective on music psychology. In D. Hodges (Ed.), *Handbook of music psychology* (2nd ed., pp. 1–28). San Antonio, TX: IMR Press.

Eagle, C. Jr., & Miniter, J. (Eds.). (1984). *Music psychology index. The international Interdisciplinary index of the influence of music on behavior: References to the literature from the natural and behavioral sciences, and the fine and therapeutic arts for the years 1978–80* (Vol. 3). Phoenix, AZ: Institute for Therapeutics Research and Oryx Press.

Economic Times. (2015, November 8). List of the most crowded music concerts in history. *The Economic Times*. Retrieved from https://economictimes.indiatimes.com/magazines/panache/list-of-the-most-crowded-music-concerts-in-history/articleshow/49702777.cms

Edwards, R., & Hodges, D. (2007). Neuromusical research: An overview of the literature. In W. Gruhn & F. Rauscher (Eds.), *Neurosciences in music pedagogy* (pp. 1–25). Hauppauge, NY: Nova Science Publishers, Inc.

Eisner, E. (1982). *Cognition and curriculum: A basis for deciding what to teach*. New York, NY: London.

Eisner, E. (1985). Aesthetic modes of knowing. In E. Eisner (Ed.), *Learning and teaching: The ways of knowing: Eight-fourth yearbook of the national society for the study of education* (pp. 23–36). Chicago: University of Chicago Press.

Ekman, P., Levenson, R., & Friesen, W. (1983). Autonomic nervous system activity distinguishes among emotions. *Science, 221*, 1208–1210.

Elbert, T., Pantev, C., Wienbruch, C., Rockstroh, B., & Taub, E. (1995). Increased cortical representation of the fingers of the left hand in string players. *Science, 270*, 305–307.

Eliot, L. (2000). *What's going on in there? How the brain and mind develop in the first five years of life*. New York, NY: Bantam.

Ellington, D. (1973). *Duke Ellington: Music is my mistress*. Garden City, NY: Doubleday Anchor Book.

Elliott, C. (1975). Attacks and releases as factors in instrument identification. *Journal of Research in Music Education, 23*(1), 35–40.

Elmer-DeWitt, P. (1987, March 16). From Mozart to megabytes. *Time Magazine*, 71.

Ember, C., & Ember, M. (1973). *Cultural anthropology*. Englewood Cliffs, NJ: Prentice-Hall.

Emmorey, K., Allen, J., Bruss, J., Schenker, N., & Damasio, H. (2003). A morphometric analysis of auditory brain regions in congenitally deaf adults. *PNAS Neuroscience (Proceedings of the National Academy of Sciences)*, 100(17), 10049–10054.

Engel, A., Hijmans, B. S., Cerliani, L., Bangert, M., Nanetti, L., Keller, P. E., & Keysers, C. (2014). Inter-individual differences in audio-motor learning of piano melodies and white matter fiber tract architecture. *Human Brain Mapping*, 35(5), 2483–2497.

Enk, R., Franzke, P., Offermanns, K., Hohenadel, M., Boehlig, A., Nitsche, I., . . . Koelsch, S. (2008). Music and the immune system. *International Journal of Psychophysiology*, 69, 207–241.

Ericsson, E. (2008). Deliberate practice and acquisition of expert performance: A general overview. *Academic Emergence Medicine*, 15, 988–994.

Ericsson, K. (1997). Deliberate practice and the acquisition of expert performance: An overview. In H. Jørgensen & A. Lehmann (Eds), *Does practice make perfect? Current theory and research on instrumental music practice* (pp. 9–52). Oslo: Norges Musikkhøgskole.

Ericsson, K., Krampe, R., & Tesch-Römer, C. (1993). The role of deliberate practice in the acquisition of expert performance. *Psychological Review*, 100(3), 363–406.

Erkkinen, M., & Berkowitz, A. (2019). Brain research in music improvisation. In M. Thaut & D. Hodges (Eds.), *The Oxford handbook on music and the brain*. Oxford: Oxford University Press.

Etzel, J., Johnsen, E., Dickerson, J., Tranel, D., & Adolphs, R. (2006). Cardiovascular and respiratory responses during musical mood induction. *International Journal of Psychophysiology*, 61, 57–69.

Evans, J., & Clynes, M. (Eds.). (1986). *Rhythm in psychological, linguistic, and musical processes*. Springfield, IL: Charles C. Thomas.

Everest, F. A. (1986). *Auditory perception: An audio training course*. Berkeley, CA: Mix Bookshelf.

Everest, F., & Pohlmann, K. (2009). *Master handbook of acoustics* (5th ed.). New York, NY: McGraw-Hill.

Evers, S., & Suhr, B. (2000). Changes of the neurotransmitter serotonin but not of hormones during short time music perception. *European Archives of Psychiatry and Clinical Neuroscience*, 250(3), 144–147.

Fabian, D., Timmers, R., & Schubert, E. (Eds.). (2014). *Expressiveness in music performance*. Oxford: Oxford University Press.

Fábián, T. (2012). *Mind-body connections: Pathways of psychosomatic coupling under meditation and other states of consciousness*. New York, NY: Nova Science.

Fabiani, M., & Friberg, A. (2011). Influence of pitch, loudness, and timbre on the perception of instrument dynamics. *The Journal of the Acoustical Society of America*, 130(4), EL193–EL199.

Fahrenberg, J. (2001). Origins and developments of ambulatory monitoring and assessment. In J. Fahrenberg & M. Myrtek (Eds.), *Progress in ambulatory assessment: Computer-assisted psychological and psychophysiological methods in monitoring and field studies* (pp. 587–614). Seattle, WA: Hogrefe & Huber.

Falk, D. (2009). New information about Albert Einstein's brain. *Frontiers in Evolutionary Neuroscience*, 1(3), doi:10.3389/neuro.18.003.2009.

Fancourt, D., Ockelford, A., & Belai, A. (2014). The psychoneuroimmunologyical effects of music: A systematic review and a new model. *Brain, Behavior, and Immunity*, 36, 15–26.

Farb, P. (1978). *Humankind*. New York, NY: Bantam Books.

Farmer, H. (1969). The music of ancient Egypt. In E. Wellesz (Ed.), *Ancient and oriental music* (pp. 255–282). London: Oxford University Press.

Farnsworth, C. (1930). *Short studies in musical psychology*. New York, NY: Oxford University Press.

Farnsworth, P. (1941). Further data on the Adlerian theory of artistry. *Journal of General Psychology*, 24, 447–450.

Farnsworth, P. (1958). *The social psychology of music*. New York, NY: Holt, Rinehart & Winston.

Farnsworth, P. (1969). *The social psychology of music* (2nd ed.). Ames, IA: Iowa State University Press.

Fasanaro, A., Spitaleri, D., Valiani, R., & Grossi, D. (1990). Dissociation in musical reading: A musician affected by alexia without agraphia. *Music Perception*, 7(3), 259–272.

Fassbender, C. (1996). Infants' auditory sensitivity towards acoustic parameters of speech and music. In I. Deliège & J. Sloboda (Eds.), *Musical beginnings: Origins and development of musical competence* (pp. 56–87). New York, NY: Oxford University Press.

References

Faulkner, R., & Davidson, J. (2006). Men in chorus: Collaboration and competition in homo-social vocal behaviour. *Psychology of Music*, *34*(2), 219–237.

Feder, S., Karmel, R., & Pollock, G. (Eds.). (1993). *Psychoanalytic explorations in music.* Madison, CT: International Universities Press.

Feld, S., & Fox, A. (1994). Music and language. *Annual Reviews of Anthropology*, *23*, 25–53.

Feldman, D. (2016). Two roads diverged in the musical wood: A coincidence appraoch to the lives and careers of Nyiregyházi and Menuhin. In G. McPherson (Ed.), *Musical prodigies* (pp. 115–133). Oxford: Oxford University Press.

Ferguson, S., & Voll, K. (2004). Burn pain and anxiety: The use of music relaxation during rehabilitation. *Journal of Burn Care Rehabilitation*, *25*(1), 8–14.

Ferreri, L., Mas-Herrero, E., Zatorre, R. J., Ripollés, P., Gomez-Andres, A., Alicart, H., . . . Riba, J. (2019). Dopamine modulates the reward experiences elicited by music. *Proceedings of the National Academy of Sciences*, 201811878.

Ferreri, L., Moussard, A., Bigand, E., & Tillmann, B. (2019). Music and the aging brain. In M. Thaut & D. Hodges (Eds.), *The Oxford handbook of music and the brain* (pp. 623–644). Oxford: Oxford University Press.

Filley, C. (2005). White matter and behavioral neurology. In J. Ulmer, L. Parsons, M. Moseley, & J. Gabrieli (Eds.), *White matter in cognitive neuroscience* (Vol. 1064, pp. 162–183). New York: Annals of the New York Academic of Sciences.

Fincher, J. (1976). *Human intelligence.* New York, NY: Putnam.

Fine, P., Berry, A., & Rosner, B. (2006). The effect of pattern recognition and tonal predictability on sight-singing ability. *Psychology of Music*, *34*(4), 431–447.

Fishbein, M., & Middlestadt, S. (1988). Medical problems among ICSOM musicians: Overview of a national survey. *Medical Problems of Performing Artists*, *3*(1), 1–9.

Fisk, J. (1997). *Composers on music: Eight centuries of writings* (2nd ed.). Boston, MA: Northeastern University Press.

Fiske, H. (1990). *Music and mind: Philosophical essays on the cognition and meaning of music.* Lewiston, NY: Edwin Mellen.

Fitch, T. (2006). The biology and evolution of music: A comparative perspective. *Cognition*, *100*, 173–215.

Fitch, T. (2009). Biology of music: Another one bites the dust. *Current Biology*, *19*(10), R403–R404.

Fletcher, H., & Munson, W. (1933). Loudness, its definition, measurement and calculation. *Journal of the Acoustical Society of America*, *5*, 82–108.

Fletcher, N., & Rossing, T. (2012). *The physics of musical instruments.* New York, NY: Springer-Verlag.

Flohr, J., & Hodges, D. (2006). Music and neuroscience. In R. Colwell (Ed.), *MENC Handbook of musical cognition and development* (pp. 7–39). New York, NY: Oxford University Press.

Flom, R., Gentile, D., & Pick, A. (2008). Infants' discrimination of happy and sad music. *Infant Behavior and Development*, *31*(4), 716–728.

Foley, E. (1975). The effects of training in conservation of tonal and rhythmic patterns on second-grade children. *Journal of Research in Music Education*, *23*(4), 240–248.

Foley, E. (Ed.). (2005). *Music and spirituality.* Basil, Switzerland: MDPI. Retrieved from www.theoretical/ philosophical explanations.

Folkestad, G. (2002). National identity and music. In R. MacDonald, D. Hargreaves, & D. Miell (Eds.), *Musical identities* (pp. 151–162). Oxford: Oxford University Press.

Forgeard, M., Winner, E., Norton, A., & Schlaug, G. (2008). Practicing a musical instrument in childhood is associated with enhanced verbal ability and nonverbal reasoning. *PLoS ONE*, *3*(10), e3566. doi:10.1371/journal.pone.0003566

Foulke, E., & Sticht, T. (1969). Review of research on the intelligibility and comprehension of accelerated speech. *Psychological Bulletin*, *72*(1), 50–62.

Fox, J. (2017, May 15). Tanglewood is a $103m economic engine for the Berkshires, study says. *The Boston Globe.* Retrieved from www.bostonglobe.com/metro/2017/05/14/tanglewood-economic-engine-for-berkshires-study-says/bCMgzSYphOQcl1q1Et2dOK/story.html?s_campaign=todaysheadlines:news letter

Frances, R. (1988). *The perception of music* (W. Dowling, Trans.). Hillsdale, NJ: Lawrence Erlbaum Associates.

Franklin, E. (1972). *Music education: Psychology and method*. London: George G. Harrap.

Fraser, C. (2004). Social psychology. In R. Gregory (Ed.), *Oxford companion to the mind* (2nd ed., pp. 850–851). New York, NY: Oxford University Press.

Freeman, W. (2000). A neurobiological role of music in social bonding. In N. Wallin, B. Merker, & S. Brown (Eds.), *The origins of music* (pp. 411–424). Cambridge, MA: The MIT Press.

Freud, S. (1910/1957). The origin and development of psychoanalysis. In J. Rickman (Ed.), *A general selection from the works of Sigmund Freud* (pp. 3–36). Garden City, NY: Doubleday Anchor Books.

Freund, H., & Hefter, H. (1990). Timing mechanisms in skilled hand movements. In F. Wilson & F. Roehmann (Eds.), *Music and child development* (pp. 179–190). St. Louis, MO: MMB Music.

Frey, B. (2018). *The SAGE encyclopedia of educational research, measurement, and evaluation* (Vols. 1–4). Thousand Oaks, CA: SAGE Publications.

Fridja, N. (1988). The laws of emotion. *American Psychologist, 43*(5), 349–358.

Fridman, R. (1973). The first cry of the newborn: Basis for the child's future musical development. *Journal of Research in Music Education, 21*(3), 264–269.

Fritz, T., Jentschke, S., Gosselin, N., Sammler, D., Peretz, I., Turner, R., . . . Koelsch, S. (2009). Universal recognition of three basic emotions in music. *Current Biology, 19*, 573–576.

Froelich, H. (2007). *Sociology for music teachers*. Upper Saddle River, NJ: Prentice-Hall.

Frolenkov, G., Belyantseva, I., Friedman, T., & Griffith, A. (2004). Genetic insights into the morphogenesis of inner hair cells. *Nature Reviews Genetics, 5*, 489–498.

Fuentes, A. (2018). How humans and apes are different, and why it matters. *Journal of Anthropological Research, 74*(2), 151–167.

Fujioka, T., Ross, B., & Trainor, L. J. (2015). Beta-band oscillations represent auditory beat and its metrical hierarchy in perception and imagery. *Journal of Neuroscience, 35*(45), 15187–15198.

Fukui, H. (2001). Music and testosterone: A new hypothesis for the origin and function of music. In R. Zatorre & I. Peretz (Eds.), *The neurosciences and music. Annals of the New York Academy of Sciences, 999*, 448–451.

Fukui, H., & Yamashita, M. (2003). The effects of music and visual stress on testosterone and cortisol in men and women. *Neuroendocrinology Letters, 24*(3–4), 173–180.

Fullagar, C. J., Knight, P. A., & Sovern, H. S. (2013). Challenge/skill balance, flow, and performance anxiety. *Applied Psychology, 62*(2), 236–259.

Fuller, L. (2004). *National days/national ways: Historical, political, and religious celebrations around the world*. Westport, CT: Praeger.

Fung, V., & Lehmberg, L. (2016). *Music for life*. Oxford: Oxford University Press.

Fyk, J. (1995). *Melodic intonation, psychoacoustics, and the violin*. Zielona Góra, Poland: Organon.

Gaab, N., Paetzold, M., Becker, M., Walker, M., & Schlaug, G. (2004). The influence of sleep on auditory learning: A behavioral study. *NeuroReport, 15*(4), 731–734.

Gabrielsson, A. (1992). The performance of music. In D. Deutsch (Ed.), *The psychology of music* (2d ed., pp. 501–602). New York, NY: Academic Press.

Gabrielsson, A. (2001). Emotions in strong experiences with music. In P. Juslin & J. Sloboda (Eds.), *Music and emotion: Theory and research* (pp. 431–449). New York, NY: Oxford University Press.

Gabrielsson, A. (2003). Music performance research at the millennium. *Psychology of Music, 31*(3), 221–272.

Gabrielsson, A. (2009). The relationship between musical structure and perceived expression. In S. Hallam, I. Cross, & M. Thaut (Eds.), *Oxford handbook of music psychology* (pp. 141–150). New York, NY: Oxford University Press.

Gabrielsson, A. (2010). Strong experiences with music. In P. Juslin & J. Sloboda (Eds.), *Handbook of music and emotion* (pp. 547–574). Oxford: Oxford University Press.

Gabrielsson, A. (2011). *Strong experiences with music*. Oxford: Oxford University Press.

Gabrielsson, A., & Juslin, P. (1996). Emotional expression in music performance: Between the performer's intention and the listener's experience. *Psychology of Music, 24*(1), 68–91.

Gabrielsson, A., & Juslin, P. (2003). Emotional expression in music. In R. Davidson, K. Scherer, & H. Goldsmith (Eds.), *Handbook of affective sciences* (pp. 503–534). New York, NY: Oxford University Press.

References

Gabrielsson, A., & Lindström, E. (1995). Emotional expression in synthesizer and sentograph expression. *Psychomusicology, 14*, 94–116.

Gabrielsson, A., & Lindström, E. (2001). The influence of musical structure on emotional expression. In P. Juslin & J. Sloboda (Eds.), *Music and emotion: Theory and research* (pp. 223–248). New York, NY: Oxford University Press.

Gabrielsson, A., & Wik, S. (2003). Strong experiences related to music: A descriptive system. *Musicae Scientiae, 7*(2), 157–217.

Gage, N., & Berliner, D. (1975). *Educational psychology*. Chicago: Rand McNally.

Gardner, H. (2006). *Multiple intelligences: New horizons*. New York, NY: Basic Books.

Gardner, H. (2011). *Creating minds: An anatomy of creativity seen through the lives of Freud, Einstein, Picasso, Stravinsky, Eliot, Graham, and Gandhi*. New York, NY: Basic Books.

Garfias, R. (1985). Music: Thinking globally, acting locally. In *Becoming human through music* (pp. 23–28). Reston, VA: Music Educators National Conference.

Garlin, F., & Owen, K. (2006). Setting the tone with the tune: A meta-anlytic review of the effects of background music in retail settings. *Journal of Business Research, 59*, 755–764.

Garofalo, R. (2010). Politics, mediation, social context, and public use. In P. Juslin & J. Sloboda (Eds.), *Handbook of music and emotion* (pp. 725–754). Oxford: Oxford University Press.

Gärtner, H., Minnerop, M., Pieperhoff, P., Schleicher, A., Zilles, K., Altenmüller, E., & Amunts, K. (2013). Brain morphometry shows effects of long-term musical practice in middle-aged keyboard players. *Frontiers in Psychology, 4*, 636.

Gaser, C., & Schlaug, G. (2003). Gray matter differences between musicians and nonmusicians. *The Neurosciences and Music: Annals of the New York Academy of Sciences, 999*, 514–517.

Gaston, E. (1951). Dynamic music factors in mood change. *Music Educators Journal, 37*, 42–44.

Gaston, E. (Ed.). (1968). *Music in therapy*. New York, NY: Palgrave Macmillan.

Gates, J. (1989). Comparison of public singing by American men and women. *Journal of Research in Music Education, 37*(1), 32–47.

Gaunt, K. (2006). *The games black girls play*. New York, NY: New York University Press.

Gazzaniga, M. (2008). *Human: The science behind what makes us unique*. New York, NY: HarperCollins.

Ge, D., & Li, Y. (2012). Songs of genes, by genes, for genes. *Leonardo, 45*(1), 96–97.

Geerdes, H. (1991). *Improving acoustics for music teaching*. Reston, VA: Music Educators National Conference.

Geissmann, T. (2000). Gibbon songs and human music from an evolutionary perspective. In N. Wallin, B. Merker, & S. Brown (Eds.), *The origins of music* (pp. 103–123). Cambridge, MA: The MIT Press.

Gembris, H. (2002). The development of musical abilities. In R. Colwell & C. Richardson (Eds.), *The new handbook of research on music teaching and learning* (pp. 487–508). New York, NY: Oxford University Press.

Gembris, H., & Davidson, J. (2002). Environmental influences. In R. Parncutt & G. McPherson (Eds.), *The science and psychology of music performance* (pp. 17–30). New York, NY: Oxford University Press.

Gendolla, G., & Krüsken, J. (2001). Mood state and cardiovascular response in active coping with an affect-regulative challenge. *International Journal of Psychophysiology, 41*(2), 169–180.

Geringer, J., & Kostka, M. (1984). An analysis of practice room behavior of college music students. *Contributions to Music Education, 11*, 24–27.

Gerling, C., & dos Santos, R. (2007). Intended versus perceived emotion. *International symposium on performance science*. Retrieved March 22, 2010, from http://www.rcm.ac.uk/cache/fl0020232.pdf

Gerra, G., Zaimovic, A., Franchini, D., Palladino, M., Giucastro, G., Reali, N., . . . Brambilla, F. (1998). Neuroendocrine responses of healthy volunteers to "techno-music": Relationships with personality traits and emotional state. *International Journal of Psychophysiology, 28*(1), 99–111.

Getzels, J. (1964). Creative thinking, problem-solving, and instruction. In E. Hilgard (Ed.), *Theories of learning and instruction: The sixty-third yearbook of the national society for the study of education* (pp. 240–267). Chicago: University of Chicago Press.

Gilbertson, S., & Aldridge, D. (2008). *Music therapy and traumatic brain injury: A light on a dark night*. London: Jessica Kingsley.

Gilboa, A., & Bodner, E. (2009). What are your thoughts when the national anthem is playing? An empirical exploration. *Psychology of Music, 37*(4), 459–484.

Gill, K., & Purves, D. (2009). A biological rationale for musical scales. *PLoS ONE, 4*(12), e8144.

Gillespie, W., & Myors, B. (2000). Personality of rock musicians. *Psychology of Music, 28*(2), 154–165.

Gilman, S. (2019). Music and psychoanalysis. In Y. Kim & S. Gilman (Eds.), *The Oxford handbook of music and the body* (pp. 112–126). Oxford: Oxford University Press. doi:10.1093/oxfordhb/9780190636234.013.8

Ginsborg, J., Spahn, C., & Williamon, A. (2012). Health promotion in higher music education. In R. MacDonald, G. Kreutz, & L. Michell (Eds.), *Music, health, and wellbeing* (pp. 356–366). Oxford: Oxford University Press.

Gjerdingen, R. (2002). The psychology of music. In T. Christensen (Ed.), *The Cambridge history of Western music theory* (pp. 956–981). Cambridge: Cambridge University Press.

Gjerdingen, R. (2007). *Music in the Galant style*. Oxford: Oxford University Press.

Gladwell, M. (2008). *Outliers: The story of success*. New York, NY: Little, Brown & Company.

Global Music Report 2017. (2017). *International federation of the phonographic industry*. Retrieved from www.ifpi.org/downloads/GMR2017.pdf

Gohl, A., Clayton, S., Strickland, K., Bufford, Y., Halle, J., & Greathouse, D. (2006). Median and ulnar neuropathies in university pianists. *Medical Problems of Performing Artists, 21*(1), 17–24.

Goldberg, P., Weiner, S., Bar-Yosef, O., Xu, Q., & Liu, J. (2001). Site formation processes at Zhoukoudian, China. *Journal of Human Evolution, 41*(5), 483–530.

Golder, S. A., Wilkinson, D. M. M., & Huberman, B. A. (2007). Rhythms of social interaction: Messaging within a massive online network. In C. Steinfield, B. Pentland, M. Ackerman, & N. Contractor (Eds.), *Communities and technologies* (pp. 41–66). London: Springer.

Goldstein, A. (1980). Thrills in response to music and other stimuli. *Physiological Psychology, 8*(1), 126–129.

Goldstein, E. (1996). *Sensation & perception* (4th ed.). New York, NY: Brooks Cole.

Goleman, D. (1986, November 9). Rethinking the value of intelligence tests. *New York Times*.

Gomez, P., & Danuser, B. (2004). Affective and physiological responses to environmental noises and music. *International Journal of Psychophysiology, 53*, 91–103.

Gomez, P., & Danuser, B. (2007). Relationships between musical structure and psychophysiological measures of emotion. *Emotion, 7*(2), 377–387.

Goolsby, T. (1989). Computer applications to eye movement research in music reading. *Psychomusicology, 8*, 111–126.

Goolsby, T. (1994a). Eye movement in music reading: Effects of reading ability, notational complexity, and encounters. *Music Perception, 12*(1), 77–96.

Goolsby, T. (1994b). Profiles of processing: Eye movements during sightreading. *Music Perception, 12*(1), 97–123.

Gopnik, A., Meltznoff, A., & Kuhl, P. (2001). *The scientist in the crib*. New York, NY: Perennial.

Gordon, E. (1961). A study to determine the effects of practice and training on Drake musical aptitude test scores. *Journal of Research in Music Education, 4*, 63–74.

Gordon, E. (1967). A comparison of the performance of culturally disadvantaged with that of culturally heterogenous students on the musical aptitude profile. *Psychology in the Schools, 15*, 260–268.

Gordon, E. (1968). A study of the efficiency of general intelligence and musical aptitude tests in predicting achievement in music. *Council for Research in Music Education, 13*, 40–45.

Gordon, E. (1971). *The psychology of music teaching*. Englewood Cliffs, NJ: Prentice-Hall.

Gordon, E. (1998). *Introduction to research and the psychology of music*. Chicago: GIA Publications.

Gordon, E. (2007). *Learning sequences in music: A contemporary music learning theory*. Chicago: GIA Publications.

Gottesman, I., & Hanson, D. (2005). Human development: Biological and genetic processes. *Annual Review of Psychology, 56*, 263–286.

Gould, G. (1956). Liner notes to the recording of Bach *Goldberg Variations*. CBS Masterworks ML 5060.

Graham, G. (2000). *Philosophy of the arts: An introduction to aesthetics* (2nd ed.). London: Routledge.

Graham, L. (2004/2005). Music in the military: It's about influence. *American Music Teacher, 54*(3), 34–36.

Gramming, P., Nord, L., Sundberg, J., & Elliot, N. (1993). Does the nose resonate during singing? In *SMAC 93: Proceedings of the Stockholm Music Acoustics Conference. Publication, 79*, 166–171.

Grant, M. J. (2014). Pathways to music torture. *Transposition: Musique et Sciences Sociales, 4*.

Grape, C., Sandgren, M., Hansson, L. O., Ericson, M., & Theorell, T. (2002). Does singing promote well-being? An empirical study of professional and amateur singers during a singing lesson. *Integrative Physiological & Behavioral Science, 38*(1), 65–74.

Gray, P., Krause, B., Atema, J., Payne, R., Krumhansl, C., & Baptista, L. (2001). The music of nature and the nature of music. *Science, 291*(5501), 52–54.

Graziano, A., & Johnson, J. (2006). Richard Wallaschek's nineteenth-century contributions to the psychology of music. *Music Perception, 23*(4), 293–303.

Greasley, A., Fulford, R., Pickard, M., & Hamilton, N. (2018). Help musicians UK hearing survey: Musicians' hearing and hearing protection. *Psychology of Music*. doi:10.1177/0305735618812238

Greasley, A., & Lamont, A. (2016). Musical preferences. In S. Hallam, I. Cross, & M. Thaut (Eds.), *The Oxford handbook of music psychology* (pp. 263–281). Oxford, UK: Oxford University Press.

Great Ape Trust. (2009). *Music perception, learning, and production in apes.* Retrieved November 6, 2009, from www.greatapetrust.org/research/programs/programNC09.php

Greeley, A. (1995). *Sociology and religion: A collection of readings.* New York, NY: HarperCollins College Publishers.

Greer, R. (1981). *An operant approach to motivation and affect: Ten years of research in music learning.* Documentary report of the Ann Arbor symposium. Reston, VA: Music Educators National Conference.

Gregersen, P., Kowalsky, E., Kohn, N., & Marvin, E. (2001). Early childhood music education and predisposition to absolute pitch: Teasing apart genes and environment. *American Journal of Human Genetics, 98*, 280–282.

Gregory, A. (1997). The roles of music in society: The ethnomusicological perspective. In D. Hargreaves & A. North (Eds.), *The social psychology of music* (pp. 123–140). Oxford: Oxford University Press.

Gregory, A., & Varney, N. (1996). Cross-cultural comparisons in the affective response to music. *Psychology of Music, 24*(1), 47–52.

Gregory, T. (1972). The effects of rhythmic notation variables on sight-reading errors. *Journal of Research in Music Education, 20*(4), 462–468.

Grewe, O., Kopiez, R., & Altenmüller, E. (2009). The chill parameter: Goose bumps and shivers as promising measures in emotion research. *Music Perception, 27*(1), 61–74.

Grewe, O., Nagel, F., Kopiez, R., & Altenmüller, E. (2007a). Emotions over time: Synchronicity and development of subjective, physiological, and facial affective reactions to music. *Emotion, 7*(4), 774–788.

Grewe, O., Nagel, F., Kopiez, R., & Altenmüller, E. (2007b). Listening to music as a re-creative process: Physiological, psychological, and psychacoustical correlates of chills and strong emotions. *Music Perception, 24*(3), 297–314.

Grey, J. (1977). Multidimensional perceptual scaling of musical timbres. *Journal of the Acoustical Society of America, 61*(5), 1270–1277.

Griesser, M. (2008). Referential calls signal predator behavior in a group-living bird species. *Current Biology, 18*(1), 69–73.

Grindea, C. (Ed.). (1995). *Tensions in the performance of music, extended edition.* New York, NY: Alexander Broude.

Grossman, S. P. (1967). *A textbook of physiological psychology.* New York, NY: John Wiley & Sons.

Gruhn, W., & Rauscher, F. (Eds.). (2007). *Neurosciences in music pedagogy.* Hauppauge, NY: Nova Science Publishers, Inc.

Gruson, L. (1988). Rehearsal skill and musical competence: Does practice make perfect? In J. Sloboda (Ed.), *Generative processes in music: The psychology of performance, improvisation, and composition* (pp. 91–112). Oxford: Clarendon Press.

Grutzmacher, P. (1987). The effects of tonal pattern training on the aural perception, reading recognition, and melodic: Sight-reading achievement of first-year instrumental music students. *Journal of Research in Music Education, 35*(3), 171–181.

Guhn, M., Hamm, A., & Zentner, M. (2007). Physiological and music-acoustic correlates of the chill response. *Music Perception, 24*(5), 473–483.

Guilford, J. (1968). Intelligence has three facets. *Science, 160*(3828), 615–620.

Guilford, J. P. (1951). *Guilford test for creativity*. Beverly Hills, CA: Sheridan Supply Company.

Gulick, W., Gescheider, G., & Frisina, R. (1989). *Hearing: Physiological acoustics, neural coding, and psychoacoustics*. New York, NY: Oxford University Press.

Gupta, U., & Gupta, B. (2005). Psychophysiological responsivity to Indian instrumental music. *Psychology of Music, 33*(4), 363–372.

Gurney, E. (1880). *The power of sound*. London: Smild, Elder, & Co.

Gustavus Adolphus College. (2007). St. Peter, Minnesota. *Information on Carl Seashore*. Retrieved April 25, 2007, from www.gustavus.edu/academics/psych/Epilogue/Seashore.html

Gute, D., & Gute, G. (2015). *How creativity works in the brain*. Washington, DC: National Endowment for the Art.

Gutheil, E. (Ed.). (1952). *Music and your emotions: A practical guide to music selections associated with desired emotional responses*. New York, NY: Liveright.

Haack, P. (1975). The influence of loudness on the discrimination of sound factors. *Journal of Research in Music Education, 23*(1), 67–77.

Haar, J. (2007). Music of the spheres. In L. Macy (Ed.), *Grove music online*. Retrieved April 27, 2007, from www.grovemusic.com

Habib, M., Lardy, C., Desiles, T., Commeiras, C., Chobert, J., & Besson, M. (2016). Music and dyslexia: A new musical training method to improve reading and related disorders. *Frontiers in Psychology, 7*, 26.

Hackney, C. M. (1987). Anatomical features of the auditory pathway from cochlea to cortex. *British Medical Bulletin, 43*(4), 780–801.

Hadjidimitriou, S., & Hadjileontiadis, L. (2012). Toward an EEG-based recognition of music liking using time-frequency analysis. *IEEE Transactions on Biomedical Engineering, 59*(12), 3498–3510.

Haider, M., & Groll-Knapp, E. (1981). Psychophysiological investigations into the stress experienced by musicians in a symphony orchestra. In M. Piperek (Ed.), *Stress and music* (pp. 15–34). Vienna: Wilhelm Braumüller.

Haier, R., Jung, R., Yeo, R., Head, K., & Alkire, M. (2004). Structural brain variation and general intelligence. *Neuroimage, 23*(1), 425–433.

Hall, D. (2002). *Musical acoustics* (3rd ed.). Boston, MA: Brooks Cole.

Hall, J. (1957). *The language of musical acoustics*. Boston, MA: Brooks Cole.

Hall, J. (2007). *New handbook of auditory evoked responses*. Boston, MA: Pearson Education, Inc.

Hall, P. C., West, J. H., & Hill, S. (2012). Sexualization in lyrics of popular music from 1959 to 2009: Implications for sexuality educators. *Sexuality & Culture, 16*(2), 103–117.

Hall, R. (2008). Geometrical music theory. *Science, 320*, 328–329.

Hallam, S. (1997). Approaches to instrumental music practice of experts and novices: Implications for education. In H. Jørgensen & A. Lehmann (Eds.), *Does practice make perfect? Current theory and research on instrumental music practice* (pp. 89–107). Oslo: Norges Musikkhøgskole.

Hallam, S. (2001). The development of metacognition in musicians: Implications for education. *British Journal of Music Education, 18*(1), 27–39.

Hallam, S. (2005). *Music psychology in education*. London: Institute of Education, University of London.

Hallam, S. (2010). The power of music: Its impact on the intellectual, social and personal development of children and young people. *International Journal of Music Education, 28*(3), 269–289.

Hallam, S. (2018). *Psychology of music*. London: Routledge.

Hallam, S., Creech, A., & Hodges, D. (Eds.). (2020). *The Routledge international handbook of music psychology in education and the community*. London: Routledge.

Hallam, S., Cross, I., & Thaut, M. (Eds.). (2009). *The Oxford handbook of music psychology*. New York, NY: Oxford University Press.

Hallam, S., Cross, I., & Thaut, M. (Eds.). (2016). *The Oxford handbook of music psychology* (2nd ed.). Oxford: Oxford University Press.

References

Hallam, S., & McDonald, R. (2009). The effects of music in community and educational settings. In S. Hallam, I. Cross, & M. Thaut (Eds.), *The Oxford handbook of music psychology* (pp. 471–480). Oxford: Oxford University Press.

Hallett, M. (2000). Transcranial magnetic stimulation and the human brain. *Nature, 406,* 147–150.

Halpern, A., Zatorre, R., Bouffard, M., & Johnson, J. (2004). Behavioral and neural correlates of perceived and imagined musical timbre. *Neuropsychologia, 42,* 1281–1292.

Hamann, D. (1982). An assessment of anxiety in instrumental and vocal performances. *Journal of Research in Music Education, 30*(2), 77–90.

Hamann, D. (1983). Anxiety and musical performance: How will it affect your students? *Update, 2*(1), 7–9.

Hamann, D., & Sobaje, M. (1983). Anxiety and the college musician: A study of performance conditions and subject variables. *Psychology of Music, 11*(1), 37–50.

Hamilton, L., Kella, J., & Hamilton, W. (1995). Personality and occupational stress in elite performers. *Medical Problems of Performing Artists, 10*(4), 86–89.

Hammel, A., & Hourigan, R. (2013). *Teaching music to students with autism.* Oxford: Oxford University Press.

Hammond, M. (1982). Unearthing the oldest known Maya. *National Geographic, 162*(1), 126–140.

Handel, S. (1989). *Listening: An introduction to the perception of auditory events.* Cambridge, MA: The MIT Press.

Hanley, B., & Montgomery, J. (2002). Contemporary curriculum practices and their theoretical bases. In R. Colwell & C. Richardson (Eds.), *The new handbook of research on music teaching and learning* (pp. 113–143). New York, NY: Oxford University Press.

Hanna, J. (1984). Towards discovering the universals of dance. *The World of Music, 26*(2), 88–101.

Hanna, W. (2007). The new Bloom's taxonomy: Implications for music education. *Arts Education Policy Review, 108*(4), 7–16.

Hannon, E. (2009). Perceiving speech rhythm in music: Listeners classify instrumental songs according to language of origin. *Cognition, 111,* 403–409.

Hannon, E., & Trehub, S. (2005). Metrical categories in infancy and adulthood. *Psychological Science, 16*(1), 48–55.

Hargreaves, D. J. (1986). *The developmental psychology of music.* Cambridge, MA: Cambridge University Press.

Hargreaves, D. J. (1996). The development of artistic and musical competence. In I. Deliège & J. Sloboda (Eds.), *Musical beginnings: Origins and development of musical competence* (pp. 145–170). Oxford: Oxford University Press.

Hargreaves, D. J., Miell, D., & MacDonald, R. (2002). What are musical identities, and why are they important? In R. MacDonald, D. Hargreaves, & D. Miell (Eds.), *Musical identities* (pp. 1–20). Oxford: Oxford University Press.

Hargreaves, D. J., Miell, D., & MacDonald, R. (Eds.). (2012). *Musical imaginations: Multidisciplinary perspectives on creativity, performance and perception.* Oxford: Oxford University Press.

Hargreaves, D. J., & North, A. (1997). *The social psychology of music.* New York, NY: Oxford University Press.

Hargreaves, D. J., North, A., & Tarrant, M. (2006). Musical preference and taste in childhood and adolescence. In G. McPherson (Ed.), *The child as musician* (pp. 135–154). Oxford: Oxford University Press.

Hari, R. (1990). The neuromagnetic method in the study of the human auditory cortex. In F. Grandori, M. Hoke, & G. Romani (Eds.), *Auditory evoked magnetic fields and electric potentials. Advances in Audiology, 6*(1), 222–282.

Harrer, G., & Harrer, H. (1977). Music, emotion, and autonomic function. In M. Critchley & R. Henson (Eds.), *Music and the brain* (pp. 202–216). London: William Heinemann Medical Books.

Hartmann, W. (2013). *Principles of musical acoustics.* New York, NY: Springer.

Haslinger, B., Erhard, P., Altenmüller, E., Schroeder, U., Boecker, H., & Ceballos-Baumann, A. (2005). Transmodal sensorimotor networks during action observation in professional pianists. *Journal of Cognitive Neuroscience, 17*(2), 282–293.

Haueisen, J., & Knösche, T. (2001). Involuntary motor activity in pianists evoked by music perception. *Journal of Cognitive Neuroscience, 13*(6), 786–792.

Hauenstein, A. (1998). *A conceptual framework for education objectives: A holistic approach to traditional taxonomies.* Lanham, MD: University Press of America.

Hauser, M. (1997). *The evolution of communication.* Cambridge, MA: The MIT Press.

Hauser, M. (2000). The sound and fury: Primate vocalizations as reflections of emotion and thought. In N. Wallin, B. Merker, & S. Brown (Eds.), *The origins of music* (pp. 77–102). Cambridge, MA: The MIT Press.

Hauser, M., & McDermott, J. (2003). The evolution of the music faculty: A comparative perspective. *Nature Neuroscience, 6,* 669–673.

Häussermann, C. (2006). Shamanism and biomedical approaches in Nepal: Dualism or synthesis? *Music Therapy Today, 7*(3), 514–622.

Heaton, P. (2003). Pitch memory, labeling and disembedding in autism. *Journal of Child Psychology and Psychiatry, 44*(4), 543–551.

Hedden, S. (1980). Psychoacoustical parameters of music. In D. Hodges (Ed.), *Handbook of music psychology* (pp. 63–92). Lawrence, KS: National Association for Music Therapy.

Hein, G., & Singer, T. (2008). I feel how you feel but not always: The empathetic brain and its modulation. *Current Opinion in Neurobiology, 18*(2), 153–158.

Hekkert, P., & Snelders, H. (1995). Prototypicality as an explanatory concept in aesthetics: A reply to Boselie (1991). *Empirical Studies of the Arts, 13*(2), 149–160.

Heller, J. (1962). *The effects of formal training on wing musical intelligence scores* (PhD dissertation). University of Iowa.

Helmholtz, H. L. F. von. (1863/1954). *On the sensations of tone as a physiological basis for the theory of music* (2nd ed., A. J. Ellis, Trans.). Reprint. New York, NY: Dover.

Heman-Ackah, Y. D., Sataloff, R. T., & Hawkshaw, M. (2013). *The voice: A medical guide for achieving and maintaining a healthy voice.* Narbeth, PA: Science & Medicine.

Henry, M. (2004). The use of targeted pitch skills for sight-singing instruction in the choral rehearsal. *Journal of Research in Music Education, 52*(3), 206–217.

Henry, M. (2008). The use of specific practice and performance strategies in sight-singing instruction. *Update: Applications of Research in Music Education, 26*(2), 11–16.

Henry, M., & Demorest, S. (1994). Individual sight-singing achievement in successful choral ensembles: A preliminary study. *Update: Applications of Research in Music Education, 13*(1), 4–8.

Henshilwood, C. S., d'Errico, F., & Watts, I. (2009). Engraved ochres from the middle stone age levels at Blombos Cave, South Africa. *Journal of Human Evolution, 57*(1), 27–47.

Henshilwood, C., d'Errico, F., Yates, R., Jacobs, Z., Tribolo, C., Duller, G. et al. (2002). Emergence of modern human behavior: Middle stone age engravings from South Africa. *Nature, 295,* 1278–1280.

Henshilwood, C., & Marean, C. (2003). The origina of moden human behavior: Critique of the models and their test implications. *Current Anthropology, 44*(5), 627–651.

Herholz, S., Lappe, C., & Pantev, C. (2009). Looking for a pattern: An MEG study on the abstract mismatch negativity in musicians and nonmusicians. *BMC Neuroscience, 10*(42). doi:10.1186/1471-2202-10-42

Hermelin, B. (2001). *Bright splinters of the mind: A personal story of research with autistic savants.* London: Jessica Kingsley Publishers.

Hernandez, P. (2018, September 20). Streaming now accounts for 75 percent of music industry revenue. *The Verge.* Retrieved from www.theverge.com/2018/9/20/17883584/streaming-record-sales-music-industry-revenue

Hevner, K. (1936). Experimental studies of the elements of expression in music. *The American Journal of Psychology, 48*(2), 246–268.

Heye, A., & Lamont, A. (2010). Mobile listening situations in everyday life: The use of MP3 players while traveling. *Musicae Scientiae, 14*(1), 95–120.

Heymans, G., & Wiersma, E. (1906–1918). Beiträge zur speziellen Psychologie [Contributions to differential psychology]. *Zeitschrift für Psychologie.* Cited in Révész, G. (1954). *Introduction to the psychology of music.* (G. deCourey, Trans.). Norman, OK: University of Oklahoma Press.

References

Hickok, G., Buchsbaum, B., Humphries, C., & Muftuler, T. (2003). Auditory-motor interaction revealed by fMRI: Speech, music, and working memory in area Spt. *Journal of Cognitive Neuroscience, 15*(5), 673–682.

Hidaka, T., Beranek, L., Masuda, S., Nishihara, N., & Okano, T. (2000). Acoustical design of the Tokyo Opera City (TOC) concert hall, Japan. *The Journal of the Acoustical Society of America, 107*(1), 340–354.

Hilgard, E., & Bower, G. (1966). *Theories of learning* (3rd ed.). New York, NY: Appleton-Century-Crofts.

Hill, E., & Stoneham, M. (2000). Practical applications of pulse oximetry. *Update in Anaesthesia, 11*(4), 1–2.

Hills, P., & Argyle, M. (1998). Musical and religious experiences and their relationship to happiness. *Personality and Individual Differences, 25*, 91–102.

Hirokawa, E., & Ohira, H. (2003). The effects of music listening after a stressful task on immune functions, neuroendocrine responses, and emotional states in college students. *Journal of Music Therapy, 40*(3), 189–211.

Hirsch, I. (1959). Auditory perception of temporal order. *Journal of the Acoustical Society of America, 31*(6), 759–767.

Ho, V., Lee, J-A., & Martin, K. (2011). The cell biology of synaptic plasticity. *Science, 334*, 623–628.

Hochberg, J. (2004). Gestalt theory. In R. Gregory (Ed.), *The Oxford companion to the mind* (2nd ed., pp. 372–375). New York, NY: Oxford University Press.

Hodges, D. (Ed.). (1980). *Handbook of music psychology*. Lawrence, KS: National Association for Music Therapy.

Hodges, D. (1996). *Handbook of music psychology* (2nd ed.). San Antonio, TX: IMR Press.

Hodges, D. (2009). Bodily responses to music. In S. Hallam, I. Cross, & M. Thaut (Eds.), *Oxford handbook of music psychology* (pp. 121–130). Oxford: Oxford University Press.

Hodges, D. (2010a). Can neuroscience help us do a better job of teaching music? *General Music Today, 23*(2), 3–12.

Hodges, D. (2010b). Psychophysiological responses to music. In P. Juslin & J. Sloboda (Eds.), *Music and emotion* (pp. 279–311). Oxford: Oxford University Press.

Hodges, D. (2016a). Bodily responses to music. In S. Hallam, I. Cross, & M. Thaut (Eds.), *Oxford handbook of music psychology* (2nd ed., pp. 183–196). Oxford: Oxford University Press.

Hodges, D. (2016b). The neuroaesthetics of music. In S. Hallam, I. Cross, & M. Thaut (Eds.), *Oxford handbook of music psychology* (2nd ed., pp. 247–262). Oxford: Oxford University Press.

Hodges, D. (2017). *A concise survey of music philosophy*. New York, NY: Routledge.

Hodges, D. (2019). Music through the lens of cultural neuroscience. In M. Thaut & D. Hodges (Eds.), *The Oxford handbook of music and the brain* (pp. 19–41). Oxford: Oxford University Press.

Hodges, D., Hairston, W., & Burdette, J. (2005). Aspects of multisensory perception: The integration of visual and auditory information in music experiences. In G. Avanzini, L. Lopez, S. Koelsch, & M. Majno (Eds.), *The neurosciences and music II: From perception to performance. Annals of the New York Academy of Sciences, 1060*, 175–185.

Hodges, D., Hairston, D., Maldjian, J., & Burdette, J. (2010). Keepng an open mind's eye: Mediation of cross-modal inhibition in music conductors. In S. Demorest, S. Morrison, & P. Campbell (Eds.), *Proceedings of the 11th international conference on music perception and cognition (ICMPC11)* (pp. 415–416). Seattle, WA: ICMPC.

Hodges, D., & Nolker, D. (2011). The acquisition of music reading skills. In R. Colwell & P. Webster (Eds.), *MENC handbook of research on music learning, Vol. II: Applications* (pp. 61–91). New York, NY: Oxford University Press.

Hodgson, D., & Verpooten, J. (2015). The evolutionary significance of the arts: Exploring the by-product hypothesis in the context of ritual, precursors, and cultural evolution. *Biological Theory, 10*(1), 73–85.

Hofmann, D. L. (1982). Music educators in Israel: Challenge to a multi-cultural society. In J. Dobbs (Ed.), *International Society for Music Education Yearbook, 9*, 148–151.

Hoffmann, D. L., Standish, C. D., García-Diez, M., Pettitt, P. B., Milton, J. A., Zilhão, J., . . . Pike, A. (2018). U-Th dating of carbonate crusts reveals Neandertal origin of Iberian cave art. *Science, 359*(6378), 912–915.

Hofstadter, D. (1979). *Gödel, Escher, Bach: An eternal golden braid*. New York, NY: Basic Books.

Hoke, K., Ryan, M., & Wilczynski, W. (2008). Candidate neural locus for sex differences in reproductive decisions. *Biology Letters, 4*(5), 518–521.

Holman, T. (2010). *Sound for film and television* (3rd ed.). New York, NY: Focal Press.

Holt, J. (1978). *It's never too late: My musical life story*. New York, NY: Delacorte.

Honing, H. (2002). Structure and interpretation of rhythm and timing. *Dutch Journal of Music Theory, 7*(3), 227–232.

Honing, H. (2014). *Musical cognition: A science of listening*. New Brunswick, NJ: Transaction Publishers.

Honing, H., Bouwer, F. L., & Háden, G. P. (2014). Perceiving temporal regularity in music: The role of auditory event-related potentials (ERPs) in probing beat perception. In H. Merchant & V. de Lafuente (Eds.), *Neurobiology of interval timing* (pp. 305–323). New York, NY: Springer.

Honing, H., & Ladinig, O. (2009). Exposure influences expressive timing judgments in music. *Journal of Experimental Psychology, 35*(1), 281–288.

Honing, H., Ladinig, O., Háden, G., & Winkler, I. (2009a). Is beat induction innate or learned? Probing emergent meter perception in adults and newborns using event-related brain potentials. *The Neurosciences and Music III—Disorders and Plasticity: Annals of the New York Academy of Sciences, 1169*, 93–96.

Honing, H., Ladinig, O., Háden, G., & Winkler, I. (2009b). Probing attentive and preattentive emergent meter in adult listeners without extensive music training. *Music Perception, 26*(4), 377–386.

Hood, L. (2001). Suppression of otoacoustic emissions in normal individuals and in patients with auditory disorders. In M. Robinette & T. Glattke (Eds.), *Otoacoustic emissions: Clinical applications* (2nd ed., pp. 325–348). New York, NY: Thieme Medical Publishers.

Hooper, J. (1981). Releasing the mystic in your brain. *Science Digest, 89*(4), 78–81, 120–122.

Hooper, J. (1982, October). Mind tripping. *Omni*, 154–160.

Horden, P. (Ed.). (2017). *Music as medicine: The history of music therapy since antiquity*. London: Routledge.

Hornbostel, E., & Sachs, C. (1992). Classification of musical instruments. In H. Meyers (Ed.), *Ethnomusicology: An introduction* (pp. 444–461). New York, NY: W. W. Norton.

Horvath, J. (2010). *Playing less hurt: An injury prevention guide for musicians*. Milwaukee, WI: Hal Leonard.

Horvath, K. (2008). Adopting a healthy approach to instrumental music making. *Music Educators Journal, 94*(3), 30–34.

Howard, D. M. (2007a). Equal or non-equal temperament in a Capella SATB singing. *Logopedics Phoniatrics Vocology, 32*(2), 87–94.

Howard, D. M. (2007b). Intonation drift in a Capella soprano, alto, tenor, bass quartet singing with key modulation. *Journal of Voice, 21*(3), 300–315.

Howard, D. M., & Angus, J. (2006). *Acoustics and psychoacoustics* (3rd ed.). Oxford: Focal Press.

Howard, D. M., Volkov, I., Mirsky, R., Garell, P., Noh, M., Granner, M., . . . Brugge, J. (2000). Auditory cortex on the human posterior superior temporal gyrus. *The Journal of Comparative Neurology, 416*, 79–92.

Howe, M., Davidson, J., & Sloboda, J. (1998). Innate talents: Reality or myth? *Behavioral and Brain Sciences, 21*(3), 399–442.

Howe, M., & Sloboda, J. (1991). Helping children to become highly competent adults: What can parents do? In J. Radford (Ed.), *Talent, teaching and achievement* (pp. 26–38). London: Jessica Kingsley Publishers.

Howell, P., Cross, I., & West, R. (Eds.). (1985). *Musical structure and cognition*. London: Academic Press.

Howell, P., West, R., & Cross, I. (Eds.). (1991). *Representing musical structure*. London: Academic Press.

Howes, F. (1927). *The borderland of music and psychology*. New York, NY: Oxford University Press.

Howle, M. (1993). Musical savants. *Update, 11*(1), 5–7.

Hudspeth, A. J. (1983). The hair cells of the inner ear. *Scientific American, 248*, 54–64.

Human Genome Project. (2017). Retrieved November 27, 2018, from www.ornl.gov/sci/techresources/Human_Genome/home.shtml

Hummelsheim, H. (1999). Rationales for improving motor function. *Current Opinion in Neurology, 12*, 697–701.

Hund-Georgiadis, M., & von Cramon, D. (1999). Motor-learning-related changes in piano players and non-musicians revealed by functional magnetic-resonance signals. *Experimental Brain Research, 125*(4), 417–425.

Hunsaker, L. (1994). Heart rate and rhythm responses during trumpet playing. *Medical Problems of Perform Artists, 9*, 69–72.

References

Hurd, R. (1933). *Musical acoustics*. London: A. Hammond.

Huron, D. (2006). *Sweet anticipation: Music and the psychology of expectation*. Cambridge, MA: The MIT Press.

Huron, D. (2009). Aesthetics. In S. Hallam, I. Cross, & M. Thaut (Eds.), *The Oxford handbook of music psychology* (pp. 151–159). Oxford: Oxford University Press.

Hutchinson, S., Lee, L., Gaab, N., & Schlaug, G. (2003). Cerebellar volume of musicians. *Cerebral Cortex*, *13*(9), 943–949.

Huttenlocher, P. (2002). *Neural plasticity: The effects of environment on the development of the cerebral cortex*. Cambridge, MA: Harvard University Press.

Hyde, K., Lerch, J., Norton, A., Forgeard, M., Winner, E., Evans, A., & Schlaug, G. (2009). Musical training shapes structural brain development. *The Journal of Neuroscience*, *29*(10), 3019–3025.

IFPI Releases 2018 Music Consumer Report. (2018). Retrieved from www.ifpi.org/news/IFPI-releases-2018-music-consumer-insight-report

IJzermans, J. (1995). Music and theory of the possession cult leaders in Chibale, Serenge District, Zambia. *Ethnomusicology*, *39*(2), 245–274.

Imberty, M. (1996). Linguistic and musical development in preschool and school-age children. In I. Deliège & J. Sloboda (Eds.), *Musical beginnings: Origins and development of musical competence* (pp. 191–213). Oxford: Oxford University Press.

Imberty, M. (2000). The question of innate competencies in musical communication. In N. Wallin, B. Merker, & S. Brown (Eds.), *The origins of music* (pp. 449–462). Cambridge, MA: The MIT Press.

Imig, D. (1997). Foreword. In V. Richardson (Ed.), *Constructivist teacher education: Building new understandings* (pp. vii–viii.). Bristol, PA: The Falmer Press.

Ingeber, D., Broudy, R., & Pearson, C. (1982). Music therapy: Tune-up for mind and body. *Science Digest*, *90*(1), 78.

Isacoff, S. (2009). *Temperament: How music became a battleground for the great minds of western civilization*. New York, NY: Knopf Doubleday.

Isbell, D. (2008). Musicians and teachers: The socialization and occupational identity of preservice music teachers. *Journal of Research in Music Education*, *56*(2), 162–178.

Istók, E., Brattico, E., Jacobsen, T., Krohn, K., Müller, M., & Tervaniemi, M. (2009). Aesthetic responses to music: A questionnaire study. *Musicæ Scientiæ*, *13*(2), 183–206.

Iverson, P., & Krumhansl, C. (1989). Pitch and timbre interaction in isolated tones and in sequences. *Journal of the Acoustical Society of America*, *86*(Suppl. 1), S58.

Iwanaga, M., Ikeda, M., & Iwaki, T. (1996). The effects of repetitive exposure to music on subjective and physiological responses. *Journal of Music Therapy*, *33*(3), 219–230.

Iyer, R. (2018). *Elements of Indian music*. Fenton, MO: Mel Bay.

Jabusch, H-C. (2006). Movement analysis in pianists. In E. Altenmüller, M. Wiesendanger, & J. Kesslring (Eds.), *Music, motor control and the brain* (pp. 109–123). Oxford: Oxford University Press.

Jabusch, H-C., & Altenmüller, E. (2006). Epidemiology, phenomenology, and therapy of musician's cramp. In E. Altenmüller, M. Wiesendanger, & J. Kesselring (Eds.), *Music, motor control, and the brain* (pp. 265–282). Oxford: Oxford University Press.

Jabusch, H-C., Alpers, H., Kopiez, R., Vauth, H., & Altenmüller, E. (2009). The influence of practice on the development of motor skills in pianists: A longitudinal study in a selected motor task. *Human Movement Science*, *28*, 74–84.

Jackendoff, R. (2009). Parallels and nonparallels between language and music. *Music Perception*, *26*(3), 195–204.

Jackendoff, R., & Lerdahl, F. (2006). The capacity for music: What is it, and what's special about it? *Cognition*, *100*, 33–72.

Jaffe, J. C. (2005). Innovative approaches to the design of symphony halls. *Acoustical Science and Technology*, *26*(2), 240–243.

Jain, R., & Bagdare, S. (2011). Music and consumption experience: A review. *International Journal of Retail & Distribution Management*, *39*(4), 289–302.

James, A. (2014). *The musical brain*. N. Charleston, SC: Createspace.

James, J. (1993). *The music of the spheres: Music, science, and the natural order of the universe*. New York, NY: Grove Press.

Janata, P. (2005). Brain networks that track musical structure. In G. Avancini, L. Lopez, S. Koelsch, & M. Majno (Eds.), *The neurosciences and music II: From perception to performance. Annals of the New York Academy of Sciences, 1060*, 111–124.

Janata, P. (2013). Cognitive neuroscience of music. In K. Ochsner & S. Kosslyn (Eds.), *The Oxford handbook of cognitive neuroscience* (Vol. 1., pp. 111–134). Oxford: Oxford University Press.

Janata, P., Birk, J., Van Horn, J., Leman, M., Tillman, B., & Bharucha, J. (2002). The cortical topography of tonal structures underlying western music. *Science, 298*, 2167–2170.

Jäncke, L., Shah, N., & Peters, M. (2000). Cortical activations in primary and secondary motor areas for complex bimanual movements in professional pianists. *Cognitive Brain Research, 10*(3), 177–183.

Jankowsky, R. (2006). Black spirits, white saints: Music, spirit possession, and sub-Saharans in Tunisia. *Ethnomusicology, 50*(3), 373–410.

Jankowsky, R. (2007). Music, spirit possession and the in-between: Ethnomusicological inquiry and the challenge of trance. *Ethnomusicology Forum, 16*(2), 185–208.

Jansens, S. Bloothooft, G., & de Krom, G. (1997). *Perception and acoustics of emotions in singing*. Proceedings of the Fifth European conference on speech communication and technology. ESCA, Rhodes, Greece, IV, 2155–2158.

Jansiewicz, E., Goldberg, M., Newschaffer, C., Denckla, M., Landa, R., & Mostofsky, S. (2006). Motor signs distinguish children with high functioning autism and Asperger's syndrome from controls. *Journal of Autism and Developmental Disorders, 36*(5), 613–621.

Järvelä, I. (2019). Genomics approaches for studying musical aptitude and related traits. In M. Thaut & D. Hodges (Eds.), *The Oxford handbook of music and the brain* Oxford: Oxford University Press.

Jeans, J. (1937/1961). *Science and music*. Reprint. Cambridge, MA: Cambridge University Press.

Jeffries, K., Fritz, J., & Braun, A. (2003). Words in melody: An H215O PET study of brain activation during singing and speaking. *NeuroReport, 14*(5), 749–754.

Jenkins, J. (1970). *Musical instruments*. London: County Hall.

Johnson, D., Tyson, A., & Winter, R. (1985). *The Beethoven sketchbooks: History, reconstruction, inventory*. Berkeley, CA: University of California Press.

Johnson, J., & Ulatowska, H. (1995). The nature of the tune and text in the production of songs. In R. Pratt & R. Spintge (Eds.), *MusicMedicine II* (pp. 153–168). St. Louis, MO: MMB Music.

Johnson, M. (1998). The neural basis of cognitive development. In E. Kuhn & S. Siegler (Eds.), *Handbook of child psychology* (Vol. 2, 5th ed., pp. 1–49). New York, NY: John Wiley & Sons.

Johnson, M. (2001). Infants' initial "knowledge" of the world: A cognitive neuroscience perspective. In F. Lacerda, C. von Hofsten, & M. Heimann (Eds.), *Emerging cognitive abilities in early infancy* (pp. 53–72). Mahwah, NJ: Lawrence Erlbaum Associates.

Johnston, I. (2002). *Measured tones: The interplay of physics and music* (2nd ed.). Philadelphia: Institute of Physics Publishing.

Jonaitis, E., & Saffran, J. (2009). Learning harmony: The role of serial statistics. *Cognitive Science, 33*, 951–968.

Jones, G. (2005, July 6). Live aid 1985: A day of magic. *CNN International.com*. Retrieved from http://edition.cnn.com/2005/SHOWBIZ/Music/07/01/liveaid.memories/index.html

Jones, M. (2009). Musical time. In S. Hallam, I. Cross, & M. Thaut (Eds.), *The Oxford handbook of music psychology* (pp. 81–92). Oxford: Oxford University Press.

Jørgensen, H. (1997). Time for practicing? Higher level music students' use of time for instrumental practicing. In H. Jørgensen & A. Lehmann (Eds.), *Does practice make perfect? Current theory and research on instrumental music practice* (pp. 123–139). Oslo: Norges Musikkhøgskole.

Jørgensen, H. (2004). Strategies for individual practice. In A. Williamon (Ed.), *Musical excellence* (pp. 85–103). Oxford: Oxford University Press.

Jørgensen, H., & Lehmann, A. (Eds.). (1997). *Does practice make perfect? Current theory and research on instrumental music practice*. Oslo: Norges musikkhøgskole.

References

Jorgensen, O. (1991). *Tuning: Containing the perfection of eighteenth-century temperament, the lost art of nineteenth-century temperament, and the science of equal temperament, complete with instructions for aural and electronic tuning.* East Lansing, MI: Michigan State University Press.

Joubart, D. (1994). Lions of darkness. *National Geographic, 18*(2), 34–53.

Juchniewicz, J. (2008). The influence of physical movement on the perception of musical performance. *Psychology of Music, 36*(4), 417–427.

Juslin, P. (2003). Five facets of musical expression: A psychologist's perspective on music performance. *Psychology of Music, 31,* 273–302.

Juslin, P. (2009a). Emotion in music performance. In S. Hallam, I. Cross, & M. Thaut (Eds.), *The Oxford handbook of music psychology* (pp. 377–389). Oxford: Oxford University Press.

Juslin, P. (2009b). Emotional responses to music. In S. Hallam, I. Cross, & M. Thaut (Eds.), *The Oxford handbook of music psychology* (pp. 131–140). Oxford: Oxford University Press.

Juslin, P. (2013). From everyday emotions to aesthetic emotions: Towards a unified theory of musical emotions. *Physics of Life Reviews, 10*(3), 235–266.

Juslin, P. (2019). *Musical emotions explained.* Oxford: Oxford University Press.

Juslin, P., & Laukka, P. (2004). Expression, perception, and introduction of musical emotions: A review and a questionnaire study of everyday listening. *Journal of New Music Research, 33*(3), 217–238.

Juslin, P., & Persson, R. (2002). Emotional communication. In R. Parncutt & G. McPherson (Eds.), *The science and psychology of music performance: Creative strategies for teaching and learning* (pp. 219–236). New York, NY: Oxford University Press.

Juslin, P., & Sakka, L. (2019). Neural correlates of music and emotion. In M. Thaut & D. Hodges (Eds.), *The Oxford handbook of music and the brain* (pp. 285–332). Oxford: Oxford University Press.

Juslin, P., & Sloboda, J. (Eds.). (2001). *Music and emotion.* New York, NY: Oxford University Press.

Juslin, P., & Sloboda, J. (Eds.). (2010a). *Handbook of music and emotion.* New York, NY: Oxford University Press.

Juslin, P., & Sloboda, J. (Eds.). (2010b). *Music and emotion* (2nd ed.). Oxford: Oxford University Press.

Juslin, P., & Västfjäll, D. (2008). Emotional responses to music: The need to consider underlying mechanisms. *Behavioral and Brain Sciences, 31*(5), 559–575.

Juslin, P., Friberg, A., Schoonderwaldt, E., & Karlsson, J. (2004). Feedback learning of musical expressivity. In A. Williamon (Ed.), *Musical excellence* (pp. 247–270). Oxford: Oxford University Press.

Juslin, P., Liljeström, S., Västfjäll, D., & Lundqvist, L-O. (2010). How does music evoke emotions? Exploring the underlying mechanisms. In P. Juslin & J. Sloboda (Eds.), *Handbook of music and emotion* (pp. 605–642). Oxford: Oxford University Press.

Juslin, P., Liljeström, S., Västfjäll, D., Barradas, G., & Silva, A. (2008). An experience sampling study of emotional reactions to music: Listener, music, and situation. *Emotion, 8*(5), 668–683.

Justus, T., & Bharucha, J. (2002). Music perception and cognition. In S. Yantis (Ed.), *Handbook of experimental psychology, vol. I: Sensation and perception* (3rd ed., pp. 453–492). New York, NY: Wiley and Sons.

Kaas, J. H. (1991). Plasticity of sensory and motor maps in adult mammals. *Annual Review of Neuroscience, 14,* 137–167.

Kageyama, N. (2019). *The bulletproof musician.* Retrieved from http://bulletproofmusician.com.

Kail, R., & Salthouse, T. (1994). Processing speed as a mental capacity. *Acta Pscyhologia, 86,* 199–225.

Kalcounis-Rueppell, M., Metheny, J., & Vonhoff, M. (2006). Production of ultrasonic vocalizations by *Peromyscus* mice in the wild. *Frontiers in Zoology, 3*(3), 1–12.

Karma, K. (2003). Technology for musicianship—Audilex the missing link? *General Music Today, 16*(3), 32–34.

Katagiri, J. (2009). The effect of background music and song texts on the emotional understanding of children with autism. *Journal of Music Therapy, 46*(1), 15–31.

Katz, R. (1982). *Boiling energy: Community healing among the Kalahari Kung.* Cambridge, MA: Harvard University Press.

Kawamura, M., Midorikawa, A., & Kezuka, M. (2000). Cerebral localization of the center for reading and writing music. *NeuroReport, 11,* 3299–3303.

Keali'inohomoku, J. (1985). Music and dance of the Hawaiian and Hopi peoples. In *Becoming human through music* (pp. 5–22). Reston, VA: Music Educators National Conference.

Keegan, S. (2013, November 2). Watch Portuguese pianist Maria João Pires play flawlessly despite orchestra playing WRONG Mozart song. *Daily Mirror*. Retrieved December 7, 2018, from www.mirror.co.uk/news/weird-news/watch-portuguese-pianist-maria-joo-2668045

Keeler, J., Roth, E., Neuser, B., Spitsbergen, J., Waters, D., & Vianney, J. (2015). The neurochemistry and social flow of singing: Bonding and oxytocin. *Frontiers in Human Neuroscience*, 9(518), 1–10.

Kemp, A. (1981). Personality differences between the players of string, woodwind, brass, and keyboard instruments, and singers. *Bulletin of the Council for Research in Music Education*, 66–67, 33–38.

Kemp, A. (1982). The personality structure of the musician. *Psychology of Music*, 10(2), 3–6.

Kemp, A. (1985). Psychological androgyny in musicians. *Bulletin of the Council for Research in Music Education*, 85, 102–108.

Kemp, A. (1996). *The musical temperament*. Oxford: Oxford University Press.

Kendall, R. (1986). The role of acoustic signal partitions in listener categorization of musical phrases. *Music Perception*, 4, 185–213.

Kendig, F., & Levitt, G. (1982). Overture: Sex, math and music. *Science Digest*, 90(1), 72–73.

Kennedy, M. (1999, February). *It's cool because we like to sing: Junior high boys' experience of choral music*. Presentation at Desert Skies Symposium on Research in Music Education. Tucson, AZ.

Kenny, D. (2011). *The psychology of music performance anxiety*. Oxford: Oxford University Press.

Kenny, D. T. (2005). A systematic review of treatments for music performance anxiety. *Anxiety, Stress, and Coping*, 18(3), 183–208.

Kenny, D. T. (2006). Music performance anxiety: Origins, phenomenology, assessment and treatment. *Context: Journal of Music Research*, 31, 51.

Kenny, D. T., Driscoll, T., & Ackermann, B. (2014). Psychological well-being in professional orchestral musicians in Australia: A descriptive population study. *Psychology of Music*, 42(2), 210–232.

Kern, P., & Humpal, M. (Eds.). (2012). *Music therapy and autism spectrum disorders*. Philadelphia: Jessica Kingsley Publishers.

Kestenbaum, D. (2004). Sounds may be of tiny 'molecular motors' hard at work. *NPR Stories*. Retrieved April 21, 2007, from www.npr.org/templates/story/story.php?storyId=3859762

Khalfa, S., Dalla Bella, S., Roy, M., Peretz, I., & Lupien, S. (2003). Effects of relaxing music on salivary cortisol level after psychological stress. In G. Avanzini, C. Faienza, D. Minciacchi, L. Lopez, & M. Majno (Eds.), *The neurosciences and music. Annals of the New York Academy of Sciences*, 999, 374–376.

Khalfa, S., Peretz, I., Blondin, J., & Manon, R. (2002). Event-related skin conductance responses to musical emotions in humans. *Neuroscience Letters*, 328, 145–149.

Khalfa, S., Roy, M., Rainville, P., Dalla Bella, S., & Peretz, I. (2008). Role of tempo entrainment in psychophysiological differentiation of happy and sad music? *International Journal of Psychophysiology*. doi:10.1016/j.ijpsycho.2007.12.001

Khenkin, Alex. (nd). *High frequency sound absorption in the air: Facts and fiction*. Retrieved January 17, 2010, from www.gearslutz.com/board/attachments/highend/119635d1240952170-capturing-ultrasonics-hf_sound.pdf

Kibler, V., & Rider, M. (1983). The effect of progressive muscle relaxation and music on stress as measured by finger temperature response. *Journal of Clinical Psychology*, 39, 213–215.

Killian, J., & Henry, M. (2005). A comparison of successful and unsuccessful strategies in individual sight-singing preparation and performance. *Journal of Research in Music Education*, 53(1), 51–65.

Kim, D-E., Shin, M-J., Lee, K-M., Chu, K., Woo, S., Kim, Y., Song, E-C., Lee, J-W., Park, S-H., & Roh, J-K. (2004). Musical training-induced functional reorganization of the adult brain: Functional magnetic resonance imaging and transcranial magnetic stimulation study on amateur string players. *Human Brain Mapping*, 23(4), 188–199.

King, E., & Waddington, C. (Eds.). (2017). *Music and empathy*. London: Routledge.

Kinsler, V., & Carpenter, R. (1995). Saccadic eye movements while reading music. *Vision Research*, 35(10), 1447–1458.

Kirchner, J. (2004–2005). Managing musical performance anxiety. *The American Music Teacher*, 54(3), 31–33.

References

Kirnarskaya, D. (2009). *The natural musician*. Oxford: Oxford University Press.

Kirschner, P. A., Sweller, J., & Clark, R. E. (2006). Why minimal guidance during instruction does not work: An analysis of the failure of constructivist, discovery, problem-based, experiential, and inquiry-based teaching. *Educational Psychologist, 41*(2), 75–86.

Kivy, P. (1989). *Sound sentiment: An essay on the musical emotions*. Philadelphia: Temple University Press.

Kivy, P. (1990). *Music alone: Philosophical reflections on the purely musical experience*. Ithaca, NY: Cornell University Press.

Kleinman, J., & Buckoke, P. (2013). *The Alexander technique for musicians*. London: Bloomsbury.

Klemish, J. (1970). A comparative study of two methods of teaching music reading to first-grade children. *Journal of Research in Music Education, 18*(3), 355–364.

Klickstein, G. (2009). *The musician's way: A guide to practice, performance, and wellness*. Oxford: Oxford University Press.

Knight, W., & Rickard, N. (2001). Relaxing music prevents stress-induced increases in subjective anxiety, systolic blood pressure, and heart rate in healthy males and females. *Journal of Music Therapy, 38*, 254–272.

Knoeferle, K. M., Paus, V. C., & Vossen, A. (2017). An upbeat crowd: Fast in-store music alleviates negative effects of high social density on customers' spending. *Journal of Retailing, 93*(4), 541–549.

Koch, S. (2014). Rhythm is it: Effects of dynamic body feedback on affect and attitudes. *Frontiers in Psychology, 5*(537), 1–11.

Kochan, A. (2003). To your health: Treating the pain of playing musical instruments. *International Musician, 101*(8), 9.

Koelsch, S. (2012). *Brain and music*. West Sussex: Wiley-Blackwell.

Koelsch, S. (2013). From social contact to social cohesion—The 7 Cs. *Music and Medicine, 5*(4), 204–209.

Koelsch, S. (2014). Brain correlates of music-evoked emotions. *Nature Reviews Neuroscience, 15*(3), 170–180.

Koelsch, S., Fritz, T., Cramon, Y., Müller, K., & Friederici, A. (2006). Investigating emotion with music: An fMRI study. *Human Brain Mapping, 27*, 239–250.

Koelsch, S., Siebel, W., & Fritz, T. (2010). Functional neuroimaging. In P. Juslin & J. Sloboda (Eds.), *Handbook of music and emotions* (pp. 314–344). Oxford: Oxford University Press.

Koelsch, S., & Skouras, S. (2014). Functional centrality of amygdala, striatum and hypothalamus in a "small-world" network underlying joy: An fMRI study with music. *Human Brain Mapping, 35*(7), 3485–3498.

Koelsch, S., Vuust, P., & Friston, K. (2018). Predictive processes and the peculiar case of music. *Trends in Cognitive Sciences, 23*(1), 63–77.

Koen, B. (2008a). *Beyond the roof of the world: Music, prayer, and healing in the Pamir mountains*. Oxford: Oxford University Press.

Koen, B. (2008b). *Oxford handbook of medical ethnomusicology*. Oxford: Oxford University Press.

Koepchen, H., Droh, R., Spintge, R., Abel, H-H., Klüssenforf, D., & Koralewski, E. (1992). Physiological rhythmicity and music in medicine. In R. Spintge & R. Droh (Eds.), *MusicMedicine* (pp. 39–70). St. Louis, MO: MMB Music.

Koeppel, D. (2012). The virtuoso. *National Geographic, 221*(5), 63–66.

Kofler, M., Müller, J., Wenning, G., Reggiani, L., Hollosi, P., Bösch, S., . . . Poewe, W. (2001). The auditory startle reaction in Parkinsonian disorders. *Movement Disorders, 16*(1), 62–71.

Koger, S., Chapin, K., & Brotons, M. (1999). Is music therapy an effective intervention for dementia? A meta-analytic review of literature. *Journal of Music Therapy, 36*(1), 2–15.

Kolinsky, R., Cuvelier, H., Goetry, V., Peretz, I., & Morais, J. (2009). Music training facilitates lexical stress processing. *Music Perception, 26*(3), 235–247.

Konečni, V. J. (2005). The aesthetic trinity: Awe, being moved, thrills. *Bulletin of Psychology and the Arts, 5*(2), 27–44.

Konečni, V. J. (2008). Does music induce emotion? A theoretical and methodological analysis. *Psychology of Aesthetics, Creativity, and the Arts, 2*, 115–129.

Konečni, V. J. (2013). Music, affect, method, data: Reflections on the Carroll v. Kivy debate. *American Journal of Psychology, 126*(2), 179–195.

Konečni, V., Brown, A., & Wanic, R. (2008). Comparative effects of music and recalled life-events on emotional state. *Psychology of Music, 36*(3), 289–308.

Konečni, V., Wanic, R., & Brown, A. (2007). Emotional and aesthetic antecedents and consequences of music-induced thrills. *American Journal of Psychology, 120*(4), 619–643.

Kopiez, R., & Galley, N. (2002). The musician's glance: A pilot study comparing eye movement parameters in musicians and non-musicians. In C. Stevens, D. Burnham, G. McPherson, E. Schubert, & J. Renwick (Eds.), *Proceedings of the 7th international conference on music perception and cognition* (pp. 683–686). Adelaide, Australia: Casual Productions – AMP.

Kopiez, R., Langner, J., & Steinhagen, P. (1999). Afrikanische trommler (Ghana) bewerten und spielen europäische Rhythmen [Cross-cultural study of the evaluation and performance of rhythm]. *Musicae Scientiae, 3,* 139–160.

Koshimori, Y. (2019). Neurochemical responses to music. In M. Thaut & D. Hodges (Eds.), *The Oxford handbook of music and the brain* (pp. 333–363). Oxford: Oxford University Press.

Kotlyar, G., & Morozov, P. (1976). Acoustical correlates of the emotional content of vocalized speech. *Soviet Physics. Acoustics, 22,* 370–376.

Koza, J. (1993). The "missing males" and other gender issues in music education: Evidence from the *Music Supervisors' Journal,* 1914–1924. *Journal of Research in Music Education, 41*(3), 212–232.

Kraeling, C., & Mowry, L. (1969). Music in the Bible. In E. Wellesz (Ed.), *Ancient and oriental music* (pp. 283–312). London: Oxford University Press.

Krakouer, L., Houghton, S., Douglas, G., & West, J. (2001). The efficacy of music therapy in effecting behaviour change in persons with cerebral palsy. *International Journal of Psychosocial Rehabilitation, 6,* 29–37.

Kramer, J. (1973). The Fibonacci series in twentieth-century music. *Journal of Music Theory, 17*(1), 110–148.

Krathwohl, D., Bloom, B., & Masia, B. (1964). *Taxonomy of education objectives. Handbook II: Affective domain.* New York, NY: McKay.

Krause, B. (1987). *The niche hypothesis: How animals taught us to dance and sing.* Retrieved April 22, 2009, from www.wildsanctuary.com

Krause, B. (1998). *Into a wild sanctuary.* Berkeley, CA: Heyday Books.

Krause, B. (2002). *Wild soundscapes: Discovering the voice of the natural world.* Berkeley, CA: Wilderness Press.

Kreutz, G., Bongard, S., Rohrmann, S., Hodapp, V., & Grebe, D. (2004). Effects of choir singing or listening on secretory immunoglobulin A, cortisol, and emotional state. *Journal of Behavioral Medicine, 27*(6), 623–635.

Kreutz, G., Murcia, C., & Bongard, S. (2012). Psychoneuroendocrine research on music and health: An overview. In R. MacDonald, G. Kreutz, & L. Mitchell (Eds.), *Music, health, and wellbeing* (pp. 457–476). Oxford: Oxford University Press.

Kries, J. von. (1926). *Wer ist musikalisch? Gedanken zur psychologie der tonkunst (Who is musical? Thoughts on the psychology of music).* Berlin: Verlag von Julius Springer.

Krings, T., Töpper, R., Foltys, H., Erberich, S., Sparing, R., Willmes, K., & Thron, A. (2000). Cortical activation patterns during complex motor tasks in piano players and control subjects. A functional magnetic resonance imaging study. *Neuroscience Letters, 278*(3), 189–193.

Kristeva, R., Chakarova, V., Schulte-Mönting, J., & Spreer, J. (2003). Activation of cortical areas in music execution and imagining: A high-resolution EEG study. *Neuroimage, 20*(3), 1872–1883.

Krumhansl, C. (1990). *Cognitive foundations of musical pitch.* New York, NY: Oxford University Press.

Krumhansl, C. (1995). Music psychology and music theory: Problems and prospects. *Music Theory Spectrum, 17*(1), 53–80.

Krumhansl, C. (1997). An exploratory study of musical emotions and psychophysiology. *Canadian Journal of Experimental Psychology, 51*(4), 336–352.

Krumhansl, C., Toivanen, P., Eerola, T., Toiviainen, P., Järvinen, T., & Louhivuori, J. (2000). Cross-cultural music cognition: Cognitive methodology applied to North Sami yoiks. *Cognition, 76*(1), 13–58.

References

Kubrin, C., & Weitzer, R. (2010). Rap music's violent and misogynistic effects: Fact of fiction? *Popular Culture, Crime and Social Control Sociology of Crime, Law and Deviance, 14,* 121–143.

Kuehn, J. (1965–66). Encounter at Leyden: Gustav Mahler consults Sigmund Freud. *The Psychoanalytic Review, 52D,* 5–25.

Kuhl, P., & Rivera-Gaxiola, M. (2008). Neural substrates of language acquisition. *Annual Review of Neuroscience, 31,* 511–534.

Kuhn, T. (1974). Discrimination of modulated beat tempo by professional musicians. *Journal of Research in Music Education, 22*(4), 270–277.

Kuhn, T. (1975). The effect of teacher approval and disapproval on attentiveness, musical achievement, and attitude of fifth-grade students. In C. Madsen, R. Greer, & C. Madsen (Eds.), *Research in music behavior: Modifying music behavior in the classroom* (pp. 40–48). New York, NY: Teachers College Press.

Kumar, A., Tims, F., Cruess, D., Mintzer, M., Ironson, G., Lowenstein, D., Cattan, R., Fernandez, B., Eisdorfer, C., & Kumar, M. (1999). Music therapy increases serum melatonin levels in patients with Alzheimer's disease. *Alternative Therapies in Health and Medicine, 5*(6), 49–57.

Kumar, V. (Ed.). (2017). *Biological timekeeping: Clocks, rhythms and behavior.* New Delhi: Springer.

Kunchur, M. (2008). Probing the temporal resolution and bandwidth of human hearing. *Proceedings of Meetings on Acoustics, Acoustical Society of America, 2*(050006), 1–12.

Kunej, D., & Turk, I. (2000). New perspectives on the beginnings of music: Archeological and musicological analysis of a middle Paleolithic bone "flute." In N. Wallin, B. Merker, & S. Brown (Eds.), *The origins of music* (pp. 235–268). Cambridge, MA: The MIT Press.

Kuriyama, K., Stickgold, R., & Walker, M. (2004). Sleep-dependent learning and motor-skill complexity. *Learning and Memory, 11,* 705–713.

Kurrle, D., & Widmer-Schnidrig, R. (2008). The horizontal hum of the Earth: A global background of spheroidal and toroidal modes. *Geophysical Research Letters, 35,* L06304.

Kwak, E. (2007). Effect of rhythmic auditory stimulation on gait performance in children with spastic cerebral palsy. *Journal of Music Therapy, 44*(3), 196–216.

Kwalwasser, J. (1927). *Tests and measurements in music.* Boston, MA: C. C. Birchard.

Kwalwasser, J. (1955). *Exploring the musical mind.* New York, NY: Coleman-Ross.

Lacey, A. (1990). *A dictionary of philosophy* (2nd ed.). New York, NY: Routledge.

Lamont, A. (1998). Music, education, and the development of pitch perception: The role of context, age and musical experience. *Psychology of Music, 26*(1), 7–25.

Lamont, A. (2002). Musical identities and the school environment. In R. MacDonald, D. Hargreaves, & D. Miell (Eds.), *Musical identities* (pp. 41–59). Oxford: Oxford University Press.

Lamont, A. (2009). Musical preferences. In S. Hallam, I. Cross, & M. Thaut (Eds.), *The Oxford handbook of music psychology* (pp. 160–168). Oxford: Oxford University Press.

Lamont, A. (2011). University students' strong experiences of music: Pleasure, engagement, and meaning. *MusicæScienti, 15*(2), 229–249.

Lamont, A. (2012). Emotion, engagement and meaning in strong experiences of music performance. *Psychology of Music, 40*(5), 574–594.

Langdon, A. (1960). *Psychosomatic music: Tonal vibrations and their affect on the mind of mankind.* Huntington, WV: Chapman Press.

Langer, S. (1967, 1972, 1982). *Mind: An essay on human feeling* (Vols. 1–3). Baltimore, MD: Johns Hopkins University Press.

Langers, D., Backes, W., & van Dijk, P. (2007). Representation of lateralization and tonotopy in primary versus secondary human auditory cortex. *NeuroImage, 34,* 264–273.

LaPine, P. (2008). The relationship between the physical aspects of voice production and optimal vocal health. *Music Educators Journal, 94*(3), 24–29.

Lardner, B., & Lakim, M. (2002). Tree-hole frogs exploit resonance effects. *Nature, 420,* 475.

Large, E., & Jones, M. (1999). The dynamics of attending: How people track time-varying events. *Psychological Review, 106*(1), 119–159.

Larsen, J., Berntson, G., Poehlmann, K., Ito, T., & Cacioppo, J. (2008). The psychophysiology of emotion. In M. Lewis, J. Haviland-Jones, & L. Barrett (Eds.), *Handbook of emotions* (3rd ed., pp. 180–195). New York, NY: Guilford Press.

Leakey, M. (1983). Tanzania's stone age art. *National Geographic, 164*(1), 84–99.

Leakey, R. (1981). *The making of mankind.* New York, NY: Dutton.

Leardi, S., Pietroletti, R., Angeloni, G., Necozione, S., Ranalletta, G., & Del Gusto, B. (2007). Randomized clinical trial examining the effect of music therapy in stress response to day surgery. *British Journal of Surgery, 94*(8), 943–947.

LeBlanc, A., Jin, Y., Obert, M., & Siivola, C. (1997). Effect of audience on music performance anxiety. *Journal of Research in Music Education, 45*(3), 480–496.

Lecanuet, J. (1996). Prenatal auditory experience. In I. Deliège & J. Sloboda (Eds.), *Musical beginnings: Origins and development of musical competence* (pp. 3–34). New York, NY: Oxford University Press.

Lederman, R. (2003). Neuromuscular and musculoskeletal problems in instrumental musicians. *Muscle Nerve, 27*(5), 549–561.

Lederman, R. (2006). Anterior interosseous neuropathy in instrumental musicians. *Medical Problems of Performing Artists, 21*(3), 137–141.

LeDoux, J. (1986). The neurobiology of emotion. In J. LeDoux & W. Hirst (Eds.), *Mind and brain* (pp. 301–354). Cambridge: Cambridge University Press.

LeDoux, J. (1994). Emotion, memory, and the brain. *Scientific American, 270*(6), 50–57.

Lee, D., Chen, Y., & Schlaug, G. (2003). Corpus callosum: Musician and gender effects. *NeuroReport, 14*(2), 205–209.

Lee, H. S., Park, H. Y., Yoon, J. O., Kim, J. S., Chun, J. M., Aminata, I. W., Cho, W-J., & Jeon, I. H. (2013). Musicians' medicine: Musculoskeletal problems in string players. *Clinics in Orthopedic Surgery, 5*(3), 155–160.

Lee, M. (1989). *Rehabilitation, music, and human well-being.* St. Louis, MO: MMB Music.

Lee, S-H., & Wolpoff, M. (2003). The pattern of evolution in Pleistocene human brain size. *Paleobiology, 29*(2), 186–196.

Lee, T. (2000). *Education in traditional China.* London: Brill.

Lefrançois, G. (1979). *Psychology for teaching* (3rd ed.) Belmont, CA: Wadsworth.

Lefrançois, G. (2006). *Theories of human learning* (5th ed.). Belmont, CA: Thomson Wadsworth.

Lehman, A., Sloboda, J., & Woody, R. (2007). *Psychology for musicians: Understanding and acquiring the skills.* New York, NY: Oxford University Press.

Lehman, P. (1968). *Tests and measurements in music.* Englewood Cliffs, NJ: Prentice-Hall.

Lehmann, A., & Davidson, J. (2002). Taking an acquired skills perspective on music performance. In R. Colwell (Ed.), *MENC handbook on musical cognition and development* (pp. 225–258). New York, NY: Oxford University Press.

Lehmann, A., & Ericsson, K. (1997). Research of expert performance and deliberate practice: Implication for the education of amateur musicians and music students. *Psychomusicology, 16,* 40–58.

Lehrer, P. (1978). Performance anxiety and how to control it: A psychologist's perspective. In C. Grindea (Ed.), *Tensions in the performance of music* (pp. 134–154). New York, NY: Alexander Broude.

Leman, M. (1997). *Music, gestalt, and computing: Studies in cognitive and systematic musicology.* Berlin: Springer.

Leman, M. (2007). *Embodied music cognition and mediation technology.* Cambridge, MA: The MIT Press.

Lennard, P. (2019). Music changes the brain. In Y. Kim & S. Gilman (Eds.), *The Oxford handbook of music and the body* (pp. 99–111). Oxford: Oxford University Press.

Leon-Guerrero, A. (2008). Self-regulation strategies used by student musicians during music practice. *Music Education Research, 10*(1), 91–106.

Lerdahl, F. (2001). *Tonal pitch space.* New York, NY: Oxford University Press.

Lerdahl, F. (2009). Genesis and architecture of the GTTM project. *Music Perception, 26*(3), 187–194.

Lerdahl, F., & Jackendoff, R. (1983). *A generative theory of tonal music.* Cambridge, MA: The MIT Press.

Lesiuk, T. (2005). The effect of music listening on work performance. *Psychology of Music, 33*(2), 173–191.

References

Levenson, R. (1992). Autonomic nervous system differences among emotions. *Psychological Science, 3*(1), 23–27.

Levenson, R. (2003). Autonomic specificity and emotion. In R. Davidson, K. Scherer, & H. Goldsmith (Eds.), *Handbook of affective sciences* (pp. 212–224). Oxford: Oxford University Press.

Levenson, R. (2007). Emotion elicitation with neurological patients. In J. Coan & J. Allen (Eds.), *Handbook of emotion elicitation and assessment* (pp. 158–168). New York, NY: Oxford University Press.

Levine, H., & Finnegan, E. (1987). Overuse and vocal disorders: Cause and effect. *Medical Problems of Performing Artists, 2*(3), 99–102.

Levinson, S., & Torreira, F. (2015). Timing in turn-taking and its implications for processing models of language. *Frontiers in Psychology, 6*(731), 1–17.

Levitin, D. (2002). *Foundations of cognitive psychology: Core readings.* Cambridge, MA: The MIT Press.

Levitin, D. (2006). *This is your brain on music: The science of a human obsession.* New York, NY: Dutton Adult.

Levitin, D., & Bellugi, U. (1998). Musical abilities in individuals with Williams syndrome. *Music Perception, 15*(4), 357–389.

Levitin, D., Menon, V., Schmitt, J., Eliez, S., White, C., Glover, G., . . . Reiss, A. (2003). Neural correlates of auditory perception in Williams syndrome: An fMRI study. *NeuroImage, 18,* 74–82.

Levy, S., Rosen, D., & Sataloff, R. (2005). Performance anxiety. In R. Sataloff (Ed.), *Professional Voice* (Vol. II, 3rd ed., pp. 585–590). San Diego, CA: Plural Publishing.

Lewis, R. (Ed.). (1963). *In praise of music.* New York, NY: Orion Press.

Lewis-Williams, D. (2002). *The mind in the cave.* London: Thames & Hudson.

Liang, Z. P., & Lauterbur, P. C. (2000). *Principles of magnetic resonance imaging: A signal processing perspective.* Bellingham, WA: SPIE Optical Engineering Press.

Libera, R., & Mace, S. (2010). Shielding sound: A study on the effectiveness of acoustic shields. *Journal of Band Research, 45*(2), 23–41.

Licht, S. (1946). *Music in medicine.* Boston, MA: New England Conservatory of Music.

Lide, D. (Ed.). (2008). *CRC handbook of chemistry and physics* (89th ed.). Boca Raton: CRC Press.

Lieberman, J. (1997). *You are your instrument: The definitive musician's guide to practice and performance* (3rd ed.). New York, NY: Huiksi Music.

Lim, S., & Lippman, L. (1991). Mental practice and memorization of piano music. *The Journal of General Psychology, 118*(1), 21–30.

Limb, C. J., & Braun, A. R. (2008). Neural substrates of spontaneous musical performance: An fMRI study of jazz improvisation. *PLoS One, 3*(2), e1679.

Lindenberger, U., Li, S-C., Gruber, W., & Muller, V. (2009). Brains swinging in concert: Cortical phase synchronization while playing guitar. *BMC Neuroscience, 10*(22). Retrieved from www.biomedcentral.com/1471-2202/10/22

Lindström, E., Juslin, P., Bresin, R., & Williamon, A. (2003). "Expressivity comes from within your soul": A questionnaire study of music students' perspectives on expressivity. *Research Studies in Music Education, 20*(1), 23–47.

Ling, Y. (1984). China recovers her past in folk songs—a report. *The World of Music, 24*(1), 44–49.

Lipps, T. (1905/1995). *Consonance and dissonance in music* (W. Thomson, Trans.). San Marino, CA: Everett Books.

Lipton, J. (1987). Stereotypes concerning musicians within symphony orchestras. *Journal of Psychology, 121*(1), 85–93.

Lisboa, T. (2008). Action and thought in cello playing: An investigation of children's practice and performance. *International Journal of Music Education, 26,* 243–267.

List, G. (1984). Concerning the concept of the universal and music. *The World Music, 26*(2), 40–47.

Liu, X., Kanduri, C., Oikkonen, J., Karma, K., Raijas, P., Ukkola-Vuoti, L., . . . Järvelä, I. (2016). Detecting signatures of positive selection associated with musical aptitude in the human genome. *Scientific Reports, 6,* 21198.

Loewy, J., Stewart, K., Dassler, A-M., Telsey, A., & Homel, P. (2013). The effects of music therapy on vital signs, feeding, and sleep in premature infants. *Pediatrics, 131,* 902–918.

Lokki, T., Pätynen, J., Peltonen, T., & Salmensaari, O. (2009, May). A rehearsal hall with virtual acoustics for symphony orchestras. *Audio Engineering Society Convention, 126.* Audio Engineering Society.

Lomax, A. (1968). *Folk song style and culture.* New Brunswick, NJ: Transaction Books.

London, J. (2004). *Hearing in time: Psychological aspects of musical meter.* New York, NY: Oxford University Press.

London, J. (2012). *Hearing in time* (2nd ed.). Oxford: Oxford University Press.

Loosen, F. (1993). Intonation of solo violin performance with reference to equally tempered, Pythagorean, and just intonations. *The Journal of the Acoustical Society of America, 93*(1), 525–539.

Lotze, M., Scheler, G., Tan, H-R., Braun, C., & Birnbaumer, N. (2003). The musician's brain: Functional imaging of amateurs and professionals during performance and imagery. *NeuroImage, 20*(3), 1817–1829.

Loui, P. (2016). Disorders of music cognition. In S. Hallam, I. Cross, & M. Thaut (Eds.), *The Oxford handbook of music psychology* (2nd ed., pp. 307–323). Oxford: Oxford University Press.

Lowenstein, O. (1966). *The senses.* Baltimore: Penguin Books.

Lowery, H. (1966). *A guide to musical acoustics.* New York, NY: Dover.

Lu, Z., Williamson, S., & Kaufman, L. (1992). Behavioral lifetime of human auditory sensory memory predicted by physiological measures. *Science, 258,* 1668–1670.

Lundin, R. (1953). *An objective psychology of music.* New York, NY: Ronald Press.

Lundin, R. (1963). Can perfect pitch be learned? *Music Educators Journal, 49,* 459–451.

Lundin, R. (1967). *An objective psychology of music* (2nd ed.). New York, NY: Ronald Press.

Lundin, R. (1985). *An objective psychology of music* (3rd ed.). Malabar, FL: Robert E. Krieger.

Lundin, R., & Allen, J. (1962). A technique for training perfect pitch. *Psychological Records, 12,* 139–146.

Lundqvist, L-O., Carlsson, F., & Hilmersson, P. (2000). Facial electromyography, autonomic activity, and emotional experience to happy and sad music. *Journal of Psychology, 35*(3–4), 225.

Lundqvist, L-O., Carlsson, F., Hilmersson, P., & Juslin, P. (2009). Emotional responses to music: Experience, expression, and physiology. *Psychology of Music, 37*(1), 61–90.

Luria, A. (2004). Vygotsky, Leo. In *Oxford companion to the mind* (2nd ed., pp. 939–940). New York, NY: Oxford University Press.

Macdonald, H. (2004). *Berlioz's orchestration treatise: A translation and commentary.* Cambridge: Cambridge University Press.

MacDonald, R., Hargreaves, D., & Miell, D. (2009). *Musical identities.* In S. Hallam, I. Cross, & M. Thaut (Eds.), *Oxford handbook of music psychology* (pp. 462–470). Oxford: Oxford University Press.

MacDonald, R., Hargreaves, D., & Miell, D. (Eds.). (2002). *Musical identities.* New York, NY: Oxford University Press.

MacDonald, R., Hargreaves, D., & Miell, D. (Eds.). (2017). *Handbook of musical identities.* Oxford: Oxford University Press.

MacDonald, R., Kreutz, G., & Mitchell, L. (2012). *Music, health, and wellbeing.* Oxford: Oxford University Press.

Mace, S. (2005). *A descriptive analysis of university music performance teachers' sound level exposures during a typical day of teaching, performing, and rehearsing* (PhD dissertation). University of North Carolina, Greensboro.

Mace, S., Wagoner, C., Teachout, D., & Hodges, D. (2012). Genre identification of very brief musical excerpts. *Psychology of Music, 40*(1), 112–128.

MacKnight, C. (1975). Music reading ability of beginning wind instrumentalists after melodic instruction. *Journal of Research in Music Education, 23*(1), 23–34.

MacLellan, C. (2011). Differences in Myers-Briggs personality types among high school band, orchestra, and choir members. *Journal of Research in Music Education, 59*(1), 85–100.

Madsen, C. (1979). Modulated beat discrimination among musicians and nonmusicians. *Journal of Research in Music Education, 27*(2), 57–67.

Madsen, C. (1997). Emotional response to music as measured by the two-dimensional CRDI. *Journal of Music Therapy, 34*(3), 187–199.

Madsen, C. (1998). Emotion versus tension in Haydn's symphony no. 104 as measured by the two-dimensional continuous response digital interface. *Journal of Research in Music Education, 46*(4), 546–554.

References

Madsen, C. (2004). A 30-year follow-up study of actual applied music practice versus estimated practice. *Journal of Research in Music Education, 52*(1), 77–88.

Madsen, C., & Forsythe, J. (1973). Effect of contingent music listening on increases of mathematical responses. *Journal of Research in Music Education, 21*(2), 176–181.

Madsen, C., & Geringer, J. (1976). Preferences for trumpet tone quality versus intonation. *Council for Research in Music Education, 46*, 13–22.

Madsen, C., Greer, R., & Madsen, Jr., C. H. (Eds.). (1975). *Research in music behavior: Modifying music behavior in the classroom.* New York, NY: Teachers College Press.

Madsen, C., & Madsen, Jr., C. H. (1970). *Experimental research in music.* Englewood Cliffs, NJ: Prentice-Hall.

Madsen, C., & Prickett, C. (1987). *Applications of research in music behavior.* Tuscaloosa, AL: University of Alabama Press.

Madsen, C., & Yarbrough, C. (1980). *Competency-based music education.* Englewood Cliffs, NJ: Prentice-Hall.

Magill, L. (2002). Spirituality in music therapy. *Music Therapy Today* (online). Retrieved from http://msictherapyworld.net

Maier, S., Watkins, L., & Fleshner, M. (1994). Psychoneuroimmunology: The interface between behavior, brain, and immunity. *American Psychologist, 49*(12), 1004–1017.

Malloch, S., & Trevarthen, C. (Eds.). (2009a). *Communicative musicality: Exploring the basis of human companionship.* Oxford: Oxford University Press.

Malloch, S., & Trevarthen, C. (2009b). Musicality: Communicating the vitality and interests of life. In S. Malloch & C. Trevarthen (Eds.), *Communicative musicality: Exploring the basis of human companionship* (pp. 1–11). Oxford: Oxford University Press.

Malm, W. (1967). *Music cultures of the pacific, the near East, and Asia.* Englewood Cliffs, NJ: Prentice-Hall.

Mampe, B., Friederici, A., Christophe, A., & Wermke, K. (2009). Newborns' cry melody is shaped by their native language. *Current Biology, 19*, 1–4.

Manchester, R. (2006). Musical instrument ergonomics. *Medical Problems of Performing Artists, 21*(4), 157–158.

Mandell, J., Schulze, K., & Schlaug, G. (2007). Congential amusia: An auditory-motor feedback disorder? *Restorative Neurology and Neuroscience, 25*(3–4), 323–324.

Manning, P. (2013). *Electronic and computer music* (4th ed.). Oxford: Oxford University Press.

Mansfield, B. (2002, September 5). Country music, in 9/11 time. *USA Today.* Retrieved May 9, 2010, from www.usatoday.com/life/music/2002-09-05-sept11-country_x.htm

Mantie, R., & Smith, G. (Eds.). (2017). *The Oxford handbook of music making and leisure.* Oxford: Oxford University Press.

Maranto, C. (1991). *Applications of music in medicine.* Washington, DC: National Association for Music Therapy.

Maranto, C., & Scartelli, J. (1992). Music in the treatment of immune-related disorders. In R. Spintge & R. Droh (Eds.), *MusicMedicine* (pp. 142–153). St. Louis, MO: MMB Music.

Marazano, R., & Kendall, J. (2007). *The new taxonomy of education objectives* (2nd ed.). Thousand Oaks, CA: Corwin Press.

Marchand, D. (1975). A study of two approaches to developing expressive performance. *Journal of Research in Music Education, 23*(1), 14–22.

Marek, G. (1975). *Toscanini.* London: Vision Press.

Margulis, E. (2013). *On repeat: How music plays the mind.* Oxford: Oxford University Press.

Margulis, E. (2019). *The psychology of music: A very short introduction.* Oxford: Oxford University Press.

Marin, M. M., & Bhattacharya, J. (2013). Getting into the musical zone: Trait emotional intelligence and amount of practice predict flow in pianists. *Frontiers in Psychology, 4*, 853.

Marinelli, L., & Mayer, A. (2006). Editors' introduction: Forgetting Freud? For a new historiography of psychoanalysis. *Science in Context, 19*(1), 1–13.

Mark, L., & Ulmer, J. (2005). Preface. In J. Ulmer, L. Parsons, M. Moseley, & J. Gabrieli (Eds.), *White matter in cognitive neuroscience. Annals of the New York Academic of Sciences, 1064*, vii–ix.

Mark, M. (1996). *Contemporary music education* (3rd ed.). New York, NY: Schirmer Books.

Marsh, K. (2008). *The musical playground: Global tradition and change in children's songs and games*. Oxford: Oxford University Press.

Marsh, K., Richardson, M., & Schmidt, R. (2009). Social connection through joint action and interpersonal coordination. *Topics in Cognitive Science*, 1, 320–339.

Martin, B. (1991). Effects of hand signs, syllables, and letters on first graders' acquisition of tonal skills. *Journal of Research in Music Education*, 39(2), 161–170.

Martindale, C. (1984). The pleasures of thought: A theory of cognitive hedonics. *Journal of Mind and Behavior*, 5(1), 49–80.

Martindale, C., & Moore, K. (1988). Priming, prototypicality, and preference. *Journal of Experimental Psychology: Human Perception and Performance*, 14(4), 661–670.

Martindale, C., Moore, K., & West, A. (1988). Relationship of preference judgments to typicality, novelty, and mere exposure. *Empirical Studies of the Arts*, 6(1), 79–96.

Martino, S. C., Collins, R. L., Elliott, M. N., Strachman, A., Kanouse, D. E., & Berry, S. H. (2006). Exposure to degrading versus nondegrading music lyrics and sexual behavior among youth. *Pediatrics*, 118(2), e430–e441.

Marvin, E., & Laprade, P. (1987). Relating musical contours: Extensions of a theory for contour. *Journal of Music Theory*, 31(2), 225–267.

Masataka, N. (1999). Preference for infant-directed singing in 2-day-old hearing infants of deaf parents. *Developmental Psychology*, 35(4), 1001–1005.

Masataka, N. (2006). Preference for consonance over dissonance by hearing newborns of deaf parents and of hearing parents. *Developmental Science*, 9(1), 46–50.

Maslow, A. (1943). A theory of human motivation. *Psychological Review*, 50(4), 370–396.

Maslow, A. (1968a). Music education and peak experience. *Music Educators Journal*, 54(6), 72–75, 163–164, 169–171.

Maslow, A. (1968b). Music, education, and peak experiences. In R. Choate (Ed.), *Documentary report of the Tanglewood symposium* (pp. 68–75). Washington, DC: Music Educators National Conference.

Maslow, A. (1968c). *Toward a psychology of being* (2nd ed.). New York, NY: Van Nostrand Reinhold Co.

Maslow, A. (1970). *Motivation and personality* (2nd ed.). New York, NY: Harper and Row.

Maslow, A. (1971). *The farther reaches of human nature*. New York, NY: Penguin Books.

Maslow, A. (1976). *Religions, values, and peak-experiences*. New York, NY: Penguin Books.

Matlin, M., & Farmer, T. (2015). *Cognition* (9th ed.). New York, NY: John Wiley & Sons.

Matthews, R. (2007). Carl, E. Seashore. In L. Macy (Ed.), *Grove music online*. Retrieved April 27, 2007, from www.grovemusic.com

Mauritz, K. (2002). Gait training in hemiplegia. *European Journal of Neurology*, 9, 23–29.

Mavridis, I. (2015). Music and the nucleus accumbens. *Surgical and Radiologic Anatomy*, 37(2), 121–125.

Mazokopaki, K., & Kugiumutzakis, G. (2009). Infant rhythms: Expressions of musical companionship. In S. Malloch & C. Trevarthen (Eds.), *Communicative musicality: Exploring the basis of human companionship* (pp. 185–208). Oxford: Oxford University Press.

Mazziotta, J. (1988). Brain metabolism in auditory perception: The PET study. In F. Roehmann & R. Wilson (Eds.), *The biology of music making* (pp. 106–111). St. Louis, MO: MMB Music.

McAdams, S. (1987). *Music and psychology: A mutual regard*. London: Harwood Academic Publishers.

McAdams, S., & Bigand, E. (1993). *Thinking in sound: The cognitive psychology of human audition*. Oxford: Oxford University Press.

McAdams, S., & Deliège, I. (Eds.). (1989). *Music and the cognitive sciences*. London: Harwood Academic Publishers.

McAdams, S., & Giordano, B. (2009). The perception of musical timbre. In S. Hallam, I. Cross, & M. Thaut (Eds.), *The Oxford handbook of music psychology* (pp. 72–80). Oxford: Oxford University Press.

McAdams, S., Winsberg, S., Donnadieu, S., De Soete, G., & Krimphoff, J. (1995). Perceptual scaling of synthesized musical timbres: Common dimensions, specificities, and latent subject classes. *Psychological Research*, 58, 177–192.

McCaffrey, R., & Freeman, E. (2003). Effect of music on chronic osteoarthritis pain in older people. *Journal of Advanced Nursing*, 44(5), 517–524.

References

McCarthy, M. (2009). Music teacher education-exploring the spiritual in music teacher education: Group musical improvisation points the way. *The Mountain Lake Reader*, 12–23.

McCarty, B., McElfresh, C., Rice, S., & Wilson, S. (1978). The effect of contingent background music on inappropriate bus behavior. *Journal of Music Therapy*, *15*, 150–156.

McClellan, E. (2007). *Relationships among parental influences, selected demographic factors, adolescent self-concept as a future music educator, and the decision to major in music education*. (PhD in Music Education), University of North Carolina, Greensboro.

McCormick, J., & McPherson, G. (2003). The role of self-efficacy in a musical performance examination: An exploratory structural equation analysis. *Psychology of Music*, *31*(1), 37–51.

McDermott, J. (2008). The evolution of music. *Nature*, *453*, 287–288.

McDonald, D., & Simons, G. (1989). *Musical growth and development: Birth through six*. New York, NY: Schirmer Books.

McFarland, R., & Kadish, R. (1991). Sex differences in finger temperature response to music. *International Journal of Psychophysiology*, *11*, 295–298.

McGraw-Hill. (2005). *McGraw-Hill concise encyclopedia of physics*. New York, NY: McGraw-Hill.

McIntosh, G., Brown, S., Rice, R., & Thaut, M. (1997). Rhythmic auditory-motor facilitation of gait patterns in patients with Parkinson's disease. *Journal of Neurology, Neurosurgery, and Psychiatry*, *62*, 22–26.

McIntosh, G., Thaut, M., & Rice, R. (1996). Rhythmic auditory stimulation as entrainment and therapy technique in gait of stroke and Parkinson's patients. In R. Pratt & R. Spintge (Eds.), *MusicMedicine II* (pp. 145–152). St. Louis, MO: MMB Music.

McKeage, K. (2004). Gender and participation in high school and college instrumental jazz ensembles. *Journal of Research in Music Education*, *52*(4), 343–356.

McKinney, C., Tims, F., Kumar, A., & Kumar, M. (1997b). The effect of selected classical music and spontaneous imagery on plasma beta-endorphin. *Journal of Behavioral Medicine*, *20*(1), 85–99.

McLaughlin, T. (1970). *Music and communication*. London: Faber and Faber.

McLellan, J. (1987, December 12). The sound of perfection. *The Washington Post*. Retrieved December 2, 2018, from www.washingtonpost.com/archive/lifestyle/1987/12/12/the-sound-of-perfection/fb73c8df-00af-4cba-8259-eeeff71b22fc/?utm_term=.011a87e8f404

McMullen, P. (1996). The musical experience and affective/aesthetic responses: A theoretical framework for empirical research. In D. Hodges (Ed.), *Handbook of music psychology* (pp. 387–400). San Antonio, TX: IMR Press.

McNair, J., & Powles, J. (2005). Hippies vs hip-hop heads: An exploration of music's ability to communicate an alternative political agenda from the perspective of two divergent musical genres. In D. Miell, R. MacDonald, & D. Hargreaves (Eds.), *Musical communication* (pp. 339–360). Oxford: Oxford University Press.

McNamara, L., & Ballard, M. (1999). Resting arousal, sensation seeking, and music preference. *Genetic, Social & General Psychology Monographs*, *125*(3), 229–251.

McPhee, E. (2011). Finding the muse: Teaching musical expression to adolsecents in the one-to-one studio environment. *International Journal of Music Education*, *29*(4), 333–346.

McPherson, G. (2005). From child to musician: Skill development during the beginning stages of learning an instrument. *Psychology of Music*, *33*(1), 5–35.

McPherson, G. (Ed.). (2006). *The child as musician: A handbook of musical development*. Oxford: Oxford University Press.

McPherson, G. (Ed.). (2014). *The child as musician* (2nd ed.). Oxford: Oxford University Press.

McPherson, G. (Ed.). (2016). *Musical prodigies*. Oxford: Oxford University Press.

McPherson, G., & Davidson, J. (2002). Musical practice: Mother and child interactions during the first year of learning an instrument. *Music Education Research*, *4*(1), 141–156.

McPherson, G., & McCormick, J. (2006). Self-efficacy and music performance. *Psychology of Music*, *34*(3), 322–336.

McPherson, G., & Renwick, J. (2001). A longitudinal study of self-regulation in children's musical practice. *Music Education Research*, *3*(2), 169–186.

McPherson, G., & Schubert, E. (2004). Measuring performance enhancement in music. In A. Williamon (Ed.), *Musical excellence* (pp. 61–82). Oxford: Oxford University Press.

McPherson, G., & Welch, G. (2012). *The Oxford handbook of music education, 2 vols.* Oxford: Oxford University Press.

McPherson, G., & Welch, G. (Eds.). (2018). *Music and music education in people's lives.* Oxford: Oxford University Press.

McPherson, G., & Zimmerman, B. (2002). Self-regulation of musical learning. In R. Colwell & C. Richardson (Eds.), *The new handbook of research on music teaching and learning* (pp. 327–347). New York, NY: Oxford University Press.

McPherson, G., Davidson, J., & Faulker, R. (Eds.). (2012). *Music in our lives.* Oxford: Oxford University Press.

McWhinnie, H. (1986). A review of the use of symmetry, the golden section and dynamic symmetry in contemporary art. *Leonardo, 19*(3), 241–245.

McWhinnie, H. (1989). A biological basis for the golden section in art and design. *Leonardo, 22*(1), 61–63.

Medina, J., & Coslett, H. B. (2010). From maps to form to space: Touch and the body schema. *Neuropsychologia, 48*(3), 645–654.

Mehl, M., & Pennebaker, J. (2003). The sounds of social life: A psychometric analysis of students' daily social environments and natural conversations. *Journal of Personality and Social Psychology, 84*(4), 857–870.

Meister, I., Krings, T., Foltys, H., Boroojerdi, B., Muller, M., Topper, R., & Thron, A. (2005). Effects of long-term practice and task complexity in musicians and nonmusicians performing simple and complex motor tasks: Implications for cortical motor organization. *Human Brain Mapping, 25*(3), 345–352.

Meltzoff, A., Kuhl, P., Movellan, J., & Sejnowski, S. (2009). Foundations for a new science of learning. *Science, 235,* 284–288.

Menon, V., & Levitin, D. (2005). The rewards of music listening: Response and physiological connectivity of the mesolimbic system. *Neuroimage, 28*(1), 175–184.

Mensah, A. (1962). Gyil: The Dagara-Lobi Xylophone. *Journal of African Studies, 9*(3), 139–154.

Menuhin, Y., & Davis, C. (1979). *The music of man.* New York, NY: Methuen.

Merker, B. (2000). Synchronous chorusing and human origins. In N. Wallin, B. Merker, & S. Brown (Eds.), *The origins of music* (pp. 315–327). Cambridge, MA: The MIT Press.

Merker, B. (2009). Ritual foundations of human uniqueness. In S. Malloch & C. Trevarten (Eds.), *Communicative musicality: Exploring the basis of human companionship* (pp. 45–59). Oxford, UK: Oxford University Press.

Merker, B. (2019). When extravagance impresses: Recasting esthetics in evolutionary terms. In M. Thaut & D. Hodges (Eds.), *The Oxford handbook of music and the brain* (pp. 66–86). Oxford: Oxford University Press.

Merriam, A. (1964). *The anthropology of music.* Chicago: Northwestern University Press.

Merrotsky, P. (2013). A note on big c-creativity and little c-creativity. *Creativity Research Journal, 25*(4), 474–476.

Meyer, L. (1956). *Emotion and meaning in music.* Chicago: The University of Chicago Press.

Meyer, L. (1973). *Explaining music.* Chicago: University of Chicago Press.

Meyer, L. (2001). Music and emotion: Distinction and uncertainties. In P. Juslin & J. Sloboda (Eds.), *Music and emotion* (pp. 341–360). New York, NY: Oxford University Press.

Meyer, M. F. (1929). *The musician's arithmetic: Drill problems for an introduction to the scientific study of musical composition.* Boston, MA: Oliver Ditson.

Meyers, H. (1992). *Ethnomusicology: An introduction.* New York, NY: W. W. Norton.

Michel, A., Baumann, C., & Gayer, L. (2017). Thank you for the music—or not? The effects of in-store music in service settings. *Journal of Retailing and Consumer Services, 36,* 21–32.

Michel, D. (1952). *Effects of stimulative and sedative music on respiration and psychogalvanic reflex as observed in seventh grade students.* Unpublished paper, University of Kansas.

Midori. (1989). *Paganini 24 Caprices, Op. 1.* CBS Masterworks, MK44944.

Miell, D., MacDonald, R., & Hargreaves, D. (Eds.). (2005). *Musical communication.* New York, NY: Oxford University Press.

Miklaszewski, K. (1989). A case study of a pianist preparing a musical performance. *Psychology of Music, 17*(2), 95–109.

References

Miksza, P. (2007). Effective practice: An investigation of observed practice behaviors, self-reported practice habits, and the performance achievement of high school wind players. *Journal of Research in Music Education, 55*(4), 359–375.

Miksza, P., Tan, L., & Dye, C. (2016). Achievement motivation for band: A cross-cultural examination of the 2× 2 achievement goal motivation framework. *Psychology of Music, 44*(6), 1372–1388.

Miller, G. (1956). The magical number seven, plus or minus two: Some limits on our capacity for processing information. *Psychological Review, 63,* 81–97.

Miller, G. (2000). Evolution of music through sexual selection. In N. Wallin, B. Merker, & S. Brown (Eds.), *The origins of music* (pp. 329–360). Cambridge, MA: The MIT Press.

Miller, J. (1993). Quick as a hair cell. *Bioscience, 43*(2), 83–84.

Miller, L. (1989). *Musical savants: Exceptional skill and mental retardation.* Hillsdale, NJ: Laurence Erlbaum.

Miller, N., & Dollard, J. (1941). *Social learning and imitation.* New Haven: Yale University Press.

Miller, R., Thaut, M., & Aunon, J. (1995). Event-related brain wave potentials in an auditory-motor synchronization task. In R. Pratt & R. Spintge (Eds.), *MusicMedicine II* (pp. 76–84). St. Louis, MO: MMB Music.

Miller, R., Thaut, M., McIntosh, G., & Rice, R. (1996). Components of EMG symmetry and variability in Parkinsonian and healthy elderly gait. *Electroencephalography and Clinical Neurophysiology, 101,* 1–7.

Miller, S. (1982). *Music therapy for handicapped children: Speech impaired* (W. Lathom & C. Eagle, Jr., Eds.). Project Music Monograph Series. Washington, DC: National Association for Music Therapy.

Miluk-Kolasa, B., Matejek, M., & Stupnicki, R. (1996). The effects of music listening on changes in selected physiological parameters in adult pre-surgical patients. *Journal of Music Therapy, 33*(3), 208–218.

Miluk-Kolasa, B., Obminski, Z., Stupnicki, R., & Golec, L. (1994). Effects of music treatment on salivary cortisol in patients exposed to pre-surgical stress. *Experimental and Clinical Endocrinology, 102*(2), 118–120.

Minagar, A., Ragheb, J., & Kelley, R. E. (2003). The Edwin Smith surgical papyrus: Description and analysis of the earliest case of aphasia. *Journal of Medical Biography, 11*(2), 114–117.

Minsky, M. (1981). Music, mind, and meaning. *Computer Music Journal, 5*(3), 28–44.

Mitchison, G. (1977). Phyllotaxis and the Fibonacci series. *Science, 196*(4287), 270–275.

Mithen, S. (2006). *The singing neaderthals: The origins of music, language, mind, and body.* Boston, MA: Harvard University Press.

Mitterschiffthaler, M., Fu, C., Dalton, J., Andrew, C., & Williams, C. (2007). A functional MRI study of happy and sad affective states induced by classical music. *Human Brain Mapping, 28,* 1150–1162.

Miyazaki, K. (1990). The speed of musical pitch identification by absolute-pitch possessors. *Music Perception, 8*(2), 177–188.

Miyazaki, K. (1992). Perception of musical intervals by absolute pitch possessors. *Music Perception, 9*(4), 413–426.

Miyazaki, K. (1993). Absolute pitch as an inability: Identification of musical intervals in a tonal context. *Music Perception, 11*(1), 55–71.

Miyazaki, K., & Ogawa, Y. (2006). Learning absolute pitch by children: A cross-sectional study. *Music Perception, 42*(1), 63–78.

Mizener, C. (1993). Attitudes of children toward singing and choir participation and assessed singing skill. *Journal of Research in Music Education, 41*(3), 233–245.

Möckel, M., Röcker, L., Störk, T., Vollert, J., Danne, O., Eichstädt, H., . . . Hochrein, H. (1994). Immediate physiological responses of healthy volunteers to different types of music: Cardiovascular, hormonal and mental changes. *European Journal of Applied Physiology, 68,* 451–459.

Moller, L. (1980). Music in Germany during the Third Reich: The use of music for propaganda. *Music Educators Journal, 67*(3), 40–44.

Monmaney, T. (1987). Key notes on the mind. *Omni, 9*(4), 45–46, 67.

Montagu, A. (1977). *Life before birth.* New York, NY: New American Library.

Montagu, A. (1978). *Touching: The human significance of the skin.* New York, NY: Harper and Row.

Montagu, A., & Matson, F. (1979). *The human connection.* New York, NY: McGraw-Hill.

Montgomery, M. (2008). The pulse of distant stars. *Science, 322*(5901), 536–537.

Moore, D. R. (1987). Physiology of the higher auditory system. *British Medical Bulletin, 43*(4), 856–870.

Moore, D. R., Burland, K., & Davidson, J. (2003). The social context of musical success: A developmental account. *British Journal of Psychology, 94*, 529–549.

Moore, G. (1984). A computer-based portable keyboard monitor for studying timing performance in pianists. *Timing and Time Perception: Annals of the New York Academy of Sciences, 423*, 651–652.

Moore, G. (1988). The study of skilled performance in musicians. In F. Roehmann & F. Wilson (Eds.), *The biology of music making* (pp. 77–91). St. Louis, MO: MMB Music.

Moore, G. (1992). Piano trills. *Music Perception, 9*, 351–360.

Moore, G., Hary, D., & Naill, R. (1988). Trills: Some initial observations. *Psychomusicology, 7*(2), 153–162.

Moore, J. (2002). Maturation of human auditory cortex: Implications for speech perception. *The Annals of Otology, Rhinology & Laryngology, 111*, 7–10.

Moore, R., Estis, J., Zhang, F., Watts, C., & Marble, E. (2007). Relations of pitch matching, pitch discrimination, and otoacoustic emission suppression in individuals not formally trained as musicians. *Perceptual and Motor Skills, 104*(3, part 1), 777–784.

Moore, R., Vadeyar, S., Fulford, J., Tyler, D., Gribben, C., Baker, P., . . . Gowland, P. (2001). Antenatal determination of fetal brain activity in response to an acoustic stimulus using functional magnetic resonance imaging. *Human Brain Mapping, 12*, 94–99.

Moravcsik, M. (1987). *Musical sound.* New York, NY: Paragon.

Moravcsik, M. (2006). *Musical sound: An introduction to the physics of music.* New York, NY: Kluwer Academic, Plenum Publishers.

Morford, J. (2007). Constructivism: Implications for postsecondary music education and beyond. *Journal of Music Teacher Education, 16*(2), 75–83.

Morgenstern, S. (1956). *Composers on music: An anthology of composer's writings from Palestrina to Copland.* New York, NY: Pantheon Books.

Morin, S., Dubé, L., & Chebat, J-C. (2007). The role of pleasant music in services capes: A test of the dual model of environmental perception. *Journal of Retailing, 83*(1), 115–130.

Morley, I. (2006). Hunter-gatherer music and its implications for identifying intentionality in the use of acoustic space. In C. Scarre & G. Lawson (Eds.), *Archaeology* (pp. 95–106). McDonald Insitute Monographs. Oxford: Oxbow Books.

Morley, I. (2013). *The prehistory of music.* Oxford: Oxford University Press.

Morris, W. (2007). David Hume. In E. Zalta (Ed.), *The Stanford encyclopedia of philosophy* (Fall ed.). Retrieved August 6, 2007, from http://plato.stanford.edu/archives/fall2007/entries/hume/

Morrison, S., & Demorest, S. (2009). Cultural constraints on music perception and cognition. In J. Chiao (Ed.), *Progress in brain research, 178, Cultural Neuroscience: Cultural influences on brain function* (pp. 67–77). Amsterdam, The Netherlands: Elsevier.

Morrison, S., & Demorest, S. (2019). Cultural distance: A computational approach to exploring cultural influences on music cognition. In M. Thaut & D. Hodges (Eds.), *The Oxford handbook of music and the brain* (pp. 42–65). Oxford: Oxford University Press.

Morrison, S., Demorest, S., Alyward, E., Cramer, C., & Maravilla, K. (2003). FMRI investigation of cross-cultural music comprehension. *NeuroImage, 20*(1), 278–284.

Morton, D., & Duriyanga, C. (1976). *The traditional music of Thailand* (Vol. 8). Berkeley, CA: University of California Press.

Mosing, M., Madison, G., Pedersen, N. L., Kuja-Halkola, R., & Ullén, F. (2014). Practice does not make perfect: No causal effect of music practice on music ability. *Psychological Science, 25*(9), 1795–1803.

Mosing, M., Peretz, I., & Ullén, F. (2018). Genetic influences on music expertise. In D. Hambrick, G. Campitelli, & B. Macnamara (Eds.), *The science of expertise: Behavioral, neural, and genetic approaches to complex skill* (pp. 272–282). New York, NY: Routledge.

Mosing, M., & Ullén, F. (2016). Genetic influences on musical giftedness, talent, and practice. In G. McPherson (Ed.), *Musical prodigies* (pp. 156–167). Oxford: Oxford University Press.

Mössler, K., Chen, K., Heldal, T., & Gold, C. (2011). Music therapy for people with schizophrenia and schizphrenia-like disorders (review). *Cochrane Database of Systematic Reviews, 12*.

Muehlenbein, M. (Ed.). (2015). *Basics in human evolution.* London: Academic Press.

Mumford, L. (1966). *The myth of the machine.* New York, NY: Harcourt Brace Javanovich.

References

Münte, T., Altenmüller, E., & Jäncke, L. (2002). The musician's brain as a model of neuroplasticity. *Nature Neuroscience, 3*, 473–378.

Murchie, G. (1961). *Music of the spheres.* Boston, MA: Houghton Mifflin Co.

Murchie, G. (1967). *Music of the spheres* (Rev. ed., Vols. 1–2). New York, NY: Dover.

Murray, M., Molholm, S., Michel, C., Heslenfield, D., Ritter, W., Javitt, D., Schroeder, C., & Foxe, J. (2005). Grabbing your ear: Rapid auditory-somatosensory multisensory interactions in low-level sensory cortices are not constrained by stimulus alignment. *Cerebral Cortex, 15*, 963–974.

Mursell, J. L. (1937/1971). *The psychology of music.* Reprint. Westport, CT: Greenwood Press.

Mursell, J. L., & Glenn, M. (1931). *The psychology of school music teaching.* New York, NY: Silver Burdett.

Music Consumer Insight Report (2018). Retrieved from https://www.ifpi.org/news/IFPI-releases-2018-music-consumer-insight-report.

Musiek, F., & Baran, J. (2018). *The auditory system: Anatomy, physiology, and clinical correlates* (2nd ed.). San Diego, CA: Plural Publishing.

Naeser, M., & Helm-Estabrooks, N. (1985). CT scan lesion localization and response to melodic intonation therapy with nonfluent aphasia cases. *Cortex, 21*(2), 203–223.

Nagarajan, S., Mahncke, H., Salz, T., Tallall, P., Roberts, T., & Merzenich, M. (1999). Cortical auditory signal processing in poor readers. *Proceedings of the National Academy of Sciences, 96*, 6483–6488.

Nagari, B. (2015). *Music as image: Analytical psychology and music in film.* London: Routledge.

Nagel, J. (2017). *Managing stage fright: A guide for musicians and music teachers.* Oxford: Oxford University Press.

Nakada, T., Fujii, Y., Suzuki, K., & Kwee, I. (1998). "Musical brain" revealed by high-field (3 Tesla) functional MRI. *NeuroReport, 19*(7), 3853–3856.

Nakahara, H., Furuya, S., Obata, S., Mauko, T., & Kinoshita, H. (2009). Emotion-related changes in heart rate and its variability during performance and perception of music. *The Neurosciences of Music III: Disorders and Plasticity: Annals of the New York Academy of Sciences, 1169*(1), 359–362.

Nakata, T., & Trehub, S. (2005). Infants' responsiveness to maternal speech and singing. *Infant Behavior and Development, 27*, 455–464.

Narmour, E. (1990). *The analysis and cognition of basic melodic structures.* Chicago: University of Chicago Press.

Narmour, E. (1992). *The analysis and cognition of melodic complexity.* Chicago: The University of Chicago Press.

Nater, U., Abbruzzese, E., Krebs, M., & Ehlert, U. (2006). Sex differences in emotional and psychophysiological responses to musical stimuli. *International Journal of Psychophysiology, 62*, 300–308.

Nater, U., Krebs, M., & Ehlert, U. (2005). Sensation seeking, music preference, and psychophysiological reactivity to music. *Musicæ Scientiæ, 9*(2), 239–254.

National Endowment for the Arts. (2018). *U.S. trends in art attendance and literary reading: 2002–2017.* Retrieved from www.arts.gov/sites/default/files/2017-sppapreviewREV-sept2018.pdf

National Institute for Occupational Safety and Health. (2018). *NIOSH sound meter.* Retrieved December 28, 2018, from www.cdc.gov/niosh/topics/noise/factsstatistics/charts/chart-lookatnoise.html

National Standards for Music Education. (2014). Retrieved July 2018, from www.musicstandfoundation.org/images/National_Standards_-_Music_Education.pdf

Nemati, S., Akrami, H., Salehi, S., Esteky, H., & Moghimi, S. (2019). Lost in music: Neural signature of pleasure and its role in modulating attentional resources. *Brain Research, 1711*, 7–15.

Nettl, B. (1977). On the question of universals. *The World of Music, 19*, 2–13.

Nettl, B. (1983). *The study of ethnomusicology.* Urbana: University of Illinois Press.

Nettl, B. (2000). An ethnomusicologist contemplates universals in musical sound and culture. In N. Wallin, B. Merker, & S. Brown (Eds.), *The origins of music* (pp. 463–472). Cambridge, MA: The MIT Press.

Nettl, B. (2005). *The study of ethnomusicology: Thirty-one issues and concepts.* Champaign, IL: The University of Illinois Press.

Nettl, B., & Bohlman, P. (1991). *Comparative musicology and anthropology of music.* Chicago: University of Chicago Press.

Neuhaus, C. (2003). Perceiving musical scale structures: A cross-cultural event-related brain potentials study. *The Neurosciences and Music: Annals of the New York Academy of Sciences, 999,* 184–188.

Nickerson, J. F. (1949). Intonation of solo and ensemble performance of the same melody. *The Journal of the Acoustical Society of America, 21*(6), 593–595.

Nielsen, F. (1983). *Oplavelse av musikalsk spænding.* [Experience of musical tension]. Copenhaen: Academisk Forlag. Cited in Gabrielsson, A., & Lindström, E. (2001). The influence of musical structure on emotional expression. In P. Juslin & J. Sloboda (Eds.), *Music and emotion: Theory and research* (pp. 223–248). Oxford: Oxford University Press.

Nielsen, F. (1987). Musical "tension" and related concepts. In T. A. Sebeok & J. Umiker-Sebeok (Eds.), *The semiotic web '86: An international yearbook* (pp. 491–513). Berlin: Mouton de Gruyler. Cited in Gabrielsson, A., & Lindström, E. (2001). The influence of musical structure on emotional expression. In P. Juslin & J. Sloboda (Eds.), *Music and emotion: Theory and research* (pp. 223–248). Oxford: Oxford University Press.

Nielsen, S. (2004). Strategies and self-efficacy beliefs in instrumental and vocal individual practice: A study of students in higher music education. *Psychology of Music, 32*(4), 418–431.

Nies, A. (1986). Clinical pharmacology of beta-adrenergic blockers. *Medical Problems of Performing Musicians, 1*(1), 25–29.

Nilsson, U. (2009). Soothing music can increase oxytocin levels during bed rest after open-heart surgery: A randomised control trial. *Journal of Clinical Nursing, 18*(15), 2153–2161.

Nilsson, U., Unosson, M., & Rawal, N. (2005). Stress reduction and analgesia in patients exposed to calming music postoperatively: A randomized controlled trial. *European Journal of Anaesthesiology, 22*(2), 96–102.

Niquette, P. (2009). Uniform hearing protection for musicians. In M. Chasin (Ed.), *Hearing loss in musicians: Prevention and management* (pp. 63–74). San Diego, CA: Plural Publishing.

Nketia, J. (1974). *The music of Africa.* New York, NY: Norton.

Nketia, J. (1984). Universal perspectives in ethnomusicology. *The World of Music, 26*(2), 3–20.

Noble, C. (1964). *The psychology of cornet and trumpet playing: Scientific principles of artistic performance.* Missoula, MT: Mountain Press.

Norman-Haignere, S., Kanwisher, N., & McDermott, J. (2015). Distinct cortical pathways for music and speech revealed by hypothesis-free voxel decomposition. *Neuron, 88,* 1281–1296.

Norris, R., & Dommerholt, J. (1998). Applied ergonomics: Adaptive equipment and instrument modification for musicians. In R. Sataloff, A. Brandfonbrener, & R. Lederman (Eds.), *Performing arts medicine* (2nd ed., pp. 261–275). San Diego, CA: Singular Publishing Group.

North, A. (2009). *People into music.* Retrieved June 12, 2009, from www.psychology.hw.ac.uk/staffDetails.php?staff_id=55

North, A., & Hargreaves, D. (1995). Eminence in pop music. *Popular Music and Society, 19*(4), 41–66.

North, A., & Hargreaves, D. (1997a). Experimental aesthetics and everyday music listening. In A. North & D. Hargreaves (Eds.) *The social psychology of music* (pp. 84–103). New York, NY: Oxford University Press.

North, A., & Hargreaves, D. (1999). Music and adolescent identity. *Music Education Research, 1*(1), 75–92.

North, A., & Hargreaves, D. (2000). Collative variables versus prototypicality. *Empirical Studies of the Arts, 8*(1), 13–17.

North, A., & Hargreaves, D. (2005). Musical communication in commercial contexts. In D. Miell, R. MacDonald, & D. Hargreaves (Eds.), *Musical communication* (pp. 405–422). Oxford: Oxford University Press.

North, A., & Hargreaves, D. (2008). *The social and applied psychology of music.* Oxford: Oxford University Press.

North, A., & Hargreaves, D. (2009). Music and consumer behavior. In S. Hallam, I. Cross, & M. Thaut (Eds.), *The Oxford handbook of music psychology* (pp. 481–490). Oxford: Oxford University Press.

North, A., & Hargreaves, D. (2010). Music and marketing. In P. Juslin & J. Sloboda (Eds.), *Handbook of music and emotion* (pp. 909–930). Oxford: Oxford University Press.

North, A., Hargreaves, D., & O'Neill, S. (2000). The importance of music to adolescents. *British Journal of Educational Psychology, 70,* 255–272.

References

North, A., Hargreaves, D., & Tarrant, M. (2002). Social psychology and music education. In R. Colwell & C. Richardson (Eds.), *The new handbook of research on music teaching and learning* (pp. 604–625). Oxford: Oxford University Press.

Norton, A., Winner, E., Cronin, K., Overy, K., Lee, D., & Schlaug, G. (2005). Are there pre-existing neural, cognitive, or motoric markers for musical ability? *Brain and Cognition, 59*(2), 124–134.

Noy, P. (1966–67). The psychodynamic meaning of music, parts 1–5. *Journal of Music Therapy, 3*(4), 116–123; 4(1), 7–23; 4(2), 45–51; 4(3), 81–94; 4(4), 117–125.

Nubé, J. (1991). Beta-blockers: Effects on performing musicians. *Medical Problems of Performing Artists, 6*(2), 61–68.

Nubé, J. (1994). Time-series analyses of the effects of propranolol on pianistic performance. *Medical Problems of Performing Artists, 9*(3), 77–88.

Nusbaum, E., Silvia, P., Burgin, C., Hodges, D., & Kwapil, T. (2014). Listening between the notes: Aesthetic chills in everyday music listening. *Psychology of Aesthetics, 8*(1), 104–109.

Nutall, P. (2008). Thank you for the music? The role and significance of music for adolescents. *Young Consumers, 9*(2), 104–111.

Nyklíček, I., Thayer, J., & Van Doornen, L. (1997). Cardiorespiratory differentiation of musically-induced emotions. *Journal of Psychophysiology, 11*, 304–321.

O'Connell, D. (2003). *The effects of prenatal music experiences on one-week-old infants' timbre discrimination of selected auditory stimuli* (Doctor of Philosophy). University of North Carolina, Greensboro. Dissertation Abstracts International, 64/06-A, 2018 (University Microfilms No. 3093879).

O'Connor, B., & Dyce, J. (1997). Interpersonal rigidity, hostility, and complementarity in musical bands. *Journal of Personality and Social Psychology, 72*(2), 362–372.

O'Neill, S. (1997a). Gender and music. In D. Hargreaves & A. North (Eds.), *The social psychology of music* (pp. 46–63). Oxford: Oxford University Press.

O'Neill, S. (1997b). The role of practice in children's early musical performance achievement. In H. Jørgensen & A. Lehmann (Eds). *Does practice make perfect? Current theory and research on instrumental music practice* (pp. 53–70). Oslo: Norges Musikkhøgskole.

O'Neill, S. (1999). Flow theory and the development of musical performance skills. *Bulletin of the Council for Research in Music Education, 141*, 129–134.

O'Neill, S., & McPherson, G. (2002). Motivation. In R. Parncutt & G. McPherson (Eds.), *The science and psychology of music performance* (pp. 31–46). Oxford: Oxford University Press.

Ochsner, K., & Kosslyn, S. (2013). *The Oxford handbook of cognitive neuroscience, 2 vols.* Oxford: Oxford University Press.

Ockelford, A. (2013a). *Applied musicology: Using zygonic theory to inform music education, therapy, and psychology research.* Oxford: Oxford University Press.

Ockelford, A. (2013b). *Music, language and autism.* London: Jessica Kingsley Publishers.

Ockelford, A. (2016). Prodigious musical talent in blind children with autism and learning difficulties: Identifying and educating potential musical savants. In G. McPherson (Ed.), *Musical prodigies* (pp. 471–495). Oxford: Oxford University Press.

Ockelford, A. (2019). The neuroscience of children on the autism spectrum with exceptional musical abilities. In M. Thaut & D. Hodges (Eds.), *The Oxford handbook of music and the brain* (pp. 671–692). Oxford: Oxford University Press.

Ohno, S. (1993, August). A song in praise of peptide palindromes. *Leukemia, 7*(Suppl 2), S157–S159.

Ohno, S., & Ohno, M. (1986). The all pervasive principle of repetitious recurrence governs not only coding sequence construction but also human endeavor in musical composition. *Immunogenetics, 24*(2), 71–78.

Oikkonen, J., Huang, Y., Onkamo, P., Ukkola-Vuoti, L., Raijas, P., Karma, K., . . . Järvelä, I. (2015). A genome-wide linkage and association study of musical aptitude identifies loci containing genes related to inner ear development and neurocognitive functions. *Molecular Psychiatry, 20*(2), 275.

Oikkonen, J., Onkamo, P., Järvelä, I., & Kanduri, C. (2016). Convergent evidence for the molecular basis of musical traits. *Scientific Reports, 6*, 39707.

Olds, C. (1985). Fetal response to music. *Midwives Chronicle, 98*(1170), 202–203.

Olejniczak, P. (2006). Neurophysiologic basis of EEG. *Journal of Clinical Neurophysiology, 23*(3), 186–189.

Olsen, D. (1980). Folk music of South America. In E. May (Ed.), *Music of many cultures—A musical mosaic* (pp. 386–425). Berkeley, CA: University of California Press.

Olson, H. (1940). *Elements of acoustical engineering.* New York, NY: D. Van Nostrand.

Olson, H. (1952). *Musical Engineering.* New York, NY: McGraw-Hill.

Olson, H. (1967). *Music, physics and engineering* (2nd ed.). New York, NY: Dover Publications.

Olson, M., & Hergenhahn, B. (2008). *An introduction to theories of learning* (8th ed.). Upper Saddle River, NJ: Pearson.

Olsson, E., von Schéele, B., & Theorell, T. (2013). Heart rate variability during choral singing. *Music and Medicine, 5*(1), 52–59.

Omar, R., Hailstone, J., Warren, J., Crutch, S., & Warren, J. (2010, February 8). The cognitive organization of music knowledge: A clinical analysis. *Brain,* available on *Brain Advance Access,* 1–14.

Ong, W. (1977). African talking drums and oral noetics. *New Literary History, 8*(3), 411–429.

Ormond, J. (1999). *Human learning* (3rd ed.). Upper Saddle River, NJ: Prentice-Hall.

Orton, A. (2004). *Learning mathematics: Issues, theory and classroom practice* (3rd ed.). New York, NY: Continuum.

Osborne, N. (2009). Towards a chronobiology of musical rhythm. In S. Malloch & C. Trevarthen (Eds.), *Communicative musicality: Exploring the basis of human companionship* (pp. 545–564). Oxford: Oxford University Press.

Osis, K., & Haraldsson, E. (1997). *At the hour of death: A new look at evidence for life after death* (3rd ed.). Norwalk, CT: Hastings House.

Ostwald, P., Avery, M., & Ostwald, L. (1998). Psychiatric problems of performing artists. In R. Sataloff, A. Brandfonbrener, & R. Lederman (Eds.), *Performing arts medicine* (2nd ed., pp. 337–348). San Diego, CA: Singular Publishing Group.

Overy, K. (2003). Dyslexia and music: From timing deficits to musical intervention. In G. Avanzini, C. Faienza, D. Minciacchi, L. Lopez, & M. Majno (Eds.), *The neurosciences of music. Annals of the New York Academy of Sciences, 999,* 497–505.

Overy, K., Norton, A., Cronin, K., Gaab, N., Alsop, D., Winner, E., & Schlaug, G. (2004). Imaging melody and rhythm processing in young children. *NeuroReport, 15,* 1723–1726.

Overy, K., Peretz, I., Zatorre, R., Lopez, L., & Majno, M. (2012). The neurosciences and music IV: Learning and memory. *Annals of the New York Academy of Sciences, 1252.*

Owens, D. (2007). Noise-induced hearing loss. *The Instrumentalist, 62*(3), 23–28.

Oyama, T., Hatano, K., Sato, Y., Kudo, M., Spintge, R., & Droh, R. (1987). Endocrine effect of anxiolytic music in dental patients. In R. Spintge & R. Droh (Eds.), *Music in Medicine* (pp. 223–226). Berlin: Springer-Verlag.

Pacholczyk, J. (1980). Secular classical music in the Arabic near East. In E. May (Ed.), *Music of many cultures—A musical mosaic* (pp. 253–268). Berkeley, CA: University of California Press.

Palac, J. (2008). Promoting musical health, enhancing musical performance: Wellness for music students. *Music Educators Journal, 94*(3), 18–22.

Palmer, A. J. (1995). Music education and spirituality: A philosophical exploration. *Philosophy of Music Education Review,* 91–106.

Palmer, A. J. (2006). Music education and spirituality: Philosophical exploration II. *Philosophy of Music Education Review, 14*(2), 143–158.

Palmer, A. J. (2010). Spirituality in music education: Transcending culture, exploration III. *Philosophy of Music Education Review, 18*(2), 152–170.

Palmer, C. (1997). Music performance. *Annual Review of Psychology, 48,* 115–138.

Palmer, C., & Meyer, R. (2000). Conceptual and motor learning in music performance. *Psychological Science, 11*(1), 63–68.

Palmer, M. (1976). Relative effectiveness of two approaches to rhythm reading for fourth-grade students. *Journal of Research in Music Education, 24*(3), 110–118.

Panksepp, J. (1995). The emotional sources of "chills" induced by music. *Music Perception, 13,* 171–201.

Panksepp, J., & Bernatzky, G. (2002). Emotional sounds and the brain: The neuro-affective foundations of musical appreciation. *Behavioural Processes, 60*(2), 133–155.

References

Panksepp, J., & Trevarthen, C. (2009). The neuroscience of emotion in music. In S. Malloch & C. Trevarthen (Eds.), *Communicative musicality: Exploring the basis of human companionship* (pp. 105–146). Oxford: Oxford University Press.

Panneton, R. (1985). *Prenatal auditory experience with melodies: Effects on postnatal auditory preferences* (Doctor of Philosophy). The University of North Carolina, Greensboro. Dissertation Abstracts International 47/09-B, 3984. University Microfilms No. 8701333).

Pantev, C., Hoke, M., Lutkenhoner, B., & Lehnertz, K. (1989). Tonotopic organization of the auditory cortex: Pitch versus frequency representation. *Science, 246*(4929), 486–488.

Papageorgi, I., & Welch, G. (2014). *Advanced musical performance*. Farnham: Ashgate.

Papousek, H. (1996). Musicality in infant research: Biological and cultural origins of early musicality. In I. Deliège & J. A. Sloboda (Eds.), *Musical beginnings: Origins and development of musical competence* (pp. 37–55). New York, NY: Oxford University Press.

Papousek, M. (1996). Intuitive parenting: A hidden source of musical stimulation in infancy. In I. Deliège & J. A. Sloboda (Eds.), *Musical beginnings: Origins and development of musical competence* (pp. 88–112). New York, NY: Oxford University Press.

Paraskeva, S., & McAdams, S. (1997). Influence of timbre, presence/absence of tonal hierarchy and musical training on the perception of musical tension and relaxation schemas. In *Proceedings of the 1997 international computer music conference, Thessaloniki* (pp. 438–441). San Francisco: International Computer Music Association.

Paraskevopoulos, E., Tsapkini, K., & Peretz, I. (2010). Cultural aspects of music perception: Validation of a Greek version of the montreal battery of evaluation of Amusias. *Journal of the International Neuropsychological Society, 16*(4), 695–704.

Park, H. (2013). The effect of individualized music on agitation for home-dwelling persons with dementia. *Open Journal of Nursing, 3*, 453–459.

Park, H., Lee, S., Kim, H-J., Ju, Y., Shin, J., Hong, D., . . . Seo, J-S. (2012). Comprehensive genomic analyses associate UGT8 variants with musical ability in a Mongolian population. *Journal of Medical Genetics, 49*, 747–752.

Parker, O. (1961). *A study of the relationship of aesthetic sensitivity to musical ability, intelligence, and socioeconomic status* (PhD dissertation). University of Kansas.

Parker, S., & Smith, A. (2013). *Musician's acoustics*. Scotts Valley, CA: CreateSpace Independent Publishing Platform.

Parncutt, R. (1989). *Harmony: A psychoacoustical approach*. Berlin: Springer-Verlag.

Parncutt, R. (2009). Prenatal development and the phylogeny and ontogeny of music. In S. Hallam, I. Cross, & M. Thaut (Eds.), *The Oxford handbook of music psychology* (pp. 219–228). Oxford: Oxford University Press.

Parncutt, R., & McPherson, G. (Eds.). (2002). *The science and psychology of music performance*. New York, NY: Oxford University Press.

Parsons, C. E., Young, K. S., Murray, L., Stein, A., & Kringelbach, M. L. (2010). The functional neuroanatomy of the evolving parent—infant relationship. *Progress in Neurobiology, 91*(3), 220–241.

Parsons, L., Sergent, J., Hodges, D., & Fox, P. (2005). The brain basis of piano performance. *Neuropsychologia, 43*, 199–215.

Parsons, M., Salgado Kent, C., Recalde-Salas, A., & McCauley, R. (2017). Fish choruses off Port Hedland, Western Australia. *Bioacoustics, 26*(2), 135–152.

Parton, D. (1995). *My life and other unfinished business*. New York, NY: Harpercollins.

Pascual-Leone, A. (2003). The brain that plays music and is changed by it. In I. Peretz & R. Zatorre (Eds.), *The cognitive neuroscience of music* (pp. 396–412). Oxford: Oxford University Press.

Pascual-Leone, A., Dang, N., Cohen, L., Brasil-Neto, J., Cammarota, A., & Hallett, M. (1995). Modulation of muscle responses evoked by transcranial magnetic stimulation during the acquisition of new fine motor skills. *Journal of Neurophysiology, 74*(3), 1037–1045.

Pascual-Leone, A., Grafman, J., & Hallett, M. (1994). Modulation of cortical motor output maps during development of implicit and explicit knowledge. *Science, 263*(5151), 1287–1289.

Pascual-Leone, A., Nguyet, D., Cohen, L. G., Brasil-Neto, J. P., Cammarota, A., & Hallett, M. (1995). Modulation of muscle responses evoked by transcranial magnetic stimulation during the acquisition of new fine motor skills. *Journal of Neurophysiology, 74*(3), 1037–1045.

Patel, A. (2008). *Music, language, and the brain*. Oxford: Oxford University Press.

Patel, A. (2009). Music and the brain: Three links to language. In S. Hallam, I. Cross, & M. Thaut (Eds.), *The Oxford handbook of music psychology* (pp. 208–216). Oxford: Oxford University Press.

Patel, A. (2011). Why would musical training benefit the neural encoding of speech? The OPERA hypothesis. *Frontiers in Psychology, 2*, 142.

Patel, A. (2014). Can nonlinguistic musical training change the way the brain processes speech? The expanded OPERA hypthesis. *Hearing Research, 308*, 98–108.

Patel, A., & Daniele, J. (2003). An empirical comparison of rhythm in language and music. *Cognition, 87*, B35–B45.

Patel, A., Iversen, J., Bregman, M., & Schulz, I. (2009). Experimental evidence for synchronization to a musical beat in a nonhuman animal. *Current Biology, 19*(10), 827–830.

Patel, A., Meltznoff, A., & Kuhl, K. (2004). Cultural differences in rhythm perception: What is the influence of native language? In S. Lipscomb, R. Ashley, R. Gjerdingen, & P. Webster (Eds.), *Proceedings of the 8th international conference on music perception and cognition*. Evanston, IL: Northwestern University. CD-ROM.

Patterson, C. (2004). Evolution: Neo-Darwinian theory. In R. Gregory (Ed.), *Oxford companion to the mind* (2nd ed., pp. 307–317). Oxford: Oxford University Press.

Pätynen, J. (2007). *Virtual acoustics in practice rooms* (Master's thesis). Helsinki University of Technology. Retrieved from https://core.ac.uk/download/pdf/80700876.pdf

Pavlov, I. (1927/2003). *Conditioned reflexes* (G. Anrep, Trans.). Mineola, NY: Dover.

Payne, K. (2000). The progressively changing songs of humpback whales: A window on the creative process in a wild animal. In N. Wallin, B. Merker, & S. Brown (Eds.), *The origins of music* (pp. 135–150). Cambridge, MA: The MIT Press.

Peach, S. (1984). Some implications for the clinical use of music facilitated imagery. *Journal of Music Therapy, 21*(1), 27–34.

Penman, J., & Becker, J. (2009). Religious ecstatics, "deep listeners," and musical emotion. *Empirical Musicology Review, 4*(2), 49–70.

Perani, D., Saccuman, M., Scifo, P., Spada, D., Andreolli, G., Rovelli, R., . . . Koelsch, S. (2010). Functional specializations for music processing in the human newborn brain. *PNAS (Proceedings of the National Academy of Sciences), 107*(10), 4758–4763.

Peretti, P., & Swenson, K. (1974). Effects of music on anxiety as determined by physiological skin responses. *Journal of Research in Music Education, 22*, 278–283.

Peretz, I. (2001). Brain specialization for music: New evidence from congenital amusia. In R. Zatorre & I. Peretz (Eds.), *The biological foundations of music. Annals of the New York Academy of Sciences, 930*, 153–165.

Peretz, I. (2010). Towards a neurobiology of musical emotions. In P. Juslin & J. Sloboda (Eds.), *Handbook of music and emotions* (pp. 99–126). Oxford: Oxford University Press.

Peretz, I., Champod, A., & Hyde, K. (2003). Varieties of musical disorders: The montreal battery of evaluation of Amusia. In G. Avanzini, C. Faienza, D. Minciacchi, L. Lopez, & M. Majno, M. (Eds.), *The neurosciences and music. Annals of the New York Academy of Sciences, 999*, 58–75.

Peretz, I., Cummings, S., & Dubé, M. P. (2007). The genetics of congenital amusia (tone deafness): A family-aggregation study. *The American Journal of Human Genetics, 81*(3), 582–588.

Peretz, I., Gagnon, L., & Bouchard, B. (1998). Music and emotion: Perceptual determinants, immediacy, and isolation after brain damage. *Cognition, 68*, 111–141.

Peretz, I., & Zatorre, R. (2003). *The cognitive neuroscience of music*. New York, NY: Oxford University Press.

Peretz, I., & Zatorre, R. (2005). Brain organization for music processing. *Annual Review of Psychology, 56*, 89–114.

Pérez, A., Carreiras, M., & Duñabeitia, J. (2017). Brain-to-brain entrainment: EEG interbrain synchronization while speaking and listening. *Scientific Reports, 7*(4190), 1–12.

References

Persson, R. (2001). The subjective world of the performer. In P. Juslin & J. Sloboda (Eds.), *Music and emotion: Theory and research* (pp. 275–289). New York, NY: Oxford University Press.

Peterson, D., & Altenmüller, E. (2019). When blue turns to gray: The enigma of musician's dystonia. In M. Thaut and D. Hodges (Eds.), *The Oxford handbook on music and the brain* (pp. 776–802). Oxford, UK: Oxford University Press.

Petit, P. (2011). *The paleolithic origins of human burial.* London: Routledge.

Petzold, R. (1963). The development of auditory perception of music sounds by children in the first six grades. *Journal of Research in Music Education, 11,* 21–43.

Pfeiffer, J. (1969). *The emergence of man.* New York: Harper and Row.

Pfeiffer, J. (1980). Icons in the shadows. *Science80, 1*(4), 72–79.

Pflederer, M. (1964). The responses of children to musical tasks embodying Piaget's principle of conservation. *Journal of Research in Music Education, 12*(3), 251–268.

Phelps, R. (1969). *A guide to research in music education.* Dubuque, IA: W. C. Brown.

Phelps, R. (1980). *A guide to research in music education* (2nd ed.). Metuchen, NJ: Scarecrow Press.

Phillips, D. (1976). An investigation of the relationship between musicality and intelligence. *Psychology of Music, 4,* 16–31.

Phillips, S., & Mace, S. (2008). Sound-level measurements in music practice rooms. *Music Performance Research, 2,* 36–47. Retrieved from www.mpr-online.net/index.html.

Phillips, S., Shoemaker, J., Mace, S., & Hodges, D. (2008). Environmental factors in susceptibility to noise-induced hearing loss in student musicians. *Medical Problems of Performing Artists, 23,* 20–28.

Phillips-Silver, J., Tolviainen, P., Gosselin, M., Piché, O., Nozaradan, S., Palmer, C., & Peretz, I. (2011). Born to dance but beat deaf: A new form of congenital amusia. *Neuropsychlogia, 49*(5), 961–969.

Piaget, J. (1947/2001). *The psychology of intelligence* (M. Piercy & D. Berlyne, Trans.). New York, NY: Routledge.

Piaget, J., & Inhelder, B. (1969/2000). *The psychology of the child* (H. Weaver, Trans.). New York, NY: Basic Books.

Pickles, J. (1988). *An introduction to the physiology of hearing* (2nd ed.). New York, NY: Academic Press.

Pierce, J. (1999). The nature of musical sound. In D. Deutsch (Ed.), *The psychology of music* (2nd ed., pp. 1–23). San Diego, CA: Elsevier Academic Press.

Pierce, J., & David Jr., E. (1958). *Man's world of sound.* Garden City, NY: Doubleday Anchor Book.

Pignatiello, M., Camp, C., Elder, S., & Rasar, L. (1989). A psychophysiological comparison of the Velten and musical mood induction techniques. *Journal of Music Therapy, 26*(3),140–154.

Pilger, A., Haslacher, H., Ponocny-Seliger, E., Perkmann, T., Böhm, K., Budinsky, A., . . . Winker, R. (2014). Affective and inflammatory responses among orchestra musicians in performance situation. *Brain, Behavior, and Immunity, 37,* 23–29.

Pincus, B. (2005). Get in tune with consumers. *Brand Strategy, 190,* 46–47.

Pinker, S. (1997). *How the mind works.* New York, NY: W. W. Norton.

Piperek, M. (1981). *Stress and music.* Vienna: Wilhelm Braumüller.

Pitts, S., Davidson, J., & McPherson, G. (2000). Developing effective practice strategies: Case studies of three young instrumentalists. *Music Education Research, 2*(1), 45–56.

Plack, C. (2005). *The sense of hearing.* Malwah, NJ: Lawrence Erlbaum.

Plomp, R. (1976). *Aspects of tone sensation: A psychophysical study.* London: Academic Press.

Plomp, R., & Bouman, M. (1959). Relation between hearing threshold and duration for tone pulses. *Journal of the Acoustical Society of America, 31*(6), 749–758.

Plotkin, H. (1994). *Darwin machines and the nature of knowledge.* Cambridge, MA: Harvard University Press.

Pohlmann, K. (1992). *The compact disc handbook.* Madison, WI: A-R Editions.

Polanka, M. (1995). Research note: Factors affecting eye movements during the reading of short melodies. *Psychology of Music, 23*(2), 177–183.

Pons, F., Lewkowicz, D., Soto-Faraco, S., & Sebastián-Gallés, N. (2009). Narrowing of intersensory speech perception in infancy. *Proceedings of the National Academy of Sciences, 106*(26), 10598–10602.

Portin, P. (2015). A comparison of biological and cultural evolution. *Journal of Genetics, 94*(1), 155–168.

Posner, M., & Keele, S. (1968). On the genesis of abstract ideas. *Journal of Experimental Psychology, 77,* 353–363.

Pottle, R. (1970). How a great orchestra resolves an intonation dilemma. *Selmer Band Wagon, 59,* 28–29.

Pouthas, V. (1996). The development of the perception of time and temporal regulation of action in infants and children. In I. Deliège & J. Sloboda (Eds.), *Musical beginnings: Origins and development of musical competence* (pp. 115–141). New York, NY: Oxford University Press.

Powell, J. (2016). *Why you love music: From Mozart to Metallica—the emotional power of beautiful sounds.* New York, NY: Little, Brown & Company.

Powell, N. (1979). Fibonacci and the gold mean: Rabbits, rumbas, and rondeaux. *Journal of Music Theory, 23*(2), 227–273.

Powers, N., & Trevarthen, C. (2009). Voices of shared emotion and meaning: Young infants and their mothers in Scotland and Japan. In S. Malloch & C. Trevarthen (Eds.), *Communicative musicality: Exploring the basis of human companionship* (pp. 209–240). Oxford: Oxford University Press.

Powers, W. (1990). *War dance: Plains Indian musical performance.* Tuscon: The University of Arizona Press.

Prassas, S., Thaut, M., McIntosh, G., & Rice, R. (1997). Effects of auditory rhythmic cuing on gait kinematic parameters in hemiparetic stroke patients. *Gait Posture, 6,* 218–223.

Pratt, C. (1931). *The meaning of music: A study in psychological aesthetics.* New York, NY: McGraw-Hill.

Pratt, R. (1996). Professionalism in music therapy and music medicine: Issues of past and future. In R. Pratt & R. Spintge (Eds.), *MusicMedicine 2* (pp. 301–308). St. Louis, MO: MMB Music.

Pratt, R. (1999). Listening to music during surgery: A program of intermountain health care. *International Journal of Arts Medicine, 6*(1), 21–30.

Pratt, R., & Grocke, D. (Eds.). (1999). *MusicMedicine 3.* Melbourne, Australia: The University of Melbourne.

Pratt, R., & Jones, R. (1987). Music and medicine: A partnership in history. In R. Spintge & R. Droh (Eds.), *Music in medicine* (pp. 377–388). Berlin: Springer-Verlag.

Pratt, R., & Spintge, R. (Eds.). (1995). *MusicMedicine 2.* St. Louis, MO: MMB.

Presley, D. (2007, August). An analysis of sound-level exposures of drum and bugle corps percussionists. *Percussive Notes,* 70–75.

Price, H. (Ed.). (1998). *Music education research.* Lanham, MD: Rowman & Littlefield Education.

Prideaux, T. (1973). *Cro-Magnon man.* New York: Time-Life Books.

Pritchard, A. (2009). *Ways of learning: Learning theories and learning styles in the classroom.* New York, NY: Routledge.

Probst, R., Lonsbury-Martin, B., & Martin, G. (1990). A review of otoacoustic emissions. *Journal of the Acoustical Society of America, 89*(5), 2027–2067.

Proops, L., McComb, K., & Reby, D. (2009). Cross-modal individual recognition in domestic horses (Equus caballus). *Proceedings of the National Academy of Sciences, 106*(3), 947–951.

Prugh, L., & Golden, C. (2014). Does moonlight increase predation risk? Meta-analysis reveals divergent responses of nocturnal mammals to lunar cycles. *Journal of Animal Ecology, 83,* 504–514.

Pujol, K. (1994). The effect of vibrotactile stimulation, instrumentation, and precomposed melodies on physiological and behavioral responses of profoundly retarded children and adults. *Journal of Music Therapy, 31,* 186–205.

Pulli, K., Karma, K., Norio, R., Sistonen, P., Göring, H. H., & Järvelä, I. (2008). Genome-wide linkage scan for loci of musical aptitude in Finnish families: Evidence for a major locus at 4q22. *Journal of Medical Genetics, 45*(7), 451–456.

Purves, D., Augustine, G., Fitzpatrik, D., Hall, W., LaMantia, A-S., Mooney, R., . . . White, L. (Eds.). (2018). *Neuroscience* (6th ed.). New York, NY: Oxford University Press.

Putman, J. (1988). The search for modern humans. *National Geographic, 174*(4), 438–477.

Quartz, S. (2003). Learning and brain development: A neural constructivist perspective. In P. Quinlan (Ed.), *Connectionist models of development* (pp. 279–309). New York, NY: Psychology Press.

Radocy, R. (1980). The perception of melody, harmony, rhythm, and form. In D. Hodges (Ed.), *Handbook of music psychology* (pp. 93–103). Lawrence, KS: National Association for Music Therapy.

Radocy, R., & Boyle, J. (1979). *Psychological foundations of musical behavior.* Springfield, IL: Charles C. Thomas.

References

Radocy, R., & Boyle, J. (1988). *Psychological foundations of musical behavior* (2nd ed.). Springfield, IL: Charles C. Thomas.

Radocy, R., & Boyle, J. (1997). *Psychological foundations of musical behavior* (2nd ed.). Springfield, IL: Charles C. Thomas.

Radocy, R., & Boyle, J. (2003). *Psychological foundations of musical behavior* (4th ed.). Springfield, IL: Charles C. Thomas.

Radocy, R., & Boyle, J. (2012). *Psychological foundations of musical behavior* (5th ed.). Springfield, IL: Charles C. Thomas.

Raeburn, S. (1987a). Occupational stress and coping in a sample of professional rock musicians: Part 1. *Medical Problems of Performing Artists, 2*(2), 41–48.

Raeburn, S. (1987b). Occupational stress and coping in a sample of professional rock musicians: Part 2. *Medical Problems of Performing Artists, 2*(3), 77–82.

Raeburn, S. (1999). Psychological issues and treatment strategies in popular musicians: A review, part 1. *Medical Problems of Performing Musicians, 14*(4), 171–179.

Raeburn, S. (2000). Psychological issues and treatment strategies in popular musicians: A review, part 2. *Medical Problems of Performing Musicians, 15*(1), 6–17.

Raffman, D. (1993). *Language, music, and mind.* Cambridge, MA: The MIT Press.

Rainbow, E., & Froehlich, H. (1987). *Research in music education: An introduction to systematic inquiry.* New York, NY: Schirmer Books.

Raloff, J. (1983). Noise: The subtle pollutant. In *Science yearbook: New illustrated encyclopedia* (pp. 194–199). New York, NY: Funk and Wagnalls.

Rapoport, E. (1996). Emotional expression code in opera and lied singing. *Journal of New Music Research, 25*(2), 109–149.

Rasch, R. (1988). Timing and synchronization in ensemble performance. In J. Sloboda (Ed.), *Generative processes in music* (pp. 70–90). Oxford: Clarendon Press.

Rasch, R., & Plomp, R. (1999). The perception of musical tones. In D. Deutsch (Ed.), *The psychology of music* (2nd ed., pp. 89–112). San Diego, CA: Elsevier Academic Press.

Rath, S., & Naik, P. (2005). Fibonacci structure and conch shell. *Current Science, 88*(4), 555–556.

Raufschecker, J. (2001). Cortical plasticity and music. In R. Zatorre & I. Peretz (Eds.), *The biological foundations of music. Annals of the New York Academy of Sciences, 930*, 330–336.

Rayner, K. (1998). Eye movements in reading and information processing: 20 years of research. *Psychological Bulletin, 124*(3), 372–422.

Rebuschat, P., Rohmeier, M., Hawkins, J., & Cross, I. (Eds.). (2012). *Language and music as cognitive systems.* Oxford: Oxford University Press.

Reck, D. (1977). *Music of the whole earth.* New York, NY: Scribner.

Reed, E. (1997). *From soul to mind: The emergence of psychology, from Erasmus Darwin to William James.* New Haven, CT: Yale University Press.

Regelski, T. (2005). Response to Philip Alperson, "robust praxialism and the ant-aesthetic turn". *Philosophy of Music Education Review, 19*(2), 196–203.

Reik, T. (1953). *The haunting melody: Psychoanalytic experiences in life and music.* New York, NY: Farrar, Strauss, and Young.

Reilly, M. (1996). Relaxation, imagery, and music as an adjunct therapy to narcotic analgesia in the perioperative period. In R. Pratt & R. Spintge (Eds.), *MusicMedicine 2* (pp. 206–217). St. Louis, MO: MMB Music.

Reilly, M. (1999). *Music, a cognitive behavioral intervention for anxiety and acute pain control in the elderly cataract patient* (Unpublished doctoral dissertation). The University of Texas Graduate School of Biomedical Sciences at San Antonio, School of Nursing.

Reimer, B. (1989). *A philosophy of music education* (2nd ed.). Englewood Cliffs, NJ: Prentice-Hall.

Reinberg, A., & Ashkenazi, I. (2003). Concepts in human biological rhythms. *Dialogues in Clinical Neuroscience, 5*(4), 327–342.

Rentfrow, P., Goldberg, L., & Levitin, D. (2011). The structure of musical preferences: A five-factor model. *Journal of Personality and Social Psychology, 100*(6), 1139–1157.

Rentfrow, P., Goldberg, L., Stillwell, D., Kosinski, M., Gosling, S., & Levitin, D. (2012). The song remains the same: A replication and extension of the MUSIC model. *Music Perception: An Interdisciplinary Journal, 30*(2), 161–185. *References*

Rentfrow, P., Goldberg, L., & Zilca, R. (2011). Listening, watching, and reading: The structure and correlates of entertainment preferences. *Journal of Personality, 79*(2), 223–258.

Rentfrow, P., & Gosling, S. (2003). The do re mi's of everyday life: The structure and personality correlates of music preferences. *Journal of Personality and Social Psychology, 84*(6), 1236–1256.

Rentfrow, P., & Gosling, S. (2006). Message in a bottle: The role of music preferences in interpersonal perception. *Psychological Science, 17*(3), 236–242.

Rentfrow, P., & Gosling, S. (2007). The content and validity of music-genre stereotypes among college students. *Psychology of Music, 35*(2), 306–326.

Rentfrow, P., & McDonald, J. A. (2010). Preference, personality, and emotion. In P. Juslin & J. Sloboda (Eds.), *Handbook of music and emotion* (pp. 669–695). Oxford: Oxford University Press.

Rentfrow, P., McDonald, J. A., & Oldmeadow, J. (2009). You are what you listen to: Young people's stereotypes about music fans. *Group Processes & Intergroup Relations, 12*(3), 329–344.

Repp, B. (1997). The aesthetic quality of a quantitatively average music performance: Two preliminary experiments. *Music Perception, 14,* 419–444.

Révész, G. (1925). *The psychology of a musical prodigy*. New York, NY: Harcourt, Brace.

Révész, G. (1954). *Introduction to the psychology of music* (C. de Courey, Trans.). Norman, OK: University of Oklahoma Press.

Reyes, A. (2009). What do ethnomusicologists do? An old question for a new century. *Ethnomusicology, 53*(1), 1–17.

Reznikoff, I. (2008). Sound resonance in prehistoric times: A study of Paleolithic painted caves and rocks. In *Proceedings of Acoustics'08 Paris* (pp. 4137–4141). Retrieved September 19, 2018, from www.researchgate.net/publication/5325208_Sound_resonance_in_prehistoric_times_A_study_of_Paleolithic_painted_caves_and_rocks

Rhodes, M. (1961). An analysis of creativity. *Phi Delta Kappan, 42*(7), 305–310.

Rhythmless Nation. (2001). *Time Magazine.* Retrieved May 6, 2010, from www.time.com/time/musicgoesglobal/asia/mtaliban.html

RIAA 2008 Consumer Profile. (2009). *Recording industry association of America.* Retrieved June 23, 2009, from www.riaa.com

Rice, T. (2014). *Ethnomusicology: A very short introduction.* Oxford: Oxford University Press.

Richardson, H. (1972). An experimental study utilizing two procedures for teaching music reading to children in second grade. Rev. by J. Klemish in *Council for Research in Music Education, 30,* 47–50.

Richardson, V. (1997). Constructivist teaching and teacher education: Theory and practice. In V. Richardson (Ed.), *Constructivist teacher education: Building new understandings* (pp. 3–14). Bristol, PA: The Falmer Press.

Richerson, P., & Boyd, R. (2008). *Not by genes alone: How culture transformed human evolution.* Chicago: The University of Chicago Press.

Rickard, N. (2004). Intense emotional responses to music: A test of the physiological arousal hypothesis. *Psychology of Music, 32*(4), 371–388.

Rideout, V., Foehr, U., & Roberts, D. (2010). *Generation M²: Media in the lives of 8- to 18-year-olds.* Menlo Park, CA: Kaiser Family Foundation.

Rider, M., & Achterberg, J. (1989). Effect of music-assisted imagery on neutrophils and lymphocytes. *Biofeedback and Self-Regulation, 14*(3), 247–257.

Ries, R. (1969). GSR and breathing amplitude related to emotional reactions to music. *Psychonomic Science, 14,* 62–64.

Rigden, J. (1996). *Macmillan encyclopedia of physics.* New York, NY: Simon and Schuster Macmillan.

Riley, P. (2008). A comparison of Mexican children's music compositions and contextual songs. *Research and Issues in Music Education, 6*(1), 6.

Rimsky-Korsakov, N. (1922/1964). *Principles of orchestration.* Mineola, NY: Dover.

Risset, J-C., & Wessel, D. (1999). Exploration of Timbre by analysis and synthesis. In D. Deutsch (Ed.), *The psychology of music* (2nd ed., pp. 113–169). San Diego, CA: Elsevier Academic Press.

424

References

Robert, D. (2009). Insect bioacoustics: Mosquitoes make an effort to listen to each other. *Current Biology, 19*(11), R446–449.

Roberts, B. (2011). Ancient technology and archaeological cultures: Understanding the earliest metallurgy in Eurasia. In B. Roberts & M. Wander Linden (Eds.), *Investigating archaeological cultures: Material culture, variability, and transmission* (p. 137). New York, NY: Springer Science+Business Media.

Roberts, D., Foehr, U., & Rideout, V. (2005). *Generation M: Media in the lives of 8–18 year-olds*. Menlo Park, CA: Kaiser Family Foundation.

Robertson, C. (1985). Process of transmission: Music education and social inclusion. In *Becoming human through music* (pp. 95–113). Reston, VA: Music Educators National Conference.

Robertson, E., Press, D., & Pascual-Leone, A. (2005). Off-line learning and the primary motor cortex. *The Journal of Neuroscience, 25*(27), 6372–6378.

Robins, R., Gosling, S., & Craik, K. (1999). An empirical analysis of trends in psychology. *American Psychologist, 54*(2), 117–128.

Robinson, R. (1983). The relationships between musical ability and intelligence. *Update: Applications of Research in Music Education, 1*(4), 19–21.

Rockwell, J. (1986, July 28). Girl, 14, conquers Tanglewood with 3 violins. *New York Times*, A1.

Roden, I., Grube, D., Bongard, S., & Kreutz, G. (2013). Does music training enhance working memory performance? Findings from a quasi-experimental longitudinal study. *Psychology of Music, 42*(2), 284–298.

Roe, K. (1999). Music and identity among European youth: Music as communication. *Journal on Media Culture, 2*. Retrieved June 10, 2009, from www.icce.rug.nl/~soundscapes/HEADER/colophon.shtml

Roederer, J. (1973). *Introduction to the physics and psychophysics of music*. New York, NY: Springer-Verlag.

Roederer, J. (1975). *Introduction to the physics and psychophysics of music* (2nd ed.). New York, NY: Springer-Verlag.

Roederer, J. (1982). Physical and neuropsychological foundations of music. In M. Clynes (Ed.), *Music, mind, and brain* (pp. 37–46). New York, NY: Plenum Press.

Roehmann, F., & Wilson, F. (Eds.). (1988). *The biology of music making*. St. Louis, MO: MMB Music.

Rogers, C. (1951). *Client-centered therapy: Its current practice, implications, and theory*. Boston, MA: Houghton Mifflin Co.

Rogers, C. (1961). *On becoming a person*. Boston, MA: Houghton Mifflin Co.

Rogers, C. (1969). *Freedom to learn*. Columbus, OH: Charles E. Merrill.

Rogers, C. (1980). *A way of being*. Boston, MA: Houghton Mifflin Co.

Rogers, G. (1996). Effect of colored rhythmic notation on music-reading skills of elementary students. *Journal of Research in Music Education, 44*(1), 15–25.

Rolls, E. (1989). The representation and storage of information in neuronal networks in the primate cerebral cortex and hippocampus. In R. Durbin, C. Miall, & G. Mitchison (Eds.), *The computing neuron* (pp. 125–159). New York, NY: Addison-Wesley.

Root-Bernstein, M., & Root-Bernstein, R. (2009). A missing piece in the economic stimulus: Hobbling arts hobbles innovation. *Imagine That! Psychology Today Blog*. Retrieved April 28, 2010, from www.psychologytoday.com/blog/imagine/200902/missing-piece-in-the-economic-stimulus-hobbling-arts-hobbles-innovation

Roschk, H., Loureiro, S. M. C., & Breitsohl, J. (2017). Calibrating 30 years of experimental research: A meta-analysis of the atmospheric effects of music, scent, and color. *Journal of Retailing, 93*(2), 228–240.

Rose, S. (2004). Memory: Biological basis. In R. Gregory (Ed.), *The Oxford companion to the mind* (2nd ed., pp. 564–568). New York, NY: Oxford University Press.

Rosenkranz, K. (2006). The neurophysiology of focal hand dystonia in musicians. In E. Altenmüller, M. Wiesendanger, & J. Kesselring (Eds.), *Music, motor control, and the brain* (pp. 283–292). Oxford: Oxford University Press.

Ross, S. (1985). The effectiveness of mental practice in improving the performance of college trombonists. *Journal of Research in Music Education, 33*(4), 221–230.

Rosset i Lobet, J., & Odam, G. (2016). *The musician's body: A maintenance manual for peak performance*. New York, NY: Routledge.

Rossing, T. (2000). *Science of percussion instruments.* Singapore: World Scientific Publishing Co.

Rossing, T. (2001). Acoustics of percussion instruments: Recent progress. *Acoustical Science and Technology, 22*(3), 177–188.

Rossing, T., & Fletcher, N. (2004). *Principles of vibration and sound* (2nd ed.). New York, NY: Springer Science+Business Media.

Roth, G., & Dicke, U. (2005). Evolution of the brain and intelligence. *Trends in Cognitive Science, 9*(95), 250–257.

Rothgeb, J. (1966). Some uses of mathematical concepts in theories of music. *Journal of Music Theory, 10*(2), 200–215.

Rothstein, E. (2006). *Emblems of mind: The inner life of music and mathematics.* Chicago: University of Chicago Press.

Rothstein, R., Alavi, A., & Reynolds, J. (1993). Electrogastrography in patients with gastroparesis and effect of long-term cisapride. *Digestive Diseases and Sciences, 38*(8), 1518–1524.

Rouget, G. (1985). *Music and trance: A theory of the relations between music and possession* (B. Biebuyck, Trans.). Chicago: University of Chicago Press.

Rowan, J. (1998). Maslow amended. *Journal of Humanistic Psychology, 38*(1), 81–92.

Rowher, D., & Polk, J. (2006). Practice behaviors of eighth-grade instrumental musicians. *Journal of Research in Music Education, 54*(4), 350–362.

Rubinstein, A. (1973). *My young years.* New York: Alfred A. Knopf.

Rumbaugh, S., & Fields, W. (2000). Linguistic, cultural and cognitive capacities of Bonobos (Pan paniscus). *Culture & Psychology, 6*(2), 131–153.

Runco, M. (2010). Divergent thinking, creativity, and ideation. In J. Kauman & R. Sternberg (Eds.), *The Cambridge handbook of creativity* (pp. 413–446). Cambridge: Cambridge University Press.

Runco, M., & Jaeger, G. (2012). The standard definition of creativity. *Creativity Research Journal, 24*, 92–96.

Russell, J. (1980). A circumplex model of affect. *Journal of Personality and Social Psychology, 39*(6), 1161–1178.

Russell, P. (1986). Experimental aesthetics of popular music recordings: Pleasingness, familiarity and chart performance. *Psychology of Music, 14*, 33–43.

Russell, P. (2007). Musical tastes and society. In D. Hargreaves & A. North (Eds.), *The social psychology of music* (pp. 141–158). Oxford: Oxford University Press.

Rutherford, E. (1911). The scattering of α and β particles by matter and the structure of the atom. *Philosophy Magazine, 21*, 669–688.

Ruthsatz, J., Detterman, D., Griscom, W., & Cirullo, B. (2008). Becoming an expert in the musical domain: It takes more than just practice. *Intelligence, 36*, 330–338.

Ryan, C. (1997). *Exploring perception.* New York, NY: Brooks/Cole.

Ryan, C., & Andrews, N. (2009). An investigation into the choral singers' experience of music performance anxiety. *Journal of Research in Music Education, 57*(2), 108–126.

Rymer, R. (1993). *Genie: An abused child's flight from silence.* New York, NY: HarperCollins Publishers.

Sachs, H. (1978). *Toscanini.* New York, NY: Harper & Row.

Sachs, M., Ellis, R., Schlaug, G., & Loui, P. (2016). Brain connectivity reflects human aesthetic responses to music. *Social Cognitive and Affective Neuroscience, 11*(6), 884–891.

Sackner, M., Watson, H., Belsito, A., Feinerman, D., Suarez, M., Gonzalez, G., . . . Krieger, B. (1989). Calibration of respiratory inductive plethysomograph during natural breathing. *Journal of Applied Physiology, 66*(1), 410–420.

Sacks, O. (1983). *Awakenings.* New York, NY: Dutton.

Sacks, O. (1987). *The man who mistook his wife for a hat.* New York, NY: Harper and Row.

Sacks, O. (2006). The power of music. *Brain, 129*, 2528–2532.

Sacks, O. (2007). *Musicophilia: Tales of music and the brain.* New York, NY: Knopf.

Sadie, S. (Ed.). (1988). *The Norton/Grove concise encyclopedia of music.* New York, NY: W. W. Norton.

Saffran, J. (2003). Musical learning and language development. In G. Avancini, C. Faienza, D. Minciacchi, L. Lopez, & M. Majno (Eds.), *The neurosciences and music. Annals of the New York Academy of Sciences, 999*, 397–401.

426

References

Saffran, J., Johnson, E., Aslin, R., & Newport, E. (1999). Statistical learning of tone sequences by human infants and adults. *Cognition, 70,* 27–52.

Saffran, J., Loman, M., & Robertson, R. (2001). Infant long-term memory for music. In R. Zatorre & I. Peretz (Eds.), *The biological foundations of music. Annals of the New York Academy of Sciences, 930,* 397–400.

Sahler, O., Hunter, B., & Liesveld, J. (2003). The effects of using music therapy with relaxation imagery in the management of patients undergoing bone marrow transplantation: A pilot feasibility study. *Alternative Therapies in Health and Medicine, 9*(6), 70–74.

Sakakibara, A. (2014). A longitudinal study of the process of acquiring absolute pitch: A practical report of training with the "chord identification method". *Psychology of Music, 42*(1), 86–111.

Saldanha, E., & Corso, J. (1964). Timbre cues and the identification of musical instruments. *Journal of the Acoustical Society of America, 36*(11), 2021–2026.

Salewski, B. (1981). *An application of observation and self-report methods to the measurement of music performance anxiety* (PhD dissertation). Michigan State University.

Salgado, A. (2006). A cognitive feedback study for improving emotional expression in solo vocal music performance. *Performance: Journal of Music Interpretation, 12*(1), 1–11.

Salimpoor, V. N., Benovoy, M., Larcher, K., Dagher, A., & Zatorre, R. (2011). Anatomically distinct dopamine release during anticipation and experience of peak emotion to music. *Nature Neuroscience, 14*(2), 257–262.

Salimpoor, V. N., van den Bosch, I., Kovacevic, N., McIntosh, A. R., Dagher, A., & Zatorre, R. J. (2013). Interactions between the nucleus accumbens and auditory cortices predict music reward value. *Science, 340*(6129), 216–219.

Salis, D. (1980). Laterality effects with visual perception of musical chords and dot patterns. *Perception and Psychophysics, 28*(4), 284–292.

Salmon, P., Schrodt, R., & Wright, J. (1989). A temporal gradient of anxiety in a stressful performance context. *Medical Problems of Performing Artists, 4*(2), 77–80.

Salzburg, R., & Wang, C. (1989). A comparison of prompts to aid rhythmic sight-reading of string students. *Psychology of Music, 17,* 123–131.

Sampras, P., & Bodo, P. (2008). *A champion's mind: Lessons from a life in tennis.* New York, NY: Crown Publishers.

Samson, S., Ehrle, N., & Baulac, M. (2001). Cerebral substrates for musical temporal processes. In R. Zatorre & I. Peretz (Eds.), *The biological foundations of music. Annals of the York Academy of Sciences, 930,* 166–178.

San Antonio Light. (1986, June 10). Argument over loud music leads to death.

Sandresky, M. (1981). The golden section in three Byzantine motets of Dufay. *Journal of Music Theory, 25*(2), 291–306.

Särkämö, T., Laitinen, S., Tervaniemi, M., Nummien, A., Kurki, M., & Rantanen, P. (2012). Music, emotion, and dementia: Insight from neuroscientific and clinical research. *Music and Medicine, 4*(3), 153–162.

Sataloff, R. (1998a). Care of the professional voice. In R. Sataloff, A. Brandfonbrener, & R. Lederman (Eds.), *Performing arts medicine* (2nd ed., pp. 137–177). San Diego, CA: Singular Publishing Group.

Sataloff, R. (1998b). *Vocal health and pedagogy.* San Diego, CA: Singular Publishing Group.

Sataloff, R. (2005). *Professional voice* (Vols. I, II, & III, 3rd ed.). San Diego, CA: Plural Publishing.

Sataloff, R., Brandfonbrener, A., & Lederman, R. (Eds.). (1991). *Textbook of performing arts medicine.* New York, NY: Raven Press.

Sataloff, R., & Hawkshaw, M. (1998). Performing arts-medicine and the professional voice user: Risks of non-voice performance. In R. Sataloff (Ed.), *Vocal health and pedagogy* (pp. 197–203). San Diego, CA: Singular Publishing Group.

Sataloff, R., Rosen, D., & Levy, S. (1999). Medical treatment of performance anxiety: A comprehensive approach. *Medical Problems of Performing Artists, 14*(3), 122–126.

Savage, W. (1977). *Problems for musical acoustics.* New York, NY: Oxford University Press.

Savan, A. (1999). The effect of background music on learning. *Psychology of Music, 27*(2), 138–146.

Sawyer, R. K. (2006). *Explaining creativity: The science of human innovation.* New York, NY: Oxford University Press.

Scarre, C., & Lawson, G. (Eds.). (2006). *Archaeouacoustics*. Oxford: Oxbow Books.

Scartelli, J. (1984). The effect of EMG biofeedback and sedative music, EMG biofeedback only, and sedative music only on frontalis muscle relaxation ability. *Journal of Music Therapy*, 21(2), 67–78.

Scartelli, J. (1992). Music therapy and psychoneuroimmunology. In R. Spintge & R. Droh (Eds.), *MusicMedicine* (pp. 137–141). St. Louis, MO: MMB Music.

Schachner, A., Brady, T., Pepperberg, I., & Hauser, M. (2009). Spontaneous motor entrainment to music in multiple vocal mimicking species. *Current Biology*, 19(10), 831–836.

Schafer, R. (1977). *The tuning of the world*. New York, NY: Alfred A. Knopf.

Schäfer, T., Smukalla, M., & Oelker, S-A. (2014). How music changes our lives: A qualitative study of the long-term effects of intense musical experiences. *Psychology of Music*, 42(4), 525–544.

Schäfer, T., Smulkalla, M., & Oelker, S-A. (2014). How music changes our lives: A qualitative study of the long-term effects of intense musical experiences. *Psychology of Music*, 42(4), 525–544.

Schellenberg, E. (1996). Expectancy in melody: Tests of the implication-realization model. *Cognition*, 58, 76–125.

Schellenberg, E. (1997). Simplifying the implication-realization model of melodic expectancy. *Music Perception*, 14(3), 295–318.

Schellenberg, E., & Trehub, S. (2008). Is there an Asian advantage for pitch memory? *Music Perception*, 25(3), 241–252.

Schink, T., Kreutz, G., Busch, V., Pigeot, I., & Ahrens, W. (2014). Incidence and relative risk of hearing disorders in professional musicians. *Occupational and Environmental Medicine*, oemed-2014.

Schlaug, G. (2006). Brain structures of musicians: Executive functions and morphological implications. In E. Altenmüller, M. Wiesendanger, & J. Kesselring (Eds.), *Music, motor control, and the brain* (pp. 141–152). Oxford: Oxford University Press.

Schlaug, G., Jäncke, L., Huang, Y., & Steinmetz, H. (1994). In vivo morphometry of interhemispheric asymmetry and connectivity in musicians. In I. Deliège (Ed.), *Proceedings of the 3rd international conference for music perception and cognition* (pp. 417–418). Liege, Belgium: ESCOM.

Schlaug, G., Jäncke, L., Huang, Y., Staiger, J., & Steinmetz, H. (1995). Increased corpus callosum size in musicians. *Neuropsychologia*, 33, 1047–1055.

Schlaug, G., Jäncke, L., Huang, Y., & Steinmetz, H. (1995). In vivo evidence of structural brain asymmetry in musicians. *Science*, 267(5198), 699–701.

Schlaug, G., Norton, A., Overy, K., & Winner, E. (2005). Effects of music training on the child's brain and cognitive development. *The Neurosciences and Music II: From Perception to Performance. Annals of the New York Academy of Sciences*, 1060, 219–230.

Schleuter, S. (1971). An investigation of the interrelation of personality traits, musical aptitude, and musical achievement. *Experimental Research in the Psychology of Music: 8. Studies in the Psychology of Music*, 90–102.

Schmidt, L., Trainor, L., & Santesso, D. (2002). Development of frontal electroencephalogram (EEG) and heart rate (ECG) responses to affective musical stimuli during the first 12 months of post-natal life. *Brain and Cognition*, 52, 27–32.

Schmuckler, M. (2009). Components of melodic processing. In S. Hallam, I. Cross, & M. Thaut (Eds.), *The Oxford handbook of music psychology* (pp. 93–106). Oxford: Oxford University Press.

Schmuckler, M., & Tomovski, R. (2005). Perceptual tests of an algorithm for musical key-finding. *Journal of Experimental Psychology: Human Perception and Performance*, 31(5), 1124–1149.

Schneck, D., & Berger, D. (2006). *The music effect: Music physiology and clinical applications*. London: Jessica Kingsley.

Schoen, M. (Ed.). (1927/1968). *The effects of music*. Reprint. Freeport, NY: Books for Libraries Press.

Schoen, M. (1940). *The psychology of music: A survey for teacher and musician*. New York, NY: Ronald Press.

Schoenberg, A. (1999). *Fundamentals of music composition*. London: Faber & Faber.

Schön, D., Boyer, M., Moreno, S., Besson, M., Peretz, I., & Kolinsky, R. (2008). Songs as an aid for language acquisition. *Cognition*, 106, 975–993.

Schreiner, C., & Winer, J. (2007). Auditory cortex mapmaking: Principles, projections, and plasticity. *Neuron*, 56(2), 356–365.

References

Schroeder, M. (1993). Listening with two ears. *Music Perception, 10*(3), 255–280.

Schullian, D. M., & Schoen, M. (Eds.). (1948). *Music and medicine*. New York, NY: Henry Schuman.

Schulz, M., Ross, B., & Pantev, C. (2003). Evidence for training-induced crossmodal reorganization of cortical functions in trumpet players. *Neuroreport, 14*(1), 157–161.

Schulz, W. (1981). Analysis of a symphony orchestra: Sociological and sociopsychological aspects. In M. Piperek (Ed.), *Music and stress* (pp. 35–56). Vienna: Wilhelm Braumüller.

Schuyler, P. (1981). Music and meaning among the Gnawa religious brotherhood of Morocco. *The World of Music, 23*(1), 3–10.

Schwaninger, J., Eisenberg, P., Schechtman, K., & Weiss, A. (2002). A prospective analysis of near-death experiences in cardiac arrest patients. *Journal of Near-Death Studies, 20*(4), 215–232.

Scott, D. (Ed.). (2000). *Music, culture, and society*. New York, NY: Oxford University Press.

Scott, S. (2006). A constructivist view of music education: Perspectives for deep learning. *General Music Today, 19*(2), 17–21.

Sears, M. (1954). *Study of the vascular changes in the capillaries as effected by music* (Unpublished master's thesis). University of Kansas.

Sears, W. (1958). The effect of music on muscle tonus. In E. Gaston (Ed.), *Music therapy 1957* (pp. 199–205). Lawrence, KS: Allen Press.

Sears, W. (1968). Processes in music therapy. In E. Gaston (Ed.), *Music in therapy* (pp. 30–44). New York, NY: Palgrave Macmillan.

Seashore, C. (1919). *The psychology of musical talent*. Boston, MA: Silver Burdett.

Seashore, C. (1932). *The vibrato: Studies in the psychology of music* (Vol. I). Iowa City: University of Iowa Press.

Seashore, C. (1936a). *Objective analysis of musical performance: Studies in the psychology of music* (Vol. IV). Iowa City: University of Iowa Press.

Seashore, C. (1936b). *Psychology of the vibrato in voice and instrument: Studies in the psychology of music* (Vol. III). Iowa City: University of Iowa Press.

Seashore, C. (1938). *Psychology of music*. New York, NY: McGraw-Hill.

Seashore, C. (1947). *In search of beauty in music: A scientific approach to musical esthetics*. New York, NY: Ronald Press.

Seashore, C. (1960). *Measures of musical talents*. New York, NY: Psychological Corporation.

Serafine, M. (1988). *Music as cognition: The development of thought in sound*. New York, NY: Columbia University Press.

Sergent, J. (1993). Mapping the musician brain. *Human Brain Mapping, 1*(1), 20–38.

Sergent, J., Zuck, E., Tenial, S., & MacDonall, B. (1992). Distributed neural network underlying musical sight reading and keyboard performance. *Science, 257*, 106–109.

Service, T. (2010, November 16). Conductors wield the baton, but orchestras wield the power. *The Guardian*. Retrieved from www.theguardian.com/music/tomserviceblog/2010/nov/16/conductors-v-orchestras

Service, T. (2015, September 30). Music as a torture weapon: Exploring the dark side. *The Guardian*. Retrieved from www.theguardian.com/music/tomserviceblog/2015/sep/30/bleak-history-music-as-torture-suzanne-cusick-morag-grant

Shadmehr, R., & Brashers-Krug, T. (1997). Functional stages in the formation of long-term motor memory. *The Journal of Neuroscience, 17*(1), 409–419.

Shehan, P. (1987). Effects of rote versus note presentations on rhythm learning and retention. *Journal of Research in Music Education, 35*(2), 117–126.

Sheldon, D. (1996). Visual representation of music: Effects of beamed and beamless notation on music performance. *Journal of Band Research, 31*(2), 87–101.

Shen, S. (1987). Acoustics of ancient Chinese bells. *Scientific American, 256*, 104–110.

Shepard, R. (1964). Circularity in judgments of relative pitch. *Journal of the Acoustical Society of America, 36*(12), 2346–2353.

Shepherd, G. (1994). *Neurobiology* (3rd ed.). New York, NY: Oxford University Press.

Sherbon, J. (1975). The association of hearing acuity, diplacusis, and discrimination with music performance. *Journal of Research in Music Education, 23*, 249–257.

Sherratt, K., Thornton, A., & Hatton, C. (2004). Music interventions for people with dementia: A review of the literature. *Aging and Mental Health, 8*(1), 3–12.

Shlain, L. (1991). *Art, and physics: Parallel visions in space, time, and light*. New York, NY: William Morrow.

Shrift, D. (1955). Galvanic skin response to two types of music. *Bulletin of National Association for Music Therapy, 10*, 5–6.

Shuter, R. (1968). *The psychology of musical ability*. London: Methuen.

Shuter, R. P. (1966). Hereditary and environmental factors in musical ability. *Eugenics Review, 58*, 149–156.

Shuter-Dyson, R. (1979). Unisex or "vive la difference"? *Bulletin of the Council for Research in Music Education, 59*, 102–106.

Shuter-Dyson, R. (2000). Profiling music students: Personality and religiosity. *Psychology of Music, 28*(2), 190–196.

Shuter-Dyson, R., & Gabriel, C. (1981). *The psychology of musical ability* (2nd ed.). London: Methuen.

Siegwart, H., & Scherer, K. (1995). Acoustic concomitants of emotional expression in operatic singing: The case of Lucia in *Ardi gli incensi*. *Journal of Voice, 9*(3), 249–260.

Silbermann, A. (1963). *The sociology of music* (C. Stewart, Trans.). London: Routledge and Kegan Paul.

Silver, D. (2001). Songs and storytelling: Bringing health messages to life in Uganda. *Education for Health, 14*(1), 51–60.

Silverman, M. (2009). The effect of single-session psychoeducational music therapy on verbalizations and perceptions in psychiatric patients. *Journal of Music Therapy, 46*(2), 105–131.

Silverstein, A., Silverstein, V., & Nunn, L. (2001). *Hearing*. Brookfield, CT: Twenty-First Century Books.

Simmons, A., & Duke, R. (2006). Effects of sleep on a performance of a keyboard melody. *Journal of Research in Music Education, 54*(3), 257–269.

Simmons-Stern, N., Budson, A., & Ally, B. (2010). Music as a memory enhancer in patients with Alzheimer's Disease. *Neuropsychologia*. doi:10.1016/j.neuropsychologia.2010.04.033

Simon, E. (2006). *Music and the human brain: The lost hypotheses*. Kaneohe, HI: Salidoña Press.

Simons, G. (1986). Early childhood musical development: A survey of selected research. *Bulletin of the Council for Research in Music Education, 86*, 36–52.

Simpson, E. (1966). *The classification of educational objectives, psychomotor domain*. Unpublished project report, University of Illinois.

Simpson, E. (1972). *The classification of educational objectives in the psychomotor domain*. Washington, DC: Gryphon House.

Sink, P. (2002). Behavioral research on direct music instruction. In R. Colwell & C. Richardson (Eds.), *The new handbook of research on music teaching and learning* (pp. 315–326). New York, NY: Oxford University Press.

Sinnamon, S., Moran, A., & O'Connell, M. (2012). Flow among musicians: Measuring peak experiences of student performers. *Journal of Research in Music Education, 60*(1), 6–25.

Skinner, B. (1953). *Science and human behavior*. New York, NY: The Free Press.

Skinner, B. (1974). *About behaviorism*. New York, NY: Alfred A. Knopf.

Skornicka, J. (1972). The function of time and rhythm in instrumental music reading. Rev. by A. Drake in *Council for Research in Music Education, 27*, 44–46.

Skov, M. (2010). The pleasure of art. In M. Kringelbach & K. Berridge (Eds.), *Pleasures of the brain* (pp. 270–283). Oxford: Oxford University Press.

Slater, P. (2000). Birdsong repertoires: Their origins and use. In N. Wallin, B. Merker, & S. Brown (Eds.), *The origins of music* (pp. 49–63). Cambridge, MA: The MIT Press.

Slaughter, F. (1954). *The effect of stimulative and sedative types of music on normal and abnormal subjects as indicated by auxillary reflexes* (Unpublished master's thesis). Lawrence, KS: University of Kansas.

Slevc, L. R., Rosenberg, J. C., & Patel, A. D. (2009). Making psycholinguistics musical: Self-paced reading time evidence for shared processing of linguistic and musical syntax. *Psychonomic Bulletin & Review, 16*(2), 374–381.

Slevc, L. R., & Miyake, A. (2006). Individual differences in second-language proficiency: Does musical ability matter? *Psychological Science, 17*(8), 675–681.

References

Sloboda, J. (1974). The eye-hand span: An approach to the study of sight-reading. *Psychology of Music, 2,* 4–10.

Sloboda, J. (1977). Phrase units as determinants of visual processing in music reading. *British Journal of Psychology, 68,* 117–124.

Sloboda, J. (1982). Music performance. In D. Deutsch (Ed.), *The psychology of music* (pp. 479–496). New York, NY: Academic Press.

Sloboda, J. (1985). *The musical mind: The cognitive psychology of music.* Oxford: Oxford University Press.

Sloboda, J. (1988). *Generative processes in music: The psychology of performance, improvisation, and composition.* Oxford: Clarendon Press.

Sloboda, J. (1991). Music structure and emotional response: Some empirical findings. *Psychology of Music, 19,* 110–120.

Sloboda, J. (2000). Music and worship: A psychologist's perspective. In J. Astely, T. Hone, & M. Savage (Eds.), *Creative chords: Studies in music, theology and Christian formation* (pp. 110–125). Leominster: Gracewing.

Sloboda, J. (2005). *Exploring the musical mind.* New York, NY: Oxford University Press.

Sloboda, J. (2010). Music in everyday life: The role of emotions. In P. Juslin & J. Sloboda (Eds.), *Handbook of music and emotion: Theory, research, applications* (pp. 493–514). Oxford: Oxford University Press.

Sloboda, J., Davidson, J., Howe, M., & Moore, D. (1996). The role of practice in the development of performing musicians. *British Journal of Psychology, 87,* 287–309.

Sloboda, J., & Howe, M. (1991). Biographical precursors of musical excellence: An interview study. *Psychology of Music, 19*(1), 3–21.

Sloboda, J., & Juslin, P. (2001). Psychological perspectives on music and emotion. In P. Juslin & J. Sloboda (Eds.), *Music and emotion: Theory and research* (pp. 71–104). New York, NY: Oxford University Press.

Sloboda, J., & Juslin, P. (2010). At the interface between the inner and outer world: Psychological perspectives. In P. Juslin & J. Sloboda (Eds.), *Handbook of music and emotion* (pp. 73–97). Oxford: Oxford University Press.

Sloboda, J., Lamont, A., & Greasley, A. (2009). Choosing to hear music: Motivation, process, and effect. In S. Hallam, I. Cross, & M. Thaut (Eds.), *The Oxford handbook of music psychology* (pp. 431–440). Oxford: Oxford University Press.

Sloboda, J., & Lehmann, A. (2001). Tracking performance correlates of changes in perceived intensity of emotion during different interpretations of a Chopin piano prelude. *Music Perception, 19*(1), 87–120.

Smith, G., & Long, M. (1980). Wilderness art: Utah's rock art. *National Geographic, 157*(1), 94–117.

Smith, H. (1953). *From fish to philosopher.* Garden City, NY: Doubleday Anchor Book.

Smith, J., & Melara, R. (1990). Aesthetic preference and syntactic prototypicality in music: Tis the gift to be simple. *Cognition, 34,* 279–298.

Smith, K. (2007). Descartes' life and works. In E. Zalta (Ed.), *The Stanford encyclopedia of philosophy* (Summer Ed.). Retrieved September 15, 2007, from http://plato.stanford.edu/archives/sum2007/entries/descartes-works/

Snyder, B. (2001). *Music and memory.* Cambridge, MA: The MIT Press.

Snyder, M. (2009). Memory for music. In S. Hallam, I. Cross, & M. Thaut (Eds.), *The Oxford handbook of music psychology* (pp. 107–117). Oxford: Oxford University Press.

Society for Ethnomusicology. *About Ethnomusicology.* Retrieved September 13, 2018, from www.ethnomusicology.org/page/AboutEthnomusicol

Soibelman, D. (1948). *Therapeutic and industrial uses of music: A review of literature.* New York, NY: Columbia University Press.

Sosniak, L. (1985). Learning to be a concert pianist. In B. Bloom (Ed.), *Developing talent in young people* (pp. 19–67). New York, NY: Ballantine Books.

Southern, E. (1975). America's black composers of classical music. *Music Educators Journal, 62*(3), 46–59.

Southern, E. (1997). *The music of Black Americans: A history* (3rd ed.). New York, NY: W. W. Norton.

Spector, J., & Brandfonbrener, A. (2005). A new method for quantification of musician's dystonia: The frequency of abnormal movements scale. *Medical Problems of Performing Musicians, 20,* 157–162.

Spintge, R. (1999). MusicMedicine: Applications, standards, and definitions. In R. Pratt & D. Grocke (Eds.), *MusicMedicine 3* (pp. 3–11). Melbourne, Australia: The University of Melbourne.

Spintge, R. (2012). Clinical use of music in operating theatres. In R. MacDonald, G. Kretutz, & L. Mitchell (Eds.), *Music, health, and wellbeing* (pp. 276–286). Oxford: Oxford University Press.

Spintge, R., & Droh, R. (Eds.). (1987). *Music in medicine: Neurophysiological basis, clinical applications, aspects in the humanities*. Berlin: Springer-Verlag.

Spintge, R., & Droh, R. (Eds.). (1992a). *MusicMedicine*. St. Louis, MO: MMB Music.

Spintge, R., & Droh, R. (1992b). The International society for music in medicine [ISMM] and the definition of Musicmedicine and music Therapy. In R. Spintge & R. Droh (Eds.), *MusicMedicine* (pp. 3–5). St. Louis, MO: MMB Music.

Spintge, R., & Droh, R. (1992c). Toward a research standard in MusicMedicine/music therapy: A proposal for a multimodal approach. In R. Spintge & R. Droh (Eds.), *MusicMedicine* (pp. 345–349). St. Louis, MO: MMB Music.

Spintge, R., & Pratt, R. (Eds.). (1995). *MusicMedicine 2*. St. Louis, MO: MMB Music.

Spire, M. (1989). The Feldenkrais method: An interview with Anat Baniel. *Medical Problems of Performing Artists, 4*(4), 159–162.

Springer, S., & Deutsch, G. (1989). *Left brain, right brain* (3rd ed.). New York: W.H. Freeman.

Stahl, B., & Kotz, S. A. (2014). Facing the music: Three issues in current research on singing and aphasia. *Frontiers in Psychology, 5*, 1033.

Stainsby, T., & Cross, I. (2009). The perception of pitch. In S. Hallam, I. Cross, & M. Thaut (Eds.), *The Oxford handbook of music psychology* (pp. 63–79). Oxford: Oxford University Press.

Staley, K., Iragui, V., & Spitz, M. (1990). The human fetal auditory evoked potential. *Electroencephalography and Clinical Neurophysiology, 77*(1), 1–5.

Standley, J. (1999). Music therapy in the NICU: Pacifier-activated-lullabies (PAL) for reinforcement of nonnutritive sucking. *International Journal of Arts Medicine, 6*(2), 17–21.

Standley, J. (2002). A meta-analysis of the efficacy of music therapy for premature infants. *Journal of Pediatric Nursing, 17*(2), 107–113.

Standley, J. (2003). The effect of music-reinforced nonnutritive sucking on feeding rate of premature infants. *Journal of Pediatric Nursing, 18*(3), 169–173.

Stanford Solar Center. (2013). *The singing sun*. Retrieved August 23, 2018, from http://solar-center.stanford.edu/singing/singing.html

Stanford, D. (1979). Bison kill by ice age hunters. *National Geographic, 155*(1), 114–121.

Steele, C., Bailey, J., Zatorre, R., & Penhune, V. (2013). Early musical training and white-matter plasticity in the corpus callosum: Evidence for a sensitive period. *The Journal of Neuroscience, 33*(3), 1282–1290.

Stefanics, G., Háden, G., Sziller, I., Balázs, L., Beke, A., & Winkler, I. (2009). Newborn infants process pitch intervals. *Clinical Neurophysiology, 120*, 304–308.

Stefano, G., Zhu, W., Cadet, P., Salamon, E., & Monatione, K. (2004). Music alters constitutively expressed opiate and cytokine processes in listeners. *Medical Science Monitor, 10*(6), MS18–MS27.

Steinbeis, N., Koelsch, S., & Sloboda, J. (2008). The role of harmonic expectancy violations in musical emotions: Evidence from subjective, physiological, and neural responses. *Journal of Cognitive Neuroscience, 18*(8), 1380–1393.

Stern, D. (1982). Some interactive functions of rhythm changes between mother and infant. In M. Davis (Ed.), *Interaction rhythms: Periodicity in communication behavior* (pp. 101–117). New York, NY: Human Sciences Press.

Sternbach, D. (2008). Stress in the lives of music students. *Music Educators Journal, 94*(3), 42–48.

Sternberg, R. (2000). The holey grail of general intelligence. *Science, 289*(5478), 399–401.

Stevens, C., & Byron, T. (2009). Universals in music processing. In S. Hallam, I. Cross, & M. Thaut (Eds.), *The Oxford handbook of music psychology* (pp. 14–23). Oxford: Oxford University Press.

Stevens, S. (1935). The relation of pitch to intensity. *Journal of the Acoustical Society of America, 6*(3), 150–154.

Stevens, S., & Warshofsky, F. (1965). *Sound and hearing*. New York, NY: Life Science Library.

References

Stewart, L. (2005). A neurocognitive approach to music reading. *The Neurosciences and Music II: From Perception to Performance. Annals of the New York Academic of Sciences, 1060*, 377–386.

Stewart, L., Henson, R., Kampe, K., Walsh, V., Turner, R., & Frith, U. (2003). Becoming a pianist: An fMRI study of musical literacy acquisition. *The Neurosciences and Music. Annals of the New York Academy of Sciences, 999*, 204–208.

Stickney, J. (1982, May). The sound of music from a lost world. *Discover*, 57–59.

Stiles, J. (2000). Neural plasticity and cognitive development. *Developmental Neuropscyhology, 18*(2), 237–272.

Storr, A. (1993). *Music and the mind*. New York, NY: Ballantine Books.

Strauser, J. (1997). The effects of music versus silence on measures of state anxiety, perceived relaxation, and physiological responses of patients receiving chiropractic interventions. *Journal of Music Therapy, 34*(2), 88–105.

Stravinsky, I. (1969). *The rite of Spring: Sketches, 1911–1913*. London: Boosey & Hawkes.

Strong, E. (1959). *Vocational interest blank for men, vocational interest blank for women*. Stanford, CA: Stanford University Press.

Strunk, O. (1965). *Source readings in music history: Antiquity and the middle ages*. New York, NY: W. W. Norton.

Stuart, G., & Garrett, W. (1981). Maya art treasures discovered in a cave. *National Geographic, 160*(2), 220–235.

Stuessy, C., & Lipscomb, S. (2019). *Rock and roll: Its history and stylistic development* (7th ed.). London: Pearson Education.

Stumpf, C. (1883). *Tonpsychologie (Tone Psychology)* (Vol. 1). Leipzig: Hirzel.

Stumpf, C. (1890). *Tonpsychologie (Tone Psychology)* (Vol. 2). Leipzig: Hirzel.

Stumpf, C. (2012). *The origins of music*. (D. Trippet, Trans.). Oxford: Oxford University Press.

Suits, B. H. (2001). Basic physics of xylophone and marimba bars. *American Journal of Physics, 69*(7), 743–750.

Sullivan, L. (1984). Sacred music and sacred time. *The World of Music, 26*(3), 33–51.

Sundberg, J., Birch, P., Gümoes, B., Stavad, H., Prytz, S., & Karle, A. (2007). Experimental findings on the nasal tract resonator in singing. *Journal of Voice, 21*(2), 127–137.

Sundberg, J., Iwarsson, J., & Hagegård, H. (1994). A singer's expression of emotions in sung performance. *Speech, Music and Hearing: Quarterly Progress and Status Report, 35*(2–3), 81–92.

Sur, S., & Sinha, V. K. (2009). Event-related potential: An overview. *Industrial Psychiatry Journal, 18*(1), 70–73.

Sutin, A., McCrae, R., & Costa, P. (2011). The neuroscience of personality traits: Descriptions and prescriptions. In J. Decety & J. Cacioppo (Eds.), *The Oxford handbook of social neuroscience* (pp. 243–251). Oxford: Oxford University Press.

Swanwick, K. (1988). *Music, mind and education*. New York, NY: Routledge.

Swisher, W. (1927). *Psychology for the music teacher*. Boston, MA: Oliver Ditson.

Sytchev, V., Vasserman, A., Kozlov, A., Spiridonov, G., & Tsymarny, V. (1987). *Thermodynamic properties of air*. New York, NY: Hemisphere Publishing Group.

Taetle, L., & Cutietta, R. (2002). Learning theories as roots of current musical practice and research. In R. Colwell & C. Richardson (Eds.), *The new handbook of research on music teaching and learning* (pp. 279–298). New York, NY: Oxford University Press.

Tait, M., & Haack, P. (1984). *Principles and processes of music education: New perspectives*. New York, NY: Teachers College Press.

Takahashi, R., & Miller, J. (2007). Conversion of amino-acid sequence in proteins to classical music: Search for auditory patterns. *Genome Biology, 8*(5), 405.

Takeuchi, H., Taki, Y., Hashizume, H., Sassa, Y., Nagase, T., Nouchi, R., & Kawashima, R. (2012). The association between resting functional connectivity and creativity. *Cerebral Cortex, 22*(12), 2921–2929.

Talavage, T., Sereno, M., Melcher, J., Ledden, P., Rosen, B., & Dale, A. (2004). Tonotopic organization in human auditory cortex revealed by progressions of frequency sensitivity. *Journal of Neurophysiology, 91*(3), 1282–1296.

Tallis, R. (2008). The limitations of a neurological approach to art. Review of neuroarthistory: From Aristotle and Pliny to Baxandall and Zeki by John Onians (Yale University Press, 2008). *The Lancet, 372*(9632), 19–20.

Tan, S-L., Cohen, A., Lipscomb, S., & Kendall, R. (Eds.). (2013). *The psychology of music in multimedia.*
Oxford: Oxford University Press.

Tan, S-L., Pfordresher, P., & Harré, R. (2010). *Psychology of music.* New York, NY: Routledge.

Tan, S-L., Pfordresher, P., & Harré, R. (2017). *Psychology of music* (2nd ed.). New York, NY: Routledge.

Tarr, B., Launay, J., & Dunbar, R. I. (2014). Music and social bonding: "Self-other" merging and neurohormonal mechanisms. *Frontiers in Psychology, 5,* 1096.

Tarrant, M., North, A., Edridge, M., Kirk, L., Smith, E., & Turner, R. (2001). Social identity in adolescence. *Journal of Adolescence, 24*(5), 597–609.

Tarrant, M., North, A., & Hargreaves, D. (2001). Social categorization, self-esteem, and the estimated musical preferences of male adolescents. *Journal of Social Psychology, 141*(5), 565–581.

Tarrell, V. (1965). An investigation of the validity of the musical aptitude profile. *Journal of Research in Music Education, 13,* 195–206.

Tau, G., & Peterson, B. (2010). Normal development of brain circuits. *Neuropsychopharmacology, 35*(1), 147–168.

Tavassoli, N. (2009). Climate, psychological homeostasis, and individual behaviors. In R. Wyer, C-Y. Chiu, & Y-Y. Hong, Eds., *Understanding culture: Theory, research, and application* (pp. 211–222). New York, NY: Psychology Press.

Tchaikovsky, M. (1906). *The life and letters of Peter Ilich Tchaikovsky* (R. Newmarch, Trans.). New York, NY: John Lane Co.

Teffera, T. (2011). Musical organization in traditional East African cultures: A case study of the embaire xylophone. *Guandu Music Journal, 14,* 113–142.

Temperley, D. (2001). *The cognition of basic musical structures.* Cambridge, MA: The MIT Press.

Temperley, D. (2004). *The cognition of basic musical structures.* Cambridge, MA: The MIT Press.

Temperley, D. (2007). *Music and probability.* Cambridge, MA: The MIT Press.

Temperly, D., & Marvin, E. (2008). Pitch-class distribution and the identification of key. *Music Perception, 25*(3), 193–212.

Teng, X., Wong, M., & Zhang, Y. (2007). The effect of music on hypertensive patients. *Conference Proceedings of the IEEE Engineering, Medicine, and Biology Society, 1,* 4649–4651.

Teplov, B. (1966). *Psychologie des aptitudes musicales. (The psychology of music aptitudes).* Paris: Presses Universitaires de France.

Terao, Y., Mizuno, T., Shindoh, M., Sakurai, Y., Ugawa, Y., Kobayashi, S.,. ., Tsuki, S. (2006). Vocal amusia in a professional tango singer due to a right superior temporal cortex infarction. *Neuropsychologia, 44*(3), 479–488.

Terrill, A. (2015, May). How cities benefit from helping the music industry grow. *WIPO Magazine.* Retrieved from www.wipo.int/wipo_magazine/en/2015/05/article_0009.html

Tervaniemi, M., Tao, S., & Huotilainen, M. (2018). Promises of music in education? *Frontiers in Education, 3*(74).

Thaut, M. (2000). *A scientific model of music in therapy and medicine.* San Antonio, TX: IMR Press.

Thaut, M. (2003). Neural basis of rhythmic timing networks in the human brain. *The Neurosciences and Music: Annals of the New York Academy of Sciences, 999,* 364–373.

Thaut, M. (2005a). Rhythm, human temporality, and brain function. In D. Meill, R. MacDonald, & D. Hargreaves (Eds.), *Musical communication* (pp. 171–191). Oxford: Oxford University Press.

Thaut, M. (2005b). *Rhythm, music, and the brain.* New York, NY: Routledge.

Thaut, M. (2009). History and research. In S. Hallam, I. Cross, & M. Thaut (Eds.), *Oxford handbook of music psychology* (pp. 552–560). Oxford: Oxford University Press.

Thaut, M. (2015). Music as therapy in early history. *Progress in Brain Research, 217,* 143–158.

Thaut, M., & Hodges, D. (Eds.). (2019). *The Oxford handbook on music and the brain.* Oxford: Oxford University Press.

Thaut, M., & Hoemberg, V. (2014). *Handbook of neurologic music therapy.* Oxford: Oxford University Press.

Thaut, M., Brown, S. Benjamin, J., & Cooke, J. (1996). Rhythmic facilitation of movement sequencing: Effects on spatio-temporal control and sensory modality dependence. In R. Pratt & R. Spintge (Eds.), *MusicMedicine II* (pp. 104–109). St. Louis, MO: MMB Music.

References

Thaut, M., Kenyon, G., Schauer, M., & McIntosch, G. (1999). The connection between rhythmicity and brain function: Implications for therapy of movement disorders. *IEEE Engineering in Medicine and Biology, 18*, 101–108.

Thaut, M., McIntosh, G., Rice, R., & Prassas, S. (1993). Effect of auditory rhythmic cuing on temporal stride parameters and EMG patterns in hemiparetic gait of stroke patients. *Journal of Neurologic Rehabilitation, 7*, 9–16.

Thaut, M., McIntosh, G., Rice, R., Rathbun, J., & Brault, J. (1996). Rhythmic auditory stimulation in gait training for Parkinson's disease patients. *Movement Disorders, 11*(2), 193–200.

Thaut, M., Rice, R., & McIntosh, G. (1997). Rhythmic facilitation of gait training in hemiparetic stroke rehabilitation. *Journal of Neurological Science, 151*, 207–215.

Thayer, J., & Faith, M. (2001). A dynamic systems model of musically induced emotions. In R. Zatorre & I. Peretz (Eds.), *The neurosciences and music. Annals of the New York Academy of Sciences, 999*, 452–456.

Thayer, R. (1972). The interrelation of personality traits, musical achievement, and different measures of musical aptitude. In E. Gordon (Ed.), *Research in the psychology of music* (Vol. 8, pp. 103–118). Iowa City: University of Iowa Press.

Theiler, A., & Lippman, L. (1995). Effects of mental practice and modeling on guitar and vocal performance. *The Journal of General Psychology, 122*(4), 329–343.

Thewlis, J. (1962). *Encyclopaedic dictionary of physics*. New York, NY: Pergamon Press.

Thomas, R. (1970). *Manhattanville music curriculum program: Final report*. Washington, DC: U.S. Office of Education, Bureau of Research. ERIC Document ED 045 865.

Thompson, P., Giedd, J., Woods, R., MacDonald, D., Evans, A., & Toga, A. (2000). Growth patterns in the developing brain detected by using continuum mechanical tensor maps. *Nature, 404*(9), 190–193.

Thompson, W. (1987). Music sight-reading skill in flute players. *Journal of General Psychology, 114*(4), 345–352.

Thompson, W. (2009). *Music, thought, and feeling: Understanding the psychology of music*. Oxford: Oxford University Press.

Thompson, W. (2014). *Music, thought, and feeling* (2nd ed.). Oxford: Oxford University Press.

Thompson, W., Graham, P., & Russo, F. (2005). Seeing music performance: Visual influences on perception and experience. *Semiotica, 156*(1–4), 203–227.

Thompson, W., & Robitaille, B. (1992). Can composers express emotions through music? *Empirical Studies of the Arts, 10*(1), 79–89.

Thompson, W., & Russo, F. (2007). Facing the music. *Psychological Science, 18*(9), 756–757.

Thompson, W., & Schellenberg, E. (2002). Cognitive constraints on music listening. In R. Colwell & C. Richardson (Eds.), *The new handbook of research on music teaching and learning* (pp. 461–486). New York, NY: Oxford University Press.

Tillman, B., Bharucha, J., & Bigand, E. (2000). Implicit learning of tonality: A self-organizing approach. *Psychological Review, 107*(4), 885–913.

Timmerman, L. M., Allen, M., Jorgensen, J., Herrett-Skjellum, J., Kramer, M. R., & Ryan, D. J. (2008). A review and meta-analysis examining the relationship of music content with sex, race, priming, and attitudes. *Communication Quarterly, 56*(3), 303–324.

Timmers, R., & Ashley, R. (2007). Emotional ornamentation in performances of a Handel sonata. *Music Perception, 25*(2), 117–134.

Titon, J. (2009a). Ecology, phenomenology, and biocultural thinking. *Ethnomusicology, 53*(1), 502–509.

Titon, J. (Ed.). (2009b). *Worlds of music: An introduction to the music of the world's peoples* (5th ed.). Belmont, CA: Schirmer Cengage Learning. One can listen to an aural example at. Retrieved January 30, 2010, from http://lint.vox.com/library/post/postal-workers-canceling-stamps-at-the-university-of-ghana-post-office.html

Titze, I. (2001). Acoustic interpretation of resonant voice. *Journal of Voice, 15*(4), 519–528.

Todd, P., & Loy, D. (1991). *Music and connectionism*. Cambridge, MA: The MIT Press.

Toga, A., & Thompson, P. (2003). Mapping brain asymmetry. *Nature Reviews Neuroscience, 4*(1), 37–48.

Toppila, E., Koskinen, H., & Pyykkö, I. (2011). Hearing loss among classical-orchestra musicians. *Noise and Health, 13*(50), 45.

Touma, H. (2009). *The music of the Arabs*. (L. Schwarts, Trans.). Portland, OR: Amadeus Press.

bibliography

Trainor, L., & Marsh-Rollo, S. (2019). Rhythm, meter, and timing: The heartbeat of musical development. In M. Thaut & D. Hodges (Eds.), *The Oxford handbook of music and the brain* (pp. 592–622). Oxford: Oxford University Press.

Trainor, L., McFadden, M., Hodgson, L., Darragh, L., Barlow, J., Matsos, L., & Sonnadara, R. (2003). Changes in auditory cortex and the development of mismatch negativity between 2 and 6 months of age. *International Journal of Psychophysiology, 51,* 5–15.

Trainor, L., Shahin, A., & Roberts, L. (2009). Understanding the benefits of musical training effects on oscillatory brain activity. In S. Dalla Bella, N. Kraus, K. Overy, C. Pantev, J. Snyder, M. Tervaniemi, . . . G. Schlaug (Eds.), *The neurosciences of music III: Disorders and plasticity. Annals of the New York Academy of Sciences, 1169,* 133–142.

Trainor, L., Tsang, C., & Cheung, V. (2002). Preference for consonance in two-month-old infants. *Music Perception, 20*(2), 185–192.

Trainor, L., & Zatorre, R. (2016). The neurobiology of musical expectations from perception to emotion. In S. Hallam, I. Cross, &M. Thaut (Eds.), *The Oxford handbook of music psychology* (pp. 285–305). Oxford: Oxford University Press.

Trehub, S. (2000). Human processing predispositions and musical universals. In N. Wallin, B. Merker, & S. Brown (Eds.), *The origins of music* (pp. 428–448). Cambridge, MA: The MIT Press.

Trehub, S. (2001). Musical predispositions in infancy. In R. Zatorre & I. Peretz (Eds.), *The biological foundations of music. Annals of the New York Academy of Sciences, 930,* 1–16.

Trehub, S. (2003). The developmental origins of musicality. *Nature Neuroscience, 6*(7), 669–673.

Trehub, S. (2004). Foundations: Music perception in infancy. In J. Flohr (Ed.), *The musical lives of young children* (pp. 24–29). Upper Saddle River, NJ: Prentice-Hall.

Trehub, S. (2006). Infants as musical connoisseurs. In G. McPherson (Ed.), *The child as musician* (pp. 33–50). Oxford: Oxford University Press.

Trehub, S. (2009). Music lessons from infants. In S. Hallam, I. Cross, & M. Thaut (Eds.), *The Oxford handbook of music psychology* (pp. 229–234). Oxford: Oxford University Press.

Trehub, S., & Trainor, L. (1998). Singing to infants: Lullabies and play songs. In C. Rovee-Collier, L. Lipsitt, & H. Hayne (Eds.), *Advances in Infancy Research, 12,* 43–78.

Trehub, S., Unyk, A., & Trainor, L. (1993). Adults identify infant-direct music across cultures. *Infant Behavior and Development, 16,* 193–211.

Trost, W., Ethofer, T., Zentner, M., & Vuilleumier, P. (2012). Mapping aesthetic musical emotions in the brain. *Cerebral Cortex, 22,* 2769–2783.

Tsang, C., & Trainor, L. (2002). Spectral slope discrimination in infancy: Sensitivity to socially important timbres. *Infant Behavior & Development, 25,* 183–194.

Tsay, C. J. (2013). Sight over sound in the judgment of music performance. *Proceedings of the National Academy of Sciences, 110*(36), 14580–14585.

Tubiana, R., & Amadio, P. (Eds.). (2000). *Medical problems of the instrumentalist musician.* London: Martin Dunitz.

Turnbull, W. (1944). Pitch discrimination as a function of tonal duration. *Journal of Experimental Psychology, 34*(4), 302–316.

Turner, G., & Kenny, D. (2010). A preliminary investigation into the association between body movement patterns and dynamic variation in western contemporary popular singing. *Musicae Scientiae, 14*(1), 143–164.

Turner, R., & Ioannides, A. (2009). Brain, music and musicality: Inferences from neuroimaging. In S. Malloch & C. Trevarthen (Eds.), *Communicative musicality: Exploring the basis of human companionship* (pp. 147–181). Oxford: Oxford University Press.

Turner, V. (1982). *Celebration: Studies in festivity and ritual.* Washington, DC: Smithsonian Institution Press.

U.S. Music Industry's Jobs & Benefits Report. (2018). Retrieved from www.riaa.com/u-s-music-industries-jobs-benefits-report/

Ukkola-Vuoti, L., Oikkonen, J., Onkamo, P., Karma, K., Raijas, P., & Järvelä, I. (2011). Association of the arginine vasopressin receptor 1a (avpr1a) haplotypes with listening to music. *Journal of Human Genetics, 56,* 324–329.

References

Ukkola-Vuoti, L., Kanduri, C., Oikkonen, J., Buck, G., Blancher, C., Raijas, P., . . . Järvelä, I. (2013). Genome-wide copy number variation analysis in extended families and unrelated individuals characterized for musical aptitude and creativity in music. *PLoS One, 8*(2), e56356.

Ullén, F., Hambrick, D., & Mosing, M. (2016). Rethinking expertise: A multifactorial gene-environment interaction model of expert performance. *Psychological Bulletin, 142*(4), 427–446.

Ullmann, Y., Fodor, L., Schwarzberg, I., Carmi, N., Ullmann, A., & Ramon, Y. (2008). The sounds of music in the operating room. *Injury, International Journal of the Care of the Injured, 39*, 592–597.

Utttal, W. (2000). *The war between mentalism and behaviorism: On the accessibility of mental processes.* Mahwah, NJ: Lawrence Erlbaum Associates.

Vaitl, D. Vehrs, W., & Sternagel, S. (1993). Prompts—leitmotif—emotion: Play it again, Richard Wagner. In N. Birbaumer & A. Öhman (Eds.), *The structure of emotion: psychophysiological, cognitive, and clinical aspects* (pp. 169–189). Seattle, WA: Hogrefe & Hüber.

Valentine, C. (1962). *The experimental psychology of beauty.* London: Methuen.

VandenBos, G. R. (Ed.). (2007). *APA dictionary of psychology.* Washington, DC: American Psychological Association.

VanderArk, S., & Ely, D. (1992). Biochemical and galvanic skin responses to music stimuli by college students in biology and music. *Perceptual and Motor Skills, 74*, 1079–1090.

VanderArk, S., & Ely, D. (1993). Cortisol, biochemical and galvanic skin responses to music stimuli of different preference values by college students in biology and music. *Perceptual and Motor Skills, 77*, 227–234.

Vandervert, L. (2016). Working memory in musical prodigies: A 10,000-year-old story, one million years in the making. In G. McPherson (Ed.), *Musical prodigies* (pp. 224–244). Oxford: Oxford University Press.

Vandiver, P., Soffer, O., Klima, B., & Svoboda, J. (1989). The origins of ceramic technology at Dolni Vestonice, Czechosklovakia. *Science, 246*(4933), 1002–1008.

Van Khe, T. (1984). Buddhist music in Eastern Asia. *The World of Music, 26*(3), 22–30.

Varki, A., & Gagneux, P. (2017). How different are humans and "great apes"? A matrix of comparative anthropogeny. In M. Tibayrenc & F. Ayala (Eds.), *On human nature: Biology, psychology, ethics, politics, and religion* (pp. 151–160). London: Academic Press.

Vaughn, B. (2007). *The impact of singing styles on tension in the adolescent voice* (PhD dissertation). The University of North Carolina, Greensboro.

Vaughn, K. (2000). Music and mathematics: Modest support for the oft-claimed relationship. *Journal of Aesthetic Education, 34*(3–4), 149–166.

Venables, P. (1987). Electrodermal activity. In R. Gregory (Ed.), *The Oxford companion to the mind.* Oxford: Oxford University Press.

Vennard, W. (1964). An experiment to evaluate the importance of nasal resonance in singing. *Folia Phoniatrica et Logopaedica, 16*(2), 146–153.

Verghese, J., Lipton, R. B., Katz, M. J., Hall, C. B., Derby, C. A., Kuslansky, G., . . . Buschke, H. (2003). Leisure activities and the risk of dementia in the elderly. *New England Journal of Medicine, 348*(25), 2508–2516.

Vickers, B. (1995). The pianist as orator: Bethoven and the transformation of keyboard style by George Barth. *Rhetorica, 13*(1), 98–101.

Vickhoff, B., Malmgren, H., Åström, R., Nyberg, G., Ekström, S-R., Engwall, M., . . . Jörnsten, R. (2013). Music structure determines heart rate variability of singers. *Frontiers in Psychology, 4*(334), 1–16.

Vidor, M. (1931). *Was ist musikalität? (What is musicality?)* Munich: Beck.

Viladot, L., Gómez, I., & Malagarriga, T. (2010). Sharing meanings in the music classroom. *European Journal of Psychology of Education, 25*(1), 49–65.

Visser, B., Ashton, M., & Vernon, P. (2006). Beyond *g*: Putting multiple intelligences theory to the test. *Intelligence, 34*, 487–502.

Vogel, I., van de Looij-Jansen, P. M., Mieloo, C. L., Burdorf, A., & de Waart, F. (2012). Risky music-listening behaviors and associated health-risk behaviors. *Pediatrics, 129*, 1097–1103.

Vogel, I., Verschuure, H., van der Ploeg, C., Burg, J., & Raat, H. (2009). Adolescents and MP3 players: Too many risks, too few precautions. *Pediatrics, 123*(6), 3953–3958.

Volkov, S. (2004). *Shostakovich and Stalin: The extraordinary relationship between the great composer and the brutal dictator*. New York, NY: Alfred A. Knopf.

Voloshinov, A. (1996). Symmetry as a superprinciple of science and art. *Leonardo, 29*(2), 109–113.

Voltmer, E., Fischer, J. E., Richter, B., & Spahn, C. (2012). Physical and mental health of different types of orchestra musicians compared to other professions. *Medical Problems of Performing Artists, 27*(1), 9.

von Puttkamer, W. (1979). Man in the Amazon: Stone age present meets stone age past. *National Geographic, 155*(1), 60–83.

Vuust, P., Brattico, E., Seppänen, M., Näätänen, R., & Tervaniemi, M. (2012). The sound of music: Differentiating musicians using a fast, musical multi-feature mismatch negativity paradigm. *Neuropsychologia, 50*(7), 1432–1443.

Vuust, P., & Kringelbach, M. (2010). The pleasure of music. In M. Kringelbach & K. Berridge (Eds.), *Pleasures of the brain* (pp. 255–269). Oxford: Oxford University Press.

Wachi, M., Koyama, M., Utsuyama, M., Bittman, B., Kitagawa, M., & Hirokawa, K. (2007). Recreational music-making modulates natural killer cell activity, cytokines, and mood states in corporate employees. *Medical Science Monitor, 13*(2), CR57–CR70.

Wade, B. (2009). *Thinking musically: Experiencing music, expressing culture* (2nd ed.). New York, NY: Oxford University Press.

Wager, T., Barrett, L., Bliss-Moreau, E., Lindquist, K., Duncan, S., Kober, H. Joseph, . . . Mize, J. (2008). The neuroimaging of emotion. In M. Lewis, J. Haviland-Jones, & L. Barrett (Eds.), *Handbook of emotions* (3rd ed., pp. 249–267). New York, NY: Guilford Press.

Wagner, M. (1975). The effect of a practice report on practice time and musical performance. In C. Madsen, R. Greer, & C. H. Madsen, Jr. (Eds.), *Research in music behavior* (pp. 125–130). New York, NY: Teachers College Press, Columbia University.

Waite, A. K., & Diaz, F. M. (2012). The effect of skill level on instrumentalists' perceptions of flow: An exploratory study. *Missouri Journal of Research in Music Education, 49*, 1–23.

Walker, J. (2002). *Physics*. Upper Saddle River, NJ: Prentice Hall.

Walker, M., Brakefield, T., Seidman, J., Morgan, A., Hobson, J., & Stickgold, R. (2003). Sleep and the time course of motor skill learning. *Learning and Memory, 10*, 275–284.

Walker, R. (1990). *Musical beliefs: Psychoacoustic, mythical, and educational perspectives*. New York, NY: Teachers College Press.

Wallaschek, R. (1886). *Ästhetik der Tonkunst (Aesthetics of music)*. Stuttgart, Germany: Druck und Verlag von W. Kohlhammer.

Wallaschek, R. (1893). *Primitive music*. London: Longmans, Green and Co.

Wallin, N. (1991). *Biomusicology: Neurophysiological, neuropsychological, and evolutionary perspectives on the origins and purposes of music*. Stuyvesant, NY: Pendragon Press.

Wallin, N., Merker, B., & Brown, S. (Eds.). (2000). *Origins of music*. Cambridge, MA: The MIT Press.

Walter, J. (2009). Sound exposure levels experienced by university band members. *Medical Problems of Performing Artists, 24*(2), 63–70.

Walter, J., Mace, S., & Phillips, S. (2008). Preventing hearing loss. *Published proceedings from the national association of schools of music annual meeting* (pp. 101–105). Chicago, IL.: National Association of Schools of Music.

Wantanabe, D., Savion-Lemiux, T., & Penhune, V. (2007). The effect of early musical training on adult motor performance: Evidence for a sensitive period in motor learning. *Experimental Brain Research, 176*(3), 332–340.

Ward, D. (1999). Absolute pitch. In D. Deutsch (Ed.), *The psychology of music* (2nd ed., pp. 265–298). New York, NY: Academic Press.

Ward-Steinman, P. (Ed.). (2011). *Advances in social-psychology and music education research*. Surrey: Ashgate.

Wass, H., Miller, M., & Redditt, C. (1991). Adolescents and destructive themes in rock music: A follow-up. *Omega: Journal of Death and Dying, 23*(3), 199–206.

Waterman, C. (1993). Africa. In H. Meyers (Ed.), *Ethnomusicology: Historical and regional studies*. New York, NY: W. W. Norton.

References

Waterman, M. (1996). Emotional responses to music: Implicit and explicit effects in listeners and performers. *Psychology of Music, 24*, 53–67.

Waters, A., & Underwood, G. (1998). Eye movements in a simple music reading task: A study of expert and novice musicians. *Psychology of Music, 26*(1), 46–60.

Watson, A. (2009). *The biology of musical performance and performance-related injury.* Lanham, MD: The Scarecrow Press.

Watson, J. B. (1924). *Behaviorism.* New York, NY: W. W. Norton.

Watson, J. D. (1968). *The double helix.* New York, NY: Mentor Books.

Webb, S., Monk, C., & Nelson, C. (2001). Mechanisms of postnatal neurobiological development: Implications for human development. *Developmental Neuropsychology, 19*(2), 147–171.

Weber, M. (1958). *The rational and social foundations of music* (D. Martindale, J. Riedel, & G. Neuwirth, Trans. & Ed.). Carbondale, IL: Southern Illinois University Press.

Webster, P. (1990). Creativity as creative thinking. *Music Educators Journal, 76*(9), 22–28.

Webster, P. (1994). *Measures of creative thinking in music.* Retrieved from http://peterrwebster.com

Webster, P. (2002). Creative thinking in music: Advancing a model. In T. Sullivan & L. Willingham (Eds.), *Creativity and music education* (pp. 16–33). Edmonton, AB: Canadian Music Educators' Association.

Webster, P. (2012). Towards pedagogies of revision: Guiding a student's music composition. In O. Odena (Ed.), *Musical creativity: Insights from music education research* (pp. 93–112). Farnham: Ashgate.

Wei, D., Yang, J., Li, W., Wang, K., Zhang, Q., & Qiu, J. (2014). Increased resting functional connectivity of the medial prefrontal cortex in creativity by means of cognitive stimulation. *Cortex, 51*, 92–102.

Weidenfeller, E., & Zimny, G. (1962). Effects of music upon GSR of depressives and schizophrenics. *Journal of Abnormal Social Psychology, 64*, 307–312.

Weinberger, N. (1999). Music and the auditory system. In D. Deutsch (Ed.), *The psychology of music* (2nd ed., pp. 47–87). New York, NY: Academic Press.

Weinberger, N. (2006, December 12). Music and the brain. *Scientific American, Special Edition: Secrets of the Senses*, 38–43.

Weinberger, N., Ashe, J., & Edeline, J. (1994). Learning-induced receptive field plasticity in the auditory cortex: Specificity of information storage. In J. Delacour (Ed.), *Neural bases of learning and memory* (pp. 530–635). Singapore: World Scientific Publishing.

Weisblatt, S. (1986). A psychoanalytic view of performance anxiety. *Medical Problems of Performing Musicians, 1*(2), 64–67.

Weisser, S., & Quanten, M. (2011). Rethinking musical instrument classification: Towards a modular approach to the Hornbostel-Sachs system. *Yearbook for Traditional Music, 43*, 122–146.

Welch, G. (2005). Singing as communication. In D. Miell, R. MacDonald, & D. Hargreaves (Eds.), *Musical communication* (pp. 239–259). Oxford: Oxford University Press.

Welch, G. (2006). Singing and vocal development. In G. McPherson (Ed.), *The child as musician* (pp. 311–329). Oxford: Oxford University Press.

Wertheimer, M. (1959). *Productive thinking* (Rev. Ed.). New York, NY: Harper & Row.

Wessel, D. (1989). Timbre and the perceptual organization of musical patterns. *Journal of the Acoustical Society of America, Supplement 1, 86*, S58–S59.

West, M. (1994). The Babylonian musical notation and the Hurrian melodic texts. *Music and Letters, 75*(2), 161–179.

West, M., King, A., & Goldstein, M. (2004). Singing, socializing, and the music effect. In P. Marler, H. Slabbekoorn, & S. Hope (Eds.), *Nature's music: The science of birdsong* (pp. 374–387). San Diego, CA: Elsevier Academic Press.

Western, D. (1999). The scientific status of unconscious processes: Is Freud really dead? *Journal of the American Psychoanalytic Association, 47*(4), 1061–1106.

Whaling, C. (2000). What's behind a song? The neural basis of song learning in birds. In N. Wallin, B. Merker, & S. Brown (Eds.), *The origins of music* (pp. 65–76). Cambridge, MA: The MIT Press.

Wheeler, B. (Ed.). (1995). *Music therapy research: Quantitative and qualitative perspectives.* Phoenixville, PA: Barcelona Publishers.

Wheeler, B. (Ed.). (2005). *Music therapy research* (2nd ed.). Gilsum, NH: Barcelona Publishers.

Wheeler, B., & Murphy, K. (2016). *Music therapy research* (3rd ed.). Dallas: Barcelona Publishers.

White, B. (1960). Recognition of distorted melodies. *The American Journal of Psychology, 73*(1), 100–107.

White, R., Mensan, R., Bourrillon, R., Cretin, C., Higham, T., Clark, A., . . . Chiotti, L. (2012). Context and dating of Aurignacian vulvar representations from Abri Castanet, France. *Proceedings of the National Academy of Sciences, 109*(22), 8450–8455.

White, T., Su, S., Schmidt, M., Kao, C. Y., & Sapiro, G. (2010). The development of gyrification in childhood and adolescence. *Brain and Cognition, 72*(1), 36–45.

Whitfield, T. (1983). Predicting preference for familiar, everyday objects: An experimental confrontation between two theories of aesthetic behaviour. *Journal of Experimental Psychology, 3,* 221–237.

Whitfield, T. (2000). Beyond prototypicality: Toward a categorical-motivation model of aesthetics. *Empirical Studies of the Arts, 18*(1), 1–11.

Whitfield, T. (2009). Theory confrontation: Testing the categorical-motivation model. *Empirical Studies of the Arts, 27*(1), 43–59.

Whitfield, T., & Slatter, P. (1979). The effect of categorization and prototypicality on aesthetic choice in a furniture selection task. *British Journal of Psychology, 70,* 65–75.

Whitley, D. (2009). *Cave paintings and the human spirit: The origin of creativity and belief.* Amherst, NY: Prometheus Books.

Whittall, A. (2010). Consonance and dissonance. In A. Latham (Ed.), *The Oxford companion to music. Oxford music online.* Retrieved February 26, 2010, from www.oxfordmusiconline.com/subscriber/article/opr/t114/e1581

Whybrew, W. (1962). *Measurement and evaluation in music.* Dubuque, IA: W. C. Brown.

Whybrew, W. (1971). *Measurement and evaluation in music* (2nd ed.). Dubuque, IA: W. C. Brown.

Wiggins, J. (2004). Letting go—Moving forward. *Mountain Lake Reader, 3,* 81–91.

Wilford, J. (1986, October 2). Artistry of the ice age. *New York Times Magazine,* 46–60.

Wilkins, R., Hodges, D., Laurienti, P., & Steen, M. (2012). Network science: A new method for investigating the complexity of musical experiences in the brain. *Leonardo, 45*(3), 282–283.

Wilkins, R., Hodges, D., Laurienti, P., Steen, M., & Burdette, J. (2014). Network science and the effects of music preference on functional brain connectivity: From Beethoven to Eminem. *Nature Scientific Reports, 4,* 6130.

Williamon, A. (Ed.). (2004). *Musical excellence: Strategies and techniques to enhance performance.* New York, NY: Oxford University Press.

Williamon, A., Aufegger, L., & Eiholzer, H. (2014). Simulating and stimulating performance: Introducing distributed simulation to enhance musical learning and performance. *Frontiers in Psychology, 5,* 25.

Williamon, A., & Valentine, E. (2000). Quantity and quality of musical practice as predictors of performance quality. *British Journal of Psychology, 91,* 353–376.

Williams, E., Winter, C., & Wood, J. (1938). Tests of literary appreciation. *British Journal of Educational Psychology, 8,* 265–284.

Williams, H. (2004). Birdsong and singing behavior. In H. Zeigler & P. Marler (Eds.), *Behavioral neurobiology of birdsong. Annals of the New York Academy of Sciences, 1016,* 1–30.

Williams, W., & Sternberg, R. (1993). Seven lessons for helping children make the most of their abilities. *Educational Psychology, 13*(3–4), 317–331.

Williamson, S., & Kaufman, L. (1988). Auditory evoked magnetic fields. In A. Jahn & J. Santos-Sacchi (Eds.), *Physiology of the ear* (pp. 497–505). New York, NY: Raven Press.

Williamson, V. (2014). *You are the music: How music reveals what it means to be human.* London: Icon.

Wills, G. I. (2003). Forty lives in the bebop business: Mental health in a group of eminent jazz musicians. *The British Journal of Psychiatry, 183*(3), 255–259.

Wilson, C., & Aiken, L. (1977). The effect of intensity levels upon physiological and subjective affective response to rock music. *Journal of Music Therapy, 13,* 60–76.

Wilson, E., & Davey, N. (2002). Musical beat influences corticospinal drive to ankle flexor and extensor muscles in man. *International Journal of Psychophysiology, 44*(2), 177–184.

References

Wilson, F. (1986a). Music and medicine: Inderal for stage fright? *Piano Quarterly, 134*, 30–35.

Wilson, F. (1986b). *Tone deaf and all thumbs? An invitation to music-making for late bloomers and non-prodigies.* New York, NY: Vintage Books.

Wilson, F. (1988). Brain mechanisms in highly skilled movements. In F. Roehmann & F. Wilson (Eds.), *The biology of music making* (pp. 92–99). St. Louis, MO: MMB Music.

Wilson, F. (1989). Acquisition and loss of skilled movement in musicians. *Seminars in Neurology, 9*(2), 146–151.

Wilson, F. (1991). Music and the neurology of time. *Music Educators Journal, 77*(5), 26–30.

Wilson, F. (1993). Digitizing digital dexterity: A novel application for MIDI recordings of keyboard performance. *Psychomusicology, 11*, 79–95.

Wilson, F. (1998). *The hand.* New York, NY: Vintage Books.

Wilson, F., & Roehmann, F. (Eds.). (1990). *Music and child development.* St. Louis, MO: MMB Music.

Wilson, F., & Roehmann, F. (1992). The study of biomechanical and physiological processes in relation to musical performance. In R. Colwell (Ed.), *Handbook of research on music teaching and learning* (pp. 509–524). New York, NY: Schirmer Books.

Wilson, G., & Roland, D. (2002). Performance anxiety. In R. Parncutt & G. McPherson (Eds.), *The science and psychology of music performance* (pp. 47–61). Oxford: Oxford University Press.

Wilson, R. S., Boyle, P. A., Yang, J., James, B. D., & Bennett, D. A. (2015). Early life instruction in foreign language and music and incidence of mild cognitive impairment. *Neuropsychology, 29*(2), 292.

Winckel, F. (1962). Optimum acoustic criteria of concert halls for the performance of classical music. *Journal of the Acoustical Society of America, 34*(1), 81–86.

Windsor, L. (1993). Dynamic accents and the categorical perception of metre. *Psychology of Music, 21*, 127–140.

Wingood, G., DiClemente, R., Bernhardt, J., Harrington, K., Davies, S., Robillard, A., & Hook III, E. (2003). A prospective study of exposure to rap music videos an African American female adolescents' health. *American Journal of Public Health, 93*(3), 437–439.

Winhold, H. (1988). High speed photography of cello playing. In F. Wilson & F. Roehmann (Eds.), *Biology of music making* (pp. 180–182). St. Louis, MO: MMB Music.

Winhold, H., & Thelen, E. (1988). Study in perceptual, cognitive, and motor aspects of highly skilled cellists. *Psychomusicology, 7*(2), 163–164.

Winkler, I., Háden, G., Ladinig, O., Sziller, I., & Honing, H. (2009). Newborn infants detect the beat in music. *PNAS (Proceedings of the National Academy of Sciences), 106*(7), 2468–2471.

Winkler, I., Kushnerenko, E., Horváth, J., Ceponiene, R., Fellman, V., Huotilainen, M., . . . Sussman, E. (2003). Newborn infants can organize the auditory world. *PNAS (Proceedings of the National Academy of Sciences), 100*(20), 11812–11815.

Witten, E. (2002, June). The universe on a string. *Astronomy Magazine,* 42–47. Retrieved April 22, 2007, from www.sns.ias.edu/~witten/papers/string.pdf

Wittengenstein, L. (1967). *Lecures and conversations on aesthetics, psychology, and religious belief.* Ed. by C. Barrett. Berkeley, CA: University of California Press.

Witvliet, C., & Vrana, S. (2007). Play it again Sam: Repeated exposure to emotionally evocative music polarizes liking and smiling responses, and influences other affects reports, facial EMG, and heart rate. *Cognition and Emotion, 21*(1), 3–25.

Wolfe, M. (1989). Correlates of adaptive and maladaptive musical performance anxiety. *Medical Problems of Performing Artists, 4*(1), 49–56.

Wolfe, M. (1990a). Coping with musical performance anxiety: Problem-focused and emotion-focused strategies. *Medical Problems of Performing Artists, 5*(1), 33–36.

Wolfe, M. (1990b). Relationships between dimensions of musical performance anxiety and behavioral coping strategies. *Medical Problems of Performing Artists, 5*(4), 139–144.

Wolpert, D., Ghahramani, Z., & Flanagan, J. (2001). Perspectives and problems in motor learning. *Trends in Cognitive Sciences, 5*(11), 487–494.

Wood, A. (1980). *The physics of music.* (J. Bowsher, Rev. Ed.). Westport, CT: Greenwood Press.

Woodrow, H. (1951). Time perception. In S. Stevens (Ed.), *Handbook of experimental psychology* (pp. 1224–1236). New York, NY: Wiley.

Woods, R., & Martin, L. (1943). Testing in music education. *Education and Psychological Measurement, 3*, 29–42.

Woody, R. (1999a). The musician's personality. *Creativity Research Journal, 12*(4), 241–250.

Woody, R. (1999b). The relationship between advanced musicians' explicit planning and their expressive performance of dynamic variations in an aural modeling task. *Journal of Research in Music Education, 47*, 331–342.

Woody, R. (2000). Learning expressivity in music performance: An exploratory study. *Research Studies in Music Education, 14*, 14–23.

Woody, R. (2002). The relationship between musician's expectations and their perception of expressive features in an aural model. *Research Studies in Music Education, 18*, 57–65.

WorldBlu. (2018). *Meet the most freedom-centered organizations in the world*. Retrieved from www.worldblu.com/certified

Worth, J. (2013). *Shadows of the workhouse*. Glasgow: Harper Collins.

Wu, S. (2007). Occupational risk factors for musculoskeletal disorders in musicians: A systematic review. *Medical Problems of Performing Artists, 22*(2), 43–51.

Wu, X., Zhang, C., Goldberg, P., Cohen, D., Pan, Y., Arpin, T., & Bar-Yosef, O. (2012). Early pottery at 20,000 years ago in Xianrendong cave, China. *Science, 336*(6089), 1696–1700.

Xenakis, I. (1992). *Formalized music: Thought and mathematics in composition*. Stuyvesant, NY: Pendragon Press.

Xu, Y. (1997). Contextual tonal variations in Mandarin. *Journal of Phonetics, 25*(1), 61–83.

Yamamoto, M., Naga, S., & Shimizu, J. (2007). Positive musical effects of two types of negative stressful conditions. *Psychology of Music, 35*(2), 249–275.

Yarbrough, C. (1975). Effect of magnitude of conductor behavior on students in selected mixed choruses. *Journal of Research in Music Education, 23*(2), 134–146.

Yarbrough, C., & Price, H. (1981). Prediction of performer attentiveness based on rehearsal activity and teacher behavior. *Journal of Research in Music Education, 29*(3), 209–217.

Yerkes, R., & Dodson, J. (1908). The relation of strength of stimulus to rapidity of habit-formation. *Journal of Comparative Neurology and Psychology, 18*(5), 459–482.

Yi, T., McPherson, G., Peretz, I., Berkovic, S., & Wilson, S. (2014). The genetic basis of music ability. *Frontiers in Psychology, 5*(658), 1–19.

Yi, T., McPherson, G., & Wilson, S. (2018). The molecular genetic basis of music ability and music-related phenotypes. In D. Hambrick, G. Campitelli, & B. Macnamara (Eds.), *The science of expertise: Behavioral, neural, and genetic approaches to complex skill* (pp. 283–303). New York, NY: Routledge.

Yoshino, I., & Abe, J-I. (2004). Cognitive modeling of key interpretation in melody perception. *Japanese Psychological Research, 46*(4), 283–297.

Young, C. (2008). Minding music and movies (music in advertising). *Admap, 43*(494), 45–48.

Yu, H-B., Liu, Y-F., & Wu, L-X. (2009). Acupuncture combined with music therapy for treatment of 30 cases of cerebral palsy. *Journal of Traditional Chinese Medicine, 29*(4), 243–248.

Zajonc, R., & McIntosh, D. (1992). Emotions research: Some promising questions and some questionable promises. *Psychological Science, 3*(1), 70–74.

Zander, M. F. (2006). Musical influences in advertising: How music modifies first impressions of product endorsers and brands. *Psychology of Music, 34*(4), 465–480.

Zangwill, O. (2004). Freud, Sigmund. In R. Gregory (Ed.), *The Oxford companion to the mind* (pp. 357–358). Oxford: Oxford University Press.

Zatorre, R. (2001). Neural specializations for tonal processing. In R. Zatorre & I. Peretz (Eds.), *The biological foundations of music. Annals of the New York Academy Sciences, 930*, 193–210.

Zatorre, R. (2003). Absolute pitch: A model for understanding the influence of genes and development on neural and cognitive function. *Nature Neuroscience, 6*, 692–695.

Zatorre, R., & McGill, J. (2005). Music, the food of neuroscience? *Nature, 434*(7031), 312–315.

References

Zatorre, R., & Peretz, I. (Eds.). (2001). *The biological foundations of music.* New York, NY: New York Academy of Sciences.

Zatorre, R., Chen, J., & Penhune, V. (2007). When the brain plays music: Auditory-motor interactions in music perception. *Nature Reviews Neuroscience, 8*(7), 547–558.

Zbikowski, L. (2002). *Conceptualizing music.* New York, NY: Oxford University Press.

Zdzinski, S. (1992). Relationships among parental involvement, music aptitude, and musical achievement of instrumental music students. *Journal of Research in Music Education, 40*(2), 114–125.

Zdzinski, S. (1996). Parental involvement, selected student attributes, and learning outcomes in instrumental music. *Journal of Research in Music Education, 44*(1), 34–38.

Zentner, M., & Eerola, T. (2010a). Rhythmic engagement with music in infancy. *PNAS (Proceedings of the National Academy of Sciences), 107*(13), 5768–5773.

Zentner, M., & Eerola, T. (2010b). Self-report measures and models. In P. Juslin & J. Sloboda (Eds.), *Handbook of music and emotions* (pp. 188–221). Oxford: Oxford University Press.

Zentner, M., Grandjean, D., & Scherer, K. R. (2008). Emotions evoked by the sound of music: Characterization, classification, and measurement. *Emotion, 8*(4), 494–521.

Zervoudakes, J., & Tanur, J. (1994). Gender and musical instruments: Winds of change? *Journal of Research in Music Education, 42*(1), 58–67.

Zillmann, D., & Gan, S. (1997). Musical taste in adolescence. In D. Hargreaves & A. North (Eds.), *The social psychology of music* (pp. 161–187). Oxford: Oxford University Press.

Zimny, G., & Weidenfeller, E. (1962). Effects of music upon GSR of children. *Child Development, 33,* 891–896.

Zimny, G., & Weidenfeller, E. (1963). Effect of music upon GSR and heartrate. *American Journal of Psychology, 76,* 311–314.

Zuckerkandl, V. (1956). *Sound and symbol: Music and the external world* (W. Trask, Trans.). Princeton, NJ: Princeton University Press.

Zuckerkandl, V. (1959). *The sense of music.* Princeton, NJ: Princeton University Press.

Zuckerkandl, V. (1969). *Sound and symbol, Vol. 1: Music and the external world* (W. Trask, Trans.). Princeton, NJ: Princeton University Press.

Zuckerkandl, V. (1973). *Sound and symbol, vol. 2: Man the musician* (N. Guterman, Trans.). Princeton, NJ: Princeton University Press.

Zull, J. (2002). *The art of changing the brain: Enriching the practice of teaching by exploring the biology of learning.* Sterling, VA: Stylus Publishing.

Zweigenhaft, R. (2008). A do re mi encore: A closer look at the personality correlates of music preferences. *Journal of Individual Differences, 29*(1), 45–55.

Index

Note: *Italicized* page numbers refer to figures; **bold** page numbers refer to tables.